The Old Testament

E. W. Hengstenberg, John Robertson and Co.

BIBLIOLIFE

CLARK'S

FOREIGN

THEOLOGICAL LIBRARY

SECOND SERIES.

VOL. 1.

Hengstenberg's Christology of the Old Testament.

VOL. I.

EDINBURGH:

T. & T. CLARK, 38, GEORGE STREET.

LONDON: J. GLADDING.   DUBLIN: JOHN ROBERTSON & CO.

MDCCCLXVIII.

CHRISTOLOGY

OF

THE OLD TESTAMENT,

AND A

COMMENTARY ON THE MESSIANIC PREDICTIONS

BY

E. W. HENGSTENBERG,

DR. AND PROF. OF THEOL. IN BERLIN.

SECOND EDITION, GREATLY IMPROVED.

Translated from the German,

BY THE

REV. THEODORE MEYER.

VOLUME I.

EDINBURGH:

T. AND T. CLARK, 38, GEORGE STREET.

LONDON: HAMILTON, ADAMS, & CO. DUBLIN: JOHN ROBERTSON & CO.

MDCCCLXVIII.

LIST OF CONTENTS.

TRANSLATOR'S PREFACE.

THE Translator avails himself of his privilege of offering a few prefatory words, chiefly in order to express the deep obligation under which he lies to the Rev. JOHN LAING, Librarian in the New College, Edinburgh, for the valuable assistance which he afforded to him in the translation of this work. Any observation on the work itself or its Author would be superfluous, if not presumptuous, considering the high position which Dr HENGSTENBERG holds as a Biblical Scholar. High, however, as this position is, the Translator feels confident that it will be raised by the present work, the Author's *latest* and *first;* and not only revering Dr HENGSTENBERG as a beloved Teacher, but being under many obligations to him for proofs of personal kindness and friendship, the Translator sincerely rejoices in this prospect.

As regards the translation itself, it was the Translator's aim to bring out fully the Author's meaning. This object, which ought to be the first in every translation, has been kept steadily in view, and preferred to all others. In rendering Dr HENGSTENBERG'S translation of Scripture-passages, the expressions in our Authorized Version have, as far as possible, been retained. Wherever the division of the text in the latter differed from that of the original text, it has been added in a parenthesis; an exception in this respect having been made in quotations from the Psalms only, in which this difference is almost constant, the inscriptions not being counted in our English Version, while they are in the Hebrew Text.

EDINBURGH, January 1854.

THE AUTHOR'S PREFACE.

————————◆————————

THE first edition of the Christology, although the impression was unusually large, had been for years out of print. It was impossible that the work could appear a second time in its original form. The first volume of it—written twenty-five years ago—was a juvenile performance, to which the Author himself had become rather a stranger; and the succeeding volumes required references to, and comparisons with, a large number of publications which subsequently appeared. But for the remodelling and revising which these circumstances rendered necessary, the Author could not find leisure, because new tasks were ever and anon presenting themselves to him; and these he felt himself, as it were, involuntarily impelled to undertake. But now he is led to believe that he could no longer delay. A powerful inclination urges him to comment on the Gospel of St John; but he thinks that the right to gratify this inclination must first be purchased by him by answering a call which proceeds from the more immediate sphere of his vocation, and which he is the less at liberty to disregard, as manifold facts give indication that the Christology has not yet completed its course. The Author dislikes to return to regions which have been already visited by him. He prefers the opening up to himself of paths which are new. It cost him therefore, at first, no little struggle to devote himself for years to the work of mere revision and emendation; but very soon, even here, he learned the truth of the proverb: "If there be obedience in the heart, love will soon enter."

The arrangement in the present edition differs from that which was adopted in the former. It bears a closer resemblance to that which has been followed in the Commentaries on the Psalms, Revelation, and the Song of Solomon. The work opens with a discussion and commentary on the particular Messianic prophecies, in their historical order and connection. The general investigations with which, in the first edition, the work commenced, are, in the present edition, to appear in the form

of comprehensive treatises, at the close. The latter have thus
obtained a more solid foundation; while the objections which
might be raised against this arrangement will have force only
until the completion of the whole, which, if it please the Lord,
will not be very long delayed. The reader will then, of course,
be at liberty, before he enters upon the particular portions, to
go over, cursorily in the meantime, the closing treatises,—the
proper study of which will be appropriate, however, only after
he has made himself acquainted with the particular portions of
the main body of the work.

The matter of the two sections of the first part has been
entirely rewritten. That of the two last parts appears more as
a revisal only,—so executed, however, that not a single line has
been reprinted without a renewed and careful examination.

The Author shall take care that the new edition shall not
exceed the former one in size. The space intended to be occupied by the enlarged discussions, and by the new investigations,
will be gained by omissions. These, however, will be limited to
such matters as now clearly appear to be superfluous; *so that the
old will not retain any value when compared with the new edition.*
The Author, had he pursued his usual method of representation,
would have curtailed many points, particularly the history of
the interpretation. But the mode of treating the subject which
he had previously adopted, is not without its advantages, and
has a certain right to be retained. The former character of the
work, in so far as the avoidance of everything properly ascetic
is concerned, has been, in the present edition, also retained.

Scientific Theology is at present threatened by serious dangers in our Church. Works of an immediately practical interest
more and more exclusively occupy the noblest minds, since the
problems which present themselves in this field are indeed un-
fathomable. But the Lord of the Church will take care that
an excellent gift, which He has bestowed upon German Christendom especially, shall not, for any length of time, continue to
be neglected. If such were to be the case, a more general decay
would be gradually brought on; and even those interests would
be injured to which at present, with a zeal, noble indeed, but
little thoughtful, solid theological learning is sacrificed.

"Not unto us, O Lord, not unto us, but to Thy name give
glory."

THE

MESSIANIC PROPHECIES IN THE PENTATEUCH.

In the Messianic prophecies contained in Genesis we cannot fail to perceive a remarkable progress in clearness and definiteness.

The first Messianic prediction, which was uttered immediately after the fall of Adam, is also the most indefinite. Opposed to the awful threatening there stands the consolatory promise, that the dominion of sin, and of the evil arising from sin, shall not last for ever, but that the seed of the woman shall, at some future time, overthrow their dreaded conqueror. With the exception of the victory itself, everything is here left undetermined. We are told neither the mode in which it is to be achieved, nor whether it shall be accomplished by some peculiarly gifted race, or family of the progeny of the woman, or by some single individual from among her descendants. There is nothing more than a very slight hint that the latter will be the case.

After the destruction of a whole sinful world, when only Noah with his three sons had been left, the *general* promise is, to a certain extent, defined. Deliverance is to come from the descendants of Shem; Japhet shall become a partaker of this deliverance; Ham is passed over in silence.

The prophecy becomes still more definite when the Lord begins to prepare the way for the appearance of this deliverance, by separating from the corrupt mass a single individual—Abraham—in order to make him the depositary of His revelations. The Lord, moreover, according to the good pleasure of His will, further specifies which of the descendants of Abraham, to the exclusion of all the rest, is to inherit this dignity, with all its accompanying blessings. From among the posterity of Shem, the Lord sets apart first the family of Abraham, then that of

Isaac, and lastly that of Jacob, as the family from which salvation is to come. Yet even these predictions, distinct though they be when compared with those previously uttered, are still very indefinite when compared with those subsequently given, and when seen in the light of the actual fulfilment. Even in these, the blessing only is foretold, but not its author. It still remained a matter of uncertainty whether salvation should be extended to all the other nations of the earth through a single individual, or through an entire people descended from the Patriarchs. The former is obscurely indicated; but the mode in which the blessing was to be imparted was left in darkness.

This obscurity is partially removed by the last Messianic prophecy contained in Gen. xlix. 10. After what had previously taken place, we might well expect that the question as to which of Jacob's twelve sons should have the privilege of becoming the source of deliverance to the whole earth, would not be left undetermined; nor could we imagine that Jacob, when, just before his death, and with the spirit of a prophet, he transferred to his sons the promises which had been given to his ancestors and himself, should have passed over in silence the most important part of them. On the contrary, by being transferred to Judah, the promise of the Messiah acquires not only the expected limitation, but an unexpected increase of clearness and precision. Here, for the first time, the *person* of the Messiah is brought before us; here also the *nature* of His kingdom is more distinctly pointed out by His being represented as the peaceful one, and the peacemaker who will unite, under His mild sceptre, all the nations of the whole earth. Judah is, in this passage, placed in the centre of the world's history; he shall obtain dominion, and not lose it until it has been realized to its fullest extent by means of the *Shiloh* descending from him, to whom all the nations of the earth shall render a willing obedience.

The subject-matter of the last four books of the Pentateuch would naturally prevent us from expecting that the Messianic prophecies should occupy so prominent a place in them as they do in Genesis. The object contemplated in these books is rather to prepare effectually the way for the Messiah, by laying the theocratic institutions on a firm foundation, and by establishing the law which is intended to produce the knowledge of sin, and

MESSIANIC PROPHECIES IN THE PENTATEUCH.

to settle discipline, and by means of which the image of God is to be impressed on the whole national life. If the hope of the Messiah was to be realized in a proper manner, and to produce its legitimate effect, it was necessary that the people should first 'be accustomed to this new order of life; that, for the present, their regards should not be too much drawn away from this their proximate and immediate vocation. Yet, even in the last four books there are not wanting allusions to Him who, as the end of the law, was, from the very beginning, to be set before the eyes of the people.

In Num. xxiv. 17–19, Balaam beholds an Israelitish kingdom raised absolutely above the kingdoms of the world, extending over the whole earth, and all-powerful; and he sees it in the form of an *ideal* king, with reference to Jacob's prophecy contained in Gen. xlix. 10, according to which the kingdom rising in Judah shall find its full and final realization in the person of one king—the Messiah.

We have here the future King of the Jews saluted from the midst of the heathen world, corresponding to the salutation of the manifested one by the wise men from the East: compare Matt. ii. 1, 2.

From the whole position of Moses in the economy of the revelations of God, it is, *a priori*, scarcely conceivable that he should have contented himself with communicating a prophecy of the Messiah uttered by a non-Israelite. We expect that, as a prefiguration of the testimony which, in the presence of the chief among the apostles, he bore to the Messiah after He had appeared (compare Matt. xvii. 3), he should, on his own behalf, testify his faith in Him, and direct the people to Him. This testimony we have in Deut. xviii. 15–19. It is natural that Moses' attestation should have reference to Christ in so far as He is his antitype. He bears witness to Christ as the true Prophet, as the Mediator of the divine revelation—thus enlarging the slender indications of Christ's prophetical office given in Gen. xlix. 10. A new and important feature of Messianic prophecy is here, for the first time, brought forward; and because of this, the character of the prophecy is that of a germ. Behind the person of the future Prophet, which is as yet *ideal*, the *real* person of Him who is the Prophet in an absolute sense, is, in the meantime, concealed. It is reserved for the future development of the prophetic prediction to separate that which is here beheld as still blended in a single picture.

Finally, the doctrine of the Divine Mediator of the unseen God, of the Angel of the Lord, or of the Logos, which forms the theological foundation for the Christology, is already found pervading the Books of Moses.

After this survey, we now proceed to an exposition of the particular passages.

---◆---

THE PROTEVANGELIUM.

As the mission of Christ was rendered necessary by the fall of man, so the first dark intimation of Him was given immediately after the fall. It is found in the sentence of punishment which was passed upon the tempter, Gen. iii. 14, 15. A correct understanding of it, however, can be obtained only after we have ascertained who the tempter was.

It is, in the first place, unquestionable that a real serpent was engaged in the temptation; so that the opinion of those who maintain that the serpent is only a symbolical signification of the evil spirit, cannot be admitted.[1] There must be unity and uniformity in the interpretation of a connected passage. But the allegorical interpretation of the *whole* is rendered impossible by the following considerations :—The passage stands in a book of a strictly historical character; it is connected with what follows, where the history of the same pair who, in this section appear as actors, is carried forward; the condition of mankind announced to them in this passage as a punishment, actually exists; there is the absence of every indication from which it might be inferred that the author intended to write an allegory, and not a history; there exist various passages of the New Testament (*e.g.*, 2 Cor. xi. 3; 1 Tim. ii. 13, 14; Rom. v. 12), in which the context of the passage before us is referred to as a real historical fact;— and there are the embarrassment, ambiguity, and arbitrariness shown by the allegorical interpreters whenever they attempt to exhibit the truth intended to be conveyed; whereas perspicuity is a characteristic essential to an allegory.—The subtlety of the

[1] So, *e.g.*, *Cramer* in the *Nebenarbeiten zur Theologischen Literatur*, St. 2.

serpent, pointed out in chap. iii. 1, is a natural attribute of that animal; and the comparison, in this respect, of the serpent with the other beasts, clearly indicates that a real serpent is spoken of. To such an one the denunciation of the punishment must necessarily, in the first instance, be referred. The last two reasons also exclude the opinion that Satan assumed merely the semblance of a serpent.

The serpent itself cannot, however, have acted independently; it can only have served as an instrument to the evil spirit. The position which the serpent would occupy, in the event of our considering it as the self-acting, independent seducer, would be in direct contradiction to the position assigned to the animal creation throughout Holy Scripture—especially in the history of the creation—and would break down the limits which, according to it, separate man and beast. By such an assumption we should be transferred from the Israelitish territory—which is distinguished by the most sharply defined limitations of the respective spheres of God, angels, men, and beasts —to the heathenish, were these are all mixed up together, and where all the distinctions disappear in the confusion. Such a fact would be altogether isolated and without a parallel in Holy Scripture. Nor is it legitimate to adduce the argument, that the conditions and circumstances of the paradisaic period were different from those of subsequent times. It is indeed true, according to the statements contained in the Mosaic account itself, that the animal world of that time was different from that of the present; but whatever, and how great soever, this difference may have been, it had no reference to the fundamental relation of the beasts; and hence we cannot, from it, explain the high intellectual powers with which the serpent appears endowed, and by the abuse of which it succeeded in seducing men. Man, as the only being on earth created in the likeness and image of God, is, in Gen. i., strictly distinguished from all other living beings, and invested with the dominion over them. Into man alone did God breathe the breath of life (ii. 7); and, according to ii. 19, 20, man recognises the great gulf which is fixed betwixt him and the world of beasts. This gulf would be entirely filled up, the serpent would altogether step beyond the sphere appointed by the Creator to the world of beasts, if there were no *background* in Gen. iii. 1–5. *Further,* The words of the serpent are an effect of wickedness: they raise in man doubts as to the love of God, in order thereby to seduce him to apostasy, and bring about the execution upon him of the fearful threatening, " On the day that thou eatest thereof thou shalt surely die." The serpent does not stand in the truth; it speaks lies; it represents to man as the highest good, that which in truth is the highest evil. Such language cannot proceed spontaneously from a being, the creation of which falls within the work of the six days during which the whole animal creation was made. For everything created within this space of time was *good,* according to the remark constantly repeated in the history of creation. To this we must add the nature of the curse itself, in which a higher reference to an invisible author of the temptation shines clearly through the lower reference to the visible one; and, further, the remark in iii. 1, " Now the serpent was more subtle," etc., evidently points to something beyond the natural subtlety of the serpent, as the result of which the subsequent words cannot be understood, but behind which we may discover the intimation: let him who reads, understand.

The view, that the serpent was the sole independent agent in this transaction, is thus refuted by internal reasons. It is set aside by the testimony of tradition also. It was an opinion universally prevalent among the Jews, that Satan himself had been active in the temptation of the first man. It is found in *Philo;* and in the Book of Wisdom, ii. 24, it is said, " By the envy of *Satan,* death came into the world." In the later Jewish writings, *Sammael,* the head of the evil spirits, is called הנחש הקדמוני " the old serpent," or simply נחש " serpent," because in the form of a serpent he tempted Eve. (See the passage in *Eisenmenger's entdecktes Judenthum* i. S. 822.) In the sacred books of the Persians also, the agency of Satan in the fall of our first parents is taught. According to the *Zendavesta* (ed. by *Kleuker,* Th. 3, S. 84, 85), the first men, Meshia and Meshianeh, were created by God in a state of purity and goodness, and destined for happiness, on condition of humility of heart, obedience to the requirements of the law, and purity in thoughts, words, and actions. But they were deceived by Ahriman, " this mischievous one who from the beginning sought only to deceive, were induced to rebel against God, and forfeited their happiness by the eating of fruits." According to the same book (Th. iii.

S. 62), Ahriman in the form of a serpent springs down from heaven to earth; and another evil spirit is called (Th. ii. S. 217) the serpent—*Dew*. (Compare *Rhode, die heilige Sage des Zendvolkes*, S. 392.) These facts prove that at the time when the Persian religion received Jewish elements (compare *Stuhr, die Religionssysteme des Orientes*, S. 373), and hence, soon after the captivity, the doctrine of Satan's agency in the temptation of our first parents was prevalent among the Jews.

But of decisive weight upon this point is the evidence furnished by the New Testament. We must here above all consider the important testimony supplied by the fact of the history of the first and second Adam being parallel (Rom. v. 12 sqq.; 1 Cor. xv. 45 sqq.),—a testimony, the weight and importance of which have, in modern times, been again pointed out by *Hahn* in his *Dogmatik*. The necessity of Christ's temptation by the prince of this world, in order that He, by His firm resistance, might deprive him of his dominion over mankind, indicates that Adam was assailed by the same tempter, and, by being overcome, laid the foundation of that dominion.

Among the express verbal testimonies of the New Testament, we must first consider the declarations of the Lord Himself; and among these the passage John viii. 44 requires, above all, to be examined. In that passage the Lord says: ὑμεῖς ἐκ τοῦ πατρὸς τοῦ διαβόλου ἐστὲ, καὶ τὰς ἐπιθυμίας τοῦ πατρὸς ὑμῶν θέλετε ποιεῖν. Ἐκεῖνος ἀνθρωποκτόνος ἦν ἀπ' ἀρχῆς, καὶ ἐν τῇ ἀληθείᾳ οὐχ ἕστηκεν· ὅτι οὐκ ἔστιν ἀλήθεια ἐν αὐτῷ. Ὅταν λαλῇ τὸ ψεῦδος, ἐκ τῶν ἰδίων λαλεῖ· ὅτι ψεύστης ἐστὶ καὶ ὁ πατὴρ αὐτοῦ. There is, indeed, an element of truth in the opinion, that Satan is in this passage called the murderer of men from the beginning, with reference to the murder by Cain—an opinion lately brought forward again by *Nitzsch, Lücke*, and others. This is evident from a comparison of 1 John iii. 12, 15, and of Rev. xii. 3. (See my commentary on this passage.) Moreover, the words in ver. 40, " Ye seek to kill Me," have a more direct parallelism in Cain's murder of his brother, than in the death which Satan brought upon our first parents; although it is altogether wrong to maintain, as *Lücke* does, that Satan at that time committed only a *spiritual* murder, which could not have come under notice. Bodily death also came upon mankind through the

B

temptation. (Compare Gen. ii. 17, iii. 19; Wisd. ii. 24; Rom. v. 12.) But when the reference to Cain's slaying his brother is brought forward as the sole, or even as the principal one, we must absolutely reject it. Cain's murder of his brother comes into consideration only as an effect of the evil principle which was introduced into human nature by the first temptation; as, indeed, it appears in the book of Genesis itself as the fruit of the poisonous tree, the planting of which is detailed in chap. iii. The same murderous spirit which impelled Satan to bring man under the dominion of death by the lie, "Ye shall not surely die," was busy in Cain also, and seduced him to slay his pious brother. The following reasons forbid an exclusive reference to the deed of Cain:—1. The murdering of man by Satan is brought into the closest connection with his *lie*. In connection with Cain's deed, however, there was not even the appearance of falsehood; while, in the case before us, lies, false and deceitful promises of high blessings to be attained, and the raising of suspicions against God, were the very means by which he seduced man, and brought him under the power of sin. The words of Jesus, when they are understood according to their simple meaning, carry us back to an event in the primitive times, in which murder and the spirit of falsehood went hand in hand. 2. The co-operation of Satan in Cain's deed is not expressly mentioned in Genesis. That there was any such we can with certainty infer, only if this event be viewed in close connection with what Satan did against our first parents,—if, behind the serpent, Satan be concealed. Whensoever Jesus has to deal with Jews, He does not teach any mysterious doctrines, but makes an open appeal to the events narrated in Scripture. 3. The words, "Ye are of your father the devil," point to the seed of the serpent spoken of in Gen. iii. 15. 4. The words, "From the beginning," direct to an event which happened at the first beginnings of mankind, and in which our first parents took a part. Whatever this may be, the event in question must be the first in which the devil manifested himself as the murderer of man. Now, as by the Jews of that time the temptation of the first man, in consequence of which death entered the world, was attributed to sin—and this appears not only from what has been already said, but also from a passage in the *Sohar Chadash*, referred to by *Tholuck*, in which the wicked are called "The children of the old serpent which has slain Adam and all who are descended from him"—it is evident that, by "the murderer of men from the beginning," Jesus can mean only the first tempter of men. That the words, "from the beginning," refer to the fall of the first man, is also clearly shown by the parallel passages 1 John iii. 8, and Rev. xii. 9, xx. 2. 5. Jesus says: Satan stands not in the truth, does not move in its element, because there is no truth in him. This points to a well-known event, in which Satan displayed his lying nature; and such is found only in the account of man's fall. 6. Jesus calls Satan not only a liar, but, by way of emphasis, He designates him as the father of lies. But Satan can be designated thus, only with reference to a lie of his which is charged against him by Scripture, and which preceded all lies on earth. Now that is the lie of which we have an account in Gen. iii. 4, 5. The words, "and the father of it," correspond with the words, "from the beginning."

Another declaration of our Lord is found in St Matthew xiii. 38: τὰ δὲ ζιζάνιά εἰσιν οἱ υἱοὶ τοῦ πονηροῦ (i.e., mali, masculinum, according to Bengel), compared with ver. 39: ὁ δὲ ἐχθρὸς ὁ σπείρας αὐτά ἐστιν ὁ διάβολος. The children of the wicked one, or of the devil, who are spoken of in this passage, are the seed of the serpent who is mentioned in Gen. iii. 15, and to whom allusion is made in the words ὁ σπείρας αὐτά also. Less incontrovertible is the passage in St Matthew xxiii. 33, where the Lord addressed the Pharisees as ὄφεις, γεννήματα ἐχιδνῶν. (Compare Matt. xii. 34, iii. 7.) Olshausen, in his commentary on Matt. iii. 7, gives it as his opinion that the serpent designates the diabolic nature. But, according to Matt. xii. 34, the point of comparison is only the wickedness (πονηροὶ ὄντες), and it is quite sufficient to refer it to Ps. cxl. 4, where David says of the future enemies of his dynasty and family foreseen by him, "They have sharpened their tongues like a serpent; adders' poison is under their lips" (compare also Ps. lviii. 5; Deut. xxxii. 33; Isa. lix. 5),—a passage to which special allusion is made in the words, πῶς δύνασθε ἀγαθὰ λαλεῖν, Matt. xii. 34, and in the connection of serpents with vipers, which would be strange when referred to the history of the fall of the first man.

Let us now turn from the Lord to His disciples. Just as is done in the account of the transaction itself, Paul, in 2 Cor.

xi. 3 (ὡς ὁ ὄφις Εὔαν ἐξηπάτησεν ἐν τῇ πανουργίᾳ αὐτοῦ), places the invisible cause of the temptation in the background, and speaks of the visible one only. But that behind the serpent he beholds Satan, appears immediately from ver. 14 and 15: Καὶ οὐ θαυμαστόν· αὐτὸς γὰρ ὁ Σατανᾶς μετασχηματίζεται εἰς ἄγγελον φωτός. Οὐ μέγα οὖν εἰ καὶ οἱ διάκονοι αὐτοῦ μετασχηματίζονται ὡς διάκονοι δικαιοσύνης, where the μετασχηματίζεται is explained by *Bengel*: " *Transformat se: Præsens, i.e., solet se transformare. Fecit id jam in Paradiso.*" The Apostle alludes to an event narrated in Scripture, where Satan shows himself in this character. But such an occurrence is not found anywhere else than in Gen. iii. 4, 5, the only passage where Satan represents himself as the friend and saviour of men. We have here the explanation of the ἐξηπάτησεν in ver. 3.—In Rom. xvi. 20, the words, Ὁ δὲ Θεὸς τῆς εἰρήνης συντρίψει τὸν Σατανᾶν ὑπὸ τοὺς πόδας ὑμῶν, contain an allusion to Gen. iii. 15, too plain to be mistaken. The Apostle recognises, in the promise of the victory over the serpent given there, a pledge of the victory over Satan. The words of Paul to Elymas in Acts xiii. 10, "O thou child of the devil," likewise contain a distinct reference to that which, in the history of man's fall, is written concerning the serpent. In the charge of subtlety, mischief, and enmity to all righteousness which he brings against him, there is an evident allusion to Genesis.

In 1 John iii. 8, Ὁ ποιῶν τὴν ἁμαρτίαν, ἐκ τοῦ διαβόλου ἐστίν· ὅτι ἀπ᾽ ἀρχῆς ὁ διάβολος ἁμαρτάνει, allusion is made to a most heinous sin committed by Satan at the first beginnings of the human race. But of such a sin there is no account, unless Satan be concealed behind the serpent.—In Rev. xii. 9 (comp. xx. 2), Satan is called the great dragon, and the *old serpent;* the last of which designations refers to the passage now under consideration.

The agency of Satan in the fall of man has been controverted, on the plea that, had such been in operation, it ought to have been mentioned. But the absence of any such mention may be explained on the ground that it is not the intention of the holy writers to give any information respecting the existence of the devil, but rather to give an account of his *real* manifestation, to which, afterwards, the doctrine connected itself. The judgment of the reader should not, as it were, be anticipated. The simple fact is communicated to him, in order that, from it, he may form his own opinion.

Further,—It has been asserted that in the entire Old Testament, and until the time of the Babylonian captivity, no trace of an evil spirit is to be found, and that, hence, it cannot be conceived that his existence is here presupposed. But this assertion may now be regarded as obsolete and without foundation. Closely connected with the affirmation, to which allusion has just been made, is the opinion which assigns the Book of Job to the time of the captivity, an opinion which is now almost universally abandoned. This book must necessarily have been written before the time of the captivity, because Jeremiah refers to it, both in his Prophecies (*e.g.,* Jer. xx. 15 sq., which passage evidently rests on Job iii.) and in his Lamentations. (Compare, for a fuller discussion of this subject, *Küper's* "*Jeremias libror. Sacrorum interpres atque Vindex.*") The reference in Amos iv. 3 to Job ix. 8, and several allusions occurring in the Prophecies of Isaiah (*e.g.,* chap. xl. 2 and lxi. 7, which refer to the issue of Job's history, which is here viewed as a prophecy of the future fate of the Church; the peculiar use of צבא in xl. 2, which alludes to Job vii. 1; chap. li. 9, which rests on Job xxvi. 13), lead us still farther back. The assertion of those also who feel themselves compelled to acknowledge the pre-exilic origin of the book, but who maintain, at the same time, that the Satan of this book is not the Satan of the later books of the Old Testament, but rather a good angel who only holds an odious office, is more and more admitted to be futile; so that we must indeed wonder how even *Beck* (*Lehrwissenschaft* i. S. 249) could be carried away by it, and could make the attempt to support this pretended fact by the supposition, that the apostasy of part of the angels from God, and their kingdom of darkness, are ever advancing and progressing. The principal evil spirit is, in Zech. iii. 1, introduced as the adversary of the holy ones of God; and this very name is sufficient to contradict such a supposition, for the name is descriptive of the wickedness of the character. He who, under all circumstances, is an "adversary," must certainly carry the principle of hatred in his heart. He moves about on the earth for the purpose of finding materials for his accusations, and grounds on which he may raise suspicions. It is a cha-

racteristic feature, that he whose darkness does not comprehend
the light, knows of no other piety but that which has its origin
in the hope of reward.   It is quite evident that it is the desire
of his heart to destroy Job by sufferings.   The only circumstance which seems to give any countenance to the supposition
is, that he appears in the midst of the angels, before the throne
of God.   But this circumstance is deprived of all its significancy, if the fact be kept in view—which, indeed, is most
evident—that the book is, from beginning to end, of a purely
poetical character.   The form of it is easily accounted for by
the intention to impress this most important thought: that
Satan stands in absolute dependence upon God; that, with all
his hatred to the children of God, he can do nothing against
them, but must, on the contrary, rather subserve the accomplishment of the thoughts of God's love regarding them.—
Isaiah likewise points to evil-spirits in chap. xiii. 21, xxxiv. 14.
(Compare my Comment. on Rev. xviii. 2.)—But even in some
passages of the Pentateuch itself, the doctrine regarding Satan
is brought before us.   It is true that it has been erroneously
supposed to be contained in Deut. xxxii. 17 (compare on this
opinion, my Comment. on Ps. cvi. 37); but only bigotry and
prejudice can refuse to admit that, under the *Asael*, to whom,
according to Lev. xvi., a goat was sent into the wilderness,
Satan is to be understood.   (The arguments in support of this
view will be found in the author's "*Egypt and the Books of
Moses*," p. 168 ff.)[1]

But we must advert to two additional considerations. *First*,
—To every one who is in the least familiar with the territory

---

[1] The positive reasons by which I there proved the reference to Satan,
have not been invalidated by the objections of *Hofmann* in his *Schriftbeweis* i. 379.   He says: As an adjective formed in a manner similar to
לְכַלְכַל (Num. xxi. 5) must have an intransitive signification, it cannot mean
"separated," but according to its derivation from אָזַל = עָזַל, it means:
"altogether gone away."   But this argument has no force.   The real import of the form of the word is gradation, and frequent repetition.   Instances of a passive signification are given in *Ewald's Lehrbuch der Hebr.
Sprache*, § 157 c.: compare, *e.g.*, Deut. xxxii. 5.   There is so much the
stronger reason for adopting the passive signification, that in Arabic also,
—which alone can be consulted, as the comparison with the Hebrew אָזַל
has no sure foundation on which to rest,—the root has the signification:
remotus, sepositus fuit, and the participle: *a ceteris se sejungens*.   Compare
Egypt and the B. M., p. 169.

of divine revelation, and who has any conception of the relation in which the Books of Moses stand to the whole succeeding revelation, it will, *a priori*, be inconceivable, that a doctrine which afterwards occupies so prominent a position in the revealed books should not have already existed, in the germ at least, in the Books of Moses. *Secondly*,—We should altogether lose the origin and foundation of the doctrine concerning Satan, if he be removed from, or explained away in, the history of the fall. That the first indication of this doctrine cannot by any means be found in the Book of Job, has already been pointed out by *Hofmann*, who remarks in the *Schriftbeweis* i. S. 378, that Satan appears in this book as a well-known being, as much so as are the sons of God. Nor is Lev. xvi. an appropriate place for introducing, for the first time, this doctrine into the knowledge of the people. The doctrinal essence of the symbolical action there prescribed is this :—that Satan, the enemy of the Congregation of God, has no power over those who are reconciled to God ; that, with their sins forgiven by God, they may joyfully appear before, and mock and triumph over, him. The whole ritual must have had in it something altogether strange for the Congregation of the Lord, if they had not already known of Satan from some other source. The questions : Who is Asael ? What have we to do with him ? must have forced themselves upon every one's mind. It is not the custom of Scripture to introduce its doctrines so abruptly, to prescribe any duty which is destitute of the solid foundation of previous instruction.

If thus we may consider it as proved, (1) that the serpent was an agent in the temptation, and (2) that it served only as an instrument to Satan, the real tempter,—then we have also thereby proved that the curse denounced against the tempter must have a double sense. It must, in the first place, refer to the instrument ; but, in its chief import, it must bear upon the real tempter, for it was properly he alone who had done that which merited the punishment and the curse. Let us now, upon this principle, proceed to the interpretation of our passage.

It is said in ver. 14 : " *And Jehovah Elohim said unto the serpent, Because thou hast done this, thou shalt be cursed above all cattle and above every beast of the field ; upon thy belly shalt thou go, and dust thou shalt eat all the days of thy life.*"—If we do not look beyond the serpent, these words have in them something incomprehensible, inasmuch as the serpent is destitute of that responsibility which alone could justify so severe a sentence. There is no difficulty attached to the idea that the serpent must suffer. It shares this fate along with all the other irrational earthly creation, which is made subject to vanity (Rom. viii. 20), and which must accompany man, for whose sake it was created, through all the stages of his existence. But the question here at issue is not about mere suffering, but about well-merited punishment. The serpent is not, like the whole remaining earth, cursed for the sake of man (Gen. iii. 17), but it is cursed because " it has done this." Punishment presupposes being created in the image of God, and, according to chap. i., such a creation is peculiar only to man. But as soon as we assume the co-operation of an invisible author of the temptation, by whom the serpent was animated, everything which is here threatened against the visible instrument acquires a symbolical meaning. The degradation inflicted upon the latter, — the announcement of the defeat which it is to sustain in the warfare with man,—represent in a figure the fate of the real tempter only. The instrument used by him in the temptation is at the same time the symbol of the punishment which he is destined to endure.

Although it be said that the serpent should be " cursed above all cattle," etc., this does not necessarily imply that the other animals are also cursed, any more than the words, " subtle above all the beasts," imply that all other beasts are subtle. It is certainly not always necessary that the whole existing difference should be pointed out. The sense is simply : Thou shalt be more cursed than all cattle. In a similar manner it is said, in the song of Deborah, concerning Jael, " Blessed above women shall Jael be," Judges v. 24 ; for this does not imply that all other women are blessed, but means only that, whether they be blessed or not, Jael, at all events, is the most blessed.

The *eating of dust* must not be interpreted literally, as if the serpent were to feed upon dust ; but, since it is to creep on the ground, it cannot be but that it swallow dust along with its food. Thus we find in Ps. cii., in "the prayer of the afflicted," ver. 10, "For I have eaten ashes like bread," used of occasional swallowing of ashes. As an expression of deepest humiliation, the licking of dust is used in Mic. vii. 17, where it is said of the enemies of the Church, " They shall lick dust like the serpent." In Is. xlix. 23, compared with Ps. lii. 9, the licking up the dust of the feet is likewise inflicted upon the humbled enemies. If, undoubtedly, there be, even in these passages, a slight reference to the one before us, the allusion to it is still plainer in Is. lxv. 25, where it is said, " And dust shall be the serpent's meat." Of the denunciation in Gen. iii. 14, 15, the eating of dust alone shall remain, while the bruising of the heel shall come to an end. And while all other creatures shall escape from the doom which has come upon them in consequence of the fall of man, the serpent—the instrument used in the temptation—shall, agreeably to the words in the sentence of punishment, " All the days of thy life," remain condemned to a perpetual abasement, thus prefiguring the fate of the real tempter, for whom there is no share in the redemption.

The opinion which has been again of late defended by *Hofmann* and *Baumgarten*, that the serpent had before the fall the same shape as after it, only that after the fall it possesses as a punishment what before the fall was its nature, stands plainly opposed to the context. Even *a priori*, and in accordance with Satan's usual mode of proceeding, it is probable that he, who loves to transform himself into an angel of light, should have chosen an attractive and charming instrument of temptation. This view loses all that is strange in it, if only we consider the change of the serpent, not as an isolated thing, but in connection with the great change which, after the fall of man, affected the whole nature (comp. Gen. i. 31, according to which the entire animal creation had, previously to the fall, impressed upon it the image of man's innocence and peace, and the law of destruction did not pervade it, Gen. iii. 17; Rom. viii. 20); and if only we keep in mind that, before the fall, the whole animal world was essentially different from what it is now, so that we cannot by any means think of forming to ourselves a distinct image of the serpent, as *Luther* and others have done.

The serpent is thus, by its disgusting form, and by the degradation of its whole being, doomed to be the visible representative of the kingdom of darkness, and of its head, to whom it had served as an instrument. But the words, when applied to the head himself, give expression to the idea: " extreme contempt, shame, and abasement shall be thy lot." Thus *Calmet* remarks on this passage: "This enemy of mankind crawls, as it were, on his belly, on account of the shame and disgrace to which he is reduced." Satan imagined that, by means of the fall of man, he would enlarge his kingdom and extend his power. But to the eye of God the matter appeared in a totally different light, because, along with the fall, He beheld the redemption.

Ver. 15. "*And I will put enmity between thee and the woman, and between thy seed and her seed; and it shall bruise thy head, and thou shalt bruise its heel.*" In the two other passages where the word שׁוּף occurs (Ps. cxxxix. 11 [compare my commentary on that passage] and Job ix. 17), it undeniably signifies: "to crush," "to bruise." This signification, therefore, which is confirmed by the Chaldee Paraphrast, and which Paul also follows in Rom. xvi. 20 (συντρίψει, whilst the LXX. have τηρήσει), must here also be retained. It is only in appearance that, in the second passage referred to, the signification "to crush" seems to be inappropriate; for there, "to crush" is used in the sense of "to destroy," "to annihilate," just as in Jonah iv. 7, "to strike" is used of the sting of an insect, because its effect is similar to that produced by a stroke. The words ראֹשׁ and עָקֵב are a second accusative governed by the verb, whereby the place of the action is more distinctly marked out. That by "head" and "heel"—a *majus* and a *minus*—a victory of mankind over the seed of the serpent should be signified, was seen by *Calvin*, who says, "Meanwhile we see how graciously the Lord deals even in the punishment of men, inasmuch as He does not give the serpent power to do more than wound the heel, while to man is given the power of wounding its head. For the words 'head' and 'heel' point out only what is superior and what is inferior." That these words are by no means intended to describe the mutual antipathy between men and serpents, is rendered evident by the consideration, that, if such were the intention, no special punishment would be denounced against the serpent, while, according to the context, such denunciation is certainly designed by the writer. The words treat of the punishment of the serpent; it is only in ver. 16 that the sentence against man is proclaimed. It is true that the bite of a serpent is dangerous when it is applied even to the heel, for the poison thence penetrates the whole body; but to this fact in natural history there is here no allusion, nor is the *biting* of the serpent at all the point here in question. The contrast between head and heel is simply that which exists between the noble and less noble parts,—those parts of which the injury is commonly curable or incurable. The objection: "The serpent creeps, man walks upright; if then an enmity exists between them, how can it be otherwise than that man wounds its head, and that it wounds his heel?" entirely overlooks the consideration, that, according to ver. 14, it is in consequence of the divine curse that the serpent creeps in the dust. In this degraded condition—a condition which is not natural, but inflicted as a punishment—it is implied that the serpent can attack man at his heel only. This plain connection between ver. 15 and 14 is evidently overlooked by those who hold the opinion, that this mutual enmity is pernicious equally to man and serpent. The very circumstance that the serpent is condemned to go on its belly, and to eat dust, whilst man retains that erect walk in which the image of God is reflected, paves the way for the announcement of the victory in ver. 16.

Experience bears ample witness to the truth of the divine sentence, that there shall, in future, be enmity between the seed of the serpent and mankind, in so far as this sentence refers to the instrument of the temptation; for abhorrence of the serpent is natural to man. Thus *Calvin* remarks: "It is in consequence of a secret natural instinct that man abhors them; and as often as the sight of a serpent fills us with horror, the recollection of our apostasy is renewed."

But, in the fate of the serpent which is here announced, there is an indication of the doom of the spiritual author of the temptation. It has been objected that any reference to Satan is inadmissible, because the "seed of the serpent" here spoken of cannot designate wicked men, who are "children of the devil;" for these, too, belong to the seed of the woman, and cannot, therefore, be put in opposition to it. But against this objection *Storr*, in his treatise, *de Protevangelio*, remarks: "We easily see that many of the seed of the woman likewise belong to the seed of the serpent; but they have become unworthy of that name, since they apostatized to the common enemy of their race." It is quite true that, by the seed of the woman, her whole progeny is designated; but they who enter into commu-

nion with the hereditary enemy of the human race are viewed
as having excommunicated themselves.   Compare Gen. xxi. 12,
where Isaac alone is declared to be the true descendant of
Abraham, and his other sons are, as false descendants, excluded.
Moreover, not only wicked men, but also the angels of Satan
(Matt. xxv. 41; Rev. xii. 7–9), belong to the seed of the serpent.
The greater number of the earlier Christian interpreters
were of opinion that, by the seed of the woman, the Messiah is
directly pointed at.   But to this opinion it may be objected,
that it does violence to the language to understand, by the seed
of the woman, any single individual; and the more so, since we
are compelled to understand, by the seed of the serpent, a plurality of individuals, viz., the spiritual children of Satan, the
heads and members of the kingdom of darkness.   *Further*,—As
far as the sentence has reference to the serpent, the human race
alone can be understood by the seed of the woman; and to this,
therefore, the victory over the invisible author of the temptation
must also be adjudged.   The reference to the human race is
also indicated by the connection between "her seed" in this
verse, and the words, "Thou shalt bring forth sons," in ver. 16.
Finally,—As the person of the Messiah does not yet distinctly
appear even in the promises to the Patriarchs, this passage cannot well be explained of a personal Messiah; inasmuch as, by
such an explanation, the progressive expansion of the Messianic
prophecy in Genesis would be destroyed.
If, however, by the seed of the woman we understand the
entire progeny of the woman, we obtain the following sense:
"It is true that thou hast now inflicted upon the woman a severe
wound, and that thou and thine associates will continue to assail
her: but, notwithstanding thine eager desire to injure, thou
shalt be able to inflict on mankind only such wounds as are
curable; while, on the contrary, the posterity of the woman
shall, at some future period, vanquish thee, and make thee feel
all thy weakness."
This interpretation is found as early as in the Targum of
Jonathan, and in that of Jerusalem, where, by the seed of the
woman, are understood the Jews, who, at the time of the Messiah, shall overcome Sammael.   Thus, too, does Paul explain it
in Rom. xvi. 20, where the promise is regarded as referring to
Christians as a body.   It has found, subsequently, an able de-

fender in *Calvin*,[1] and, in modern times, in *Herder*.[2] The treatise of *Storr*, too (in the *Opusc.* ii.), is devoted to its defence.

Even according to this interpretation, the passage justly bears the name of the *Protevangelium*, which has been given to it by the Church. It is only in general terms, indeed, that the future victory of the kingdom of light over that of darkness is foretold, and not the person of the Redeemer who should lead in the warfare, and bestow the strength which should be necessary for maintaining it. Anything beyond this we are not even entitled to expect at the first beginnings of the human race; a gradual progress is observable in the kingdom of grace, as well as in that of nature.

It is certainly, however, not a matter of chance that the posterity of the woman is not broken up into a plurality, but that, in order to designate it, expressions in the singular (זרע and הוא) are chosen. This unity, which, in the meanwhile, it is true, is only *ideal*, was chosen with regard to the person of the Redeemer, who comprehends within Himself the whole human race. And it is not less significant, and has certainly a deeper ground, that the victory over the serpent is assigned to the seed of the woman, not to the posterity of Adam; and though, in-

---

[1] He says,—This, therefore, is the sense of the passage: "The human race, whom Satan had endeavoured to destroy, shall at length be victorious. But, meanwhile, we must bear in mind the mode in which, according to Scripture, that victory is to be achieved. According to his own pleasure, Satan has, through all centuries, led captive the sons of men, and even to this day he continues that sad victory. But, since a stronger one has come down from heaven to subdue him, the whole Church of God shall, under her Head, and like Him, be victorious."

[2] *Briefe das Studium der Theologie betr.* ii. S. 225 (Tüb. 1808): "The serpent had injured them; it had become to them a symbol of evil, of seduction, and at the same time of God's curse, of contempt and punishment. To men the encouraging prospect was held out, that they, the seed of the woman, were stronger and nobler than the serpent, and all evil. They should tread upon the head of the serpent, while the latter should be able to avenge itself only by a slight wound in their heel. In short, the good should gain the ascendancy over the evil. Such was the prospect. How clear or how obscure it was to the first human pair, it is not our present purpose to inquire. It is enough that the noblest warrior against evil, the most valiant bruiser of the serpent's head from among the descendants of Eve, was comprehended in this prospect, and indeed pre-eminently referred to. Thus, then, only an outline, as it were, was given to them in a figure, the import of which only future times saw more clearly developed."

deed, the circumstance that the woman was first deceived may have been the proximate cause of it, yet it cannot be exclusively referred to, and derived from, it. By these remarks we come still nearer to the view of the ancient Church.

THE BLESSINGS OF NOAH UPON SHEM AND JAPHETH.

(GEN. ix. 18–27.)

Ver. 20. "*And Noah began and became an husbandman, and planted vineyards.*"—This does not imply that Noah was the first who began to till the ground, and, more especially, to cultivate the vine; for Cain, too, was a tiller of the ground, Gen. iv. 2. The sense rather is, that Noah, after the flood, again took up this calling. Moreover, the remark has not an independent import; it serves only to prepare the way for the communication of the subsequent account of Noah's drunkenness. By this remark, a defence of Noah on account of his drunkenness is entirely cut off. Against such a defence *Luther* expressed himself in very strong terms: "They," says he, "who would defend the Patriarch in this, wantonly reject the consolation which the Holy Ghost considered to be necessary to the Church—the consolation, namely, that even the greatest saints may, at times, stumble and fall."[1]

Ver. 21. "*And he drank of the wine, and was drunken; and he was uncovered within his tent.*"

Ver. 22. "*And Ham, the father of Canaan, saw the nakedness of his father, and told his two brethren without.*"—David is reproved in 2 Sam. xii. 14, for having given occasion to the enemies of God to blaspheme. The same reproof might justly be administered to Noah also. Ham rejoiced to find a nakedness in him whose reproving earnestness had often been a burden to his sinful soul. *Luther* remarks: "There is no doubt

---

[1] The object of this event, as pointed out by *Calvin*, viz., that God intended to give to all coming ages, in the person of Noah, a warning and an exhortation to temperance, would likewise be frustrated by this unwarrantable apology.

that he (Noah) must have done much which was offensive to his proud, high-minded, and presumptuous son. . . . For this reason we must not regard this deed of Ham as mere child's play, as an action destitute of all significance ; but as the result of the bitterest hatred and resentment of Satan, by which he prepares and excites his members against the true Church, and specially against those who are in the ministry. Let them, therefore, give earnest heed as to whether, either in their persons or in their offices, they give any occasion for blasphemy. We have in this history an example of divine terrors and judgment, that we may take warning from the danger of Ham, and not venture to be rash in judging, though we should see that a secular or ecclesiastical authority, or even our parents, do err and fall."

Ver. 23. *"And Shem and Japheth took the garment."*— *Luther* says : "Such an outward and lovely reverence they could not have shown to their father, if they had not, inwardly and in their hearts, been rightly disposed towards God, and had not considered their father as a high priest and king set over them by divine appointment." The mode of expression indicates that the real impulse proceeded from Shem, and that, as a prefiguration of what was to take place, Japheth only showed susceptibility for the good, and a willingness to join with him. It is true that the singular ויקח is not, by itself, decisive. When the verb precedes, it is not absolutely necessary that it should agree with the *subject* in gender and number ; but the use of the singular is, nevertheless, remarkable. If Shem and Japheth had been equally active, the latter also would, at once, have been present to the mind of the writer. Under these circumstances, there is the less reason for supposing that the use of the singular can be merely accidental, especially as the words, "and he told his *two brethren* without," immediately precede. But all doubt is removed by a second allusion, which goes hand in hand with the first, and which is contained in the following verse.

Ver. 24. *" And Noah awoke from his wine, and knew what his younger son had done unto him."*—That Ham was older than Japheth, appears from the circumstance that the order in which the sons of Noah are introduced is uniformly thus : Shem, Ham, Japheth ; or, beginning, as in chap. x., from the youngest,

Japheth, Ham, Shem,—where, however, in ver. 21, the words added immediately after Shem—"the elder brother of Japheth," expressly indicate that, for a certain purpose, the writer has proceeded in order from the youngest to the oldest. It is altogether in vain that some have attempted to prove from chap. xi. 10 (according to which Shem was, two years after the flood, only a hundred years old), compared with chap. v. 32 (according to which Noah began to beget when he was five hundred years old), that Shem was not the first-born. The words in chap. v. 32 are: "And Noah was five hundred years old, and Noah begat Shem, Ham, and Japheth." That the chronology can here be determined in a way which only approximates to the truth, is implied, as a matter of course, in the statement, that all the three sons were begotten when Noah was five hundred years of age; nothing more is meant than that Noah begat them after he had finished his fifth, or at the beginning of his sixth, century. (Compare *Ranke's Untersuchungen*.) It is just an indefinite statement of time which points forward to another genealogy, in which the details will be given with greater precision. Ham everywhere stands between the two; but that, nevertheless, he is, in this passage, called the younger son, can be explained only on the ground that, in the case before us, Shem and Ham are the two more especially noticed—Shem as positively good, and Ham as positively evil, while Japheth only takes part with Shem. We have thus laid an excellent foundation for the right understanding of the subsequent prophetic utterance of Noah—for the announcement, namely, of Japheth's dwelling in the tents of Shem.

Ver. 25. "*And he said, Cursed be Canaan; a servant of servants shall he be to his brethren.*"—*Luther* says: "Good old Noah, who is regarded by his son as a foolish and stupid old man, deserving only of mockery, appears here in truly prophetic majesty, and announces to his sons a divine revelation of what shall come to pass in future days; thus verifying what Paul says in 2 Cor. xii., that God's strength is made perfect in weakness."

According to the opinion now current, Canaan is said to mean "lowland," and to be transferred from the land to the people, and from the people to the pretended ancestor. But this opinion is shown to be untenable by the considerations, that, according to historical tradition, Canaan appears first as the name of the ancestor;—that the verb כנע is never used of natural lowness, but always of humiliation;—that in our passage, where the name first occurs, it stands in connection with servitude;—that the masculine form of the noun (on the adjective termination *an*, compare *Ewald's Lehrb. d. Heb. Spr.* § 163, b.) is not applicable to the country;—that the country Canaan is so far from being a lowland, that it appears, everywhere in the Pentateuch, as a land of hills (see Deut. xi. 2, iii. 25, where the land itself is even called, " that goodly mountain ") ;[1]—and, finally, that, from all appearance, Canaan is primarily the name, not of the country, but of the people—the former being called ארץ כנען, the land of Canaan.

The real etymology of the name is almost expressly given in Judges iv. 23 ; ויכנע, " and God bowed down, or *humbled*, on that day Jabin the king of *Canaan.*" Compare also Deut. ix. 3, where, in reference to the Canaanites, it is said, הוא יכניעם, " He will humble or subdue them;" and Nehem. ix. 24 : " Thou bowedest down before them the inhabitants of the land—the Canaanites." Our passage also proceeds upon this interpretation of the name. We are the rather induced to assume a connection betwixt the name " Canaan," and the words, " a servant of servants shall he be," as in the case of Japheth also there is certainly an allusion to the signification of the name, and probably in the case of Shem also. Perhaps even the name Ham, *i.e.*, " the blackish one," may be connected with the character which he here displays—a suggestion which we do not here follow up. We refer, however, for an analogy, to what has been remarked in our Commentary on the Psalms, in the Introduction of Ps. vii.

Canaan means : " the submissive one." It is a name which the people themselves, on whose monuments it appears, would never have appropriated to themselves (just as in the case of the Egyptians also, on which point *Gesenius* in the *Thesaurus,* and my work *Egypt,* etc., p. 210, may be compared), unless it had been proper to them from their very origin. Ham gave this name to his son from the obedience which he demanded, but

---

[1] The reverse is the case with reference to Aram, which is essentially a lowland, while these critics would have us to believe that it means " highland." (Compare *Baur* on Amos, S. 229.)

did not himself yield. The son was to be the servant of the father (for the name suggests servile obedience), who was as despotical to his inferiors as he was rebellious against his superiors. When the father gave that name to his son, he thought only of submissiveness to *his* orders; but God, who, in His mysterious providence, disposes of all these matters, had another submissiveness in view.

But why is Canaan cursed and not Ham? For an answer to this question, we are at liberty neither to fall back upon the sovereign decree of God, as *Calvin* does, nor to say with *Hofmann*: "Canaan is the youngest son of Ham (Gen. x. 6); and because Ham, the youngest son of Noah, had caused so much grief to the father, he, in return, is to experience great grief from his youngest son." This latter view rests upon false historical suppositions. We have already proved that Ham was not the youngest son of Noah; and it by no means follows from Gen. x. 6, that Canaan was the youngest son of Ham. Canaan's name is mentioned last among the sons of Ham, because the whole account of Ham's family was to be combined with the detailed enumeration of Canaan's descendants, who stood in so important a relation to Israel. The boundary line as regards Shem is formed, quite naturally, by that branch of Ham's family which stood in so 'important a relation to the main branch of the family of Shem. But, as little reliance can be placed upon the theological grounds of that conjecture; for the question at issue is not the withdrawal of outward advantages. Canaan is *cursed*, and it is just the sting of his servitude that it is the consequence of the curse. It would indeed sadly affect the biblical doctrine of recompense, if cursing and blessing were dependent upon such external reasons as, in the case before us, upon the circumstance that Canaan was so unfortunate as to be the youngest son.

The right answer to the question is without doubt this :— Ham is punished in his son, just as he himself had sinned against his father. He is punished in *this* son, because he followed most decidedly the example of his father's impiety and wickedness. To this view we are led by the whole doctrine of Holy Scripture concerning the visitation of the guilt of the fathers upon the children. (Compare the author's "*Dissertations on the Genuineness of the Pentateuch*, vol. ii. p. 373.)

To this view we are also led by the passage in Gen. xv. 16:
" But in the fourth generation they shall come hither again, for
the iniquity of the Amorites is not yet full." According to
this passage, the curse on Canaan can be realized upon him,
only when his own iniquity has been fully matured. This his
iniquity is presupposed by his curse. If he were to be punished
on account of the guilt of the father,—a guilt in which he had
no share,—then indeed no delay would have been necessary.
To this view we are farther led by what is reported in Genesis
concerning the moral depravity of Sodom and Gomorrah, which,
in the development of the sinful germ inherent in the race, had
outrun all others, and were, therefore, before all others, overtaken by punishment. (To this view we are further led by
what is reported in Genesis concerning the moral depravity of
Sodom and Gomorrah, which, in the development of the sinful
germ inherent in the race, had outrun all others, and were
therefore, before all others, overtaken by punishment) To this
view we are led, *further*, by Lev. xviii. and the parallel passages, where the Canaanites appear as a nation of abominations
which the land spues out; and, *finally*, by what ancient heathen
writers report regarding the deep corruption of the Phœnicians
and Carthaginians.

The remainder of Ham's posterity are passed over in silence;
it is only in the sequel that we expect information regarding
them. But the foreboding arises, that their deliverance will be
more difficult of accomplishment than that of Japheth, although
the circumstance that Canaan is singled out from among them
affords us decided hope for the rest.

But not even the exclusion of Ham is to be considered as an
unavoidable fate resting upon him. Heathenism alone knows
such a curse. The subjective conditions of the curse imply the
possibility of becoming free from it. To this, there is an express testimony in the circumstance, that the promise to the
Patriarchs is not limited. David received the remnant of the
Canaanitish Jebusites into the congregation of the Lord. (Compare remarks on Zech. ix. 7.) And, in the Gospels, the Canaanitish woman appears as a representative of her nation, and
as a proof the possibility, granted to them, of breaking through
the fetters of the curse. (Compare also the remarkable passage, Ezek. xvi. 46.)

" The curse is contrasted with the blessing pronounced on Shem and Japheth, and the second member of ver. 25 is, in vers. 26, 27, used as a repetition in reference to each of the two brethren, who were, in it, viewed together."—(*Tuch.*)

Ver. 26. " *And he said: Blessed be Jehovah, the God of Shem; and Canaan shall be a servant to them.*"—The Patriarch Noah,—a just man, and one who walked before God (Gen. vi. 9),—a man raised on high, as David says of himself in 2 Sam. xxiii. 1,—a man whose utterances are not mere individual wishes, but, at the same time, prophecies,—sees such rich blessings in store for his son, that, instead of announcing them to him, he immediately breaks out into the praise of God, who is the Author of them, and from whom the piety of Shem,[1] the foundation of this salvation, was derived, just as Moses, in Deut. xxx. 20, instead of blessing Gad, blesses him by whom Gad is enlarged. The manner in which God is here spoken of indicates, *indirectly*, what that is in which the blessing consists. *First*,—God is not called by the name *Elohim* (which is expressive of merely the most general outlines of His nature), but by the name *Jehovah*, which has reference to His manifested personality, to His revelations, and to His institutions for salvation.[2] *Secondly*,—Jehovah is called the God of Shem,— the first passage of Holy Scripture in which God is called the God of some person. Both these circumstances indicate that God is to enter into an altogether peculiar relation to the descendants of Shem; that He will reveal Himself to them; establish His kingdom among them, and make them partakers of both His earthly and His heavenly blessings. Thus *Luther* says: " This is indeed perceptible and clear, that he thus binds closely together God and his son Shem, and, as it were, commits the one to the other. In this, he indeed indicates the mystery of which Paul treats in Rom. xi. 11 sq., and Christ, in John iv. 22, that salvation cometh from the Jews, but that, nevertheless, the heathen shall become partakers of it. For

---

[1] *Bochart* remarks : " He cursed the guilty one in his own person, because the source and nourishment of evil is in man himself. But, rejoiced at Shem's piety, he rather blessed the Lord, because he knew that God is the Author of everything which is good."

[2] With reference to the difference between these two names, compare the disquisitions in the author's " *Genuineness of the Pent.*," vol. i. p. 213 ff.

although Shem alone be the real root and trunk, yet into this tree the Gentiles are, as a strange branch, graffed, and enjoy the fatness and sap which are in the elect tree. This light Noah, through the Holy Spirit, sees, and although he speaks dark words, he yet prophesies very plainly, that the kingdom of the Lord Jesus Christ shall be planted in the world, and shall grow up among the race of Shem, and not among that of Japheth." As yet Shem and Japheth were on an equal footing. In the preceding part of the narrative, nothing had been communicated by which God had, in His relation to Shem, given up His nature as Elohim, and had become his God. It is only by anticipation, then, that God can, in His relation to Shem, be designated as Jehovah, and as the God of Shem. The thought can, when fully brought out, be this alone: " Blessed be God, who will, in future, reveal Himself as Jehovah, and as the God of Shem."

If it be overlooked that, in this appellation of God, there is implied the indirect designation of the blessings which are to be conferred on Shem (just as in Gen. xxiv. 27 the words, " Blessed be Jehovah, the God of my master Abraham," imply the thought : because. He has manifested Himself as Jehovah, and as the God of my master ; which thought is then further carried out in the subsequent words : " And who hath not left destitute my master of His mercy and His truth ;"—and just as it is also in the utterance of Zacharias in Luke i. 68, where the words, " Blessed be the Lord [κύριος], the God of Israel," imply the thought : because He has manifested Himself as the Lord [in the New Testament, κύριος is used where the Old has Jehovah], the God of Israel),—if this be overlooked, we obtain only a weak and inadequate thought, very unsuitable to the context, the purport of which evidently is to celebrate Shem, and to mark him out as worthy of his name. So it is according to *Hofmann*, who, in the words, " Blessed—Shem," finds only an expression of gratitude for the gift of this good son, and who limits the announcement of blessings to the single one— that Canaan shall be Shem's servant. Against this feeble interpretation we must adduce these considerations also : that nowhere does the gift of the good son form, even indirectly, the subject in question ;—that thus we should lose the opposition of the curse and the blessing (which requires that, under the " Blessed be Jehovah," we should have concealed the " Blessed be Shem"), just as we should, the contrast between Jehovah here and Elohim in the following verse;—and, lastly, that what, in the following verse, is said of Japheth's dwelling in the tents of Shem, would thus be deprived of its necessary foundation.

It is said: " Canaan shall be a servant to *them*." The suffix ‏מוֹ‎, which cannot be used for the singular, any more than can the suffix ‏ם‎, for which it is only the fuller poetical form (the instances of a different use, adduced by *Ewald*, § 247, d., can easily be explained in accordance with the rule), indicates that the announcement has no reference to the personal relation of Shem and Ham, but that they come into view solely as the heads of families.

Ver. 27. *May God enlarge Japheth, and may he dwell in the tents of Shem; and Canaan shall be a servant to them.*"—These words, in the first instance, contain the blessing pronounced upon Japheth; but they entitle us to infer from them, at the same time, a glorious blessing destined for Shem, which is the source of blessing to Japheth also. They thus complete the promise of the preceding verse, which directly refers to Shem.

The first clause of this verse has received a great variety of interpretations. The word ‏יַפְתְּ‎, which refers to, and is explanatory of, the name ‏יֶפֶת‎ (i.e. Japheth), is the future apoc. *Hiphil* of ‏פָּתָה‎. The *Piel* of this verb has in Hebrew commonly the signification: " to persuade, or prevail upon any one to do anything." Hence many interpreters translate with *Calvin*: " May God allure Japheth that he may dwell in the tents of Shem." *Luther* also, in his Commentary, thus explains it: " God will kindly speak to Japheth;" while, in his translation, he has: " May God enlarge Japheth."—But to this interpretation it has been rightly objected, that the verb ‏פתה‎ is found only in Piel, not in Hiphil, with the signification " to persuade;" that, commonly, it signifies " to persuade" only in a bad sense; and that, in this sense, it is never construed with ‏ל‎, but always with the accusative.—All interpreters now agree that (in conformity with the LXX. [πλατύναι ὁ Θεὸς τῷ Ἰάφεθ], the *Vulgate* [dilatet Deus Japhet], and *Onkelos*) ‏יַפְתְּ‎ must be derived from ‏פתה‎ in its primary signification, " to be wide, large," in which it is found in Prov. xx. 19 (where ‏שֹׂפָתָיו‎

is accusative denoting the place), and which signification is the common one in Aramaic.   But they then again disagree, inasmuch as some think of a local extension : God shall give to Japheth a numerous posterity, which shall take possession of extended territories ; while others find here expressed the idea of general prosperity : God shall prosper Japheth, shall bring him into a free and unstraitened position.

Both of these views partake of a like mistake from regarding the words *per se*, and as disconnected from the following announcement of Japheth's dwelling in the tents of Shem.   It must also be objected to them, that in the case of Shem, only one feature of the blessing is pointed out, viz., that God will be to him Jehovah, *his* God ; and so, likewise, only one feature of the curse in the case of Ham.   When those words are isolated, separated from what follows, and understood of extension, this difficulty arises, that Ham enjoys this extension in common with Japheth, as is shown by a glance at Gen. x.   If, on the other hand, we understand them as expressive of prosperity (according to *Hofmann* : " general prosperity in the affairs of outward life"), this explanation is destitute of a sufficient foundation, and there is nothing reported in the sequel regarding the fulfilment of such a promise.   To this we must further add, that the verb יפת is, on account of its immediate nearness to the proper name, too little expressive, and that, hence, we must expect to find its meaning more fully brought out in what follows.

But if it be acknowledged that the extension appears here as a blessing, in so far only as it leads to the dwelling in the tents of Shem, mentioned in the subsequent clause of the verse, and that the blessing can consist in nothing else, there is then no essential difference betwixt the two interpretations.   But we decide in favour of the *latter* view, because the corresponding verb הרחיב, " to make wide, to enlarge," when construed with ל, is always used in the signification : " to bring into a free, unstraitened, easy, happy position."   (See, *e.g.*, Gen. xxvi. 22 ; Ps. iv. 2 ; Prov. xviii. 16 ; 2 Sam. xxii. 20.)   Even when followed by an accusative, the verb is found with this signification in Deut. xxxiii. 20 : " Blessed be He that enlargeth Gad."   (In this passage, too, the word has been understood as denoting extension ; and Deut. xii. 20, xix. 8, have been appealed to in support of the opinion ; but this appeal is inadmissible, because extension of the borders is the thing which is there spoken of. The allusion to the signification of the name *Gad* = good luck [Gen. xxx. 11 : " And Leah said, For good luck ;[1] and she called his name Gad "], is favourable to our view, as well as the circumstance, that in this case the subsequent words are only an expansion of the general thought, and more closely determine the happiness. Jehovah, who enlarges Gad, according to the words which follow, " He dwelleth like a lion, and teareth the arm with the crown of the head," is contrasted with the enemies who wish to drive him into a strait. If room be made for him, he becomes happy, as it were, by enlargement.) To understand יַפְתְּ of prosperity and happiness, is countenanced also by the consideration that, in such circumstances, the name Japheth appears much more appropriate in the mouth of Noah, by whom it was uttered at a time when extension could be but little thought of, and that it corresponds much better with the name Shem.

Elohim is to enlarge Japheth. Elohim here stands in strict contrast with Jehovah, the God of Shem. It is only by dwelling in the tents of Shem, that Japheth passes over into the territory of Jehovah,—up to that time, he belongs to the territory of Elohim. But Elohim leads him to Jehovah. It is a contrast in all respects similar to that which we have in Gen. xiv., where, in verse 19, Melchizedek speaks of " the most high God," whose priest he is, according to verse 20 ; while Abraham, on the contrary, speaks, in verse 22, of " Jehovah the most high God."

There is a difference of opinion regarding the determination of the subject in the second clause of the verse : " and he shall dwell in the tents of Shem." According to a very ancient interpretation, Elohim is to be supplied as such ; from which the following sense would be obtained : " God shall indeed enlarge and prosper Japheth, but He shall dwell in the tents of Shem."

[1] Our English authorized version translates the first clause of this verse thus : " And Leah said, A troop cometh,"—a rendering which cannot be objected to on etymological grounds, and which receives some support from Gen. xlix. 19. The ancient versions, however, are quite unanimous in assigning to the נד in בגד the signification of "fortune," " good luck ;" and render it either : " in or for good luck ;" " luckily," " happily " (so the LXX. et Vulg.), or, following *Onkelos* and the Mazorets : " good luck has come."—(Tr.)

The inferior blessing of Japheth would thus be contrasted with the superior one of Shem, among whose posterity God should, by His gracious presence, glorify Himself,—first in the tabernacle, then in the temple, and lastly, should, in the highest sense, dwell by the incarnation of His Son. Thus *Onkelos*: "God shall extend Japheth, and His Shechinah shall dwell in the tents of Shem." The ancient book *Breshith Rabba* remarks on this passage: "The Shechinah dwells only in the tents of Shem." (See *Schöttgen, de Messia*, p. 441.) *Theodoret* also (Interrog. 58 in Genesin) advances this explanation, and ably brings out this sense. It has of late been again defended by *Hofmann* and *Baumgarten*. But against this view there are decisive arguments, which show that Japheth alone can be the subject. To mention only a few:—It cannot be doubted that it is on purpose that Noah, when speaking of Shem, has chosen the name Jehovah, and that, as soon as he comes to Japheth, he makes use of the name Elohim. We cannot, therefore, suppose that here, where, according to this interpretation, he would just touch upon the essential point in the peculiar relation of Jehovah to the descendants of Shem—the Israelites, he should have made use of the general name of Elohim, as in the case of Japheth. The subject—Jehovah—could not in this case have been omitted before ישכן. *Further*,—By such an interpretation we are involved in inextricable difficulties as regards the last clause of the verse. The words, "And Canaan shall be a servant to them," can neither be referred to Shem alone—for, in that case, they would be an useless repetition, as in ver. 25 Canaan had been doomed to be a servant to *his brethren*—nor can they be referred to Shem and Japheth at the same time; the analogy of the למו in the preceding verse, where the plural referred to the plurality represented by the one Shem, forbids this. If, then, the last clause can refer to Japheth only, the clause in which the dwelling in the tents of Shem is spoken of, must likewise be referred to Japheth. To these arguments we may *further* add, that there is something altogether strange in the expression: "God shall dwell in the tents of Shem." There is, in Holy Scripture, frequent mention of God's dwelling in His tabernacle, on His holy hill, in Zion, in the midst of the children of Israel. Believers also are said to dwell in the tabernacle or temple of God; but nowhere is

God spoken of as dwelling in the tents of Israel. *Further,*— If we refer the second clause to Shem, the first, in its detached position, would be too general, too indefinite, and too loose to admit of the blessing of Japheth being concluded with it. We must not, moreover, lose sight of the consideration, that when we refer the second clause also to Japheth, there springs up a beautiful connection between the relation of Shem and Japheth to each other in the present, and during their future progress. As the reaction against the corruption of Ham had originated with Shem, and Japheth had only joined him in it; so in future also, the real home of piety and salvation will be with Shem, to whom Japheth, in the felt need of salvation, shall come near. *Finally,*—The analogy of the promise made to the Patriarch, according to which all the nations of the earth shall be blessed by the seed of Abraham, is in favour of our referring the second clause to Japheth. And if the Lord, alluding to our passage, says, in Luke xvi. 9, "Make to yourselves friends of the mammon of unrighteousness, that when ye fail they may receive you into everlasting habitations" (σκηνή = אהל), He expresses the view which we are now defending. For, in that passage, it is not God who receives, but man: they who, by their prayers, are more advanced, come to the help of those who have made less progress; those who have already attained to the enjoyment of salvation, make them partakers who stand in need of salvation.

Of those who correctly consider Japheth to be the subject, several (*J. D. Michaelis, Vater, Gesenius, Winer, Knobel*) give the translation: "and he shall dwell in renowned habitations." But it is quite evident that this sense is admissible only as a secondary one: as such, we must indeed admit it in a context in which the appellative signification of the proper names is never lost sight of. That שם is here, however, primarily a proper name, is shown by the preceding verse.

The translation, "Japheth shall dwell in the tents of Shem," is, then, the correct one. But now the question is,—How are these words to be understood? According to the views of many interpreters, it is intimated by Japheth's dwelling in the tents of Shem, that the true religion would be preserved among the posterity of Shem, and would pass over from them to the descendants of Japheth, who should be received into the community of the worshippers of the true God. So *Jonathan* explained its meaning: "The Lord shall make glorious the end of Japheth; his sons shall be proselytes, and shall dwell in the schools of Shem." So also *Jerome:* "Since it is said, And he shall dwell in the tents of *Shem,* this is a prophecy concerning us, who, after the rejection of Israel, enjoy the instruction and knowledge of the Scriptures." *Augustine* also (*c. Faustum* xii. 24) understands by the tents of Shem, "the churches which the apostles, the sons of the prophets, have built up."

But although this explanation be, in the main, correct, it cannot, *per se,* satisfy us. It must be reconciled with that other explanation given by *Bochart* (*Phaleg.* iii. 1 c. 147 sqq.), *Calmet, Clericus,* and others, according to which the passage is to be understood literally, as foretelling that the posterity of Japheth should, at some future time, gain possession of the country belonging to the descendants of Shem, and should reduce them to subjection.

The phrase, "and they dwelt in their tents," is, in 1 Chron. v. 10, used to express the relation of conquerors and conquered. There is no parallel passage which could indubitably prove that "dwelling in the tents of some one" could ever, by itself, denote spiritual communion with him. If Shem had come to Japheth with the announcement of salvation only, it is not likely that a dwelling of Japheth in the tents of Shem would have been spoken of. Even the last clause of the verse—"and Canaan shall be a servant to them"—when compared with the preceding verse, according to which Canaan is, in the first place, to be Shem's servant only, supposes that Japheth will step beyond his borders, and will invade the territory naturally belonging to Shem. If Japheth assume the dominion of Shem over Canaan, he must then dwell in the tents of Shem in a sense different from the merely spiritual one. *Finally*—Even in other passages of the Pentateuch, an invasion of Shem's territory by Japheth is foretold. In Num. xxiv. 24, Balaam says: "And ships shall come from the coast of Chittim and shall afflict Asshur, and shall afflict Eber, and he also shall perish." "We have here (compare my monography on Balaam) the announcement of a future conquest of the Asiatic kingdoms by nations from Europe, such as was historically realized in the Asiatic dominion of the Greeks and Romans."

On the other hand, however, it must not by any means be supposed that Noah should, in favour of Japheth, have weakened the power of the brilliant promise given to Shem by the announcement of such a sad event; for it is evidently his intention to exalt Shem above his brethren, as highly as he had excelled them both in his piety towards his father.

The difficulties which stand in the way of either explanation are easily removed by the following consideration. The occupation of the land of Shem by Japheth is the condition of Japheth's dwelling in the tents of Shem. Why this dwelling is a blessing to Japheth—"God shall enlarge Japheth, and he shall dwell," etc.—appears from what precedes, according to which, God reveals Himself to Shem as Jehovah, and becomes *his* God. To be received into the fellowship of Jehovah—to find Him in the tents of Shem—constitutes the blessing promised to Japheth. But if such be the case, there can be no more room for speaking of an announcement of any event adverse to Shem. Underneath the adversity, joy is hidden. It will here be fulfilled in its highest sense, that the conquered give laws to the conquerors.

"And Canaan shall be a servant to them." The servitude of Canaan was completed by Japheth, among whose sons (Gen. x. 2) Madai also appears; so that even the Medo-Persian kingdom is one of Japheth's. Phœnicia was completely overthrown by him. Haughty Tyrus fell to the ground. Zech. ix. 3, 4, when announcing the Greek dominion (compare ver. 13), says: "And Tyrus did build herself a stronghold, and heaped up silver like dust, and fine gold as the mire of the streets. Behold, the Lord will cast her out, and He will smite her power in the sea, and she shall be devoured with fire."

The objection raised by *Tuch* and *Hofmann*, that the Greeks and Romans made Shem also their servant, is, after what has been remarked, destitute of all weight, inasmuch as the servitude then had reference only to the lower territory. Shem and Judah were not injured in that which, in ver. 26, had been pointed at as their chief and peculiar good. On the contrary, it shone out, on that occasion, in its highest glory. Canaan, however, lost that upon which he set the highest value. In the case of Canaan, the servitude was the consequence of the curse; but in the case of Shem, the outward servitude was a consequence of the blessing, the most emphatic verification of the words: "Blessed be Jehovah, the God of Shem."

It must indeed fill us with adoring wonder when we see how clearly and distinctly the outlines of the world's history, as well as of the history of Salvation, are here traced. "This," says *Calvin*, "is indeed a support to our faith of no common strength, that the calling of the Gentiles was not only predestined in God's eternal decree, but also publicly proclaimed by the mouth of the Patriarch; so that we are not required to believe that by a sudden and fortuitous event merely, the inheritance of eternal life was proclaimed to all men in common."

It is not a matter of *chance* that this prophecy was given immediately after the deluge, which stands out as so great an event in the history of the fallen human race,—the first event, indeed, subsequent to the fall, with which the *Protevangelium* was connected. A new period begins with the calling of Abraham, and in it we obtain another link in the chain of the prophecies, —a link which fits as exactly into that which is now under consideration, as did this into the *Protevangelium*. The import of this prophecy is: "The kingdom of God shall be established in Shem, and Japheth shall be received into its community."—The meaning of the prophecy which is now to engage our attention is: "By the posterity of the Patriarchs all the nations of the earth shall be blessed." The promise to the Patriarchs differs, however, from the prophecy upon which we have just commented, not only in the natural progress—that from among the descendants of Shem a narrower circle is separated—but in this circumstance also, that in the former the blessing is extended to all the nations of the earth, while in the latter Ham is passed over in silence. This difference, however, has its main foundation in the historical circumstances of the latter prophecy; although, it is true, the complete silence which is observed regarding him, calls forth apprehensions about his being less susceptible of salvation, or, at least, of his not occupying any prominent position in the development of the kingdom of God. Here, where the object was to punish Ham for his wickedness, not the prosperous, but the adverse events impending upon him in his posterity, are brought prominently out; while, on the other hand, to Shem and Japheth blessings alone are foretold.

THE PROMISE TO THE PATRIARCHS.

A GREAT epoch is, in Genesis, ushered in with the history of
the time of the Patriarchs. *Luther* says : "This is the third
period in which Holy Scripture begins the history of the Church
with a new family." In a befitting manner, the representation
is opened in Gen. xii. 1–3 by an account of the first revelation
of God, given to Abraham at Haran, in which the way is opened
up for all that follows, and in which the dispensations of God
are brought before us in a rapid survey. Abraham is to forsake
everything, and then God will give him everything.

Gen. xii. 1. "*And the Lord said unto Abraham, Get thee
out of thy country, and from thy home, and from thy father's
house, into a land that I will show thee. Ver. 2. And I will make
of thee a great nation, and I will bless thee, and make thy name
great ; and thou shalt be a blessing. Ver. 3. And I will bless them
that bless thee, and him who curseth thee I will curse : and in thee
all the families of the earth shall be blessed.*"

"*Into a land that I will show thee.*" From what follows, it
appears that, in the very same revelation, the country was afterwards *more definitely* pointed out ; for Abraham, without having
received any new revelation, goes to Canaan. For the sake of
brevity, the writer gives the details only afterwards, when he has
occasion to report how they were carried out. The land which
God will show to Abraham, stands contrasted with that in which
he is at home,—in which he and his whole being had taken root.
This contrast points out the greatness of the sacrifice which God
demands of Abraham. With a like intent we have the accumu-
lation of expressions—" out of thy land," etc.—corresponding to
a similar one when the command was given to sacrifice Isaac
(Gen. xxii. 2), and forming the condition of the promise which
follows. This promise is intended to make the sacrifice a light
thing to Abraham, by pointing out what he is to receive if he
give up everything which stands in the way of his living to
God. A similar call comes to all who feel impelled to renounce
the world in order to serve God. This call to Abraham is peculiar only as to its form ; as to its essence, it is ever repeating
itself. This will appear the more distinctly, when we inquire
into the true reason of the *outward* separation here demanded of

Abraham. It can be intended only as a means of the *internal* separation. In the circle in which he lived, sin had already made a mighty progress, as appears from Josh. xxiv. 2,—a passage which shows us that idolatry had already made its way into the family of Abraham. In order to withdraw him from the influences of this corruption, Abraham is removed from the circle in which he had grown up, and in which he had hitherto moved. That the special thing here demanded is only the result of the general duty of renunciation and self-denial, which is here, in Abraham, laid upon the whole Church, appears from the circumstance, that the promise was renewed at a subsequent period, when, with a willing heart, he had offered up his son Isaac as a spiritual sacrifice to his God. The carnal, ungodly love to Isaac is thus placed on a level with the attachment to the land, etc., which came betwixt him and his God. The general idea, that self-renunciation lies at the foundation, is brought out in Psalm xlv. 11.

The words, *"And thou shalt be a blessing,"* imply more than the words, "I will bless thee :" they are intentionally placed in the centre of the whole promise. Abraham shall, as it were, be an embodied blessing—himself blessed, and the cause of blessing to all those who bless him—to all the generations of the earth who shall, at some future period, enter into this loving and grateful relation to him. On the ground of Abraham's self-denial, and unreserved surrender, blessing is poured out *upon him*, blessing also *on his account* and *through him*. The blessing connected with him begins with himself, and extends over all the families of the earth.

"And I will bless them that bless thee, and him that curseth thee I will curse." The blessing is based upon the turning to Him who has appointed Abraham for a blessing, as we may learn from the example of Melchizedek, Gen. xiv. 19. They who bless are themselves not far from the kingdom of God ; blessing, therefore, is the preparatory step towards being blessed. (Compare Matt. x. 40–42.)

"And in thee shall all the families of the earth be blessed." *Luther* says : "Now there follows the right promise, which ought to be written in golden letters, and proclaimed in all lands, and for which we ought to praise and glorify."

The promise stands here in close connection with the Mosaic

history of the creation. According to that, man, as such, bears upon him the impress of the divine image, Gen. i. 26, and is the depository of the divine breath, Gen. ii. 7. From such a beginning, we cannot conceive of any limitation of salvation which is not, at the same time, a means of its universal extension. It must therefore be in entire accordance with the nature of the thing, that even here, where the setting apart of a particular chosen race takes its rise, there should be an intimation of its universally comprehensive object. There is, in the circumstance of *families* being spoken of, a distinct reference to the history of creation ; משפחה everywhere corresponds exactly with our word "family." It is everywhere used only of the subdivisions in the greater body of the nation or tribe. The expression, then, points to the higher unity of the whole human race, as it has its foundation in the fact that all partake in common of the divine image.

The announcement of the blessing in this passage leads us back to the curse pronounced in consequence of sin, Gen. iii. 17: "Cursed is the ground (*Adamah*) for thy sake." (Compare Gen. v. 29.) This curse is, at some future time, to be abolished by Abraham. We can account for the mention of the families of the "Adamah" only by supposing that a reference to this passage was fully intended; for it was just the "Adamah" (primarily, "land") which had there been designated as the object of the curse.

In announcing that all the families shall be blessed in Abraham, the writer refers also to the judgment described in Gen. xi., by which the family of mankind,—which, according to the intention of God, ought to have been united,—was dispersed and separated. When viewed in this connection, we expect that the blessing will manifest itself in the healing of the deep wound inflicted upon mankind, in the re-establishment of the lost unity, and in the gathering again of the scattered human race around Abraham as their centre.

Beyond this, no other disclosure about the nature of this salvation is given. But that it consisted essentially in the union with God accomplished through the medium of Abraham, and that everything else could be viewed as emanating only from this source, was implied simply in the circumstance, that all the blessing which Abraham enjoyed for himself had its origin in this, that he could call God *his God;* just as, in Gen. ix., it had been declared as the blessing of Shem, that Jehovah should be his God, and as the blessing of Japheth, that he was called to become a partaker of this blessing. The blessings which were either bestowed upon or promised to the Patriarchs and their descendants, had for their object the advancement of knowledge and the practice of true religion, and had been bestowed or promised only under this condition (compare Gen. xvii. 1, xvii. 17–19, xxii. 16–18, xxvi. 5); they could not hence expect anything else than that their posterity would, in so far, be the cause of the salvation of the heathen nations, that the latter should, by means of the former, be made partakers of the blessings of true religion.

With regard to the manner in which this blessing was to come to the Gentiles, no intimation was given by the words themselves. The person of the Redeemer is not yet brought before us in them; the indication of that was reserved for a later stage in the progress of revelation.[1]

The last clause of ver. 3 cannot, by any means, take away from the import of the preceding one; the announcement of the blessing which, through Abraham, is to come upon all the families of the earth, does not repeal the foregoing one, according to which all shall be cursed who curse him. This view is confirmed by an allusion to this announcement in Zech. xiv. 16–19, where the words, "the families of the earth," must be regarded as a quotation. In ver. 16, the prophet says that *all the Gentiles* shall go up to Jerusalem to celebrate the Feast of Tabernacles; but then, in vers. 17–19, he intimates the punishment of those who should refuse to go up. *Luther* says: "If you wish to

---

[1] *Herder* says, in his *Briefe das Studium der Theol.* betr. ii. S. 278: "If, in Abraham's descendants, all the nations of the earth were to be blessed, Abraham might and should have conceived of this blessing in all its generality, so that everything whereby his nation deserved well of the nations of the earth, was implied in it. If, then, Christ also belongs to the number of those noble individuals who deserved so well, the blessing refers to Him, not *indirectly,* but *directly;* and if Christ be the chief of all this number, it then most directly, and in preference to all others, refers to Him; —although, in this germ, Abraham did not distinctly perceive His person, did not, nor could, except by special revelation, in this bud, so plainly discover the full growth of His merits."

D

comprehend in a few words the history of the Church from the time of Abraham down to our days, then consider diligently these four verses. For in them you will find the blessing; but you will see also, that those who curse the Church are cursed, in turn, by God; so that they must perish, while the eternal seed of the Church stands unmoved and unshaken. For which reason, this text agrees with the first promise given in Paradise, concerning the seed which is to bruise the serpent's head. For the Church is not without enemies, but is assailed and harassed so that she groans under it; but yet, by this seed, she is invincible, and shall at length be victorious, and triumphant over all her enemies, in eternity."

References to this fundamental prophecy are found in other parts of the Old Testament, besides the passage just quoted from Zechariah. In the 28th verse of Ps. xxii., which was written by David, it is said: "All the ends of the world shall remember, and turn unto the Lord; and all the *families* of the Gentiles shall worship before Thee." The realization of the blessing announced in Genesis, to all the families of the earth, appears in this psalm as being connected with the wonderful deliverance of the just. Another reference is in Ps. lxxii., which was written by Solomon. In ver. 17 of this psalm it is said of Solomon's great Antitype: "And they shall bless themselves in Him, all nations shall bless Him." In these words the realization of the Abrahamitic blessing is distinctly connected with the person of the Redeemer.

Among the New Testament references, the most remarkable is in John viii. There, in ver. 53, the Jews say to Christ: "Art thou greater than our father Abraham, which is dead? Whom makest thou thyself?" Jesus, in ver. 56, answers: "Your father Abraham rejoiced to see My day; and he saw it, and was glad." In ver. 57 the Jews reply: "Thou art not yet fifty years old, and hast thou seen Abraham?" In ver. 58 Jesus thus says to them: "Verily, verily, I say unto you, Before Abraham was, I am."

Let us here, in the first place, consider only the declaration of Jesus, that Abraham rejoiced to see His day, and was glad. It is altogether out of the question to think of any such explanation of this as the one given by *Lücke*, after the example of *Lampe* namely: "that Abraham, in the heavenly life, as a blessed spirit with God, saw the day of the Lord, and in heaven rejoiced in the fulfilment." For it is the custom of Jesus to argue with the Jews from *Scripture;* and He cannot, therefore, here be appealing to an assumed fact which could not be proved from it. The answer of the Jews, in ver. 57, is likewise opposed to such an explanation, inasmuch as it proceeds from a supposition which Jesus had acknowledged to be true, namely, that the question at issue was a meeting of Christ with Abraham not mentioned in history; and in ver. 58 Christ sets aside their argument, "Thou art not yet fifty years old." But *Lücke* must himself bear testimony against his own interpretation, inasmuch as, according to it, he is obliged to speak of "the very foolish question of the adversaries."[1]

Jesus saw Abraham, and Abraham saw Jesus. Not the person, but the day of Christ, was future to Abraham. And this can be explained only by Jesus' being concealed behind Jehovah who appeared to him, and gave him the promise, that in him and his seed all the nations of the earth should be blessed. This blessing of all the families of the earth is the day of Jehovah,—the day when He will be glorified on the earth.

The key to the right understanding of this is furnished by the doctrine of the Angel of the Lord, which meets us as early as in Genesis. From the passages in which, at the appearances and revelations of Jehovah, the mediation of the Angel is expressly mentioned, we infer that it (the mediation) took place even when Jehovah by Himself is spoken of; and the more so, since, even in the former series of passages, the simple name of Jehovah is commonly varied by that of the Angel of Jehovah. The Evangelist John's whole doctrine of the *Logos* points to the personal identity of Jesus with the Angel of the Lord. Not less so does the passage, John xii. 41; and there is unquestionably a purpose which cannot be misunderstood in the fact, that, throughout the discourses of Jesus, as reported by John, the declaration that God *sent* Him occurs with such frequency and regularity. But we can scarcely conceive of any other purpose than that of marking out Jesus as the Angel or Messenger of Jehovah spoken of in the writings of the Old Testament. Compare, *e.g.*, xii. 44,

---

[1] Even in this he was preceded by *Lampe,* who remarks: "Christ had spoken of seeing the day; the Jews speak about seeing the person. He had spoken of Abraham's seeing; they speak of Christ's seeing."

45 : " Jesus cried and said, He that believeth on Me, believeth not on Me, but on Him that *sent* Me ; and he that seeth Me, seeth Him that *sent* Me." So also iv. 34, v. 23, 24, 30, 37, vi. 38–40, vii. 16, 28, 33, viii. 16, 18, 26, 29, ix. 4, xii. 49, xiii. 20, xiv. 24, xv. 21, xvi. 5.

Let us now, in addition, turn to the words, "Abraham rejoiced to see (literally, that he might see) My day." It cannot be liable to any doubt, that these words express the heartfelt, joyful desire of Abraham to see that day, and that *Bengel* correctly explains it by the words: *gestivit cum desiderio*. It is true, ἀγαλλιάομαι signifies, by itself, only "to rejoice;" but it has added to it the idea of joyful desire by its being connected with ἵνα. The words now under consideration are expressive of Abraham's joy and longing in the spirit for the manifestation of the day of Jehovah and of Christ, while those in the last clause of the verse express the gratification of this longing, which was produced by his receiving the promise that all the families of the earth should be blessed.

The ardent desire of Abraham to see the day of Christ implies that he already *knew* Christ, which can be the case only on the supposition of Christ's concealment in Jehovah. This longing desire is not expressly mentioned in Genesis, but it is most intimately connected with all living faith, and must necessarily precede such divine communications. The seed of the divine promises is everywhere sown only in a well prepared soil. That the promise in 2 Sam. vii. was to David, in like manner, a gratification of his anxious desire—an answer to prayer—we are not, it is true, expressly told in the historical record; and yet, that it was so, is evident from the words of Ps. xxi. 3: "Thou hast given him his heart's desire, and hast not withholden the request of his lips." There is here, then, express mention made of that which is a matter of course, and which forms the necessary condition of that which was reported in Genesis.

We are furnished by the Book of Genesis itself with the right explanation of what is meant by the day of Christ, about which interpreters have so frequently erred. It is not the time of His first appearing, but, in accordance with the New Testament mode of expression (*e.g.*, Phil. i. 10), the time of His glorification. The day of Christ is the time when the promise, "In thee shall all the families of the earth be blessed," shall be fulfilled.

Peter quotes this promise in Acts iii. 25, 26. Among the families of the earth he enumerates, first and chiefly, the people of the Old Testament dispensation; and he does so with perfect propriety, since there is no warrant whatever for limiting it to the Gentiles.

Paul probably refers to this promise when, in Rom. iv. 13, he speaks of a promise given to Abraham and his seed that he should be the heir of the world. A blessing imparted to the whole world is a spiritual victory obtained over the world. The world is, in a spiritual sense, conquered by Abraham and his seed. Express references are found in Gal. iii. 8, 14, 16.

The same promise is repeated to Abraham in Gen. xviii. 18. Instead of the משפחות האדמה (the families of the earth), the גויי הארץ (the nations of the earth) are there mentioned; the family-connection is lost sight of, and the comprehensiveness only—the catholic character of the blessing—is prominently brought out. This promise is a third time repeated to Abraham in chap. xxii. 18, on a very appropriate occasion, even that on which, by his endurance of the greatest trial, and by his willingness to sacrifice to God even what was dearest to him, he had proved himself a worthy heir of it. It is certainly not a matter of mere accident that this promise is just three times given to Abraham. There is in this a correspondence with the three individuals to whom the same promise is addressed. Abraham, however, as the first of them, and as the father of the faithful, could not be put on the same footing with the others. Instead of "in thee, or "by thee" (בך), we read in xxii. 18, "in" or "by thy seed" (בזרעך). The same promise is confirmed to Isaac in chap. xxvi. 14, and it is transferred to Jacob in chap. xxviii. 14. But while, in the first and second passages, it is said, "by thee," and in the third and fourth, "by thy seed," we read, in the passage last mentioned, "by thee and thy seed." This evidently shows that, in those passages where we find "by thee" standing alone, we are not at liberty to explain it as meaning simply: "by thy seed." It is not only the seed of Abraham, but Abraham himself also, who is to be the medium of blessing to the nations, as the foundation-stone of the large building of the Church of God, as the father of our Lord Jesus Christ according to the flesh, and as the father of all believers.

There is a deep reason for the fact that, wherever the pos-

terity of the Patriarchs are spoken of as the instruments of blessing, the singular is always used. This circumstance is pointed
out by Paul in Gal. iii. 16. The Apostle does not in the least
think of maintaining that, by זֶרַע "seed," only a single individual could be signified. Such an opinion, no one who understood Hebrew could for a moment entertain; and Rom. iv. 13
shows that Paul was indeed very far from doing so. The
further development of the promise (which took place within
the limits of Genesis itself, in chap. xlix. 10), as well as its fulfilment (it is, indeed, with reference to the promise now under
consideration that the lineal descent of Christ from Abraham is
established at the commencement of Matthew's Gospel), showed
that the real cause of the salvation bestowed upon the Gentiles
was not the seed of Abraham as a whole, but one from among
them, or rather He, in whom this whole posterity was comprehended and concentrated. Now, all to which Paul intends to
draw our attention is the fact, that the Lord, who, when He gave
the promise, had already in view its fulfilment which He had
Himself to accomplish, did not unintentionally choose an expression which, besides the comprehensive meaning which would
most naturally suggest itself to the Patriarchs, admitted also of
the more restricted one which was confirmed by the fulfilment.
In the *Protevangelium*, and in the promise of the Prophet in
Deut. xviii., we have a case quite analogous to this; and in
2 Sam. vii. there is likewise a case which is, to a certain extent,
parallel.

In two passages out of the five—in chap. xxii. 18 and xxvi. 4
—the Hithpael of the verb בָּרַך instead of the Niphal is found.
We meet with it also again in the derived passage in Ps. lxxii.
17, where it is said of the great King to come, "And they shall
bless themselves in Him, all nations shall bless Him." In xxii.
18 and xxvi. 4, we shall be allowed to translate only thus:
"They shall bless themselves in thy seed." For the Hithpael
of בָּרַך always signifies "to bless oneself;" and the person from
whom the blessing is derived (Isa. lxv. 16; Jer. iv. 2), or
whose blessing is desired, is connected with it by means of the
preposition בְּ. (Compare Gen. xlviii. 20: "In thee shall Israel
bless, saying, God make thee as Ephraim and as Manasseh.")
From the nature of the case, it is evident that only the latter
can be meant here. This is shown also by the derived passage

in Ps. lxxii. 17, where the words, "they shall bless themselves in Him," are explained by the subsequent expression, " they shall bless Him."

But it is certainly not accidental that the Hithpael is on both sides inclosed by the Niphal, and that the latter stands not only twice at the beginning, but also at the end. Hence we are not at liberty to force upon the Hithpael the signification of the Niphal; but the passages in which the Hithpael occurs must be supplemented from the real fundamental passages. " To bless oneself *in*" is the preparatory step to being "blessed *by*." The acknowledgment of the blessing calls forth the wish to be a partaker of it. (Compare Isa. xlv. 14, where, in consequence of the rich blessings poured out upon Israel, the nations make the request to be received among them.) Oftentimes in the Psalms utterance is given to the expectation that, through the blessing resting on the people of God, the Gentiles will be allowed to seek communion in it. See my Commentary on Ps. vol. iii. p. lxxvii.) But especially in Ps. lxxii. does it clearly appear how "blessing oneself in" is connected with " being blessed by." The very same people who bless themselves in the glorious King to come, hasten to Him to partake in the fulness of the blessings which He dispenses. He has dominion from sea to sea; they that dwell in the wilderness bow before Him; all kings worship Him; all nations serve Him.

Several commentators (*Clericus, Gesenius, de Wette, Maurer, Knobel,* and, in substance, *Hofmann* also) attempt to explain the fundamental passage by the derived ones, and force upon Niphal the signification of Hithpael; so that the sense would be only that a great and, as it were, proverbial happiness and prosperity belonged to Abraham: " Holding up this name as a pattern, most of the eastern nations will comprehend all blessings in these or similar words: ' God bless thee as He blessed Abraham.'" But this explanation is, according to the *usus loquendi*, incorrect, inasmuch as the Niphal is used only in the signification " to be blessed," and never means "to bless oneself," or " to have or find one's blessing in something." To a difference in the significations of the Niphal and the Hithpael, we are led also by the circumstance that the Hithpael is connected only with the seed—" they shall bless themselves in thy seed,"—and the Niphal only with the person of the Patriarch:

" they shall be blessed in thee," and " in thee and thy seed."
The Patriarchs themselves are the source of blessing, but, if
these nations *blessed themselves*, they wish for themselves the
blessing of their descendants exhibited before their eyes. The
reference in Zech. xiv. 17, 18 to the promise made to the Patriarchs presupposes the Messianic character, and the passive
signification of נברכו. In like manner, all the quotations of it
in the New Testament rest on the passive signification. It is
from this view of it that the Lord says that Abraham saw His
day ; that, in Rom. iv. 13, Paul finds, in this promise, the prophecy of His conquering the world ; and that, in Gal. iii. 14, he
speaks of the blessing of Abraham upon the Gentiles through
Christ Jesus.   Gal. iii. 8 and Acts iii. 25 render נברכו by
ἐνευλογηθήσονται. The explanation, " they shall wish prosperity
or happiness to each other," is destructive of the gradation, so
evident in the fundamental passage,—blessing *for, on account
of*, and *by* Abraham ; it cannot account for the constant, solemn
repetition of this proclamation which everywhere appears as the
acme of the promises given to the Patriarch ; it destroys the
correspondence existing between this blessing upon all the families of the earth, and the curse which, after the fall, was inflicted upon the earth ; it does away with the contrast, so clearly
marked, between the union of the families of the earth effected
by the blessing, and their dispersion, narrated in chap. xi.; it
demolishes the connection existing between the prophecy of
Japheth's dwelling in the tents of Shem (ix. 27), on the one
hand, and the Ruler proceeding from Judah, to whom shall be
the obedience of the nations (xlix. 10), on the other ; and it
severs all the necessary connecting links which unite these prophecies with one another.

Another attempt to deprive this promise of its Messianic
character—that, namely, made by *Bertholdt (de ortu theol. Vet.
Hebr.* p. 102) and others, who would have us to understand, by
the families and nations of the earth, the Canaanitish nations—
does not require any minute examination, as the weakness of
these productions of rationalistic tendency are so glaringly
manifest.

THE BLESSING OF JACOB UPON JUDAH.

(GEN. xlix. 8–10.)

Ver. 8. *" Judah, thou, thy brethren shall praise thee ; thy hand shall be on the neck of thine enemies ; before thee shall bow down the sons of thy father. Ver. 9. A lion's whelp is Judah ; from the prey, my son, thou goest up ; he stoopeth down, he coucheth as a lion, and as a full-grown lion, who shall rouse him up? Ver. 10. The sceptre shall not depart from Judah, nor lawgiver from between his feet, until Shiloh come, and unto Him the people shall adhere."*

Thus does dying Jacob, in announcing " what shall befall his sons in the end of the days" (ver. 1), speak to Judah, after having dismissed those of his sons to whom, in the name of the Lord, he must tell hard things—things which did not, however, exclude them from the salvation common to all of them (ver. 28), although their shadow made the light of Judah shine so much the more brightly.[1]

In ver. 8 everything depends upon a right determination of the meaning of the name Judah. Being formed from the Future in Hophal, it signifies : " He (viz., God) shall be praised." This explanation rests upon Gen. xxix. 35, where Leah, after the birth of Judah, says, " Now will I praise the Lord ;" and then follow the words : " therefore she called his name Judah." It rests likewise on the common use of the verb ידה, the Hiphil of which is, according to *Maurer,* almost constantly used of " praising God," and is, as it were, set apart and sanctified for that purpose. After having enumerated a multitude of passages, *Gesenius* says, in his *Thesaurus :* " In all these passages it refers

---

[1] *Luther* says : " No doubt the sons of Jacob will have waited with anxious desire, and with weeping and groaning, for what their father had yet to say ; for, after having heard curses so hard and severe, they were very much confounded and afraid. And Judah, too, will certainly not have been able to refrain from weeping, and will have been afraid, when thinking of what should now become of him. There will have arisen in his heart very sad recollections of his sins, of his whoredom with Thamar, and of the advice which he had given to sell Joseph. Certainly, I should have died with sorrow and tears. But there soon follow a fine dew and a lovely balm, refreshing the heart again."

to the praise of God, and it is only rarely (Gen. xlix. 8 compared with Job xl. 14) that it refers to the praise of men." Even these few exceptions are such only in appearance. In Job xl. 14, he whom God will praise is not an ordinary man, but a *god-man*. By the subsequent words in Gen. xlix. 8, "Before thee shall bow down," something divine is ascribed to Judah; we need not therefore be astonished that, by the word יודוך, he is raised above the merely human standing. They only who do not know the Lion of the tribe of Judah, have any reason to explain away, by a forced exposition, the slight allusion to a superhuman dignity of the tribe of Judah. The greater number of expositors, referring to the subsequent words, " thy brethren shall praise thee," explain the name by the expression, " blessed one." But, even though we should retain the sure explanation which has been given above, the idea now mentioned falls very naturally in with it. He who, in the fullest sense, is a " God's-praise" (*Gottlob*), whose very existence becomes the cause of exclaiming, δόξα τῷ Θεῷ, praise be to God, will assuredly receive praise from the brethren.—"Judah thou " stands (according to Gen. xxvii. 36; Matt. xvi. 18) either for, " Thou art Judah," *i.e.*, thou art rightly called so, or, according to Gen. xxiv. 60, for, " Thou Judah," *i.e.*, I have something particular to tell thee (compare the emphatic " I " in Gen. xxiv. 27).—On the expression, " Thine hand shall be in the neck of thine enemies," *i.e.*, thou shalt put to flight all thine enemies, and press them hard while they are fleeing, compare Exod. xxiii. 27, " I will make all thine enemies (turn their) backs unto thee," and Ps. xviii. 41, where David says, in the name of his family, in which Judah centred, as did Israel in Judah, " Thou hast given me mine enemies (to be) a back." If, however, we inquire how this prophecy was fulfilled, we must not overlook the circumstance that the subjects of it are sinful men, and that, for this reason, God could never give up the right of visiting their iniquity,— a right which has its foundation in His very nature. Three sentences of condemnation precede the blessing upon Judah, and this indicates that Judah too will be weighed in the balance of justice. " The excellency of dignity and the excellency of power," which, in ver. 3, were taken from Reuben, are here adjudged to Judah. The circumstance of his being the first-born could not protect the former against the loss of his privileges; and just as little will the divine election deliver Judah from a visitation for his sins, although, by that election, the total loss of his privileges is rendered impossible. These two ordinations—the election and the visitation of sin in the elect —stand by the side of each other; and the latter could not be stayed, even at the time when Judah had reached its height in the Lion from out of his tribe; for although the Shepherd was blameless, yet the flock was not so. The ordination of election is, however, far from being thereby darkened; it only shines by a brighter light. Often painful indeed were the defeats which Judah had to sustain; often enough—as during the centuries which elapsed between the destruction of David's kingdom and the coming of Christ—was the promise, "Thy hand shall be in the necks of thine enemies," reversed. But when we behold Judah ever and anon returning and rising to the dignity here bestowed upon him,—when the advance then always keeps equal pace with the preceding depths of humiliation (we need think only of David's time, and compare it with the period of the Judges),—then indeed it appears all the more clearly, that the hand of God is ever active in bringing this promise to a sure and firm fulfilment. In the history of the world there is only one power—that of Judah—in which, notwithstanding all defeats, the promise, "Thy hand shall be in the necks of thine enemies," is ever, after all, fulfilled anew; only one power, the victorious energy of which may indeed be overcome by sleep, but never by death; only one power which can speak as does David in the name of his family in Ps. xviii. 38–40: "I pursue mine enemies and overtake them, I do not return till they are consumed; I crush them, and they cannot rise: they fall under my feet. And Thou girdest me with strength for the war, Thou bowest down those that rise against me."—Luther remarks on this passage: "These promises must be understood in spirit and faith. This may be seen from the history of David, where it often appears as if God had altogether forgotten him, and what He had promised to him. After he had already been elected, he was, for ten years, not able to obtain a fixed place, or residence in the whole kingdom; and when at last he took hold of the reins of government, he fell into great, grievous, heinous sin, and was sore vexed when he had to bear the punishment of it. Therefore these two things—promise and faith—must always be combined; and it is necessary that a man who has a divine promise know well the art which Paul teaches in Rom. iv. 18, to believe in hope even against hope.—The kingdom of Israel, too, was assailed by so great weakness, and pressed down by so many burdens, that it appeared as if every moment it would fall; and this was especially the case when sin, and punishment in consequence of sin, broke in upon them, as, for instance, after David's adultery with Bathsheba, and oftentimes besides. Yet, even in all such temptations, it always remains, on account of the promise."—It must be carefully observed that the words, "Thy hand shall be in the neck of thine enemies," are placed between, "Thy brethren shall praise thee," and "Before thee shall bow down the sons of thy father," and that, immediately after this, Judah's victorious power against the enemies of God's people is again pointed out. This teaches us that the exalted position which Judah, when compared with his brethren, occupies, rests mainly on this:—that he is their fore-champion in the warfare against the world, and that God has endowed him with conquering power against the enemies of His kingdom. The history of David is best calculated to show and convince us, how closely these two things are connected with each other. That he was called to verify the truth of the promise given to Judah, "Thy hand shall be in the neck of thine enemies," was first seen in his victory over Goliath the Philistine, fore-champion of the world's power. After David's word had been fulfilled, "The Lord who delivered me out of the paw of the lion, and out of the paw of the bear, He will deliver me out of the hand of this Philistine," and the Philistines had fled, seeing that their champion was dead (1 Sam. xvii. 37–51), then also were fulfilled the other words: "Thy brethren shall praise thee, the sons of thy father shall bow before thee." "And it came to pass as they came, when David was returned from the slaughter of the Philistine, that the women came out of all the cities of Israel, singing and dancing, to meet King Saul, with tabrets, with joy, and with instruments of music. And the women answered one another as they played, and said, Saul has slain his thousands, and David his ten thousands."—And in Sam. xviii. 16, it is said: "But all Israel and Judah *loved* David, *because* he went out and came in before them;"—and in 2 Sam. v. 2, when the ten tribes acknowledged David as their king, they said: " Also in time past, when Saul was king over us, thou wast he that leddest out and broughtest in Israel." David would never have succeeded in overcoming the jealousy and envy of the other tribes, unless the promise, "Thy hand shall be in the neck of thine enemies," had been fulfilled in him.—*Before Judah shall bow down the sons of his father*. I have already remarked, in my commentary on Rev. xix. 10, that there is very little ground for the common distinction between religious and civil προσκύνησις (bowing down, worship). The true distinction is between that προσκύνησις which is given to God, either directly or indirectly, in those who bear His image, in the representatives of His gifts and offices,—and that προσκύνησις which is exacted apart from, and against God. "The God of Scripture demands to be honoured in those who bear His image, who hold His offices,—in father and mother and old men (Lev. xiv. 32), in princes (Exod. xxii. 28), in the office of the judge (Deut. i. 17; Exod. xxi. 6, xxii. 7, 8). It is wicked to refuse this honour, and its natural expression in the bowing of the body, under the pretext, that it is due to *God* alone. It is to be refused only where there is some danger that, thereby, any independent honour would be ascribed to the mere vessel of the divine glory." In what the προσκύνησις consists, which Judah is to receive from his brethren, we see distinctly from Isa. xlv. 14, where the heathen, at the time of the salvation, fall down before Israel: "Thus saith the Lord, The labour of Egypt and merchandise of Ethiopia, and the Sabeans, men of stature, shall come over unto thee, and be thine: they shall go behind thee; in chains they shall walk; *and they shall fall down before thee, and they shall make supplication unto thee* (saying), *Only in thee is God, and there is no God else.*" The ground of Judah's adoration on the part of his brethren is this:—that God's glory is visibly upon him, that by glorious deeds and victories the seal is impressed upon him: "with us is God" (*Immanuel*). And this found its most glorious fulfilment in the Lion of the tribe of Judah, in Christ, of whom it is said in Phil. ii. 9—11: "Wherefore God has highly exalted Him, and given Him a name which is above every name; that at the name of Jesus every knee should bow, of all those who are in heaven, and on earth, and under the earth; and that every tongue should confess that Jesus Christ is the Lord, to the glory of God the Father." That, in its final accomplishment, this prophecy referred to Christ, was known to Jacob as certainly as he makes Judah centre in the Shiloh. This Solomon also knew, when, in Ps. lxxii. 11 (compare Ps. xlv. 12), he ascribes to his great Antitype what is here ascribed to Judah: "All kings shall worship Him, and all nations shall serve Him." The consequence of the worship "by kings and nations" is the worshipping "by the sons of the father." Jacob thus transfers to Judah that which Isaac had promised to *him*: "People shall serve thee, and nations shall worship thee: be lord over thy brethren, and thy mother's sons shall worship before thee:" Gen. xxvii. 29.

In ver. 9 Judah is first designated a young lion,—a name which is intended to indicate, that the victorious power ascribed to Judah exists, as yet, only in the *germ*. It required that centuries should pass away before he grew up to be a lion, a full-grown lion. By the long period which thus intervened between the promise and its fulfilment, the divine election is the more strikingly manifested. (Several interpreters have been of opinion that there is no difference between the young lion, the lion, and the full-grown lion. But it is shown by Ezek. xix. 3—"And she brought up one of her גורים, and it became a כפיר, and it learnt to tear prey,"—that גור אריה is a young lion not yet able to catch prey.[1]) In the words, "From the prey, my son, thou art gone up," the *prey* is the *terminus a quo*: for עלה with מן is always used of the place from which it is gone up (see Josh. iv. 17, x. 9; Song of Sol. iv. 2): the *terminus ad quem* is the usual abode, as is shown by what follows. The residence of the conqueror and ruler is conceived of as being *elevated*. Joseph, according to Gen. xlvi. 31, goes up to Pharaoh, and in ver. 29 of the same chapter he goes up to meet his father. The expression "to go up" is commonly used of those who come from

---

[1] *Bochart* says: "When the whelp of a lion is weaned, and begins to go out for prey, and to seek his own food without the help of his mother, he then ceases to be a גור, and is called a כפיר." Deut. xxxiii. 22 must, therefore, not be translated, "Dan is a lion's whelp leaping from Bashan" —as if the גור אריה were already active—but thus, "Dan is a lion's whelp; he shall leap (*i.e.*, after he shall have grown up) from Bashan." Dan is in that place styled a lion's whelp, just as is Judah in Gen. xlix. 9, because, as yet, he is only a candidate for future victories.

other countries to Canaan. But the " going up " in the passage
under review implies also the " going down " into the lower
regions to seek for prey, just as in Ps. lxviii. 19, where it is said
of the Lord, after He had fought for His people, and had been
victorious, " Thou hast ascended on high, Thou hast led captivity captive: Thou hast received gifts for men; yea, for the
rebellious also, that the Lord God might dwell among them."
" *To dwell* " means there, that, after having accomplished all
this, thou mayest dwell gloriously, and be inaccessible to the
vengeance of the conquered, in thy usual place of abode. The
sense is the same in the passage before us. Luther is therefore
wrong in explaining it thus : " Thou hast risen high, my son,
by great victories,"—as are others also who translate it, " From
the prey thou growest up." Such a view of this clause would,
moreover, break up the connection, and all that follows would
appear without preparation.[1]

The words, " He stoopeth down, he croucheth as a lion, and
as a full-grown lion; who shall rouse him up?" contain a transition and allusion to what we are subsequently told concerning
Shiloh. Even here we are presented with a picture of peace,—
a peace, however, which is not to the prejudice of victorious
power, as in the case of Issachar (vers. 14, 15), but which, on the
contrary, preserves it undiminished. If the promise, " From
the prey, my son, thou art gone up," found its first glorious,
although only preliminary, fulfilment in the reign of David
(compare the enumeration of his victories in 2 Sam. viii.), the
words, " He stoopeth down, he coucheth," etc., are the most
appropriate inscription for the portal of Solomon's reign. But,
in Christ, the pre-eminence in the reign both of war and peace
is united.—That לביא is not " the lioness," but only the poetical
designation of the lion, appears from just the very passage
which is so commonly adduced in support of the former signification, viz., Job iv. 11 ; for the sons of the lion spoken of in that
passage are the sons of the wicked (compare Job xxvii. 14).

A parallel to the words in ver. 10, " The sceptre shall not
depart from Judah," is formed by the departing of the sceptre
from Egypt, in Zech. x. 11 : " And the pride of Assyria shall

---

[1] The LXX. translate, ἐκ βλαστοῦ υἱέ μου ἀνέβης, " from a shoot, my
son, thou hast grown up." They explain טרף by an inappropriate reference to Ezek. xvii. 9, where it is used of a fresh green leaf.

be brought down, and the sceptre of Egypt shall depart away."
All dominion of the world over the people of God is only temporary; and so also, the dominion of the people of God over the
world, as it centres in Judah, can sustain only a temporary
interruption: its departure is everywhere in appearance only;
and when it departs, it is only that it may return with enhanced
weight.—The *sceptre* is the emblem of dominion. The words,
"A sceptre rises out of Israel" (Num. xxiv. 17), are explained
in chap. xxiv. 19 by the words, "*Dominion* shall come out of
Jacob." The question as to the subjects of this dominion must
be determined from the preceding words; for there shall not
depart from Judah what Judah, according to these words, possesses. Hence they are (1) the brethren of Judah, and (2)
the enemies of Israel. The latter can the less properly be excluded, because of these alone the whole of the preceding verse
treated. In the words of Balaam, in Num. xxiv. 17 (which
refer to the passage under consideration), "There cometh a
star out of Jacob, and a sceptre riseth out of Israel, and smiteth
the territories of Moab, and destroyeth all the sons of the
tumult," there is viewed, in the sceptre, only the victorious and
destructive power which he shall display in his relation to the
world; but the subjects of dominion are, in that passage, according to ver. 19, the heathens also. The sceptre is pre-eminently an ensign of kings. Hence, to the sceptre and star out
of Israel (Num. xxiv. 17) corresponds, in ver. 7, his *king*: "And
his king shall be higher than Agag, and his kingdom shall be
exalted,"—*i.e.*, not merely a single royal person, but the Israelitish kingdom. But we can here the less legitimately separate
sceptre and kingdom from each other, because, even in the
earlier promises made to the Patriarch, there is the prophecy of
the rising of a kingdom among their descendants,—of a kingdom, too, that shall extend beyond the boundary of that posterity
itself. (Compare Gen. xvii. 6, "Kings shall come out of thee;"
ver. 16, "And she shall become nations, *kings* of nations shall
be of her." See also Gen. xxxv. 11.) In vol. ii. of the *Dissertations on the Genuineness of the Pentateuch*, p. 166 f., we
detailed the natural foundations which there existed for foresee-
ing the establishment of a kingdom in Israel. It is evident that
the promise which was formally given to the whole posterity of
the Patriarchs, is here appropriated specially to Judah, who, for

the benefit of the whole people, is to have the sceptre.[1] From what has been remarked, it appears that the fulfilment of this prophecy began first with David; up to that time Judah had been only " a lion's whelp." " In the person of Saul," as Calvin remarks, " there was an abortive effort; but there came out at length in David, under the authority and legitimate arrangement of God, the sovereignty of Judah, according to the prophecy of Jacob." It also appears, from what has been observed, that *Reinke*, S. 45 of his Monography, *Die Weissagung Jacobs über Schilo*, Münster 1849 (a work written with great diligence), is mistaken in determining the sense to be,[2] that Judah as a tribe would not perish, and his superiority not cease, until out of him Shiloh, etc.; and that he is wrong, too, in maintaining, S. 133, that the continuance of the royal dignity, and the superiority over all the tribes until the time of Christ, were not required by these words. From the remarks which we have made, even more than that is required,—the *continuance*, namely, *of Judah's dominion over the Gentiles;* for otherwise it would be necessary to make a violent separation of these words from the preceding ones. That which has given rise to such interpretations and assertions, viz., the apparent difficulty encountered in pointing out the fulfilment,[3] is by no means removed by such an explanation. For, if we look to the surface only, what had been left of the superiority of the tribe of Judah, at the time when Christ appeared? But if we look deeper, we shall find no reason for such feeble interpretations. The fulness of strength which, notwithstanding the deepest humiliation, still dwelt in the sceptre of Judah at the time when Christ appeared, is made manifest by the very appearance of Christ—the Lion of the tribe of Judah. Although faint-heartedness, perceiving only what is immediately before the eyes, might have said, " The sceptre has departed from

[1] Calvin says: " This dignity is bestowed upon Judah only with a view to benefit the whole of the people."

[2] In the first edition of this work, the author had likewise maintained that view.

[3] It was this difficulty which led *Grotius* to adopt the feeble exposition, " That teachers out of Judah's posterity would lead the people until the times of the Messiah, who would be the highest leader and commander of Jews and Gentiles."

E

Judah," to every one who was not blinded it must have been
evident, at the very moment when Christ appeared, that the
sceptre had not departed from Judah.   We must not allow ourselves to be perplexed by any events and arguments adduced
to prove that the sceptre *has departed* from Judah; for the very
same events and arguments would militate against the eternal
dominion of his house which had been promised to David, and
would therefore make us doubtful of that also.   All these events
and arguments lose their significancy, when we remark, that
this departing is only an *apparent,* not a *definitive* one;—that
God never, by His promises, binds the hands of His punitive
justice;—that His election goes always hand-in-hand with the
visitation of the sins of the elected; but that, in the end, the
election will stand in all its validity.[1]   To Judah applies exactly what in Ps. lxxxix. 31–35 is said of David: "If his children forsake My law, and walk not in My judgments; if they
break My statutes, and keep not My commandments; then will
I visit their transgression with the rod, and their iniquity with
stripes.   Nevertheless, My loving-kindness will I not utterly take
from him, nor suffer My faithfulness to fail.   My covenant will
I not break, nor alter the thing that is gone out of My lips."
But the greater the degradation that had come upon Judah,
the more consoling is this promise.   If we see that neither the
decline of David's and Judah's dominion after Solomon, nor
the apparently total disappearance of David's kingdom which
took place after the Chaldee catastrophe, and continued for
centuries; nor the altogether comfortless condition (when

---

[1] Calvin says: "If any one should object, that the words of Jacob
convey a different meaning, we would answer him, that whatever promises
God gave concerning the outward condition of the Church, they were so
far limited that God might, in the meantime, exercise His judgments in
the punishment of men's sins, and prove the faith of His people.   And indeed
it was not a light trial when, at the third succession, the tribe of Judah was
deprived of the greater part of his territory.   A more severe one followed
when, before the eyes of the father, the sons of the king were slain, his own
eyes put out, and himself was carried to Babylon, and given over to servitude
and exile along with the whole royal family.   But the heaviest trial of all
came, when the people returned to their land, and were so far from seeing
their expectations fulfilled, that they were, on the contrary, subjected to a
sad dispersion.   But even then, the saints beheld with the eye of faith the
sceptre hidden under ground; neither did their hearts fail, nor their
courage give way, so that they desisted not from continuing their course."

looking only at what is visible) which Jeremiah describes in the words: "Judah is captive in affliction and great servitude: she dwelleth among the heathen, and findeth no rest. The anointed of the Lord, who was our consolation, is taken in their pits, he of whom we said, Under his shadow we shall live among the heathen. Slaves are ruling over us, and there is none to deliver us from their hand;"—if we see that all these things did not prevent the fulfilment of the words, "The sceptre shall not depart from Judah until Shiloh come;"—that, notwithstanding all these things, it most gloriously manifested itself in the appearance of Christ, that the dominion remained still with Judah;—why should we be dismayed though the river of the kingdom of God should sometimes lose itself in the sand? Why should we not be firmly confident that in due time it shall spring forth again with its clear and powerful waters?—But the *Jews* are not benefited by this distinction betwixt the *definitive* departing of the sceptre, and one which is merely *temporary*. The latter must necessarily be distinguished from the former by this :—that even in the times of abasement, there must be single symptoms which still indicate the continuance of the sceptre; and this was evidently the case in the times before Christ. In Jehoshaphat, Uzziah, and Hezekiah, the sceptre of Judah brought forth new leaves; after their return from the captivity, the place, at least, was pointed out by Zerubbabel, which the Davidic kingdom would, at some future period, again occupy. The victories of the times of the Maccabees, though they themselves were not of the tribe of Judah, served to manifest clearly that the lion's strength and the lion's courage had not yet departed from Judah. It is not without significance that *Judas Maccabeus* had his name thus. And under all these events the family of David always remained distinct, and capable of being traced out. But nothing of all this is to be found with the Jews during the 1800 years after Christ; and hence the vanity of their hope that, in some future time, it will be made evident by the appearance of Shiloh, that the supremacy and dominion of Judah are not lost.

Along with the *sceptre* which shall not depart from Judah, the *lawgiver* is mentioned, for whom many would, quite arbitrarily, substitute the *commander's staff*. Is. xxxiii. 22 is explanatory of this passage: "For the Lord our Judge, the

Lord our Lawgiver, the Lord our King, He will save us"—
where the *lawgiver* is put on a level with the *judge* and *king*.
Gesenius translates it by : our *commander*.

The lawgiver shall not depart " from between his feet."
This is a poetical expression for " from him." He is, as it were,
to have the lawgiver wherever he moves or stands. Explanatory of this is the passage in Judges v. 27, where, in the Song
of Deborah, it is said of Jael, " He bowed between her feet,
he fell, he lay down." That which any one has between his
feet, is accordingly his territory on which he moves, that within
his reach. In the latter passage the prose expression would
have been, " beside her," and in the passage under consideration, " from him." [1]

Sceptre and lawgiver shall not depart from Judah until
Shiloh come. Here everything depends upon fixing the derivation and signification of this word. There cannot be any
doubt, and, indeed, it is now almost universally admitted, that
it is derived from שלה, " to rest." In the first edition of this
work, the author gave it as his opinion, that its formation was
analogous to that of בידור, " tumult of war," from בדר, " to be
troubled," קיטר, " smoke," from קטר, שֵׁלֹה from שלה ; and many
(*Hofmann, Kurtz, Reinke*) have stedfastly maintained this opinion even until now. But the author must confess that the
objections raised against this derivation by *Tuch* are well-
founded. "In the first place," *Tuch* remarks, " it is well
known that forms like קיטר do not constitute any special class in
the etymology, but have originated from *Piel* forms (*Ewald,*
Lehrb. d. Hebr. Spr. § 156 b), as is very clearly shown by
קימוש, being found by the side of קמוש. But the *o* in the final
syllable of these words is not an *o* unchangeable, according to
the rules of etymology, and could, therefore, not remain in a
root לה; *and there is not found, in general, any form of a root*
לה *analogous to* קיטר." But far more decisive is another reason.
" The *nomina Gentilia* גילני (2 Sam. xv. 12), שילני (1 Kings

---

[1] Many expositors, following the LXX. (ἐκ τῶν μηρῶν αὐτοῦ), the
Vulgate (*de femore ejus*), and the Chaldee Paraphrast, understand this
expression as a designation of origin and production. But in that case,
we must assume a very hard ellipsis, viz., " he who is to proceed." Moreover, this explanation is destructive of the parallelism, according to which,
" from between his feet" must correspond with " from Judah."

xi. 29, xii. 15), lead us from the supposed form to the substantive termination ןֹ- which a *liquida* may drop, and express the remaining vowel ו by ה." (Compare *Ewald*, § 163.) Now that *Shiloh* is an abbreviation of *Shilon* is proved, not only by the *nomen gentile*, but also by the fact, that the ruins of the town which received its name from the Shiloh in our passage, are, up to the present moment, called *Seilun*, and that Josephus writes *Silo* as well as *Silun*, Σιλοῦν (compare *Robinson*, Travels iii. 1, p. 305); and, *finally*, by the analogy of the name שלמה, which is formed after the manner of שילה, and likewise shortened from שלמון. We must confess that *Tuch* is right also when he asserts: "That it is quite impossible to give the word the signification of an appellative noun, since it is only in proper names, in which the signification of the suffix of derivation is of less consequence, that *on* is shortened into *o*." The only exception is that of אבדה, " hell," in Prov. xxvii. 20; but even this is only an *apparent* exception, and is quite in accordance with the rule laid down, inasmuch as " hell " is, in this passage, personified,—as is frequently the case in other passages. (Compare Rev. ix. 11.) But this case very plainly shows that we are not at liberty to apply, as *Tuch* does, the measure of our proper names to those of Scripture, which are used in a more comprehensive sense. The Samaritan translation is, therefore, right in retaining the " Shiloh." As the passage under review is the first in which the person of the Redeemer meets us, so Shiloh is also the first *name* of the Redeemer,—a name expressive of His nature, and quite in correspondence with the names in Is. ix. 5, and with the name Immanuel in Is. vii. 14. With respect to the *signification* of the name, the termination *on*, according to *Ewald*, § 163, forms adjectives and abstract nouns. The analogy of the name שלמה, which is formed after the manner of שילה, indicates that it has here *an adjective* signification, and, like Solomon, Shiloh denotes " the man of rest," corresponds to the " Prince of Peace " in Is. ix. 5, and, viewed in its character of a proper name, is like the German " *Friedrich* " = Frederick, *i.e.*, " rich in peace," " the Peaceful one."

To Shiloh the nations shall adhere. The word יקהה is commonly understood as meaning " obedience."[1] But it does not

---

[1] The signification, " expectation," given to this word by the LXX. (καὶ αὐτὸς προσδοκία ἐθνῶν), *Jerome*, and other translators, is founded upon

denote every kind of obedience, but only that which is spontaneous, and has its root in piety.   This is clearly shown by the
only passage in which, besides the one under consideration, the
word יקהה is found, Prov. xxx. 17 : " An eye that mocketh at
his father, and despises the יקהה of his mother."[1]   To this view
we are led also by the Arabic, where the word وَقِهَ, does not
denote obedience in general, but willing obedience, docility, in
the viii. sq. لِ *dicto audientem se præbuit more discipuli.*   (Compare *Camus* in *Schulten,* on Prov. l. c.)   Cognate is وَقَى, " to
take care," " to guard oneself," specially of the conflict with the
higher powers of life, in the viii. *semet custodivit ab aliqua re, et
absolute timuit coluitque Deum, pius fuit.*   From it is derived
יקה *pius* in Prov. xxx. 1, where the son of Jakeh speaks to
" With me is God, and I prevail" (*Heb.* Itheal and Ucal.)

Luther, although he has misunderstood the right meaning
of Shiloh, has yet beautifully comprehended the sense of the
whole passage.   " This is a golden text," he says, " and well
worthy of remembrance, namely : that the kingdom of Christ
will not be such a kingdom as that of David was, of whom it is
said, 1 Chron. xxviii. 3, that he was a man of war and had shed
much blood.   The kingdom of Shiloh, which succeeded it, is
not a kingdom so powerful and bloody, but consists in this,—
that the word, by which it is ruled or administered, is heard,
believed, and obeyed.   All will be done by means of preaching;
and this will just be the sign by which the kingdom of Christ
is distinguished from the other kingdoms of this world, which
are governed by the sword and by physical power."   To this
point also Luther draws attention, that our prophecy affords a
powerful support to the ministers of the Word : " It will be
done by the proclamation of the promise, and Shiloh will be

---

the erroneous derivation of the word from קוה.   In the other passage
(Prov. xxx. 17), where the LXX. translate, " the age of his mother," they
have confounded the root יקה with קהה, " to be blunted."

[1] *Gousset* says : The word can signify something good only, on account
of the passage, Prov. xxx. 17, namely, something which adorns the relation of the son to his mother, the despising of which is a crime on the part
of the son, and which deserves that he should be sent εἰς κόρακας.   And
not less so from its being used in Gen. xlix. 10 in reference to the Shiloh,
where, thereby, not one or a few, but all the nations without exception,
are bound to Him by a tie similar to that which exists betwixt mother
and son.

present with it, and will be efficient and powerful through our tongue and mouth."

That by the *nations* are not meant either the Canaanites in particular, or the tribes of Israel, but the nations in general, appears, partly, from the connection with what precedes—those who now willingly obey are evidently the enemies spoken of in vers. 8, 9,—and, partly, from the reference to the earlier promises of Genesis, all of which refer to nations in general. If a limitation had been intended, an express indication of it would have been necessary. The analogy of the parallel Messianic passages likewise militates against such a limitation; *e.g.*, Ps. lxxii. 8 : " He shall have dominion from sea to sea, and from the river unto the ends of the earth." (Compare also Is. xi. 10.)

In the Shiloh, the whole dignity of Judah as Lord and Ruler is to be concentrated. It hence follows, that the nations who will not willingly obey Him as Shiloh, must experience the destructive power of His sceptre (Num. xxiv. 17 ; Ps. ii. 9), and that behind the attractive kingdom of peace, there is concealed the destructive dominion of the lion.

Several interpreters have determined the sense as follows :— The dominion of Judah should continue until the appearing of Shiloh; but that then he should lose it.[1] We, on the contrary, conceive the sense to be this : " That the tribe of Judah should not lose the dominion until he attain to its highest realization by Shiloh, who should be descended from him, and to whom all the nations of the earth should render obedience."

Against this interpretation no difficulty can be raised from the עַד כִּי. It is true that this term has always a reference to the *terminus ad quem* only, and includes it ; but it is as certain that, very frequently, a *terminus ad quem* is mentioned which is not intended to be the last, but only one of special importance ; so that what lies beyond it is lost sight of. (Compare the author's *Dissert. on the Genuin. of Daniel*, pp. 55–56.) If

---

[1] Thus Luther says : " This sceptre of Judah shall continue, and shall not be taken from him, till the hero come ; but when He comes, then the sceptre also shall depart. The kingdom or sceptre has fallen ; the Jews are scattered throughout the whole world, and, therefore, the Messiah has certainly come ; for, at His appearing, the sceptre should be taken from Judah."

only sceptre and lawgiver were secured to Judah up to the time of Shiloh's coming, then, as a matter of course, they were so afterwards. That, previous to the coming of Shiloh, great dangers would threaten the sceptre of Judah, is indicated by Jacob, since he lays so much stress upon the sceptre's not departing *until* that time. *Hence we expect circumstances that will almost amount to a departing of the sceptre.*

But the positive reason for this interpretation is, that if, according to the other opinion, Judah were told that the dominion of his tribe were, at some future period, to cease, this would not be in harmony with the tone of the remainder of the address to Judah, which is altogether of a cheerful character. And *then*,—Jacob would, in that case, not have allowed the Messianic promise to remain in its indefinite state; from former analogies, we should have been induced to expect that he would transfer it to one of his sons. And *finally*,—from the analogy of the other Messianic prophecies, as well as from history, it seems not to be admissible to contrast the dominion of Judah with the kingdom of the Messiah. The dominion of Judah does not by any means *terminate* in Christ; it rather *centres* in Him.

We are not expressly told that the Shiloh will be descended from Judah; but this is supposed to be self-evident, and is not, therefore, expressly mentioned. If it were otherwise, the Shiloh would not have been alluded to in connection with Judah at all. A restriction of the promise to Judah, such as would take place if the Shiloh did not belong to him, is the less legitimate, inasmuch as, in vers. 8, 9, victory and dominion, without any limitation, are promised to Judah.

Having thus adduced the positive arguments in support of our view of this passage, let us now further examine the opinions of those who differ from us. Here, then, we must first of all consider those which are at one with us in the acknowledgment that this passage contains the promise of a personal Messiah.

1. Some interpreters (*Jonathan, Luther, Calvin, Knapp, Dogm.*) are of opinion that שׁילה is compounded of the noun שׁי, "child," and the suffix of the third person: " Until his (*i.e.*, Judah's) son or descendant, the Messiah, shall come." (Luther, somewhat differently.) But this supposed signification of שׁי

is destitute of any tenable foundation. That by such an explanation, moreover, there is a dissolution of the connection betwixt the Shiloh in this passage, and Shiloh the name of a place, which is written in precisely the same manner, is decisive against both the view just given forth and that which follows.

2. Others (the last of them, *Sack* in the second edition of his *Apolog.*) suppose the word to be erroneously pointed. They propose to read שֶׁלֹּה, compounded of שׁ for אֲשֶׁר, and the suffix ה for וֹ. They suppose the language to be elliptical: "Until He come to whom the dominion or sceptre belongs, or is due." The principal argument in support of this exposition is, that most of the ancient translators seem to have followed this punctuation. It is true that this is doubtful as regards *Onkelos* and the *Targum* of Jerusalem, which translate, "*Donec veniat Messias, cujus est regnum;*" for we may well suppose that here שׁילה is simply rendered by מְשִׁיחָא, while the following clause adds a complement from Ezek. xxi. 32, which is founded upon the passage now under review. But it is certain that the LXX. supposed the punctuation to be שֶׁלֹּה. They translate: ἕως ἂν ἔλθῃ τὰ ἀποκείμενα αὐτῷ. (Thus read the two oldest manuscripts—the Vatican and Alexandrian. The other reading, ᾧ ἀπόκειται, has no doubt crept in from the later Greek translations, notwithstanding the charge which *Justinus* [*Dial. c. Tryph.* § 120] raises against the Jews, that they had substituted the τὰ ἀποκείμενα αὐτῷ for the earlier ᾧ ἀπόκειται. Comp. *Stroth* in *Eichhorn's* Repert. ii. 95; *Holme's* edition of the LXX.) *Aquila* and *Symmachus*, who translate, ᾧ ἀπόκειται, as well as the Syriac and Saadias, who translate, *Ille cujus est*, follow the same reading. But the defenders of this exposition are wrong in inferring, from the circumstance of the ancient translations having followed this punctuation, that it was generally received. Had such been the case, how could it be explained that it should no more be found in any of our manuscripts? For the circumstance that forty manuscripts collected by *de Rossi* have שׁלה written without a וֹ, cannot be considered as of great weight; since it is merely a defective way of writing, occurring frequently in similar words. But if we consider the fact, which may be established upon historical grounds, that the Jews watched with most anxious care the uncorrupted preservation of the received

text of Holy Scripture, according to its consonants and pronunciation; that they did not even venture to receive into the text any emendation, though it should have recommended itself as in the highest degree probable; while, on the other hand, the ancient Jewish and Christian translators took great liberties in this respect, and, in the manifold perplexities into which, owing to their insufficient resources and knowledge, they fell, helped themselves as best they could;—it will certainly appear to us most probable, that even the ancient translators found our vocalization of the word as the received one, but felt themselves obliged to depart from it, because they could, in accordance with it, give no suitable derivation; whilst the punctuation adopted by them agreed perfectly with the traditional reference of the passage to the Messiah. But if this be the case, the authority of the ancient translations can here be of no greater weight than that of any modern interpreter; and, in the case under review, we are at liberty to urge all those considerations which are, in general, advanced against any change in the vocalization, unless there be most urgent reasons for it. The ancient translators, moreover, can have less weight with us, because we can distinctly perceive that a misapprehension of Ezek. xxi. 32 (27)—on which passage we shall afterwards comment—gave rise to their error. Against this explanation it may be further urged, not only that the ש *prefix* occurs nowhere else in the Pentateuch—an objection which is not in itself sufficient, since it occurs so early as in the song of Deborah, Judges v. 7—but also, that the supposed ellipsis would be exceedingly hard. (Compare *Stange, Theol. Symm.* i. S. 238 ff.)

Before we pass on to a consideration of the non-Messianic interpretation, we shall first state the reasons which bear us out in assuming that the passage under review contains a prophecy of a personal Messiah.

It is certainly, with respect to this, a matter of no slight importance that, with a rare agreement, exegetical tradition finds a promise to this effect here expressed; and this circumstance has a significance so much the greater, the less that this agreement extends to the interpretation of the particulars, especially as regards the Shiloh. How manifold soever these differences may be, *all antiquity agrees in interpreting this passage of a personal Messiah;* and we could scarcely conceive of such an agreement,

unless there had been some objective foundation for it. As
regards, first, the exegetical tradition of the Jews,—how far
soever we may follow it, it finds, in ver. 10, the Messiah. Thus
the LXX. explained it; for, that by " what is destined to Judah"
(ἕως ἂν ἔλθῃ τὰ ἀποκείμενα αὐτῷ) they understood nothing else
than the sending of the Messiah, is shown by the words following—καὶ αὐτὸς προσδοκία ἐθνῶν,—which can refer only to the
Messiah. (Compare Is. xlii. 4 according to the LXX.) In
the same manner the passage was understood by *Aquila*, the
Chaldee Paraphrasts, the *Targum* of *Onkelos*, of *Jonathan*, and
of *Jerusalem*, the *Talmud*, the *Sohar*, and the ancient book of
Breshith Rabba. Several even of the modern commentators,
e.g., *Jarchi*, have retained this explanation, although a strong
doctrinal interest, to which others yielded, tempted them to
give another interpretation to this passage, which occupied so
prominent a place in the polemics of the Christians. (Compare
the passage in *Raim. Martini Pug. Fid.* ed. *Carpzov; Jac.
Alting's* Shiloh, Franc. 1660, 4to [also in the opp. t. v.];
Schöttgen, hor. Hebr. ii. p. 146; and, most completely, in "*Jac.
Patriarch. de Schiloh vatic. a depravatione Clerici assertum,* op.
Seb. Edzardi, Londini 1698, p. 103 sq.") The Samaritans,
too, understood the passage as referring to the Messiah.
(Compare *Samarit. Briefwechsel*, communicated by *Schnurrer*
in *Eichhorn's Repert.* ix. S. 27.) It is true that from other
passages ("*Epist. Samarit. ad Jobum Ludolfum*," in *Eichhorn's
Repert.* xiii. S. 281-9, compared with *de Sacy* "*de Vers.
Samarit. Arab. Pentateuchi* in *Eichhorn's Biblioth.*" x. S. 54) it
appears that, in accordance with their doctrine of a double
Messiah—one who had already appeared, and one who was
still to come—they referred our passage, *partly* to the former,
and denied its reference to the real Messiah. But this is of no
importance. For, as Gesenius also has remarked (*Carmina
Samaritana*, p. 75), the doctrine of a double Messiah is of
recent origin with the Samaritans as well as with the Jews;
and hence, it is very probable that the reference to the real
Messiah was, formerly, the generally prevailing one, which was,
even afterwards, to a large extent retained, as is shown by the
passage first quoted.—*Finally*, In the Christian Church the
Messianic interpretation has been the prevailing one ever
since the earliest times. We find it as early as *Justin Martyr*.

The Greek and Latin Fathers agree in it. (Compare the statements in *Reinke*.) Even *Grotius* could not but admit that this passage referred to the Messiah; and *Clericus* stands quite alone and isolated, in his time, as an objector against the Messianic interpretation of it.

But even in the Canon itself, this passage is understood of a personal Messiah. David, Solomon, Isaiah, Ezekiel, look upon it in this light. (Concerning this point, compare the inquiries in the subsequent portions of this work.)

The entire relation of the Pentateuch to the succeeding sacred literature, and the circumstance that the former constitutes the foundation of the latter, and contains, in the germ, all that is afterwards more fully developed, entitle us to expect, that the Messianic idea has also found its expression in those books. The more prominent the place occupied, in the later books, by the announcement of a personal Messiah, the more unlikely it will be to him who has acquired right fundamental views regarding the Pentateuch, to conceive that this announcement should be wanting in it—the announcement, especially, of the Messiah in His kingly office; for it is this office of the Messiah which, in the Old Testament, generally takes a prominent place, and is, before all others, represented in the subsequent books. But there cannot be any doubt, that the promise of a personal Messiah in His kingly office, if it be found in the Old Testament at all, must exist in the passage which we are now considering.

The promises which first were given to Jacob's parents, and thereafter transferred to him, included two things:—*first*, a numerous progeny, and the possession of Canaan for them;—and *secondly*, the blessing which, through them, was to come upon all nations. How, then, could it be expected that Jacob, in transferring these blessings to his sons, and while in spirit seeing them already in possession of the promised land, and describing the places of abode which they would occupy, and what should befall them, should have entirely lost sight of the second object, which was much the more important, and as often repeated? Is it not, on the contrary, probable that, as formerly, from among the sons of Abraham and Isaac, so now, from among the sons of Jacob, *he* should be pointed out who should, according to the will of God, become the depositary of this promise, which was acquiring more and more of a definite shape? The contrary of this we can the less imagine, because, according to ver. 2, Jacob is to tell his sons that which shall befall them "at the end of the days." The expression, "the end of the days," is always used of that only which lies at the end of the course which is seen by the speaker. (Compare my work on Balaam,[1] p. 465 f.) Accordingly, it indicates, in this passage, that Jacob's announcement must comprehend the whole of the future sphere which was accessible to him. But if we do not admit the reference, in this passage, to the Messiah, then a whole territory of future time, notoriously accessible to Jacob, is left untouched by his announcement.—From the beginning of Genesis, we find the expectation of an universal salvation; and at every new separation, the depositary of this salvation, and its mediator for the whole remaining world, are regularly pointed out. At first, salvation is promised to the whole human race, then to the family of Shem, then to Abraham, then to Isaac, then to Jacob. "Now that the patriarchal *trias*, since Jacob, has extended into a *dodekas* forming the historical transition from the family of the promise to the nation of the promise, the question arises, from which of the twelve tribes salvation, *i.e.*, the victory of mankind, and the blessing of the nations, is to come." (*Delitzsch, Prophetische Theologie*, S. 293.) Should Genesis become to such a degree inconsistent with itself as not to answer a question which itself has called forth? But that answer is contained in the passage under consideration, only if Shiloh be taken for the personal name of the Redeemer. Unless we have recourse to artificial explanations, the announcement of Judah's being the bearer of salvation is to be found in our passage, only when, at the same time, the first indication of the person of the Messiah is perceived in it.

If the reference of the passage to a personal Messiah be explained away, we should certainly be at a loss to discover where the fundamental prophecy of such an one could possibly be found. We should then, in the first place, be thrown upon the Messianic Psalms, especially Ps. ii. and cx. But as it is the office of prophecy only to introduce to the knowledge of the congregation

[1] In the volume containing the *Dissertations on the Genuineness of Daniel, etc.* Edinburgh, T. and T. Clark.

truths absolutely new, it would subvert the whole relation of psalm-poetry to prophecy, if in these psalms we were to seek for the origin of the expectations of a personal Messiah. These psalms become intelligible, only if in Shiloh we recognise the first name of the Messiah. The passage in question, in combination with the prophetical announcement of the eternal dominion of the house of David, afforded the complete objective foundation for the subjective poetry of the Psalms. The eternity of dominion here promised to Judah was, as we learn from 2 Sam. vii., transferred to David. The exalted person in whom, according to our passage, the dominion of Judah was to culminate, must then necessarily belong to the house of David. *Further,*—If the passage under review be understood of the Messiah, we have an excellent fountainhead for all the prophecies of a personal Messiah; in its significant, enigmatical, and expressive brevity, it is most suitable for such a purpose. But if its reference to the Messiah be explained away, we are deprived altogether of a suitable starting-point. In the Davidic psalms, the Messianic prophecy already more strongly resembles a stream than a fountain.

So great is the weight of these reasons for the Messianic interpretation, that we might reasonably have expected that such expositors at least as stand on the ground of positive Christianity should abandon it only from overwhelming reasons, or, at least, from such only as are in the highest degree probable. But in this expectation we have been disappointed. The most superficial objections have been considered sufficient by *Hofmann, Kurtz,* and others, to induce them to disregard the *consensus* of the whole Christian Church. We cannot, indeed, but be astonished at this.

Kurtz, following the example of *Hofmann,* says: " The organic progress of prophecy, and its correlative connection with history, which must be maintained in all its stages, forbid us, most decidedly, to assign to the expectation of a personal Messiah, a period so early as that of the Patriarchs. The clearly expressed aim of the whole history of this period is the expansion into a great nation; its whole tendency is directed towards the growth of the multiplicity of a people from the unity of the Patriarchs. As long as the subject of the history was the increase into a nation, the idea of a single personal Saviour could not, by any means, take root. Such could occur only after they had actually expanded into a great nation in history, and the necessity had been felt of concentrating the multiplicity of the expanded, into the unity of a single, individual, *i.e.*, after one had appeared as the deliverer and saviour, as the leader and ruler of the whole nation. It is therefore only after Moses, Joshua, and David, that the expectation of a personal Messiah could arise."—Do you mean to teach God wisdom? we might ask, in answer to such argumentation. To chain prophecy to history in such a manner, is in reality nothing short of destroying it. How much soever people may choose to varnish it, this is but another form of Naturalism, against the influence of which no one is secure, because it is in the atmosphere of our day. Men who occupy a ground of argumentation so narrow-minded and trifling,—who would rather shape history than heartily surrender themselves to it, and find out, meditate upon, and follow the footsteps of God in it,—will be compelled to erase even the promise in Gen. xii. 3, "In thee all the families of the earth shall be blessed," yea, even the words, "I will make of thee a great nation," with which the promise begins; for even *that* violates the natural order. But the historical point of connection for the announcement of a personal Messiah, which here at once, like a flash of lightning, illuminates the darkness, is not at all wanting to such a degree as is commonly asserted. On the contrary, if the blessing upon the heathen be allowed to stand, the expectation of a personal Saviour must necessarily arise from a consideration of the known events of history, and meet the immediate revelation of such an one by God. The whole history of the time of the Patriarchs bears a *biographical* character. Single individuals are, in it, the depositaries of the divine promises, the channels of the divine life. All the blessings of salvation which the congregation possessed at the time when Jacob's blessing was uttered, had come to them through single individuals. Why, then, should the highest Salvation come to them in any other way? Why should not Abraham be as fit a type of the Messiah as Moses, Joshua, and David,—Abraham, of whom God, in Gen. xx. 7, says to Abimelech, the heathen king, "Now therefore restore the man his wife, for he is a prophet; and if he prays for thee, thou shalt live?" Or why not Joseph, who, according to Gen. xlvii. 12, "nourished his father and his brethren, and all his father's household," and whom the grateful Egyptians called "the Saviour of the World?"

Just as untenable is a second argument against the Messianic explanation,—namely, that there is no parallelism between the two clauses, "until Shiloh comes," "and to Him shall be the obedience of the nations," but only a pure progress of thought. The laws of parallelism are not iron fetters; and, moreover, the parallelism in substance fully exists here, if only it be acknowledged that יקהת does not signify any kind of obedience, but only a willing surrender. The words, "until Shiloh comes, and to Him shall be the obedience of the nations," are identical in meaning with, "until He cometh, who bringeth rest, and whom the nations shall willingly obey." The second member thus serves to explain the first; the sense would be substantially preserved although one of the members were wanting. The parallelism is slightly concealed only by the circumstance that the words run, "to Him the obedience of the nations,"—instead of, "He to whom shall be the obedience of the nations."

Let us now take a survey of the principal non-Messianic interpretations. A suspicion as to their having any foundation at all in the subject itself must surely be raised by their variety and multiplicity, as well as by the circumstance, that they who object to the Messianic explanation can never, in any way, succeed in uniting with each other, but that, with them, one interpretation is sure to be overthrown by another. Such is, in every case, a sure indication of error.

Moreover, it is possible, in every case, to trace out some interest, apart from the merits of the question, which has led to the objections against the Messianic interpretation. With the Jews, it was because they were driven to a strait by the argumentation of the Christians, that the Messiah must long ago have come, since sceptre and lawgiver had long ago departed from Judah. The rationalistic interpreters have evidently been determined by their antipathy to any Messianic prophecies in the Old Testament. *Hofmann* and his followers do not in the least conceal that they are guided by their principle of a concatenation of prophecy with history.

The opinion, according to which it is maintained that Shiloh is the name of the well-known locality in Ephraim, has found not a few defenders. Among these, several, and last of all

Bleek, in the *Observ.*; *Hitzig*, on Ps. ii. 2; *Diestel*, "der Segen Jacobs," translate: "Until he or they come to Shiloh." The sense is thus supposed to be: "Judah will be the leader of the tribes, in the journey to Canaan, until they come to Shiloh." There, in consequence of the tribes being dispersed to the boundaries assigned to them, he would then lose his leadership.[1] But such an explanation is, in every point of view, inadmissible. It is very probable that the town Shiloh did not exist at all, under this name, at the time of Jacob. The name nowhere occurs in the Pentateuch; and the Book of Joshua (as we shall show at a subsequent time) contains traces, far from indistinct, that it arose only after the occupation of the land by the Israelites. But even supposing that the town of Shiloh already existed at the time of Jacob, yet the abrupt mention of a place so little known would be something strange and unaccountable. It would be out of the range of Jacob's visions, which nowhere regard mere details, but have everywhere for their object only the future in its general outlines. *Further*,—The temporary limitation thus put to the superiority of Judah would be in glaring contradiction to vers. 8 and 9, where Judah is exalted to be the Lion of God without any limitation as to time. And, *finally*, —Up to the time of their arival in Shiloh, Judah was never in possession of the sceptre and lawgiver;—and this reason would alone be sufficient to overthrow the opinion which we are now combating. We have already proved that, by these terms, royal power and dominion are designated, and that, for this reason, the *beginning* of the fulfilment cannot be sought for in any period previous to the time of David. But even if we were to come down to the mere *leadership* of Judah, we could demonstrate that even this did not belong to him. His marching in front of the others cannot, even in the remotest degree, be considered as a leadership. Moses, who belonged to another tribe, had been solemnly called by God to the chief command. Nor was Joshua

---

[1] *Delitzsch* (who had formerly been a defender of the explanation of a personal Messiah) differs, in his Commentary on Genesis, from this view, only in so far, that he supposes that, while Judah's dominion over the tribes comes to an end in Shiloh, his dominion over the nations dates from that period. But this explanation must be objected to on the ground, that the dominion bestowed upon Judah is not merely a dominion over the tribes, but over the world.

F

of the tribe of Judah. In him, on the contrary, there appeared the germ of Ephraim's superiority, which continued through the whole period of the Judges, and which came to an end only by David's having been raised to the royal dignity. (Compare my commentary on Ps. lxxviii.)

Others (*Tuch, Maurer*) give the explanation : "As long as they come to Shiloh." This, according to them, the "poet" meant to be identical with : "in all eternity." They think that his (the "poet's") meaning was, that the holy tabernacle, which at his time (*Tuch* assigns the composition of Jacob's blessing to the period of Samuel) was at Shiloh, would remain there to all eternity. To this exposition it would be alone sufficient to object that, according to it, the phrase עד כי, which uniformly means only "until," is taken in the signification "as long as." *Further,*—History plainly enough shows how little the sanctuary was considered to be bound to Shiloh; to which place it had been brought, not in consequence of an express divine declaration, but only in accordance with Joshua's own views. When the ark of the covenant was carried away by the Philistines, this was considered as an express declaration of God, that He would no longer dwell in Shiloh. How different was the case as regards Jerusalem ! Notwithstanding the destruction by the Chaldees, the city continued to be the seat of the sanctuary. *Further,*—This view implies a strange blending of gross error—viz., the supposition that the sanctuary would remain for ever in Shiloh—and of true prophecy, viz., the announcement, uttered at the time of Ephraim's leadership, of the dominion of the tribe of Judah, which was first realized in David's royalty. The only ground in support of the Ephraimitic Shiloh—the fact, namely, that Shiloh, wherever else it occurs in the Old Testament, always signifies the name of the place—we hope to invalidate by and by ; when it will be seen that the town received its name only on the ground of the passage now under consideration.

Other opponents of the Messianic interpretation take Shiloh as a *nomen appellativum*, in the signification of *rest*. They translate either, "Until rest cometh and people obey him" (thus *Vater, Gesenius, Knobel*), or, "Until he comes (or, they come) to rest" (thus *Hofmann, Kurtz*, and others). By "rest," they understand either the political rest enjoyed under David and Solomon, or they find here expressed the idea of eternal rest in the expected Messianic time. Thus do *Gesenius, Hofmann,* and *Kurtz* understand it. The last-named determines the sense thus : "Judah shall remain in the uninterrupted possession of a princely position among his brethren, until through warfare and by victory he shall have realized the aim, object, and consummation of his sovereignty in the attained enjoyment of happy rest and undisturbed peace, and in the willing and joyful obedience of the nations." But this explanation is to be suspected, simply from the circumstance, that, in whatever other place Shiloh occurs, it is used as a *nomen proprium;* while it is entirely overthrown by the circumstance, that, according to its form, as already deduced, Shiloh can be nothing else than a *nomen proprium.*[1] We here only remark, by way of anticipation, that David, Solomon, Isaiah, and Ezekiel bear testimony against this explanation. An interpretation which dissevers the connection betwixt Shiloh and Shiloh, betwixt Shiloh and Solomon, betwixt Shiloh and the Prince of Peace, betwixt Shiloh and Him "whose is the judgment," must be, thereby, self-condemned. Against the explanation, "Until he comes to rest," it may also be urged, that the Accusative could not here stand after a verb of motion ; it was too natural to consider Shiloh as the subject. If it had been intended in any other sense, a preposition would have been absolutely requisite.

We further remark, that vers. 11 and 12, which ancient and modern interpreters, *e.g., Kurtz,* have attempted to bring into artificial connection with ver. 10, simply "finish the picture of Judah's happiness by a description of the luxurious fulness of his rich territory" *(Tuch).* Their tenor is quite different from that which precedes, where a pre-eminence was assigned to Judah ; for they contain nothing beyond a simple, positive declaration. What is in them assigned to Judah, belongs to him only as a part of the whole, as a fellow-heir of the country flowing with milk and honey, and corresponds entirely with the blessings upon the other sons, which are, almost all of them, only individual applications of the general blessing. It is evidently parallel to what, in vers. 25, 26, is said of Joseph, and in ver 20 of Asher. That which Jacob here assigns to Judah, was

---

[1] *Knobel* knows of no other expedient by which to escape from the force of this argument, than by changing the punctuation. He proposes to read שִׁלֹּה, a word which nowhere occurs.

formerly, in Gen. xxvii. 28, assigned by Isaac to Jacob, and in him to the whole people: "God give thee of the dew of heaven, and the fatness of the earth, and plenty of corn and wine." Hence, it is not at all necessary to examine history for the purpose of ascertaining whether Judah was distinguished above the other tribes, by plenty of wine and milk.

We need not lose much time in discussing the attempts which have been made to assign the blessing of Jacob to a later period. The futility of all of them is proved by the circumstance, that we have not here before us any special predictions, such as are peculiar to *vaticinia post eventum*, but general prophetical outlines, individual applications of the general blessings, exemplifications. Whatever seems, at first sight, to be different, melts away while handling it. Thus, for example, the blessings which Israel enjoyed by his dwelling on the sea-side, are pointed out in the blessing upon Zebulun, because he had his name from the *dwelling*, Gen. xxi. 20. That Zebulun is here viewed only as a part of the whole, appears from the fact that, afterwards, he did not live by the sea at all. In the case of Issachar, it was the individuality of the ancestor Jacob which gave him occasion to describe, from his own example, the dangers of an indolent rest. History does not say anything of Issachar alone having yielded to these dangers in a peculiar degree. In the case of Joseph, the events personal to the son are transferred to the tribe, and in the tribe, to the whole nation. In an inimitable manner the tender love of the father towards his son and provider meets us here. The only thing which goes beyond the human sphere of Jacob, is the prediction by which Judah is placed in the centre of the world's history. But it is just this which, even in its beginnings, goes beyond the time at which this pretended *vaticinium post eventum* is placed by *Tuch, Bleek*, and *Ewald;* for, by this assumption of theirs, they are necessarily limited to the time before David, if they wish to avoid the insurmountable difficulties which arise from what is said of Levi and of Joseph. But to the man who looks deeper, vers. 8-10 are just the seal of the divinity, and hence of the genuineness also, of this prophecy, and, with all his heart, he will hate such miserable conjectures.[1]

[1] The rationalistic objection, that at so great an age, and on the brink of the grave, man is not wont to compose poems, may be refuted by a

Let us now follow through history Jacob's blessing upon
Judah. From this inquiry it will appear how deep has been
the impression made by it upon the people of the covenant.
On this occasion also, it will be seen still more distinctly what
the right is which rationalistic criticism has to declare this
fundamental prophecy to be the recent production of an obscure
poet. The chain-like character of Holy Scripture will be seen
in a very striking light.

In Num. ii. regulations are laid down respecting the order
in which the tribes are to encamp about the tabernacle, and in
which they are to set forth. " On the east side, towards which
the entrance of the sanctuary is directed, and hence in the
front, Judah, as the principal tribe, is encamped; and the two
sons of his mother—Issachar and Zebulun—who were born
immediately after him, pitch next to him. On the south side
there is the camp, with the standard, of Reuben ; and next to him
are his brother Simeon, who was born immediately after him,
and Gad, one of the sons of his mother's maid. The west side
is assigned to the sons of Rachel, with Ephraim at their head.
And, *finally*, on the north side, the three other sons of the maids,
viz., Dan, Asher, and Naphtali, have their position. In the same
order as they encamp they are also to set forth." (*Baumgarten.*)

Judah is the chief tribe on the chief side. This distinction
reference to the history of the ancient Arabic poetry. The Arabic poets
before the time of Mohammed often recited long poems extempore,—so
natural to them was poetry. (Compare *Tharaphæ Moallakah*, ed. *Reiske*,
p. xl.; *Antaræ Moallakah*, ed. *Menil.* p. 18.) The poet *Lebid*, who
attained to the age of 157 years (compare *Reiske prolegg. ad Thar. Moall.*
p. xxx. ; *De Sacy, Memoires de l'Academie des inscriptions*, p. 403 ff.),
composed a poem when he was dying ; compare *Herbelot Bibl. Or.* p. 513.
The poet *Hareth* was 135 years old when he recited extempore his *Moallakah*, which is still extant ; compare *Reiske* l.c. The objection, too, that it
is inconceivable how the blessing spoken by Jacob could have been handed
down *verbatim* to Moses, finds its best refutation in the history of Arabic
poetry. The art of writing was introduced among the Arabs only a short
time before Mohammed. (Compare *de Sacy* l.c. pp. 306, 348 ; *Amrulkeisi
Moall.* ed. *Hengstenberg*, p. 3.) Up to that time, even the longest poems,
of which some consisted of more than a hundred verses, were preserved by
mere oral tradition (compare *Nuweiri* in *Rosenmüller, Zoheiri Moall.* p.
11) ; and the internal condition of those which have been preserved to us
bears the best testimony to their having been faithfully handed down.
But in the case before us, something altogether different from a poem was
concerned.

is not based on the deeds hitherto performed by Judah, nòr is it the result of any revelation which Moses received upon the subject. It is regarded as a matter of course. And yet, there must necessarily have been some foundation for such a distinction, because, otherwise, it would have called forth the opposition of the other tribes, especially of that of Ephraim. Such a foundation, however, is afforded only by the blessing of Jacob, in which the tribe of Judah appears as the leading one. The complete realization of this prediction is left, indeed, in the hand of God; but the bearer of honours so great, even although future, must, in the prospect of that future, enjoy, even in the present, a certain distinction; such distinction, however, as does not at all imply sovereignty.

But we are compelled to have recourse to Genesis, and especially to chap. xlix., the more because the whole arrangement of the camp has evidently its foundation in Genesis, and the key to a whole series of facts in it can be found only in chap. xlix. If we ask why it is that the tribes of Issachar and Zebulun are subordinate to Judah; that Reuben, Simeon, and Gad, that Ephraim and Benjamin, that Dan, Asher, and Naphtali are encamped by each other; it is in Genesis alone that we are furnished with the answer.

The position which Reuben occupies specially points to Gen. xlix. As the first-born, he ought to stand at the head; but here we find him occupying the second place. In Gen. xlix. Jacob says to him, on account of his guilt, "Thou shalt not excel;" and "the excellency of dignity, and the excellency of power," which up to that time he had possessed, are transferred to Judah. Yet Moses has so much regard to his original dignity, that he places him immediately after Judah; the utterance of Jacob did not entitle him to assign to him a lower position. *Further*,—The reason why Dan stands at the head of the sons of the maids is explained only in Gen. xlix. 16–18, where Dan is specially distinguished among them, and where it is specially said of him, "Dan shall judge his people."

If the blessing of Jacob be the production of a later time, then the order of the encampment, which rests upon it, must necessarily be so also; but such an idea will at once be discarded by every man of sound judgment. Even they who refuse to acknowledge Moses as the author of the Pentateuch, admit that those regulations which bear reference only to the condition of things in the wilderness must have originated from him.

But exactly the same order which Moses in Num. ii. prescribes for the encampment and setting forth of the tribes, is found again in chap. vii., where there is described the offerings which the princes of the tribes offered at the dedication of the altar. Every prince has here a day to himself, and here also does Judah occupy the first place: "And he that offered his offering the first day was Nahshon, the son of Amminadab, of the tribe of Judah."—If any one should venture to set down this chapter also, with all its details, as a fabrication of later times, he would only betray an utter absence of all scientific judgment.

According to Num. x. 14, Judah led the march when they set forth from Sinai.

Balaam's prophecies, the genuineness of which is proved by so many weighty arguments (compare the enumeration of them in my work on Balaam), rest, in general, on the fundamental prophecies of Genesis, but especially on the blessing of Jacob upon Judah.

In Num. xxiii. 24, Balaam says: "Behold, a people, like a full-grown lion he rises, and like a lion he lifts himself up. Not shall he lie down until he eat of the prey, and drink the blood of the slain." This conclusion of Balaam's second prophecy, which at once demolishes Balak's vain hopes of victory, by pointing out the dreadful power of Israel, unconquerable by all his enemies, and crushing them all, has an intentional reference to Gen. xlix. 9,—a reference specially suitable for such a conclusion. What was there ascribed to Judah is here transferred to Israel, whose fore-champion Judah is. "Dost thou think," says Balaam to Balak, "of being able to overcome them, to stop them in their course towards the mark held out to them? Behold, according to an old revelation of their God, they are a people destroying their enemies with the lion's strength. Therefore, get thee out of their way, lest such a fate befall thee."

In Num. xxiv. 9, Balaam says, "He couches, he lies as a lion, and as a great lion, who shall stir him up?" As in the preceding prophecy he had pointed out Israel's dreadful power which secures to him victory in the battle, so here he shows how, even after having finished the battle, this power so intimidates his enemies, that they do not venture to disturb his peace.

That which Jacob had said of Judah, is, with intended literality, here transferred to Israel.

In Num. xxiv. 17, we read: "I see him, but not now; I behold him, but not nigh: a star goeth out of Jacob, and a sceptre riseth out of Israel, and smiteth the borders of Moab, and destroyeth all the sons of the tumult."—As the two preceding utterances carry us back to Gen. xlix. 9, so this one refers to ver. 10, where the sceptre, the emblem of dominion, denotes, just as it does in this passage, dominion itself, and where to Judah, and in him to all Israel, the kingdom is promised which shall at last be consummated in the Shiloh. The meaning of the words, "A sceptre riseth out of Israel," is explained in ver. 19 by the words, "Dominion shall come out of Jacob." Jacob has in view the internal relations among his descendants, and hence he speaks specially of Judah; but Balaam, in accordance with his object, speaks of Israel only. Jacob points, at the close, to Shiloh's just and peaceful dominion; but Balaam, who has to do with the enraged and obstinate enemies of Israel, points out, from among the effects produced by the star and sceptre, only the victorious might, and destructive power which these will display in the conflict with the enemies of Israel.

In the blessing of Moses, Deut. xxxiii. 7, it is said of Judah: "Hear, Lord, the voice of Judah, and bring him unto his people; with his hands he fights for himself, and be Thou an help to him from his enemies." Even the remarkable brevity of this utterance points back to the blessing of Jacob. With this brevity, the length of the blessing upon Levi, who had been treated too summarily by Jacob, forms a striking contrast. In the case of Reuben also, the attempt to pour oil into the wounds then inflicted is visible. The whole announcement is based upon the supposition that Judah is the fore-champion of Israel; and this supposition refers us back to Gen. xlix. This appears especially in the words, "Bring him to his people," on which light is thrown only by Gen. xlix. It is for his people that Judah engages in foreign wars, and the Lord, fulfilling the words, "From the prey, my son, thou goest up," brings him safely to his people.[1]

[1] *Onkelos* paraphrases these words very correctly, thus: "Hear, O Lord, the prayers of Judah when he goes out to war, and bring him safely back to his people."

There can be no doubt that in Shiloh, as the name of a place, there is a reference to Gen. xlix. 10. They who rightly denied that Shiloh could, in that passage, be understood as the name of the place, could, nevertheless, not feel satisfied as long as they allowed a twofold Shiloh to exist unconnected with each other. The agreement in the very rare and peculiar form, which nowhere else occurs, cannot well be a matter of accident.

In the Pentateuch, Shiloh does not occur at all as the name of a place. In the passage where Shiloh is first mentioned—in Josh. xvi. 6—another name is beside it, and prefixed to it. According to that passage, the former name was Taanah. (They who are of opinion that this place was different from Shiloh, can find no support from the authority of *Eusebius;* it is not said Taanah by Shiloh, but Taanath-Shiloh.) After that place had become the seat of the Sanctuary, the holy name *Shiloh* took the place of the former natural one. The reason why this name was given to it is indicated in Josh. xviii. 1 : " And the whole congregation of the children of Israel assembled together at Shiloh, and set up the tabernacle of the congregation there ; *and the land was subdued before them."* Compare also xxi. 44, xxii. 4, where it is remarked that at that time " the Lord gave them rest round about." (See *Bachiene, Palestina* ii. 3, S. 409 ff.) In the subjection of the country,—in the rest which the Lord had given them from all round about, they saw an earnest of, and a prelude to, the obedience of the nations in general, and to the state of perfect rest which should take place at some future time with the appearing of Shiloh. Victory, peace ! (*Siegfried!*) such was the watchword corresponding to the elevated consciousness of the people. It is an elevation quite similar to that which we so often perceive in the Psalms. " Sometimes there rises the hope that the Gentiles shall, at some future period, be received among the people of God—a hope based upon the experience of the Lord's victorious power in the present, in which faith perceives a pledge of the future subjection of the world's power under His sceptre. Thus, in vers. 29–32 of Ps. lxviii., which was composed by David on the occasion of his having, by the help of the Lord, conquered his most dangerous enemies, the Aramites and Ammonites ; in Ps. xlvii., written on the occasion of Jehoshaphat's victory over several heathen nations ; and in Ps. lxxxvii., composed on the ground of the joyful events under Hezekiah, the germ of the hope for the conversion of the heathen, which had all along lain dormant in the people, was developed."[1]

After the main power of the Canaanites had been broken by the expeditions of all Israel under Joshua, Judah begins, at the command of God, to expel the Canaanites from the territory assigned to him. In Judges i. 1, 2, we read: "And the children of Israel asked the Lord, Who shall go up for us against the Canaanites at the beginning to fight against them? And the Lord said, Judah shall go up; behold, I deliver the land into his hands." They were concerned to find out the tribe who, by the decree of God, had been destined to be the fore-champion for his brethren, and with whom they might be sure of a happy commencement of the war. The short answer, "Judah shall go up," would scarcely have been justified, had it not had a foundation in a previous declaration of God's will. It indicates that Jacob's blessing upon Judah still possessed its power.

In like manner, in the war against Benjamin, according to divine direction, Judah goes up first to the battle, forms the vanguard, Judges xx. 18. The intentional identity of the expression used here and in chap. i., leads us to the supposition that the words, "Judah shall go up," have, in both passages, the same foundation.

From both of these events, we are led to expect that Judah may be called to occupy a still more important position. The announcement of Jacob regarding Judah, to which the words, "Judah shall go up," refer, finds, in these events, evidently but a poor beginning of its complete fulfilment. All, however, which was required in the meantime, was the indication, by gentle touches, of the position which Judah was called to occupy in future times. It is just God's way to take time in carrying out

---

[1] It is probable also, that in the passage, Josh. xvi. 6, where Shiloh occurs for the first time as the name of a place, and which we have already discussed, there is not, as we assumed, a connection of the former name with the latter, but the complete appellation, of which the latter—Shiloh —is only an abbreviation. From the well ascertained and common signification of the verb אָנָה, we are entitled to explain Taanath-Shiloh: "the futurity, or the appearance of Shiloh." Shiloh shall come! Such was the watchword at that time. The word תֵּאָנֶה would then correspond to the יָבֹא of the fundamental passage.

His elections; all human conditions must first disappear. After these two intimations, at the end of the time of Joshua (for Judges i. 1, 2, belongs to that period; the words, " And it came to pass after the death of Joshua," do not refer to what follows immediately after, but only to the contents of the book as a whole), and at the beginning of the time of the Judges, Judah retires out of view. During the whole period of the Judges, Ephraim held the supremacy. Under David, the validity of the election suddenly appeared, and the announcement of Jacob found a glorious fulfilment; but again, such an one only as pointed to a still more glorious fulfilment in the future. Before this took place, however,—before Shiloh came, to whom the obedience of the people was promised, the lamp of Judah was once more to be extinguished, so that, to human eyes, it should be invisible for many centuries.

In 1 Chron. xxviii. 4, David says: " And the Lord God of Israel chose me out of all the house of my father to be king over Israel for ever; for He hath chosen Judah to be the ruler, and in the house of Judah, the house of my father, and in the house of my father, He liked me to make me king over all Israel." David here points to an event by which Judah was raised to be the ruling tribe; and such an election is nowhere else to be found than in Gen. xlix. We cannot for a moment suppose that Judah was elected only in, and with, the election of David. Against such a supposition militates the fact, that even the election of David's house is represented in history as being distinct from the election of David himself; for in 1 Sam. xvi. the decree of God is first made known, that one of Jesse's sons is to be king; and it is only afterwards that we are told which of them is to be chosen. The expression too, " He hath chosen Judah to be the *ruler*," is decisive against it; for this expression has an evident reference to the sceptre and lawgiver in Gen. xlix. But if any doubt should still remain, it would be entirely removed by the parallel passage in 1 Chron. v. 2, where, in the words, " For Judah was mighty among his brethren, and of him the prince was to come," there is an allusion, which cannot be mistaken, to Gen. xlix.

There cannot be a doubt that David gave to his son the name Solomon, because he hoped that, in his just and peaceful reign, he would be a type of the Shiloh whom the nation should will-

ingly obey, just as, in his own reign, there had been the first
grand fulfilment of what Jacob had prophesied of Judah's lion-
courage, and lion-strength,—of Judah's sceptre and lawgiver.
We have here the counterpart of the fact, that the children of
Israel, after the first occupation of the country, gave to the seat
of the sanctuary the name of Shiloh.   In the case of Solomon,
both the name and the substance point to Shiloh.   With regard
to the *name*, three out of the four letters of which the name
שלמה consists, are common to it with Shiloh.   The signification
is precisely the same; so also is the form.   In שלמה as well as
in שילה we meet with the very rare case of the ן at the end
being thrown off.   In *Ewald's* Grammar, § 163, these two names
are, for this reason, pointed out and placed immediately beside
each other.   And, with regard to the agreement in the *substance*,
we refer to 1 Chron. xxii. 9, where Nathan says to David:
"Behold, a son shall be born to thee, who shall be a man of
rest, and I will give him *rest* from all his enemies round about;
for his name shall be Solomon, and I will give peace and quiet-
ness unto Israel in his days."   We refer, *further*, to 1 Kings
v. 4, where Solomon says to Hiram: "And now the Lord my
God hath given me *rest* round about; there is neither adversary
nor evil obstacle."   We refer, *finally*, to 1 Kings v. 4, 5 (iv.
24, 25): "He had dominion over all the region on the other
side of the river, from Tiphsah even to Gaza, over all the kings
on the other side of the river, and he had peace from all his
servants round about.   And Judah and Israel dwelt safely,
every man under his vine and fig-tree, from Dan even to Beersheba, all the days of Solomon."[1]

But if any further doubt should remain as regards the typical
relation in which Solomon stands to Shiloh, it would be removed
by Ps. lxxii., which discards the very idea that Solomon could
be anything more than a type,—that any hope had ever been
entertained of his being himself the Shiloh.   Even David's
Messianic Psalms bear witness against such an opinion... In
harmony with the words of our Lord in Matt. xii. 42, "A

---

[1] That there exists a connection between Shiloh and Solomon has often
been guessed at and expressed; but expositors have not succeeded well in
determining it more closely.   The Samarit. Arab. Translation here says
expressly: "Until Solomon cometh." (Comp. *Lib. Genes. sec. Arab. Pent.
Samarit. vers. ed. Kuenen. Leyden*, 51.)

greater than Solomon is here," Solomon in this Psalm points beyond himself. In his own just and peaceful dominion, he beholds a type of the kingdom of the Prince of Peace, who, by His justice and love, shall obtain dominion, over the world, and whom all kings shall worship, and all the heathen shall serve. How closely this Psalm is connected with Gen. xlix. is pointed out by Ezekiel, in a passage of which we shall immediately treat.

In ver. 9 of Ps. lx., which was composed by David, the words, "Judah is my lawgiver"—equivalent to, Judah is my, *i.e.*, Israel's ruling tribe—point to Gen. xlix. 10, according to which the lawgiver shall not depart from Judah; just as ver. 13, "Give us help from the enemy," alludes to Deut. xxxiii. 7, where it is said of Judah, "Be thou a help to him from his enemies," and ver. 14, to Num. xxiv. 18.

That the Prince of Peace spoken of in Is. ix. 5, under whom there is "no end to the increase of government and of peace," refers to the Peaceful One, to whom the nations render obedience, will not be doubted by those who have recognised the connection in which Solomon and Ps. lxxii. stand to the Shiloh. Nor will such fail to recognise an allusion to the Shiloh in all the other passages of the Prophets, in which the Messiah is described as the Author of rest and peace; *e.g.*, Mic. iv. 1–4; Is. ii. 2–4; Zech. ix. 10; and the less so, the more clearly it appears, from passages of Ezekiel, what influence Gen. xlix. exercised over the prophetic consciousness. Isaiah significantly alludes to it in other passages also. In chap. xxix. 1, 2, he says: "Woe to Ariel, (*i.e.*, Lion of God), the city where David encamped! Add ye year to year, let the feasts revolve. And I distress Ariel, and there shall be heaviness and affliction, but it shall be unto me as Ariel;"—the meaning of which is: Jerusalem will, in times to come, endure heavy affliction (through Asshur), but the world-conquering power of the kingdom of God will manifest itself in her deliverance. The name Ariel is emphatically placed at the beginning, and, in it, the Prophet gives to the congregation of God a guarantee for her deliverance. That which Jacob had said of Judah, who, to him, appeared as the invincible lion of God, is here applied to Zion, the city where David encamped, the centre of the kingdom of Judah.

Ezekiel, in his lamentation over the princes of Israel who,

in his time, were standing just at the brink of the abyss, says
in chap. xix. 2 : "Thy mother was a lioness, who lay down
among lionesses, and brought up her whelps among young lions."
The mother is the congregation of Judah. The image of the
lion points to the blessing of Jacob, and its fulfilment in history.
"Judah once couched in a threatening position, endangering his
adversaries,[1] in the midst of lions, *i.e.*, among the other powerful
kingdoms fond of conquests." (*Hävernick.*)

In Ezek. xxi. 15, 18 (10-15), the Lord, with an evident
allusion to Gen. xlix. 10, announces the (temporary) destruction
of the sceptre of His son (*i.e.*, Israel or Judah), a sceptre which
despises all other sceptres.

In vers. 30-32 (25-27) of the same chapter, Ezekiel foretells,
in the name of the Lord, a complete overturning of all relations,
a total revolution, in which the Davidic kingdom especially
is brought down, a condition of affairs in which rest and safety
will not anywhere be found. This state of things is to continue
"until He comes to whom is the judgment; to Him I will
give it."

The reference of this passage to Gen. xlix. cannot be mistaken. It was recognised, indeed, by the ancient translators ;
only that most of them erroneously found in it an explanation
instead of an allusion.

Instead of the words, "to whom is the judgment," we
should, from the expression used in Gen. xlix. 10, "Until
Shiloh cometh," have expected, "to whom is peace ;" but
Ezekiel has filled up Gen. xlix. 10 from Ps. lxxii. 1-5, where
judgment and righteousness appear as the basis of the peace
which the Anointed One shall bring. And *peace* occupies the
background in Ezekiel also. The advent of Him to whom is
the judgment, in contrast with the injustice and wickedness of
those who were hitherto the bearers of the sceptre, puts an end
to strife, confusion, and destruction. That, in like manner, in
Gen. xlix., the *judgment* occupies the background, we see plainly,
from the commentary upon that passage furnished by Ps. lxxii.,
as well as from Is. ix. and ii. In Ps. lxxii., peace comes into
consideration, only in so far as it is a product and consequence
of justice, which is an attribute of the King, and is by him

---

[1] *Kimchi* says : " As long as the Jews were doing the will of God, they
could lie down like the lion without fear."

infused into the life of the nation. In vers. 1–50, the thought is : "God gives righteousness to His King, and in consequence of it, righteousness and the fear of God become indigenous to the people, and these again bring peace in their train."

Every word in Ezekiel is taken from Gen. xlix. and Ps. lxxii. From the latter are taken the words, "judgment," and "I will give it." (Compare Ps. lxxii. 1 : "Give the King thy judgments.") The combination of these two passages points out their close connection, and indicates that Ps. lxxii. is to be viewed as a comment. *Onkelos*, who thus translates the passage in Gen. xlix., "Until Messiah comes, to whom the kingdom is due, and Him the people shall obey," has very properly only supplemented the declaration of Jacob from Ezekiel, or, at least, has taken thence the explanation of Shiloh.

But, at the same time, the words אשר לו המשפט, which, on the basis of Ps. lxxii., Ezekiel puts in the place of שילה, allude to the letters of the latter word which forms the initials of the words in Ezekiel. That שׁ is the main letter in אשר, is shown by the common abbreviation of it into שׁ; and that the י in שילה is unessential, is proved by the circumstance that the name of the place is often written שלה, and that even in Gen. xlix. 10, a number of manuscripts have this orthography.

"From the allusion to a prophecy so well known, and so frequently used, the brevity of the prophecy in Ezekiel is to be explained. It forms a most powerful conclusion and resting-point for the prophetic discourse." (*Hävernick.*)

There cannot be any doubt that Ezekiel found in Gen. xlix. 10, the prophecy of a personal Messiah. They, therefore, who assert that no such prophecy is contained in our passage, must, at the same time, assert that Ezekiel misunderstood it; yea, even more, that, even as early as at that period, a false view of that passage was generally prevalent. For, the manner in which Ezekiel alludes to it presupposes that, at that time, the view which found in it a personal Messiah was generally held. If we observe still further, that Ezekiel connected the allusion to Ps. lxxii. with that to Gen. xlix., we cannot hesitate for a moment to admit that he understood the name Shiloh to be Rest-maker, Peace-maker; only, that on the ground of Ps. lxxii., he mentions the cause instead of the effect. He had, moreover, the stronger reason for designating the bearer of peace as the bearer of judgment, because, in his time, the want of judgment had evidently produced the absence of peace, and the general confusion, misery, and destruction.

" As in Gen. xlix. the Patriarch sees a light rising at a far distance, and spreading its brightness over the darkness of centuries, so in Ezekiel also, the same ray of glorious hope lightens through the dark night of confusion and unutterable misery in which he sees himself enveloped."

Kurtz, S. 266, has altogether denied the connection of the passage in Ezekiel with Gen. xlix. These two passages are, as he thinks, altogether different, inasmuch as Ezekiel announces destruction and desolation which shall continue until He comes to whom is the judgment, while Gen. xlix., when understood of a personal Messiah, announces dominion which shall continue until Shiloh comes. But Ezekiel does not contradict Gen. xlix. 10. He gives only the supplement necessary for preventing this passage from being considered as a permission to sin, and from becoming a support of false security. Ezekiel, too, assumes a continuation of the dominion. If that were not concealed behind the destruction, how could " the coming of Him to whom is the judgment" be pointed out as the limit of that destruction? The tree indeed is cut down, but the root remains in its full vigour.

When Jacob announces that the sceptre shall not depart until Shiloh, the prince of peace, cometh, he can thereby mean only that it would not depart *definitively ;* for, otherwise, he would have belied his own experience. From the way by which the Lord had led him, he had sufficiently learnt that God's promises to sinful men must be taken *cum grano salis ;* that they never exclude the visitation of the elect on account of their sins, and that it is only in the end that God will bring all to a glorious fulfilment. When he went to Mesopotamia, God had said to him, " I am with thee, and I will keep thee in all places whither thou goest," Gen. xxviii. 15 ; and yet the deceit which he had practised upon his father and brother was recompensed to him there by the deceit of Laban, and he was obliged to say, " In the day the drought consumed me, and the frost by night, and my sleep departed from mine eyes," Gen. xxxi. 40. When he came from the land of the two rivers, God blessed him and gave him the honourable name of Israel, Gen. xxxii. ; and yet he had soon thereafter to experience grievous distress on account of Dinah and Joseph; and in chap. xxxvii. 34, 35, we are told concerning him: " And Jacob rent his clothes, and put sackcloth upon his loins, and mourned for his son many days. And all his sons and all his daughters rose up to comfort him ; but he refused to be comforted, and he said, I shall go down into the grave unto my son in sorrow." In the kingdom of God there are no other promises than such as resemble those rivers which flow alternately above and below ground. since it is certain that all the subjects of the promises are affected by sin.

Ezekiel xliii. 15 likewise refers to the blessing of Jacob upon Judah. The altar for the burnt-offerings in the new temple is first called *Harel* == the mountain of God, and afterwards *Ariel* == the Lion of God,—indicating that what had been promised to Judah in Gen. xlix., viz., the Lion's nature and invincible power, victorious over all enemies, has its root in the altar,—in the circumstance that the people of God are a people whose sins are forgiven, who dedicate themselves to God, and give Him thanks and praise.

A very remarkable reference to Gen. xlix. meets us at the very threshold of the New Testament. In Luke ii. 13, 14, the heavenly host praise God, saying: " Glory be to God in the highest, and on earth peace." The words, " glory" or " praise be to God," are an allusion to Judah, and to the glorious things foretold in Gen. xlix. of him who centres in Christ. Christ is the true Judah,—He by whom God is glorified, John xiv. 13. The words, " on earth peace," contain the explanation of the name Shiloh, the first name under which the Saviour is celebrated in the Old Testament.

As the words with which the Saviour is first introduced into the world allude to Gen. xlix., so the Lord Himself, before His departure, alludes to this fundamental Messianic prophecy in John xiv. 27: " Peace I leave with you, My peace I give unto you ;" and in xvi. 33: " These things I have spoken unto you, that in Me ye might have peace." So also, after His resurrection, Christ says, in the circle of His disciples, " Peace be unto you," John xx. 19, 21, 26.

The last book of the entire Holy Scripture—the Apocalypse

G

—likewise points back to the remarkable prophecy of Christ at the close of its first book. In Rev. v. 5, we read : " And one of the elders saith unto me, Weep not : behold, the Lion of the tribe of Judah, the Root of David, hath prevailed." " The designation of Christ as the Lion of the tribe of Judah, rests on Gen. xlix. 9. Judah appears there as a lion, in order to denote his warlike and victorious powers. But Judah himself, according to the blessing of dying Jacob, is at some future period to centre in the Messiah. As a type, he had formerly centred already in David, in whom the lion-nature of the tribe of Judah was manifested." This allusion shows that even what is said in vers. 8, 9, found its complete fulfilment only in Christ, and that vers. 8, 9, are parallel to the entire ver. 10, and not to its first half only.

Bengel remarks on Rev. v. 6 : " The elder had pointed John to a Lion, and yet John beheld a Lamb. The Lord Jesus is called a Lion only once in this prophecy, and that, at the very beginning, before the appellation Lamb appears. This indicates that as often as the Lamb is remembered, we should also remember Him as the Lion of the tribe of Judah."

As the designation of Christ as the Lion refers to what, in the blessing of Jacob, is said of the lion-nature of the tribe of Judah, so, in the "Lamb"—the emblem of innocence, justice, silent patience and gentleness—the name Shiloh is embodied.

BALAAM'S PROPHECY.

(NUMB. xxiv. 17–19.)

CARRIED by the Spirit into the far distant future, Balaam sees here how a star goeth out of Jacob and a sceptre riseth out of Israel, and how this sceptre smiteth Moab, by whose enmity the Seer had been brought from a distant region for the destruction of Israel. And not Moab only shall be smitten, but its southern neighbour, Edom, too shall be subdued, whose hatred against Israel had already been prefigured in its ancestor, and had now begun to display itself; and in general, all the enemies of the people of God shall be cast down to the ground by the Ruler out of Jacob.

Ver. 17. "*I see him, but not now; I behold him, but not nigh. A star goeth out of Jacob, and a sceptre riseth out of Israel, and smiteth the borders of Moab, and destroyeth all the sons of the tumult.* Ver. 18. *And Edom shall be a possession, and Seir shall be a possession—his enemies, and Israel acquireth might.* Ver. 19. *And a Ruler shall come out of Jacob, and destroyeth what remaineth out of the city.*"

The star is, in Scripture, the symbol of the splendour of power. The sceptre leads us back to Gen. xlix. 10; and, in general, the announcements of Balaam have, throughout, the promises and hopes of the Patriarchs for their foundation. As in the fundamental passage, so here also, the sceptre, the symbol of dominion, stands for dominion itself. The substance of the two figurative expressions is briefly stated in ver. 19, in the words, "They shall rule out of Jacob," which are tantamount to, "A Ruler shall come out of Jacob."

A difference of opinion exists regarding the glorious King who is here announced. From the earliest times, the Jews understood thereby the Messiah, either exclusively, or, at least, principally, so as to admit of a secondary reference to David. *Onkelos* translates: "When a King shall rise out of Jacob, and out of Israel Messiah shall be anointed;"—*Jonathan:* "When a valiant King shall rise out of the house of Jacob, and out of Israel, Messiah, and a strong Sceptre shall be anointed." The Book of Sohar remarks on the words, "I see him, but now:" "This was in part fulfilled at that time; it will be completely fulfilled in the days of Messiah." (Compare the passages in *Jos. de Voisin*, in the *Prooem.* on *R. Martini Pugio fid.* p. 68; *R. Martini* iii. 3, c. 11; *Schöttgen*, "*Jesus Messias*," S. 151.) How widely this opinion was spread among the Jews, is sufficiently apparent from the circumstance, that the renowned pseudo-Messiah in the time of Hadrian adopted, with reference to the passage under review, the surname *Barcochba, i.e.,* Son of the Star.—From the Jews, this interpretation very soon passed over to the Christians, who rightly found a warrant for it in the narrative of the star of the wise men from the East. *Cyril* of Jerusalem defended the Messianic interpretation against *Julian*. (Compare *Julian*, ed. *Spanh.* p. 263 c. See other passages from the fathers of the Church in *Calov.*) According to *Theodoret* (Quest. 44 in Numb.), there were, indeed, some to whom "Balaam appeared to have foretold nothing concerning our Saviour;" but this opinion was rejected as profane. The Messianic interpretation has, in a narrower and wider sense—*i.e.*, as referring in the first instance to David, but in the highest and proper sense to Christ—become the prevailing one in the Evangelical Church also. It was defended even by such interpreters as *Calvin* and *Clericus*, who, as to other passages, differed from the prevailing Messianic interpretation. (Compare especially *Mieg, de Stella et Sceptro Baleamitico* in the *Thes. Nov.* p. 423 sqq., and *Boullier, Dissert. Syll. Amsterdam* 1750, *Diss* I.) On the other hand, the Messianic interpretation found a zealous and ingenious opponent, first in *Verschuir* in the *Bibl. Brem. nova*, reprinted in his *Opusc.* He was joined by the rationalistic interpreters, who maintained an exclusive reference to David. But *Rosenmüller* and *Baumgarten-Crusius* (bibl. Theol. S. 369) returned to the Messianic interpretation.

The question at issue is chiefly this :—Whether by the star and sceptre some single Israelitish king is designated, or rather, an *ideal* person—the personified Israelitish kingdom. The latter view I proved, in my work on Balaam, to be the correct one, for the following reasons :—1. The reference to a certain Israelitish king is against the analogy of the other prophecies of the Pentateuch. A single person, especially a single king of future time, is nowhere announced in it,—except the Messiah, whose announcement, however, is different from that of David. But, on the other hand, the rise of the *kingdom* in Israel is announced as early as in the promise to the Patriarchs, on which all of Balaam's declarations rest throughout. It is only to this that the words, "A star goeth out of Jacob, and a sceptre riseth out of Israel," can refer,—according to the analogy of Gen. xvii. 6 : "Kings shall come out of thee;" ver. 16 : "And she shall become nations, *kings* of people shall be of her;" and xxxv. 11 : "Kings shall come out of thy loins." 2. The reference to a single king would be against the *analogy* of *Balaam's* prophecies, inasmuch as these nowhere refer to a single individual. 3. The *sceptre* does not, in itself, lead us to think of an individual, since it does not designate a ruler, but dominion in general. But that which especially militates against the reference to an individual is the comparison with the fundamental passage, Gen. xlix. 10, in which Judah, and in him all Israel, does not receive the promise of a single king, but of the kingdom which shall at last be consummated in the Shiloh. 4. In favour of this general interpretation is also ver. 19, in which the words, "And dominion shall come out of Jacob," or literally, "They shall rule out of Jacob," may be considered as just a commentary on the words, "A sceptre riseth out of Israel." So also is ver. 7, "More elevated than Agag be his king," where the king of Israel is an *ideal* person—the personification of the kingdom. Agag, *i.e.*, the fiery one, is not a proper name, but a surname of all Amalekite kings. The Amalekite kingdom— which here represents the world's power, opposed to the kingdom of God, because at the time of the Seer the Amalekites were the most powerful among the people who were hostile to Israel (compare ver. 20, where they are called the *beginning* of the heathen nations, *i.e.*, the most powerful of them)—is here put in opposition to the Israelitish kingdom, and the latter will show itself superior to all worldly power.

The arguments which thus prove the reference of Balaam's prophecy to an Israelitish kingdom, disprove also, not only the exclusive reference to David, but also the exclusive reference to Christ; although they imply at the same time that the prophecy, in its final reference, has Christ for its subject. The Israelitish kingdom, indeed, attained to the full height of its destiny only in and with the Messiah; without the Messiah, the Israelitish kingdom is a trunk without a head. The prophecy thus centres in Christ. We are, however, not entitled to suppose that the prophet himself was not aware of this; on the contrary, we cannot but assume that Balaam must have known it. It is with intention that he does not speak of a plurality of Israelitish kings. The Israelitish kingdom, on the contrary, appears to him in the from of an *ideal* king, because he knows that, at some period, it will find its full realization in the person of one king. For the same reason, Moses also describes the prophetic order, in the first instance, as an *ideal* prophet. That Balaam knew that the Israelitish kingdom would centre in the Messiah, is shown by the reference which his prophecy has to that of dying Jacob, in Gen. xlix. 10, from which the figure of the sceptre is borrowed. According to the latter passage, the whole dignity of Judah as ruler and lord over the whole heathen world is to centre in one elevated individual—the Shiloh. As to the letter, Balaam's prophecy falls short of the prophecy to which it refers, and on which it is founded, in two points. Instead of Judah, it mentions Israel; and instead of the invincible kingdom which is at last to centre in the Messiah, it represents the invincible kingdom only in general. But in both cases, this generality is easily accounted for by the *external* direction of Balaam's prophecy: a more definite tendency was of importance only for those who were *within*. We are fully entitled to suppose that Balaam himself knew what was contained in the fundamental passage. To the same result we are led by the contents of the prophecy itself. Balaam here brings into view an Israelitish kingdom, all-powerful on earth, and raised absolutely above the world's power. He does not stop with the victory over Moab and Edom —even this victory appears to him as an absolute and lasting one, and hence, essentially different from the temporary submission to David—but, from the particular, which only serves to exemplify the idea in reference to the historical relations existing at the present, he passes on, in ver. 19, to the general, the total overthrow of the whole hostile world's power. Indeed, such a progress is probably found even in ver. 17 itself. If at the close of it we read, "And destroyeth all the sons of the tumult," the word *all*, which is wanting in Jer. xlviii. 45, indicates that by the sons of the tumult we are to understand not only the Moabites, but the whole *species* to which they belonged, the whole heathen world, whose nature is restlessness, desire for strife, and the spirit of conquest,—the opposites of meekness and gentleness, which are the virtues characteristic of the subjects of the kingdom of God. In ver. 18, the particular is likewise followed by the general. But while ver. 17 and 18 contain, in each of the two particular features, a previous short allusion to the general, ver. 19 most expressly and intentionally reduces the particular to the general. The absolute elevation above the world's power, attributed by Balaam to the Israelitish kingdom, leads not only beyond the idea of a single king of the ordinary stamp, but also beyond that of the entire ordinary kingdom.

The objections urged against the Messianic interpretation are based either on a misunderstanding, or upon a superficial view of the passage. They who maintain that the judging activity of the Messiah is here brought forward in a manner too one-sided, forget that this part only could here be treated of. As Balaam's discourse formed the answer to Balak's message—"Come, curse me this people; peradventure we shall prevail to smite them and drive them out of the land,"—its natural subject was: *Israel's position towards their enemies;* and Balaam had expressly stated, in ver. 14, that he would treat of that subject. Balaam had to do with an enemy of Israel, and his chief aim was to represent to him the vanity of all his hostile efforts. The partial view arises, therefore, from the nature of the case; and only *in that case* could doubts arise as to the ultimate reference to the Messiah, if the other view were altogether *denied.* But such is by no means the case; for the words in ver. 9, "Blessed is he that blesseth thee," distinctly point it out. They who object to the Messianic interpretation on the ground that, at the time of Christ, the Moabites had disappeared from the stage of history, overlook the circumstance, that the Moabites here, as well as in Is. xi., where the complete destruction of Moab is likewise assigned to the times of the Messiah, are viewed only in their character as enemies to the congregation of God. If the prophecy were fulfilled upon the Moabites, even at the time when they still existed as a nation, not as Moabites, but as the enemies of the people of God; then the limit of their national existence cannot be the limit of the fulfilment of the prophecy. A case quite analogous is found in Mic. v. 4, 5, where the prophet characterizes the enemies of the kingdom of God at the time of the Messiah by the name of Asshur, although it appears, from other passages, that he distinctly knew that Asshur must, long ere that time, have disappeared from the scene of history.

The Messianic character of the prophecy being thus established, it will be impossible to misunderstand the internal relation between the star of Balaam and the star of the wise men from the East. The star of Balaam is the emblem of the kingdom which will rise in Israel. The star of the Magi is the symbol of the Ruler in whom the kingly power appears concentrated. The appearance of the star embodying the image of the prophet, indicates that the last and highest fulfilment of his prophecies is now to take place.

MOSES' PROMISE OF THE PROPHET.

(DEUT. xviii. 15–19.)

Ver. 15. "*A prophet from the midst of thee, of thy brethren, like unto me, Jehovah thy God will raise up : unto him ye shall hearken.* Ver. 16. *According to all that thou desiredst of Jehovah thy God in Horeb, in the day of the assembly, when thou didst say, I will not hear any farther the voice of Jehovah my God, and will not see this great fire any more, that I die not.* Ver. 17. *Then Jehovah said unto me, They have well spoken.* Ver. 18. *A prophet I will raise them up from among their brethren, like unto thee; and I will put My words into his mouth, and he shall speak unto them all that I shall command him.* Ver. 19. *And it shall come to pass, that whosoever will not hearken unto My words which he shall speak in My name, I will require it of him.*"

If we leave out of view the unfortunate attempts of those who would understand by the prophet here promised, either Joshua—as is done by *Abenezra, Bechai,* and *von Ammon* (*Christol.* S. 29)—or Jeremiah—as is the case in *Baal Hatturim* and *Jalkut* out of the book *Pesikta,* and in *Abarbanel*—we may reduce the expositions of this passage to three classes. 1. Several consider the "prophet" as a collective noun, and understand thereby the prophets of all times. Such was the opinion of *Origen* (*c. Celsum* i. 9, § 5, *Mosh.*), of the Arabic translator, and of most of the modern Jewish interpreters,— especially *Kimchi, Alshech,* and *Lipman* (*Nizachon* 137) ; while *Abenezra* and *Bechai* conjoin this view with that according to which Jeremiah is meant. Among recent expositors, it is defended by *Rosenmüller, Vater, Baumgarten-Crusius* (*Bibl. Theol.* S. 369), and others. 2. Some see in it an exclusive reference to Christ,—a view which has been held by most interpreters in the Christian Church, and from the earliest times. It is found as early as in *Justin Martyr, Tertullian, Athanasius, Eusebius* (*Demonstr.* iii. 2, ix. 11), *Lactantius* (iv. 17), *Augustine* (*c. Faustum,* xvi. c. 15, 18, 19), and *Isidore* of *Pelusium* (c. iii. ep. 49). It was held by *Luther* (t. 3. *Jen. Lat.* f. 123), became the prevailing one in the Lutheran Church, and was approved of by most of the Reformed interpreters. Among its earliest defenders, the most eminent are *Deyling* (*Misc.* ii. 175), *Frischmuth* (in the *Thesaurus theol.-philol.* i. 354), and *Hasaeus* (in the *Thes. theol.-philol.* nov. i. S. 439.) In recent times it has been defended by *Pareau* (in the *Inst. interpr. V. T.* p. 506), by *Knapp* (*Dogm.* ii. 138). 3. Others have steered a middle course, inasmuch as they consider the " prophet" to be a collective noun, but, at the same time, maintain that only by the mission of Christ, in whom the idea of the prophetic order was perfectly realized, the promise was completely fulfilled. Thus did *Nicolaus de Lyra, Calvin,* several Roman Catholic interpreters, *Grotius, Clericus,* and others.

In favour of the Messianic interpretation, the authority of tradition has been, first of all, appealed to. It is true that modern Jewish interpreters differ from it; but this has been the result of polemical considerations alone. It can be satisfactorily proved that the Messianic interpretation was the prevailing one among the older Jews. 1 Mac. xiv. 41—" Also that the Jews and priests resolved that Simon should be commander and high priest for ever, until a *credible prophet* should arise,"—has been frequently appealed to in proof of this, but erroneously. For, that by the " credible prophet," *i.e.,* one sufficiently attested by miracles or fulfilled prophecies, we are not to understand the prophet promised by Moses (as was done by Luther, and many older expositors who followed him), is shown, partly by the absence of the article, and partly by the circumstance that a *credible* prophet is spoken of. The sense is rather this : Simon and his family should continue to hold the highest dignity until God Himself should make another arrangement by a future prophet, as there was none at that time (comp. Ps. lxxiv. 9 : " There is no more any prophet"), and thus put an end to a state of things which, on the one hand, was in contradiction to the law, and, on the other, to the promise,—a state of things unto which they had been led by the force of circumstances, and which could, at all events, be only a provisional one. (Compare *J. D. Michaelis* on that passage.) It is not on the passage under review that the expectation of a prophet there rests, but rather on Mal. iii. 1, 23, where a prophet is promised as the precursor of the Messiah. But the New Testament furnishes sufficient materials for proving the

Messianic interpretation. The very manner in which Peter and Stephen quote this passage shows that the Messianic interpretation was, at that time, the prevailing one. . They do not deem it at all necessary to prove it ; they proceed on the supposition of its being universally acknowledged. It was, no doubt, chiefly our passage which Philip had in view when, in John i. 46, he said to Nathanael : ὃν ἔγραψε Μωϋσῆς ἐν τῷ νόμῳ, εὑρήκαμεν, Ἰησοῦν. For, besides the passage under consideration, there is only one other personal Messianic prophecy in the Pentateuch, namely, Gen. xlix. 10 ; and the marks of the Shiloh did not so distinctly appear in Jesus, as did those of the Prophet. The mention of the person of Moses[1] (which in Gen. xlix. 10 is less concerned), and of the law, clearly point to the passage under review. After the feeding of the five thousand, the people say, in John vi. 14 : Ὅτι οὗτός ἐστιν ἀληθῶς ὁ προφήτης, ὁ ἐρχόμενος εἰς τὸν κόσμον. The Messianic interpretation was, accordingly, not peculiar to a few learned men, but to the whole people. Even with the Samaritans the Messianic explanation was the prevailing one,—based, no doubt, upon the tradition which had come to them from the Jews. The Samaritan woman says, in John iv. 25 : οἶδα ὅτι Μεσσίας ἔρχεται, ὁ λεγόμενος Χριστός· ὅταν ἔλθῃ ἐκεῖνος, ἀναγγελεῖ ἡμῖν πάντα. Now, as the Samaritans acknowledged only the Pentateuch, there is no other passage than that under review from which the idea of the Messiah as a divinely enlightened teacher, which is here expressed, could have been derived. The last words agree in a remarkable manner with Deut. xviii. 18 : "And he shall speak unto them all that I shall command him." That too great weight, however, must not be attached to tradition, is shown by John i. 21, and vii. 40, 41 ; for these passages clearly prove that there were also many who thought it possible that Deut. xviii. contained not only the announcement of the Messiah, but of some distinguished prophet also, besides Him, who should be His precursor or companion. At the same time, we must not overlook the circumstance that, in both passages, the people are at a loss, and are thereby induced to deviate from the pre-

---

[1] *Lampe* says : He has preserved to us not only what, in Paradise, and afterwards to and through the Patriarchs, had been told about this Redeemer ; but he himself, under divine inspiration, has prophesied of Him, —especially in Deut. xviii. 15-18.

vailing opinion. Their uncertainty and wavering, however, is only about the person. In this they agree, notwithstanding, that in Deut. xviii. they find the announcement of one distinguished person.

But the Messianic interpretation may appeal, with still greater confidence, to the direct evidence of the New Testament. The declaration of the Lord in John v. 45-47 is here to be noticed above all : *Μὴ δοκεῖτε ὅτι ἐγὼ κατηγορήσω ὑμῶν πρὸς τὸν πατέρα· ἔστιν ὁ κατηγορῶν ὑμῶν, Μωϋσῆς, εἰς ὃν ὑμεῖς ἠλπίκατε. Εἰ γὰρ ἐπιστεύετε Μωϋσῇ, ἐπιστεύετε ἂν ἐμοί· περὶ γὰρ ἐμοῦ ἐκεῖνος ἔγραψεν. Εἰ δὲ τοῖς ἐκείνου γράμμασιν οὐ πιστεύετε, πῶς τοῖς ἐμοῖς ῥήμασι πιστεύσετε;*—It is clear that the Lord must here have had in view a distinct passage of the Pentateuch,—a clear and definite declaration of Moses. Dexterous explanations (*Bengel: Nunquam non ; Tholuck:* The prophetical and typical element implied in the whole form of worship) are of no apologetic value, and it is not possible summarily, on such grounds, to call the enemies before the judgment-seat of God. It was not enough to allude, in a way so general, to what could not be at once perceptible ; greater distinctness and particularity would have been required. But if a single declaration—a direct Messianic prophecy—form the question at issue, our passage only can be meant ; for it is the only prophecy of Christ which Moses, on whose person great stress is laid, uttered in his own name. Moreover, Christ would more readily expect that the Jews would acknowledge our prophecy to be fulfilled in Him, than the prophecy in Gen. xlix., which refers rather to the Messiah in glory. The preceding words of Jesus likewise contain references to the passage now under consideration. Ver. 38—"And ye have not His word abiding in you ; for whom He hath sent, Him ye believe not,"—contains an allusion to Deut. xviii. 18 : "And I will put My words into his mouth, and he shall speak unto them all that I shall command him ;" so that whosoever rejects the Ambassador of God, rejects His word at the same time. John v. 43—"I am come in My Father's name, and ye receive Me not,"—acquires both its significance and earnestness from its reference to ver. 19 of our passage : " Whosoever will not hearken unto My words, which he shall speak in My name, I will require it of him." *Further,*—The point at issue in this discourse of Christ is an accusation of the Jews against Christ, that He had violated the Mosaic law. (Compare John v. 10–16, and v. 18, which states the second apparent violation of the law.) It was thus highly appropriate that Jesus should throw back upon the Jews the charge which they brought against Him, and should prove to them that it was just they who were in fatal opposition to the enactments of the Mosaic law. *Finally,* —It is this same Moses in whom they trusted, whom they considered as their patron, and whom to please the more, they were so zealous for his law against Jesus,—it is this same Moses whom Jesus represents as their accuser. And he is such an accuser as renders every other superfluous, so that Christ did not need specially to come forward in such a character. The accusation of Moses must, then, according to this declaration, and in accordance with what follows, refer to the cause of Christ. But the passage under review is the only Messianic prophecy of a *threatening character* which the Pentateuch contains,—the only one in which divine judgments are threatened to the despisers of the Messiah,—the only Mosaic foundation for the denunciation : " Woe to the people that despiseth thee." If it be denied that Christ refers to it,—if its Messianic character be not acknowledged, the first words of Christ are destitute of foundation. But if it be thus undeniable that Christ declared Himself to be the prophet of our passage, it must be considered an indirect attack upon His divinity to say, as *Dr Lücke* does, that Christ did so by way of " adaptation to the interpretation of that time." It is just this appeal which forms the pith of Christ's discourse ; it is the real death-blow inflicted by Him upon His adversaries. If this blow was a mere feint, His honour is endangered,—which may God forbid !—The Lord further marks Himself out as the prophet announced by Moses, and that, too, in a very distinct manner, in John xii. 48–50,—a passage which is evidently based upon vers. 18 and 19 of the text under review. (Compare John xiv. 24–31.)—To this we may add, further, that, according to St Luke xxiv. 44, the Lord Himself explains to His disciples the prophecies in the Pentateuch concerning Him ; and we cannot well expect that Christ should have made no reference to a passage which one of the Apostles points out as being of greater weight than all others. This is done by Peter in Acts iii. 22, 23. The manner in which he quotes it, entirely excludes the notion that Moses was speaking of Christ, only in so far as He belonged to the collective body of the prophets. Peter says expressly, that Moses and the later prophets foretold τὰς ἡμέρας ταύτας; and the words, τοῦ προφήτου ἐκείνου, show that he did not understand the singular in a collective sense. The circumstance that Stephen, in Acts vii. 37, likewise refers the passage to Christ, would not be, in itself, conclusive, because Stephen's 'case is different from that of the Apostles. But we must not overlook the passage Matt. xvii. 5, according to which, at Christ's transfiguration, a voice was heard from heaven which said: οὗτός ἐστιν ὁ υἱός μου ὁ ἀγαπητός, ἐν ᾧ εὐδόκησα· αὐτοῦ ἀκούετε. As the first part of this declaration is taken from the Messianic prediction in Is. xlii., so is the second from the passage under consideration; and, by this use of its words, the sense is clearly shown. It is a very significant fact, that our passage is thus connected just with Is. xlii.—the first prophetic announcement in which it is specially resumed, and in which the prophetic order itself is the proclaimer of *the* Prophet. And it is not less significant that this reference to our text, with which all the other announcements by Isaiah concerning the Great Prophet to come are so immediately connected, should precede chapters xlix., l., and lxi. It thus serves as a commentary upon the declaration of Moses. The beginning and the outlines receive light from the progress and completion.

He, however, who believes in Christ, will, after these details, expect that internal reasons also should prove the reference to Christ; and this expectation is fully confirmed.

That Moses did not intend by the word נָבִיא, "prophet," to designate a collective body merely, but that he had at least some special individual in view, appears, partly, from the word itself being constantly in the singular, and, partly, from the constant use of the singular suffixes in reference to it; while, in the case of collective nouns, it is usual to interchange the singular with the plural. The force of this argument is abundantly evident in the fact, that not a few of even non-Messianic interpreters have been thereby compelled to make some single individual the subject of this prophecy. But we must hesitate the more to adopt the opinion that נָבִיא stands here simply in the singular instead of the plural, because neither does this word anywhere else occur as a collective noun, nor is the prophetic order ever spoken of in the manner alleged. The expectation of a Messiah was already at that time current among the people. In what way, then, could they understand a promise, in which one individual only was spoken of, except by referring it, at least chiefly, to the one whom they expected?—*Hofmann* (*Weissagung und Erfüllung* i. S. 253) objects that the prophet here spoken of was, in no respect, different from the *king* in Deut. xvii. 14–20. But the king mentioned there is no collective noun. An individual who, in future times, should first attain to royal dignity, forms there the subject throughout. This appears especially from ver. 20, where he and his *sons* are spoken of. The first king is held up as an example, to show in him what was applicable to the royal dignity in general. On the other hand, it is in favour of our view, that, in the verses immediately preceding (vers. 8–13), the priests are, at first, spoken of only in the plural, although the priestly order had much more of the character of a collective body than the prophetic order.

A comparison between this prophecy and that of the Shiloh in Gen. xlix. 10 is likewise in favour of the Messianic interpretation. Even there, His prophetic office is alluded to in the kingly office. The ruler out of Judah is the Peaceful One, to whom the nations yield a spontaneous obedience, an obedience flowing from a pious source,—and He rules not by compulsion, but by the word.

The prophet is moreover contrasted with a single individual —with Moses; and this compels us to refer the prophecy to some distinguished individual. In ver. 15, Moses promises to the people a prophet *like unto himself*; and thus also does the Lord say, in ver. 18: "A prophet *like unto thee* I will raise up." We cannot for a moment suppose that this likeness should refer to the prophetic calling only,—to the words: "I will put My words into his mouth, and he shall speak unto them all that I shall command him." It must at the same time be implied in it, that the future prophet shall be as thoroughly competent for his work, as Moses was for that which was committed to him. If it were not so, the promise would be deficient in that consolatory and elevating character which, according to the context, it is evidently intended to possess. If we were to paraphrase thus, "The Lord will raise up a prophet, inferior, indeed, to myself, but yet the bearer of divine revelations," we should at once perceive how unsuitable it were. *Further,*—It is quite evident that the "Prophet" here is the main instrument of divine agency among the covenant-people of the future,—that He is the real support and anchor of the kingdom of God. But now the difficulties of the future were, as Moses himself saw, so great, that gifts in any way short of those of Moses would by no means have been sufficient. Moses foresees that the spirit of apostasy, which, even in his time, began to manifest itself, would, in future times, increase to a fearful extent. (Compare especially Deut. xxxii.) Against this, ordinary gifts and powers would be of no avail. A successful and enduring reaction could be brought about only by one who should be, for the more difficult circumstances of the future, such as Moses was for his times. But— and this circumstance is of still greater weight—it forms the task of the future to translate the whole heathen world into the kingdom of God. · In it, Japheth is to dwell in the tents of Shem; all the nations of the earth are to become partakers in the blessing resting on Abraham. In the view of such a task, a prophet of ordinary dimensions, as well as the collective body of such, would dwindle down to the appearance of a dwarf. They would have been less than Moses. In Deut. xxxiv. 10, it is said, "There arose not a prophet since in Israel like unto Moses, whom the Lord knew face to face;"—a passage which not only plainly refers to the experience acquired at that time, but which expresses also what might be expected of that portion of the future which was more immediately at hand. When Miriam and Aaron said, "Doth the Lord indeed speak only by Moses, doth He not speak by us also?" the Lord immediately, Num. xii. 6-8, reproves their presumption of thinking themselves *like unto Moses,* as respects the prophetical gift, in these words: "If some one be your prophet,"—*i.e.,* if some one be a prophet according to your way, with prophets of your class,—"I, the Lord, make myself known unto him in a vision, in a dream I speak unto him. Not so my servant Moses; in all My house he is faithful. Mouth to mouth I speak to him, and face to face, and not in dark speeches; and the appearance of the Lord he beholds." Moses, as a prophet, is here contrasted with the whole order of prophets of ordinary gifts. A higher dignity among them is claimed for him on the ground that not some special mission, but the care of the whole economy of the Old Testament, was entrusted to him; compare Heb. iii. 5. His is a specially close relation to the Lord, a specially high degree of illumination. The collective body of ordinary prophets cannot, therefore, by any possibility be the "prophet" who is *like unto Moses*, as completely equal to the task of the future as Moses was for that of his day. But the greater the work of the future, the more necessary is it that the prophet of the future, in order to be *like unto Moses*, should, in his whole individuality, and in all his gifts, be far superior to him; compare Heb. iii. 6.

Finally,—The common prophetic order itself refuses the honour of being the prophet like unto Moses. The prophecies of Isaiah, in chapters xlii., xlix., l., and lxi., are based upon our passage, and in all of them the Messiah appears as the prophet κατ' ἐξοχήν. It is to Him that the mission is entrusted of being the restorer of Jacob, and the salvation of the Lord, even unto the end of the world.

Whilst these reasons demand the reference of this prophecy to Christ, there are, on the other hand, weighty considerations which make it appear that a reference to the prophetic order of the Old Testament cannot be excluded. These considerations are, 1. The wider context. Deuteronomy is distinguished from the preceding books by this, that provisions are made in it for the time subsequent to the death of Moses, which was now at hand. From chap. xvii. 8, the magistrates and powers—the superiors, to whose authority in secular and spiritual affairs the people shall submit—are introduced. First, the civil magistrates are brought before them, xvii. 8–20; and then the ecclesiastical superiors, chap. xviii. Vers. 1–8 treat of the priests as the ordinary servants of the Lord in spiritual things. Everywhere else, offices, institutions, orders, are spoken of. In such a connection, it is not probable that *the prophet* should be only an individual; and the less so, because evidently the prophet, as the organ of the immediate revelation of God, is placed by the side of the priests, the teachers of the law (compare xvii. 10, 11, 18; xxxiv. 10), as their corrective, as a thorn in their flesh, to make up for their inability. It is true that this wider connection is also against those who would here *exclude* Christ. If it be certain that Moses already knew the Messianic promises (compare the remarks on Gen. xlix.), then, just in this context, the reference to Christ, the head of the authorities of the future, could not be wanting.

2. An exclusive reference to Christ is opposed by the more immediate context. This connection is twofold. In ver. 15, Moses first utters the promise in his own name, and here it stands connected with what precedes. Moses had forbidden to the people the use of all the means by which those who were given to idolatry endeavoured to penetrate the boundaries of human knowledge: "Thou shalt not do so," is his language; for that which these are vainly seeking after in this sinful manner, shall, in reality, be granted to thee by thy God. Here, it was not only appropriate to remind them of the Messiah, inasmuch as His appearance, as being the most perfect revelation of God, satisfies most perfectly the desire after higher communications; but it would have been very strange if here, where so suitable an opportunity presented itself, the founder of the Old Economy had omitted all reference to the founder of the New Economy, and had limited himself to the intervening, more imperfect divine communications. But, on the other hand, it would have been as strange if Moses had taken no notice of them at all,—if, supposing that a series of false prophets would appear, he had been satisfied to lay down in chap. xiii. 2 sqq. the distinctive marks of true and false prophets, and had then, in the passage under review, referred to the divine revelations to be expected in the distant future, without noticing those to be expected in the more immediate future,—thus neglecting to employ means peculiarly fitted for gaining admission for his exhortations. The word נתן in ver. 14 is especially opposed to such a view. "And thou (shalt) not (do) so, Jehovah thy God *gave* thee." *J. D. Michaelis* says: "What He gave to the Israelites is specified in vers. 15 and 18." The past tense suggests the idea of a gift which had already taken its beginning in the present.—The promise stands in a different connection in ver. 18. Moses had already given it in his own name in ver. 15. In order to give it greater authority, he reports, in the following verses, when and how he had received it from God. It was delivered to him on Sinai, where God had directly revealed Himself to the people at the promulgation of the Law, partly in order to strengthen their confidence in Moses the mediator, and

partly to show them the folly of their desiring any other mode of divine communication. But the people were seized with terror before the dreadful majesty of God, and prayed that God would no longer speak to them directly, but through *a* mediator, as He had hitherto done; compare Exod. xx.; Deut. v. The Lord then said to Moses, "They have well spoken; a prophet," etc. The words here, in ver. 17, agree very well with Deut. v. 28. The agreement in the words indicates that *here* we have an addition to that which is *there* communicated regarding what was spoken by God on that occasion. *There,* we are told only what had an immediate reference to the present—viz., the appointment of Moses as mediator; *here,* we are told what was at that time fixed in reference to the future of the people. We cannot fail to perceive that *here,* if ever, a divine revelation was appropriate concerning the coming of Christ, who, as the Mediator between God and man, veiled His Godhead, and in human form, brought God nearer to man. But we should, at the same time, expect here an allusion to the inferior messengers of God, who were to precede Him.

3. The exclusive reference to the Messiah is inconsistent with vers. 20–22. The marks of a false prophet are given in them. If, however, that which precedes had no reference at all to true prophets, it would be almost impossible to trace any suitable connection of the thoughts.

4. If the passage were referred to Christ exclusively, the prophetic institution would then be without any legitimate authority; and from the whole character of the Mosaic legislation, as laying the foundation for the future progress and development of the Theocracy, we could not well conceive that so important an institution should be deficient in this point. Moreover, the whole historical existence of the prophetic order necessarily presupposes such a foundation. Deut. xiii. 2 sq. was not fitted to afford such a foundation, as it refers, only indirectly and by implication, to true prophets.

5. *Finally,*—There are not wanting slight hints in the New Testament that the reference to Christ is not an exclusive one. These are found in Luke xi. 50, 51: Ἵνα ἐκζητηθῇ τὸ αἷμα πάντων τῶν προφητῶν . . . ἀπὸ τῆς γενεᾶς ταύτης . . . ναὶ λέγω ὑμῖν ἐκζητηθήσεται ἀπὸ τῆς γενεᾶς ταύτης. The emphatic repetition of ἐκζητεῖν in that passage shows plainly its connection

with the words, " I will require it of him," in the passage under review ; just as the יררש, which, according to 2 Chron. xxiv. 22, the prophet Zechariah, who was unjustly slain, uttered when dying, alludes not only to Gen. ix. 5, but to our passage also. But here we must remark that, in consequence of the sin committed against the Prophet κατ᾽ ἐξοχήν—Christ—vengeance for the crimes committed against the inferior prophets is executed at the same time, so that, in the first instance, *His* blood is required, and, on this occasion, all the blood also which was formerly shed.

But how can these two facts be reconciled :—that Moses had, undeniably, the Messiah in view, and that, notwithstanding, there seems at the same time to be a reference to the prophets in general ? The simplest mode of reconciling them is the following.   The prophet here is an *ideal* person, comprehending all the true prophets who had appeared from Moses to Christ, including the latter. But Moses does not here speak of the prophets as a collective body, to which, at the close, Christ also belonged, as it were, incidentally, and as one among the many, —as *Calvin* and other interpreters mentioned above suppose ; but rather, the plurality of prophets is, for this reason only, comprehended by Moses in an *ideal* unity, that, on the authority of Gen. xlix. 10, and by the illumination of the Holy Spirit, he knew that the prophetical order would, at some future time, centre in a real person,—in Christ.   But there is so much the more of truth in thus viewing the prophetic order as a whole, since, according to 1 Peter i. 11, the Spirit of Christ spoke in the prophets.   Thus, in a certain sense, Christ is the only Prophet.

THE ANGEL OF THE LORD IN THE PENTATEUCH, AND THE BOOK OF JOSHUA.

The New Testament distinguishes between the hidden God and the revealed God—the Son or Logos—who is connected with the former by oneness of nature, and who from everlasting, and even at the creation itself, filled up the immeasurable distance between the Creator and the creation ;—who has been the Mediator in all God's relations to the world ;—who at all times, and even before He became man in Christ, has been the light of

the world,—and to whom, specially, was committed the direction
of the economy of the Old Covenant.

It is evident that this doctrine stands in the closest connection with the Christology,—that it forms, indeed, its theological foundation and ground-work.   Until the Christology
has attained to a knowledge of the true divinity of the Saviour,
its results cannot be otherwise than very meagre and unsatis-
factory.   Wheresoever the true state of human nature is seen
in the light of Holy Scripture, no high expectations can be
entertained from a merely human Saviour, although he were
endowed even with as full a measure of the gifts of the Spirit
of God as human nature, in its finite and sinful condition, is
able to bear.   But unless there exist in the one divine Being
itself, such a distinction of persons, the divinity of the Saviour
cannot be acknowledged, without endangering the unity of God
which the Scriptures so emphatically teach.   If, however, there
be such a distinction,—if the Word be indeed with God, we
cannot avoid ascribing to God the desire of revealing Himself ;
nor, in such a case, can we conceive that He should content
Himself with inferior forms of revelation, with merely transitory
manifestations.   We can recognise in these only preparations,
and preludes of the highest and truest revelation.

The question then is, whether any insight into this doctrine
is to be found as early as in the Books of the Old Testament.
Sound Christian Theology has discovered the outlines of such
a distinction betwixt the hidden and the revealed God, in many
passages of the Old Testament, in which mention is made of
the Angel or Messenger of God.   The general tenor of these
passages will be best exemplified by the first among them,—the
narrative of Hagar in Gen. xvi.   In ver. 7, we are told that
the Angel of Jehovah found Hagar.   In ver. 10, this Angel
ascribes to Himself a divine work, viz., the innumerable increase
of Hagar's posterity.   In ver. 11, He says that Jehovah had
heard her distress.   He thus asserts of Jehovah what, shortly
before, He had said of Himself.   Moreover, in ver. 13, Hagar
expresses her astonishment that she had seen GOD, and yet had
remained alive.—The opinion that these passages form the Old
Testament foundation for the Proemium of St John's Gospel,
has not remained uncontroverted.· From the very times of the
Church-fathers it has been asserted by many, that where the

Angel of the Lord is spoken of, we must not think of a person connected with God by unity of nature, but of a lower angel, by whom God executes His commands, and through whom He acts and speaks. The latest defenders of the view are *Hofmann* in "*Weissagung und Erfüllung*," and in the "*Schriftbeweis*," and *Delitzsch* in his commentary on Genesis.—Others are of opinion, that the Angel of Jehovah is identical with Jehovah Himself,—not denoting a person distinct from Him, but only the form in which He manifests Himself. We shall not here discuss the question in its whole extent; we shall, in the meantime, consider only what the principal passages of the Pentateuch and of the adjacent Book of Joshua teach upon this point, and how far their teaching coincides with, or is in opposition to, these various views. For it is only to this extent that the inquiry belongs to our present object.

In Gen. xvi. 13, these words are of special importance: "*And she called the name of the Lord who spoke unto her, Thou art a God of sight: for she said, Do I now* (properly *here*, in the place where such a sight was vouchsafed to me) *still see after my seeing?*" "Do I see" is equivalent to, "Do I live," because death threatened, as it were, to enter through the eyes. (Compare the expression, "Mine eyes have seen," in Is. vi.) רֹאִי is the pausal form for רְאִי; see Job xxxiii. 21, where, however, the accent is on the penultimate. Then follows ver. 14: *They called the well, "Well of the living sight;"* i.e., where a person had a sight of God, and remained alive.

Hagar must have been convinced that she had seen God without the mediation of a created angel; for, otherwise, she could not have wondered that her life was preserved. Man, entangled by the visible world, is terrified when he comes in contact with the invisible world, even with angels. (Compare Dan. viii. 17, 18; Luke ii. 9.) But this terror rises to fear of death only when man comes into contact with the Lord Himself. (Compare the remarks on Rev. i. 17.) In Gen. xxxii. 31—a passage which bears the closest resemblance to the one now under review, and from which it receives its explanation—it is said: "And Jacob called the name of the place *Peniel*, for I have seen GOD face to face, and my life has been preserved." In Exod. xx. 19, the children of Israel said to Moses, "Speak thou with us, and we will hear; and let not GOD speak with us, lest we die;" compared with Deut. v. 21: "Now therefore why should we die? for this great fire will consume us; if we hear the voice of the Lord our God any more, then we shall die." (Compare also Deut. xviii. 16.)   And it is Jehovah who, in Exod. xxxiii. 20, says, "There shall no man see Me and live." Israel's Lord and God is, in the absolute energy of His nature, a "consuming fire," Deut. iv. 24. (Compare Deut. ix. 3; Is. xxxiii. 14: "Who among us would dwell with the devouring fire? who among us would dwell with everlasting burning?" Heb. xii. 29.)   It is not the reflected light, even in the most exalted creatures, nor the sight of the saints of whom it is said, "Behold, He puts no trust in His servants, and His angels He chargeth with folly,"—but the sight of the thrice Holy One, which makes Isaiah exclaim, "Woe is me, for I am undone; for I am a man of unclean lips, and dwell in the midst of a people of unclean lips."

So much then is clear,—that the opinion which considers the Angel of the Lord to be a created angel is overthrown by the first passage where that angel is mentioned, if the exposition which we have given of vers. 13, 14—an exposition which is now generally received, and which was last advanced by *Knobel*—be correct.   But *Delitzsch* gives another exposition: "Thou art a God of sight," *i.e.*, one whose all-seeing eye does not overlook the helpless and destitute, even in the remotest corner of the wilderness."   Against this we remark, that ראי never denotes the act of seeing, but the sight itself.   "Have I not even here (even in the desert land of destitution) looked after Him who saw me?"   "Well of the living one who seeth me," *i.e.*, of the omnipresent divine providence.   In opposition to this exposition, however, we must remark, that God is nowhere else in Genesis called the Living One.   But our chief objection is, that these expositions destroy the connection which so evidently exists between our passage and those already quoted, —especially Gen. xxxii. 31; Exod. xxxiii. 20. (Compare, moreover, Jud. xiii. 22: "And Manoah said unto his wife, We shall surely die, because we have seen GOD.")

It has been asked, Why should the Logos have appeared first to the Egyptian maid?   But the low condition of Hagar cannot here come into consideration; for the appearance is in reality intended, not for her, but for Abraham.   Immediately before, in chap. xii. 7, it is said, "And the Lord appeared unto Abraham;" and immediately after, in chap. xvii. 1, "And when Abraham was ninety years old and nine, the Lord appeared to him;" the appearance of the Lord Himself is mentioned in order that every thought of a lower angel may be warded off.   The passage under consideration, then, contains the indication, that such appearances must only be conceived of as manifestations of the Deity Himself to the world.   Just as our passage is preserved from erroneous interpretations by such passages as Gen. xii. 7, xvii. 1, so these receive from ours, in return, their most distinct definition.   We learn from this, that wherever appearances of Jehovah are mentioned, we must conceive of them as effected by the mediation of His Angel.   There is no substantial difference betwixt the passages in which Jehovah Himself is mentioned, and those in which the Angel of Jehovah is spoken of.   They serve to supplement and to explain one another.   The words, "In His Angel," in chap. xvi. 7, furnish us with the supplement to the succeeding statement, "And *Jehovah* appeared to him" (so, *e.g.*, also in chap. xviii. 1), just as the writer in Gen. chap. ii. iii. makes use of the name Jehovah-Elohim, in order that henceforth every one may understand that where only Jehovah is spoken of, He is yet personally identical with Elohim.

Let us now turn to Gen. xviii. xix.   According to *Delitzsch*, all the three men who appeared to Abraham were "finite spirits made visible."   *Hofmann* (*Schriftb.* S. 87) says : "Jehovah is present on earth in His angels, in the two with Lot, as in the three with Abraham."   We, however, hold fast by the view of the ancient Church, that in chap. xviii. the Logos appeared accompanied by two inferior angels.

Abraham's regards are, from the very first, involuntarily directed to one from among the three, and whom he addresses by אֲדֹנָי, O Lord (xviii. 3) ; the two others are considered by him as companions only.   But Lot has to do with both equally, and addresses them first by אֲדֹנַי, my Lords.—In chap. xviii., it is always one only of the three who speaks; the two others are mute;[1] while in chap. xix. everything comes from the two

---

[1] The words in ver. 9, "And they said to him," are to be understood only thus:—that one spoke at the same time in the name of the others ; in the question thus put, it is, in the first instance, only the general relation

equally. He with whom Abraham has to do, always, and without exception, speaks as God Himself; while the two with whom Lot has to do speak at first, as λειτουργικὰ πνεύματα, distinguishing themselves from the Lord who sent them (compare ver. 13); and it is only after they have thus drawn the line of separation between themselves and Jehovah, that they appear, in vers. 21, 22, as speaking in His name. They do so, moreover, only after Lot, in the anxiety of his heart and in his excitement, had previously addressed, in them, Him who sent them, and with whom he desired to have to do as immediately as possible. The scene bears, throughout, a character of excitement, and is not fitted to afford data for general conclusions. We cannot infer from it that it was, in general, customary to address, in the angels, the Lord who sent them, or that the angels acted in the name of the Lord. In chap. xviii., from ver. 1, where the narrative begins with the words, "And Jehovah appeared unto him," Moses always speaks of him with whom Abraham had to do as Jehovah only, excepting where he introduces the three men. (He with whom Abraham has to do is called, not fewer than eight times, Jehovah, and six times אֲדוֹנָי.) But in chap. xix., Jehovah, who is concealed behind the two angels, appears only twice in the expression, "And He said," in vers. 17, 21, for which ver. 13 suggests the supplement: "through His two angels."— Even in ver. 16, the narrative distinguishes Jehovah from the two men,—and all this in an exciting scene which must have influenced even the narrator. If he who spoke to Abraham was an angel like the other two, we could scarcely perceive any reason why he should not have taken part in the mission to Sodom; but if he was the Angel of the Lord κατ' ἐξοχήν, the reason is quite obvious; it would have been inconsistent with divine propriety. —In chap. xviii. Moses speaks of three men; it is evidently on

of the guests to the hostess that comes into consideration. That such is the case, appears from ver. 10, where the use of the plural could not be continued, because a work was on hand which was peculiar to the one among them, and in which the others were not equally concerned. If the words in ver. 9 were spoken by all the three, then the one in ver. 10 ought to have been singled out thus: "And one from among them thus spoke." On account of the suffix in אַחֲרָיו, "And the door was behind him," the וַיֹּאמֶר in ver. 10 can be referred only to the one, and not to the Jehovah concealed behind all the three. This shows how the preceding, "And they said," is to be understood.

purpose that he avoids speaking of three angels. In chap. xix. 1, on the contrary, we are at once told: "And there came the two angels." (Compare ver. 15.) The reason why in chap. xviii. the use of the name *angels* is avoided can only be, because it might easily have led to a misunderstanding, if the Angel of the Lord had been comprehended in that one designation along with the two inferior angels, although it would not, in itself, have been inadmissible.—If we suppose that he, with whom Abraham had to do, was some created angel, we cannot well understand how, in chap. xviii. 17 seq., the judgment over Sodom could, throughout, be ascribed to him. *He* could not, in the name of the Lord, speak of that judgment, as not he, but the two other angels who went to Sodom, were the instruments of its execution. Hence it only remains to ascribe the judgment to him as the *causa principalis*.—If the three angels were equals, it would be impossible to explain the adversative clause in chap. xviii. 22 : "And the men turned from thence and went to Sodom ; *but Abraham stood yet before the Lord*." Jehovah and the two angels are here contrasted. It is true that, in the two angels also, it is Jehovah who acts. This is evident from xviii. 21 : "I will go down and see"—where the going down does not refer to descending to the valley of Jordan, the position of which was lower (thus *Delitzsch*) ; but, according to xi. 7, it refers to a descent from heaven to earth. That Jehovah, though on earth, should declare His resolution to go down, as in xi. 7, may be explained from the ὁ ὢν ἐν τῷ οὐρανῷ in John iii. 13. God, even when He is on earth, remains in heaven, and it is thence that He manifests Himself. Moreover, the words immediately following show in what sense this going down is to be understood,—that it is not in His own person, but through the medium of His messengers. The resolution, "I will go down," is carried into effect by the going down of the angels to Sodom.

By the Jehovah who, from Jehovah out of heaven, caused brimstone and fire to rain upon Sodom and Gomorrah (xix. 24), we are not at liberty to understand the two angels only,[1] but,

---

[1] *Delitzsch* says : "As the two are really sent to destroy Sodom and Gomorrah, it is evident that Jehovah, in ver. 24, who causes brimstone and fire to rain from Jehovah out of heaven, is viewed as being present in the two on earth, but in such a manner that, nevertheless, His real judicial throne is in heaven."

agreeably to the views of sound Christian expositors generally, Christ,—with this modification, however, that the two angels are to be considered as His servants, and that what they do is His work also. It is true that the angels say, in xix. 13, "We will destroy," etc. ; but much more emphatically and frequently does he with whom Abraham has to do, ascribe the work of destruction to himself. (Compare xviii. 17, where Jehovah says, "How can I hide from Abraham that thing which I am doing?" vers. 24–28, etc.) If in xix. 24 there be involved the contrast between, so to speak, the heavenly and earthly Jehovah, —between the hidden God and Him who manifests Himself on earth,—then so much the more must we seek the latter in chap. xviii., as in ver. 22, compared with ver. 21, the angels are distinctly pointed out as His Messengers.

Delitzsch asserts that in Heb. xiii. 2, the words, ἔλαθόν τινες ξενίσαντες ἀγγέλους, clearly indicate that " all three were finite spirits made visible." This assertion, however, which was long before made by the Socinian *Crellius*, has been sufficiently refuted by *Ode de Angelis*, p. 1001. The author of the Epistle to the Hebrews intends to connect the events which happened to Abraham and Lot equally—τίνες ; and for this reason he did not go beyond what was common to them both. Moreover, the Angel of the Lord is likewise comprehended in the appellation " angels," for the name has no reference to the nature, but to the mission.

———

Of no less importance and significance is the passage Gen. xxxi. 11 seq. According to ver. 11, the Angel of God, מלאך האלהים, appears to Jacob in a dream. In ver. 13, the same person calls himself the God of Bethel, with reference to the event recorded in chap. xxviii. 11–22. It cannot be supposed that in chap xxviii. the mediation of a common angel took place, who, however, had not been expressly mentioned ; for Jehovah is there contrasted with the angels. In ver. 12, we read : "And behold the angels of God ascending and descending on it." In ver. 13, there is another sight : "And behold Jehovah stood by him and said, I am Jehovah, the God of Abraham thy father, and the God of Isaac ; the land whereon thou liest, to thee will I give it, and to thy seed."

This passage is also in so far of importance, because, agreeably to what has been remarked in p. 119, it follows from it that even there, where Jehovah simply is mentioned, the mediation through His Angel is to be assumed.

He with whom Jacob wrestles, in Gen. xxxii. 24, makes himself known as God, partly by giving him the name Israel, *i.e.*, one who wrestles with God, and partly by bestowing a blessing upon him. Jacob calls the place *Peniel*, *i.e.*, face of God, because he had seen God face to face, and wonders that his life was preserved. The answer which Elohim gives here to Jacob's question regarding His name, remarkably coincides with that which in Judges xiii. 17, 18, is given by *the* Angel of the Lord to a similar question. In Hosea xii. 4 (comp. the remarks on this passage in the Author's "*Genuineness of the Pentateuch*," vol. i. p. 128 ff.), he who wrestled with Jacob is called Elohim, as in Genesis; but in ver. 5, he is called מלאך, a word which is more distinctly defined by the preceding Elohim; so that we can, accordingly, think only of the Angel of God. As it was certainly not the intention of the prophet to state a new historical circumstance, the mention of the Angel must be founded upon the supposition, that all revelations of God are made by the mediation of His Angel,—a supposition which we have already proved to have its foundation in the book of Genesis itself.

Delitzsch says, S. 256, "Jehovah reveals Himself in the מלאך, but just by means of a finite spirit becoming visible, and therefore in a manner more tolerable to him who occupies a lower place of communion with God." And similarly, *Hofmann* expresses himself, S. 335: "It is quite the same thing whether it be said, he saw God, or an angel, as is testified by Hosea also; and nowhere have we less right to explain it as if it were an appearance of God the Son, in contrast with the appearance of an angel."

But since it is an essentially different matter, whether Jacob wrestled with God Himself, or, in the first instance, with an ordinary angel merely, we have, as regards this opinion, only the choice between accusing the prophet Hosea, who brought in the angel, of an Euhemerismus, or of raising against sacred history the charge that it cannot be relied on, because it omitted so important a circumstance. The name Israel, by which, "at the same time, the innermost nature of the covenant-people was fixed, and the divine law of their history was established" (*Delitzsch*), is, in that case, a falsehood. Jacob has overcome omnipotence, and, in this one adversary, all others who might oppose him,—as he is expressly assured in ver. 29 : " Thou hast wrestled with God and *with men*, and hast prevailed." Can God invest a creature with omnipotence? Jacob would certainly not have gone so cheerfully to meet Esau, if in Him over whom he prevailed with weeping and supplication, he himself had recognised only an angel, and not Jehovah the God of hosts, as Hosea, in ver. 6, calls the very same, of whom in ver. 5 he had spoken as the angel. The consolatory import of the event for the Church of all times is destroyed, if Jacob had to do with a created angel only. With such an one, Jacob had not to reckon on account of his sinfulness, and it is just the humiliating consciousness of this his sinfulness which forms the point at issue in his wrestling. Moreover, with such a view, the New Testament Antitype would be altogether lost. Jesus, the true Israel, does not wrestle with an angel,—such an one only appears to strengthen Him in His struggle, Luke xxii. 43—but with God, Heb. v. 7.—The occurrence would, according to this opinion, furnish a strong argument for the worship of angels: "He wept and made *supplication* unto him," Hos. xii. 5 (compare Deut. iii. 23). The ἀγωνίζεσθαι ἐν ταῖς προσευχαῖς, mentioned in Col. iv. 12, in allusion to our passage, would, in that case, besides God, have the angels for its object.

If an ordinary angel were here to be understood, we must likewise believe that an angel is spoken of in Gen. xxxv. 9 seq. For, of the same angel with whom Jacob wrestled, Hosea says that Jacob found him in Bethel: "And he wrestled with the Angel and prevailed, he wept and made supplication unto him; he found him in Bethel, and there he spake with *us*." (*Tarnov:* "*Nobiscum qui in lumbis Jacobi hærebamus.*") Then, it must have been a common angel, too, who appeared to Jacob in Gen. xxviii. 10 ff.; for chap. xxxv. 9, compared with ver. 7, does not allow us to doubt of the identity of him who appeared on these two occasions. But such an idea cannot be entertained for a moment; for in chap. xxviii. 13, Jehovah is contrasted with the angels ascending and descending on the ladder.

In Gen. xlviii. 15, 16, we read of Jacob: "*And he blessed Joseph, and said, The God before whom my fathers Abraham and Isaac did walk, and the God which fed me all my life long unto this day, the Angel which redeemed me from all evil, bless the lads.*"

In this passage, God first appears, twice in the indefiniteness of His nature, and then, specially, as the Angel concerned for Jacob and his posterity.

By the Angel, we cannot here understand a divine emanation and messenger, because no permanent character belongs to such; while here the whole sum of the preservations of Jacob, and of the blessings upon Ephraim and Manasseh, is derived from the Angel. And just as little can we thereby understand a created angel, according to the view of *Hofmann*, who, in S. 87, says: "Jacob here makes mention of God, not thrice, but twice only; first as the God of his fathers, and then as the God of his own experience, but in such a way that in ver. 16 he names, instead of God, the Angel who watched over him; and he does so for the purpose of denoting the special providence of which he had been the object."

The analogy of the threefold blessing of Aaron in Num. vi. 24–26 would lead us to expect that the name of God should be three times mentioned. No created angel could in this manner be placed by the side of God, or be introduced as being independent of, and co-ordinate with, Him. Such an angel can only be meant as is connected with God by oneness of nature, and whose activity is implied in that of God. The singular יברך is here of very special significance. It indicates that the Angel is joined to God by an inseparable oneness, and that his territory is just as wide as that of Elohim.[1] If by the angel we understand some created one, we cannot then avoid the startling inference, that God is, in all His manifestations, bound

[1] This significance of the singular was pointed out as early as in the third century by *Novatianus*, who, *de Trinitate* c. xv. (p. 1016 in *Ode*), says: "So constant is he in mentioning that Angel whom he had called God, that even at the close of his speech he again refers, in an emphatic manner, to the same person, by saying, 'God bless these lads.' For had he intended that some other angel should be understood, he would have used the plural number in order to comprehend the two persons. But since, in his blessing, he made use of the singular, he would have us to understand that God and the Angel are quite identical."

absolutely to the mediation of the lower angels. In the history upon which Jacob looks back, the inferior angels do not appear at all as taking any part in all the preservations of Jacob. Twice only are they mentioned in his whole history,—in chap. xxviii. 12, and xxxii. 2. *Lastly,*—The angel cannot well be a collective noun ; for we nowhere meet with the *ideal* person of the angel, as comprehending within himself a real plurality. (Compare remarks on Ps. xxxiv. 8.) We should therefore be compelled to think of Jacob's protecting angel. But this, again, would be in opposition to the fact, that Scripture nowhere says anything of the guardian angels of any individual. Moreover, it is a plurality of angels that in xxviii. 12, xxxii. 2, serves for the protection of Jacob, and we nowhere find the slightest trace of one inferior angel being attached to Jacob for his protection.

In Exod. xxiii. 20, 21, Jehovah says to the children of Israel : " *Behold, I send an angel before thee, to keep thee in the way, and to bring thee into the place which I have prepared. Beware of him, and obey his voice; do not rebel against him, for he will not pardon your transgressions : for My name is in him.*"

As the people are here told to beware of the Angel, because he will not pardon their transgressions, so Joshua xxiv. 19 warns them as regards the most high God : " Ye will not be able to serve Jehovah : for He is a holy (*i.e.,* a glorious, exalted) God ; He is a jealous God; He will not forgive your transgressions nor your sins." The energetic character of the reaction proceeding from the angel against all violations of His honour, is founded upon the words, "For My name is in him." By the " name of God " all His deeds are understood and comprehended, His glory testified by history, the display and testimony of His nature which history gives. (Compare the remarks in my commentary on Ps. xxiii. 2, xlviii. 11, lxxxiii. 17–19, lxxxvi. 11.) " My name is him;" *i.e.,* according to Calvin, " My glory and majesty dwell in him." Compare here what in the New Testament is said of Christ : ἃ γὰρ ἂν ἐκεῖνος ποιῇ, ταῦτα καὶ ὁ υἱὸς ὁμοίως ποιεῖ, John v. 19 ; ἵνα πάντες τιμῶσι τὸν υἱὸν καθὼς τιμῶσι τὸν πατέρα, John v. 23 ; ἐγὼ καὶ ὁ πατὴρ ἕν ἐσμεν, John x. 30 ; ἵνα γνῶτε καὶ πιστεύσητε ὅτι ἐν ἐμοὶ ὁ πατὴρ κἀγὼ ἐν αὐτῷ,

John x. 38 ; οὐ πιστεύεις ὅτι ἐγὼ ἐν τῷ πατρὶ καὶ ὁ πατὴρ ἐν ἐμοί ἐστι, John xiv. 10 ; καθὼς σὺ πάτερ ἐν ἐμοὶ κᾀγὼ ἐν σοί, John xvii. 21 ; ἐν αὐτῷ κατοικεῖ πᾶν τὸ πλήρωμα τῆς θεότητος σωματικῶς, Col. ii. 9.—It is impossible that the name of God could be communicated to any other, Is. xlii. 8.   The name of God can dwell in Him only, who is originally of the same nature with God.

After Israel had contracted guilt by the worship of the golden calf, He who had hitherto led them—Jehovah = the Angel of Jehovah—says, in Exod. xxxii. 34, that He would no more lead them Himself, but send before them His Angel, מלאכי : "*For I (myself) will not go up in the midst of thee, for thou art a stiff-necked people, lest I consume thee in the way;*" xxxiii. 3, compared with xxiii. 21.   The people are quite inconsolable on account of this sad intelligence, ver. 4.

The threatening of the Lord becomes unintelligible, and the grief of the people incomprehensible, if by the Angel in chap. xxiii. an ordinary angel be understood.   But everything becomes clear and intelligible, if we admit that in chap. xxiii. there is an allusion to the Angel of the Lord κατ᾽ ἐξοχήν, who is connected with Him by oneness of nature, and who, because the name of God is in Him, is as zealous as Himself in inflicting punishment as well as in bestowing salvation ; whilst in chap. xxxii. 34, the allusion is to an inferior angel, who is added to the highest revealer of God as His companion and messenger, and who appears in the Book of Daniel under the name of Gabriel, while the Angel of the Lord appears under the name of Michael.

On account of the sincere repentance of the people, and the intercession of Moses, the Lord revokes the threatening, and says in xxxiii. 14, "My face shall go."   But Moses said unto Him, "If Thy face go not, carry us not up hence."

That פנים, *face*, signifies here the *person*, is granted by *Gesenius:* "The face of some one means often his personal presence, —himself in his own person."   A similar use of the word occurs in 2 Sam. xvii. 11: "Thy face go to battle" (*Michaelis:* "Thou thyself be present, not some commander only"); and in Deut. iv. 37, where בפניו means *in*, or *with, his personal presence:* " He brought them out with His face, with His mighty power out of Egypt."

The state of things has in xxxiii. 14, 15, evidently become again what it was in xxiii. 20, 21. The face of the Lord in the former passage, is the Angel of the Lord in the latter. Hence, we cannot here admit the idea of some inferior angel; we can think only of that Angel who is connected with the Lord by oneness of nature.

The connection between the face of the Lord in xxxiii. 14, 15, and the Angel in whom is the name of the Lord, in xxiii., becomes still more evident by Is. lxiii. 8, 9: "And He (Jehovah) became their Saviour. In all their affliction (they were) not afflicted, and the Angel of His face saved them; in His love and in His pity He redeemed them, and He bore and carried them all the days of old." The Angel of the face, in this text, is an expression which, by its very darkness, points back to some fundamental passage—a passage, too, in the Pentateuch—as facts are alluded to, of which the authentic report is given in that book. The expression, "Angel of the face," arose from a combination of Exod. xxiii. 20—from which the "Angel" is taken—and Exod. xxxiii. 14, whence he took the "face." To explain "Angel of the face" by "the angel who sees His face," as several have done, would give an inadequate meaning; for by the whole context, an expression is demanded which would elevate the angel to the height of God. Now, as in Exod. xxxiii. 14, "the face of Jehovah" is tantamount to "Jehovah in His own person," the Angel of the face can be none other than He in whom Jehovah appears personally, in contrast with inferior created angels. The Angel of the face is the Angel in whom is the name of the Lord.

When Joshua was standing with the army before Jericho, in a state of despondency at the sight of the strongly fortified city, a man appeared to him, with his sword drawn; and when he was asked by Joshua, "Art thou for us or for our adversaries?" he answers, in chap. v. 14, "Nay, for I am the Captain of the host of Jehovah, שר צבא יהוה; now I have come." This Captain claims for himself divine honour, in ver. 15, precisely in the same manner as the Angel of Jehovah in Exod. iii., by com-

manding Joshua to put off his shoes, because the place on which
he stood was holy. In chap. vi. 2 he is called Jehovah. For it
is evident that we are not to think of another divine revelation there given to Joshua in any other way—as some interpreters suppose; because, in that case, the appearance of the
Captain, who only now gives command to Joshua, would
have been without an object. In chap. v. the directions would
be wanting; in chap. vi. we should have no report of the appearance.

There can be no doubt that, by the host of the Lord, the
heavenly host is to be understood; and *Hofmann* (S. 291) has
not done well in reviving the opinion of some older expositors
(*Calvin, Masius*) which has been long ago refuted, viz., that the
host of the Lord is "Israel standing at the beginning of his
warfare," and in asserting that the prince of this host is some
inferior angel. The Israelites cannot be the host of the Lord,
that explanation is excluded by the comparison with the host of
the Lord mentioned at the very threshold of revelation, in Gen.
ii. 1; that which is commonly (Gen. xxxii. 2; 1 Kings xxii. 19;
Neh. ix. 6; Ps. ciii. 21, cxlviii. 2, compared with 2 Kings vi.
27) so called, infinitely surpasses the earthly one in glory, and of
it the Lord has the name JEHOVAH ZEBAOTH. It is only in two
isolated passages of the Pentateuch that the appellation which
properly belongs to the heavenly hosts of God is transferred to
the earthly ones; and that is done in order to point out their
correspondence, and thereby to elevate the mind. In the first
of these passages, Exod. vii. 4, the "host of the Lord" is not
spoken of absolutely, but it is expressly said what host is intended: "And I bring forth My host, My people, the children
of Israel." The second passage, in Exod. xii. 41, is similarly
qualified, and refers to the first. According to this view of
Hofmann, the words, "now I have come," are quite inexplicable.[1] The Captain of the host of the Lord expresses Himself
in such a manner as if, by His coming, everything were accomplished. But if he was only the commander of Israel—an in-

---

[1] *Seb. Schmid* says: "I have now come with my heavenly host to attack
the Canaanites, and to help thee and thy people. Be thou of good cheer;
prepare thyself for war along with me, and I will now explain to thee in
what manner thou must carry it on:" vi. 2 ff.

I

ferior angel—-his coming was no guarantee for success, for his limited power might be checked by a higher one. But if the Captain of the host of Jehovah be the Prince of angels, we cannot by any means refer the divine honour which He demands and receives, to Him who sent Him, in contrast with Him who is sent; the higher the dignity, the more necessary is the limitation. If the honour be ascribed to Him, He must be a partaker of a divine nature.

Jesus not at all indistinctly designates Himself as the Captain of the Lord's host spoken of in our passage, in Matt. xxvi. 53 : Ἢ δοκεῖς ὅτι οὐ δύναμαι ἄρτι παρακαλέσαι τὸν πατέρα μου, καὶ παραστήσει μοι πλείους ἢ δώδεκα λεγεῶνας ἀγγέλων ; This passage alone would be sufficient to refute the view which conceives of the Angel of the Lord as a mere emanation and messenger. It also overthrows the opinion that he is an inferior angel, inasmuch as the Angel of the Lord here appears as raised above all inferior angels.

Thus there existed, even in the time of Moses, the most important foundation for the doctrine concerning Christ. He who knows the general relation which the Pentateuch bears to the later development of doctrine, will, a priori, think it impossible that it should have been otherwise; and, instead of neglecting these small beginnings, appearing, as it were, in the shape of germs, he will cultivate them with love and care.

It is only at a late period, in Malachi iii. 1, that the doctrine of the Angel of the Lord is expressly brought into connection with that of Christ. But a knowledge of the divine nature of the Messiah is found at a much earlier period; and we can certainly not suppose that the doctrine of the Angel of the Lord, and that of a truly divine Saviour, should have existed by the side of each other, and yet that manifold forebodings regarding their close obvious connection should not have been awakened in the mind.

THE PROMISE IN 2 SAMUEL, CHAP. VII.

The Messianic prophecy, as we have seen, began at a time long anterior to that of David. Even in Genesis, we perceived it, increasing more and more in distinctness. There is at first only the general promise that the seed of the woman should obtain the victory over the kingdom of the evil one;—then, that the salvation should come through the descendants of Shem;—then, from among them Abraham is marked out,—of his sons, Isaac,—from among his sons, Jacob,—and from among the twelve sons of Jacob, Judah is singled out as the bearer of dominion, and marked out as the person from whom, at length, should proceed the glorious King whose peaceful dominion is destined to extend over all the nations of the earth.

Whilst, hitherto, the tribe only had been pointed out, in the midst of which an imperishable dominion should be established, and out of which the Saviour was at last to come,—under David another feature was added by the determination of the *family*. This was done in the prophetic announcement which the Lord, by the prophet Nathan, addressed in 2 Sam. vii. to David, when he had adopted the resolution of building to the Lord a fixed temple, instead of the moveable tabernacle which had hitherto been used.

Ver. 1. "*And it happened when the king sat in his house, and the Lord had given him rest from all his enemies round about.* Ver. 2. *And the king said unto Nathan the prophet, See, now, I dwell in a house of cedar, and the ark of God dwelleth within curtains.*"

The question here is:—To what time is the occurrence to be assigned? The answer is:—To the time not long after David had obtained the dominion over all Israel. To this opinion we are led by the position which the report occupies in the Books both of Chronicles and of Samuel. The supposition is so very probable, that nothing short of very cogent reasons could induce us to abandon it. A narrative, in which David's accession to the throne is followed by the conquest of Jerusalem, and this by the building of his palace,—and this again by the bringing up of the ark of the covenant,—and this, still further, by David's anxiety for a fixed sanctuary, evidently agrees with the order in which these events followed each other. We can the less entertain any doubt concerning it, because we are expressly told, that the wars and victories of David reported in chap. viii. were subsequent to what is reported in chap. vii.; compare viii. 1. That the conquest of Jerusalem and the building of his palace belong to the period soon after his accession to the throne, is both evident, and generally acknowledged; but that David's anxiety for a fixed sanctuary was awakened in him soon after the completion of his palace, is expressly stated in 1 Chron. xvii. 1.   Instead of כי ישב in ver. 1 of our passage, we find there כאשר ישב, "when," or "as soon as" he dwelt.   We cannot well think of any later period, as David's zeal for the building of the house of the Lord was closely connected with the question regarding the duration of his own family, which was so readily suggested by the fate of Saul, and which must necessarily have engaged his attention at a very early period.   If he obtained the divine sanction for the building of the temple, that question also was thereby answered.   *Further,*—It appears from ver. 12, that Solomon was not yet born at the time when David received the promise. The circumstance, too, that there are so many allusions to it in the Psalms of David, proves that this promise had been already given to him at the beginning of his reign.—One circumstance only has been adduced against assigning to it so early a period, viz., that the event is here placed within the time when the Lord had given David rest from all his enemies round about. But there is not one word which affirms that this rest was a definitive one; while, on the other hand, the contrary is alluded to by the circumstance that the Books of Chronicles make no mention at all of David's rest from his enemies, and is distinctly indicated by viii. 1.   In 1 Chron. xiv. 17 it is said, after the account of David's victory over the Philistines (on which event the Books of Samuel report previous to chap. vii., viz. in v. 17–25): "And the name of David went out into all lands, and the Lord gave his fear upon all the heathen."   This previous result was so much the more important, as the Philistines had been, for a long time, the most dangerous enemies of Israel, and David himself may have considered it as a definitive one, —may have imagined this truce to be a peace,—may not have been aware that he had yet to bear the burden of the most trying wars.   Looking, then, to the passage in Deut. xii. 10, 11—in which the choice of a place where the Lord will cause His name to dwell, is connected with the giving of rest from all enemies round about—he might think that the present circumstance formed a call upon him to erect a sanctuary to the Lord.[1] But the issue (compare viii. 1) soon made it manifest to him, that the supposition on which he proceeded was an erroneous one. We have a tacit correction of David's mistake in 1 Kings v. 17, 18: "Thou knowest how that David my father could not build an house unto the name of the Lord his God, for the wars with which they surrounded him, until the Lord put them under the soles of his feet. And now the Lord my God hath given me rest on every side, and there is neither adversary nor evil occurrence." It was only under Solomon that the period provided for by Deut. xii. really arrived. (Compare 1 Chron. xxii. 19.)

Ver. 3. "*And Nathan said to the king, Go, do all that is in thine heart, for the Lord is with thee. Ver. 4. And it came to pass that night that the word of the Lord came unto Nathan, saying: Ver. 5. Go and tell My servant David, Thus saith the Lord, Shalt thou build Me a house to dwell in?*"

In ver. 5 the question is stated, the answer to which is the point at issue. In ver. 6, the exposition begins with כִּי, which refers to the whole of it, and not merely to the clause which immediately follows. Hitherto, the Lord has not had a fixed temple (ver. 6), nor has any such been wished for or desired by Him (ver. 7). By the grace of God, David has been raised to be ruler over the people (ver. 8), and the Lord has helped him gloriously (ver. 9), and, through him, His people (ver. 10). This mercy the Lord had already bestowed upon him, that, since the beginning of the period of the Judges, it was through him, first of all, that the people had obtained rest from all their enemies round about; but to this favour the Lord is now adding another, by announcing to him that He would make him an house (ver. 11). When David dies, his seed shall occupy the throne, and be established in the kingdom (ver. 12). It is he who shall build an house for the Lord who will establish for ever the throne of his kingdom, vers. 13–16.

David's zeal for the house of the Lord is thus acknowledged (compare Ps. cxxxii. 1), and so also is the correctness of his supposition, that the building of the fixed temple is intimately

---

[1] *Seb. Schmid* says: "He thought that this duty was imposed upon him by the Word of God. For, as the state enjoyed peace, the royal palace was finished, and his family established, there seemed to be nothing wanting but to build a temple to the Lord."

connected with his being raised to be ruler over Israel. The first answer of Nathan remains correct; it is only more distinctly and closely defined and modified. David is to build the house, —not, however, in his own person, but in his seed, and after the Lord has begun to fulfil His promise, that He would make him an house.

But why was it that David himself was not permitted to build the house to the Lord? In this passage we obtain no answer. In Solomon's message to Hiram (1 Kings v. 17) an external reason only is stated—viz., that, by his numerous wars, David had been prevented from building a house to the Lord. There was a deeper reason than this; but the heathen could not comprehend it. It is contained in the words which, according to 1 Chron. xxviii. 3, David spoke to the people: "And God said unto me, Thou shalt not build an house for My name, because thou hast been a man of war, and hast shed blood;" and in the words of the Lord which, according to 1 Chron. xxii. 8, David repeated to Solomon: "Thou hast shed blood abundantly, and hast made great wars; thou shalt not build an house unto My name, because thou hast shed much blood upon the earth in My sight,"—a disclosure which David could have obtained only at a later period, and as a supplement to the divine communication which had been made to him through Nathan. For it is only after the revelation in 2 Sam. vii. that David had to carry on his most bloody wars. We must not, by any means, entertain the idea that these words express anything *blameworthy* in David, and that the permission to build the temple was refused to him on account of his personal unworthiness. David stood in a closer relation to God than did Solomon. His wars were wars of the Lord, 1 Sam. xxv. 28. It is in this light that David himself regarded them; and that he was conscious of his being divinely commissioned for them, is seen, *e.g.*, from Ps. xviii.: it was the Lord who taught his hands to war (ver. 35) and who gave him vengeance, and subdued the people unto him, ver. 48. The passages 1 Chron. xxii. 8, xxvii. 3, do not, in themselves, contain one reproachful word against David. On the contrary, the words, *in My sight*, in the former of these passages, rather lead us to suppose that David is, in his wars, to be considered only as a servant of the Lord (*Michaelis*: "*In My sight—i.e.*, who am, as it were, the highest judge, and the commander"). The reason is rather of a symbolical character. How necessary soever, under certain conditions, war may be for the kingdom of God,—as indeed the Saviour also says that (in the first instance) He had not come to send peace, but a sword,—it is after all only something accidental, and rendered needful by human corruption. The real nature of the kingdom of God is peace. Even in the Old Testament, the Lord of the Church appears as the Prince of Peace, Is. ix. 5. According to Luke ix. 56, the Son of Man is not come to destroy men's lives, but to save them. In order to impress upon the mind this view of the nature and aim of the Church, the Temple—the symbol of the Church—must not be built by David the man of war, but by Solomon, the peaceful, the man of rest, 1 Chron. xxii. 9.

Ver. 6. *"For I have not dwelt in any house from the day that I brought up the children of Israel out of Egypt even to this day, and have walked in a tent and in a tabernacle. Ver. 7. In all that I have walked among the children of Israel, have I spoken one word with any of the tribes of Israel whom I commanded to feed My people Israel, saying, Why build ye Me not a house of cedar?"*

According to several interpreters, these words are intended as a consolation to David for the delay in building the temple, and convey this sense: that God did not require the temple, that the building of it was of no consequence,—as sufficiently appears from the circumstance of His not having hitherto urged it. But such a view would ill agree with the great importance which David continues, even afterwards, to ascribe to the building of the temple,—with the grand efforts of Solomon towards it,—and with the exulting words which are uttered by the latter, in 1 Kings viii. 13, after the work has been accomplished: "I have built Thee an house to dwell in, a settled place for Thee to abide in for ever." A comparison of 1 Kings viii. 16-20 furnishes us with a clue to the right interpretation. In that passage, the period before David is contrasted with that during which David lived. (Compare the עתה, *now*, in ver. 8.) Hitherto, everything in the government had borne a provisional character, and, hence, the sanctuary also. But now that, after the unsettled state of things under the Judges and Saul, *the definitive government* has been called into existence with David, to whom the Lord will make an house, the *definitive sanctuary* also shall be built,—only, that it shall not be founded by David, but by his seed.[1] The words, *I have walked*—literally, I have been walking, I have continued walking—*in a tent and in a tabernacle*, indicate not only that the Lord dwelt in a portable sanctuary, but also, that the place of this sanctuary was oftentimes changed, from one station to another in the wilderness, then to Gilgal, Shiloh, Nob and Gibeon. This changing of the place of the tabernacle is still more distinctly pointed out, in the parallel passage in 1 Chron. xvii. 5: "And I have been from tent to tent, from tabernacle to tabernacle;" *i.e.*, I went from one tent into the other, *e.g.*, from the dwelling-place of Shiloh into that of Nob,—a mode of expression which pays no attention to the circumstance whether or not the tent was materially the same. Instead of, "With any of the tribes of Israel," we find in 1 Chron. xvii. 6, "With any of the judges of Israel,"—a parallel passage which very well explains the main text. The tribes come into consideration through their judges, who, in the Book of Judges, always appear as judges in Israel, and procured a temporary

---

[1] In 1 Kings viii. 16, Solomon thus reports what, in 2 Sam. vii., had been spoken to David, in reference to the house of the Lord: "Since the day that I brought up My people Israel out of Egypt, I chose no city out of all the tribes of Israel to build an house that My name might be in it; and I chose David to be over My people Israel." The comment on this passage is given by the parallel one, 2 Chron. vi. 5, 6: "I did not choose any man to be a ruler over My people Israel. And I have chosen Jerusalem that My name might be there, and I have chosen David to be over My people Israel." Since David resided in Jerusalem, the election of David, announced in 2 Sam. vii., implies also the choice of Jerusalem as the place of the sanctuary. Hence, we must add to 1 Kings viii. 16, the supplement: "And in connection with this choice, David (the Davidic dynasty) is to build Me an house at the place of his residence." The Vulgate translates very correctly: *Sed elegi*. Solomon then continues, *Ver.* 17: "And it was in the heart of David my father (namely, before he received this divine revelation) to build an house for the name of the Lord, the God of Israel. *Ver.* 18. And the Lord said unto David my father, Whereas it was in thine heart to build an house unto My name, thou didst well that it was in thine heart. *Ver.* 19. And thou shalt not build the house; but thy son that shall come forth out of thy loins, he shall build the house unto My name."

superiority to the tribe from which they proceeded.[1] The שֵׁבֶט,
which has been doubted, is rendered certain by 1 Kings viii. 16.
(Compare, moreover, Ps. lxxviii. 67, 68.)—The reason why no
such word came to any one of these tribes is, that the superiority
of none of them was permanent; the election of all of them
was merely temporary. The continuance of the tent-temple
was intended to indicate that the state of things was, in general,
provisional only, and that a new order of things was at hand.
The creation of a settled sanctuary was to be coincident with
the establishment of an abiding kingdom, to which the grace of
God was vouchsafed. It was an evil omen for Saul that the
erection of a fixed sanctuary was not even mooted under him.
The close of Ps. lxxviii. likewise points out the intimate connection of the kingdom and the sanctuary.

Ver. 8. "*And now, thus shalt thou say unto David My
servant: Thus saith the Lord of hosts, I took thee from the
sheep-cote,*[2] *from behind the sheep, to be ruler over My people,
over Israel.* Ver. 9. *And I was with thee whithersoever thou
wentest, and have cut off all thine enemies from before thee, and
have made thee a great name like unto the name of the great men
that are upon the earth.* Ver. 10. *And I gave room unto My
people Israel, and planted them, and they dwell in their place,
and they shall no more be frightened, and the sons of wickedness
shall afflict them no more as heretofore.*"

Seven divine benefits are here enumerated,—one in ver. 8,
which forms the foundation of all the others, and three in each
of the two following verses,—in ver. 9, what the Lord has
given to David,—in ver. 10, what, through him, He has given
to Israel. These benefits are so many symptoms that a *definitive* order of things has now taken the place of the *provisional* one, and that, hence, the moveable sanctuary will now
be soon followed by the settled one. In the first member of
ver. 10, there is an enumeration of the benefits which the

---

[1] *Seb. Schmid* says: " He rightly considers the tribes and the judges as
one. For the tribes are viewed in the judges who had sprung from them,
and *vice versa*, the judge, in his paternal tribe. And that the matter is
thus to be understood, is clear, because, in Chronicles, where the judge is
spoken of, he is introduced in the plural: ' Why have *ye* not built Me an
house,' etc.? viz., thou, judge, with thy tribe."

[2] That נָוֶה, properly "habitation," "abode," is used here, as frequently, of
the sheep-cote, is shown by Ps. lxxviii. 70, which is based upon our passage.

people have already received through David; in the second and third members, an enumeration of the benefits to be constantly bestowed upon them through him. A commentary upon it is formed by Ps. lxxxix. 22–24, in which it is said of David: "With whom My hand shall be continually, Mine arm also shall strengthen him. The enemy shall not exact upon him, nor the son of wickedness afflict him. And I crush his enemies before him, and will smite those who hate him."

Ver. 11. "*And since the day that I commanded judges over My people Israel, I have given thee rest from all thine enemies. And the Lord telleth thee, that the Lord will make thee an house.*"

The first part of this verse comprehends all the benefits formerly enumerated;—the second adds another, which, however, is closely connected with the previous ones. The circumstance that the Lord first gave rest to David, and, in him, to the people, was a sign of his election which could not but manifest itself afterwards in the care for his house. The promise, "The Lord will make thee an house," was to David an answer to prayer, as is shown by Ps. xxi. 3, 5, lxi. 6, cxxxviii. 3. Even the thought of building the temple was a question put to the Lord, as to whether He would, in harmony with His past conduct, give a duration to his house, different from that of the house of Saul.

Ver. 12. "*And when thy days be fulfilled, and thou shalt sleep with thy fathers, I shall cause thy seed to rise up after thee which shall proceed out of thy bowels, and I will establish his kingdom.*"

The הקים does not signify the beginning of existence, but the elevation to the royal dignity. זרע, *seed*, denotes the posterity, which, however, may consist of one only, or be represented by a single individual. In the parallel passage, 1 Chron. xvii. 11, the words run thus: "Thy seed which shall be of thy sons," *i.e.*, who shall be one of thy sons (Luther). The truth of the promise, "I shall establish his kingdom," became manifest, *e.g.*, in the vain machinations of Adonijah. That the fulfilment of this promise must be sought in the history of Solomon, in whom the difference between the house of David and that of Saul first became evident (instead of, "I establish," in ver. 12, we find, in the second member of ver. 13, "I establish for ever"), is seen from 1 Kings viii. 20, where Solomon says, "And the Lord hath performed His word which

He spake; for I am risen up in the room of David my father, and sit on the throne of Israel, as the Lord promised." (Compare 1 Kings ii. 12: "And Solomon sat upon the throne of David his father, and his kingdom was established greatly.")

Ver. 13. " *He shall build an house for My name, and I establish the throne of his kingdom for ever.*"

The general establishment which was spoken of in ver. 12 precedes the building of the temple; the eternal establishment mentioned in ver. 13 follows the building of the temple, or is coincident with it. It is evident, that the first clause of the verse refers, in the first instance, to the building of the temple which was undertaken by Solomon. (Compare 1 Kings v. 19, where Solomon says, "Behold, I purpose to build an house unto the name of the Lord my God, as the Lord spake unto David my father, saying, Thy son whom I will set upon thy throne in thy stead, he shall build the house unto My name.") We shall not, however, be at liberty to confine ourselves to what Solomon, as an individual, did for the house of the Lord. The building of the house here goes hand in hand with the eternity of the kingdom. We expect, therefore, that the question is not about a building of limited duration. If a building of only a limited duration were meant, such, surely, might have been erected long ago, even in the period of the Judges. The contrary, however, is quite distinctly brought out in 1 Kings viii. 13, where, at the dedication of the temple, Solomon says, "I have built Thee an house to dwell in, a fixed place for Thee to abide in *for ever.*" If, then, with the eternity of the kingdom of David's house the eternity of the temple to be built by him be closely bound up, the destruction of the latter can be only *temporary,* and the consequence of the apostasy and punishment of the Davidic race, —of which vers. 14 and 15 treat. Or, if it be definitive, it can concern the *form* only. If the building of the temple fall into ruins, it is only the Davidic race from which its restoration can proceed; the local relation of the royal palace to the temple prefigured their close union. Hence, the building of the temple by Zerubbabel was likewise comprehended in the words, " He shall build an house for My name." It was impossible that the second temple could be reared otherwise than under the direction of David's family. But we must go still farther. The essence of the temple consists in its being a symbol, an outward representation of the kingdom of God under Israel. The real import of our passage then is,—that henceforth the kingdom of David and the kingdom of God should be closely and insepa- rably linked together. As the third phase, therefore, in the fulfilment of our prophecy, John ii. 19 must come under con- sideration : λύσατε τὸν ναὸν τοῦτον, καὶ ἐν τρισὶν ἡμέραις ἐγερῶ αὐτόν. (Regarding the sense of this passage, and the symbolical meaning of the tabernacle and temple, compare " *Dissertations on the Genuineness of the Pent.*," vol. ii. p. 514 ff.) "House of God" is, in ver. 14 of the parallel text, used of the Church, and in parallelism with "kingdom of God,"—a sense in which it occurs as early as in Num. xii. 7.[1] This *usus loquendi* is quite common in the New Testament; compare 1 Tim. iii. 15; 2 Cor. vi. 16; Heb. iii. 6. In the first two phases of the temple of Solomon, the house consists in the first instance of ordinary stones,— although, even at that time, the *spiritual* is concealed behind the *material ;* but in its third phase, the material is altogether thrown off, and the house is entirely spiritual—consisting of living stones, 1 Pet. ii. 5.—That the expression, " for ever," in the second clause of the verse, is to be taken in its strict and full sense, is proved not only by the threefold repetition, but also by a comparison with the numerous secondary passages, in which the duration of the Davidic dominion appears as abso- lutely unlimited. In Ps. lxxxix., for example, where the pro- mise is repeated, " for ever " corresponds with, " as the days of heaven " in ver. 30,—with " as the sun " in ver. 37,—and with " as the moon " in ver. 38. The final fulfilment of this promise is pointed out by the words of the angel to Mary, in Luke i. 32, 33 : οὗτος ἔσται μέγας (compare ver. 9 here), καὶ υἱὸς ὑψίστου κληθήσεται (compare ver. 14), καὶ δώσει αὐτῷ κύριος ὁ Θεὸς τὸν θρόνον Δαυὶδ τοῦ πατρὸς αὐτοῦ. Καὶ βασιλεύσει ἐπὶ τὸν οἶκον Ἰακὼβ εἰς τοὺς αἰῶνας, καὶ τῆς βασιλείας αὐτοῦ οὐκ ἔσται τέλος.

Ver. 14. "*And I will be a father to him, and he shall be a son to Me. If he commit sin, I will chastise him with the rod of men, and with the stripes of the children of men. Ver. 15. And My mercy shall not depart away from him, as I caused it to depart away from Saul, whom I put away before thee.*"

[1] Michaelis says : "Just as in the preceding verses also, the house of David did not mean a heap of stones and wood brought together, but a congregation of people."

Wheresoever God is, in the Old Testament, designated as *Father*, there is a reference to the deepest intensity of His love, —a love which is similar to that of a father towards his son. (Compare remarks on Ps. ii. 7.) Sonship to God has this significancy here also, as is shown by what immediately follows, where, in explanation of it, the promise of indestructible love is connected with it. But this relationship, in its highest and closest form, cannot exist betwixt God and a mere man. It is only when the Davidic family is viewed as centring in Christ, that the words can acquire their full truth. To this, the quotation in Heb. i. 5 points: Τίνι γὰρ εἶπέ ποτε τῶν ἀγγέλων, Υἱός μου εἶ σύ, ἐγὼ σήμερον γεγέννηκά σε; Καὶ πάλιν· Ἐγὼ ἔσομαι αὐτῷ εἰς πατέρα, καὶ αὐτὸς ἔσται μοι εἰς υἱόν; The depth of meaning which is contained in these words appears plainly from their expansion in Ps. lxxxix. 26: "And I place his hand on the sea, and his right hand on the rivers. He shall call Me thus: Thou art my Father, my God, and the rock of my salvation. And I will also make him My first-born, the highest of the kings of the earth." The sonship accordingly implies the dominion over the world, which in Ps. ii. 7–9 appears, indeed, as inseparably connected with it.—If the race of David commit sin, it shall be chastened with the rods of men, and with the stripes of the children of men. Ps. xvii. 4 distinctly and unambiguously designates corrupt actions—walking in the ways of transgressors—as "the works of men." (Compare 1 Sam. xxiv. 10; Hos. vi. 7; Job xxxi. 33, xxiii. 12.) Hence, the rods of men, and the stripes of the children of men, are punishments to which all men are subject, because they are sinners, and at which no man needs to be surprised. Grace is not to free the Davidic family from this common lot of mankind, is not to afford to them the privilege of sinning. The mitigation only follows in ver. 15, in which the close resumes the beginning: "I will be a father to him." But this mitigation must not be misunderstood by being conceived of as referring to the individuals. Such a conception of it would be opposed to the nature of the thing itself, would be in opposition to 1 Chron. xxviii. 9, where David says to Solomon, "If thou seek Him, He will be found of thee; and if thou forsake Him, He will cast thee off *for ever*;" and would be against history, which shows that the rebellious members of the Davidic dynasty were visited with destroying judgments. The contrast is rather thus to be understood : sin is to be visited upon the individuals, while the grace abides continually upon the race,—so that the divine promise is raised to an absolute one. The commentary on it is furnished by Ps. lxxxix. 31 seq.: "If his children forsake My law, and walk not in My judgments . . . then I will visit their transgression with the rod, and their iniquity with stripes. But My loving-kindness will I not withdraw from him, nor will I break My faithfulness." —The words from "if he commit sin" to "children of men" are awanting in the parallel passage. This omission is intended to make the continuance of the mercy appear the more distinctly, and to show, as indeed is the case, that the main stress is to be laid upon it. We cannot for a moment conceive that any unworthy motive prompted this omission; for the Chronicles were written at a time when the chastening rod of the Lord had already fallen heavily upon the Davidic race. There would have been stronger reasons for adding the words than for omitting them, inasmuch as, under these circumstances, they were full of consolation. It is just upon these words that the penman of Ps. lxxiv. dwells at particular length.

Ver. 16. "*And thine house and thy kingdom shall be sure for ever before thee, thy throne shall be firm for ever.*"

The extent to which this prophecy of Nathan bears the character of a fundamental one, appears from the circumstance that almost every word of the verse under review has called forth an echo in later times. נאמן, *sure, certain, constant*, occurs again in Ps. lxxxix. 29, compared with ver. 38, and in Is. lv. 3. The *sure (constant)* mercies of David, spoken of in the last of these passages, shall be bestowed upon the people of the covenant, in the coming of Christ, by which the perpetuity of the house of David was most fully manifested. The נכון, *constant, firm*, occurs in Mic. iv. 1, and the לעולם, *for ever*, in Ps. lxxii. 17, lxxxix. 37, xlv. 7, and cx. 4. The saying of the people in John xii. 34, ἡμεῖς ἠκούσαμεν ἐκ τοῦ νόμου ὅτι ὁ Χριστὸς μένει εἰς τὸν αἰῶνα, refers, in the first instance, to our passage, and all the other texts quoted may be considered as a commentary.

It is certainly not the result of mere accident, that the twelve verses of Nathan's prophecy are divided into two sections of seven and of five verses respectively, and that the former again is subdivided into sections of three and four verses. Its closing words, " The Lord will make thee an house," are further expanded in vers. 12–16.

We subjoin to the exposition of Nathan's prophecy, that of David's prayer of thanks, because, by means of the thanks, the promise itself is more clearly brought out.

The Lord has done great things for His servant in his low estate, and has promised things still more glorious, vers. 18–21. By doing such glorious things to His servant, He has manifested Himself as a faithful God, in harmony with His revelations in ancient times, vers. 22–24. The thanksgivings for the promise are followed in vers. 25–29 by a prayer for its fulfilment, intermingled with expressions of hope.

As the promise was expressed in twelve verses, so are the thanks. These twelve verses are again divided into seven and five, and the seven into four and three.

The name of Jehovah occurs twelve times. Ten times is the address directed to Jehovah. Once He is addressed by the simple name of Jehovah, six times by that of Adonai Jehovah, twice by that of Jehovah Elohim, and once by that of Jehovah Zebaoth. The address, Adonai Jehovah, occurs at the beginning and the close. The third division first takes up the name of God which is used in the second, and returns, at the close, to that which is used in the first division. In the parallel passage in Chronicles, Jehovah occurs seven times, and Elohim three times.—Ten times the servant of the Lord is mentioned in David's prayer, and seven times, the house of David. The servant of the Lord occurs three times in vers. 18–21, and seven times in vers. 25–29; the house of David twice in 18–21, and five times in vers. 25–29. In vers. 22–24, where the manifestation of the mercies to David are brought into connection with the glorious revelations of God in ancient times, neither the servant nor the house is mentioned.

Ver. 18. " *And King David came and sat before the Lord, and said : Who am I, Lord Jehovah, and what my house* (literally, *who* my house,—the house being conceived of as an *ideal* person), *that Thou hast brought me hitherto ?* "

Moses also was sitting in long-continued prayer, Exod. xvii. 12. David, as a true descendant of Jacob (Gen. xxxii. 10), acknowledges his unworthiness of the great mercies bestowed upon him. The comparison of Ps. cxliv. 3 is still more striking than that of Ps. viii. 5 ; for, in the former, the words, "Lord, what is man, that Thou takest knowledge of him; the son of mortal man, that Thou hast regard to him?" were uttered in praise of the adorable mercy which the Lord had shown to his house.

Ver. 19. "*And this is yet too little in Thy sight, Lord Jehovah; and Thou speakest also to the house of Thy servant of things far distant; and this is the law of man, Lord Jehovah.*"

The word תורה has only the signification of *law*. Gesenius, in assigning to it the signification of *mos, consuetudo*, has no other warrant for it than our passage. The law of any one is the law which has been given for him, or which concerns him; compare Lev. vi. 2 (9) : "This is the law of the burnt-offering;" Lev. xiii. 7 : "This is the law for her that hath born ;" Lev. xiv. 2 : "This shall be the law of the leper," etc. Hence the law of man can only be the law regulating the conduct of man. Man is commanded in the law : "Thou shalt love thy neighbour as thyself ;" compare Mic. vi. 8 : "He hath showed, O man, what is good; and what doth the Lord require of thee but to do justice, and to *love kindness*, and to walk humbly before thy God?" The fact that God should, in His conduct towards poor mortals, follow the rule which He hath given to men for their conduct towards one another, and that He shows. Himself to be full of mercy and love, cannot but fill him who knows God and himself with adoring wonder. The words in Ps. xviii. 36 are parallel: "Thou givest me the shield of Thy salvation, and Thy right hand holdeth me up, and Thy meekness (the parallel passage in 2 Sam. has : 'Thy being low') maketh me great." In the parallel passage in Chronicles the words are these : "And Thou hast regarded me according to the law of man (concerning תורה = תור compare remarks on Song of Sol. i. 10), Thou height, Jehovah God." The essential agreement of the sense of the parallel passage with that of the fundamental passage, may be applied as a test to prove the correctness of our exposition. "To regard some one" is used for "to visit some one," "to have intercourse with some one;" compare 2 Sam. iii. 13, xiii. 5, xiv. 24, 28 ; 2 Kings viii. 29. The words, "Thou height" (God is represented as personified height in Ps. xcii. 9 : "And Thou art a height for evermore, O Lord"), bring out still more prominently the contrast with human lowness, which was already implied in the names of

God, Adonai Jehovah, and Jehovah Elohim, and serves therefore to show still more distinctly the condescension of God,
whose revelation on this occasion was a prelude to ὁ λόγος σὰρξ
ἐγένετο. *Luther* has introduced into the main text a direct
allusion to the incarnation of God in Christ. He translates,
"This is the manner of a man who is God the Lord;" and adds,
in a marginal note, the following remark: "This means, Thou
speakest to me of such an eternal kingdom, in which no one
can be king unless he be God and man at the same time, because he is to be my son and yet a king for evermore—which
belongs to God alone." But this single circumstance is sufficient
to overthrow this view :—that in the preceding, as well as in the
subsequent context, Adonai Jehovah is always used in the
vocative sense.

Ver. 20. "*And what shall David say more unto Thee?* (In
the parallel passage: 'As regards the honour for Thy servant.')
And Thou knowest Thy servant, Lord Jehovah."

It is not necessary that David should make many words, in
order to express his thanks, as his thankful heart lies open before
God. In Ps. xl. 10, David also appeals to the testimony of the
Omniscient as regards his thankful heart: "I preach righteousness in the great congregation; lo, I will not refrain my lips, O
Lord, Thou knowest,"—knowest how with my whole heart I
am thankful for Thy great mercy. It is, in general, David's
practice to appeal to God, the Searcher of hearts; compare, *e.g.*,
Ps. xvii. 3.

Ver. 21. "*For Thy word's sake, and according to Thine own
heart, hast Thou done all these great things to make Thy servant
know them.*"

In 1 Chron. xvii. 19, the words run thus: "Lord, on
account of Thy *servant*, and according to Thine own heart, hast
Thou done all these great things, to make known all the glorious
things." Hence, by the "word," a promise given to David can
alone be intended,—a word formerly spoken to David, which
contained the germ of the present one. There is, no doubt, a
special allusion to the word in 1 Sam. xvi. 12: "And the Lord
said, Arise and anoint him, for this is he." (Compare 2 Sam.
xii. 7; Ps. lxxxix. 21; Acts xiii. 22.) *According to Thine
heart:* "The Lord is merciful and gracious, slow to anger and

K

plenteous in mercy," Ps. ciii. 8.' *All these great things,—i.e.* the promise of the eternal dominion of his house. גְדֻלָּה and גְּדֻלָּה —words in which David takes special delight—never mean "greatness," but always "great things." (Compare remarks on Ps. lxxi. 21, cxlv. 3.) The words, "To make know," etc., indicate that the *making* refers, in the meantime, only to the divine decree.

Ver. 22. " *Wherefore Thou art great, Lord God: for there is none like Thee, neither is there any God besides Thee, according to all that we have heard with our ears.*"

Wherefore—in the first instance, on account of the great things which Thou hast done unto me. *According to all*, etc., *i.e.*, as this is confirmed by all, etc. Of this David has been reminded anew by his personal experience. Just as he does here, David, in Ps. xl. 6, rises from his personal experience to the whole series of God's glorious manifestations in the history of His people. As to the words, "There is none like Thee, neither is there any God besides Thee," compare the fundamental passages Exod. xv. 11; Deut. iii. 24, iv. 35.

Ver. 23. " *And where is there a nation on earth like Thy people Israel, for whose sake God went to redeem them for a people to Himself, and make Him a name, and to do for you great things, and terrible things for Thy land, putting away from before Thy people, whom Thou redeemedst to Thee out of Egypt, heathen and their gods?*"

We must here compare the fundamental passages, Deut. iv. 7, 34, xxxiii. 29, in which that which Israel has received from his God is praised, as being without precedent and parallel. In לכם and לארצך the address is, with poetical liveliness, directed to Israel. *For you great things*—instead of, To do for them great things, as the Lord has done for you. The phrase מפני עמך means, literally, only, "away from before Thy people;" "putting" must be supplied from the preceding לעשות, and from a comparison of the fundamental passages, Exod. xxiii. 28, 29, xxxiv. 11; Deut. xxxiii. 27, to which the concise expression refers. The text in Chronicles, which expressly adds what we have here to supply, לגרש מפני, "to drive out before," is, in this case also, merely a parallel passage which, by the addition of a word, serves as a commentary.

Ver. 24. " *And Thou hast confirmed to Thyself Thy people*

Israel to be a people for ever, and Thou, Lord, art become their God."

Ver. 25. *" And now, Jehovah God, the word that Thou hast spoken concerning Thy servant, and concerning his house, establish it for ever, and do as Thou hast said."*

Praise and thanks for the promise are followed by the prayer for its fulfilment.

Ver. 26. *" And let Thy name be magnified for ever, so that it may be said, Jehovah Zebaoth (is) God over Israel. And the house of Thy servant shall be firm before Thee."*

Let Thy name be magnified, instead of, Give cause for its being glorified; compare Ps. xxxv. 27, xl. 17.—*Is God over Israel, i.e.*, proves Himself to be such, by protecting the house of the king, on whom the salvation of Israel depends. In Chronicles it is thus expressed: " Jehovah Zebaoth, the God of Israel, is God for Israel," *i.e.*, He fulfils to Israel what He promised (Jarchi). The prayer for the establishment of David's house is expressed in the form of confidence, in the conviction based upon the word of God, that such is according to the will of God.

Ver. 27. *" For Thou, Jehovah Zebaoth, God of Israel, hast opened the ear of Thy servant, saying, I will build thee an house. Therefore Thy servant found (in) his heart to pray this prayer unto Thee."* (Otherwise, his heart would have failed him; he would have had neither the desire nor the courage.) Ver. 28. *" And now, Lord Jehovah, Thou art God, and Thy words are truth, and Thou hast promised unto Thy servant these good things.* Ver. 29. *And now let it please Thee to bless the house of Thy servant, that it may continue for ever before Thee; for Thou, Lord Jehovah, hast spoken, and, by Thy blessing, the house of Thy servant shall be blessed for ever."*

To whom does this promise refer, which David received through Nathan? Some Rabbins, and *Grotius*, would fain restrict it to Solomon and his more immediate posterity. This opinion, however, is refuted by the single circumstance, that they are compelled to assume merely a long duration of time, instead of the eternity which is here promised to the house of David. And that such cannot be the meaning of the words "for ever," is abundantly confirmed by a comparison with

Ps. lxxxix. 30, "And I place his seed for ever, and his throne as the days of heaven." In these words of the Psalm there is a reference to Deut. xi. 21, where the *people* of the Lord are promised a duration " as the days of heaven and of earth." An absolute perpetuity is everywhere ascribed to the people of God. If, then, the house of David is placed on the same level as they, its perpetuity must likewise be absolute. *Further,*—with such a view, it is impossible to comprehend what David here says in his prayer, regarding the greatness of the promise, and also what he says in Ps. cxxxviii. 2: "For Thou hast magnified Thy word above all Thy name." The giving of the promise is there placed on a loftier elevation than all the former deeds of the Lord.

Others—as *Calovius*—would refer the promise to Christ alone. But vers. 14, 15 are decisive against this view; for, according to them, God will not, by a total rejection, punish the posterity of David, if they commit sin,—from which the reference is evident to a posterity merely human, and hence sinful. According to ver. 13, David's posterity is to build a temple to the Lord,—a declaration which, with reference to David's plan of building a temple to the Lord, can, in the first instance, be understood in no other way than as relating to the earthly temple to be built by Solomon. To this consideration it may be added, that, in 1 Chron. xxii. 9 seqq., David himself refers this announcement primarily to Solomon, and that Solomon, in 1 Kings v. 5 seqq., and in 2 Chron. vi. 7 seqq., refers it to himself.

Nor is there entire soundness in the view of those who, following *Augustine* (*de Civitate Dei* xvii. 8, 9), assume the existence of a double reference,—to Solomon and his earthly successors on the one hand, and to Christ on the other. Thus *Brentius:* " Solomon is not altogether excluded, but Christ is chiefly intended." It is true that these interpreters are substantially right in their view; but they err as to the manner in which they give expression to it. The promise has not a reference to two subjects simultaneously.[1] It views David's house as an *ideal* unity.

---

[1] This mistake was corrected by *Seb. Schmid.* He says: " The promises here given to David have, of course, a reference to Solomon; but not such as if they were to be fulfilled only in the person of Solomon, and not also in his posterity, and, most of all, in the Messiah to be descended from David and Solomon."

The promise is given to the house of David, vers. 11, 16, 19, 25, 26, 27, 29; to his seed, ver. 12. It is to the house of David that the absolute perpetuity of existence, the unchangeable possession of the grace of God—a relation to God similar to that of a son to his father—and the inseparable connection of their dominion with the kingdom of God in Israel, are guaranteed.

There is no direct mention of the person of the Messiah; and yet the words, when considered in their full import, point, indirectly, to Him. The absolute perpetuity of the race can be conceived of, only when at last it centres in some superhuman person. But still more decisive is the connection in which this promise stands to Gen. xlix. The dominion which is there promised to Judah is here transferred to David. It is then to David's race that the exalted individual must belong, in whom, according to Gen. xlix. 10, Judah's dominion is to centre at some future period. That David really connected the promise which he received with Gen. xlix. 10, is shown by 1 Chron. xxviii. 4 (compare p. 91), and also by the name, Solomon, which he gave to his son; compare ibid. That Solomon also founded his hopes regarding the future upon a combination of Gen. xlix. and 2 Sam. vii., is shown by Ps. lxxii., which was composed by him; compare pp. 91, 92.

But, as respects this combination, David was not left to himself. He received further light from the source from which the promise had come to him. Although his mission was not properly a prophetic one,—although, in the main, it belonged to him to describe poetically what had come to him through prophetic inspiration, yet prophetic inspiration and sacred lyric are frequently commingled in him. The man who is " the sweet psalmist of Israel" claims a נאם in 2 Sam. xxiii. 1, and, in ver. 2, says that the Spirit of God spake by him, and His word was upon his tongue. In Acts ii. 30, 31, Peter declares that, by the divine promise, David received, first the impulse, and afterwards further illumination, by the prophetic spirit dwelling in him. The latter declaration, moreover, rests on the testimony of the Lord Himself, in Matt. xxii. 43, where He says that in Ps. cx., David had spoken ἐν πνεύματι, i.e., seized with the Holy Spirit.

It is true that, in a series of Psalms, David is not any more explicit and definite than the fundamental prophecy, but speaks only of the grace which the Lord had conferred upon the Davidic race by the promise of a dominion which should outlast all earthly things. Thus it is in Ps. xviii., where, in the presence of the congregation, he offers those thanks which previously he had, as it were, privately expressed, for the glorious promise made to him;—in Ps. xi., where, in the name of the people, he expresses thankful joy for this same promise;—in Ps. lxi. and in the cycle of Psalms from Ps. cxxxviii. to cxlv.—the prophetic legacy of David—in which, at the beginning, in Ps. cxxxviii., he praises the Lord for His promise of eternal mercy given to him, and then, with the torch of promise, lightens up the darkness of the sufferings that are to fall upon this house,—Psalms with which Ps. lxxxix. and cxxxix., which were composed at a later period, and by other writers, are closely connected.

But there are other Psalms (ii. and cx.) in which David, with a distinctness which can be accounted for only by divine revelation, beholds the Messiah in whose coming the promise in 2 Sam. vii. should find its final and complete fulfilment. Whilst David, in these Psalms, represents the Messiah as his antitype, as the mighty conqueror, who will not rest until He shall have subjected the whole earth to His sway, Solomon, in Ps. lxxii., represents Him as the true Prince of Peace, and His dominion. as a just and peaceful rule. The circumstances of the time of Solomon form, in a similar way, the foundation for the description of the Messiah in Ps. xlv., which was written by the sons of Korah.

A personal Messianic element is contained in some of those Davidic Psalms also which refer to the *ideal* person of the *righteous one*, whose image we at last find fully portrayed in the Book of Wisdom. In these the sufferings of the righteous one in a world of sin are described, as well as the glorious issue to which he attains by the help of the Lord. After his own experience, David could not have doubted that, notwithstanding the glorious promise of the Lord, severe sufferings were impending over his family, and over Him in whom that family was, at some future time, to centre. But his own experience likewise promised a glorious issue to these sufferings. The Psalms in which, besides the reference to the righteous one, and to the people, the allusion to the afflictions of the Davidic race, and to the suffering Messiah, most plainly appear, are the xxii., the cii., and the cix.

There cannot be any doubt that the Messianic promise made considerable progress in the time of David. It is, in itself, a circumstance of great importance that the eyes of the people were henceforth directed to a definite family; for, thereby, their hopes acquired greater consistency. *Further,*—The former prophecies were, all of them, much shorter, and more in the shape of hints; but, now, their hopes could become detailed descriptions, because a *substratum* was given to them in the present. The Messiah had been foretold to David as a successor to his throne,—as a King. Hence it was, that, in the view of David himself and of the other psalmists, the earthly head of the Congregation of the Lord formed the *substratum* for the future Saviour. The naked thought now clothed itself with flesh and blood. The hope gained thereby in clearness and distinctness, as well as in practical significance.

The slight hint of a higher nature of the Messiah, given in Gen. xlix. 8, forms the main ground for the advancing and more definite knowledge, which we find in the days of David and Solomon. Grand and lofty expectations could, henceforth, not fail to be connected with the promise in 2 Sam. vii. 14, "I will be a father to him, and he shall be a son to Me," and with the prophecy of the absolute perpetuity of dominion, in the same passage. In Ps. ii. 12, the Messiah appears as the Son of God κατ᾽ ἐξοχήν,—as He, in whom to trust is to be saved, and whose anger brings destruction. In Ps. cx. 1, He appears as the Lord of the Congregation and of David himself,—as sitting at the right hand of omnipotence, and as invested with a full participation in the divine power over heaven and earth. In Ps. lxxi. eternity of dominion is ascribed to Him. In Ps. xlv. 7, 8, He is called God, Elohim.

Among the offices of Christ, it is especially the *Regal* office on which a clear light has been shed. The Messiah appears prominently as He " who has dominion from sea to sea, and from the river unto the.ends of the earth," Ps. lxxii. 8. In Ps. cx., however, the office of the Messiah as the eternal *High Priest* is first revealed to the congregation. He appears as the person who atones for whatever sins cleave to His people, as their Intercessor and Advocate with God, and as the Mediator of the closest communion with God. We have here the outlines, for the filling up of which Isaiah was, at a later period, called. The *Prophetic* office of the Saviour does not distinctly appear in the Psalms. It was reserved for Isaiah to bring out into a clearer light the allusion given, on this subject, by Moses, after it had been taken up again, for the first time since Moses' day, by the prophet Joel.

It was quite natural that David, who himself was exercised and proved by the cross, should be the first to introduce to the knowledge of the Church a *suffering Messiah*. But the doctrine has with him still the character of a germ; he still mixes up the references to the Messiah with the allusions to His types. It was from these that David rose to Him; it was from their destiny that David, by the Holy Spirit, inferred what would befall Him. Nowhere, however, has David directly and exclusively to do with a suffering Messiah, as had, afterwards, the prophet Isaiah.

In all that respects the Psalms, we must content ourselves with merely a passing glance, lest we encroach too much upon the territory which belongs to the Commentary on the Psalms. But "the last words of David," preserved to us in the Books of Samuel, we shall make the subject of a more minute consideration, inasmuch as they form a connecting link between the two classes of Psalms which rest on the promise in 2 Sam. vii., viz., those referring to David's house and family, and those relating to the personal Messiah. The "ruler among men" whom we meet in these "last words," is, in the first instance, an *ideal* person,—viz., the Davidic race conceived of as a person; but the *ideal* points to the *real* person, in whom all that had been foretold of the Davidic family should, at some future period, find its full realization. It is with a view to this person, that the personification has been employed.

2 SAMUEL XXIII. 1–7.

The last words of David are comprehended in seven verses; and these, again, are subdivided into sections of five and two verses respectively. First, there is a description of the fulness of blessings which the dominion of the just ruler shall carry along with it, and then of the destruction which shall overtake hostile wickedness.

It is not by accident that these last words are not found in the collection of Psalms. The reason is indicated by the נאם There is a prophetic element in the lyric poetry of David wheresoever it refers to the future destiny of his house; but this prophetic element rises, here, at the close of his life, to pure prophetic inspiration and utterance, which stand on an equal footing with the prophecy of Nathan in 2 Sam. vii., and claim an equal authority.

Ver. 1. "*And these are the last words of David. David, the son of Jesse, prophesies, and the man prophesies who was raised up on high, the anointed of the God of Jacob, and sweet in the Psalms of Israel.*"

It is substantially the same thing, whether we understand: "the last words of David" or "the latter words of David"—later in reference to xxi. 1. For even Ps. xviii., which precedes in chap. xxii., belongs, according to its inscription and contents, to the last times of David; it is, as it were, "a grand Hallelujah with which he withdraws from the scene of life." But, at all events, there is a closer connection with that Psalm; in it, too, David has in view the future destiny of his race, and we have here, in the last words, the prophetic conclusion of the lyrical effusion there. From this connection with chap. xxii., the closer limitation of the "words" follows. We learn from it that *holy* words only can be meant. The solemn introduction, and the parallelism with the blessings of Jacob and Moses, fully agree with and confirm this our introductory remark regarding the chronological position of these "words."—There can be no doubt that, in this introduction, there is a reference to Balaam's prophecy in Num. xxiv. 3,—and this goes far to prove how much David was occupied with the views which men of God had formerly opened up into future times :—"And he took up his parable and said : Balaam the son of Beor prophesies, and the man who had his eyes shut, prophesies : He prophesies who hears the words of God, who sees the vision of the Almighty, falling down and having his eyes open." The remarks which we made on that passage find here also a strict application :

"Balaam begins with a simple designation of his person, and then, in the following members, adds designations of such qualities of this person as here come into consideration, and serve for affording a foundation to the נאם with which he opens his discourse." As נאם always has the signification, "word of God," "revelation," it can here be ascribed to David, as it was in the fundamental passage to Balaam, only in as far as the word has been received by, and communicated to, him. The על, "upon," "over," stands here for "on high,"[1]—those over whom David has been raised up being omitted in order to express the absolute sovereignty bestowed upon David, more, however, in his posterity, than in his own person. (Compare Ps. xviii. 44: "Thou makest me the head of the heathen;" and in ver. 48: "God who avengeth me, and subdueth people under me.") *He who was raised up on high*—With the exception of the bodily ancestor and the lawgiver, of none under the Old Testament could this be with so much truth affirmed, as of David, the founder of the royal house, which, in all eternity, was to be the channel of blessings for the Congregation of the Lord, and to which, at last, all power in heaven and on earth was to be given. *The anointed of the God of Jacob*—Such is David, not only as an individual, but also as the representative of his race; compare Ps. xviii. 51. He is pre-eminently the anointed, the Christ of God.—זמיר, plur. זמירות, signifies, according to derivation and usage, not *song* or *hymn* in general, but the hymn in the higher strain, the skilful, solemn song of praise; compare my commentary on Song of Sol. ii. 12. David's Psalms are called זמירות of Israel, because he sang them as the organ of the congregation, and because they were appointed to be used in public worship; compare Comment. on Psalms, vol. iii. p. vi. *Sweet in Psalms of Israel* here finds its place only on the supposition that David, in his Psalms, spoke in the Spirit, Matt. xxii. 41–46; compare Commentary on Psalms, vol. iii. p. vii. viii. The most distinguished excellence in poetry which is

---

[1] תחת, "below," "beneath," "under," is often used adverbially, *e.g.*, Gen. xlix. 25. על, in the signification "on high," occurs also in Hosea xi. 7,—less certainly in Hos. vii. 16. For, according to 2 Chron. xxx. 9, that passage may be explained: "they return, not *to*," *i.e.*, there is the mere commencement of conversion, but not the attainment of the end. On הוקם Deut. xxviii. 36 is to be compared.

merely human cannot form a foundation for the assertion in ver. 2. But if, on the other hand, David be an often times tried organ of the Spirit for the Church, it cannot surprise us that in ver. 2 he even declares that, in the Spirit, he there foretells the future. Thus the נאם in our verse also has a good foundation.

Ver. 2. "*The Spirit of the Lord spake to me, and His word is upon my tongue.*"

That דבר refers to the communication which David promulgates in the sequel, and not to other revelations which he had formerly received, appears from its relation to the נאם in ver. 1. We should lose the new revelation announced in ver. 1, if ver. 2, and, hence, ver. 3 also—for the אמר there evidently resumes the דבר—refer to divine revelations which David, or, as *Thenius* supposes, even some other person, had formerly received.—בי is not "through me," for in that case the Participle would have been used instead of the Preterite; nor "in me," for that is contradicted by the parallel passages in which דבר occurs with ב; but "into me," which is stronger than "to me," and marks the deeply penetrating power of the revelation by the Spirit; compare remarks on Hosea i. 2. Such being the case, the Preterite is quite in its proper place; for the inward revelation, the נאם יהוה, precedes the communication—the נאם דוד. (On the whole verse, 1 Pet. i. 11, 2 Pet. i. 21, are to be compared.)

Ver. 3. "*The God of Israel said, the Rock of Israel spake to me: a Ruler over men—just; a Ruler—fear of God.*"

The omission of the verb, "will be or rise," is quite suited to the concise and abrupt style of the divine word. The mention of God, the Rock of Israel, shows that the revelation has a reference to what is done for the good of the people of God,—of His Church. For her good, the glorious Ruler shall be raised. (Compare the words, ἀντελάβετο Ἰσραὴλ παιδὸς αὐτοῦ, in Luke i. 54, as also ver. 68, and ii. 32.) The appellation, Rock of Israel, indicates God's immutability, trustworthiness, and inviolable faithfulness; compare my comment. on Psalm xviii. 3, 32–47. The connection betwixt Ps. xviii. and the "last words of David" here also clearly appears. The fundamental passage is Deut. xxxii. 4.—That *men* must be conceived of as the subjects of dominion, is proved by Ps. xviii. 44, where David is made the head of nations, and people whom he has not known serve him,—and by ver. 45, where the sons of the stranger do homage to him,—and by ver. 48 : " Who subdues people under me."—*A Ruler—fear* of God, *i.e.*, a Ruler who shall, as it were, be fear of God itself—personified fear of God. We must here compare the expression, " This man is the peace," Mic. v. 4, and, as to the substance of the expression, Is. xi. 2, " And the Spirit of the Lord rests upon him . . . the spirit of knowledge and of the fear of the Lord." We might be disposed to refer this exclusively to the person of the Messiah, especially when those Psalms are compared which refer to a personal Messiah. But Ps. xviii.—which here receives, as it were, its prophetic seal—and especially the relation of ver. 3 and 4 to ver. 5, where David speaks of his house, prove that the Ruler here is, primarily, only an ideal person, viz., the seed of David spoken of in Ps. xviii. 51. Things so glorious can, however, be ascribed to it only with a reference to the august personage in whom that seed will centre at the end of days,—the righteous Branch, whom the Lord will raise up unto David (Jer. xxiii. 5), who executeth judgment and righteousness on earth, Jer. xxxiii. 15. David knew too well what human nature is, and what is in man, to have expected any such thing from the collective body, as such.

Ver. 4. " *And as the light of the morning when the sun riseth, a morning without clouds ; by brightness, by rain,—grass out of the earth.*"

In the first hemistich we have to supply: will be His appearance in its loveliness and saving importance. The morning elsewhere also, especially in the Psalms (compare remarks on Ps. lix. 17 ; Song of Sol. iii. 1), is used as the emblem of salvation. The condition of men before the appearance of the Ruler among them, is, in its destitution, like dark night.—The *brightness* is that of the Ruler, as the spiritual Sun, the Sun of Salvation. (Compare Mal. iii. 20 [iv. 2], where righteousness is represented as the sun rising to those who fear God.) The *rain*—the warm, mild rain, not the winter's rain which, in the Song of Sol. ii. 11, and elsewhere, occurs as an emblem of affliction and judgment—is the emblem of blessing (compare Is. xliv. 3, where " rain" is explained by " blessing "). The *grass*, which springs up out of the earth by means of sunshine and rain, is emblematical of the fruits and effects of salvation.

(Compare Is. xlv. 8, where, in consequence of the rain of salvation pouring down from the skies, the earth brings forth salvation and righteousness.) The passage in Ps. lxxii. 6 is parallel, where Solomon says of his Antitype, "He shall come down like rain upon the mown grass, as showers watering the earth." The figure of the rain making fresh grass to spring up is there likewise employed to designate the blessings of the Messianic time.

Ver. 5. *"For is not thus my house with God? For He has made with me an everlasting covenant, ordered in all things and kept; for all my salvation, and all pleasure,—should He not make it to grow?"*

The special revelation which David received at the close of his life (compare the remarks on נאם in ver. 1) is here connected with the fundamental promise in 2 Sam. vii., which was thereby anew confirmed to him. Those who, like *De Wette* and *Thenius*, mistake the correct sense of vers. 3 and 4, are not a little perplexed by the *"for"* at the beginning of this verse, and attempt in vain to account for it.—*Thus, i.e.,* as it had been told in what precedes.—ערוכה, "prepared," "ordered," forms the contrast to what is only half finished, indefinite, depending upon circumstances and conditions, admitting of provisions and exceptions. The extent to which all interposing obstacles were excluded, or rather, had been considered and calculated upon beforehand, appears especially from 2 Sam. vii. 14, 15, according to which, even the most fatal of all interpositions—the apostasy of the bearers of the covenant—should not destroy the covenant,—should not annul the gracious promise made to the race. *Kept, i.e.,* firm, inviolable, because given by Him who keepeth covenant and mercy, Deut. vii. 9; Dan. ix. 4. In 1 Kings viii. 25, Solomon prays, "And now, Lord God of Israel, keep with Thy servant David my father what Thou promisedst him when Thou saidst, There shall not be cut off unto thee a man from My sight to sit on the throne of Israel." The second *"for"* points out the cause of *kept. All pleasure, i.e.,* all that is well-pleasing to me, all that my heart desires. The preceding ישעי serves the purpose of qualifying it more definitely. The object of David's desires is, accordingly, his salvation, the glory of his house.

Ver. 6. *"And wickedness, like thorns, they will all be driven away; for not will any one take them into his hands."*

The subject treated of in this verse is: the Ruler among men

in His relation to His enemies. To those He is as formidable
as His appearance is blessed to those who surrender themselves
to Him. In Ps. xviii. also, there is a celebration of the indomi-
table power which the Lord grants to David, His anointed, and
to his seed against all their enemies; compare ver. 38: "I pursue mine enemies and overtake them, and do not turn again till
they are consumed; ver. 39, I crush them and they cannot rise,
they fall under my feet." In the cycle of Psalms from cxxxviii.
to cxlv., David likewise speaks of the dangers which threaten
his house from enemies, and the leading thought of Ps. ii. is:
the Messiah as the conqueror of His enemies. The eyes of
David were the more opened to this circumstance, the more he
himself had had to contend against adversaries.—בליעל always
means unworthiness in a moral point of view, "wickedness,"
"vileness." *Wickedness* is here used in the concrete sense = the
wicked ones, the sons of wickedness, Deut. xiii. 14. The wicked
ones, the enemies of the Church, are compared to the thorns, on
account of their pricking nature; and therefore their end is like
that of thorns, they will be thrown aside like them. In Ezek.
xxiv. 28, after the judgment upon the neighbouring people has
been proclaimed, it is said, "And there shall remain no more a
pricking brier everywhere round about the house of Israel, where
their enemies are, nor a grieving thorn;" compare Num. xxxiii.
55; Song of Sol. ii. 2; Is. xxvii. 4; Nahum i. 10.—מנד, the
Partic. Hoph. of נוד, "thrust out," "put to flight" (compare
Ps. xxxvi. 12), cannot be applied to the thorns, but only to the
men. *Like thorns, i.e.,* so that they become like thorns, of
which the land is cleared. *For not will any one take them into
his hands—Michaelis: Intractabiles sunt.*

Ver. 7. "*And if any one toucheth them, he is filled with iron,
and the staff of a spear; and they shall be utterly burnt with fire
where they dwell.*"

The two members of vers. 6 and 7 stand in an inverted
relation to each other. In ver. 6, we have, first, the punishment
described, and then their hostile nature, by which the punishment was called forth. In ver. 7, we have, first, the cause, and
then the consequence. The thought in the first member is:
every touch of them bears a hostile character. *Iron*—instead
of weapons fabricated of iron; comp. 1 Sam. xvii. 7; Job
xx. 24, xli. 19 compared with vers. 18, 20; Jer. xv. 12.

בשבת, literally, "in the dwelling" (compare Ps. xxiii. 6, xxvii. 4; Deut. xxx. 20) instead of "where they dwell," shows that in their own borders they shall be visited and overtaken by retribution. בשבת cannot have the signification, "without delay," ascribed to it by *Thenius*.

------◆------

THE SONG OF SOLOMON.

An important link in the chain of the Messianic hopes is formed by the Song of Solomon. It is intimately associated with Ps. lxxii., which was written by Solomon, and represents the Messiah as the Prince of Peace, imperfectly prefigured by Solomon as His type. As in this Psalm, so also in the Song of Solomon, the coming of the Messiah forms the subject throughout, and He is introduced there under the name of Solomon, the Peaceful One. His coming shall be preceded by severe afflictions, represented under the emblems of the scorching heat of the sun, of winter, of rain, of dark nights, and of the desert. Connected with this coming is the reception of the heathen nations into His kingdom, and this, through the medium of the old Covenant-people.

Thus far the first part, down to chap. v. 1. The subjects contained in the second part are, the sin of the daughter of Zion against the heavenly Solomon and the judgment; then, repentance and reunion, which will be accomplished by the co-operation of the daughters of Jerusalem, *i.e.*, of the very heathen nations who had formerly received salvation through them; the complete re-establishment of the old relation of love, in consequence of which the daughter of Zion again occupies the centre of the kingdom of God; and the indissoluble nature of this covenant of love now anew entered into, in contrast with the instability of the former.

The Song of Solomon does not, strictly speaking, possess a prophetical character. It does not communicate any new revelations; like the Psalms, it only represents, in a poetical form, things already known. It sufficiently appears from our former statement, that, in the first part of this book, not one feature occurs which did not form a part of those Messianic prophecies which we can prove to have been known at the time of Solomon. In the second part, however, it is somewhat different. No corresponding parallel can be adduced from any former time to the view, that a great part of the people would reject the salvation offered to them in Christ, and, thereby, draw down judgment upon themselves. Yet, all that the book under consideration contains upon this point, is only the application of a general truth, the knowledge of which the covenant-people had received at the very beginning of their history. A consideration of human nature in general, and more especially of Israel's character, as it had been deeply and firmly impressed upon the people by the Mosaic law, joined to the ample experience which history had afforded in this respect, sufficiently convinced those who were more enlightened, that it could not be by any means expected—that, indeed, it was even impossible—that, at the coming of the Messiah, the whole people would sincerely and heartily receive Him, and do homage to Him. And there existed, on the other hand, at the time of Solomon also, the foundation for the doctrine of the final restoration of the people. For, even in the Pentateuch, the election of Israel by God is represented as irrevocable and absolute, and which, therefore, must at last triumph over all apostasy and covenant-breaking on the part of the people.

The Song of Solomon, then, is no *apocalypsis*, no revelation of mysteries till then unknown. There is in it no such disclosure as is, *e.g.*, that in 2 Sam. vii., on the descent of the Messiah from David; or, as is that in Mic. v. 1 (2), on His being born at Bethlehem; or even as is that in Is. liii. on His office as a High Priest, and His vicarious satisfaction. But, nevertheless, we must not imagine the case to have been thus, that the contents of the Song of Solomon could have originated merely from reflection on the part of Solomon. The truths hitherto revealed had too much of the character of mere germs to allow us to suppose that from them, and in such a way, we could account for the clearness and certainty with which they have been blended into one whole. Another element, moreover, must be joined to the historical ground—viz., an elevated condition of the soul, a "being in the Spirit,"—a breathing of the divine Spirit upon the human. History bears witness that such prophetic states, in the wider sense, were not strange to Solomon. It twice reports about the Lord's having appeared to him, 1 Kings iii. 5, ix. 2. From such an elevated state of soul, his dedicatory prayer, in 1 Kings viii., and Ps. lxxii., also originated.

We must content ourselves with these hints as regards Solomon's Song. As it moves throughout on Messianic ground, the Author must consider his commentary on this book (Berlin, 1853) as an appendix to the Christology.

MESSIANIC PREDICTIONS IN THE PROPHETS.

AFTER the time of Solomon, the Messianic prediction was for a considerable time discontinued. It was first resumed, and farther expanded, by the Canonical prophecy which began under Uzziah. There cannot be any doubt that that which *appears* as an interval was *really* such. There is no ground for the supposition that any important connecting links have been lost. The Messianic prediction in the oldest canonical prophets is immediately connected with that which existed previously at the time of David and Solomon.

It is not a matter of chance that, whilst the blossom of prophetism appeared as early as Samuel, the canonical prophetism took its rise at a much later date. Nor is it the result of accident, that we do not possess any written prophecies, either by Elijah, who, at the transfiguration of the Lord, appeared as the representative of all the Old Testament prophets, or by Elisha. Nor is it merely accidental that, at the time of Uzziah, there appears all at once, and simultaneously, a whole series of prophets. All these things are connected with the circumstance, that it was only at that time that great events for the Covenant-people were in preparation,—that, only then, those catastrophes were impending which were to be brought about by the Asiatic kingdoms, and which kept equal pace with the sin of Israel, the measure of which was being more and more filled up. Canonical prophecy is closely linked with these catastrophes. It is called to disclose to the Church the meaning of these judgments, and, thereby, to secure to them their effects in all time coming. The Messianic predictions uttered by the prophets are likewise closely connected with the announcement of these judgments. Whilst false security was shaken by the threatenings, despondency—which is as hostile to true conversion—was prevented by pointing to the future coming of the Saviour.

The prophets do not deliver the Messianic prediction in its whole compass, any more than do the writers of the Messianic Psalms. On the contrary, it is always only certain individual aspects which they exhibit. The writers of the Messianic Psalms take up those features which presented points of contact with their own lives and their own experiences, or at least the circumstances of their times. This is quite in keeping with the more subjective origin of Psalm-poetry. Thus David describes the suffering Messiah surrounded by powerful enemies, and who, after severe struggles, at length obtains victory and dominion. To Solomon, He appears as the Ruler of a great and peaceful kingdom, and he beholds the most distant nations reverentially offering presents to Him and doing Him allegiance. But the Prophets, in pointing out this or that feature, are not so much guided by their own experience, disposition of mind, and peculiar circumstances, as by the wants of those whom they are addressing, and by the effect which they are anxious to produce on them. When they have to do with pusillanimity, desponding at the sight of the heathen world as it seems to be all-powerful,—they then represent the Messiah as the invincible conqueror of the heathen world, who shall subject the whole earth to the kingdom of God. When they have to deal with pride, trusting in imaginary prerogatives of the Covenant-people, and boldly challenging the judgments of God upon the heathen,—they then represent the Messiah as Him who shall make a great separation among the Covenant-people themselves, and who shall be a consolation to the godly, while He brings inexorable judgments upon the wicked when they have to do with those who mourn in Zion, who through the inflicted judgments of the Lord have been brought to a deep sorrow on account of their sins,—they then represent the Messiah as Him who shall one day take away the sins of the land, who is to bear their griefs and carry their sorrows. Now, as canonical prophecy extends over several centuries, during which circumstances, wants, and dispositions the most diverse, must have taken place, and as the Messianic prophecy is in harmony with these, it displayed, more and more fully, its riches, and did so in a manner far more effective and vivid than it could possibly have done had it been proclaimed in the form of a discussion or treatise. As the Messiah was thus represented from the most various points of view, and in the way of direct perception, and divine confidence,—as He was thus everywhere pointed out as the end of the development, He could not but become more and more the soul of the nation's life.

In the Messianic announcements by the prophets, no such gradual progress in clearness and distinctness can be traced, as in those of the Pentateuch. The assertion that there existed with them at first, only a general hope of better times, unconnected with any person, rests on the unfounded hypothesis that Joel is the oldest among all the prophets,—and at the same time on the erroneous assumption that he was ignorant of a personal Messiah,—and, *further*, on the incorrect supposition that the prophets, who write only what presents itself immediately to their view, have not in their creed all that they omit to say. It is, *moreover*, opposed by the prospect of a personal Messiah held out in the Pentateuch, the Psalms, and the Song of Solomon. How very slender is the ground for inferring that, because many essential points are not touched upon by Hosea, Joel, and Amos, they, therefore, did not know them, is shown by the fact that neither do several among the later prophets—as Jeremiah and Ezekiel—touch upon them, although the previous more distinct prophecies of Isaiah were certainly known and acknowledged by them. We must never forget that it is from above that each of the prophets received his share of the prophetic spirit, and that this depended partly upon the measure of his receptivity, which might have been greater with the former than with the latter prophets,—and, partly, upon the wants and capacities of those for whom the prophecy was destined.

A central position, as regards the Messianic predictions, is occupied by Isaiah. Even his Messianic prophecies, however, when viewed detached and isolated, bear the character of one-sidedness. He nowhere gives us a complete image of the Messiah. But, whilst the other prophets were permitted to give only single disclosures, he gives us, in the whole body of his Messianic prophecies, the materials for a full and entire image, although not the image itself. The Fathers of the Church have, therefore, rightly designated him as the Evangelist among the prophets. But the transition to him from the Psalms and the Song of Solomon could not be immediate. Hosea, Joel, Amos, Obadiah, Jonah, and Micah form, as it were, the connecting links. Proceeding from the Messianic promise, in the shape which it had received at the time of David and Solomon, they give it a standing in the prophetic message, and infuse into it new life by means of the connection into which it is brought by them, and supplement it by adding single new features.

It is our intention to give an exposition of the Messianic passages in the prophets, according to their chronological order. In placing Hosea at the head, we follow the example of those who collected the Canon, and who, regarding not so much the succession of years as that of the governments, may have assigned the first place to Hosea, because he is the most important among the prophets at the time of Jeroboam in Israel, and of Uzziah in Judah, or because he really appeared first, and the prophecy in chap. i.-iii. is the beginning of written prophecies. The latter supposition most naturally suggests itself; the analogies are in its favour, and no decisive argument has been brought forward against it.

THE PROPHET HOSEA.

GENERAL PRELIMINARY REMARKS.

That the kingdom of Israel was the object of the prophet's ministry is so evident, that upon this point all are, and cannot but be, agreed. But there is a difference of opinion as to whether the prophet was a fellow-countryman of those to whom he preached, or was called by God out of the kingdom of Judah. The latter has been asserted with great confidence by *Maurer*, among others, in his *Observ. in Hos.*, in the *Commentat. Theol.* ii. i. p. 293. But the arguments by which he supports this view will not stand the test. He appeals (1) to the inscription. The circumstance that, in this, there is mention made of the kings of Judah under whom Hosea exercised his ministry,—that they are mentioned *at all*,—and that they are mentioned *first* and *completely*, while only one of the kings of Israel is named, proves, according to him—especially on a comparison with the inscription of Amos—that the prophet acknowledged the kings of Judah as his superiors. But this mode of argumentation entirely overlooks the position which the pious in Israel generally, and the prophets especially, occupied in reference to Judah. They considered the whole separation—the civil as well as the religious—as an apostasy from God. And how could they do otherwise, since the eternal dominion over the people of God had been granted, by God, to the house of David? The closeness of the connection between the religious and the civil sufficiently appears from the fact, that Jeroboam and all his successors despaired of being able to maintain their power, unless they made the breach, in religious matters also, as wide as possible. The chief of the prophets in the kingdom of the ten tribes—Elijah—by taking twelve stones according to the number of the tribes of Israel (1 Kings xviii. 31), plainly enough declared, that he considered the separation as one not consistent with the idea of the Jewish kingdom, and that therefore, in reality, it must at some future period be done away with; that he considered the government in Israel as existing *de facto*, but not *de jure*.

By none do we find this view so distinctly brought out as by Hosea. "They have set up kings, and not by Me"—says the Lord by him, chap. viii. 4—"they have made princes, and I knew it not." In his view, then, the whole basis of the government in Israel is ungodliness. Because they have chosen kings and princes without God, and against the will of God, they shall be taken from them by God, chap. iii. 4. Salvation cannot come to the people until Israel and Judah set over themselves one head, ii. 2 (i. 11), until the children of Israel seek Jehovah their Lord, and David their king, iii. 5. These two things are, in his view, intimately connected; no true return to the invisible head of the Theocracy is possible without, at the same time, a return to the visible one—the house of David. What, at some future time, the mass of the people, when converted, were to do, the converted individual must do even now. He even now recognised the kings of the tribe of Judah as truly his sovereigns, although he yielded civil obedience to the rulers of Israel, until God should again abolish the government which He gave to the people in wrath, and set

up in opposition to the government of the house of David in
His anger, on account of their apostasy. From all this, it
clearly appears that, in order to account for the peculiarity of
the inscription, we need not have recourse to the conjecture,
that Hosea was a native of Judah. One might, with as much
reason, maintain that all the prophets in the kingdom of Israel,
who rejected the worship of the calves—and hence all the
prophets without exception—were natives of the kingdom of
Judah. For the worship of the calves is quite on a par with
the apostasy from the anointed of God. Hosea mentions, first
and completely, the kings of the legitimate family. He then
further adds the name of one of the rulers of the kingdom of
Israel, under whom his ministry began, because it was of importance to fix precisely the time of its commencement. Uzziah,
the first in the series of the kings of Judah mentioned by him,
survived Jeroboam nearly twenty-six years; compare *Maurer*,
l. c. p. 284. Now, had the latter not been mentioned along with
him, the thought might easily have suggested itself, that it was
only during the latter period of Uzziah's reign that the prophet
entered upon his office; in which case all that he said about the
overthrow of Jeroboam's family would have appeared to be a
vaticinium post eventum, inasmuch as it took place very soon
after Jeroboam's death. The same applies to what was said
by him regarding the total decay of the kingdom which was so
flourishing under Jeroboam; for, from the moment of Jeroboam's death, it hastened with rapid strides towards its destruction. If, therefore, it was to be seen that future things lie
open before God and His servants "before they spring forth"
(Is. xlii. 9), it was necessary that the commencement of the
prophet's ministry should be the more accurately determined;
and this is effected by the statement, that it happened within
the period of the fourteen years during which Uzziah and Jeroboam reigned contemporaneously. That this is the main reason
for mentioning Jeroboam's name, is seen from the relation of
ver. 2 to ver. 1. The remark there made,—that Hosea received
the subsequent revelation at the very beginning of his prophetic
ministry, corresponds with the mention of Jeroboam's name in
ver. 1. But this is not all; nor can we say that, had it not
been for this reason, Hosea would not have mentioned any king
of Israel at all, in order that, from the outset, he might exhibit

his disposition. There was a considerable difference between Jeroboam and the subsequent kings. *Cocceius* remarked very strikingly : "The other kings of Israel are not considered as kings, but as robbers." Jeroboam possessed a *quasi* legitimacy. The house of Jehu, to which he belonged, had opposed the extreme of religious apostasy. It was, to a certain degree, acknowledged, even by the prophets. Jeroboam had obtained the throne, not by usurpation, but by birth. He was the last king by whom the Lord sent deliverance to the people of the ten tribes ; compare 2 Kings xiv. 27 : "And the Lord would not blot out the name of Israel from under heaven ; and He saved them by the hand of Jeroboam, the son of Joash." (2.) The *internal* reason adduced by *Maurer* (S. 294) is equally insignificant. "The *morum magistri*," he says, "are wont more slightly to reprove, in the case of strangers, that which they severely condemn in their own people ; but Hosea rebukes with as much severity the inhabitants of Judah, when he comes to speak of them, as he does the Israelites." But no certain inferences can be drawn from such commonplaces ; for, in this way we might as reasonably infer, that Isaiah and the writer of the Books of Kings were natives of the kingdom of the ten tribes, because they censure the sins of the Israelites as severely as they do those of the inhabitants of Judah. To this commonplace we might as easily oppose another equally true, viz., the "*morum magistri*, from a partiality for their own people, are wont to judge more leniently of their faults than of those of strangers." Such maxims require to be applied with the utmost caution, even in the territory to which they belong, because one consideration may be so easily outweighed by another. Here, however, its application is altogether out of the question. The prophets, as the instruments of the Spirit, spoke pure and plain truth without any regard to persons. Whether Hosea was a native of Judah or of Israel, he would express himself in the same way concerning the inhabitants of Judah. He would severely rebuke their sins, and at the same time readily acknowledge, as he does, their advantages,—for "Salvation cometh of the Jews."

If, then, these be the arguments in favour of the Judean origin of Hosea, it readily appears that the probabilities of such an origin, compared with that of his Israelitish descent, are not even in the proportion of one to a hundred. The prophets were almost more numerous in the kingdom of Israel than in that of Judah; and yet the entire history knows of only two instances of prophets being sent from the kingdom of Judah to that of Israel, viz., the prophet spoken of in 1 Kings xiii. and Amos. And the former of these even scarcely belongs to this class, inasmuch as he received only a single mission into the kingdom of Israel, and *that*, at a time when the prophetic institution was not as yet organized there. In the case of Amos likewise, it is manifest not only that he was only an exception to the rule,— as appears from the transactions with the priest Amaziah, reported in Amos vii. (compare especially ver. 12),—but still more plainly, from the mention in the inscription of his having been a native of Judah.

With regard to the *time* of the prophet, the inscription places his ministry in the reigns of the kings Uzziah, Jotham, Ahaz, and Hezekiah. A long period is, no doubt, thus assigned to it, —a period embracing at least twenty-six years of Uzziah's reign, and, in addition, the sixteen years of that of Jotham, the sixteen years during which Ahaz reigned, and at least one or two years of the reign of Hezekiah, making, at the lowest calculation, a period of sixty years in all.

This exceedingly long duration of the prophet's ministry might easily excite suspicion regarding the genuineness and correctness of the inscription; but such suspicion is at once set at rest by the fact, that the statements contained in the book itself lead us to assume a period equally extended. The *beginning* of the prophet's ministry cannot be assigned to any *later* period; for, in chap. i. 4, the fall of Jeroboam's house, which took place soon after his death, is announced as a future event. *Moreover*, the condition of the kingdom appears still, throughout the whole first discourse, as a very flourishing one. Nor can the *end* of his ministry be assigned to any earlier period. For in chap. x. 14, an expedition of Shalman or Shalmaneser against the kingdom of Israel (*Vitringa, Proleg. in Is.* p. 6) is described as being already past, and a second invasion is threatened. But the first expedition of Shalmaneser, reported in 2 Kings xvii. 1 seqq., is almost contemporaneous with the beginning of Hezekiah's reign. For it was directed against Hoshea, king of Israel, who began his reign in the twelfth year of that of Ahaz, which lasted sixteen years. The exact harmony of the passage in Hosea with that in 2 Kings xvii. is very evident. In 2 Kings xvii. 3, it is said: "Against him came up Shalmaneser, king of Assyria, and Hoshea became his servant and gave him tribute." This was the first expedition of Shalmaneser. Then followed the second expedition, which was caused by the rebellion of Hoshea,—in consequence of which Samaria was taken and the people carried away. In Hos. x. 14, 15, it is said: "And tumult ariseth against thy people, and all thy fortresses shall be spoiled, as Shalman spoiled Beth-arbel in the day of battle; the mother was dashed in pieces upon (her) children. So shall he do unto you, Bethel, because of your great wickedness in the dawn of the morning, destroyed, destroyed shall be the king of Israel." Hosea here declares that the beginning of the destruction by Shalmaneser is the prophecy of the end of the kingdom of Israel. The " morning dawn" is the time of apparently reappearing prosperity, when, according to *Cocceius*, a time of peace begins to shine. In Amos iv. 13, v. 8, the prosperity again dawning upon the kingdom of Israel is likewise expressed by "morning" and "morning dawn." The identity of Beth-arbel and Arbelah in Galilee can the less be doubted, because recent researches have rendered it certain that this place, now called *Irbid*, was an important fortress. (Compare *Münchener gelehrte Anzeigen* 1836, S. 870 ff.; *Robinson*, iii. 2, p. 534; *v. Raumer*, S. 108.) The use of Beth-arbel, instead of the more common Arbelah, as well as that of Shalman instead of Shalmaneser, belongs to the higher style. At the first expedition, the decisive battle had, no doubt, taken place at Arbelah. They who disconnect this passage from 2 Kings xvii. do not know what to make of it. *Simson* complains of the darkness resting on the passage under consideration.—But Hos. xii. 2 (1) likewise leads us to the very last times of the kingdom of Israel,—those times when Hoshea endeavoured to free himself from the Assyrian servitude by the help of Egypt. " Ephraim feedeth on wind, and followeth after the east-wind; he daily increaseth lies and desolation; and they do make a covenant with Assyria, and oil is carried into Egypt." Their sending oil to Egypt, notwithstanding the covenant made with Assyria, is the lie, which goes hand in hand with desolation, while they imagine thereby to work deliverance. This explanation has been already given by *J. H. Manger*, of whose *Commentarius in Hoseam, Campen,* 1782—a commentary in many respects excellent—most of the recent commentators, and, lastly, *Simson*, have, to their great disadvantage, not availed themselves. *Manger* says: "These words refer to the ambassadors who were sent with splendid presents by king Hoshea to the king of Egypt, in order to win him over to himself, and induce him to assist him against the Assyrians, to whom he had become subject by a solemn treaty."—To the last times of the kingdom of Israel we are likewise led by what occurs in other passages concerning the relation of Israel to Egypt and Asshur. The matter has been falsely represented by very many as if two parties among the people were spoken of,—an Assyrian and an Egyptian party. Nor is it so, that the whole people turn at one time to Egypt in order to free themselves from the Assyrians, and at another time to Assyria to assist them against Egypt. The position is rather thus: The people, heavily oppressed by Asshur, at one time seek help from Egypt against Asshur, and, at another, attempt to conciliate the latter. Precisely thus is the situation described in vii. 11: "They call to Egypt, they go to Asshur." That by which Israel was threatened, was, according to viii. 10, "the burden of the king of princes, the king of Asshur," ver. 9. This they seek to turn off, partly by artifices, and partly by calling to their help the king of Egypt. Asshur alone is the king "warrior" (*Jareb*), v. 13, x. 6; he only has received the divine mission to execute judgment; compare xi. 5: "He, *i.e.,* Israel, shall not return to the land of Egypt, and Asshur, he is his king." As an ally not to be trusted, Egypt is described in vii. 16, where, after the announcement of their destruction on account of their rebellion against the Lord, it is said: "This shall be their derision on account of the land of Egypt," *i.e.,* thus they shall be put to shame in the hope which they place on Egypt. Is. xxx. 1–5 is quite analogous. In that passage the prophet announces that Judah's attempt to protect themselves against Asshur by means of Egypt would be vain; compare, especially, ver. 3: "And the fortress of Pharaoh shall be your shame, and the trust in the shadow of Egypt, your confusion;" and ver. 5: "Not for help nor for profit, but for shame and for reproach." Such historical circumstances, however, had not yet occurred under Menahem. At that time, Israel was not yet placed in the midst betwixt Asshur and Egypt. It is expressly mentioned in 2 Kings xv. 20, that the invasion of Pul was only transitory, and that not conquest, but spoil, was its aim. The real commencement of the Assyrian oppression is formed by the invasion of Tiglathpileser at the time of Ahaz. Isaiah, in chap. vii., points out the pernicious consequences of Ahaz's calling the Assyrians to his assistance against Syria and Israel. The very fact of this war carried on against Judah by Syria and Ephraim shows, that up to that time, Asshur had not laid his hand upon these regions. It was only with the invasion under Ahaz that there was any display of Asshur's tendency to make permanent conquests on the other side of Euphrates, which could not fail to bring about the conflict with the Egyptian power.—"King Jareb,"—such had already become the historical character of the king of Asshur, at the time when Hosea wrote; but prior to the times of Ahaz and Hezekiah, he did not stand out as such.

There is no decisive weight to be attached to what *Simson* advances in order to prove that we must fix an earlier date. He argues thus: "Gilead, which, according to 2 Kings xv. 29, was taken and depopulated by Tiglathpileser, whom Ahaz had called to his assistance, appears in vi. 8, xii. 12 (11) to be still in the possession of Israel. Hence, the ministry of the prophet cannot have extended beyond the invasion of Judah by the Syrians and Ephraim." But since the book gives the sum and substance of Hosea's prophecies during a prolonged period, there must necessarily occur in it references to events which already belonged to the past, at the time when the prophet wrote. In chap. i. 4, even the overthrow of the house of Jeroboam appears as being still future.

But even although we could not establish, from other sources, the statement contained in the inscription, the inscription itself would nevertheless be a guarantee for it; and the more so, because there are other analogies in favour of so long a duration of the prophetic office, which was sometimes entered upon even in early youth. The inscription has the same authority in its favour as every other part of the book; and it is hardly possible to understand the levity with which it has, in recent times, been pretty generally designated as spurious, or, at least, suspicious.

It is altogether impossible to sever it from the other parts of the book. There must certainly have been some object in view when, in ver. 2, it is expressly remarked, that what follows took place at the *beginning* of Hosea's ministry. But such an object it will be possible to point out, only in the event of its being more accurately determined at what time this beginning took place—viz., still under the reign of Jeroboam, when the state of things as it appeared to the eye did not yet offer any occasion for such views of the future as are opened up in the first three chapters. Ver. 1 cannot, therefore, be regarded as an addition subsequently made, unless the words in ver. 2, from תחלת to בהושע be so likewise. But these again are most closely connected with what follows by the *Future* with *Vav convers.*, which never can begin a narrative. There remains, therefore, only this alternative:—either to regard the whole as having been written at a later period, or to claim for Hosea the inscription also. We cannot agree with the view of *Simson*, that the remark by which the beginning of the book is assigned to the beginning of the prophet's ministry, originated from a chronological interest only; and we can the less do so, because the prophet does not pay any attention to chronology in any other place, but is anxious to give only the sum and substance of what he had prophesied during a series of years. The only exception which he makes in this respect must have originated from strong reasons; and such do not exist, if the inscription in ver. 1, or the mention of the kings in it, be spurious. The mention of the beginning in ver. 2 would, in that case, be so much the more groundless, as we could know nothing at all regarding the length of his ministry.

Much more fruitful, certainly, than all such vain doubts, are the reflections of Calvin on the long duration of the prophet's ministry: "How grievous is it to us when God requires our services for twenty or thirty years; and, especially, when we have to contend with ungodly people, who would not willingly take upon them the yoke, yea, who even obstinately resist us! we then wish to be freed at once, and to become pensioned soldiers. But, seeing this prophet's long protracted ministry, let us take from it an example of patience, that we may not despair although the Lord should not at once free us from our burden."

Many interpreters have zealously attempted to determine the

particular portions of this lengthened period to which the particular portions of this book belong. But such an undertaking is wholly vain in the case before us, as well as in that of Micah, and most of the minor prophets generally. The supposition upon which it rests is false—viz., that the collection consists of a number of single, detached portions. We do not possess the whole of Hosea's prophecies, but only the substance of their essential contents,—a survey which he himself gave towards the end of his ministry. This appears (1) from the דבר יהוה in the inscription. In itself, this would not be a decisive argument, as the prophet might also have comprehended in an *ideal* unity, discourses outwardly distinct; but, nevertheless, as long as no reason appears for the contrary, it is more naturally referred to a continuous discourse with an external unity also. (2.) It appears from the entire omission of all chronological data. The only exception is in ver. 2; but this exception serves only to strengthen the argument drawn from the omission everywhere else. (3.) It is proved by the absence of all certain indications about the beginning and ending of the particular portions. There occur, just as in the second part of Isaiah, new starting points only; but, with these exceptions, the discourse always moves on in the same manner. (4.) It is seen from the indefiniteness and generality of the historical references, which must necessarily arise if the prophet referred, in like manner, to the whole of this lengthened period. That the facts, upon which the last two arguments rest, really exist, is made sufficiently apparent from the immense diversity of opinions as to the number and extent of the particular portions, and as to the time of their composition. There are not even two of the more important interpreters who agree in the main points alone. Such a diversity does not exist in reference to any of the prophetical books which actually consist of detached prophecies. (5.) The style and language are too much the same throughout the whole, to admit of the idea that any long period could have elapsed between the particular prophecies. This, indeed, is only a subordinate argument; but it acquires its full importance, when connected with the foundation of the third and fourth proofs.

It now only remains to give a survey of the historical circumstances at the time of the prophet. This is the more necessary, as a knowledge of these is required for the exposition of the Messianic prophecies, not only of Hosea, but also of Amos, his contemporary.

The kingdom of Israel carried within it, from its very commencement, a twofold element of destruction—viz., the establishment of the worship of the calves, and the rebellion against the dynasty of David. With regard to the former,—the consequence of this apparently so much isolated transgression of a Mosaic ordinance extended much further than would appear upon a superficial view. In this case also it was seen that a little leaven leaveneth the whole lump. Of far higher importance than the low conceptions of God produced by this symbolical representation of Him, was another aspect of the transaction. The prohibition of image-worship in the Pentateuch was as distinct and clear as it was possible to make it. The kings of Israel were far from rejecting it; but still, how difficult soever it may appear, they found out an interpretation by which they evaded the application of it to their institution. Such a course once entered upon, could only lead them further and further astray. As, in so important a case, they had, in opposition to their own better convictions, allowed themselves to pervert and explain away the law—asserting, probably, that it was given only on account of the coarse sensuality of former generations —the same was done in other things also, as often as it was called for by the disposition of the corrupted heart. All unfaithfulness which is known to be so, and yet is cherished, and excused to the conscience and before men, must draw after it entire ruin, in a community, not less than in an individual. As a reason for this ruin, it is very strikingly said in 2 Kings xvii. 9 : " And they *covered* (this is the only ascertained signification of חפא) words that were not so, over the Lord their God;" *i.e.*, they ventured, by a number of perversions and false interpretations of His word, to veil its true form. To this, the following consideration must be added :—That first change of the religious institutions proceeded from the political power which secured to itself, for the future, an absolute influence upon the religious affairs, by subjecting to its control the ecclesiastical power, which had hitherto been independent of it. Those Levites who, having no regard to the miserable sophisms invented by the king as an excuse, declared against the worship of calves, were expelled, and, in their stead, creatures of the king were made ministers of the sanctuary. This became now the king's sanctuary (compare the remarkable passage, Amos vii. 13), and all the ecclesiastical affairs were, in strict contradiction to the Mosaic law, submitted to his arbitrary power. The consequences of this must necessarily have been all the sadder, the worse the kings were; and they must inevitably have become so, because of the bad foundation on which the royal power rested.

Image-worship was very speedily followed by idolatry,—which is, however, in like manner, not to be looked upon in the light of an undisguised opposition to the true God. Such an opposition took place during the reign of only one king—Ahab—under whom the matter was carried to an extreme. Holy Scripture, however, with a total disregard of the whole multitude of miserable excuses ordinarily made, designates as *direct* apostasy from God, everything which was substantially such, although it did not outwardly manifest itself as such. Externally, they remained faithful to Jehovah; they celebrated His feasts,—they offered the sacrifices prescribed in the Pentateuch,—they regulated, in general, all the religious institutions according to the requirements there laid down, as may be proved from the Books of Kings, and, still more plainly, from Amos and Hosea. But in all this they discovered a method by which light and darkness, the worship of idols with that of the Lord, might be combined. Nor was this discovery so very difficult, since their eye was not single. They had before them the examples of heathen nations, who were quite prepared reciprocally to acknowledge their deities, in all of whom they recognised only different forms of manifestation of one and the same divine being; and they were quite willing to extend this acknowledgment even to the God of Israel also, as long as they did not meet with intolerance on the part of those who professed to worship Him, and were therefore not roused to the practice of intolerance in return. This reciprocal recognition of their deities by the nations in the midst of whom the Israelites lived, is sufficiently evident from the circumstance, that they all called their highest deity by the same name—Baal—and expressed, by some epithet, only the form of manifestation peculiar to each. Now, the Israelites imagined that they might be able, at one and the same time, to satisfy the demands of their God, and to propitiate the idols of the neighbouring mighty nations—especially of the Phœnicians—if they removed the wall of separation betwixt the two. Jehovah and Baal were, in their view, identical as to their essence. The former was that mode of manifestation peculiar to them, and the main object of their worship according to the method prescribed by Himself in His revelation. But the latter was not to be neglected; inasmuch as they imagined that they might thereby become partakers of the blessings which this form of manifestation of the deity was able to bestow. And thus to Jehovah they gave the name of Baal also, Hos. ii. 18 (16); they celebrated the days appointed by Jehovah, ver. 13 (11), but those also devoted to Baalim, ver. 15 (13). In this way we receive an explanation of the fact which, at first sight, is so startling, viz., that according to Hosea and Amos, all is filled with the service of Baal; while the Books of Kings would lead us to think that, with the reign of Ahab, the dominion of this worship had ceased. But it was only its hostile opposition to the worship of Jehovah that had disappeared, while a far more dangerous religious compromise took its place. No doubt can be entertained as to the party on whose side lay the advantage in this compromise. It was plainly on that side on which it always lies, whensoever the heart is divided betwixt truth and falsehood. Externally, the worship of Jehovah remained the prevailing one; but, inwardly, idolatry obtained almost the sole dominion. If only the limits betwixt the two religions were removed, that religion would of course come with the highest recommendation, the spirit of which was most in accordance with the spirit of the people. But, owing to the corrupt condition of human nature, this would not be the strict religion of Jehovah, which, as coming from God, did not bring God down to the level of human debasement, but demanded that man should be raised to His elevation,—which placed the holiness of God in the centre, and founded upon it the requirement that its possessors should be holy;—but it would be the soft, sensual, idolatrous doctrine which flattered human corruption, because from that it had its origin. Thus the Jehovah of the Israelites became in reality what they sometimes called Him by way of alternation—a Baal. And the matter was now much more dangerous than if they had deserted Him externally also, inasmuch as they now continued to trust in His covenant and promises, and to boast of their external services, —thus strengthening themselves in their false security.

The *natural* consequence of this apostasy from the Lord was a frightful corruption of manners. The next result of spiritual adultery was the carnal one. Voluptuousness formed the fundamental characteristic of the Asiatic religions in general, and, in particular, of those with which the Israelites came in contact. But the pernicious influence extended still further over the whole moral territory. Where there is no holy God, neither will there be any effort of man after holiness. All divine and human laws will be trampled under foot. All the bonds of love, law, and order, will be broken. And, as such, the condition of the country in a moral point of view is described by its two prophets throughout. Compare, *e.g.*, Hosea iv. 1, 2 : "There is no truth, nor mercy, nor knowledge of God in the land. Swearing, and lying, and killing, and stealing, and committing adultery—they break through, and blood toucheth blood." There then followed, from the moral corruption, the internal dissolution of the state, and its external weakness.

The *supernatural* consequences of the apostasy from the Lord, were the severe punishments which He inflicted upon the people. With whomsoever God has entered into a closer connection, whomsoever He thinks worthy of His grace, in him the Lord will be glorified by the infliction of punishment upon him, if, through his own guilt, He has not been glorified by sanctification in him. Just because Israel formed part of the Covenant-people, they could not be allowed to continue to retain the outward appearance of it, when, inwardly, they did not retain a vestige.

As the second element of the ruin, we mentioned the rebellion against the dynasty of David. Their dominion rested on divine right, while the new Israelitish kingdom rested upon the sandy foundation of human caprice. The first king had raised himself to the throne by his own power and prudence, and through the favour of the people. Whosoever had the same means at his disposal, imagined that these gave him the right to do likewise. And thus dynasty supplanted dynasty, regicide followed regicide. In the bloody struggles thereby occasioned, the people became more and more lawless. Sometimes interregna, and periods of total anarchy took place; and by these internal struggles the power to resist external enemies was more and more broken. No king was able to stop this source of mischief, for such an effort would have required him to lay aside his position as a king. And as little was any one able to put a stop to that source of evil formerly mentioned: for, if the religious wall of partition which was erected between Israel and Judah were once removed, the civil one likewise threatened to fall.

Such were, in general, the circumstances under which Hosea, like the other prophets of the kingdom of Israel, appeared. There cannot be any doubt that these were much more difficult than those of the kingdom of Judah. There, too, the corruption was indeed very great; but it was not so firmly intertwined with the foundation of the whole state. Thorough-going reforms, like those under Hezekiah and Josiah, were possible. The interest of a whole tribe was closely bound up with the preservation of true religion.

The reign of Jeroboam II., which was externally so prosperous, and in which Hosea entered upon his prophetic ministry, had still more increased the apostasy from the Lord, and the corruption of manners, and thus laid the foundation for the series of disastrous events which began soon after his death, and which, in quick succession, brought the people to total ruin. The prosperity only confirmed them still more in their security. Instead of being led to repentance by the unmerited mercy of God (compare 2 Kings xiv. 26, 27), they considered this prosperity as a reward of their apostasy, as the seal by which Jehovah-Baal confirmed the rectitude of their ways. The false prophets, too, did what was in their power to strengthen them in their delusion, whilst the true prophets preached to deaf ears.

Immediately after the death of Jeroboam, it soon became apparent on which side the truth lay. There followed an interregnum of from eleven to twelve years.[1] After the termination

---

[1] *Ewald, Thenius,* and others, will not grant that such an interregnum took place. As numbers were originally expressed by letters, in which an interchange might easily happen, we cannot deny the possibility of such an error having occurred in 2 Kings xiv. 23. It is quite possible that the duration of Jeroboam's reign was there originally stated at fifty-two or

of it, Zachariah, the son of Jeroboam, succeeded to the throne; but he was murdered by Shallum, after a short reign of six months, 2 Kings xv. 10. Shallum, after he had reigned only one month, was slain by Menahem, ver. 14. Menahem reigned ten years at Samaria. Under him, the catastrophe was already preparing which brought the kingdom to utter destruction. He became tributary to the Assyrian king Pul, vers. 19–21. He was succeeded by his son Pekahiah, in the fiftieth year of Uzziah. After a reign of two months, he was slain by Pekah, the son of Remaliah, who held the government for twenty years (ver. 27), and, by his alliance with the kings of Syria against his brethren the people of Judah (comp. Is. vii.), hastened on the destruction of Israel. The Assyrians, under Tiglathpileser, called to his assistance by Ahaz, even at that time carried away into captivity part of its citizens,—the tribes who lived on the other side of the Jordan. In the fourth year of Ahaz, Pekah was slain by Hoshea, who, after an interregnum of eight years, began to reign in the twelfth year of Ahaz, xvii. 1. He became tributary to Shalmaneser; and the end of his government of nine years was also the end of the kingdom of the ten tribes. His having sought for an alliance with Egypt drew down, upon himself and his people, the vengeance of the king of Assyria.

We have already proved that the historical references in the prophecies of Hosea extend to the time when the last king of Israel attempted to secure himself against Asshur, by the alliance with Egypt. It is very probable that the book was written at

fifty-three, instead of forty-one years. But strong reasons would be required for rendering such a supposition admissible,—the more so, as the interchange would not have been limited to one letter, as *Thenius* supposes, but must have extended to both. But no such reasons exist. The silence of the Books of Kings upon the subject of this interregnum cannot be urged as a reason, since these books are so exceedingly short as regards the history of the last times of the kingdom of Israel. Sacred historiography has no interest in the details of this process of decay, which began with the death of Jeroboam, —which also is represented by Amos as if it were the day of Israel's death (Amos vii. 11 : "Jeroboam shall die by the sword, and Israel shall be led away captive out of their own land"), although bare existence is still, for some time, spared. By the rejection of this interregnum, Hosea's ministry would be shortened by twelve years; but this gain—if such it be—can be purchased only at the expense of a most improbable extension of the duration of Jeroboam's reign. *Simson*, S. 201, has defended the interregnum.

that time. At the time when the sword of the Lord was just
being raised to inflict upon Israel the death-blow, Hosea wrote
down the sum and substance of what he had prophesied during
a long series of years, beginning in the last times of Jeroboam,
when, to a superficial view, the people were in the enjoyment of
the fullest prosperity. When at the threshold of their final
fulfilment, he condensed and wrote down his prophecies, just
as, in the *annus fatalis*, the fourth year of Jehoiakim, Jeremiah,
according to chap. xxv., gave a survey of what he had prophesied
over Judah during twenty-three years.

In the prophecies of Hosea, as in those of Amos, the *threatening* character prevails. The number of the elect in Israel was
small, and the judgment was at hand. In Jeremiah and Ezekiel,
too, the prophecies, previous to the destruction, are mainly
minatory. It was only after the wrath of God had been manifested in deeds, that the stream of promise brake forth without
hindrance. Hosea, nevertheless, does not belie his name, by
which he had been dedicated to the helping and saving God,
and which he had received, *non sine numine*. (הושע, properly
the Inf. Abs. of ישע, is, in substance, equivalent to Joshua, *i.e.*,
the Lord is help.) Zeal for the Lord fills and animates him,
not only in the energy of his threatenings, but also in the
intensity and strength of his conviction of the pardoning mercy
and healing love of the Lord, which will, in the end, prevail.
In this respect, Hosea is closely connected with the Song of
Solomon—that link in the chain of Holy Scripture into which
he had, in the first instance, to fit. There are in Hosea undeniable references to the Song of Solomon. (Compare my Comment. on the Song of Solomon, on chap. i. 4, ii. 3.) It is
certainly not by accident that the brighter views appear with
special clearness at the beginning, in chap. i. 3 (compare ii. 1–3,
16–25 [i. 10, ii. 1, 14–23], iii. 5), and at the close, xiv. 2–10
(1–9), where the fundamental thought is expressed in ver. 4 (3):
"For in Thee the fatherless findeth mercy." But even in the
darker middle portions, they sometimes suddenly break through;
compare v. 15, vi. 3, where the subject is : " He teareth and He
healeth us; He smiteth and He bindeth up;" vi. 11, where,
after the threatening against Israel, we suddenly find the words :
"Nevertheless, O Judah ! He grants thee a harvest, when I
(*i.e.*, the Lord) return to the prison of My people." (Judah is

here mentioned as the main portion of the people, in whom mercy is bestowed upon the whole, and in whose salvation the other tribes also share.)   Compare also xi. 8–11, where we have this thought: After wrath, mercy; the Covenant-people can never, like the world, be altogether borne down by destructive judgments; xiii. 14, where the strong conviction of the absolutely imperishable nature of the Congregation of the Lord finds utterance in the words, "I will ransom them from the hand of hell; I will redeem them from death: O death! where is thy plague? O hell! where is thy pestilence? repentance is hid from Mine eyes." *Simson* is perplexed "by the sudden transition of the discourse, in this passage, from threatening to promise,—and this without even any particle to indicate the mutual relation of the sentences and thoughts." But the same phenomenon occurs also in vi. 11 (compare Micah ii. 12, 13), where, likewise, several expositors are perplexed by the suddenness and abruptness of the transition. It is explained from the circumstance, that behind even the darkest clouds of wrath which have gathered over the Congregation of the Lord, there is, nevertheless, concealed the sun of mercy. In the prophets, it sometimes breaks through suddenly and abruptly; but in this they are at one with history, in which the deepest darkness of the night is oftentimes suddenly illuminated by the shining of the Lord: "And at midnight there was a cry made: Behold, the bridegroom cometh."

The sum and substance of Hosea's prophetic announcement is the following:—Israel falls, through Asshur: Judah, the main tribe, shall be preserved from destruction in this catastrophe. (The prophet's tender care for Judah is strikingly brought out in his exhortation to Israel, in iv. 15, that they should desist from their compromises in religion, and that, if they chose to commit sin, they should rather desert the Lord altogether, lest by their hypocrisy Judah also should be seduced and infected.) But at a later period, Judah too is to fall under the divine judgment (ii. 2 [i. 11], where it is supposed that Judah shall also be carried away into captivity; v. 5: "Israel and Ephraim fall by their iniquity, Judah also falleth with them;" v. 12: "I am unto Ephraim as a moth, and to the house of Judah as rottenness;" compare also xii. 1, 3), although the immediate instruments of the judgment upon Judah are not mentioned by Hosea. But the judgments which the two houses of Israel draw upon themselves by their works (ii. 2 [i. 11], iii. 5, indicate that even Judah will, at some future time, rebel against the house of David) shall be followed by the deliverance to be accomplished by grace. Judah and Israel shall, in the future, be again gathered together under one head, ii. 2 (i. 11); a glorious king out of David's house not only restores what was lost, but also raises the Congregation of the Lord to a degree of glory never before conceived of, iii. 5: " Afterwards shall the children of Israel return and seek the Lord their God, and David their King, and shall fear the Lord and His goodness in the latter days."

The peculiarity of the Messianic prophecies of Hosea, as compared with those of the time of David and Solomon, consists in the connection of the promise with threatenings of judgments, and in the Messiah's appearing as the light of those who walk in the deepest darkness of the divine judgments. It was necessary that this progress should have been made in the Messianic announcements, before the breaking in of the divine judgments; for, otherwise, the hope of the Messiah would have been extinguished by them, because it was but too natural to consider the former as, *in fact*, an annihilation of these dreamy hopes. But now there was offered to the elect a staff on which they might support themselves, and walk with confidence through the dark valley of the shadow of death.

The Book of Hosea may be divided into two parts, according to the two principal periods of the prophet's ministry,—under Jeroboam, when the external condition was as yet prosperous, and the bodily eye did not as yet perceive anything of the storms of divine wrath which were gathering,—and under the following kings, down to Hosea, when the punishment had already begun, and was hastening, by rapid strides, towards its consummation. — Another difference, although a subordinate one, is this:—that the first part, which comprehends the first three chapters, contains prophecies connected with a symbol , while the second part contains direct prophecies which have no such connection. A similar division occurs in Amos also,—with this difference, that there, the symbolical prophecies form the conclusion. The first part may be considered as a kind of outline, which all the subsequent prophecies served to fill up; just as may the 6th chapter in Isaiah, and the first and second in Ezekiel. We shall give a complete exposition of this section, as it will afford us a vivid view of the whole position of Hosea, and as it is just there that the Messianic announcement meets us in its most developed form.

THE SECTION CHAP. I.–III.

The question which here above all engages our attention, and requires to be answered, is this: Whether that which is reported in these chapters did, or did not, actually and outwardly take place. The history of the inquiries connected with this question is found most fully in *Marckius's " Diatribe de uxore fornicationum,"* Leyden, 1696, reprinted in the Commentary on the Minor Prophets by the same author. The various views may be divided into three classes.

1. It is maintained by very many interpreters, that all the events here narrated took place <u>actually</u> and <u>outwardly</u>. This opinion was advanced with the greatest confidence by *Theodoret, Cyril* of Alexandria, and *Augustine* from among the Fathers of the Church; by most interpreters belonging to the Lutheran and Reformed Churches (*e.g. Manger*); most recently, by *Stuck, Hofmann* (*Weissag u. Erf.* S. 206), and, to a certain extent, by *Ewald* also, who supposes "a free representation of an event actually experienced by the prophet."

2. Others consider it as a parabolical representation. Thus does Calvin, who expressly opposes the supposition not only of an external, but also of an internal event. He explains it thus: "When the prophet began to teach, he commenced thus: The Lord has placed me here as on a stage, that I might tell you, I have taken à wife," etc. Entirely similar was the opinion of the Chaldee Paraphrast, by whom the words, " Go," etc., are thus paraphrased: "Go and prophesy against the inhabitants of the adulterous city." Of a like purport is the view held, from among recent interpreters, by *Rosenmüller, Hitzig* ("that which the prophet describes as actual, is only a fiction"), *Simson* and others. The strange opinion of Luther, which, out of too great respect, was adopted by a few later theologians (*Osiander,*

Gerhard, Tarnovius), is only a modification of this. It is to the effect, that the prophet had only ascribed to his own chaste wife the name and works of an adulteress, and, hence, had performed with her, before the people, a kind of play. (Compare, against this view, *Buddeus, de peccatis typicis* in the *Misc. s. t.* i. p. 262.) The same opinion is expressed by *Umbreit*: "His own wife is implicated in the general guilt, and hence she is a representative of the whole people." In opposition to this view, compare *Simson's* Commentary.

3. Others suppose that the prophet narrates events which took place *actually*, indeed, but *not outwardly*. This opinion was, considering the time at which it was advanced, very ably defended by *Jerome* in *Epist. ad Pammachium*, and in his commentary on chap. i. 8. According to *Rufinus*, all those in Palestine and Egypt who respected the authority of *Origen*, asserted that the marriage took place only in spirit. The difficulties attaching to the first view were made especially obvious by the ridicule of the Manicheans (*Faustus* and *Secundinus* in *Augustine*, t. vi. p. 575) on this narrative. The most accomplished Jewish scholars (*Maimonides* in the *More Nebuch.* p. ii. c. 46, *Abenezra, Kimchi*) support this opinion. Some new arguments in defence of it have been adduced by *Marckius*.

Of these three views:—actually and outwardly; neither outwardly nor actually; actually, but not outwardly,—the second must be at once rejected. Those who hold it supply, "God has commanded me to tell you." But there is not the slightest intimation of such an ellipsis; and those interpreters have no better right to supply it in this, than in any other narrative. There is before us action, and nothing but action, without any intimation whatsoever that it is merely an invention.

But the following arguments are decisive in favour of the third, and against the first view.

1. The defenders of an outward transaction rely, in support of their view, upon the supposition, that their interpretation is most obvious and natural;—that they are thus, as it were, in the *possession* of the ground, and in a position from which they can be driven only by the most cogent reasons;—that if the transaction had been internal, it would have been necessary for the prophet to have expressly marked it as such. But precisely the reverse of all this is the case. The most obvious supposi-

tion is, that the symbolical action took place in vision. If *certain* actions of the prophets, especially seeing, hearing, and their speaking to the Lord, etc., must be conceived of as having taken place inwardly, unless there be distinct indications of the opposite, why not the remainder also? For the former presupposes that the world in which the prophets move, is altogether different from the ordinary one; that it is not the outward, but the spiritual world. It is certainly not a matter of chance, that the *seeing* in the case of the prophets must be understood spiritually; and if there be a reason for this, the same reason entitles us to assert that the walking, etc., also took place inwardly only. By what right could we make any difference between the actions of others, described by the prophet, and his own? Vision and symbolical action are not opposed to each other; the former is only the *genus* comprehending the latter as a *species*. By this we do not at all mean to assert, that *all* the symbolical actions of the prophets took place in inward vision only. An inward transaction always lay at the foundation; but sometimes, and when it was appropriate, they embodied it in an outward representation also (1 Kings xx. 35 seq., xxii. 11; Jer. xix. xxviii.; and a similar remarkable instance from modern times, in *Croesi Hist. Quakeriana*, p. 13). For this very reason, however, this argument cannot be altogether decisive by itself; but it furnishes, at least, a presumptive proof, and that by no means unimportant. If regularly and naturally the transaction be internal only, then the opposite requires to be proved in this case. If this had been admitted, no attempt would have been made elsewhere also, *e.g.*, Is. xx., by false and forced interpretations to explain away the supposition of a merely internal transaction.

2. No one will certainly venture to assert that a merely internal transaction would have missed its aim, since there exists a multitude of symbolical actions, in regard to which it is undeniable, and universally admitted, that they took place internally only. For the inward action, being narrated and committed to writing, retained the advantage of vividness and impressiveness over the naked representation of the same truth. Sometimes, in the case of actions concentrated into a single moment, this advantage may be still further increased by the inward transaction being represented outwardly also. But, here, just the

opposite would take place. We have here before us a symbolical transaction which, if it had been performed outwardly, would have continued for several years. The separation of the single events would have prevented its being taken in at a single view, and have thus deprived it of its impressiveness. But, what is still more important, the natural *substratum* would have occupied the attention so much more than the *idea*, that the latter would have been thereby altogether overlooked. The domestic affairs of the prophet would have become the subject of a large amount of *tittle-tattle*, and the idea would have been remembered only to give greater point to the ridicule.

3. The command of God, when considered as referring to an outward transaction, cannot be, by any means, justified. This is most glaringly obvious, if we understand this command, as several do, to mean that the prophet should beget children with an unchaste woman, and without legitimate marriage. Every one will sympathize with the indignation expressed by *Buddeus* (l. c. p. 206) against *Thomas Aquinas*, who, following this view, maintains that the law of God had been, in this special case, repealed by His command. God Himself cannot set us free from His commands; they are an expression of His nature, an image of His holiness. To ascribe arbitrariness to God in this respect, would be to annihilate the idea of God, and the idea of the Law at the same time. This view, it is true, is so decidedly erroneous as to require no further refutation; but even the opinion of *Buddeus* and others presents insurmountable difficulties. They suppose that the prophet had married a woman who was formerly unchaste. In opposition to this, Calvin very strikingly remarks: " It seems not to be consistent with reason, that God should spontaneously have rendered His prophet contemptible; for how could he ever have appeared in public after such ignominy had been inflicted upon him? If he had married such a wife, as here described, he ought rather to have hidden himself all his lifetime than have assumed the prophetic office." In Lev. xxi. 7 the law forbids the priests to take a wife that is a whore, or profane. That which, according to the letter, referred to the priests only, is applicable, in its spirit, to the prophets also,—yea, to them in a higher degree, as will be seen immediately, when the ordinance is reduced to its *idea*. The latter is easily inferred from the reason stated,

viz., that the priests should be holy to their God. The servants of God must represent His holiness; they are, therefore, not allowed, by so close a contact with sin, to defile or desecrate themselves either inwardly or outwardly. Although the inward pollution may be prevented in individual cases by a specially effective assistance of divine grace, yet there always remains the outward pollution.

It is inconceivable that, at the very commencement of his ministry, God should have commanded to the prophet anything, the inevitable effect of which was to mar its successful execution. Several—and especially *Manger*—who felt the difficulties of this interpretation, substituted for it another, by which, as they imagined, all objections were removed. The prophet, they say, married a person who had formerly been chaste, and fell only after her marriage. This view is no doubt the correct one, as is obvious from the relation of the figure to the reality. According to ver. 2, it is to be expressed figuratively that the people went a-whoring from Jehovah. The spiritual adultery presupposes that the spiritual marriage had already been concluded. Hence, the wife can be called a whoring wife, only on account of the whoredom which she practised after her marriage. This is confirmed by chap. iii. 1, where the more limited expression "to commit adultery" is substituted for "to whore," which has a wider sense, and comprehends adultery also. The former unchastity of the wife would be without any meaning, yea, would be in direct contradiction to the real state of the case. For before the marriage concluded at Sinai, Israel was devoted to the Lord in faithful love; comp. Jer. ii. 2: "I remember thee, the kindness of thy youth, the love of thine espousals, thy walking after Me in the wilderness, in a land not sown." Compare also Ezek. xvi., where Israel, before her marriage, appears as a *virgo intacta*. But how correct soever this view may be—and every other view perverts the whole position—it is, nevertheless, erroneous to suppose that thereby all difficulties are removed. All which has been urged against the former view, may be urged here also. It might have been better for the prophet to have married one who was previously unchaste, in the hope that her subsequent better life might wipe out her former shame, than one previously chaste, who *was required* to become unchaste, and to remain so for a long time, because,

otherwise, the symbolical action would have lost all its significance. The objection brought forward, that whatever is un-
becoming as an outward action, is so likewise though it were
only an internal action, can scarcely be meant to be in earnest.
For, in this case, every one knew that the prophet was a mere
type; and, with regard to his wife, this circumstance was so
obvious, that mockery certainly gave way to shame and confusion. But a marriage outwardly entered into is never purely
typical. It has always its significance apart from the typical
import, and must be justifiable, independently of its typical
character. Ridicule would, in this case, have been not only too
obvious, but to a certain extent also well founded.

4. If the action had taken place only outwardly, it would
have been impossible to explain the abrupt transition from the
symbolical action to the mere figure, and again to the entirely
naked representation as we find it here, and *vice versa*. In the
first chapter, the symbolical action is pretty well maintained;
but in the. prophecy ii. 1–3 (i. 10–ii. 1), which belongs to the
same section, it is almost entirely lost sight of. As the corporeal adultery, and rejection in consequence of it, were to be
the type of the spiritual adultery and rejection, so the receiving
again of the wife, rejected on account of her faithlessness, but
now reformed, was to typify the Lord's granting mercy to the
people. But of this, not a trace is found. And yet, we are
not at liberty to say that the ground of it lies in a difference
betwixt the type and the thing typified,—in the circumstance
that the wife of the prophet did not reform. If there existed
such a difference, the type could not have been chosen at all.
The contrary appears also from ii. 9 (7).—In the whole second
section, ii. 4–25 (ii. 2–23), regard is indeed had to the symbolical
action; but in a manner so free, that it dwindles away to a
mere figure, from behind which the thing itself is continually
coming into view. In chap. iii. the symbolical action again
acquires greater prominence. These phenomena can be accounted for, only if the transaction be viewed as an inward
one. In the case of an outward transaction, the transition
from the symbolical action to the figure, and from the figure
to the thing itself, would not have been so easy. The substratum of the idea is, in that case, far more material, and the
idea itself too closely bound to it.

5. When the transaction is viewed as an outward one, insurmountable difficulties are presented by the third chapter; and the argument drawn from this would, in itself, be quite sufficient to settle the question: " Then the Lord said unto me, Go again, love a woman beloved of her friend and an adulteress." Interpreters who have adopted that view, find themselves here in no little embarrassment. Several suppose that the woman, whom the prophet is here commanded to love, is his former wife, Gomer,—with her he should get reconciled. But this is quite out of the question. In opposition to it, there is, *first*, the indefinite signification by אשה; *then*, in ver. 2, there is the purchase of the woman,—which supposes that she had not yet been in the possession of the husband; and, *further*, the words, " beloved of her friend, and an adulteress," can, according to a sound interpretation, mean only, " who, although she is beloved by her faithful husband, will yet commit adultery;" so that, if it be referred to the reunion with Gomer, we should be compelled to suppose that, after being received again, she again became unfaithful,—and in favour of this opinion, no corresponding feature can be pointed out in the thing typified. *Lastly,*—The word " love" cannot mean " love again," "*restitue amoris signa.*" For the love of the prophet to his wife must correspond with the love of God to the people of Israel. That this love, however, cannot be limited to the love which God will show to the Congregation *after* her conversion, is seen from the additional clause, " And they turn themselves to other gods, and love grape-cakes." Hence it appears that the love of.GOD continues even during the unfaithfulness, and consequently, also, the love of the prophet, by which it is typified.—Equally untenable is the other opinion, that the prophet is here called upon, by his entering into a new marriage, to prefigure the relation of God to the Covenant-people a second time. In that case, it is supposed either that Gomer had been rejected, because she would not return, or that she had died. In either case, however, she would not have been chosen by God to be a type of the people of Israel. The ground of this choice can be no other than the correspondence with the antitype. But this would be wanting just in the most important point. If the ungodly part of the nation were not to be deprived of all hope, nor the pious of all consolation, it was of special importance to

point out that even the rejected congregation would receive mercy; that the Lo-Ruhamah should be the Ruhamah. Just the reverse of all this, however, would, according to this view, have been typified. Two different women would, quite naturally, suggest the thought of two different nations. Moreover, the non-conversion of Gomer would be in direct opposition to the prophet's own expressions. There cannot be any doubt, that her relation to the prophet still lies at the foundation of the description in ii. 4 seqq. For they are her three children whose former names, announcing disaster, are changed, in ver. 25 (23), into such as are significant of salvation. In vers. 4–6 (2–4) the whole relation, as previously described, is presupposed. But now, she who, in ver. 9 (7), says, " I will go and return to my first husband, for then was it better with me than now," is the same who said in ver. 7 (5), " I will go after my lovers that give me my bread and my water, my wool and my flax." To the same result we are also led by the showing of mercy to her children, announced in the first section, ii. 1–3 (i. 10–ii. 1), where the prophet alludes to their names; and still more distinctly in the second section; compare ver. 25 (23). But now, the showing of mercy to the children cannot be conceived of without the conversion of the mother, and mercy being subsequently shown to her also. As they are to be rejected on account of the unfaithfulness of the mother (compare ii. 6 [4], and, specially, the כי at the commencement of ver. 7), so the ground of their being received into favour can only be the faithfulness of the mother. Being begotten in adultery, they stand in connection with the prophet only through the mother; as soon as he has rejected the mother, he has nothing further to do with them.— The supposition that Gomer had died, is evidently the result of an embarrassment which finds itself compelled to invent such fictions.—*Finally,*—Several interpreters, after the example of *Augustine,* suppose that no marriage at all is here spoken of, but only a certain kindness which the prophet should manifest to some woman, in order to encourage her conversion. But this opinion is contradicted by these circumstances :—that the prophet's love towards the woman must necessarily be of the same extent, and of the same nature, as the love of God towards the people of Israel, since the אהב and the כאהבת exactly correspond with each other; that only conjugal love is suitable to the image; that this view falls, of itself, to the ground when יֵ is referred to the prophet, as it must be; that, in such circumstances, no satisfactory account can be given of the purchase of the woman, etc. To all these suppositions there is, moreover, the common objection that, according to them, no account can be given of the omission of very important circumstances which the prophet leaves to his hearers and readers to supply from the preceding symbolical action. Two things only are pointed out, viz., the appropriation of the woman by the prophet, ver. 2, and the course which he pursues for her reformation, ver. 3. Every intervening circumstance—the criminal, long-continued unfaithfulness of the wife—is passed over in silence. If we suppose an outward action, this circumstance cannot be accounted for. For we are not at liberty to draw, from the first case, any inference bearing upon the second. The latter would again have required a complete account. But if we suppose an inward transaction, everything is easily explained. The question as to whether it was Gomer, or some other person, does not come up at all. If Gomer was only an *ideal* person, that which applied to her was equally applicable to the second *ideal* wife of the prophet; since both typified the same thing, and without having an independent existence of their own, came into consideration as types only. Thus, very naturally, the second description was supplemented from the first, and the prophet was allowed abruptly to point out those circumstances only which were of special importance in the case before him.

6. If the whole be viewed as an outward transaction, there arises a difficulty, by no means inconsiderable, as regards the children mentioned in chap. i. These had been begotten in adultery. Even although the mother did reform, they could yet never be considered by the prophet as, in the full sense, his own. There would then arise a great difference between the type and the thing typified. But if we suppose a transaction merely inward, this difficulty vanishes. The physical impossibility then no longer comes into consideration. That which is possible in the thing typified, viz., that those who formerly were not children of God, become children of God, is transferred to the type. In point of fact, the mother does not exist beside, and apart from, the children; she stands related to them as the whole to the parts; and hence it is, that in ii. 25 (23), the

mother and children are imperceptibly blended in the prophet's description.

7. We are led to the idea of a mere inward transaction by the symbolical names of the first wife, and of her father. On the other hand, if such a symbolical signification could not be proved, this might be used as an argument for the literal interpretation,—although, indeed, it would be only a single argument which would be obliged to yield to other counter-arguments. For it may well be conceived that the prophet, in order to give to the inward transaction more of the appearance of an outward one, should have chosen names usual at that time; just as, in a similar manner, poetry would not be satisfied with invented names used only in certain formulas and proverbs, but makes use of names which would not, at once, be recognised by every one as mere fictions.—גֹּמֶר can only mean "completion" in the passive sense. For *Segolate-forms* in *o* are only used to express passive and intransitive notions, and the verb נמר is found in the signification "to be completed," in Ps. vii. 10, xii. 2. The sense in which the woman, the type of the Israelitish people, is called *completion*,—*i.e.*, one who, in her whoredom, had proceeded to the highest pitch,—is so obvious from the context, as to render nugatory the argument which *Maurer* (p. 360) has drawn from the omission of express statements on this point, in order thereby to recommend his own interpretation, which is altogether opposed to the laws of the language. A significant proper name can, in any case, convey only an allusion; but such an allusion was here quite sufficient, inasmuch as the mention of the wife's whoredom had preceded. Compare, moreover, Zech. v. 5-11, where the thought, that Israel had filled up the measure of their sins, is represented by a woman sitting in an Ephah. *Hofmann* explains the name Gomer by "end," "utmost ruin:" "By luxury, Israel has become wanton, and hence it must come to an end, to utter ruin." But this interpretation is at variance with the context, from which it must necessarily be derived; for it is not the *punishment*, but the *guilt* which is spoken of in the context. נמר, "Completion" (compare the גמיר, "*perfectus*," "*absolutus*," in Ezra vii. 12), is equivalent to אשׁת זנונים, "a wife of whoredom." The בת דבלים can only mean, "daughter of the two fig-cakes," = *filia deliciarum* = *deliciis*

N

dedita. The word "daughter" serves to indicate every relation of dependence and submission: *Gesenius, Thesaurus*, p. 220. Fig-cakes were considered as one of the greatest dainties; compare *Faber* on *Harmar.* i. p. 320 ff. Sensuality was the ground of the Israelites' apostasy from the severe and strict religion of Jehovah to the idolatry of their neighbours, which was soft, sensual, and licentious. The occasion which had called it forth with their neighbours was one which rendered them favourably disposed towards it. The masculine form can offer no difficulty as to the derivation from דבלה, "fig-cake;" for the masculine form of the plural occurs also in 1 Sam. xxv. 18; 1 Chron. xii. 40. As little difficulty can arise from the Dual form, which may be explained from the circumstance that fig-cakes commonly consisted of a double layer of figs, or of double cakes (*Hesych.* παλάθη—which Greek word is a corruption of the Hebrew דבלה—ἡ τῶν σύκων ἐπάλληλος θέσις), and the Dual is used in reference to objects which are commonly conceived of as a whole, consisting of two parts, even when several of them are spoken of. That this explanation of the Dual is correct, is proved from the circumstance, that it occurs also as the name of a Moabitish town, *Beth-Dibhlathaim*, Jer. xlviii. 22, and *Dibhlathaim*, Num. xxxiii. 46, which, probably, was famous for its fig-cakes.—There existed another special reason for the prophet's choosing the Dual in the masculine form, viz., that there was the analogy of other proper names of men—as Ephraim, etc.—in its favour; and such an analogy was required, —for, otherwise, the name would not have been, as it was intended to be, a riddle. Our whole exposition, however, which was already in substance, although without proper foundation and justification, advanced by *Jerome*, is raised above the condition of a mere hypothesis, by its being compared with chap. iii. There, the words, "They turn themselves to other gods, and love grape-cakes," are a mere paraphrase of "*Gomer Bath Dibhlaim.*" It scarcely needs to be remarked, that the difference betwixt grape-cakes and fig-cakes does not here come into consideration at all, inasmuch as both belonged to the choicest dainties; and it is as evident, that "to love," and "to be the daughter of," express the same idea. But if thus the symbolical signification of the name be established, the correctness of the supposition of a merely internal transaction is established at the same time. The symbolical names of the children alone could not have furnished a sufficient foundation for this supposition. Against this an appeal might, with the most perfect propriety, have been made to *Shear-Jashub*, and *Maher-shalal-hash-baz*, neither of whom can, by any means, have been an *ideal* person. The prophet *gave* them these names; but the matter is quite different in the case of the wife, who already had her name when the prophet took her. All that we can grant to *Hofmann* is, that such a providential coincidence was *possible;* but *probable* it could be, only if other decisive arguments favoured the view of the transaction having been an outward one. If the name were not symbolical—if it belonged to the real wife of the prophet, it cannot be easily explained, why he did not afterwards mention the name of his second wife also, but content himself with the general term, "a wife."

8. A main argument against the literal interpretation is further furnished by iii. 2. The verse is commonly translated: " And then I bought her to me for fifteen pieces of silver, and an homer of barley, and a lethech of barley;" and is explained from the custom prevalent in the East of purchasing wives from their parents. But it is very doubtful whether the verb כרה has the signification " to purchase." There is no necessity for deviating from the common signification " to dig," in Deut. ii. 6: " And water also ye shall dig from them for money, and drink" (compare Exod. xxi. 33); the existing wells were not sufficient for so great a multitude, compare Gen. xxvi. 19, 21, 22. To this philological reason, we must *further* add, that the circumstance would be here altogether destitute of significance, while every other feature in the description is full of meaning. We base our interpretation upon the supposition, already sufficiently established by *J. D. Michaelis*, that the whole purchase-money amounted to thirty shekels, of which the prophet paid one-half in money, and the other half in the value of money. According to Ezek. xlv. 11, the homer contained ten ephahs, and a lethech was the half of an homer. We have thus fifteen pieces of silver, and also fifteen ephahs; and the supposition is very probable that, at that time, an ephah of barley cost a shekel,—the more so, as according to 2 Kings vii. 1, 16, 18, in the time of a declining famine, and only relative cheapness, two-thirds of an ephah of barley cost a shekel. We are unable

to say with certainty, why one-half was paid in money, and the other half in natural productions; but a reason certainly exists, as no other feature is without significance. Perhaps it was determined by custom, that the sum by which servants were purchased was paid after this manner. The lowness of their condition was thereby indicated; for barley, *vile hordeum*, was, in all antiquity, very little esteemed. Upon this estimate of it was based its use at the jealousy offering (Num. v. 11 seqq.; compare *Bähr's Symb.* ii. S. 445), and the symbolical use of the barley-bread in Judg. vii. 13. The statement of the sum leads us, involuntarily, to think of slaves or servants. It is the same sum which was commonly given for a man-servant, or a maid-servant, as is expressly mentioned in Exod. xxi. 32; compare the remarks on Zech. xi. 12. And this opinion is confirmed by the use of ואכרה. The ears of a servant who was bound to his master to *perpetual* obedience, were bored; compare Exod. xxxi. 5, 6; Deut. xv. 17, where it is added: "And also unto thy maid-servant thou shalt do likewise." In conformity with the custom of omitting the special members of the body, in expressions frequently occurring, it is said simply "to bore." The meaning then is: I made her my slave. It was not a free woman, then, whom the prophet desired in marriage, but a servant, whom he was obliged, previous to marriage, to redeem from servitude; who was therefore under a double obligation to him, and over whom he had a double claim. The reference to the thing to be typified is quite apparent. It was not a free, independent people whom the Lord chose, but a people whom He was obliged first to redeem from vile servitude, before He entered into a nearer relation to them. This redemption appears, throughout, as a ransoming from the house of bondage,— and the wonderful dealings of the Lord, as the price which He paid. Compare, *e.g.*, Deut. vii. 8: "But because the Lord loved you, and because He kept His oath which He had sworn to your fathers, He has brought you out with a mighty hand, and redeemed thee (ויפדך) from the house of bondmen (מבית עבדים), from the hand of Pharaoh, king of Egypt." See also Deut. ix. 26. It is upon this redemption that the exhortation to the people is founded—that, as the Lord's servants, they should serve Him alone; comp., *e.g.*, the introduction to the Decalogue. Thus, we have here also a feature so evidently typical, so plainly transferred from the thing typified to the type, that we cannot any longer think of an outward transaction. This argument, however, is, in the main point, quite independent of the philological interpretation of כרה. Even if it be translated "I bought her to me," the circumstance, notwithstanding, always remains, that the wife was redeemed from slavery, unless there be a denial of the connection of the sum mentioned with Exod. xxi. 32, and Zech. xi. 12, where the thirty pieces of silver likewise appear as the estimate of a servant's value; and this circumstance evidently suggests the inward character of the transaction.

The first germs of the representation of God's relation to Israel under the figure of marriage, are found so early as in the Pentateuch, Exod. xxxiv. 15, 16; Lev. xx. 5, 6, xvii. 7; Num. xiv. 33—where idolatry, and apostasy from the Lord in general, are represented as whoredom—Deut. xxxii. 16, 21; compare the author's *Dissertations on the Genuineness of the Pent.* vol. i. p. 107 ff.; and commentary on the Song of Solomon, S. 261. But it was only through the Song of Solomon that it became quite a common thing to represent the higher love under the figure of the lower. It is not through accident that this representation appears so prominent just in Hosea, where it not only pervades the first three chapters, but returns continually in the second part also. Hosea, being one of the oldest prophets, was specially called to fit, as a new link, into the Song of Solomon, which was the last link in the chain of Sacred Literature. There are, moreover, in the details, other undeniable references to the Song of Solomon, which coincide with this connection with it, as regards the fundamental idea. The basis, however, for this whole figurative representation is Gen. ii. 24, where marriage appears as the most intimate of all earthly relations of love, and must, for this very reason, have a character of absolute exclusiveness.

———◆———

CHAP. I.–II. 3 (II. 1).

The section chap. i.–iii. is distinguished from the other prophecies by this,—that, in it, the relation of the Lord to the people of Israel is represented, *throughout*, under the figure and symbol of marriage, whilst this same mode of representation is soon relinquished wherever else it occurs in the book. By this closer limitation, the objections of *Böckel* and *Stuck* to the common division of the collection into two parts, are set aside. This first portion may be divided into three parts, which are, in one respect, closely connected, as is shown by the *Fut.* with the *Vav Conv.* in iii. 1, and likewise by the fact that this chapter requires to be supplemented from the two preceding ones, while, in another respect, they may be considered as wholes, complete in themselves. They do not, by any means, so distribute the contents among themselves, as that the first describes the apostasy; the second, the punishment; and the third, the return and restoration; but each of them contains all these three features, and yet in such a manner, that here the one feature, and there the other, is more fully expanded; so that the whole description is complete, only when all the three parts are taken together. In the portion now before us, the covenant relation into which the Lord entered with Israel is typified by a marriage which the prophet contracted at the command of the Lord; the apostasy of the people, and especially of the ten tribes, to whom the prophet was sent in the first instance, is typified by the adultery of the wife, by the divine punishment, and the unpropitious names which he gives to the children born by the adulterous wife. In chap. ii. 1–3, there follows the announcement of salvation more directly, and only with a simple allusion to the symbol.

———

Ver. 1. " *The word of the Lord that came unto Hosea, the son of Beeri, in the days of Uzziah, Jotham, Ahaz, Hezekiah, kings of Judah, and in the days of Jeroboam, the son of Joash, king of Israel.   Ver. 2. At the beginning when the Lord spake to Hosea, the Lord said to Hosea: Go take unto thee a wife of whoredoms, and children of whoredoms; for the land is whoring away from the Lord.*"

דִּבֶּר is never a noun—not even in Jer. v. 13—but always the 3d pers. *Pret. Piel.* The *status constr.* תְּחִלַּת is explained by the fact, that the whole of the following sentence is treated as one substantive idea: the beginning " of the Lord hath spoken," etc., for "the beginning of speaking." יום דבר יהוה, *the day of "the Lord spoke,"* instead of, "the day on which the Lord spoke." Similar constructions occur also in Is. xxix. 1, and Jer. xlviii. 6.—The *Fut.* with *Vav Conv.*, ויאמר, "and then He spoke," carries forward the discourse, as if there had preceded: the Lord began to speak to Hosea. There is here a *constructio ad sensum*. It is intentionally, and in order the more distinctly to point out the idea of the beginning, that the prophet has made use of the noun תחלת, not of the verb. The construction of דבר with ב, with the signification "to speak to some one," may be explained thus:—that the words are, as it were, put into the mind of the hearer in order that they may remain there. Several interpreters erroneously translate, "spoke through;" others, following *Jerome* (the last is *Simson*), "spoke in;" as if thereby the act of speaking were to be designated as an inward one. The difference between outward and inward speaking disappears in the vision; and, for this reason, we cannot imagine that there is any intention of here noticing it particularly. Everything which takes place in the vision is substantially, indeed, internal, but in point of form it is external. Moreover, דבר with ב several times occurs in other passages also, where the signification, "to speak to some one," is alone admissible. Thus 1 Sam. xxv. 39, where *Simson's* explanation, "David sent and *ordered* to speak *about* Abigail," is set aside by ver. 40. The analogy of the construction of the verbs of hearing and seeing with ב is likewise in favour of our explanation.[1]—A wife of *whoredoms* and *children of whoredoms.* The wife belongs to whoredoms in so far as she is *devoted to them;* the children, in

[1] In Hab. ii. 1, where the prophet is standing upon his watch, and watches to see what the Lord will say *unto* him, it would be rather strange to translate "in me." There is nothing else to lead us to conceive that the apparition of angels in Zech. is internal. But Num. xii. 8 is quite decisive. The Lord there says, with reference to His relation to Moses, "Mouth to mouth I speak to him (בו);" and immediately afterwards it is said, "Wherefore, then, were ye not afraid to speak to My servant (בעבדי), to Moses?" It is evident that the ב cannot be explained by "in" in the one case, and by "through" in the other. It is remarkable, however, that דבר with ב occurs very frequently when the Lord Himself, or, as in Zechariah, *the Angel,* speaks. This may, perhaps, be explained from the circumstance, that the heavenly discourses have an especially penetrating power, and sink very deeply into the heart.

so far as they *proceed* from them. For we cannot suppose that the children themselves are described as given to whoredom. Such a thought would here be altogether out of place. For whoredom is here only the general designation of adultery, as, by way of applying it to the case in question, it is immediately subjoined, "away from Jehovah." The subject of consideration is only the relation of the wife and children to the prophet, as the type of the Lord; and with this view, it is only the origin of the children from an adulterous wife which can be of importance. That this alone is regarded, appears from ii. 6 (4), compared with ver. 7 (5). That the children, as children of whoredoms, deserve no compassion, is founded upon the fact that their mother plays the harlot. אשת זנונים is stronger than זונה; it expresses the idea that the woman is given, soul and body, to whoredoms. The same emphasis is expressed also by the analogous designations: man of blood, of deceit, etc.— Calvin says, " She is called a wife of whoredoms, because she was long accustomed to them, gave herself over to the lusts of all indiscriminately, did not prostitute herself once, or twice, or to a few, but to the debauchery of every one." It is not without reason that "*take*" is connected with the children also. The prophet shall, as it were, receive and take, along with the wife, those who, without his agency, have been born of her. It is self-evident, and has been, moreover, formerly proved, that we cannot speak of children who were previously born of the prophet's wife; but that, on the contrary, the children are they whose birth is narrated in ver. 4 seqq. And that we cannot consider these children as children of the prophet, as is done by several interpreters (*Drus.*: " *Accipe uxorem et suscipe ex eâ liberos*"), is obvious from their being designated "children of whoredoms;" from the word "take" itself, which is expressive of the passive conduct of the prophet; from the fact that, in the subsequent verses, the conceiving and bearing of the wife are alone constantly spoken of, but never, as in Is. viii. 3, the begetting by the prophet; and, *finally*, from the relation of the type to the thing typified. By the latter, it is absolutely required that children and mother stand in the same relation of alienation from the legitimate husband and father. The words in ver. 3, " She bare him a son," are not indeed in opposition to it, for these words are only intended to mark the deceit of the wife who offers to her husband the children begotten in adultery, as if they were his, and, at the same time, to bring out the patience and forbearance of the husband who receives them, and brings them up as if they were his, although he knows that they are not. In like manner, the Lord treated, for centuries, the rebellious Israelites as if they were His children, and granted to them the inheritance which was destined only for the children, along with so many other blessings, until at length He declared them to be bastards, by carrying them away into captivity. The last words state the ground of the symbolical action. The causal כי is explained from the fact that the import of a symbolical action is also its ground. The *Inf. absol.* preceding the *tempus finitum* gives special emphasis to the verbal idea. The prophet thereby indicates that, in using the expression "to whore," he does so deliberately, and because it corresponds exactly to the thing, and wishes us to understand it in its full strength and compass. In calling the thing by its right name, he silences, beforehand, every attempt at palliating and extenuating it. Of such palliations and extenuations the Jews had abundance. They had not the slightest notion that they had become unfaithful to their God, but considered their intercourse with idols as trifling and allowable attentions which they paid to them.— *Manger* understands by whoredoms, their placing, at the same time, their confidence in man; but from what follows, where idolatry alone is constantly spoken of, it is obvious that this is inadmissible. If this special thing be reduced to its idea, it is true that trusting in men is, then, not less comprehended under it than idolatry, inasmuch as this idea is the turning away from God to that which is not God. And, from this dependence of what is special upon the idea, it follows that the description has its eternal truth, and does not become antiquated, even where the folly of gross idolatry has been long since perceived.—הארץ, the definite land, the land of the prophet, the land of Israel.—Concerning the last words, Ps. lxxiii. 27 may be compared, where זנה מן occurs with a similar signification. This phrase contains an allusion to the common expression, "to walk with, or after, God;" compare 2 Kings xxiii. 3. According to *Calvin*, the spiritual chastity of the people of God consists in their following the Lord.

Ver. 3. "*And he went and took Gomer the daughter of Dibhlaim, and she conceived and bare him a son.*

Many interpreters suppose that, by the three children, three different generations are designated, and the gradual degeneracy of the people, which sinks deeper and deeper. But this opinion must certainly be rejected. There is no gradation perceptible. On the contrary, the announcement of the total destruction of the kingdom of Israel is connected immediately with the name of the first child, ver. 4. Nor is it legitimate to say, as *Rückert* does, that the three children are a designation of the "conditions" in which the Israelites would be placed in consequence of their apostasy from the Lord. For, how could mercy be shown to *conditions?* The right view rather is, that the wife and children are both the people of Israel, viewed only in different relations. In the first designation, they are viewed as a unity; in the latter, as a plurality proceeding from, and depending upon, this unity. The circumstance that the prophet mentions the birth of children at all, and the birth of three only, is accounted for by their names. The children exist only that they may receive a name. The three names must, therefore, not be considered separately, but must be viewed together. In that case they present a corresponding picture of the fate impending upon Israel. The circumstance that the mother and sons are distinguished in Hosea, rests upon the Song of Solomon. (Compare the more copious remarks in my commentary on the Song of Sol. iii. 4: "By the mother, the people is designated according to its historical continuity,—by the daughter or sons, according to its existence at any moment.")

Ver. 4. "*And the Lord said unto him, Call his name Jezreel; for yet a little* (while), *and I visit the blood of Jezreel upon the house of Jehu, and cause to cease the kingdom of the house of Israel.*"

The name "Jezreel" is, by most expositors, explained in this passage as meaning: "God disperses." This they maintain to be its real signification, according to the etymology, and that all the rest is only an allusion. But this exposition is erroneous, as *Manger* has correctly perceived. For, 1. No instance occurs where the verb יָרַע has this signification. When applied to men, it is always used only in a good sense: compare ii. 25, Ezek. xxxvi. 9, and the subsequent remarks on Zech. x. 9. The idea of *scattering* is not at all the fundamental one; so that the signification, to *disperse,* is much further from the fundamental signification than might, at first sight, appear. 2. The subsequent words must be considered as an explanation of the name Jezreel, as is obvious from the corresponding explanations of the names Lo-Ruhamah in ver. 6, and Lo-Ammi in ver. 9, which are intimately connected with these names. But in this explanation, not even a single word is said on the subject of the dispersion of the people of Israel. The circumstance that, in this explanation, Jezreel occurs as a proper name, without any regard being paid to its appellative signification[1]—an allusion to which occurs only in the announcement of the salvation—shows that here too it must be viewed in the same way. The correct view is this. Jezreel was the place where the last great judgment of God upon the kingdom of Israel had been executed. The apostasy from the Lord, and the innocent blood of His servants, shed by Jezebel and the whole house of Ahab, had been there avenged upon them by Jehu, the founder of the dynasty which was reigning at the time of the prophet. At the command of God, Jehu is anointed as king by one of the sons of the prophets sent by Elisha, 2 Kings ix. In vers. 6—9 the Lord says to him through the latter: "I anoint thee king over the people of the Lord, over Israel. And thou shalt smite the house of Ahab thy master; and *I avenge the blood of My servants the prophets, and the blood of all the servants of the Lord at the hand of Jezebel, and the whole house of Ahab shall perish.* And I give the house of Ahab like the house of Jeroboam the son of Nebat, and like the house of Baasha the son of Ahijah." The execution corresponded with the command. When Jehu approached Jezreel, Joram the son of Ahab went out against him, and met him in the portion of Naboth the Jezreelite, ver. 21. Appealing to the declaration of the Lord,

---

[1] This is very natural, for the proper name has originally a cheering signification. It is apparent from the remarks of *Schubert (Reise* iii. S. 164–166), and of *Ritter (Erdkunde* 16, i. S. 693), on the natural condition of the plain of Jezreel, how it happened that it received this name, which means: "God sows." *Schubert* calls the soil of Jezreel a field of corn, the seed of which is not sown by any man's hand, the ripe ears of which are not reaped by any reaper. The various kinds of corn appeared to him to be wild plants; the mules walked in them with half their bodies covered by them; the ears of wheat were sown by themselves. "All travellers," says *Ritter,* "agree in their descriptions of the extraordinary beauty and fertility of the plain."

"Surely I have seen the blood of Naboth, and the blood of his sons, and I will requite thee in this portion of ground" (ver. 26), Jehu orders the corpse of the slain king to be cast thither. At Jezreel, Jezebel too found a disgraceful death. Thither, as to the central point of vengeance, were sent the heads of the seventy royal princes, who had been slain, x. 1–10, and there Jehu slew all that remained of the house of Ahab, ver. 11.— The royal house, and, along with it, all Israel, are now anew to become a Jezreel; *i.e.*, the same divine punitive justice which, at that time, was manifested at Jezreel, is to be exhibited anew. The reason why this should be, is stated in the explanation. The house of Jehu, and all Israel, shall become a Jezreel, in as far as punishment is concerned, because they have become a Jezreel with respect to guilt, and because, as in former times at Jezreel, so now again, blood that has been shed cries to the Lord for vengeance. Where a new carcase is, there the eagles must anew be gathered together.—It must have already appeared from this, how we understand the words, "I visit the blood of Jezreel," used in the explanation of the name of Jezreel, in the verse under consideration. According to the prophet's custom of designating, by the name of an old thing, any new thing which is substantially similar to it, the new guilt is marked by the name of the old; and it is marked as *blood*, because the former guilt was pre-eminently blood-guiltiness;[1] and as the blood of Jezreel, because the former blood-guiltiness had been especially contracted there, and it was there where the punishment was executed. The deep impression, which just this mode of representation must have produced, must not be overlooked. The sins formerly committed at Jezreel were acknowledged as such by the whole people, and especially by the royal house, whose whole rights were based upon this acknowledgment. The recollection of the fearful punishment was still in the minds of all; but they did not by any means imagine that they were implicated in the same guilt, and had to expect the same punishment. That which they considered as already

---

[1] This transference was so much the more natural, as, under the government of the house of Jehu, guilt had certainly been frequently concentrated in the form of blood-guiltiness. Compare Is. i. 21, where the prophet, in order to mark out the reigning sin in its highest degree, represents Jerusalem as being full of murderers.

absolutely past, the prophet, by a single word, brings again into the present, and the immediate future. By a single word of dreadful sound he terrified and aroused them out of their self-deception (which will not recognise its own sin in the picture of the sins of others), and out of their carnal security. Entirely analogous are 2 Kings ix. 31, where Jezebel says to Jehu, "Hast thou peace, Zimri, murderer of his master?" which *Schmid* well explains by—"It is time for thee to desist, that thou mayest not experience the same punishment as Zimri;" Zech. v. 11, where the prophet mentions Shinar as the place of Israel's future banishment; and x. 11, where he calls their future oppressors by the names of Asshur and Egypt, and describes a new passing through the Red Sea. In Revelation, the degenerate church is called by the names of Sodom and Egypt (xi. 18); the true Church, by Jerusalem; Rome, by Babylon. —The explanation which we have given will be its own defence against the current, and evidently erroneous, expositions. Many interpreters understand, by the blood of Jezreel, the slaughter of the family of Ahab which was accomplished there by Jehu. It is, indeed, quite correct to say that a deed objectively good does not thereby become one which is subjectively so. That which has been willed and commanded by God may itself become an object of divine punishment, if it be not performed from love and obedience to God, but from culpable selfishness. But that Jehu was actuated by motives so bad, is sufficiently obvious from the circumstance, that he himself did the very thing which he had punished in the house of Ahab. *Calvin* rightly remarks: "That slaughter is, as far as God is concerned, a just vengeance; but, as far as Jehu is concerned, it is open murder." But yet, this deed cannot be regarded as the principal crime of Jehu and his family. We must not overlook other crimes far more heinous, and consider the guilty blood shed by them as the sole ground of their punishment. That this was indeed considered as guilt, but only as a lower degree of it, is clearly seen from 1 Kings xvi. 7, where destruction is announced to Baasha, who had destroyed the house of Jeroboam I., "on account of all the evil which he did in the sight of the Lord, in provoking Him to anger with the works of his hands, so that he may be like the house of Jeroboam, and because he killed him." The main crime is, that Baasha had become like the house of Jeroboam. What he perpetrated against this house is the minor crime, and becomes a crime only through the former.—It is worthy of notice that "the blood of Jezreel" exactly corresponds, according to our explanation, with the expression, "so that he may be like the house of Jeroboam." It may be further noticed, that, in the deed of Jehu, every better feeling cannot be excluded. If the command of God had been used by him merely as a pretext, we could not account for the praise and the promises given to him on account of this very deed, 2 Kings x. 30. It is true that the limitation of the promise shows that pure motives alone did not prevail with him.[1]—"The bloody deed to which the house of Jehu owed its elevation" nowhere else appears as the cause of the catastrophe which befell this house. That which he had done against the house of Ahab, whose sins were crying to heaven for vengeance far more than those of Baasha, is, in 2 Kings x. 30, 31, represented as his *merit*. His *guilt* consisted in his not departing from the ways of Jeroboam, and in his making Israel to sin. It is this guilt alone which, in the Book of Kings, is charged against all the members of his family,—against Jehoahaz, the son of Jehu, in 2 Kings xiii. 2; against Jehoash, in 2 Kings xiii. 11; against Jeroboam, in 2 Kings xiv. 24; against Zechariah, under whom the catastrophe took place, in 2 Kings xv. 9: "And he did that which was evil in the eyes of the Lord, as his fathers had done, and departed not from the sins of Jeroboam the son of Nebat, who had made Israel to sin." According to the context, we must, in the first place, think of the *religious guilt*; the blood of Jezreel, in the verse under consideration, must correspond with the *whoredoms* in ver. 2.—Moreover, the extension of the punishment to all Israel could not, according to this explanation, be understood; for the deed was only that of Jehu and his assistants. How, then, could not only the house of Jehu be punished, but also

---

[1] *Hitzig* is of opinion that "the prophet cannot blame him for the death of Joram and Jezebel, but may well do so for the murder of Ahaziah, king of Judah, and of his brethren, and for the carnage described in 2 Kings x. 11." But Ahaziah was not killed at Jezreel: compare 2 Kings ix. 27; 2 Chron. xxii. 9. And "the carnage in 2 Kings xii." likewise took place at Jezreel to a small extent only, in so far, namely, as it concerned the princes of the house of Ahab, who still remained in Jezreel. Compare *Thenius* on this passage.

the kingdom of the house of Israel be destroyed, and its bow broken in the valley of Jezreel?

According to another interpretation still more prevalent, "the blood of Jezreel" denotes "all the evil deeds committed by the Israelitish kings in Jezreel." But this interpretation is sufficiently invalidated by the single circumstance, that the residence of the family of Jehu, which, after all, alone comes into consideration in this place, was, from the very beginning, not Jezreel, but Samaria; compare 2 Kings x. 36, xiii. 10, xiv. 23.

Two particulars are contained in the announcement of punishment. *First*,—The whole house of Jehu, and *then* all Israel, are to become a Jezreel as regards punishment, as they are even now in point of guilt; and, in this announcement, the significant *paronomasia* must not be overlooked between *Israel* —the designation of the dignity of the people, and *Jezreel*— that which is base in deeds and condition. Calvin makes prominent the last-mentioned feature only: "You are," he explains, "a degenerate people, you differ in nothing from your king Ahab." We cannot, however, follow him in this explanation; the words, "I cause to cease the kingdom of the house of Israel," cannot, as several interpreters suppose, mean merely, "I will put an end to the dominion of the family of Jehu over Israel." That these words rather announce the cessation of every native regal government, and hence of the entire national independence, is so evident, that it stands in need of no proof. Both of these features are, in their fulfilment, separated indeed by a long period of time (see the Introduction); but they are nevertheless closely connected. With the ruin of the house of Jehu, the strength of the kingdom of Israel was broken; from that time it was only a living corpse. The fall of the house of Jehu was the beginning of the end,—the commencement of the process of putrefaction. The omission, in the inscription, of all mention of any of the kings after Jeroboam, coincides with the circumstance that the fall of the house of Jehu is connected with the fall of the kingdom. With regard, however, to the former event, Hosea had an earlier prophecy before him. It had been prophesied to Jehu (2 Kings x. 30) that his children should sit on the throne until the fourth generation. Now, since Jeroboam was the great-grandson of Jehu, the glory of this family must come to an end with his son. But at no period did the house of Jehu, and the kingdom of Israel, seem to be so far from destruction as under the reign of Jeroboam; and, hence, it was time that the forgotten prophecy should be revived, and, at the same time, expanded.

Ver. 5. "*And it shall come to pass at that day, that I break the bow of Israel in the valley of Jezreel.*"

Of this, Calvin gives the following paraphrase: "Ye are puffed up with pride; ye oppose your fierceness to God, because ye excel in weapons and strength; because ye are warlike men, ye believe that God can do nothing against you. But surely your bows shall not prevent His hands from destroying you."— In the valley of Jezreel, Israel shall become, as to punishment, what they already are, as to guilt, viz., a "Jezreel." The verse is a further expansion of the last words of the preceding one, to which the words, "at that day," refer. He whose bow is broken is defenceless and powerless; compare Gen. xlix. 24; 1 Sam. ii. 4; Jer. xlix. 35. It is evident that we can here think only of the defeat of Israel by the Assyrians, the consequence of which was the total overthrow of the kingdom of Israel. But it is not to be overlooked, that the Assyrians, who in the second section of Hosea are frequently mentioned in express terms, as the instruments of God's punishment, are not spoken of at all as such in the first section, which belongs to the reign of Jeroboam. Amos likewise abstains from mentioning any name of the enemies. The Assyrians had not at that time appeared on the historical horizon. But the prophecy was to evince itself as such, by the fact of the announcement of the judgment at a time when its instruments were not as yet prepared; just as Elijah, in 1 Kings xviii. 41, hears the rushing of the rain before there was even a cloud in the sky.—We are not told in the historical books at what place Israel was defeated by the Assyrians. *Jerome,* in his remarks on our passage, says that it took place in the valley of Jezreel. It is very probable, however, that this is only an inference clothed in the garb of history. But even apart from the passage under review, the matter is very probable. The valley of Jezreel or Esdrelon "is the largest, and at the same time the most fertile, plain of Palestine. The brook of Kishon, which is, next to Jordan, the most important river of Palestine, waters and fructifies it, and, with its tributaries, flows through it in all directions." (*Ritter*, S. 689.) In all the wars which were carried on within the territories of the ten tribes, especially when the enemies came from the North, it was the natural battle-field. "It was, in the first centuries, the station of a legion (μέγα πεδίον λεγεῶνος); it is the place where the troops of Nebuchadnezzar, Vespasian, Justinian, the Sultan Saladdin, and many other conquering armies were encamped, down to the unsuccessful expedition of *Buonaparte*, whose success in Syria here terminated. *Clarke* found erected here the tents of the troops of the Pacha of Damascus. In later times, it was the scene of the skirmishes between the parties of hostile hordes of Arabs and Turkish pachas. In the political relations of Asia Minor, it is to this locality that there must be ascribed the total devastation and depopulation of Galilee, which once was so flourishing, full of towns, and thickly populated." (*Ritter, Erdk.* 1 *Ausg.* ii. S. 387.) We may add, that, in the same plain also, the battle was fought in which Saul and Jonathan perished (for the plain of Esdrelon is bounded on the south-east by the mountains of Gilboa), and so likewise was the battle between Ahab and the Syrians. To it also belonged the plain near the town of Megiddo, where Josiah, in the battle against Pharaoh-Necho, was mortally wounded. Compare *Rosenmüller, Alt.* ii. 1, p. 149.

Ver. 6. " *And she conceived again, and bare a daughter. And He said to him, Call her name Lo-Ruhamah* (*i.e.*, one who has not obtained mercy): *for I will not continue any more to have mercy upon the house of Israel; for I will take away from them.*" —Interpreters ask why the second child was a female; and this question is by no means an idle one, since the prophet everywhere else adheres closely to the subject-matter, and adds no feature, merely for the sake of giving vividness to the picture. We cannot for a moment suppose, as *Jerome* and others do, that the female child denotes a more degraded generation. For why, then, is the third again a male child? The supposition proceeds from the altogether unfounded notion that the three children denote different generations. The reason must, on the contrary, be sought for in the name. *Schmid* says: "It seems to have reference to the weakness of the sex. For the female sex finds greater sympathy than the male." The verb רחם does not denote any kind of love, but only the love of him who is high to him who is low, of the strong to the weak; and hence the LXX., whom Peter follows in 1 Pet. ii. 10 (οὐκ ἠλεημένη), render the word more accurately than Paul, in Rom. ix. 25 (οὐκ ἠγαπημένη). Hence it is never used of man's love to God, but only of the love of God to man,—of His mercy. The only passage which seems to contradict this, Ps. xviii. 2, is not to the purpose, as, there, the *Kal* is used. But the female sex, being weaker, stands in greater need of the compassion of men, than does the male, Is. ix. 16. The female child places the neediness and helplessness of the people in more striking contrast with the refusal of help from Him who alone can bestow it. The רחמה is either *Participle* in *Pual* which has cast off the מ, or the 3d fem. *Pret. in pause;* thus *Cocceius,* who explains it by: "She has not obtained mercy." It is in favour of the latter view, that according to *Ewald,* § 310 b, לא does not often stand before a *Participle.* The words, "*I will not continue,*" refer to the former great manifestations of divine mercy, and especially the last under Jeroboam, which the people still, at that time, enjoyed; compare 2 Kings xiii. 23: "And the Lord was gracious unto them, and had *mercy* upon them, and turned towards them because of His covenant with Abraham, Isaac, and Jacob, and would not destroy them, neither cast them from His presence." Upon this contrast, also, rests the mild expression, "I will not have mercy,"—an expression which, in virtue of this contrast, becomes stronger than any other. Several interpreters here lay peculiar stress upon the circumstance, that "the *house* of Israel" is spoken of. This, the kingdom of Israel, they say, as an independent state, is given over to everlasting destruction; it is only single individuals who shall obtain mercy after they have joined the house of David. But the supposition that "house of Israel" is used in this sense, is altogether unfounded. The house is equivalent to the family; and the prophets speak of "a house of Israel" after the destruction, no less than before it. The words in ii. 6 (4), "I will not have mercy upon her children," and the circumstance that she who is here called Lo-Ruhamah is afterwards called Ruhamah, also militate against referring "house of Israel" to the state. The right view rather is, that the denial of mercy must not be understood absolutely, but relatively. It is not for ever that mercy shall be denied to them, but for a time,—until God's punitive justice shall have been satisfied. Just as Israel shall not always remain Jezreel, Lo-Ammi shall, at some future time, become again Ammi.—The last words are, by the greater number of recent interpreters, almost unanimously explained: "That I should forgive them." But, in that case, we can perceive no reason why the *Inf. abs.* should be placed before the *tempus finitum*. Why should the verbal idea here be rendered so emphatic? In addition to this, the extreme feebleness of the sense would be remarkable. Nothing would be said that would not be already implied in the words, "I will not continue any more to have mercy." But, on the other hand, we obtain a very suitable sense if we translate thus: "I will take away from them." The object is not mentioned, just because *every thing* is to be understood. The prominence given to the verbal idea is then accounted for from its being contrasted with the *having mercy*, which implies *giving*. There is then, moreover, a very striking contrast with the standing phrase נשׂא עָוֹן ל, or also simply נשׂא ל: I shall take away from them, not, however, as hitherto, their guilt (compare Amos vii. 8), but all that they have. *Calvin* had previously directed attention to the circumstance that the following verse also is in favour of the translation by *tollere*: "*Servare et tollere inter se opponit propheta.*" Chap. v. 14 may also be compared, where נשׂא is used in a similar manner, the object being likewise omitted: "I will tear and go away, I will take away, and there is none that delivereth."

Ver. 7. "*And I will have mercy upon the house of Judah, and I save them by the Lord their God; and I do not save them by bow, and by sword, and by war, and by horses, and by horsemen.*"

Several interpreters suppose that mercy is here promised to Judah as a *consolation* to Israel, inasmuch as the latter should partake in it. But this view is erroneous. From the antithesis to ver. 6, it is evident that mercy is here promised to Judah for the time when Israel shall not find mercy; and we are not at liberty to anticipate the time described in ii. 1–3, when both become partakers of mercy. This is apparent also from the circumstance that in vers. 8, 9, the threatening of punishment to Israel is still continued. It can then only be the intention of the prophet, by describing the mercy which Judah their brethren should experience, to sharpen the goad, more effectually to rouse Israel from their false security, and to direct their attention to the bad foundation of the entire constitution of their political and ecclesiastical affairs, in consequence of which they considered as legitimate that which, in Judah, was only an abuse. As the showing of mercy to Judah runs parallel with the withholding of it from Israel, we can, primarily and chiefly, think only of the different fates of the two, during the Assyrian dominion. The wonderful deliverance of Judah on that occasion is foretold by Isaiah, xxxi. 8, in a similar manner : "And Asshur falls through the sword not of a man, and the sword not of a man devours him." We must not, however, limit ourselves to this event; a preference of Judah over Israel, a remnant of divine mercy appeared, even when they were carried away into captivity. During its continuance, they were not altogether deprived of marks of the continuance of the divine election. Prophets continued to labour among them, as immediate ambassadors of God. Wonderful events showed them in the midst of the Gentiles the superiority of their God, and prepared the way for their deliverance. They maintained, in a far greater degree, their national constitution; and, *lastly*, their affliction lasted for a far shorter time than did that of the Israelites. Contrary to all human expectation, their affairs soon took a favourable turn, in which only a comparatively small number of their Israelitish brethren partook, while, for the rest, the withholding of mercy continued. But it is just by means of this contrast with the lot of Judah, that the announcement of the lot of Israel appears in its true light. Without this contrast, one might have imagined, that the announcement of the prophet did not go beyond his human vision. It would, of course, appear highly probable that a kingdom so weak as that of Israel,—weak, especially when compared with those great Asiatic kingdoms which were great already, and yet were continually striving after enlargement,— a kingdom, moreover, placed in the midst between these kingdoms, and their natural enemy and rival, Egypt—should not have been able to maintain its existence for any length of time. But this probability existed in a far higher degree in the case of the kingdom of

Judah, which was smaller and weaker still, and which had suffered much through Jehoash the father of Jeroboam (2 Kings xiv. 13), under the latter of whom, the splendour and glory of Israel had been so greatly increased. But that which prevented this probability from becoming a reality lay altogether beyond the sphere of human calculation, as Hosea himself here so emphatically expresses. And by *such* help, the kingdom of Israel would have been delivered, no less than the kingdom of Judah. It is true that this prediction of Hosea is no prediction of some accidental event, but has its foundation in the idea. The lots of Israel and Judah could not be otherwise than so different, after their different position in reference to the Covenant-God was once fixed. Nor is this prediction one which has ceased after its first and literal fulfilment, but is constantly and anew realizing itself. The proceeding of God towards the different Churches and States is regulated by their conduct towards Him. The history of the world is a judgment of the world. But even to know this truth is, in itself, a supernatural gift; and they only are able to use it with safety, to whom God has given an insight into the mysteries of His government of the world. This becomes very evident, if we observe how often the predictions of those who knew the truth in general, down to *Bengel* and his followers, have been put to shame by the result. God's ways are not our ways. No one knows them except Himself, and those to whom He will reveal them. The extent to which the prophecy rests on the idea is, moreover, clearly seen by the words, "And I save them *by Jehovah their God.*" Here we have the ground of their deliverance. Jehovah is the God of Judah, and, hence, the source of their salvation, which does not cease to flow although all human sources be dried up. The reason why Israel does not obtain mercy must then be, that Jehovah is not their God. That this contrast is implied here, is confirmed by iii. 5: "Afterwards shall the children of Israel return and seek the *Lord their God,* and David their king." That which in aftertimes they shall seek, and thereby obtain salvation, they must have lost now; and this loss must be the source of their affliction. Calvin makes the following pertinent remark: "The antithesis between the false gods and Jehovah must here be kept in mind. Jehovah was the God of the house of Judah; and hence, it is just as if the prophet had said, 'Ye indeed profess the name of God, but ye worship the devil, and not God. Ye have no part in Jehovah. He resides in His temple, and has pledged His faithfulness to David when He commanded him to build Him a temple on Mount Zion; but from you, the true God has departed!'" (Compare Amos ii. 8, where the prophet speaks of the god of the ten tribes as one who belongs to them alone, and with whom he has nothing to do.) In contrast with Him who alone could grant help, and whom Israel did not possess, but Judah did, the prophet enumerates, in the remaining part of the verse under consideration, the aids which could not afford any real help, in which Israel was, at that time, much richer than Judah, and in which they placed a false confidence. Compare x. 13: "Thou didst trust in thy way, in the multitude of thy mighty men;" Ps. xx. 8; Mic. v. 9 seqq.; and Deut. xxxiii. 29, where the Lord is spoken of as the only true bulwark and armour: "Happy art thou, Israel: who is like unto thee? a people saved by the Lord, the shield of thy help, thy proud sword: thine enemies shall be liars unto thee, and thou shalt tread upon their high places." Calvin says, "God does not require any other aids; His own strength is quite sufficient. The sum and substance is therefore this, that although the weakness of the kingdom of Judah excites the contempt of all, this shall be no obstacle to its deliverance by the grace of God, although there be no help at all from men."—The prophet has, at the same time, before his eyes the great events of former history, where, when all human resources failed, the power of God had shown itself to be alone quite sufficient.—We cannot assert with *Gesenius*, that " war" should here be quite identical with " weapons of war;" it rather comprehends everything which is required for war, viz., the prudence of the commanders, the valour of the heroes, the strength of the army, etc. "Heroes and horsemen " are, however, specially mentioned, because in ancient times the main strength of the armies lay in these. Even Mahommed thought himself entitled to hold up a victory which he had obtained without cavalry—by infantry alone—as a miracle wrought immediately by God; comp. *Abulf. vit. Moh.* pp. 72, 91.

Ver. 8. "*And she weaned Lo-Ruhamah, and conceived, and bare a son.*"

Ver. 9. "*And He said, Call his name, Lo-Ammi (i.e.,* not

my people); *for you are not My people, and I, not will I be yours.*"

As the prophet everywhere else adheres closely to his subject-matter, as, indeed, he allows the figure to recede behind the subject of his discourse, but never the opposite, we cannot well imagine that the weaning is mentioned merely for the purpose of making the description more graphic. Calvin says, "I do not doubt that the prophet intends here to commend the Lord's long-continued mercy and forbearance towards that people." The unfaithfulness of the wife, and the forbearance of the prophet, do indeed continue for years. But it is better to suppose that the mention of the weaning is intended to separate the territory of Lo-Ruhamah from the following birth, and to call forth the idea that, now, there may follow one of better import. —The literal translation of the close of the verse is, " And I will not be to you"—equivalent to, "I will not any longer belong to you." We cannot assume, as *Manger* does, that לאלהים has been here left out, nor, as others do, that it must be supplied. Since it is God who speaks, "to you," or " yours," is sufficiently definite. Similar is Ezek. xvi. 8: "And I entered into a covenant with thee, and thou becamest Mine," ותהיי לי; Ps. cxviii. 6: " The Lord is mine, יהוה לי, I will not fear." The explanation given by some, "I shall not be among you," is too limited. It is the highest happiness to possess God Himself, with all His gifts and blessings, and the greatest misery to lose Him. The fulfilment of this threatening is reported in 2 Kings xvii. 18: " And the Lord was very angry with Israel, and removed them out of His sight; and there was none left but the tribe of Judah alone ;" comp. also Is. vii.

The first three verses of the following chapter ought to have been connected with the first chapter; for they contain the announcement of salvation which is necessary to complete the first prophecy.

Chap. ii. 1. "*And the number of the children of Israel shall be as the sand of the sea, which is not measured nor numbered. And it shall come to pass, in the place where it was said unto them, Not my people ye, it shall be said unto them, Sons of the living God.*"

The first point which requires to be determined, is the subject of the verse. Every other reference except that to the

ten tribes is here out of the question; inasmuch as the same
who, in the preceding verse, were called Lo-Ammi, are now to
be called sons of the living God. Several of the ancient expositors here assume a sudden transition to the Christian Church;
but such would be a *salto mortale*. Nor are we to understand
by the children of Israel, all the descendants of Jacob; for the
children of Judah are distinguished from them in ver. 2. Substantially, however, those too are included, as appears from this
very verse; for both shall then form one nation of brethren.
But here the prophet views only one portion, because to this
only did the preceding threatening, and the mission of the
prophet in general, refer. From this, also, it may be explained
how the prophet may apply to the *part* the promises of Genesis,
which there refer to the *whole*. The reference to these promises,
in the first part of the verse, cannot be at all mistaken. Compare especially, as agreeing most literally, the passage in Gen.
xxii. 17: "I will multiply thy seed as the stars of heaven, and
as the sand which is on the shore of the sea;" and xxxii. 13
(12): "I make thy seed as the sand of the sea, which is not
numbered for multitude." A similar literal reference is in
Jer. xxxiii. 22: "As the host of heaven is not numbered, neither
the sand of the sea measured; so will I multiply the seed of
David My servant." Now, the reference here cannot be accidental. It supposes that these promises were at that time
generally known in the kingdom of Israel. They served to
strengthen the ungodly in their false security. Relying on
them, they charged the prophets with making God a liar in thus
announcing the impending destruction of the kingdom, inasmuch as the prophecy had not yet been fulfilled in all its extent.
The prophet, however, by his almost literal repetition of the
promise, shows that thereby his threatenings are not excluded—
"teaches that the visitation of which he had spoken would be
such that, nevertheless, God would not forget His word; that the
rejection of the people would be such that, nevertheless, its election should stand firm and sure,—and, finally, that the adoption
should not be invalid by which He had chosen Abraham's progeny
as His people" (*Calvin*).—The case is quite analogous, when
corrupted Christian churches harden themselves in trusting in
the promise that the Lord would be with them all the days, and
that the gates of hell should not prevail against His Church. The

Lord knoweth how to execute His judgments so that His promises shall not suffer thereby, yea, that their fulfilment is thereby rendered possible. The relation of our passage to Is. x. 22 requires *further* to be considered: "For though thy people Israel be as the sand of the sea, the remnant only shall return." Here, too, the reference to the promises in Genesis cannot be mistaken. But there is this difference,—that in the time of Isaiah, the people, viewing the partial fulfilment of the promises of God in their then prosperous condition, as a sure pledge of divine mercy, founded thereupon their false security. To this, however, the prophet replies, that even the perfect fulfilment would give no warrant for it. In Hosea, however, they rely on the perfect fulfilment, which had, as yet, no existence at all. But Hosea has in view the godly as much as the ungodly. To the former he shows that here also there would be a fulfilment of what is written in Num. xxiii. 19: "God is not a man, that He should lie; neither the son of man, that He should repent. Should He say, and not do it; and speak, and not fulfil it?" Moreover, we cannot fail to see that, in the verse under review, as also in ver. 2, there is an allusion to the first child, Jezreel,— that in the second member of the verse there is an allusion to Lo-Ammi, and in ver. 3, to Lo-Ruhamah. But the name Jezreel is now taken in a good sense, probably in the sense in which it was first given to the valley (compare remarks on i. 4), and also to the town by its founders. Jezreel means "God sows." The founders of the town thereby expressed the hope that God would cause an abundant harvest to proceed from a small sowing—a glorious end from a small beginning. Thus God will now sow the small seed of Israel, and an infinitely rich harvest shall be gained from this sowing; compare remarks on ver. 25.—But if now we seek for the historical reference of the announcement, we are compelled to go back to the sense of those declarations in Genesis. By many, these are referred merely to the bodily descendants of the Patriarchs; by many, also, to their spiritual descendants, their successors in the faith. But the latter reference is altogether arbitrary; and the former could be well-founded only, if the Congregation of the Lord had been destined solely for the natural descendants, and if all the Gentiles had been refused admittance into it. But that such is not the case, is evident from the command to circumcise every bond-servant; for, by circumcision, a man was received among the people of God. This appears, *further*, from the command in Exod. xii. 48, that every stranger who wished to partake of the Passover must be previously circumcised; and this implies that strangers might partake in the sign and feast of the covenant if they wished; compare *Michaelis, Mos. Recht.* Th. iv. § 184. This appears, *moreover*, from Deut. xxiii. 1–8, where the Edomites and Egyptians are expressly declared to be capable of being received into the Congregation of the Lord. It appears, *still further*, from the circumstance that, in the same passage, the command to exclude the Ammonites and Moabites is founded upon a special reason. And, *finally*, it appears from the Jewish practice at all times. But the heathens who were received among the people of God were considered as belonging to the posterity of the Patriarchs, as their sons by adoption. How indeed could it be otherwise, since, by intermarriage, every difference must have very soon disappeared? They were called children of Israel, and children of Jacob, no less than were the others. It now appears to what extent the promise to the Patriarchs refers to the Gentiles also—viz., in so far as they became believers in the God of Israel, and joined themselves to Israel. Compare Is. xliv. 5: "One shall say, I am Jehovah's, and another shall call the name of Jacob, and another shall write with his hand, Unto the Lord! and boast of the name of Israel." Such an eager desire of the Gentiles towards the kingdom of God regularly took place, either when the God of Israel had revealed Himself by specially distinguishing manifestations of His omnipotence and glory, as, *e.g.*, in the deliverance from the Egyptian and Babylonish captivities, in both of which events we find a number of those who had previously been heathens, ערב, in the train of the Israelites;—or when a feeling of the vanity of the idols of the heathen world had been awakened with special vividness, as in the times after Alexander the Great, in which Roman and Greek heathenism became more and more *effete*, and rapidly hastened on towards ruin. In the time of Christ, both of these causes co-operated. If there were soundness in the opinion now generally prevalent, according to which the Church of the New Testament stands quite independent of the Congregation of Israel, having originated from a free and equal union of believers from Israel, and of those from among the Gentiles,

then indeed the promise now before us would have no longer
any reference to New Testament times. The New Testament
Church would be a generation altogether different, and no
longer acknowledge Abraham, Isaac, and Jacob as their fathers.
But, according to the constant doctrine of the Old as well as of
the New Testament, there is only one Church of God from
Abraham to the end of the days—only one house under two
dispensations. John the Baptist proceeds upon the supposition that the members of the New Testament also must be
children of Abraham, else the covenant and promise of God
would come to nought. But as the bodily descent from Abraham
is no security against the danger of exclusion from his posterity
—of which Ishmael was the first example—and as, so early as
in the Pentateuch, it is said, with reference to every greater
transgression, "This soul is cut off from its people," so, on the
other hand, God, in the exercise of His sovereign liberty,
may give to Abraham, in the room of his degenerate children
after the flesh, adopted children without number, who shall
sit down with him, and Isaac, and Jacob, in the kingdom
of God, whilst the sons of the kingdom are cast out.—After
these remarks on the promise to the Patriarchs, there can be
no longer any difficulty in making out the historical reference
of the announcement before us. It cannot refer to the bodily
descendants of Abraham, as such, any more than the promise
of a son to Abraham was fulfilled in the birth of Ishmael, or
than the Arabs stand related to the promise of the innumerable multitude of his descendants,—a promise which is repeated,
in the same extent, to Isaac and Jacob, although they were not
the ancestors of the Arabs. Degenerate sons are not a blessing;
they are no objects of promise, no sons in the full sense. Every
one is a son of Abraham, only in so far as he is a son of God.
For this reason the phrases "sons of Israel" and "sons of the
living God" are, in the passage before us, connected with each
other. Not as though the corporeal descent were altogether a
matter of indifference. The corporeal descendants of the Patriarchs had the nearest claims to becoming their children in
the full sense. It was to them that the means of becoming so
were first granted. To them pertained the covenants, the
promises, and the adoption, Rom. ix. 4. But all these external
advantages were of no avail to them when they allowed them to

remain unused; in these circumstances, neither the promise to Abraham, nor the announcement before us, had any reference to them. Both of them would have remained to this day unfulfilled, although the unconverted children of Israel had increased so as to have become the most populous nation on the face of the whole earth. It thus appears that the announcement before us was first truly realized in the time of the Messiah; inasmuch as it was at that time that the family of the Patriarchs was so mightily increased; and that it will yet be more fully realized, partly by the reception of an innumerable multitude of adopted sons, and partly by the elevation of those who were sons only in a lower sense, to be sons in the highest. That which occurred at the time after the Babylonish captivity, when the Lord stirred up a number of Israelites to return to Palestine, we can regard as only an insignificant prelude; partly because this number was too small to correspond, even in any degree, to the infinite extent of the promise, and partly because there were among them certainly a few only who, in the fullest sense, deserved the name of "Children of Israel." "Israel"—which is the higher name, and has reference to the relation to God—is here used emphatically, as appears especially from a comparison with ver. 4, where it is taken from the degenerate children, and exchanged for the name "Jezreel."—In the second part of the verse, we must first set aside the false interpretation of במקום אשר by "instead of," which is given by *Grotius* and others. It has arisen from an inappropriate reference to the Latin, which has, however, no support in the Hebrew *usus loquendi*. The words can only mean (compare Lev. iv. 24, 33; Jer. xxii. 12; Ezek. xxi. 35; Neh. iv. 14): "in the place where," or, more literally still, "in the place that"—the wider designation instead of the narrower. The *status constr.* is explained by the circumstance that the whole succeeding sentence together expresses only one substantive idea, equivalent to: "in the place of the being said unto them." The place may here be, either that where the people first received the name Lo-Ammi, *i.e.*, Palestine, or the place of the exile, where they first felt the full meaning of it, —the misery being a *sermo realis* of God. Decisive in favour of the latter reference is the following verse, where the הארץ, the land of the exile, corresponds with מקום in the verse before us. (According to *Jonathan*, the sense is: "In the place to which they have been carried away among the Gentiles.") It is intentionally that both times the Future יֹאמַר is used, which is to be understood as the Present. The difference of time being thus disregarded, the contrast becomes so much the more striking.—By "people" and "children" of God, the same thing is expressed according to different relations. The Israelites were the people of God, inasmuch as He was their King; and children of God, in as far as He was their Father,—their Father, it is true, in the first place, not, as in the New Testament (John i. 12, 13), in reference to the spiritual generation, but in relation to heartfelt love, similar to the love of a father for a son. With regard to the Old Testament idea of sonship to God, compare the remarks on Ps. ii. 7. In this relation, sometimes all Israel is personified as the son of God; thus, *e.g.*, Exod. iv. 22: "Thus thou shalt say unto Pharaoh: My son, My first-born is Israel." Sometimes the Israelites are also called the *children* or *sons* of God; *e.g.*, Deut. xiv. 1: "Ye are children to the Lord your God" (compare also Deut. xxxii. 19), although not every single individual could on this account be called "son of God." In this sense, that designation is never used, evidently because the sonship under the Old Testament does not rest so much on the personal relation of the single individual to God,—as is the case in the New Testament,—but the individual rather partakes in it only as a part of the whole. But there is an easy transition from the sonship as viewed in the Old Testament, to the sonship as seen in the New. The former, in its highest perfection, cannot exist at all without the latter. It is only when its single members are born of God, that the Congregation can be regarded and treated as the child of God in the full sense of the word, and that the whole fulness of His love can be poured out upon it; for this is the only way of attaining to likeness with God, which is the condition of admission to the rights of children. Hence it appears that the υἱοθεσία under the Old Testament was an actual prophecy of the times of the New Testament; and from it, it follows also that the announcement under consideration has its ultimate reference to these times. Earlier fulfilments—especially at the return from the Babylonish captivity—are not to be excluded, inasmuch as the idea comprehends in it everything in which it is, even in the least degree, realized; but they can be considered only as a slight prelude to its real fulfilment, which takes place only when the reality fully coincides with the idea; so that we are not at liberty to limit ourselves to the commencement of the Messianic time, but must include the Messianic time in its last consummation.—Another question still remains :—Why is God here called the "*living?*" Plainly, to point out the antithesis of the true God to dead idols, which cannot love, because they do not live; and thus to bring out the greatness of the privilege of being the child of such a God. The same antithesis is found in Deut. xxxii. 3 seqq.: "Where are now their gods, the rock in whom they trusted, which did eat the fat of their sacrifices, and drank the wine of their drink-offerings? Let them rise up and help you; let it be a covering to you. See now that I, I am He, and not is a God beside Me. I kill and I make alive. I wound and I heal." This antithesis still continues; the world has only changed its idols. It still always seeks the life from the dead, from the gross idol of sin up to the refined idol of a self-made abstract god, whether he be formed from logical notions or from emotions and feelings. But how much soever they may strive to give life to their idols, they remain dead, although they should even attain to a semblance of life. The true God, on the contrary, lives and continues to live, how much soever they may strive to slay Him. He manifests Himself as the living one, either by smiting and killing them, if they continue in their impenitence, or by healing and quickening them, if they become His children.— *Finally,*—we must still consider the two citations, in the New Testament, of the passage before us. One in 1 Pet. ii. 10, *οἱ ποτὲ οὐ λαὸς, νῦν δὲ λαὸς Θεοῦ· οἱ οὐκ ἠλεημένοι, νῦν δὲ ἐλεη-θέντες,* must certainly strike us, inasmuch as this epistle, on conclusive grounds (compare *Steiger* S. 14 ff.), cannot be considered as being addressed to Jewish Christians exclusively. But still more striking is the second quotation in Rom. ix. 25, 26: *ὡς καὶ ἐν τῷ Ὡσηὲ λέγει· Καλέσω τὸν οὐ λαόν μου, λαόν μου· καὶ τὴν οὐκ ἠγαπημένην, ἠγαπημένην. Καὶ ἔσται, ἐν τῷ τόπῳ οὗ ἐρρήθη αὐτοῖς οὐ λαός μου ὑμεῖς, ἐκεῖ κληθήσονται υἱοὶ Θεοῦ ζῶντος.* Here our passage is not only alluded to, but expressly quoted, and, in opposition to the Jews, the calling of the Gentiles is proved from it. But how can a passage which, according to the whole context, can refer to Israel only, be applied directly to the Gentiles? The answer very readily suggests itself when we reduce the prophecy to its fundamental idea. This is none other than that of divine mercy, which may indeed, by apostasy and unfaithfulness, be prevented from manifesting itself, but can never be extinguished, because it has its foundation in God's nature. Compare Jer. xxxi. 20: " Is Ephraim a dear son to Me, a child of joy? For as often as I speak of him, I must still remember him. Therefore My bowels sound for him, *I will have mercy* upon him, saith the Lord." Now, in the same manner as this truth was realized in the restoration of the children of Israel to be again the children of God, so it is in the reception of the Gentiles. It is not at all a mere application, but a real proof which here forms the question at issue. It is *because* God had promised to receive again the children of Israel, that He must receive the Gentiles also; for otherwise that divine decree would have its foundation in mere caprice, which cannot be conceived to have any existence in God. Although the Gentiles are not so near as Israel, yet He must satisfy the claims of those who are more remote, just because He acknowledges the claims of those who are near. The necessity of going back to the fundamental idea appears in the promises as well as in the commandments. We cite only one instance which is especially fitted to serve as a parallel to the case before us. There is no doubt, and prejudice alone could have denied, that in the Pentateuch, by *friend* and *brother* the Israelite is to be understood throughout; it is in the New Testament that the command of Christian brotherly love is given. After having commended truthfulness, Paul adds: " Because ye are members of one another"—a reason which can refer to those only who have Christ as their common head. From this limitation, can anything be inferred to the prejudice of love towards the whole human race, or of the duties towards all without any distinction? Just the reverse. It is just because the Israelite is bound to love the Israelite, and the Christian the Christian, that he should embrace all men in love. If the special relation to God as the common Redeemer afford the foundation for the *special* love, then the *general* relation to God as the Creator and Preserver must also afford the foundation of *universal* love; just as from the command to honour father and mother, it necessarily follows that we must also honour uncle and aunt, king and magistrate. This is the only correct view of the laws and prophecies; and if it be consistently followed out, it will make water to flow out of the rock, and will create streams in the wilderness.

Ver. 2. *"And the children of Judah and the children of Israel assemble themselves together, and set over themselves one head, and go up out of the land; for great is the day of Jezreel."*

The words, "They appoint themselves a king," appear strange at first sight. For it is not, in general, the union of Judah and Israel which the prophet expects from better times;—a *perverse* union of both, one, it may be, in which the house of Judah shall also give up Jehovah his God, and David his King, only in order to be able to live on a right brotherly footing with Israel, would have been anything but a progress and a blessing; —but such a union as has for its foundation the return of Israel to the true God, and to the Davidic dynasty. This appears clearly from iii. 5. The difficulty is removed by a comparison with the passage of the Pentateuch to which the prophet seems to allude: "Thou shalt set over thee a king, whom the Lord thy God shall choose," Deut. xvii. 15. The prophet seems to have these words before his eyes, as it appears elsewhere also, where he describes the hitherto opposite conduct of the Israelites; compare the remarks on iii. 4. From these it appears that the election of the king by God, who had promised eternal dominion to the house of David, and his election by the people, do not in the least exclude one another. On the contrary, it is *because* God had elected the king, that now the people also elect him. *Calvin* remarks: "There appears to be transferred to men what properly belongs to God alone—viz., the appointment of a king; but the prophet expresses, by this word, the obedience of faith; for it is not enough that Christ be given, and placed before men as a King, but they must also acknowledge and reverently receive Him as a King. From this we infer, that when we believe the Gospel, we choose, as it were by our own vote, Christ as our King." That the prophet understands the "setting of a head" in this sense, appears also from the circumstance that the whole verse is based upon the reference to the Exodus from Egypt, which is now to be repeated. To this the words, "They assemble themselves together," likewise refer; for the departure from Egypt was preceded by the assembling together of the

whole people.   The mention of a "head" refers back to Moses.
In his case, as well as that of David subsequently, the election
by the people was only the acknowledgment of his having
been divinely called.—Another question is, How are the words,
"They go up out of the land," to be understood?   There can
be no doubt that by "land," the land of captivity is designated.
For the words are borrowed from Exod. i. 10, where Pharaoh
says, "When there falleth out any war, they will join our
enemies, and fight against us, and go up out of the land," ועלה מן
הארץ.   The prophet, moreover, is his own interpreter in ii. 17,
where he expressly compares this new going up to the promised
land with the former going up 'from Egypt: "*As in the day
when she went up out of the land of Egypt;*" just as, in other
passages, he describes their being carried away, under the figure
of their being carried away to Egypt—Assyria being considered
as another Egypt.   Compare viii. 13 : "Now will He remember
their iniquity and visit their sins; they shall return to Egypt;"
ix. 3: "They shall not dwell in the Lord's land, and Ephraim
returns to Egypt."   (Compare, on this passage, the Author's
Dissertations on the Genuineness of the Pentateuch, vol. i. p. 121 ff.)
Moreover, in the other prophets also, the going up from, or
deliverance out of, Egypt, forms throughout the basis of the
second great deliverance.   And this is quite natural; for both
of those events stand in the closest actual connection with each
other;—both proceeded from the same Divine Being; and the
former was a prophecy *by fact,* and a pledge of the latter.   The
deliverance of the people of God from Egypt sealed their election; and from the latter the new deliverance necessarily followed;—a relation which repeats itself in individuals also.   From
this we may explain the fact that in the Psalms, they who celebrate God's former mercies, prove from them to Him and to
themselves, throughout, that He must now also be their helper.
It is then by no means a mere external similarity which induces
the prophets ever and anon to refer to the deliverance from
Egypt (compare the passages Mic. ii. 12, 13; Jer. xxiii. 7, 8,
which bear so close a resemblance to the passage before us),
any more than that the Passover is a mere memorial.   Such
cannot occur in the true religion which has a living God, and
hence knows nothing of anything absolutely past.   *Ewald's*

P

exposition, that they go up out of the country for the purpose of further conquest, and that of *Simson*, that they go up to Jerusalem, sever the three events which, as the example of previous history shows, are evidently so closely allied; and these expositors, moreover, give, by an addition of their own, that definiteness to the words, "And they shall go up out of the land," which they can obtain only by a reference to the history of the past. In their ambiguity, they almost expressly point to such a commentary.—The article in הארץ, *the* (*i.e.*, the definite) land, is explained from the circumstance that, in the previous context, there had been an indirect allusion to their being carried away into a strange land. If Israel was no more the people of God,—if they no longer enjoyed His mercy, then it is supposed that they could not remain in the land which they had received only as the people of God, and had hitherto retained only through His mercy. But, primarily, the article refers to "the place where it was said unto them," in the preceding verse.—That along with the children of Israel, the children of Judah also assemble themselves and go up, implies a fact which the prophet had not expressly mentioned, because it did not stand immediately connected with his purpose—viz., that Judah too should be carried into captivity. It thus supplements chap. i. 7, by showing that the mercy there promised to the inhabitants of Judah is to be understood relatively only. Such suppositions, indeed, show very plainly how distinctly the future lay before the eyes of the prophet.[1]—With regard, now, to the historical reference,—it must, in the first place, be remarked, that whatever is here determined concerning it, must be applicable to all other

---

[1] That the carrying away of Judah, which is here supposed, is a total and future one, and not, as *Hofmann* (*Weiss. u. Erf.* i. S. 210) asserts, one which is partial and already past (Joel iv. [iii.] 2–8; Amos i. 6, 9), appears from the analogy of the children of Israel,—from the reference to the type of the Egyptian conditions,—from a comparison of chap. v. 5, 12, xii. 1–3, —from the fact that the carrying away is placed in the view of the *whole people* as early as in the Pentateuch, *e.g.*, Deut. xxviii. 36, iv. 26, 27,—and, finally, from the fact, that the other prophets also, even from the most ancient times, manifest a clear knowledge of the catastrophe which threatened Judah also; compare, *e.g.*, Amos ii. 4, 5. Moreover, in Is. xi. 11, 12, also, the return of Judah is prophesied, although no express announcement of the carrying away precedes. In like manner, in Amos ix. 11, the restoration of the fallen tabernacle of David is foretold, although no express mention is made of its fall.

parallel passages also, in which a future reunion of Israel and Judah, and their common return to the promised land, are announced; *e.g.*, Jer. iii. 18 : "In those days the house of Judah shall walk with the house of Israel, and they come together out of the land of the north to the land that I have given to their fathers;" l. 4 : "In those days the children of Israel shall come, they and the children of Judah together, weeping shall they come and seek the Lord their God." Compare also Is. xi.; Ezek. xxxvii. 19, 20. In the passage under consideration, several interpreters, as *Theodoret*, think of the return from Babylon, and refer the "one head" to Zerubbabel. Now we certainly cannot deny that, in that event, there is a small beginning of the fulfilment. But if that had been the entire fulfilment, Hosea would more resemble a dreamer and an enthusiast than a true prophet of the living God. The objection which immediately presents itself—viz., that, after all, the greatest portion of the ten tribes, and a very considerable part of Judah, remained in captivity—is by no means the strongest. Although the whole both of Judah and Israel had returned, the real and final fulfilment could not be sought for in that event. It is not the renewed possession of the country, as such, which the prophet promises, but rather a certain kind of possession,—such a possession as that the land is completely the land of God, partaking in all the fulness of His blessings, and thus a worthy residence for the people of God, and for their children. One may be in Canaan, and yet, at the same time, in Babylon or in Assyria. Had not the threatened punishment of God been indeed as fully executed upon those who, during the Assyrian and Babylonish captivities, wandered about the country in sorrow and misery, as upon those who were carried away? Can the circumstance that Jews are even now living in Jerusalem in the deepest misery, be adduced as a proof that the loss of the promised land, with which the people were threatened, had not been completely fulfilled? It is true that, during the times of the Old Covenant, there existed a certain connection betwixt the lower and the higher kinds of possession. As soon as the people ceased to be the people of the Lord, they lost with the former, after being often previously warned by the decrease of it, the latter also. As soon as they obtained again the lower kind of possession, which could happen only in the case of a return to the Lord, they recovered, to a certain degree, in proportion to the earnestness and sincerity of their conversion, the higher kind of possession also. A commencement of the fulfilment must, therefore, be at all events assumed in the return from the Babylonish captivity; but a very feeble commencement only. Just as the conversion was very superficial, so was the degree of the higher kind of possession but a very small one. The manifestations of mercy were very sparing; the condition of the new colony was, upon the whole, very poor; they did not possess the land as a free property, but only under the dominion of a foreigner. That which was, in one respect, the termination of the captivity, was, in another, much rather a continuation of it. It was certainly not the true Canaan which they possessed, any more than one still possesses the beloved object while he embraces only his corpse. Where the Lord is not present with His gifts and blessings, there Canaan cannot be. It was just as the land of the presence of the Lord, that it was so dear and valuable to all believers.—From what has now been said, it appears that, as regards the historical reference, we need not limit ourselves to the times of the Old Covenant, nor dream of a return of Israel to Canaan to take place at some future time. Luther's explanation, "They will go up from this place of pilgrimage to the heavenly father-land," is quite correct, —not indeed according to the letter, but according to the spirit. It is not the form, but the essence of the divine inheritance, which the prophet has in view. The form is a different one under the New Covenant, where the whole earth has become a Canaan; but the essence remains. To cling here to the form, would be just as absurd as if one, who, for Christ's sake, has forsaken all, were to upbraid Him because he had not received again, according to the letter of His promise, precisely an hundred-fold, lands, brothers, sisters, mothers, etc., Mark x. 30. The words of God, which are spirit and life, must be understood with spirit and life.—Suppose that the children of Israel were, at some future time, to return to Canaan, this would have nothing to do with our prophecy. In a religious point of view, it would be a matter of no consequence, and could not serve to prove the covenant-faithfulness of God. Under the New Covenant it finds its fulfilment, that " Canaan must, even in the North, bloom joyfully around the beloved." The three stations

—Egypt, the wilderness, and Canaan—will continue to exist for ever; but we go from the one to the other only with the feet of the spirit, and not, as in the Old Covenant, with the feet of the body at the same time. The grossly literal explanation which knows not to separate the thought from its drapery, the essential from the accidental, agrees, just in the main point, with the allegorical explanation—viz., in interpolating, instead of interpreting.—The fulfilment of the prophecy before us is, therefore, a continuous and progressive one, which will not cease until God's whole plan of salvation be consummated. It began at Babylon, and was carried forward at the appearance of Christ, whom many out of Judah and Israel set over themselves as their head, to be their common leader to Canaan. It is, even now, realized every day before our eyes in every Israelite who follows their example. It will, at some future time, find its final fulfilment in the last and greatest manifestation of God's covenant-faithfulness towards Israel, which, happily, is as strongly guaranteed by the New as it is by the Old Testament.—The last words of the verse have been already explained, substantially, in ver. 1. The name " Jezreel" is here used with a reference to its appellative signification. Israel appears here (compare ver. 25 [23], which serves as a commentary and as a refutation of differing interpretations) as a seed which is sown by God in fruitful land, and which shall produce a rich harvest. The figure appears, with a somewhat different turn, in Jer. xxxi. 27; Ezek. xxxvi. 9, where the house of Israel, and the house of Judah, appear as the soil in which the seed is sown by God. Analogous is also Ps. lxxii. 16: "They of the city shall flourish up like the grass of the earth."—The כִּי is explained by the circumstance that the sowing, which can take place only in the land of the Lord (compare ver. 25), supposes the going up from the land of the captivity. But if the day of sowing be great, .if it be regarded by God as high and important, then the going up, which is the condition of sowing, must necessarily take place.

Ver. 3. " *Say ye unto your brethren, My people (Ammi); and to your sisters, Who has obtained mercy (Ruhamah).*"

The words, "My people," are a concise expression for: "You whom the Lord has called, My people." The mention of the brothers and sisters is explained by the reference to the male and female members of the prophet's family. The phrase, "Say ye," is in substance equivalent to: "Then will ye be able to say." The prophet sees before him the people of the Lord who have experienced mercy; and calls upon the members to salute one another joyfully with the new name given to them by God. Such is the simple meaning of the verse, which has been darkened by a multitude of forced interpretations.

CHAP. II. 4–25 (2–23).

"The significant couple"—*Rückert* remarks—"disappears in the thing signified by it; Israel itself appears as the wife of whoredoms." This is the only essential difference between this and the preceding sections; and it is the less marked, because even there, in the last part of it, the symbolical action passed over into a mere figure. With this exception, this section also contains the alternation of punishment and threatening, and of promise,—the latter beginning with ver. 16 (14). The features of the image, which were less attended to in the preceding portion, but are here more carefully portrayed, are the rejection of the unfaithful wife, and her gradual restoration. *Calvin* says: "After God has laid open their sins before men, He adds some consolation, and tempers the severity, lest they should despair. But then He returns again to threatenings, and He must do so necessarily; for though men may have been terrified by the fear of punishment, yet they do not recover, and become wise for ever." "By a new impetus as it were," says *Manger*, "he suddenly returns to expand the same argument, and sets out again from things more sad."

Ver. 4. "*Contend with your mother, contend; for she is not my wife, and I am not her husband: and let her put away her whoredoms from her face, and her adultery from her breasts.*"

Calvin is of opinion that a contrast is here intended, inasmuch as the Israelites were striving with God, and attributed to Him the cause of their misfortune: "Do not contend with Me, but rather with your mother, who, by her adultery, has brought down *righteous* punishment upon herself and upon you." But this interpretation is inadmissible; because it proceeds from the unfounded supposition that the divorce is to be considered as having already taken place outwardly, whilst the contending here clearly appears as one by which divorce may yet be averted. The words, "Contend with your mother," rather mean, on the contrary, that it is high time to call her to account, if they would not go to destruction along with her. From this, however, we are not entitled to infer that the moral condition of the children was better than that of the mother. Without any regard to their moral condition, the prophet only wishes to say that their interest required them to do this. If it were not his intention just to carry out the image of adultery, he might as well have called upon the mother to contend against the children, as it is said in Is. li. 1: "Behold, for your iniquities you have been sold, and for your transgression your mother has been put away." In point of fact, the mother has no standing-place apart from the children. *Vitringa* says: "One and the same people is called 'mother' when viewed in their collective character; and 'children' when viewed in the individuals who are born of that people. For a people is born from the people. For the whole people is considered according to that which is radical in it, which constitutes its nature and substance,—and, in this respect, it is called the 'mother of its citizens.'" But we are as little entitled to infer from this exhortation, that a reform, and an averting of the threatened judgments, may still be hoped for. This is opposed by what follows, where the wife appears as incorrigible, and her rejection as unavoidable. The fundamental thought is, on the contrary, only this:—that a reform is necessary if the threatened judgments are to be averted. That this necessity, however, would not become a reality, the prophet foresaw; and for this reason he speaks unconditionally in the sequel. But from this again it must not be inferred that, in that case, his exhortations and threatenings would be altogether in vain. Though no reform was to be expected from the people, single individuals might, nevertheless, be converted. At the same time, it was of great importance for the future, that before the calamity should break in, a right view of it should be opened up to the whole people. It is of great importance, that if any one be smitten, he should know for what reason. The instructions in the doctrines of Christianity, which a criminal has received in childhood, may often seem for a long series of years to have been altogether in vain; but afterwards, notwithstanding, when punishment has softened his heart, they bring forth their fruits.—In the words, "For she is not my wife, and I am not her husband," the ground of the exhortation is stated.   Even for this reason, the words cannot be referred to the *external* dissolution of the marriage, to the punishment of the wife; they signify rather the *moral* dissolution of the marriage—the guilt of the wife— and are equivalent to: "our marriage is dissolved *de facto.*" But in the case of the spiritual marriage, this dissolution *de facto* is always, sooner or later, according to the greater or smaller measure of God's forbearance, followed by the dissolution *de jure;* or, to speak without figure, wherever there is sin, punishment will always follow.   God bears with much weakness on the part of His people; but wherever, through this weakness, the relation to Him is essentially dissolved, He there annuls the relation altogether.   The παρεκτὸς λόγου πορνείας applies to spiritual marriages also.   The surrender of the main faculties and powers of our nature to something which is not God, stands on a par with carnal adultery.   Thus, then, the connection betwixt "contend" and "for" clearly appears. —Many interpreters, viewing the clause beginning with כי as parenthetical, would connect the last words of the verse with ריבו: "Contend with your mother that she may put away." But the words are rather to be considered as parallel with the first member; for "contend," etc., is equivalent to: "seek to bring your mother to a better way," or: "let your mother reform herself."   Her crime is designated first as whoredom, and then as adultery.   The relation in which the two stand to one another is plainly seen from chap. i. 2, where the notion of adultery is paraphrased by: "whoring away from the Lord." By "whoredom," the *genus*—carnal crimes in general—is designated; by "adultery," the *species*, or carnal crime by which the sacred rights of another person are, at the same time, violated.   The idea of whoredom, when transferred to a spiritual relation, implies chiefly the worldliness of those with whom God has not entered into any special relation; whilst the idea of adultery implies the worldliness of individuals and communities with whom God has entered into a special marriage, and whose apostasy is, for this reason, far more culpable.   Leaving out of view the more aggravating circumstance, the prophet first speaks of whoredom in the case of the children of Israel also.—The reason why the whoredom is here attributed to the face, and the adultery to the breasts, is well given by *Manger:* " We need not have any difficulty about seeing adultery attributed to the very face and breasts. There is a certain expressiveness in this conciseness which demonstrates, as it were before our eyes, that, in her whole deportment, the wife was given over to sensuality, and that her whole aim was only to excite to it, and to practise it. For the face is, with women, the sign of dissolute lasciviousness—as *Horace* expresses it in his Odes, I. 19 :—

> Urit grata protervitas
> Et vultus nimium lubricus aspici.

Ezekiel, too, in chap. xxiii. 3, speaks of 'the pressed breasts of Israel in Egypt.'" *Schmid* states as the reason why just the face and breasts are mentioned, " that Scripture, in order not to offend modesty, forbears to mention the worse and grosser deeds of fornication." But this is very little in harmony with the manner of Scripture—as may be seen from a comparison of Ezek. xvi. and xxiii., and of ver. 12 of the chapter before us. The reason rather is, that those parts are here specially to be mentioned, in which the whoring nature openly manifests itself ; so that the highest degree of impudence is thereby expressed. This then shows that there is no longer any halting, no longer any struggle of the better against the evil principle. Such an impudent whore he resembles who, without shame or concern, publicly exhibits his devotedness to the world. In this way has *Calvin* also explained it. "There is no doubt," says he, " that the prophet here expresses the impudence of the people, who in their hardihood, in their contempt of God, in their sinful superstitions, and in every kind of wickedness, had gone to such lengths, that they were like whores who do not conceal their turpitude, but publicly prostitute themselves, yea, try to exhibit the signs of their wickedness in their eyes, as well as in their whole body."

Ver. 5. "*Lest I strip her naked and expose her as in the day of her birth, and make her like the wilderness, and set her like dry land, and slay her by thirst.*"

In the marriage here spoken of, there was this peculiarity, that the husband first redeemed the wife from a condition the most wretched and miserable, before he united himself to her; and hence became her benefactor, before he became her husband. Compare iii. 2, where the Lord redeems the wife from slavery; and Ezek. xvi. 4, where the people appear as a child exposed, naked, and covered with filth, upon whom the Lord has mercy, —whom He provides with precious clothing and splendid ornaments, and destines for His spouse. During the marriage, the husband continues his liberality towards his wife. But now, the gifts, all of which had been bestowed upon her only with a view to the marriage which was to take place or was already entered upon, are to cease, because the marriage-tie has been broken by her guilt. She now returns to the condition of the deepest misery in which she had been sunk before her union to the Lord.—There is, in this, an allusion to that which, in the case of actual marriage, the husband was bound to give to his wife, viz., clothing and food; compare Is. iv. 1. If God withdraws His gifts, the consequences are infinitely awful, because, altogether unlike the natural husband, He has everything in His possession; if He does not give anything to drink, He then slays by thirst. If we keep in view this aggravation of the punishment, which has its ground only in the person of the husband, it is evident that we have here before us only a reference to the withdrawal of the marriage-gifts which is the consequence of the divorce, and not, as several interpreters—e.g., *Manger*—suppose, to a punishment of adultery, alleged by them to have been common at that time, "that the wife was stripped of her clothes, exposed to public mockery, and killed by hunger and thirst." The eternal and universal truth which, in the verse before us, is expressed with a special reference to Israel, is, that all the gifts of God are bestowed upon individuals, as well as upon whole nations, either in order to lead them to the communion of life with Him, or because this communion already exists; just as our Saviour says that to him who has successfully sought for the kingdom of heaven, all other things shall be added, without any labour on his part. If we overlook the truth that the gifts of God have this object—if they be not received and enjoyed as the gifts of God—if the spiritual marriage be refused, or if, having been already entered into, it be broken,—sooner or later the gifts will be withdrawn.—The word "naked" properly includes a whole clause: "I shall strip

her so that she shall become naked." The verb הִצִּיג, "to place,"
"to set," has the secondary signification of public exhibition;
compare Job xvii. 6. The literal translation ought to be, "I
shall expose her as *the day* of her birth;" and we must assume
that there is here the occurrence of one of those numerous cases,
in which the comparison is merely alluded to, without being carried out; compare, *e.g.*, "Like the day of Midian," Is. ix. 3;
"Their heart rejoiceth like wine," Zech. x. 7. The *tertium
comparationis* between the day of her birth and her future condition is only the entire nakedness; compare Job i. 21. Any
allusion to the filth, etc., is less obvious; the prophet would
have been required to give an intimation of this in some manner.
The two parts of the first hemistich of the verse correspond
with each other; just as do the three parts of the second hemistich. In the first, the withdrawal of clothing, and nakedness;
in the second, the withdrawal of food, and hunger and thirst.
It is questionable whether the mention of the birth-day here
belongs merely to the imagery, is a mere designation of entire
nakedness, because man is never more naked than when he
comes into the world; or whether it is to be understood as belonging to the thing itself, and refers to the condition of the
people in Egypt to which they are now to be reduced. In
favour of the latter explanation, there is not only the comparison of the parallel passage in Ezekiel, but, still more, the purely
matter-of-fact character of the entire description. Israel is, in
this section, not *compared* to a wife, so that *figure* and *thing*
would be co-ordinate, but appears as the wife herself. Ver. 17
also is in favour of this interpretation.—The words, "I make
her like the wilderness," which, by *Hitzig* and others, are erroneously referred to the country instead of the people, are perti-
nently explained by *Manger:* "The prophet depicts a horrible
and desperate condition, where everything necessary for sustaining life is awanting,—where she has to endure a thirst
peculiar to an altogether uncultivated and sunburnt wilderness."
The comparison appears so much the more suitable, when we
remark that wilderness and desert are here personified, and appear as hungry and thirsty. This, however, was too poetical
for several prosaic interpreters. Hence they would in both instances supply a כ after the כ, "as in the wilderness"="I
place her in the condition in which she was formerly, in the

wilderness." But it is self-evident that such a supplying of the ב is inadmissible. If we were to receive this interpretation, we must rather assume that here also there is merely a comparison intimated: "as the wilderness,"—for, "as she was in the wilderness." But even then, the interpretation cannot, for another reason, be admitted. The impending condition of the people did not, in the least, correspond to what it was in the wilderness. The natural condition of the wilderness was not then seen in all its reality; the people of the Lord received bread from heaven, and water from the rock. It has its antitype rather in such a condition as that which is to follow upon the punishment, ver. 16. The Article indicates that, by "the wilderness," we are here to understand, specially, the Desert of Arabia,—the desert κατ᾽ ἐξοχήν. But that this comes into consideration only as one especially desolate, and not as the former abode of the Israelites, appears from the following—"in dry land," without the Article, and not, as otherwise we would expect, "in *the* dry land." *Finally,*—We have a parallel to this in the threatening in Deut. xxviii. 48: "And thou servest thine enemy whom the Lord thy God will send upon thee, in hunger, and in thirst, and in nakedness, and in great want."

Ver. 6. "*And I will not have mercy upon her children, for they are children of whoredoms.*"

It appears from ver. 7, that the children are to be repudiated on account of their origin (compare the remarks on i. 2), and not on account of their morals. *Michaelis* says, "They have the same disposition, and follow the same course as their adulterous mother; for a viper bringeth forth a viper, and a bad raven lays a bad egg." The cause of their rejection is, that they are children of whoredoms. That they are such, is proved by the circumstance that their mother is whoring. Compare also v. 7: "They have become faithless to the Lord, for they have born strange children." In point of fact, however, a sinful origin and a sinful nature are identical.

Ver. 7. "*For their mother has been whoring, she who bore them has been put to shame; for she has said, I will go after my lovers, the givers of my bread and my water, of my wool and my flax, of my oil and my drink.*"

הובישה is explained in a two-fold way. The common explanation is: "She has practised what is disgraceful, she has acted shamefully." Others, on the contrary, explain: "She has been put to shame, she has been disgraced." In this latter way it is explained by *Manger*, who remarks, "that this word is stronger than זנה; that it implies not only an accusation of vile whoredom, but also that she has been convicted of this crime, and as it were apprehended *in flagranti;* so that, even if she were yet impudent enough, she could no longer deny it, but must sink down in confusion and perplexity." This latter exposition is, without doubt, the preferable one; for, 1. הוביש never occurs in the first-mentioned signification. *Winer* contents himself with quoting the passage before us. *Gesenius* refers, moreover, to Prov. x. 5. But the בן מביש of that passage is evidently a son bringing disgrace upon his parents,—in xxix. 15 אמו is added,— or making them ashamed, disappointing their hopes. On the other hand, the signification, "to be put to shame," "to be convicted of a disgraceful deed," is quite an established one. Compare, *e.g.,* Jer. ii. 26: "As the disgrace of a thief when he is found, thus the whole house of Israel is *put to shame;*" Jer. vi. 15: "They are put to shame, for they have committed abomination; they shamed not themselves, they felt no shame;" compare also Jer. viii. 9. In all these passages, הוביש signifies the shame forced upon those who have no sense of shame.—2. The signification, "to act disgracefully," does not admit of a regular grammatical derivation. *Gesenius* refers to analogies such as הרע, היטיב; but these would be admissible only if the *Kal* בוש signified, "to be infamous," while it means only "to be ashamed." Being derived from בוש, the verb can mean only "to put to shame," in which signification it occurs, *e.g.,* in 2 Sam. xix. 6. But, on the other hand, the signification, "to be put to shame," can be well defended. As the *Hiphil* cannot have an intransitive signification, it must, with this signification, be considered as derived from בשת, "*pudorem, ignominiam contraxit,*"—a view which is favoured by Jer. ii. 26.—The "lovers" are the idols; compare the remarks on Zech. xiii. 6. The כי confirms the statement, that she who bare them has been whoring, and has been put to shame by a further exposure of the crime and its origin. The same delusion which appears here as the cause of the spiritual adultery, is stated as such also in Jer. xlix. 17, 18. Jeremiah there warns the people not to contract sin by idolatry, because that was the cause of all their present misery, and would bring upon them greater misery still. But they answer him, that they would continue to offer incense and drink-offerings to the Queen of heaven, as they and their fathers had formerly done in their native land ; for, "since we left off to do so, we have wanted all things, and were consumed by hunger and sword." The antithesis in Jer. ii. 13 of the fountain of living waters, and the broken cisterns that hold no water, has reference likewise to this delusion. But that which is the *cause* of the gross whoredom, is the *consequence* of the refined one. The inward apostasy must already have taken place, when one speaks as the wife does in the verse before us. As long as man continues faithfully with God in communion of life, he perceives, by the eye of faith, the hand in the clouds from which he receives everything, which guides him, and upon which everything—even that which is apparently the most independent and powerful—depends. As soon as, through unbelief, he has lost this communion with God, and heaven is shut against him, he allows his eye to wander over every visible object, looks out for everything in the world which appears to manifest independence and superior power, makes this an object to which he shows his love, soliciting its favour, and making it his god. In thus looking around, the Israelites would, necessarily and chiefly, have their eyes attracted by the idols. For they saw the neighbouring nations wealthy and powerful ; and these nations themselves derived their power and wealth from the idols. To these also the Israelites now ascribed the gifts which they had hitherto received; and this so much the rather, because it was easier to satisfy the demands of these idols, than those of the true God, who requires just that which it is most difficult to give—the heart, and nothing else. And, being determined not to give it to Him, they felt deeply that they could expect no good from Him. Whatever good He had still left to them, they could consider as only a gift of unmerited mercy, and destined to lead them to repentance,—a consideration which makes a natural man recoil and draw back, inasmuch as, in his relation to God, he always thinks only of merit. That which we thus perceive in them is even now repeated daily. We need only put in the place of idols, the abstract God of the Rationalists and Deists, man's own power, or the power of other men, and many other things besides, and it will at once be seen that the words, "I will go after my lovers that give me my bread," etc., are, up to the present moment, the watch-word of the world.—"Bread and water" signify the necessaries of life; "oil and (strong) drink," those things which serve rather for luxuries.—"My bread," etc., is an expression of affection, indicating that she regards these as most necessary, and to be sought after, in preference to everything else.

Ver. 8. " *Therefore, behold, I hedge up thy way with thorns, and I wall her wall, and her paths she shall not find.*"

The apostate woman is first addressed: " *thy* way;" but the discourse then passes to the third person,—"her wall, her paths." We must not conceive of this, as if the wife were to be shut up in a two-fold way:—first, by a hedge of thorns, and then, by a wall; but the same thing is expressed here by a double figure, as is also done in Is. v. 5. First, the shutting up is alone spoken of; it is afterwards brought into connection with the effects to be thereby produced; and because she is enclosed by a wall, she cannot find her path. " I wall her wall " is tantamount to, " I make a wall for her." The words of the husband in the verse under consideration form an evident contrast to those of the wife in the preceding verse. *Schmid* says: " The punishment is by the law of retaliation. She had said, ' I will go to my lovers;' but God threatens, on the contrary, that He will obstruct the way so that she cannot go. The הנני points to the unexpectedness of the result. The wife imagined that she would be able to carry out her purpose with great safety and ease; it does not even occur to her to think of her husband, who had hitherto allowed her, from weakness, as she imagines, to go on her way undisturbed; but she sees herself *at once* firmly enclosed by a wall.—There can be no doubt, that, by the hedging and walling about, severe sufferings are intended, by which the people are encompassed, straitened, and hindered in every free movement. For sufferings regularly appear as the specific against Israel's apostasy from their God. Compare, *e.g.*, Deut. iv. 30: " In the tribulation to thee, and when all these things come upon thee, thou returnest in the end of the days to the Lord thy God, and hearest His voice;" Hosea v. 15: " I will go and return to My place till they become guilty; in the affliction to them, they will seek Me." The figure of enclosing has elsewhere also, undeniably, the meaning of inflicting sufferings. Thus in Job iii. 23: " To the man whose way is hid, and whom God has hedged in round about;" xix. 8: "He hath fenced up my way and I cannot pass, and upon my paths He sets darkness;" Lam. iii. 7: "He hath hedged me about, and I cannot get out; He hath made my chain heavy;" compare also ibid. ver. 9; Ps. lxxxviii. 9.—The object of the walling about is to cut her off from the lovers; the infliction of heavy sufferings is to put an end to idolatrous tendencies.—The words, "thy way," clearly refer to, "I will go after my lovers," in ver. 7; and by "her paths which she cannot find," her whole previous conduct in general is indeed to be understood, but chiefly, from the connection with ver. 7, her former intercourse with idols. But here the question arises:—How far is the remedy suited for the attainment of this end? We can by no means think of an external obstacle. Outwardly, there was, during the exile, and in the midst of idolatrous nations, a stronger temptation to idolatry than they had in their native land. Hence, we can think of an internal obstacle only; and then again we can think only of the absolute incapacity of the idols to grant to the people consolation and relief in their sufferings. If this incapacity has been first ascertained by experience, we begin to lose our confidence in them, and seek help where alone it can be found. As early as in Deut. xxxii. we are told how misery proves the nothingness of false gods, and shows that the Lord alone is God; compare especially ver. 36 sqq. Jeremiah says in ii. 28, "And where are thy gods that thou hast made thee? Let them arise and help thee in the time of trouble." That which the gods cannot turn away, they cannot have sent; and if the suffering be sent by the Lord, it is natural that help should be sought from Him also. Compare vi. 1: "Come and let us return unto the Lord, for He hath torn and He healeth us, He smiteth and He bindeth us up."

Ver. 9. "*And she runs after her lovers and shall not overtake, and she seeks them and shall not find; then she saith: I will go and return to my first husband, for it was better with me then than now.*"

רדף has, in *Piel*, not a transitive, but an intensive meaning. *Calvin* remarks: "By the verb, insane fervour is indicated, as indeed we see that idolaters are like madmen; it shows that such is the perverseness of their hearts, that they will not at once return to a sound mind." The distress at first only increases the zeal in idolatry; compare Jer. xliv. 17. Every effort is made to move the idols to help. But if help be, not-withstanding, refused—and how could it be otherwise, since they from whom it is sought are *Elilim, i.e.*, nothings?—they by and by begin to bethink themselves, and to recover their senses. They discover the nothingness of their idols, and return to the true God. This apostasy and return are in a touching manner described by our prophet in xiv. 2–4 also. The words, " I will go and return to my first husband," form a beautiful con-trast to, " I will go after my lovers," in ver. 7. This statement of the result shows that God's mercy is then greatest and most effective, just when it seems to have disappeared altogether, and when His punitive justice seems alone to be in active exercise. For the latter is by no means to be excluded, inasmuch as there is no suffering which does not, at the same time, proceed from it, and no punishment which is inflicted solely on account of the reformation.

Ver. 10. *" And she, she does not know that I gave her the corn, and the must, and the oil, and silver I multiplied unto her, and gold which upon Baal they spent."*

The prophet, starting anew, here returns to a description of her guilt and punishment; and it is only from ver. 16 that he expands what, in ver. 9, he had intimated concerning her con-version, and her obtaining mercy. The words, " She saith," in that verse, belong thus to a period more remote than the words, " She does not know," in the verse before us. The things which are here enumerated were, in the case of Israel, in a peculiar sense, the gift of God. He bestowed them upon the Congre-gation as her Covenant-God, as her husband. They are thus announced as early as in the Pentateuch; compare, *e.g.*, Deut. vii. 13: " And He loveth thee, and blesseth thee, and multi-plieth thee, and blesseth the fruit of thy womb, and the fruit of thy land, thy corn, thy must, and thy oil;" xi. 14: " And I give the rain of your land in due season, and thou gatherest in thy corn, thy must, and thy oil." It is certainly not accidental that Hosea enumerates the three objects, just in the same order in which they occur in these two passages. By the celebration of the feasts, and by the offering of the first-fruits, the Israelites were to give expression to the acknowledgment,

that they derived these gifts of God from His special providence—from the covenant relation. The relative clause עשׂו
לבעל is subjoined, as is frequently the case, without a sign of its
relation, and without a *pron. suff.*, which is manifest from the
preceding substantive. Several interpreters, from the Chaldee
Paraphrast down to *Ewald*, give the explanation, "which they
have made for a Baal," *i.e.*, from which they have made images
of Baal, and appeal to viii. 4: "Their silver and their gold
they have made into idols for themselves." But we must object
to this opinion on the following grounds. 1. עשׂה, with ל following, is a religious *terminus technicus*, with the sense of, "to make
to any one," "to appropriate," "to dedicate," as appears from
its frequent repetition in Exod. x. 25 sqq., and also from the
fact that ליהוה is frequently omitted. The phrase is used with
a reference to idolatry in 2 Kings xvii. 32; 2 Chron. xxiv. 7.—
2. It cannot be proved that הבעל, in the singular and with the
Article, could be used for "statues of Baal."—3. By this explanation we lose the striking contrast between that which the
Israelites *were doing*, and that which they *were to do*. That
which the Lord gave to them, they consecrated to Baal, instead
of to Him, to whom alone these embodied thanks were due.
And, not satisfied in withdrawing from the true God the honour
and thanks which were due to Him, they transferred them to
His enemy and worthless rival,—a proceeding which bears witness to the deep corruption of human nature, and which, up to
the present day, is continually repeated, and must be so, because
the corruption remains the same. It is substantially the same
thing that the Israelites dedicated their gold to Baal, and that
our great poets consecrate to the world and its prince the rich
intellectual gifts which they have received from God. The
words, "and she knew not," in both cases show that they are
equally guilty and equally culpable. He who bestows the gifts
has not concealed Himself; but they on whom they are bestowed
have shut their eyes, that they may not see Him to whom they
are unwilling to render thanks. They would fain wish that
their liberal benefactor were utterly annihilated, in order that
they may not be disturbed in the enjoyment of His gifts by a
disagreeable thought of Him,—in order that they may freely use
and dispose of them, without being obliged to fear their loss,—
and in order that they may be able to devote them, without any

obstruction, to a god who is like themselves, who is only their own self viewed objectively (*ihr objectivirtes Ich*). Parallel to the passage before us, and, it may be, formed after it, is Ezek. xvi. 17, 18: "And thou didst take thy ornament of My gold and of My silver which I gave thee, and madest to thyself images of men, and didst commit whoredom with them. And thou tookest thy broidered garments, and coveredst them, and My fat and Mine increase thou gavest before them." *Hitzig* understands, by the Baal here, the golden calf, appealing to the fact that the real worship of Baal had been abolished by Jehu. But no proof at all can be adduced for the assertion that the name of Baal had been transferred to the golden calf. It is self-evident, and is confirmed by 2 Kings xiii. 6, xvii. 16 (in the latter of which passages the worship of Baal appears as a continuous sin in the kingdom of the ten tribes), that the destruction of the heathenish worship by Jehu was not absolute. But so much is certain, that by the mention of Baal, the sin is here designated only with reference to its highest point, and that, in substance, the service of the calves is here included. In 1 Kings xiv. 9, it is shown that the sin of worshipping Jehovah under the image of calves is on a par with real idolatry; and in 2 Chron. xi. 15, the calves are put on a footing with the goat-deities of Egypt.

Ver. 11. "*Therefore I return, and take My corn in its time, and My must in its season, and take away My wool and My flax to cover her nakedness.*"

לכן stands here with great emphasis. It points to the eternal law of God's government of the world, according to which He is sanctified *upon* them, *in* whom He has not been sanctified; and this so much the more, the closer was His relation to them, and the greater were His gifts. From him who is not thereby moved, they will be taken away; and nothing but his natural poverty and nakedness is left to him who was formerly so richly endowed. And well is it with him if they be taken from him at a time when he is able still to recognise the giver in Him who taketh away, and may yet deeply repent of his unthankfulness, and return to Him, as is said of Israel in iii. 5. If such be done, it is seen that the ungrateful one has not yet become an object of divine justice alone, but that divine mercy is still in store for him. The longer God allows His

gifts to remain with the ungrateful, the darker are their pros-
pects for the future. That which He gave in mercy, He, in
such a case, allows to remain only in anger. The words אשיב
ולקחתי are commonly explained by expositors, "I shall take
again," inasmuch as two verbs are frequently found together
which, in their connection, are independent of each other—the
one indicating only an accessory idea of the action. But this
mode of expression occurs in general far more rarely than is
commonly assumed; and here the explanation, "I will return
and take," is to be preferred without any hesitation. Scripture
says, that God appears even when He manifests Himself only
in the effects of His omnipotence, justice, and love,—a mode of
expression which is explained by that large measure of faith
which perceives, behind the visible effect, the invisible Author
of it; compare, *e.g.*, Gen. xviii. 10, where the Lord says to
Abraham, that He would return to him at the same period in
the following year; whereas He did not return in a visible
form, as then, but only in the fulfilment of His promise. Thus
God had formerly appeared to Israel as the Giver; and now
that they did not acknowledge Him as such, He returns as the
God that takes away. "She did not know that I gave, therefore I shall return and take." That the words were to be thus
understood, the prophet, as it appears, intended to indicate by
the change of the tenses. It is quite natural that a verb, used
as an adverb, should be as closely as possible connected with
that verb which conveys the principal idea; and it would
scarcely be possible to find a single instance—at all events
there are not many instances—where, in such a case, a difference
of the tense takes place. Altogether analogous is Jer. xii. 15 :
"And it shall come to pass after I have destroyed them, אשוב
ורחמתים, I will return and have compassion on them;" where the
sense would be very much weakened if we were to translate, "I
shall *again* have compassion." There appears to be the same
design in the change of the tenses in iii. 5 also. What is there
said of Israel forms a remarkable parallel to what is here said
of God. God had formerly come, giving—Israel, taking; God
now returns, taking—Israel giving,—a relation which opens up
an insight into the whole economy of the sufferings.—"*My* corn,"
etc., forms a contrast to ver. 7, where Israel had spoken of all
these things as *theirs*. Whatever God gives, always remains

His own, because He gives only as a loan, and on certain conditions. If any one should consider himself as the absolute master of it, He makes him feel his error by taking it away.—"In its time" and "in its season" are added, because it was *then*, ordinarily, that God had appeared as *giving*, and because *then* they therefore confidently expected His gifts. But now He appears at once as *taking*, because they were already so sure of the expected gifts that they held them, as it were, already in their hands; just as if, at Christmas—which corresponds to the harvest, the ordinary season of God's granting gifts—parents should withdraw from their children the accustomed presents, and put a rod in their place. It is better thus to understand the expression, "in its time, etc.," than to follow *Jerome*, who remarks, that " it is a severe punishment, if at the time of harvest the hoped-for fruits are taken away, and wrested from our hands;" for if, even at the time of the harvest, there be a want of all things, how will it be during the remaining time of the year.—The words, " to cover, etc.," are very concise, but without any grammatical ellipsis, instead of, " which hitherto served to cover her nakedness." As to the sense, the ‧LXX. are correct in translating, τοῦ μὴ καλύπτειν τὴν ἀσχημοσύνην αὐτῆς. For that which had *hitherto* been, is mentioned by the prophet only for the purpose of drawing attention to what *in future* will *not* be.—It is the Lord who must cover the nakedness; and this leads us back to the natural poverty of man, who has not, in the whole world, a single patch or shred—not even so much as to cover his shame, which is here specially to be understood by nakedness. The same thought which is so well calculated to humble pride—what have we that we have not received, and that the Giver might not at any moment take back?—occurs also in Ezek. xvi. 8 : " I spread out My wings over thee, and covered thy nakedness."

Ver. 12. " *And now I will uncover her shame before the eyes of her lovers, and none shall deliver her out of My hands.*"

The ἄπαξ λεγόμενον נבלות is best explained by " decay," " *corpus multa stupra passum.*" Being a femin. of a Segholate-form, its signification can be derived only from the *Kal;* but נבל always signifies " to be faded, weak, feeble ;" in *Piel* it means, " to make weak," " to declare as weak," " to disgrace," " to despise." As the signification of *Kal* does not imply the idea of ignominy, we cannot explain the noun, as several interpreters do, by "*turpitudo, ignominia.*" The ἀκαθαρσία of the LXX. is probably a free translation of the word according to our view.—לְעֵינֵי is constantly used for "*coram, inspectante aliquo,*" properly, "belonging to the eyes of some one," and cannot therefore be explained here by "to the eyes," as if she were uncovered to, or for, the lovers alone; these, on the contrary, are mentioned only as fellow-witnesses. But in what respect do they come into consideration here? Several interpreters are of opinion that their powerlessness, and the folly of trusting in them, are intended to be here pointed out. Thus *Calvin* says: "The prophet alludes to the impudent women who are wont, even by terror, to prevent their husbands from using their rights. He says, therefore, this shall not prevent me from chastising thee as thou deservest." Thus also *Stuck,* who subjoins to the phrase "her lovers:" "who, if they had the strength, might be a help to her." But it is altogether erroneous thus to understand the verse. The words, "Before the eyes of the lovers," rather mean, that the Lord would make her an object of disgust and horror even to those who formerly sought after her. The idea is this: Whosoever forsakes God on account of the world, shall, by God, be put to shame, even in the eyes of the world itself, and all the more, the more nearly he formerly stood to Him. This idea is here expressed in a manner suited to the figurative representation which pervades the whole section. *Jerome* says: "All this is brought forward under the figure of the adulterous woman, who, after she has been taken in the very act, is exposed and disgraced before the eyes of all." The uncovering, as guilt, is followed by the uncovering, as punishment; and every one (and her lovers first) turns away with horror from the disgusting spectacle. They now at once see her who, hitherto, had made a show with the apparel and goods of her lawful husband, in her true shape as a withered monster. That this explanation is alone the correct one, appears from the parallel passages: compare, *e.g.,* Nah. iii. 5: "Behold, I come upon thee, saith the Lord of hosts, and uncover thy skirts upon thy face, and make the heathen to see thy nakedness, and kingdoms thy shame. And it cometh to pass, all that see thee shall flee from thee;" Lam. i. 8: "Jerusalem hath committed sin, therefore she has become a reproach; all that honoured her, despise her, for they have seen her nakedness; she sigheth and turneth away;" Jer. xiii. 26: "And I also (as thou hast formerly uncovered) uncover thy skirts over thy face, and thy shame shall be seen;" Ezek. xvi. 37, 41; Is. xlvii. 3.—But now, it might seem that, according to this explanation, not the idols, but only the nations serving them, can be understood by the lovers. But this is only in appearance. In order to make the scene more lively, the prophet ascribes to the אלילים, to them who are nothing, life and feeling. If they had these, they would act just as it is here described, and as their worshippers really acted afterwards.—The second member of the verse, "And none shall deliver," etc., is in so far parallel to the first, as both describe the dreadfulness of the divine judgment. Parallel is v. 14: "For I will be as one who roars to Ephraim, and as a lion to the house of Judah: I will tear and go away, I will take away, and there is no deliverer."

Ver. 13. *"And I make to cease all her mirth, her feast, and her new-moon, and her sabbath, and all her festival time."*

The feasts served a double purpose. They were days of sacred dedication, and days of joy; compare Num. x. 10. Israel had violated them in the former character—just as at present the sacred days have, throughout the greater part of Christendom, the name only by way of *catachresis*—and, as a merited punishment, they were taken away by God in the latter character. They had deprived the festival days of their sacredness; by God, they are deprived of their joyfulness. The prophet, in order to intimate that he announces the cessation of the festival days as days of gladness, premises "all her mirth," to which all that follows stands in the relation of *species* to *genus*. משוש does not here denote "joyful time:" it might, indeed, according to its formation, have this signification; but it is never found with it. It here means "joy" itself. (Compare the parallel passages, Jer. vii. 34; Lam. i. 4: "The ways of Zion do mourn, because none come to the feasts;" Amos viii. 10: "And I will turn your feasts into mourning, and all your songs into lamentation;" Lam. v. 15; Is. xxiv. 8, 11.) The three following nouns were very correctly distinguished by *Jerome*. חג, "feast," is the designation of the three annual principal festivals. In addition to these, there was in every month the feast of the new-moon; and in every week, the Sabbath. This connection is a standing one, which, even in the New Testament (compare Col. ii. 16), still reverts. The words, " all her festival time," comprehend the single *species* in the designation of the *genus*. That מוֹעֵד properly signifies " appointed time," then, more specially, " festival time," " feast," appears from Lev. xxiii. 4: " These are the מוֹעֲדֵי of the Lord, the sacred assemblies which you shall call בְּמוֹעֲדָם, in their appointed time." That the *feasts* are not a single species co-ordinate with the new-moons and Sabbaths, but the genus, appears from the fact that in Lev. xxiii. the Sabbath opens the series of the מוֹעֲדִים. In a wider sense, the new-moons also belonged to the מוֹעֲדִים, although they are not enumerated among them in Lev. xxiii. on account of their subordinate character. In Num. x. 10, Is. i. 14, Ezra iii. 5, the new-moons are mentioned along with the מוֹעֲדִים, only as the species by the side of the genus. But we are at liberty to think only of the feasts appointed by God; for, otherwise, there would be no room for the application of the *lex talionis:*—God takes from the Israelites only what they had taken from Him. The days of the Baalim are afterwards specially mentioned in ver. 15. The days of God are taken from them; for the days of the Baalim they are punished. This much, however, appears from the passage before us—and it is placed beyond any doubt by several other passages in Hosea as well as in Amos—that, outwardly, the worship, as regulated by the prescriptions of the Pentateuch, had all along continued. (For the arguments in proof of this assertion, the author's *Dissertations on the Genuineness of the Pentateuch*, vol. i., are to be compared.)

Ver. 14. " *And I make desolate her vine and fig-tree, whereof she said, They are the wages of whoredom to me, that my lovers have given me; and I make them a forest, and the beasts of the field eat them.*"

The vine and fig-tree, as the two noblest productions of Palestine—*Ispahan*, in the " *Excerpta ex vita Saladini*," p. 10, calls them " *ambos Francorum oculos* "—are here also connected with each other, as is commonly done in threatenings and promises, as the representatives of the rich gifts of God, wherewith He has blessed this country.—אֲשֶׁר is often placed before an entire sentence, to mark it out as being relative in general.

It is the looser, instead of the closer connection, = "of which."
—אתנה, "wages of prostitution," instead of which, in ix. 1 and
other passages, the form אתנן occurs, requires a renewed investigation. It is commonly derived from תנה, to which the signification " *largiter donavit, dona distribuit*," is ascribed. But opposed to this, there is the fact that the root תנה is, neither in
Hebrew, nor in any of the dialects, found with this signification. It has in Hebrew, Arabic, and Syriac, the signification
"to laud," "to praise," "to recount." But besides this תנה,
there occurs another תנה, not with the general signification "to
give," but in the special one, "to give a reward of whoredom;"
in which signification it cannot be a primitive word, but derived
from נתן אתנה = אתנה, in the passage under consideration, and in
Ezek. xvi. 34. The supposition of a primitive verb תנה, with the
signification "to give," is also opposed by the circumstance that
the noun which is said to be derived from it never occurs with
the general signification "gift," but always with the special
one, "reward of prostitution." אתנה is rather derived from the
first pers. Fut. Kal of the verb נתן, a "I will-give-thee," similar
to our "forget-me-not." The whore asks, in Gen. xxxviii. 16,
מה־תתן לי ("what wilt thou give me?"), and the whoremonger
answers, אתן־לך ("I will give thee"), ver. 18. From this there
originated, in the language of the brothel, a base word for such
base traffic. The sacred writers are not ashamed or afraid to
use it. They speak, throughout, of common things in a common
manner; for the vulgar word is the most suitable for the vulgar
thing. The morality of a people, or of an age, may be measured
by their speaking of vulgar things in a vulgar manner, or the
reverse. Wherever, in the language, the " *fille de joie*" or
" *Freudenmädchen*" has taken the place of the " whore," a similar change will, in reality, have taken place. Whatsoever the
people of Israel imagined that they received from their idols,
they certainly will not have designated as a "reward of prostitution," but as a "reward of true love." But the prophet at
once destroys all their pleasant imaginings by putting into their
mouths the corresponding expression,—an expression which
must certainly have sounded very rudely and vulgarly in their
tender ears; for the tongue and the ear become more tender,
in the same degree in which the heart becomes more vulgar.
She who imagined herself so tender and affectionate sees her-

self at once addressed as a common prostitute. The sweet proofs
of the heartfelt mutual love which her "lovers" gave her are
called "wages of whoredom." This is indeed a good corrective
for our language, for our whole view of things, for our own
hearts, which are so easily befooled. All love of the world, all
striving after its favour, every surrender to the spirit of the
age, is whoredom. A reward of whoredom, which must not be
brought into the temple of the Lord (for it is an *abomination*
unto the Lord thy God, Deut. xxiii. 19), is everything which
it offers and gives us in return. Like a reward of whoredom,
it will melt away; "of wages of whoredom she has collected,
and to wages of whoredom it shall return."—This derivation
from the Future has a great many analogies in its favour;
among others, the whole class of nouns with ת prefixed, in which
it is quite evident (although this has been so often overlooked) that they have arisen from the Fut. If the ת in these
forms originated from the *Hiphil*, how could it be explained
that they are more frequently connected with *Kal?* Even the
very common occurrence of the formation from the Future in
the case of proper names, induces us to expect, *a priori*, that it
will be more frequent in appellative names than is commonly
supposed. The occurrence of the phrase נתן אתנה, in the passages
quoted, is also in favour of this derivation. By it, the interchange of the two forms אתנה and אתנן is easily accounted for.
In the latter of these forms, the *Nun* which prevails in נתן, but
which had been dropped at the beginning, again reappears. A
variation in the form is, moreover, quite natural in a word which
originated from common life, which is entirely destitute of accurate analogies, and is therefore, as it were, without a model;
for the other nouns of this class are formed from the 3d pers.
of the *Fut.*—As regards, now, the substance :—Egotism, and
selfishness arising out of it, are the ground of all desire for the
love of that which is not God, especially in the case of those who
have already known the true God; for where this is not the
case, there may be, even in idolatry, a better element, which
seeks for a false gratification only because it does not know the
true one. From this, however, it appears, that the idolatry of
the Israelites (and this is only a species of the idolatry of all
those who have had opportunity to know the true God, and of
whom it is true that "the last is worse than the first") was

much lower than that of the Gentiles, whose poets and philoso-
phers, in part, zealously opposed the dispositions which are here
expressed; compare the passages in *Manger*. Egotism is here,
as it always is, folly; for it trusts in him who himself possesses
only borrowed and stolen goods, which the lawful owner may,
at every moment, take away from him. And in order that
such folly may appear as such, and very glaringly too, He appears here indeed, and takes what He had in reality given out
of His mercy, but what, according to their imagination, they
had received from the idols as a reward.—The suffix in שׂמתים
refers to the vine and fig-tree. The gardens of vines and fig-
trees carefully tended, hedged and enclosed round about, are to
be deprived of hedges, enclosures, and culture (καθυλομανεῖ γὰρ
μὴ κλαδευομένη ἡ ἄμπελος, *Clem. Alex. Paed.* i. 1, p. 115 Sylb.),
to be changed into a forest, and given over to the ravages of
wild beasts; for the words "and eat them" are by no means
to be refered to the fruits only. The same image of an entirely
devastated country is found in Is. vii. 23 ff.; Mic. iii. 12.

Ver. 15. *" And I visit upon her the days of the Baalim, to
whom she burnt incense, and put on her ring and her ornament,
and went after her lovers, and forgat Me, saith the Lord."*

The days of the Baalim are the days consecrated to their
worship, whether they were specially set apart for that purpose,
or whether they were originally devoted to the worship of the
Lord, whom they sought to confound with Baal. *Manger*, and
with him, most interpreters, are wrong in understanding by the
days of Baal, " all the time—certainly a very long one—in which
that forbidden worship flourished in this nation." Such would
be too indefinite an expression. When days of the Baalim are
spoken of, every one must think of days specially consecrated
to them,—their festivals. To this must be added, moreover, the
reference to the days of the Lord in ver. 13. In ver. 10, however, only one Baal, הבעל, is spoken of; here there are several.
This may be reconciled by the supposition that one and the same
Baal was worshipped according to his various modes of manifestation which were expressed by the epithets. But the plural
may also be explained—and this seems to be preferable—from
1 Kings xviii. 18, where Baalim is tantamount to Baal and his
associates (compare *Dissertations on the Gen. of the Pent.* vol. i.
p. 165); or from Lev. xvii. 7, where שׂעירים denotes the Goat-

idol, and others of his kind. The calves, the worship of which
was, at the time of Hosea, the prevailing one throughout the
kingdom of the ten tribes, are, in that case, comprehended in
the Baalim.—In the words, " And she put on her ring and
ornament," the figurative mode of expression has been overlooked by most interpreters. Misled by the תקטיר, which refers
directly to the spiritual adulteress, they imagined that the wear-
ing of nose-rings, and other ornaments, in honour of the idols,
was here spoken of. A more correct view was held by the
Chaldee who thus paraphrases : " The Congregation of Israel
was like a wife who deserted her husband, and adorned herself,
and ran after her lovers. Thus the Congregation of Israel was
pleased to worship idols, and to neglect My worship." A great
many false interpretations have had their origin in the circumstance, that they could not comprehend this liberty of the sacred
writers, who at one time speak plainly of the spiritual antitype,
and at another time transfer to it the peculiarities of the outward type. Had this been kept in view, it would not, e.g., have
been asserted, that David had, in Ps. xxiii. 5, relinquished the
image of the good shepherd, because he does not speak of a
trough which the actual good shepherd places before his sheep,
but of a table, placed before them by the spiritual good Shepherd.
In the passage under consideration, the תקטיר denotes an action
performed by her who is an adulteress in a spiritual point of
view. In the words, " She puts on," etc., her conduct is described under the figure of that of her outward type. The
actual correspondence is to be found in her efforts of making
herself agreeable,—in the employing of every means in order to
gain her spiritual lovers. The putting on of precious ornaments
comes into view, only in so far as it is one of these efforts, and,
indeed, a very subordinate one. The burning of incense, the
offering of sacrifices, etc., are, in this respect, of far greater
importance. The correctness of our interpretation is confirmed
by those parallel passages also, in which the same figurative
mode of expression occurs. Thus, e.g., Is. lvii. 9 : " Thou lookest
upon the king (the common translation, " thou goest to the king,"
cannot be defended on philological grounds) in oil (i.e., smelling
of ointment), and multipliest thy perfume,"—evidently a figurative designation, taken from a coquetish woman, to express the
employing of all means in order to gain favour ;—Is. iv. 30 :

" And thou desolate one, what wilt thou do ? For thou puttest
on thy purple, for thou adornest thyself with golden ornaments,
for thou rentest thine eyes with painting. In vain thou makest
thyself fair ; the lovers despise thee, they seek thy life." In
Ezek. xxii. 40–42, Jerusalem washes and paints herself, expecting her lovers, and decks herself with ornaments ; then she sits
down upon a stately couch ; a table is prepared before her, upon
which she places the incense of the Lord, and His oil. In this
last feature in Ezekiel, the type disappears behind the thing
typified, although not so completely as is the case in the passage
under consideration, in the words, " She burns incense."—From
what has been remarked, it appears that, in substance, Hos. iv.
13, " They sacrifice upon the tops of the mountains and burn
incense upon the hills," is entirely parallel. The two clauses,
" She went after her lovers," and " she forgat Me," both serve to
represent the crime in a more heinous light. Sin must certainly
have already poisoned the whole heart, if occasion for its exercise be spontaneously sought after. In reference to the latter,
Calvin remarks : " Just as when a wife has for a long time
lived with her husband, and has been kindly and liberally treated
by him, and then prostitutes herself to lovers, and does not entertain or retain any more love for him ; such a depravity is
nothing less than brutish."

Ver. 16. " *Therefore, behold, I allure her, and lead her into
the wilderness and speak to her heart.*"

The consolation and promise here begin with as great abruptness as in the first section. It is reported how the Lord gradually
leads back His unfaithful wife to reformation, and to reunion
with Him, the lawful husband. Great difficulty has been occasioned to interpreters by the לכן at the commencement. Very
easily, but at the same time very inconsiderately, the difficulty
is got over by those who give it the signification, " *utique, pro-
fecto;*" but this cannot be called interpreting. It must be, above
all, considered as settled and undoubted, that לכן can here have
that signification only which it always has ; and this all the more,
that in vers. 8 and 15 it occurred in the same signification.
This being taken for granted, the " therefore " might be referred
to the words of the wife in ver. 9, " I will go and return to my
first husband," and all which follows be considered as only a
kind of parenthesis. That the Lord begins again to show Himself

kind to His wife would then have its foundation in this :—that in her the first symptoms of a change of character manifested themselves. But this supposition is, after all, too forced. These words are too far away as that the prophet could have expected to be understood, in thus referring to them in a manner so indefinite. Several interpreters follow the explanation of *Tarnovius:* "Therefore, because she is not corrected by so great calamities, I will try the matter in another and more lenient way, by kindness." But the prophet could not expect that his hearers and readers should themselves supply the thought, which is not indicated by anything,—the thought, namely, "because that former method was of no avail, or rather, because it *alone* did not suffice ;" for it was by no means wholly in vain. When the Lord had hedged up her way with thorns, the woman speaks : " I will go and return ;" and where tribulations are of no avail—tribulations through which we must enter the kingdom of God—nothing else will. The severity of God must precede His love. And even though this train of thought should have occurred to them, they had no guarantee for its correctness. It is most natural to take the לכן as being simply co-ordinate with the לכן in vers. 8 and 11. The " *because*," which, in all the three places, corresponds to the *therefore*, is the wife's apostasy. Because she has forgotten God, He recalls Himself to her remembrance, first by the punishment, and then, after this has attained its end,—after the wife has spoken : "I will go and return,"—by proofs of His love. The leading to Egypt, into the wilderness, into the land of Canaan, rests on her unfaithfulness as its foundation. Without it, the Congregation would have remained in undisturbed possession of the promised land. By it, God is induced, both according to His justice and His mercy, to take it from her, to lead her back into the wilderness, and thence to the promised land.—פתה, in the *Piel*, is a *verbum amatorium;* it signifies " to allure by tender persuasion." There is to be a repetition of the proceeding of God, by which He formerly, in Egypt, allured the people to Himself, and induced them to follow Him into the wilderness, from the spiritual and bodily bondage in Egypt. After the sufferings, there always follows the alluring. God first takes away the objects of sinful love, and then He comes alluring and persuading us that we should choose, for the object of our love, Him who alone is worthy of, and entitled to, love. He is not satisfied with the strict prosecution of His right, but endeavours to make duty sweet to us, and, by His love, to bring it about that we perform it from love. After He has thus allured us, He leads us from Egypt into the wilderness.—The words, "I lead her into the wilderness," have been very much misunderstood by interpreters. According to *Manger*, the wilderness here is that through which the captives should pass on their return from Babylon. But one reason alone is sufficient to refute this opinion,—namely, that on account of the following verse, by *the* wilderness (the article must not be overlooked), only that wilderness can be understood which separates Egypt from Canaan. Others (*Ewald, Hitzig*), following *Grotius*, understand by the wilderness, the Assyrian captivity. *Kuehnöl* has acquired great merit for this exposition, by proving from a passage in *Herodotus*, that there were, at that time, uncultivated regions in Assyria! The same reason which militates against the former interpretation is opposed to this also. To this it may be further added, that, according to it, we can make nothing of the *alluring*. The Israelites were not *allured* into captivity by kindness and love; they were driven into it *against* their will, by God's wrath. *Moreover*, what according to this interpretation is to be done with the מִשָּׁם in ver. 17? Did, perhaps, the vineyards of Canaan begin immediately beyond Assyria, or does not even this rather lead us to the Arabian desert? It is certain, then, that this desert is the one to be thought of here, and, in addition, that it can only be as an image and type that the prophet here represents the leading through the wilderness, as a repetition of the former one in its individual form; inasmuch as it was, substantially, equal with it. For they who returned from the Assyrian captivity could not well pass through the literal Arabian desert; and the comparison expressed in the following verse, "As in the day when she went up from the land of Egypt," shows that here also a *decurtata comparatio* must take place. But, now, all depends upon determining the essential feature, the real nature and substance, of that first leading through the wilderness; because the leading spoken of in the verse before us must have that essential feature in common with it. The principal passage— which must guide us in this investigation, and which is proved to be such by the circumstance that the Lord Himself referred

to it when He was *spiritually* led through the wilderness, an
event which, for a sign, *outwardly* also took place in the wilderness—is Deut. viii. 2–5: "And thou shalt remember all the
way which the Lord thy God led thee these forty years in the
wilderness, to afflict thee and to prove thee, to know what was
in thy heart, whether thou wouldst keep His commandments,
or no.   And He afflicted thee, and suffered thee to hunger, and
fed thee with the manna which thou knewest not, neither did
thy fathers know, that He might make thee know that man
doth not live by bread only, but by everything which proceedeth
out of the mouth of the Lord doth man live.   Thy raiment
waxed not old upon thee, neither did thy foot swell these forty
years.   And thou knowest in thine heart, that as a father
chasteneth his son, so the Lord thy God chasteneth thee."
The essential feature in the leading through the wilderness is,
accordingly, the *temptation*.   By the wonderful manifestations
of the Lord's omnipotence and mercy, on the occasion of Israel's
deliverance from Egypt, a heartfelt love to Him had been
awakened in the people.   (Compare the tender expression of it
in the Song in Exod. xv.; and also the passage in Jer. ii. 2:
"I remember thee, the kindness of thy youth, the love of thine
espousals, thy going after Me in the wilderness in a land not
sown,"—which cannot but refer to the very first time of the
abode in the wilderness, before the giving of the law on Sinai,
as is evident from the mention of the youth and espousals; for
the latter ceased on Sinai, where the marriage took place.)   The
whole conduct of the people at the giving of the law,—their
great readiness in promising to do all that the Lord should
command,—likewise bear testimony to this love.   The Lord's
heartfelt delight in Israel during the first period of their
marching through the wilderness, of which Hosea speaks in
ix. 10, likewise presupposes this love.   Thus the first station
was reached.   The people now hoped to be put in immediate
possession of the inheritance promised to them by the Lord.
But, because the Lord knew the condition of human nature,
His way was a different one.   A state of temptation and trial
succeeded that of entire alienation from God.   The first love
is but too often—nay, it is, more or less, always—but a flicker-
ing flame.   Sin has not been entirely slain; it has been only
subdued for a moment, and only wants a favourable opportunity

to regain its old dominion. It would never be thoroughly destroyed, if God allowed this condition always to continue; if by always putting on new fuel, if by uninterrupted proofs of His love, He were to keep that fire burning continually. If the love of the feelings and imagination is to become a cordial, thorough moral love, it requires to be tried, in order that thus it may recognise its own nothingness hitherto, and how necessary it is that it should take deeper root. The means of this trial are God's afflicting us, concealing Himself from us, leading us in a way different from that which we expected, and, apparently, forsaking us. But because He is the merciful One who will not suffer us to be tempted above that we are able,—because He Himself has commanded us to pray, "Lead us not into temptation," *i.e.*, into such an one as we are not able to bear, and would thereby become a temptation inwardly,—He makes His gifts to go by the side of His chastisements. He who suffered Israel to hunger, gave them also to eat. He who suffered them to thirst, gave them also to drink. He who led them over the burning sand, did not suffer their shoes to wax old. But this counterpoise to tribulation becomes, in another aspect, a new temptation. As Satan tries to overthrow us by pleasure as well as by pain; so God proves us by what He gives, no less than by what He takes away. In the latter case, it will be seen whether we love God *without* His gifts; in the former, whether we love Him *in* His gifts. This second station is, to many, the last; the bodies of many fall in the wilderness. But while a multitude of individuals remain there, the Congregation of God always passes over to the third station, —the possession of Canaan. The state of temptation is, to her, always a state of sifting and purification at the same time. That which is to the individual a calamity, is to her a blessing.—That we have thus correctly defined the nature and substance of the leading through the wilderness, is confirmed by the temptation of Christ also, which immediately succeeded the bestowal of the Spirit, which again corresponded to the first love. That this temptation of Christ corresponded to the leading through the wilderness—in so far as it could do so in the case of Him who was tempted in all things, yet without sin; while in our case, there is no temptation, even when resisted

R

victoriously, that is without sin—appears sufficiently from its two external characteristics, viz., the stay in the wilderness, and the forty days; but still more so, from the internal feature,—the fact that the Saviour, in order to show the tempter that He recognised in His own case a repetition of the stay in the wilderness, opposed Him with a passage taken from the *locus classicus* concerning it, already quoted.—We now, moreover, cite the parallel passages which serve as an explanation of the passage under consideration, and as a confirmation of the explanation which we have given. The most important is Ezek. xx. 34–38: "And I bring you *out from the nations*, and gather you out of the countries wherein ye are scattered, with a mighty hand and with a stretched-out arm, and with fury poured out. And I bring you into the *wilderness of the nations*, and there will I plead with you face to face; like as I pleaded with your fathers in the wilderness of the land of Egypt, so will I plead there with you, saith the Lord God. And I cause you to pass under the rod, and bring you into the bond of the covenant, and purge out from among you the rebels, and them that transgress against Me; out of the land of your pilgrimage (the standing designation of Egypt in the Pentateuch) I will bring them forth, and into the land of Israel they shall not come, and ye shall know that I am the Lord." Here also, the stay in the wilderness appears as a state of trial, lying in the middle between the abode among the nations (corresponding to the bondage in Egypt, which was so not merely bodily, but spiritual also), and the possession of Canaan. And the result of this trial is a different one, according to the different condition of the individuals. Some shall be altogether destroyed; even the appearance of the communion with the Lord, which they hitherto maintained by having come out of the land of pilgrimage along with the others, shall be taken away; whilst the others, by the very means which brought about the destruction of the former, shall be confirmed in their communion with the Lord, and be more closely united to Him. Hosea, who, in consequence of the personification of the Congregation of Israel, has the whole more in view, regards chiefly the latter feature. A very remarkable circumstance in Ezekiel, however, requires to be still more minutely considered; because it promotes essentially the right understanding of the passage before us. What is meant

by the " wilderness of the nations?" Several interpreters think
that it is the wilderness between Babylon and Judea. Thus,
for example, *Manger*: " *I am disposed to think* that the desert
of Arabia itself is here called the wilderness of the nations, on
account of the different nomadic tribes which are accustomed
to wander through it." *Rosenmüller* says : " He *seems* to speak
here of those vast solitudes which the Jews had to pass through,
on their way from Babylon to Judea." But this " I am disposed to think," and this " he seems," on the part of these interpreters, show that they themselves felt the insufficiency of
their own explanation. That nomadic tribes are straying
through that wilderness, is not at all essential, and can therefore
not be mentioned here, where only the essential feature—the
nature and substance of the leading through the wilderness
—are concerned. And we cannot at all perceive why just the
wilderness between Babylon and Judea should be called the
wilderness of the nations. It was no more travelled by nomadic tribes than was any other wilderness. And just as little
was it characteristic of it, that it bordered upon the territories of
various nations (*Hitzig*). Such a designation would throw us
upon the territory of mere conjecture, on which we are, in Holy
Scripture, never thrown, except through our own fault. But it
is quite decisive that the words, " I bring you out of the wilderness of the nations," stand in a close relation to the words, " I
bring you out from the nations." From this it appears that the
nations, to which the Israelites are to be brought, cannot be any
other than those, out of the midst of whom they are to be led.
In the first leading out of the Israelites, the two spiritual conditions were separated externally also. The first belonged to
Egypt ; the second, to the wilderness. But it shall not be thus,
in this announced repetition of the leading. It is only spiritually
that the Israelites, at the commencement of the second condition,
shall be led out from among the nations, in the midst of whom
they, outwardly, still continue to be. The wilderness is in the
second Egypt itself. The stay in the wilderness is repeated as
to its essence only, and not as to its accidental outward form ;
just as in Zech. x. 12, the words, " And he passeth through
the sea," which apparently might imply a repetition of the outward form merely, are limited to the substance by the subjoined
" affliction." From this we obtain for our passage (*Hitzig* like-

wise remarks : Ezek. xx. 34–38 seems to depend on Hosea ii.
16) the important result, that the leading of God which is here
announced, is not limited to a definite place, and as little, to a
definite time.   And what is true of the leading through the
wilderness, must necessarily apply to the leading into Canaan
also.   Just as Egypt might begin, and actually did begin, even
in Palestine, inasmuch as Israel was there in a condition of heavy
spiritual and bodily bondage;—just as, spiritually, they might
already be in the wilderness, though, outwardly, they were still
under Asshur; so, the stay in the wilderness might, relatively,
have still continued in Canaan, even although—which did not
happen—the whole people should have returned thither with
Zerubbabel.   What is it that makes Canaan to be Canaan, the
promised land, the land of the Lord?   It is just this :—that the
Lord is there present with all His gifts and blessings.   But such
was by no means the case in the new colony.   Because the spiritual condition of those who had returned was in conformity
with the second—in part, even with the first—rather than with
the last station, their outward condition was so likewise.   John
the Baptist symbolized this continuation of the condition of the
wilderness, by his appearing *in the wilderness*, with the preaching of repentance, and with the announcement, that now the
introduction to the true Canaan was near at hand.   By proclaiming himself as the voice crying in the wilderness, announced by Isaiah, he showed with sufficient plainness how
false was that carnal view which, without being able to distinguish the thought from its drapery, understood, and still
understands, by the wilderness spoken of in this prophecy, some
piece of land, limited as to space, and then murmured that the
actual limit did not correspond with the fancied one.—As in
the case of Israel, so in ours also, these conditions are distinguished, not absolutely, but relatively only.   Even he who has,
in one respect, been already led through to Canaan, remains, in
another respect, in the wilderness still.   Canaan, in the full
sense, does not belong to the present world, but to the future,
as regards both the single individual, and the whole Church.—
Another parallel passage is Jer. xxxi. 1, 2 : " At this time, saith
the Lord, will I be the God of all the families of Israel, and
they shall be My people.   Thus saith the Lord, The people
who have escaped from the sword find mercy in the wilderness;

I go to give rest to Israel." In Rev. xii. 6, 14, the wilderness likewise designates the state of trial and temptation.—דבר על-לב, properly "to speak over the heart," because the words fall down upon the heart, signifies an affectionate and consolatory address; compare Gen. xxxiv. 3 ("And he loved the damsel, and spoke over the heart of the damsel"), l. 21; Is. xl. 2. Here they signify that the wife is comforted after she had been so deeply cast down by the consciousness of her former unfaithfulness, and by the experience of its bitter consequences. The view of those who would here think only of the comforting words of the prophets is much too limited,—although these words are, of course, included. We must chiefly think of the *sermo realis* of the Lord, of all the proofs of affectionate and tender love, whereby He gives rest to the weary and heavy-laden, and brings it about, that those who were formerly unfaithful, but who now suffer themselves to be led by Him out of the spiritual bondage into the spiritual wilderness, can now put confidence in Him; just as, formerly, He comforted Israel in the wilderness, in the waste and desolate land, in the land of drought and of the shadow of death (Jer. ii. 6), and affectionately cared for all their wants, in order that they might know that He is the Lord their God, Deut. xxix. 4, 5.

Ver. 17. *"And I give her her vineyards from thence, and the valley of Achor (trouble) for a door of hope; and she answers thither as in the days of her youth, and as in the day when she came up out of Egypt."*

The same faithful love which led into the wilderness, now leads into Canaan also; and the entrance into the promised land is immediately followed by the possession of all its gifts and blessings, which now legitimately belong to the *faithful* wife (*her* vineyards), whilst, formerly, they were taken from the unfaithful wife by the giver, ver. 14. נתן with ל of the person, always means "to give to some one." Hence *Simson* is wrong in giving the explanation: "And I make her of it, viz., the wilderness, her vineyards;" for the valley of Achor was not situated in the wilderness, but in Canaan; compare Is. lxv. 10. The signification "to give" is here suited to the second member of the verse also. The valley of Achor is given to her in its quality as a valley of hope. The *vineyards* are mentioned with reference to ver. 14, where the devastation of the vine is threatened. They are brought under notice as the noblest possession, as the finest ornament of the cultivated land, in contrast with the barren wilderness. מִשָּׁם, properly "from thence," is correctly explained by *Manger:* "As soon as she has come out of that wilderness." The explanation of *Rödiger* and others, " From that time," is unphilological ; שָׁם is never an adverb of time.—According to the opinion of many interpreters (*Calvin, Manger,* and others), the valley of Achor here comes into consideration only because of its fruitfulness, and its situation at the entrance of the promised land, but not with any reference to the event which, according to Josh. vii., happened there. But the circumstance that here, as in the whole preceding context, the prophet, in almost every word, has before his eyes the former leadings of Israel, compels us, almost involuntarily, to have respect to that event. And, in addition, there is a still more decisive argument. It cannot be denied that there is a contrast between what the valley of Achor is by nature, and what it is made by the Lord ; there is too plain a contrast between the *hope* and the *affliction.* But if thus the meaning of the name is brought into view, then certainly there must also be a reference to the event to which it owed its name. But in order to have a right understanding of this reference, we must find out what was the essential feature in the event, the repetition of which is here announced. The people, when they were entering into Canaan, were immediately deprived of the enjoyment of the divine favour by the transgression of an individual— Achan—which was only a single fruit from the tree of the sin which was common to all. But God Himself, in His mercy, made known the means by which the lost favour might be recovered ; and thus the place, which seemed to be the door of destruction, became the door of hope ; compare *Schuliens* on *Harari* iii. p. 180. The remembrance of this event was perpetuated by the name of the place ; compare ver. 25 : " And Joshua said, Why hast thou troubled us ? The Lord shall trouble thee this day. Therefore the name of the place was called, The valley of Achor, unto this day." This particular dealing of God, however, is based upon His nature, and must, therefore, repeat itself when Israel again comes into similar circumstances,—must be repeated, in general, whensoever similar conditions arise. Even they who have already entered the promised land, who have already come to the full enjoyment of salvation (*full*, in so far as it is considered as a whole, and designated as the last station ; but as this last station again has several steps and gradations, this fulness can be relative only. If it were absolute, if nothing more of the wilderness were left, then, of course, the case here in question could no more occur; for a salvation absolutely full presupposes a righteousness absolutely full);—even they who have already come to the full enjoyment of salvation, and to a degree of righteousness corresponding to this salvation, require still the mercy of God; for, without it, they would soon lose their salvation again. This mercy, however, is vouchsafed to them in abundant measure. The whole manner in which God leads those who have obtained mercy, is a changing of the valley of trouble into a door of hope. He will order all things in such a way, that the bond of union betwixt Him and those for whom all things must work together for good, instead of being broken by sin—as it would be if He were justice alone—is only the more strengthened. The same idea occurs again in ver. 21. The new marriage-covenant is there founded not on justice only, but on mercy also.—The words וענתה שמה are commonly explained, "She sings there," or, "She there raises alternative songs." But both of these interpretations are unphilological. For 1. שמה does not signify "there," but "thither." Those passages which have been appealed to for the purpose of proving that it may also sometimes signify "there," or "at yonder place," all belong to the same class. The opposite of the construction of the verbs of motion with ב takes place in them. As, in these verbs, the idea of rest is, for the sake of brevity, omitted, so here, that of motion. Thus, *e.g.*, Jer. xviii. 2, "Go down to the potter's house, and *thither* will I cause thee to hear My voice," is a concise mode of expression for, "I will send My voice thither, and cause thee to hear there ;" 1 Chron. iv. 41, "Which were found thither," instead of, "which were found there when they came thither." We might, in the case of the passage under consideration, most easily concede what we are contending against, that שמה is used instead of שם, as a kind of grammatical blunder; but that the writer knew the difference between these two forms clearly appears from the close of the verse, where, certainly, he would not have put שמה for שם. These are the instances adduced by *Winer*. *Gesenius*, further, refers

to Is. xxxiv. 15 : " *Thither* makes her nest ;" but the making of
the nest implies the placing of it. *Ewald*, moreover, appeals to
Ps. cxxii. 5 : " *Thither* sit the thrones for judgment." It is true
that ישב never signifies " to sit down," but it frequently implies it.
He appeals, further, to the Song of Solomon viii. 5 : " *Thither*
thy mother brought thee forth ;" which is tantamount to—there
she brought thee forth, and put thee down. But שמה can so much
the less signify " there," that the instances alleged for the weak-
ening of the ה *locale* in other passages, will not stand the test.
Ewald appeals to Ps. lxviii. 7 : " God makes the solitary to dwell
ביתה ;" which, however, does not mean " *in* the house," as *Ewald*
translates, but " *into* the house"—He leads them thither, and
makes them to dwell there. The idea of motion being sufficiently indicated by the ה itself, no other designation was required in poetry, which delights in brevity. *Further*—Hab. iii.
11 : " Sun and moon stand זבלה, towards their habitation," *i.e.*, go
into their habitation and stand there. 2. The verb ענה signifies
neither " to begin the discourse," nor " to sing," nor " to sing
alternately," nor " to correspond," nor " to be favourably disposed" (*Ewald*), nor " to obey" (*Hitzig*), but always, and everywhere, " to answer." All these explanations will lose their
plausibility, if we only consider, that it is not always necessary
that a question be expressed by words, but that it may be implied
in the thing itself—especially in the case of the lively Orientals,
for whom things, even the most mute, have a language. As
examples, we cite only 1 Sam. xxi. 12 :—" Did they not answer
to him in dances, saying, Saul has slain his thousands, but
David his ten thousands !" Similarly also xxix. 5. That even
here, the signification " to answer" ought to be retained, is plain
from xviii. 7, compared with ver. 6. The coming together of
David and Saul was a silent question as to which was the greater.
Ps. cxlvii. : " Answer the Lord with praise." The real addresses
of the Lord were His blessings ; compare vers. 2–6, 8 ff. By
everything which God gives He asks, What art thou doing to
Me, since I am doing that to thee ?   עָנָה is often used of God,
although no formal question or prayer preceded ; but the very
relation itself implies prayer and asking. It is in this sense that
even the ravens are said to cry to God. It is in this sense that
God *answers* His people before they cry to Him. He who has
nothing, prays by this very circumstance, even without words,

yea, even without the gestures and posture of one who is praying. Since, in these remarks, we have already refuted the arguments which seemed most plausible, we may pass over other objections which are less to the purpose. There is only the passage Exod. xv. 21, which requires to be specially noticed, as it is in that passage that the signification " to sing alternately" is supposed, beyond any doubt, to be; and many interpreters assume that there is a verbal reference to it in the passage under consideration. "And then Miriam answered to them (להם, *i.e.*, to the men), Sing ye to the Lord." Moses sings first with the children of Israel, ver. 1, " and then Miriam the prophetess took, etc., and *answered.*" The signification "to answer," is here quite evident. But, on the other hand, it appears that that passage has not the slightest relation to the one under consideration, inasmuch as there is not, in the latter, any mention of a first choir, to which the second answers.—From what has been hitherto remarked, it is settled that the translation, " And she answers thither," is alone admissible. But now, since no *verbal* question or address has preceded here, the question arises:— Which address by deeds called forth the answer ? To this question an answer is readily suggested by the reference of שמה to the preceding משם. The address must have come from that place to which the answer is sent; hence, it can consist only in the giving of the vineyards, and of the good things of the promised land generally. On entering into it, she is welcomed by this affectionate address of the Lord, her husband, and there she answers it. The following words, " As in the days," etc., show what that is in which the answer consists. If, at that time, Israel answered the Lord by a song of praise, full of thanks for the deliverance from Egypt, now also they will answer Him by a song of praise, for being led into Canaan. If history had given any report of a hymn of praise sung by Israel when they entered into Canaan, the prophet would have referred to it; but as it was, he could only remind them of that hymn. And although the occasion on which it was sung did not altogether correspond, it must be borne in mind, that in this hymn (compare ver. 12 ff.) the passing through the Red Sea is represented as a preparatory step, and as prefiguring the occupation of Canaan—the latter being contained in it as in a germ. It is, moreover, self-evident that the essential fundamental thought is

only that of the cordial and deep gratitude of the redeemed,—
that the form only is borrowed from the previous manifestation
of this thankfulness.   An image altogether similar, and arising
from the same cause, is found in Is. xii. also, where the reference
to Moses' hymn of thanks is manifested by employing the very
words; and likewise in Is. xxvi.; and, further, in Hab. iii. and
Rev. xv. 3.—יְמֵי and יוֹם are Nominatives, not Accusatives; which
latter could not be made use of here, because the discourse is not of
an action extending through the whole period, but of one happen-
ing at a particular point of that period.   The comparison is here
also merely intimated, because the *tertium comparationis* is abundantly evident from what precedes: "As the days of her youth,"
instead of, "As she once answered in the days of her youth."

Ver. 18. "*And it shall be at that day, saith the Lord, thou
shalt call Me, My husband, and shalt call Me no more, My Baal.*"

The full performance of her duties corresponds with the full
admission to her rights.   The prophet expresses this thought,
by announcing the removal of the two forms in which the
apostasy of the people from the true God—the violation of the
marriage-covenant which rested on exclusiveness—was at that
time manifested.   One of these was the mixing up of the religion
of Jehovah with heathenism, according to which they called the
true God "Baal," and worshipped Him as Baal; the other was
still grosser—was pure idolatry.   The abolition of the former
(compare above, p. 176 f.) is predicted in this verse; the abolition of the latter, in the verse following.   Both are in a similar
way placed beside each other in Zech. xiv. 9: "In that day
shall there be one Lord, and His name one;" where the first
clause refers to the abolition of polytheism, and the second to
the abolition of the mixing of religion—of the hidden apostasy—
which, without venturing to forsake the true God entirely and
openly, endeavours to mix up and identify Him with the world.
To the fundamental thought there are several parallels; *e.g.*,
Deut. xxx. 5 ff.: "And the Lord thy God bringeth thee into
the land which thy fathers possessed; and the Lord thy God
circumciseth thine heart, and the heart of thy seed, to love the
Lord thy God with all thine heart, and with all thy soul, that
thou mayest live."   This passage shows that the verse before us,
no less than that which precedes, contains a *promise*, and that
the "calling," and the "calling no more," is a work of divine

grace. To this we are led also by the words, "I shall take away," in ver. 19, as well as by the other parallel passages:— Jer. xxiv. 7: "And I give them an heart to know Me, that I am the Lord; and they shall be a people to Me, and I will be a God to them, for they shall return to Me with their whole heart;" Ezek. xi. 19: "And I give them one heart, and a new spirit I put within them, and take the stony heart out of their flesh;" compare further Zech. xiii. 2. Another interpretation of the verse recommends itself by its apparent depth. According to it, בעל is to be taken as an appellative noun, the "marriage-Lord," in contrast with איש, "husband," and that the people are henceforth to be altogether governed by love. But this interpretation must be objected to, for a whole multitude of reasons. There is, *first* of all, the relation of this verse to the following one, which does not allow that בעל, which there occurs as a proper name, should in this place be taken as an appellative. There is, *then*, the arbitrariness in defining the relation between איש and בעל, the former of which as little exclusively expresses the relation of love, as the latter excludes it. (Compare Is. liv. 5, 6, lxii. 4; 2 Sam. xi. 26.) Further, it is incorrect to say that בעל properly means "Lord;" it means "possessor." *Still further,*— There is the unsuitableness of the thought, which would be without any analogy in its favour throughout Scripture. And, *lastly*, the relation of love to God cannot, even in its highest consummation, do away with reference to Him, etc.

Ver. 19. "*And I take away the names of the Baalim out of her mouth, and they shall no more be remembered by their name.*"

The people are to conceive such an abhorrence of idolatry, that they shall be afraid of being defiled even by pronouncing the name of the idols. The words are borrowed from Exod. xxiii. 13: "Ye shall not make mention of the name of other gods, neither shall it be heard out of thy mouth." The special expression of the idea must, as a matter of course, be referred back to this idea itself, viz., the abhorrence of the former sin · and, hence, such a mention cannot here be spoken of as, like that in the passage before us, has no reference to that sin.

Ver. 20. "*And I make a covenant for them in that day with beasts of the field, and with the fowls of heaven, and with the eping things of the earth; and bow, and sword, and war I break of the land, and make them to dwell in safety.*"

On the expression, " I make a covenant," *Manger* remarks, " The cause is here put for the effect, in order to inspire with greater security." For the benefit of Israel, God makes a covenant with the beasts, *i.e.*, He imposes upon them obligations not to injure them. The phrase כרת ברית is frequently used of a transaction betwixt two parties, whereby an obligation is imposed upon only one of the parties, without the assumption of any obligation by the other. A somewhat different turn is given to the image in Job v. 23, where, by the mediation of God, the beasts themselves enter into a covenant with Job after his restoration. רמש never means " worm," but always " what moves and creeps," both small and great, as, in Ps. civ. 25, is subjoined by way of explanation. The three classes stand in the same order in Gen. ix. 2. The normal order there established, " And the fear of you and the dread of you shall be upon every beast," etc., returns, after the removal of the disturbance which has been produced by sin. Upon the words, " I break," etc., *Manger* makes the very pertinent remark : " It is an emphatic and expressive brevity, according to which breaking out of the land all instruments of war, and war itself, means that He will break them and remove them out of the land." It is self-evident that " war" can here, as little as anywhere else, mean " weapons of war." The prophet, as it appears, had in view the passage Lev. xxvi. 3 ff. : " If ye will walk in My statutes, and keep My commandments and do them, I will give you your rains in due season, and the land shall yield her increase, and the trees of the field shall yield their fruit. . . . And I give peace in the land, and you dwell, and there is none who makes you afraid ; and I destroy the wild beasts out of the land, and the sword shall not enter into your land." It is so much the more obvious that we ought to assume a reference to this passage, as Ezekiel also, in xxxiv. 25 ff., copies it almost *verbatim*. On account of the fatal *If*, that promise had hitherto been only very imperfectly fulfilled ; and frequently just the opposite of it had happened. But now that the condition is fulfilled, the promise also shall be fully realized. But we must observe, with reference to it, that, when we look to the present course of the world, this hope remains always more or less ideal, because in reference to the condition also, the idea is not yet reached by the reality. The idea is this :—As evil is, as a punishment, the inseparable concomitant of sin, so prosperity and salvation are the inseparable companions of righteousness. This is realized even in the present course of the world, in so far as everything must serve to promote the prosperity of the righteous. But the full realization belongs to the παλιν-γενεσία, where, along with sin, evil too (which is *here* still necessary even for the righteous, in order to purify them) shall be extirpated. Parallel are Is. ii. 4, xi.—xxxv. 9; Zech. ix. 10.

Ver. 21. "*And I betroth thee to Me for eternity; and I betroth thee to Me in righteousness and judgment, and in loving-kindness and mercy.*"

Ver. 22. "*And I betroth thee to Me in faithfulness, and thou knowest the Lord.*"

The word אָרַשׂ, " to espouse" (compare Deut. xx. 7, where it is contrasted with לָקַח), has reference to the entrance into a marriage entirely new, with the wife of youth, and is, for this reason, chosen on purpose. " Just as if (so *Calvin* remarks) the people had never violated conjugal fidelity, God promises that they should be His spouse, in the same manner as one marries a *virgo intacta*." It was indeed a great mercy if the unfaithful wife was only received *again*. Justly might she have been rejected for ever; for the only valid reason for a divorce existed, inasmuch as she had lived in adultery for years. But God's mercy goes still further. The old offences are not only *forgiven*, but *forgotten*. A relation entirely new begins, into which there enter, on the one side, no suspicion and no bitterness, and on the other, no painful recollections, such as may pass into similar human relationships, where the consequences of sin never disappear altogether, and where a painful remembrance always remains. The same dealing of God is still repeated daily; every believer may still say with exultation: " Old things are passed away; behold, all things are become new." It is the greatness of this promise which occasions the direct address, whilst hitherto the Lord had spoken of the wife in the third person. She shall hear face to face, the great word out of His mouth, in order that she may be assured that it is she whom it concerns; and in order to express its greatness, its joyfulness, and the difficulty of believing it, it is repeated three times. *Calvin* says: " Because it was difficult to deliver the people from fear and despair, and because they could not but be

aware how grievously they had sinned, and in how many ways
they had alienated themselves from God, it was necessary to
employ many consolations, that thus their faith might be confirmed.   One likes to hear the repetition of the intelligence of
a great and unexpected good fortune which one has some difficulty in realizing.   And what could a man, despairing on account of his sins, less readily realize than the greatest of all
miracles—viz., that all his sins should be done away with, at
once and for ever?   But the repetition is, in this case, so much
the more full of consolation, that, each time, it is accompanied
with the promise of some new blessing; that, each time, it
opens up some new prospect of new blessings from this new
connection.   First, there is the eternal duration,—then, as a
pledge of this, the attributes which God would display in
bestowing it,—and, finally, there are the blessings which He
would impart to His betrothed."   The לעולם points back
to the painful dissolution of the former marriage-covenant:
This new one shall not be liable to such a dissolution; for "the
mountains shall depart, and the hills be removed, but My
kindness shall not depart from thee, neither shall the covenant
of My peace be removed, saith the Lord:" Is. liv. 10.   The
attributes which God will display towards the wife, and the
conduct which she shall observe towards Him through His
mercy, are connected with ארשתיך לי, "I betroth thee to Me," by
means of ב, which is often used to mark the circumstances on
which some action rests.   Thus, in the case before us, the betrothment rests upon what God vouchsafes along with it, inasmuch as thereby only does it become a true betrothment.   That
the accompanying gifts must be thus distributed—as we have
done—first, the faithful discharge of all the duties of a husband
on His part, and then, the inward communication of strength
to her for the fulfilment of her obligations; and that we are
neither at liberty to refer, as do some interpreters, everything
to one of the two parties, nor to assume, as others do, that
everything refers to both at the same time—is proved not only
by the intervening repetition of " I betroth thee to Me," but also
by the internal nature of the gifts mentioned. רחמים, "mercy,"
cannot be spoken of in the relation of the wife to God, nor
knowledge of God, in the relation of God to the wife.   The
four manifestations of God which are mentioned here form

a double pair,—righteousness and judgment, loving-kindness and mercy. The two are frequently connected in a similar way; *e.g.*, Is. i. 27: "Zion shall be redeemed in judgment, and her inhabitants in righteousness." They are distinguished thus:—the former, צדק, designates the *being just*, as a subjective attribute, with the dispositions and actions flowing from it; the latter, משפט, denotes the *objective right*.[1] A man can give to another his right or judgment, and yet not be righteous; but God's righteousness, and His doing right in reference to the Congregation, consists in this:—that He faithfully performs the obligations which He took upon Himself when He entered into covenant with her. This, however, is not sufficient. The obligations entered into are reciprocal. If, then, the covenant be violated on the part of the Congregation, what hope is left for her? In order the more to relieve and comfort the wife, who, from former experience, knew full well what she might expect from righteousness and judgment alone, the Lord adds a second pair,—loving-kindness and mercy, the former being the root of the latter, and the latter being the form in which the former manifests itself, in the relation of an omnipotent and holy God to weak and sinful man. חסד, properly "love," man may also entertain towards God; although even this word is very rarely used in reference to man, because God's love infinitely exceeds human love; but God only can have רחמים, "mercy," upon man. But still a distressing thought might, and must be entertained by the wife. God's mercy and love have their limits; they extend only to the one case which dissolves even human marriage—the type of the heavenly marriage, the great mystery which the Apostle refers to Christ and the Church. What, then, if this case should again occur? Her heart, it is true, is now filled with pure love; but who knows whether this love shall not cool,—whether she shall not again yield to temptation? A new consolation is applied to the new distress. God Himself will bestow what it is not in the power of man to bestow—viz., faithfulness towards Him (compare אמונה, used of human faithfulness, in Hab. ii. 4; Jer. v. 3, vii. 28; the faithfulness in this verse forms the contrast to the whoredom in i. 2),

[1] In our authorized version משפט is almost constantly rendered by "*judgment*," although evidently in the sense pointed out by the author,—for which reason, this rendering has been retained here.—TR.

and the knowledge of Him. "Thou knowest the Lord" is tantamount to—"in My knowledge." The knowledge of God is here
substantial knowledge. Whosoever thus knows God cannot but
love Him, and be faithful to Him. All idolatry, all sin, has its
foundation in a want of the knowledge of God.

Ver. 23. *"And it comes to pass in that day, I will hear, saith
the Lord; I will hear the heavens, and they shall hear the earth ;
Ver. 24. And the earth shall hear the corn, and the must, and
the oil; and they shall hear Jezreel"* (*i.e.*, him whom God sows).

The promise in this passage forms the contrast to the
threatening in Deut. xxviii. 23, 24: "And thy heaven that is
over thy head shall be brass, and the earth that is under thee
shall be iron. The Lord will give for the rain of thy land,
dust, and dust shall come down from heaven upon thee." The
second אענה is, by most interpreters, considered as a resumption
of the first. But we obtain a far more expressive sense, if we
isolate the first אענה, "I shall hear," namely, all prayers which
will be offered up unto Me by you, and for you. Parallel,
among other passages, is Is. lviii. 9, where the reformed people
are promised: "Then shalt thou call, and the Lord shall answer; thou shalt cry, and He shall say, Here I am." By a bold
prosopopœia, the prophet makes heaven to pray that it might
be permitted to give to the earth that which is necessary for its
fruitfulness, etc. Hitherto they have been hindered from fulfilling their *destination*, since God was obliged to withdraw His
gifts from the unworthy people, ii. 11; but now, since this
obstacle has been removed, they pray for permission to resume
their vocation. The prophets in this manner give, as it were, a
visible representation of the idea, that there is in the whole
world no good independent of God,—nothing which, in accordance with its destination, is not ours, and would indeed be ours,
if we stood in the right relation to Him,—nothing that is not
His, and that will not be taken away from us, if we desire the
gift without the Giver. *Calvin* remarks: "The prophet shows
where and when the happiness of men begins, viz., when God
adopts them, when He betrothes Himself to them, after having
put away their sins. . . . He teaches, also, in these words,
that the heavens do not become dry by some secret instinct;
but it is when God withholds His grace, that there is no rain
by which the heavens water the earth." God, then, here shows

plainly that the whole *order of nature* (as men are wont to say) is so entirely in His hand, that not one drop of rain shall fall from heaven unless by His will,—that the whole earth would produce no grass,—that, in short, all nature would be sterile, unless He made it fruitful by His blessing.

Ver. 25. "*And I sow her unto Me in the land, and I have mercy upon her 'who had not obtained mercy'* (Lo-Ruhamah); *and I say to 'not My people'* (Lo-Ammi), *Thou art My people, and they say to Me, My God.*"

The three symbolical names of the children of the prophet here once more return. The *femin. suffix* in זְרַעְתִּיהָ, referring to יִזְרְעֶאל, need not at all surprise us; for, in the whole passage before us, the sign disappears in the thing signified. In point of fact, however, *Jezreel* is equivalent to Israel to be *sowed* anew. (It is not the Israel to be *planted* anew, which is a figure altogether different; the sowing has always a reference to the increase.)

———◆———

CHAPTER III.

"The significant couple returns for a new reference" (*Rückert*). First, in vers. 1–3, the symbolical action is reported. At the command of the Lord, the prophet takes a wife, who, notwithstanding his affectionate and faithful love, lives in continued adultery. He does not entirely reject her; but, in order that she may come to recovery and repentance, he puts her into a position where she must abstain from her lovers. The interpretation of the symbol is given in ver. 4: Israel, forsaken by the world, shall spend a long time in sad seclusion. A glance into the more distant future, without any symbolical imagery, forms the conclusion. The punishment will at length produce conversion. Israel returns to the Lord his God, and to David his king.

————

Ver. 1. "*Then said the Lord unto me, Go again, love a*

s

woman beloved of her friend, and an adulteress, as the Lord loveth the sons of Israel, and they turn to other gods and love grape-cakes."

The right point of view for the interpretation of this verse has been already, in many important respects, established; compare p. 183 sqq. We here take for granted the results there obtained. It is of great importance, for an insight into the whole passage, to remark, that the symbolical action in this section, just as in that to which chap. i. belongs, embraces the entire relation of the Lord to the people of Israel, and not, as some interpreters assume, one portion only, viz., the time from the beginning of the captivity. This false view—of which the futility was first completely exposed by *Manger*—has arisen from the circumstance, that the prophet, in narrating the execution of the divine commission, omits very important events. In the expectation that every one would supply them, partly from the commission itself, and partly from the preceding portions, where they had been treated of with peculiar copiousness, he rather at once passes from the first conclusion of the marriage, to that point which, in this passage, forms his main subject, namely, the disciplinary punishment to which he subjects his wife,—the Lord, Israel. The prophet's aim and purpose is to afford to the people a right view of the captivity so near at hand; to lead them to consider it neither as a merely accidental event, having no connection at all with their sins; nor as a pure effect of divine anger, aiming at their entire destruction; but rather as being at the same time a work of punitive justice, and of corrective love. Between the second verse, "I purchased her to me," etc., and the third, "Then I said unto her," etc., we must supply, And I took her in marriage and loved her; but she committed adultery. That this is the sound view, appears clearly from ver. 2. According to the right exposition (compare p. 195 sqq.), this verse can be referred only to the first beginning of the relation betwixt the Lord and the people of Israel—to that only by which He acquired the right of property in this people, on delivering them from Egypt. This is confirmed, moreover, by the second half of the verse under consideration: "As the Lord loveth," etc. Here the love of the Lord to Israel in its widest extent is spoken of. Every limitation of it to a single manifestation—be it a renewal of love after the apostasy, or the corrective discipline inflicted from love—is quite arbitrary; and the more so, because, by the addition, "And they turned," etc., the love of God is represented as running parallel with the apostasy of the people. The same result is obtained from a consideration of the first half. For what entitles us to explain "love" by "love again," or even by "*restitue amoris signa*," as is done by those who hold the opinion, already refuted, that the woman is *Gomer?* The word "love" corresponds exactly with "as the Lord loveth." If the latter must be understood of the love of the Lord in its whole extent,—if it does not designate merely the manifestation of love, but love itself,—how can a more limited view be taken of the former "love?" How could we explain, as is done by those who defend the reference to a new marriage, the words, "Beloved of her friend, and an adulteress," as referring to a former marriage of the wife, and as tantamount to—who was beloved by her former husband, and yet committed adultery? In that case, there would be the greatest dissimilarity betwixt the type and the antitype. Who, in that case, is to be the type of the Lord? Is it to be the former husband, or the prophet? If the figure is at all to correspond with the reality,—the first member with the second, the רֵעַ can be none other than the prophet himself.—Let us now proceed to particulars. אהב, "love," is stronger than קח, "take," in chap. i. 2. There, marriage only was spoken of; here, marriage from love and in love. This is still more emphatically pointed out by the subsequent words אהבת רע, and contrasted with the conduct of the wife, which is indicated by מנאפת, so that the sense is this: "In love take a wife who, although she is beloved by thee, her friend, commits adultery, and with whom—I tell it to thee beforehand—thou wilt live in a constant antagonism of love, and of ingratitude, the grossest violation of love." The word "*love*" has a reference to the love preceding and effecting the marriage; the word "*beloved*," to the love uninterruptedly continuing during the marriage, and notwithstanding the continued adultery, unless we should say—and it is quite admissible—that "love" implies, at the same time, "to take out of love," and "to love constantly." Instead of "beloved by *thee*," it is said, "beloved by her *friend*." Many have been thereby misled; but it only serves to make the contrast more prominent.[1] עֵ has only one signification—that of *friend*. It never, by itself, means "fellow-man," never "fellow-Jew," never "one with whom we have intercourse." The Pharisees were quite correct in understanding it as the opposite of enemy. In their gloss, Matt. v. 43, καὶ μισήσεις τὸν ἐχθρόν σου, there was one thing only objectionable—the most important, it is true—that by the friend, they understood only him whom their heart, void of love, loved indeed ; not him whom they ought to have loved, because God had united him to them by the sacred ties of friendship and love. Thus, what ought to have awakened them to love, just served them as a palliation for their hatred. Now this signification, which alone is the settled one, is here also very suitable. He whom the wife criminally forsakes, is not a severe husband, but her loving friend, whom she herself formerly acknowledged as such, and who always remains the same. Entirely parallel is Jer. iii. 20: "As a wife is faithless towards her *friend*, so have ye been faithless to Me;" compare ver. 4: "Hast thou not formerly called me, My father, *friend* of my youth art thou?" Compare also Song of Sol. v. 16. The correct meaning was long ago seen by *Calvin:* "There is," says he, "an expressiveness in this word. For often, when women prostitute themselves, they complain that they have done it on account of the too great severity of their husbands, and that they are not treated by their husbands with sufficient kindness. But if a husband delight in having his wife with him, if he treat her kindly and perform the duties of a husband, she is then less excusable. Hence, it is this most heinous ingratitude of the people that is here expressed, and set in opposition to the infinite mercy and kindness of the Lord." For a still better insight into the meaning of the first half of this verse, we subjoin the *paraphrasis* by *Manger:* "Seek thee a wife in whom thou art to have thy delight, and whom thou art to treat with such love, that, even if she, by her unfaithfulness, violate the sacred rights of matrimony, and thou, for that reason, canst no longer live with her,

---

[1] It is quite impossible to refer עֵ to the adulterers, and for this reason : —that it is always Israel's love to the idols that is spoken of, but never the love of the idols to Israel. In the explanation given in the words immediately following, it is not the idols that take the initiative ; it is Israel who turns to other gods.

she shall still remain dear to thee, and shall be willingly received again into thy favour, as soon as she shall have reformed her life."—In the second half of the verse, there is a verbal agreement with passages of the Pentateuch, so close that it cannot certainly be accidental. Compare on כאהבת יהוה את־בני ישראל, Deut. vii. 8, כמאהבת יהוה אתכם;—an agreement which undoubtedly deserves so much more attention, that we have already established the relationship of the passage with ver. 2. On פנים אל אלהים אחרים, compare Deut. xxxi. 18: "I will hide My face in that day for all the evil they are doing, for they turn to other gods," פנה אל אלהים אחרים.—אשישי ענבים, "grape-cakes," has, as to its substance, been already explained, p. 194 sqq. It is the result of an entire misunderstanding, that some interpreters should here think of the love of feasting and banqueting. Others (as *Geśenius*) are anxious to prove that such cakes were used at the sacrifices which were offered to idols. The grape-cakes are rather idolatry itself; but the expression, "They love grape-cakes," adds an essential feature to the words, "They turn to other gods." It points, namely, to the sinful origin of idolatry. Earnest and strict religion is substantial and wholesome food; but idolatry is soft food, which is sought only by the dainty and squeamish. That which is true of idolatry, is true also of the service of sin, and of the world in general, which, in Job xx. 12, appears under the image of meat which is, in the mouth, as sweet as honey from the comb, but which is, in the belly, changed into the gall of asps. In the symbolism of the law, honey signified the *lust* of the world; compare my work *Die Opfer der Heil. Schrift*, S. 44. It is only the derivation of אשישים, the signification of which is sufficiently established by parallel passages, which requires investigation. We have no hesitation in deriving it from אֵשׁ, "fire;" hence it means properly, "that which has been subjected to fire (compare אָשָׁה) = that which has been baked," "cakes." The derivation from אשש, "to found," has of late become current; but the objections to it are:—partly, that the transition from "founding," to "cake," is by no means an easy one; partly and mainly, that there is not the slightest trace of this root elsewhere in Hebrew. It is asserted, indeed, that אשישים itself is found in Is. xvi. 7, with a signification which renders necessary the derivation from the verb אשש. But, even in that passage, the signification of

"cakes" must be retained. The following reasons are in favour
of it, and against the signification "ruins," adopted by *Gesenius*,
Winer, and *Hitzig*.   1. The signification "cakes" deserves,
ceteris paribus, a decided preference, because it is established by
the other passages.   It is only for reasons the most cogent that
we can grant that one and the same word has two meanings,
and these not at all connected with each other.   2. The transition from the meaning "foundation," which alone can be derived
from the verb אשׁשׁ, to that of "*ruins*," is by no means so easy
as those critics would represent it.   With respect to a rebuilding,
for which the ruins afford the foundation, they might, it is true,
be called foundations, compare Is. lviii. 12, but not where destruction only is concerned.   Who would speak of howling over
foundations, instead of howling over ruins?   3. The context is
quite decisive.   If we translate אשׁישׁים by "ruins," the subsequent כי is quite inexplicable.   This little word, upon which so
much depends, performs also the office of a guide: "For this
reason Moab howls, for Moab altogether does he howl, for the
cakes of Kirhareseth you do sigh, wholly afflicted; *for* the vineyards of Heshbon are withered, the vine of Sibmah, the grapes
of which intoxicated the lord of the nations," etc.   Then, ver. 9,
"Therefore I weep with Jaeser for the vine of Sibmah."   If
there be no more grapes, neither are there any more grape-
cakes.   The destruction of the vineyards is therefore the cause
of the howling for the cakes.   That such cakes, moreover, were
prepared in many places in Moab, sufficiently appears from the
name of the place Dibhlathaim, *i.e.*, town of cakes.   It may be
remarked further, that we are not entitled to assume a sing.
אשׁישׁ as given by lexicographers along with אשׁישׁה; דבלה likewise forms the plural דבלים.

Ver. 2. "*And I bought her to me for fifteen pieces of silver,
and a homer of barley, and a lethech of barley.*"   Compare the
explanation of this verse, p. 195 sqq.

Ver. 3. "*And I said unto her, Thou art to sit for me many
days: thou art not to whore, and thou art not to belong to a man;
and so I also to thee.*"

The sitting has the accessory idea of being forsaken and
solitary, which may be explained from the circumstance, that he
who is not invited to go with us is left to sit.   Thus, *e.g.*, Gen.
xxxviii. 11 : " Sit as a widow in thy father's house, until Shelah

my son be grown ;" Is. xlvii. 8, where Babylon says, " I shall not *sit* as a widow," etc. The Fut. in this and the following verses must not be taken in an imperative sense, as meaning, thou shalt sit for me, thou shalt not whore; the explanation given in ver. 4, and in the parallel passage in chap. ii. 8, 9, are alike opposed to it. The husband will not subject his wife to a moral probation, but he will lock her up, so that she *must* sit solitary, and *cannot* whore. With reference to this, *Manger* strikingly remarks : " There is, in that very severity, the beginning of leniency ; ' sit for me,' *i.e.*, I who have been so unworthily treated by thee, and who yet am thy most affectionate husband, and who, though now at a distance from thee, will not altogether forget thee." The ‎לֹ indicates that the sitting of the wife must have reference to the prophet. Quite similar is Exod. xxiv. 14 : " And he said unto the elders, ‎שְׁבוּ לָנוּ, Sit ye here for us until we return to you." The phrase itself, which must not be explained by " to sit in expectation of some one," does not indicate in what way the sitting has reference to him. The issue of the whole proceeding, described in ver. 5, clearly shows, however, that it is not inflicted by him as a merited punishment, as an effect of his just indignation, but rather that we must think chiefly of his compassionate love, which makes use of these means in order to render the reunion possible.—The distinction between " to whore," and " to belong to a man," is obvious : the former denotes *vagos et promiscuus amores ;* the other, connubial connection with a single individual ; compare, *e.g.*, Ezek. xvi. 8 ; Lev. xxi. 3. But the question is,—Who is to be understood by the " *man ?*" Several refer it to the prophet exclusively. Thus *Jerome* says, " Thou shalt not shamefully prostitute thyself with other lovers, nor be legally connected with me, the man to whom thou art married." Others admit, at least, a co-reference to the prophet = the Lord. By the words, " Thou art not to whore," they say that the intercourse with the lovers is excluded ; but, by, " Thou art not to belong to a man," the intercourse with the husband also ; so that the sense would be, " Thou shalt not have connubial intercourse either with me, or with any other man." But the correct view is to refer both to the intercourse with the lovers ; and so, indeed, that the former designates the giving of herself up, now to one, then to another ; while the latter points to her entering into a firm relation to a single individual; just as, in point of fact, the relation of Israel to the idols hitherto was a whoring. According as it suited their inclination, they made, now this, and then that, god of the neighbouring nations an object of their worship; whilst a marriage connection would have been formed, if they had entered with any one of them into a permanent and exclusive connection, similar to that which had heretofore existed between them and the Lord. This explanation is required by the words, " And so I also to thee," at the close of the verse. If the words, " Thou shalt not belong to any man," referred to the prophet, then " thou shalt not have any intercourse with me" would imply, " I shall not have any intercourse with thee;" and did not require any new mention to be made.—The questions, however, now arise :—By what means was the state of things corresponding to the figure to be brought about? By what is adulterous Israel to be prevented from whoring, and from belonging to any man? By what means is idolatry to be extirpated from among the people? The answer has been already given in our remarks on chap. ii. 8, 9. The idols manifest themselves to Israel in their supposed gifts. If these were taken from them,—if they were entirely stripped, and plunged into want and misery, they could not fail to recognise the vanity of all their previous efforts, along with the vanity of the object of their worship, while their love to him could not but vanish. The absolute inability of the idols to afford consolation and help to the people in their sufferings must have put an end to their showing them allegiance.—The last words, " And I also to thee," are explained by the greater number of interpreters to mean, " I also will be thine." *Manger* explains them thus : " I will not altogether break the tie of our love, nor marry another wife; but I will remain thine, will at last receive thee again into my favour, and restore thee to the position of my wife." *De Wette* interprets them thus : " But then I will come to thee ;" *Umbreit :* " And I also only to thee ;" *Ewald :* " And yet I am full of love towards thee." But the words, " And I also to thee," are rather tantamount to—" I will conduct myself in a similar manner towards thee." Now two things may constitute this equality of conduct. *Either* it is conceived thus :— that the prophet is placed in parallelism with the wife. The latter has lost all claims upon the prophet; she has violated connubial fidelity, and, hence, has no title to demand that he should observe it. But that which she cannot demand from him, he does, from the necessity of his nature. He promises to her that, during the proceeding which has commenced against her, he would not enter into any new connection; and by holding out to her the hope of her returning, at some future period, to her old relation to him, he makes it more easy for her to break off the sinful connections which have destroyed it. Without a figure: The Lord, from His forbearance and mercy, waits for the reformation of those who hitherto were His people; does not drive them to despair by receiving another people in their place. *Or*, The prophet is placed in parallelism with the other man. As the wife does not enter into any relation with that man, so the prophet also abstains from any nearer intercourse with her. The latter explanation (adopted by *Simson* and *Hitzig*) is to be preferred. The exclusiveness cannot in the same sense be applicable to the prophet, representing the Lord, as to the wife, representing the people. So early as in Deut. xxxii. 21, we read: "They have moved Me to jealousy with that which is not God, they have provoked Me to anger with their vanities; and I will move them to jealousy with those which are not a people, I will provoke them to anger with a foolish nation." After all that had, in the Song of Solomon, been predicted regarding the reception of the Gentile nations into the kingdom of God and Christ, and about the receiving again into it of Israel, to be effected by their instrumentality (compare my *Comment. on Song of Sol.*, S. 239), the thought suggested by the former view would be quite incomprehensible. Quite decisive, however, is ver. 4, in which the thought, which is here in a symbolical garb, is expressed in plain language. There, however, not only the intercourse with the idols, but the connection with Jehovah also, appears to be intermitted. The reason why the prophet does not enter into a closer connection with the wife is, that her repentance is more of a negative, than of a positive character. By want and isolation, her hard heart is to be broken, true repentance to be called forth, and the flame of cordial conversion and love to her husband, whose faithful love she had so ill requited, to be enkindled in her. In favour of the explanation given by us, and in opposition to that first mentioned, the נֵם is decisive. Against this, that other explanation,

in its various modifications, tries its strength in vain. "I also
will be thine, or will adhere to thee," would require in the preceding context, "Thou shalt be mine, or adhere to me;" but
of this, there is no trace. It is only in ver. 5 that, with an
after, the conversion is reported. In favour of that false interpretation it is said, and with some plausibility, that the explanation would otherwise be more extended than the symbol:
The latter would contain the outward dealing only; while the
former, in ver. 5, would contain at the same time its salutary
effect. But, even according to this explanation, the words
would not correspond with ver. 5. *Here*, the showing of mercy
would be announced without the mention, even by a word, of
the sincere return to the husband—and this, altogether apart
from the גם, would be quite unsuitable, and would, moreover,
be opposed by the analogy of chap. ii. 9—while, in ver. 5, not
the showing of mercy, but only the reformation, would form
the subject. In that case, it ought not to have been said,
"They shall return to the Lord," but rather, "The Lord
shall return to them." But this plausible reason falls to the
ground, along with the unfounded supposition that the *two* last
verses contain the explanation. The correct view is, that the
explanation is limited to ver. 4. Ver. 5 must be considered as
an appendix, in which, without any figurative covering, the
effect is described which will be produced upon the nation by
these outward dealings. The symbol and its explanation extend
only as far as the main object of the prophet in the section
under review,—that object being to present the impending captivity in its true light, and thereby to secure against levity and
despair when it should appear.

Ver. 4. "*For many days the children of Israel shall sit
without a king, and without a prince, and without a sacrifice, and
without a pillar, and without an Ephod and Teraphim.*"

כי is used because the reason of the performance of the
symbolical action lies in its signification. Concerning ישב, see
the remarks on ver. 3; compare, moreover, Lament. i. 1: "How
does the city sit solitary that was full of people! she has become
as a widow."—The question is, whether, by the religious objects
here mentioned, such only are to be understood as belonged to
the worship of the idols, or such also as belonged to the worship
of Jehovah. The following furnishes the reply. The מצבה only

can be considered as belonging exclusively to the idolatrous
worship. Such pillars always occur only as being consecrated
to the idols—especially to Baal. It cannot be proved in any
way that, contrary to the express command in Lev. xxvi. 1,
Deut. xvi. 22, they were, in the kingdom of Israel, consecrated
to the Lord also; compare 2 Kings iii. 2, xvii. 10, x. 26–28.
On the other hand, among the objects mentioned, there is also
one, the אֵפוֹד, the mantle for the shoulders of the high priest,
on which the Urim and Thummim were placed, which must be
considered as belonging exclusively to the worship of Jehovah;
at least there is not the smallest trace to be found that it was
part of any idolatrous worship. It is true that *Gesenius*, in the
Thesaurus, p. 135, gives *s. v.* אפוד, under 2, the signification *statua,
simulacrum idoli*, and, besides the passages under consideration,
refers to Jud. viii. 27, xvii. 5, xviii. 14, 17. But one requires
only to examine these passages a little more minutely, to be
convinced that the metamorphosis of Jehovah into an idol is as
little justified as the changing of the mantle into a statue.
From the personal character of Gideon, who was so zealous for
the Lord against the idols, we cannot at all think of idolatry in
Jud. viii. 27. In the *Dissertations on the Genuineness of the
Pentateuch*, vol. ii. p. 80, it has been proved that the Ephod of
Gideon was a precious imitation of that of the high priest. In
chap. xvii. 5, we need only to consider these words: "And the
man Micah had an house of God, and made an Ephod and
Teraphim, and consecrated one of his sons, and he became a
priest to him." Afterwards, Micah took a *Levite* for a priest.
But for what reason should he have been better suited for that
purpose than any other man? The answer is given in ver. 13:
"Then said Micah, Now I know that Jehovah will do me good,
for the Levite has become a priest to me." The ignorant man
knows after all thus much, that the Levites alone are the only
legitimate servants of Jehovah, and he rejoices, therefore, that
he had now remedied the former irregularity. Jud. xviii. 14
does not require any particular illustration, for it is the same
Ephod which is spoken of in that passage; but we must still
direct attention to vers. 5 and 6 of that chapter. "Then they
(the Danites) said unto him (the Levite), Ask God, we pray
thee, in order that we may know whether our way in which we
go shall be prosperous. And the priest said unto them, Go in

peace, before *Jehovah* is the way wherein ye go." Here, then, we have a revelation given to the priest, as is alleged, by means of Ephod and Teraphim; and this revelation is not ascribed to the idols, but to Jehovah, whom alone the Levite wished to serve. From this it appears that the graven image and the molten image—which, besides Ephod and Teraphim, according to ver. 14, exist in the house of Micah—must be considered as representations of Jehovah, similar to the calves in the kingdom of the ten tribes. In vol. ii. pp. 78, 79, of my *Dissertations on the Genuineness of the Pentateuch*, it has been demonstrated that the Ephod of Micah was, along with the Teraphim, an apeing of the high-priestly Ephod with the Urim and Thummim. The four objects mentioned in Judges xvii. and xviii. are such as were separable although connected, and connected although separable. The *molten work* is the pedestal under the image; the image is clothed with the Ephod, and in the Ephod were the Teraphim, from whom information and good counsel for the future were expected. For, that this is the object of the whole contrivance, is plain from chap. xviii. 5, 6, where the priest asks counsel of God for the Danites.—With regard to the other two objects mentioned in the verse before us, viz., the sacrifice and Teraphim, a reference, at least exclusive, to idolatrous worship, cannot be by any means maintained. As sacrifices are mentioned in the widest generality, without any limitation in the preceding context, there is certainly nothing which could in the least entitle us to exclude the sacrifices which were offered to Jehovah. The Teraphim are intermediate deities, by means of which the future is to be disclosed (compare the remarks on Zech. x. 2); they might be brought into connection with every religious system, but are found only once in connection with any other religion than that of Jehovah,—and this in a case where a non-Israelite is spoken of. It is true, however, that, in substance, the Teraphim belong to the side of idolatry; for, wherever they occur within the religion of Jehovah, they belong to a degenerate condition of it only, which is on a par with idolatry. It would appear that they are here contrasted with the Ephod, as the illegal means for ascertaining the future, in opposition to the legal means. That the Ephod was used for discovering the divine will, is seen from 1 Sam. xxiii. 9, xxx. 7. The Teraphim, in like manner, served to explore the future. A closer connection of the two seems to be indicated by the circumstance that אין is omitted before תרפים.——But how can we account for this strange intermingling of what belonged to the idols with what belonged to Jehovah, since it cannot but be done intentionally? It points to the dark mixture which at that time existed among the people, and is a kind of ironical reflection upon it.—The Lord makes them disgusted with idolatry, and all that belongs to it, through His visitations, in which they seek in vain the help of the idols, and become thoroughly acquainted with their vanity; compare remarks in ver. 3. At the same time, however, all the pledges of His grace are taken from them, so that they get into an altogether isolated position. He withdraws from them their independent government, the altar and priesthood—the former as a just punishment for their rebellion against the dynasty ordained by God (compare chap. viii. 4), of which, first Israel, and then Judah, had made themselves guilty.—As regards the historical reference of this prophecy, interpreters are divided, and refer it either to the Assyrian, the Babylonish, or the Romish exile. The greater number of them, however, refer it exclusively to the last. This is especially the case with the Jewish interpreters; e.g., Kimchi, who says: "These are the days of the exile, in which we are now; we have neither an Israelitish king nor an Israelitish prince, but are under the dominion of the Gentiles and their kings." The principal defenders of a direct reference to the Assyrian captivity, are Venema (Dissert. p. 232) and Manger. The decision depends chiefly upon what we are to understand by "the children of Israel." If these are the whole people, it is arbitrary to assign any narrower limits to the Word of God, than to His deed. The prophecy must, in that case, comprehend everything in which the idea is realized; and this so much the more, as the spiritual eye of the prophet, directed to the idea only, does not generally regard the intervals which, in the fulfilment, lie between the various realizations of the idea. But now, ver. 5 would seem to lead us to entertain the opinion, that, in the first instance, the prophet has in view the children of Israel in the more limited sense only. The words, "They shall return and seek David their king," imply a reference to the then existing apostasy of the ten tribes from the dynasty of David. But the future apostasy of the sons of Judah also from

David their king may be as well *presupposed* here, as, in chapter
ii. 2, their being carried away; and this so much the rather, as
in chap. ii. 2, the words, "They appoint themselves a king,"
suggest that the sons of Judah also, no less than the sons of
Israel, are without a head, and hence have apostatized from
David the king.   And it is so much the more natural to adopt
such a supposition, as the Song of Solomon had already described
so minutely the rebellion of the whole people against the glorious
descendant of David—the heavenly Solomon—to which the
apostasy of the ten tribes from the house of David was only a
prelude. Considering the whole relation in which Hosea stands
to the Song of Solomon, we could scarcely imagine that, in
this respect, he should not have alluded to, and resumed its
contents. *In the whole third chapter there is nothing which
refers exclusively to the ten tribes.* Chap. iii. 2 has reference to
all Israel.   Throughout the whole Book of Hosea also, as well
as by the second Israelitish prophet Amos (compare the remarks
on Amos, chap ix.), Judah and Israel are viewed together, both
as regards apostasy and punishment (v. 5, 12, viii. 14, x. 11, etc.),
and as regards salvation, vi. 1–4, etc.   Of special importance
is the comparison of the remarkable prophecy of Azariah in
2 Chron. xv. 2–4, which was uttered at the time of Asa, king
of Judah, and which so nearly coincides with the one before us,
that the idea suggests itself of an allusion to it by Hosea: "Hear
ye me, Asa, and all Judah and Benjamin : The Lord will be
with you, if you are with Him; and if ye seek Him, He will
be found of you; and if ye forsake Him, He will forsake you.
And many days will be to Israel when there is no true God,[1]
and no teaching priest,[2] and no law.   Then they return in their
trouble unto Jehovah the God of Israel, and they seek Him,
and He is found of them."   If the fundamental prophecy refer
to all Israel, the same must be the case with the prophecy under
consideration.   The condition in which the Jews are, up to the
present day, is described in both of these prophecies with remarkable clearness; and hence we may most confidently enter-

---

[1] *J. D. Michaelis* remarks : " In the present captivity they do not,
indeed, worship idols, but nevertheless they do not know, nor worship,
the true God, since they reject the Son, without whom the Father will not
be worshipped, John xvii. 3 ; 1 John ii. 23 ; 2 John 9."

[2] The " priest " here corresponds with the " Ephod " in Hosea.

tain the hope, that there shall be a fulfilment also of that which, in them as well as in the Song of Solomon, has been foretold regarding the glorious issue of these dealings of God.

Ver. 5. "*Afterwards shall the children of Israel return and seek the Lord their God, and David their king, and shall tremble to the Lord and to His goodness in the end of the days.*"

וּבִקְשׁוּ must not by any means be regarded as modifying בקשו, so that both the verbs would constitute only one verbal idea. This must be objected to, not only from the arguments already stated in the remarks on chap. ii. 11, but, most decidedly, on account of the parallel passage, chap. ii. 9, "I will go and return to my first husband." Compare chap. vi. 1: "Come and let us return unto the Lord;" v. 15, where the Lord says, "I will go and return to My place until they become guilty and seek My face; in their affliction they will seek Me;" Jer. l. 4: "In those days, and in that time, saith the Lord, the children of Israel shall *come*, they and the children of Judah together, weeping will they come, and seek the Lord their God,"—a passage which, like Jer. xxx. 9, points to the one before us in a manner not to be mistaken; Is. x. 21: "The remnant shall *return*, the remnant of Jacob, unto the mighty God." The text, and the parallel passages, most clearly indicate what is to be considered as the object of their return, namely, the Lord their God, and David their king, from whom they had so shamefully apostatized; so that those interpreters who here think of a return to Canaan do not deserve a refutation. The words, "Jehovah their God," at the same time lay open the delusion of the Israelites (who imagined that they could still possess the true God, in the idol which they called Jehovah), and rebuke their ingratitude. *Calvin* says, "God had offered Himself to them, yea, He had had familiar intercourse with them,—He had, as it were, brought them up on His bosom just as a father does his sons. The prophet, therefore, indirectly rebukes, in these words, their stupendous wickedness." The God of the Israelites, as well as the God of the Jews after they had rejected Christ, stood to the God of Israel in the same relation as does the God of the Deists and Rationalists to the God of the Christians. The question here arises, Who is to be understood here by "David their king?" Some interpreters refer it, after the example of *Theodoret* (t. ii. p. 2, p. 1326), to

Zerubbabel; but by far the greater number of them, following the Chaldee ("And they shall obey the Messiah, the son of David their king"), understand, thereby, the Messiah. It is true that the latter exposition is quite correct as to its substance, but not as to the form in which it is commonly expressed. From the words, "They shall return and seek," it is evident that the Messiah is here not called David as an individual, as is done in other passages, *e.g.*, Jer. xxx. 9. For the return presupposes their having been there formerly, and their having departed; just as the seeking implies neglecting. The expression, "their king," also requires special attention. In contrast to the "king" in ver. 4 (compare viii. 4, "They have made a king, and not by Me, a prince, and I knew it not"), it shows that the subject of discourse is not by any means a new king to be elected, but such an one as the Israelites ought to obey, even now, as the king ordained for them by God. The sound view is this: By the "king David" the whole Davidic house is to be understood, which is here to be considered as an unity, in the same manner as is done in 2 Sam. vii., and in a whole series of Psalms which celebrate the mercies shown, and to be shown, to David and his house.[1] These mercies are most fully concentrated in Christ, in whose appearance and everlasting dominion the promises given to David were first to be fully realized. The prophet mentions the whole—the Davidic family—because it was only thus that the contrast between the apostasy and the return could be fully brought out; but that, in so doing, he has Christ especially in view—that he expected a return of the children of Israel to David in Christ, is shown by the term באחרית הימים, which, in the prophets, never occurs in any other sense than the times of the Messiah. (Compare, regarding this expression, the remarks on Amos ix. 1.) This reason is alone sufficient to refute the reference to Zerubbabel; although so much must indeed be conceded, that the circumstance of part of the citizens of the kingdom of the ten tribes adhering to him, the descendant of the house of David, may be considered as a prelude of that general return. The close connection betwixt the seeking of Jehovah their God and David their king, likewise claims our attention. David and his family had been elected by God to be the mediator between Him and the

---

[1] In 1 Kings xii. 16, also, David stands for the Davidic dynasty.

people—the channel through which all His blessings flowed down upon the people—the visible image of the invisible King, who, at the end of the days, was, in Christ, most perfectly to reflect His glory. The Israelites, in turning away from David their king, turned away, at the same time, from Jehovah their God,—as was but too soon manifested by the other signs of apostasy from Him, by the introduction of the worship of calves, etc. He who refuses to acknowledge God in that which He has Himself declared to be His visible image (from Christ down to every relation which represents Him in any respect, *e.g.*, that of the father to the son, of the king to the subject), will soon cease to acknowledge Himself. But as, first, the ten tribes, and afterwards, the entire people, apostatized from God, by apostatizing from David, so, by their apostasy from him, they excluded themselves from all participation in the privileges of the people of God, which could flow to them only through him. It is only when they return to David by returning to Christ, that, from their self-made God, they come to the true God, and within the sphere of His blessings. That the same thing is repeated among ourselves in the case of those who have forsaken Christ their King, and yet imagine still to possess God, and that it is only by their returning to the brightness of His glory that they can attain to a true union with the Lord their God, and to a participation in the blessings which He bestows,— all this is so obvious as to require nothing beyond a simple suggestion. A perfectly sound interpretation of this passage is to be found in *Calvin*, who remarks: "David was, as it were, a messenger of the Lord, and, hence, that defection of the ten tribes was tantamount to a rejection of the living God. The Lord had, on a former occasion, said to Samuel (1 Sam. viii. 7), 'They have not rejected thee, but they have rejected Me.' But how much more was this applicable in the case of David, whom Samuel had anointed at the command of God, and whom the Lord had adorned with so many glorious attributes, that they could not reject his rule without, at the same time, publicly rejecting, to a certain extent, the Lord Himself! It is true, indeed, that David was then dead; but Hosea here represents, in his person, his everlasting dominion, which the Jews knew would last as long as the sun and moon." The expression,

T

"They tremble to the Lord," graphically describes the disposition of heart in him, who, trembling with terror and anxiety on account of the surrounding danger and distress, flees to Him who can alone afford help and deliverance. That we must thus explain it,—that we cannot entertain the idea of any trembling which proceeds from the inconceivable greatness of the blessing —a disposition of heart so graphically described by *Claudian* in the words,

> "Horret adhuc animus, manifestaque gaudia differt
> Dum stupet et tanto cunctatur credere voto,"—

and that we can as little think of a fearing or trembling which is the consequence of the knowledge of deep sinfulness and unworthiness, is shown by the parallel passage in chap. xi. 11: "They tremble as a bird out of Egypt, and as a dove out of the land of Assyria." The bird and the dove are here an emblem of helplessness. Substantially parallel is also chap. v. 15: "In their affliction they will seek Me." Their trembling is not voluntary; it is forced upon them by the Lord. But that they tremble *to the Lord*—that, through fear, they suffer themselves to be led to the Lord—is their free act, although possible only by the assistance of grace. The manner in which the words, "and to His goodness," are to be understood, is most plainly shown by the words, "I will return to my first husband, for it was *better* with me then than now," chap. ii. 9. Along with the Lord, they have lost His goodness also, and the gifts flowing from it. But distress again drives them to *seek* the Lord, and His goodness, which is inseparable from Himself. This explanation is confirmed by other parallel passages also; *e.g.*, Jer. xxxi. 12: "And they come and exult on the height of Zion, and flow together to the goodness of the Lord (טוב יהוה), to corn, and must, and oil, and lambs, and cattle;" ver. 14: "My people shall be satisfied with My goodness." Compare also Ps. xxvii. 13, xxxi. 20; Zech. ix. 17. We would therefore object to the opinion of several interpreters, who would explain טוב יהוה as being equivalent to כבוד יהוה, to His manifestation in the Angel of the Lord, the Λόγος, by whom His glory and goodness are made known.

THE PROPHET JOEL.

PRELIMINARY REMARKS.

The position which has been assigned to Joel in the collection of the Minor Prophets, furnishes an external argument for the determination of the time at which Joel wrote. There cannot be any doubt that the Collectors were guided by a consideration of the chronology. The circumstance, that they placed the prophecies of Joel just between the two prophets who, according to the inscriptions and contents of their prophecies, belonged to the time of Jeroboam and Uzziah, is thus equivalent to an express testimony that he also lived, and exercised his ministry, during that time.

By this testimony we have, in the meanwhile, obtained a firm standing-point; and it must remain firm, as long as it is not overthrown by other unquestionable facts, and the Collectors are not convicted of an historical error. But, as regards the latter point, there is the greater room for caution, because all the other statements which they have made are, upon a careful examination, found to stand the test; for none of the other Minor Prophets is found to occupy a place to which he is not entitled. But no such facts are to be found; on the contrary, everything serves to confirm their testimony.

It will not be possible to assign the prophecies of Joel to a later period; for Amos places at the head of one of his prophecies one of the utterances of Joel (compare Amos i. 2 with Joel iv. 16 [iii. 16]), as the text, as it were, on which he is to comment. That we are not thereby precluded from considering the two prophets as contemporaneous, is shown by the altogether similar case of Isaiah, in his relation to Micah. Isaiah, too, borrows, in chap. xiii. 6, a sentence from Joel i. 15, the peculiarity of which proves that the coincidence is not accidental. Such verbal repetitions must not be, by any means, considered as unintentional reminiscences. They served to exhibit that the prophets acknowledged one another as the organs of the Holy Spirit,—to testify the ἀκριβῆ διαδοχήν, the want of which in the times after Ezra and Nehemiah is mentioned by Josephus as one of the reasons why none of the writings of that period could be acknowledged as sacred. (See the Author's *Dissertations on the Genuineness of Daniel*, p. 199.) *Further,*— The description of the threatening judgment in chap. i. and ii. is, in Joel, kept just in that very same generality in which we find it in the oldest prophecies that have been preserved to us, viz., in Amos, in the first chapters of Isaiah and of Hosea; whilst in later times, the threatening is, throughout, particularized by the express mention of the instruments who were, in the first instance, to serve for its fulfilment, viz., the Assyrians and Babylonians. That which Judah had to suffer from the former was so severe, that Joel, in chap. iv. 4 ff.—where he mentions, although, as it were, only in the way of example, nations with which Judah had hitherto already come into hostile contact— would scarcely have passed them over in silence, in order to mention only the far lesser calamity inflicted by other nations.

But just as little can we think of an earlier period. It is certainly not accidental, that among all the prophets whose writings have been preserved to us, no one appeared at an earlier period; any more than it is accidental, that no prophecies are extant of the distinguished men of God in earlier times, of whom the historical books make mention, especially Elijah and Elisha. It was only when the great divine judgments were being prepared, and were approaching, that it was time, through their announcement, to waken from the slumber of security those who had forgotten God, and to open the treasures of hope and consolation to the faithful. Formerly, the living, oral word of the prophets was the principal thing; but now that God opened up to them a wider view,—that their calling had regard not only to the present, but also to the future time, the written word was raised to an equal dignity. Nothing, then, but the most cogent reasons could induce us to make, in the case of Joel only, an exception to so established a rule.

But we cannot acknowledge as such, what *Credner* (in his *Comment. on Joel*, p. 41 sqq.) has brought forward to prove that Joel committed to writing his prophecies as early as under the reign of Joash, *i.e.*, about 870–65 B.C., or from seventy to eighty years earlier than any of the other prophecies which have come down to us. If we do not allow ourselves to be carried away by the multitude of his words, we shall find that the only remaining plausible argument is—that the Syrians of Damascus are not mentioned among the enemies of the Covenant-people, as they are in Amos. From this, *Credner* infers that Joel must have prophesied before the first inroad of the Syrians on Judea, which, according to 2 Kings xii. 18 ff.; 2 Chron. xxiv. 23 ff., took place under Jehoash. But we need only look at that passage, in order to be convinced that the mention of that event could not be expected in Joel. The expedition of the Syrians was not directed against Judea, but against the Philistines. It was only a single detached corps which, according to Chronicles, incidentally, and on their return, made an inroad on Judah; but Jerusalem itself was not taken. This single act of hostility could not but be soon forgotten in the course of time. It was of quite a different character from that of the Phœnicians and Philistines mentioned by Joel, which were only particular outbreaks of the hatred and envy which they continually cherished against the Covenant-people, and which, as such, were preeminently the object of punitive divine justice. But on what ground does the supposition rest, that Joel must necessarily mention all those nations, with which the Covenant-people came, at any time, into hostile contact? The context certainly does not favour such an idea. The mention of former hostile attacks in chap. iv. (iii.) 4–8 is altogether incidental, as *Vitringa*, in his *Typ. Doctr. Proph.* p. 189 sqq., has admitted: "The prophet," says he, "was describing the heavy judgments with which God would, after the effusion of the Spirit, successively, and especially in the latter days, visit the enemies of the Church, and overthrow them, on account of the injuries which they had inflicted upon it. And while he was doing so, those injuries presented themselves to his mind, which in his own time, and in the immediate past, were inflicted upon the Jewish people—a portion of the universal Church—by the neighbouring nations, the Tyrians, Sidonians, and Philistines. To them he addresses his discourse *in passing* (*in transitu*), and announces to them, in the name of God, that they themselves also would not remain unpunished." The correctness of *Vitringa*, with his " *in transitu*," is proved by the גם, as well as by the circumstance, that vers. 9 ff. are closely connected with ver. 3; so that vers. 4 ff. form a real parenthesis. How entirely out of place would here have been any mention of the Syrians! There was necessarily something required which was very striking, and which, having but recently occurred, was still vividly remembered. But the matter was altogether different in the case of Amos. Joel has to do with the enemies of Judah only; Amos, with those of the kingdom of Israel also, among whom the Syrians were the most dangerous. Hence, he begins with them at once. The crime with which he charges them in chap. i. 3, that they had threshed the inhabitants of Gilead with threshing instruments of iron, concerns the kingdom of Israel only. The same applies to the Ammonites and Moabites also, who, in like manner, are mentioned by Amos, and not by Joel. The Ammonites are charged in Amos i. 13 with ripping up the women with child of Gilead, that they might enlarge their border; and the crime of the Moabites, rebuked in chap. ii. 1, occurred, very probably, during the time of, or after, the expedition against them, mentioned in 2 Kings iii.—the real instigator of which was the king of Israel.

We must indeed be astonished that *Hitzig, Ewald, Meier, Baur*, and others, after the example of *Credner*, have likewise declared in favour of the view that the prophecies of Joel were composed under Joash. None of the arguments, however, by which they attempt to support their view, can stand examination.

"There is nowhere, as yet, the slightest allusion to the Assyrians," says *Ewald*. But neither is any such found in Amos, nor in the first part of Hosea. An irruption, however, such as former times had not known,—an overflowing, as it were, by the heathen, such as could by no means proceed from the small neighbouring nations, but from extensive kingdoms only, is here also brought into view. Joel is, in this respect, in strict agreement with Amos, who embodies his prophecy concerning this event, in chap. vi. 14, in these words: "For, behold, I raise up against you, O house of Israel, Gentile people, saith the Lord, the God of hosts, and they shall afflict you from Hamath unto the river of the wilderness."

"There breathes here still the unbroken warlike spirit of the times of Deborah and David," *Ewald* further remarks. But is there in the fourth (third) chapter any trace of self-help on the part of the people? Judgment upon the Gentiles is executed without any human instrumentality, by God,—not by His earthly, but by His heavenly "heroes," who are sent down from heaven to earth, and who make short work with these fancied earthly heroes. Compare chap. iv. (iii.) 11–13, where the address is directed to the heavenly ministers of God, at the head of whom the Angel of the Covenant must be supposed to be: Ps. ciii. 20; Rev. xix. 14. *Such* a victory of the kingdom of God, all the prophets announce,—not only Isaiah and Micah, but also Ezekiel, *e.g.*, in chap. xxxviii. and xxxix.

"We perceive here the prophetic order in Jerusalem, still in the same ancient greatness as when Nathan and Gad may have exercised their office at the time of David. A whole people, without contradicting or murmuring, still depend upon the prophet. He desires the observance of a grievous ordinance, and willingly it is performed; his word is still like a higher command which all cheerfully obey. Nor is any discord to be seen in the nation, nor any wicked idolatry or superstition; the ancient simple faith still lives in them, unbroken and undivided." So *Ewald* still further remarks. But this argument rests upon a false supposition; a conversion of the people at the time of the prophet is not at all spoken of. The pretended repentance is to take place *in future*,—which, according to chap. i. 4, we must conceive of as being still afar off, namely, in the time after the divine judgments have broken in. And as to a progress in the apostasy of the people, it can scarcely be proved that such took place in the time betwixt Joash and Uzziah. Between these two, we do not find any new stage of corruption. The idolatry of Solomon, and the abominations of Athaliah, had exercised their influence, even as early as under Joash. How deep the rent was which, even then, went through the nation, is shown by the fact, that, according to 2 Chron. xxiv. 17, 18, after the death of Jehoiada, Joash gave way to the *urgent demands of the princes of Judah*, and allowed free scope to idolatry. Moreover, the threatening announcement of a judgment, which is to extend even to the destruction of the temple, proves how deep the apostasy was at the time of Joel. Where a judgment is thus threatened, which, in its terrors, far surpasses all former judgments, the "ancient faith" certainly cannot have been very vigorous.

"The Messianic idea appears here in its generality and indefiniteness, without being as yet concentrated in the person of an ideal king," *Hitzig* remarks. But if this argument were at all valid, we should have to go back even beyond the time of Joash. Solomon, David, and Jacob already knew the personal Messiah. The prophets, however, do not everywhere proclaim everything which they know. Even in Isaiah, there occur long Messianic descriptions, in which the Messiah Himself is not to be found. In Joel, moreover, everything is collected around the person of the " Teacher of righteousness."

" Joel," it is further remarked, " must have prophesied at a time when the Philistine and other nations, who had become so haughty under Jehoram, had but lately ventured upon destructive plundering expeditions as far as Jerusalem, 2 Chron. xxi. 10 ff." This argument would be plausible, if the injuries inflicted by the Philistines and the inhabitants of Tyrus had not appeared in equally lively colours before the mind of Amos (chap. i. 6–10), who, at all events, prophesied between seventy and eighty years after these events. It is just this fact which should teach caution in the application of such arguments. The recollection of such facts could not be lost, as long as the disposition continued from which they originated. It was as if they had happened in the present; for, under similar circumstances, similar events would have again immediately taken place. The passage chap. iv. 19, " Egypt shall be a desolation, and Edom shall be a desolate wilderness, for the violence against the children of Judah, because they have shed innocent blood in the land," shows also how lively was the recollection of injuries sustained long ago. Egypt and Edom in that passage are mentioned individually, in order to designate the enemies of the people of God in general, and yet with an allusion to deeds perpetrated by the Egyptians and Edomites properly so called. As the suffix in ארצם must be referred to the sons of Judah— for we have no historical account of a bloody deed perpetrated against Judah by the Edomites in their own land, and it was the land of Judah which was invaded and devastated by the host of locusts—we can think, in the case of the Egyptians, only of the invasion under Rehoboam (1 Kings xiv.), and in the case of the Edomites, only of the great carnage which they made in Judah, during the time at which David carried on war with Aram in Arabia and on the Euphrates,—probably at a time when he had sustained heavy losses in that warfare; compare my Comment. on Ps. xliv. and lx. Of any similar later occurrence there is no account extant. It is only by a fanciful exposition that "the innocent blood" can be found in 2 Kings viii. 20-22. The Edomites at that time kept only a defensive position, and did not come into the land of Judah. "The innocent blood" implies a war of conquest, and a hostile inroad.

"In chap. iv. (iii.) 4-7, Joel promises a return to the citizens of Judah, who had been carried away by the Philistines under Jehoram; and, hence, an age cannot have elapsed since that event." Thus *Meier* argues. But the words, "Behold, I raise them out of the place whither ye have sold them," contain no special prediction, but only the application of the general truth, that God gathers together the dispersed of Judah, and brings back again the exiled of Israel; and it is only requisite to compare concerning them, Gen. xv. 16, "In the fourth generation they shall come hither again," and l. 24, "God will visit you, and bring you out of this land."

We thus arrive at the conclusion that Joel occupies the right place in the Canon.

The assertion that Joel belonged to the priestly order, is as baseless as the similar one regarding Habakkuk, and as the supposition that the author of the Chronicles was a musician.

The book contains a connected description. It begins with a graphic account of the ruin which God will bring upon His apostate Congregation, by means of foreign enemies. These latter represent themselves to the prophet in his spiritual vision as an all-destroying swarm of locusts. The fundamental thought is this:—"Wheresoever the carcase is, there will the eagles be gathered together,"—wherever corruption manifests itself in the Congregation of the Lord, punishment will be inflicted. Because God has sanctified Himself *in* the Congregation, and has graciously imparted to her His holiness, He must therefore sanctify Himself upon her,—must manifest His holiness in her punishment, if she has become like the profane world. He cannot allow that, after the Spirit has departed, the dead body should still continue to appear as His kingdom, but strips off the mask of hypocrisy from His degenerate Church, by representing her outwardly as that which, by her guilt, she has become inwardly. This thought commonly appears in a special application, by the mention of the name of the particular people whom the Lord is, in the immediate future, to employ for the realization of it. In the case before us, however, He is satisfied with pointing to the dignity and power inherent in Him. The enemies are designated only as *people from the North*. But it was from the North—from Syria—that all the principal invasions of Palestine proceeded. Hence there is no reason either to think of one of them exclusively, or to exclude one. On the contrary, the comprehensive character of the description distinctly appears in i. 4. It is there, at the very threshold, intimated, that the heathenish invasion will be a fourfold one,—that Israel shall become the prey of four successive extensive empires. Joel's mission fell at the commencement of the written prophecy; and in harmony with this, he gives only an outline of that which it was reserved for the later prophets to fill up, and to carry out in its details, by the mention of the name of each single empire, as the times moved on. It was enough that Joel prophesied the destruction by these great empires, even before any one of them had appeared on the stage of history, and that he was enabled to point even to the fourfold number of them.

The threat of punishment, joined with exhortations to repentance, to which the people willingly listened, and humbled themselves before the Lord, continues down to chap. ii. 17. With this is connected the proclamation of salvation—which extends down to chap. iii. 2 (ii. 29). The showing of mercy begins with the fact, that God sends the *Teacher of righteousness*. He directs the attention of the people to the design of their sufferings, and invites the weary and heavy laden to come to the Lord, that He may refresh them. His voice is heard by those who are of a broken heart; and there then follows rich divine blessing, with its consummation—the outpouring of the Spirit. Both—the sending of the Teacher of righteousness, and the outpouring of the Spirit—had their preliminary fulfilments; the first of which took place soon after the commencement of the devastation by the locusts, in the time of the Assyrians,—a second, after the destruction by the Babylonians had come upon the people,—a third, after the visitation by the Greek tyranny under the Maccabees. But the chief reference of the prophecy is, throughout, to Christ, and to the vouchsafe-

ment of the blessing, and to the outpouring of the Spirit, origi-
nating in His mediation.

The announcement of salvation for the Covenant-people is,
in the third and last part, followed by the opposite of it, viz.,
the announcement of judgments upon the enemies of the Congregation of God. Their hatred of it, proceeding from hatred
to God, is employed by Him, indeed, as a means of chastising
and purifying His Church; but it does not, for that reason,
cease to be an object of His punitive justice. The fundamental idea of this part of the book is expressed in 1 Pet. iv. 17 by
the words : " For the time is come that judgment must begin
at the house of God. And if it first begin at us, what shall
the end be of them that obey not the Gospel of God ? And if
the righteous scarcely be saved, where shall the ungodly and
the sinner appear ?" The description bears here also, as in
the second and first parts, a comprehensive character. That
which, in the course of history, is realized in a long series of
single acts of divine interposition against the enemies of the
Church, is here brought together in a single scene. The overthrow of Assyria, Babylon, the Persian and Grecian monarchies, is comprehended in this prophecy. But its final fulfilment must be sought for only in the Messianic time. This is
sufficiently evident from the relation of this part to the second.
Having given ear to the Teacher of righteousness, and the
Spirit having been poured out upon her, the Congregation has
become an object of the loving providence of God. From this
flows the judgment upon her enemies. If, then, the promise of
the Teacher of righteousness and of the outpouring of the Spirit
be, in substance, Messianic, so, the judgment too must, in substance, bear a Messianic character. The same appears from iv.
(iii.) 18, according to which passage, simultaneously with the
judgments, there cometh forth, from the house of the Lord, a
fountain which watereth the valley of Shittim—the waters of
salvation which water the dry land of human need. (Compare
the remarks on Ezek. xlvii.; Zech. xiv. 8; and my *Comment. on
Revel.* xxii. 1.) This feature, however, clearly points to the
Messianic time.

We must here, however, avoid confounding the substance
with the form,—the idea with the temporary clothing which the
prophet puts upon it, in accordance with the nature of prophetic

vision, in which, necessarily, all that is spiritual must be represented in outward sketches and forms. This form is as follows:—In the place nearest to the temple, and which was able to contain a great multitude of people, in the valley of Jehoshaphat, all nations are gathered. (The valley very probably received its name from the appellation which, in the passage under consideration, the prophet gives to it, in order to mark its destination; for Jehoshaphat means, " the Lord judges," or " Valley of Judgment."[1]) The Lord, enthroned in the temple, exercises judgment upon them. In this manner—in outward forms of perception—the idea is brought out, that the judgment upon the Gentiles is an effect of the kingdom of God; that they are not punished on account of their violation of the natural law, but because of the hostile position which they had occupied against the teachers of God's revealed truth,—against the Lord Himself who is in His Church. Every violation of the natural law may be pardoned to those who have not stood in any other relation to God, even although they should have

---

[1] *Hofmann* (*Weissag. u. Erfül.* i. S. 203) has revived the explanation, according to which the valley of Jehoshaphat is to be understood as the valley in which, under Jehoshaphat, judgment was executed upon several Gentile nations. But this locality, the desert of Thekoa, which was about three hours distance from Jerusalem (compare my *Comment. on the Psalms*, in the *Introduction to Ps.* xlvi. xlviii. lxxxiii.), is at too great a distance from the temple, where, according to vers. 16 and 17, the Lord holds His judgment upon the nations. Tradition has rightly perceived that the valley of Jehoshaphat can be sought for only in the immediate vicinity of the temple. In favour of the valley of Jehoshaphat now so called, " at the high east brink of Moriah, the temple-hill " (*Ritter, Erdk.* xv. 1, S. 559; xvi. 1, S. 329), is also Zech. vi. 1–8 (compare the remarks on that passage). From the circumstance that there is, first, the mention of the name, and, then, the statement of its signification, " And I gather all nations, and bring them down into the valley of Jehoshaphat, and *plead* with them there," *Hofmann* infers that the name must have already existed as a proper name. There is, however, an analogy in Num. xx. 1: " And the people encamped at Kadesh ; "—but the place received the name Kadesh only because of the event to be subsequently related : previous to that, its name was Barnea. (Compare *Dissert. on Gen. of the Pent.* vol. ii. p. 310 ff.) The two theological names of the place, which arose only from the event recorded in Num. xx., occur even as early as Gen. xiv. 7. The natural name of the valley of Jehoshaphat is, moreover, in all likelihood, *King's Dale*; compare Gen. xiv. 17; 2 Sam. xviii. 18; and *Thenius* on this passage.

proceeded to the most fearful extent in depravity. They who were once disobedient, when the long-suffering of God waited in the days of Noah, were not as yet given over to complete condemnation, but were kept in prison until Christ came and preached to them. "This was the iniquity of Sodom: fulness of bread, and abundance of peace, were in her and her daughters; yet the hand of the poor and needy they did not assist; but they were haughty and committed abomination before the Lord: therefore He took them away as He saw good." But, nevertheless, the Lord will, at some future time, turn the captivity (the misery) of this Sodom and her daughters, and they shall be restored as they were before,—not corporeally, for their seed is utterly rooted out from the earth, and even their place is destroyed, but spiritually; compare Ezek. xvi. 49 ff. But, on the other hand, far more severe punishments are inflicted upon those who have rejected, not the abstract, but the concrete God,—not the God who is shut up in the heavens, but the God who powerfully manifests Himself on earth, in His Church. It is true, that as long as this revelation is still an imperfect one—as it was under the Old Testament dispensation—and hence the guilt of rejecting Him less, mercy may still be shown. External destruction does not involve spiritual ruin. Moab, indeed, is destroyed, so that it is no longer a people, because it has exalted itself against the Lord; yet, "in the latter days I will turn the captivity of Moab, saith the Lord," Jer. xlviii. 47. But when the revelation of the grace of God has become perfect, His justice also will be perfectly revealed against all who reject it, and rise in hostility against those who are the bearers of it: "Their worm shall not die, neither shall their fire be quenched, and they shall be an abhorring unto all flesh," Is. lxvi. 24. These remarks contain the key to all which the Lord declares as to the future judgment which, in its completion, belongs only to the future world. It is not the world as such, but that world to which the Gospel has been declared, and in the midst of which the Church has been founded, which forms the object of it; compare Matt. xxiv. 14.

JOEL I.–II. 17.

We shall not dwell here for any length of time upon the history of the expositions of this passage. It has been given with sufficient minuteness by *Pococke* and *Marckius* among older writers, and by *Credner* among the more modern. We content ourselves with remarking that the figurative exposition is the more ancient, having been adopted by the Chaldee Paraphrast, and by the Jews mentioned by *Jerome*, and that we cannot by any means, as *Credner* does, derive it from doctrinal considerations only ; for many, with whom such considerations weighed, as *Bochart*, *Pococke*, and *J. D. Michaelis*, do not approve of it ; whilst, on the other hand, there are among its defenders not a few who were guided by just the opposite motives, such as *Grotius*, *Eckermann*, *Berthold* (Einl. S. 1607 ff.), and *Theiner*. Two preliminary questions, however, require to be answered, before we can proceed to the main investigation.

1. Does Joel here describe a present, or a future calamity? The former has been asserted, in former times, by *Luther* and *Calvin* (compare, especially, his commentary on chap. i. 4), and in more recent times, with special confidence, by *Credner*. But there is nothing to favour this view. The frequent use of the Preterites would prove something in support of it, provided only we were not standing on prophetical ground. They are, moreover, found quite in the same manner in chap. iv.—in that portion which, by all interpreters unanimously, is referred to the future. And yet, if this view were to be acknowledged as sound, it ought to commend itself by stringent considerations, inasmuch as the prophetic analogy is, *a priori*, against it. There is not found anywhere in the prophets so long and so detailed a description of the present or the past. But, moreover, if we once give up the reference to the future, we could think of the past only ; for in chap. ii. 18, 19, the description of the salvation following upon the misery, is connected with the preceding context by the Future with *vav conversivum*. If, then, the scene of inward vision be forsaken, and everything referred to external reality, the calamity described in the preceding context must likewise be viewed as one already entirely past, and the salvation as already actually existing. It can be proved, how-

ever, from the contents, by incontrovertible special reasons, that the reference to the future is alone the correct one. The day of the Lord is several times spoken of as being at hand, which may be explained from the circumstance, that God's judgment upon His Church is a necessary effect of His justice, which never rests, but always shows itself as active. When, therefore, its object—the sinful apostasy of the people—is already in existence, its manifestation must also of necessity be expected; and although not the last and highest manifestation, yet such an one as serves for a prelude to it. The day of the Lord is, therefore, continually coming, is never absolutely distant; and its being spoken of as *at hand* is a necessary consequence of the saying, "Wheresoever the carcase is, there will the eagles be gathered together,"—a declaration founded upon the divine nature, and therefore ever true. (Compare my *Commentary on the Apocalypse* i. 1.) This designation is first found in i. 15: "Alas! for the day, for the day of the Lord is *at hand*, and as a destruction from the Almighty does it come." Here, two expedients for evasion have been tried. *Justi* maintained that "the day is at hand" was equivalent to "the day is there,"—an opinion which does not deserve any further refutation. *Holzhausen, Credner*, and *Hitzig* suppose that, by "the day of the Lord," we are not to understand the devastation by the locusts, but some severe judgment, to which that served as a prelude. This supposition is, however, opposed, first of all, by the verbal parallel passage in Isa. xiii. 6: "Howl ye, for the day of the Lord is at hand; it cometh as a destruction from the Almighty,"—where the day of the Lord cannot be any other than that which is described in the preceding context. But this opinion is further opposed by the circumstance, that, in the subsequent context, there is not the slightest trace of any other judgment than that of the devastation by the locusts; on the contrary, with its termination, the whole period of suffering comes to an end, as regards the Covenant-people, and the time of blessing upon them and of judgment upon their enemies begins. But the necessity for understanding, by "the day of the Lord at hand," the devastation by the locusts, and hence, for viewing the latter as still future, is even more clearly seen from the second passage, chap. ii. 1, 2: "Blow ye the trumpet in Zion, and sound an alarm in My holy mountain; let all the inhabitants of the land tremble, for the day of the Lord *hath come*, for *nigh at hand*, a day of darkness and gloominess, a day of clouds and fogs, as the morning-red spread upon the mountains, a people numerous and strong; there hath not been the like from eternity, neither shall there be any more after it, even through the years of all generations." That, by "the day of the Lord," which the prophet, from the standing-point of his inward vision, here speaks of as having already come, and as being in reality nigh at hand, we must understand the same day as that which is minutely described in the preceding and subsequent context, viz., the devastation by the locusts, appears, in the first place, from the verbal parallel passage, Ezek. xxx. 2, which likewise speaks of one day only: "Thou son of man, prophesy and say, Thus saith the Lord, Howl ye, woe for the day! For the day is near, a day to the Lord, a day of clouds, the time of the heathen it shall be." But what places the matter beyond all doubt are the words: "A people numerous and strong." These words, by which, according to what follows, the locusts only can be understood, form an explanatory apposition to "the day of the Lord," "the day of darkness," etc. To this we may further add, that, by the last words, this judgment is represented as the most formidable, and the last by which Judea shall be visited; so that we cannot by any means think of a subsequent later day of the Lord. 2. Are the different names of the locusts designations of various species of locusts, or are these, beside the common name of the locusts, only poetical names, which denote the qualities coming into consideration? *Credner* has attempted to prove the former. He maintains that Joel's description has to do with two generations of locusts,—the first belonging to the end of one year,—the second, to the beginning of the year following. The latter he thinks to be the offspring of the former. In accordance with this hypothesis, he explains the different names. גזם is, according to him, the migratory locust, which visits Palestine chiefly in autumn; ארבה, elsewhere the general name of locusts, here the young brood; ילק, the young locust in the last stage of its transformation, or between the third and fourth casting of the skin; חסיל, the perfect locust, proceeding from the last trans-formation, and, hence, as the brood proceeded from the גזם, חסיל would be the same גזם.

It forms a general argument against this hypothesis, that, according to it, the prophet should enter so deeply and minutely into the natural history of locusts, that a Professor of that science might learn from him. There is nothing analogous to this, either in Scripture generally, or in the Prophets particularly. The difficulty, moreover, increases, when we assume—what has been already proved—that the description refers to the future. The religious impression which the prophet has, after all, solely in view, would not gain, but suffer by such a minute detail in the description of a future natural event,—especially such as a devastation by locusts.

A closer examination proves that the whole explanation of the names of the locusts, upon which the hypothesis is built, is untenable. It appears, then, that the prophet knows of only one kind of locusts, which he divides into four hosts; and that, with the exception of ארבה, the names are not those of natural history, but poetical, and taken from the qualities of the locusts.

Let us first demonstrate that the interpretation of ילק, upon which *Credner* founds that of the other names, is inadmissible. This interpretation, he maintains (S. 295), is put beyond all doubt by the passage, Nah. iii. 16: "The ילק casts its skin and flies away." The merchants, who constituted the principal part of the population of Nineveh, are, according to him, compared to a ילק which flies away, after having cast his skin for the third or last time. But this passage of Nahum, when minutely examined and correctly interpreted, is by itself sufficient to refute that opinion concerning the ילק. In ver. 15, it is said concerning Nineveh: "There shall the fire devour thee, the sword shall cut thee off, it shall eat thee up, as the *licker* (כילק): make thyself many as the *lickers*, make thyself many as the locusts. Ver. 16: Thou hast multiplied thy merchants like the stars of heaven; *lickers broke through and flew away.* Ver. 17: Thy princes are like locusts, and thy captains are as a host of grasshoppers, which camp on the hedges in the day of cold. The sun has risen, and they flee away, and their place is not known where they are." This passage just proves that ילק must be *winged* locusts. The inhabitants of Nineveh are numerous like the locusts; numerous are her rich merchants; but suddenly there cometh upon them a numberless host of locusts, who rob

U

them of everything, and fly away. They who rob and fly away, in ver. 16, are not the merchants, but the enemies. This becomes quite evident from the comparison of ver. 15, where quite the same antithesis is found between—"The sword shall eat thee up as the lickers" (Nominat.), and "Make thyself many as the lickers." The verb פשט, in its common signification, *irruit, invasit ad praedam agendam*, is here, in reference to the merchants, very significant. But what is decisive against the explanation of *Credner* is this:—that the signification "to cast the skin" cannot be established at all, and that the whole sense is utterly unsuitable. For the discourse is not here, by any means, of mercenaries or foreign traders, but of the native merchants of Nineveh, just as, in the subsequent verses, the discourse is about her own nobles. How then could that image be suitable, which must certainly denote a safe transition from one state into a better?—*Credner* moreover refers to Jer. li. 27, where to ילק the quality סמר, *horridus*, is ascribed. This, according to him, is to be referred to the rough, horn-like coverings of the wings of the young locusts. But, according to the context, and to the analogy of the parallel passage, li. 14, we should rather expect that "horrid" is here a designation of the multitude. (Compare the ὡς ἀκρίδων πλῆθος of the LXX.) But it is still more natural to give to סמר the signification of "awful," "terrible." (Compare Ps. cxix. 120, where the verb occurs with the meaning "to shudder.")—That by ילק, not the young brood, but the winged locusts are to be understood, appears also from a comparison of Ps. cv. 34 with Exod. x. 12 ff. In Exod. a single army of *flying* locusts overspread Egypt; the Psalmist, in recalling this event to memory, says: "He spake, and the locusts came, and ילק without number." From this passage, especially when compared with Ps. lxxvii. 46, where, instead of ילק, חסיל is interchanged with ארבה, which alone is found in Exod., it is very clearly seen that ילק, the *licker*, is nothing else than a poetical epithet of the locusts. It never occurs, indeed, in prose; and this can be the less accidental, as גזם, the *gnawer*, is also never found in prose writings, and חסיל only once, in the prayer of Solomon, 1 Kings viii. 37—as that which it is in reality, as a mere attribute to ארבה. That ילק has its name from the eating, is shown by Nah. iii. 15: "The sword shall eat thee up as the ילק." And, in addition to this, we may further urge, that the exposition of אַרְבֶּה is altogether fictitious, and contradicted by all the passages;—that the prophet in ii. 25 inverts the order, and puts the גָזָם last, from which it is certainly to be safely inferred that the arrangement in i. 4 is not a chronological one;—that *Credner* himself, by his being obliged to grant that גָזָם and חָסִיל do not signify a particular kind of locusts, raises suspicions against his interpreting the two other names of particular kinds;—and that if this interpretation were to be considered as correct, גָזָם and חָסִיל must denote the locusts as fully grown. But that is by no means the case. The origin of the name גָזָם is, moreover, clearly shown by Amos iv. 9: "Your vineyards, your fig-trees, and your olive-trees,—הַגָּזָם devours them." As regards the corn, other divine means of destruction had been mentioned immediately before; the trees alone then remained for the locusts, and they received a name corresponding to this special destination, viz., הַגָּזָם, *the gnawer.* —The verb חָסַל is, in Deut. xxviii. 38, used of the devouring of the locusts, and חָסִיל never occurs excepting where the locusts are viewed in this capacity. (Besides the passages already quoted, compare Is. xxxiii. 4.)

The following also may be considered. The description of the ravages of the second brood is, according to *Credner*, to begin in chap. ii. 4. But the suffix in ver. 4 refers directly to the winged locusts spoken of in vers. 1–3; and in the verb יְרֻצוּן they are the subject.

And now, every one may judge what value is to be attached to a hypothesis which has everything against it, and nothing in its favour, and the essential suppositions of which—such as the departure of the swarms, their leaving their eggs behind, their death in the Red Sea—are, as the author of the hypothesis himself confesses, passed over in silence by the prophet.

We may now proceed to the solution of our proper problem. There are no general reasons, either against the figurative, or against the literal interpretation; neither of them has any unfavourable prejudice which can be urged against it. A devastation by real locusts is threatened, in the Pentateuch, against the transgressors of the law, Deut. xxviii. 38, 39; against the Egyptians, the Lord actually made use of this, among other methods of punishment; and a devastation in Israel by locusts is, in Amos iv. 9, represented as an effect of divine anger.—

On the other hand, figurative representations of that kind are of very common occurrence. In Isaiah, *e.g.*, the invading Assyrians and Egyptians appear, in a continuous description, as swarms of flies and bees. The comparison of hostile armies with locusts is very common, not only on account of their multitude (from which circumstance the locusts received their name in Hebrew), but also on account of the sudden surprise, and the devastation: compare Judges vi. 5; Jer. xlvi. 23, li. 27; Judith ii. 11. Several times a hostile invasion also is represented under the *image* and *symbol* of the plague of the locusts. In Nah. iii. 15–17, the Assyrians appear in the form of locusts, —and that this is not only on account of their numbers, but also on account of the devastations which they make, is shown by the comparison with the יֶלֶק in ver. 15;—and just in the same manner are the enemies described who accomplish their overthrow. And,—what is completely analogous,—in Amos vii. 1–3, the prophet beholds the approaching divine judgment under the image of a swarm of locusts, just as, in ver. 4, under that of a fire, and in ver 7, under that of a plumb-line. All these three images are in substance identical; their meaning is expressed in ver. 9 by the words: "The high places of Isaac shall be desolate, and the sanctuaries of Israel shall be destroyed." The locusts denote destroying hostile armies; the fire denotes war; and the plumb-line, the destruction to be accomplished by the enemies. It was so much the more natural to represent the divine judgment under the image of a devastation by locusts— as is done also in Rev. ix. 3 ff.—because, formerly, it had actually manifested itself in this way in Egypt. The figurative representation had therefore a significant substratum in the history of the past. But it is, throughout, the custom of the prophets to describe the future under the image of the analogous past, which, as it were, is revived in it.—It ought to be still further remarked, that we must, *a priori*, be the less indisposed to admit a detailed symbolical representation in Joel, as the two prophets, betwixt whom he is placed, have likewise such symbolical portions.

The decision depends, therefore, upon the internal character of the description itself. An allegory must betray itself as such, by significant hints; where these are wanting, it is arbitrary to assume its existence. Following the order of the text, we shall bring together everything of this kind which we find in it.

The words, even, of the introduction,—" Hath any such thing happened in your days, and in the days of your fathers? Of it you shall tell your sons, and your sons to their sons, and their sons to the succeeding generation,"—scarcely permit us to think of a devastation by locusts in the literal sense. It could only be by means of the grossest exaggeration—which, if it were far from any prophet, was certainly so from the simple and mild Joel—that he could represent, as the greatest disaster which ever befell, or should ever befall the nation, a devastation by locusts which was, after all, only a transitory evil. For it is the greatness of the disaster which is implied in the call to relate it to the latest posterity; no later suffering should be so great as to cause this one to be forgotten.

We must not overlook the expression in ver. 6 : "*For a nation* (גוי) has come up over my land." " Nation," according to most interpreters, is thought to signify the mere multitude; but in that case, עם would certainly have been used, as is done in Prov. xxx. 25, 26, concerning the ants. In גוי there is implied not only the idea of what is hostile—this *Credner* too acknowledges—but also of what is profane. This, indeed, is the principal idea; and, on this account, even the degenerate Covenant-people several times receive the name גוי. That this principal idea is here likewise applicable, is evident from the antithesis : " Over my land." It is true, that the suffix cannot be referred to Jehovah, as is done by *J. H. Michaelis* and others, although the antithesis would thus most strikingly appear; but as little can we refer it, as is done by modern interpreters, to the prophet as an individual; for, in this case the antithesis would be lost altogether. The comparison of vers. 7 and 19 clearly shows that, according to a common practice (compare the Introduction to Micah, and the whole prophecy of Habakkuk), the prophet speaks in the name of the people of God. A strange, unheard-of event! A heathen host has invaded the land of the people of God! The antithesis is in ii. 18 : " Then the Lord was jealous for His land, and spared His people." We do not think that the prophet loses sight of his image. He designates the locust as the heathen host; but he would not have chosen this designation, which, when literally understood, is very strange, unless the matter had induced him to do so. If it be understood figuratively, Amos vi. 14 entirely harmonizes with it.—In the same verse (Joel i. 6) it is said: " His teeth, the teeth of a lion, cheek teeth of a lion to him ;" on which Rev. ix. 8 is to be compared. This comparison is quite suitable to figurative locusts, to furious enemies (compare Is. v. 29; Nah. ii. 12, 13; Jer. ii. 15, iv. 7, xlix. 19; Ezek. xxxii. 2; Dan. vii. 4), but not to natural locusts; for the lion cannot possibly be the symbol of mere voracity.

It is remarkable, that in the description of the locusts in this verse, and throughout, their flying is not mentioned at all. It is only in chap. ii. **2,** " Day of darkness and gloominess, day of clouds and thick darkness," that *Credner* supposes such an allusion to exist. The darkness is, according to him, in consequence of the swarm of locusts coming up in the skies. But the incorrectness of such a supposition is immediately perceived, upon a comparison of chap. ii. 10. Before the host, and before it arrives, the earth quakes, the heavens tremble, sun and moon cover themselves with darkness, and the stars withdraw their shining. It is only after all this has happened, that the Lord approaches at the head of His host. It is not from this host, therefore, that the darkness can proceed. On the contrary, the darkening of the heavens, as is quite conclusively shown by the numerous almost literally agreeing parallel passages (compare the remarks on Zech. xiv. 6), is the symbol of the anger of God, the sign that He approaches as a Judge, and an Avenger. But in what way could the omission of every reference to the flying of the locusts, in a description so minute, be accounted for other than this: that the reality presented nothing corresponding to this feature?

It is only the heaviest and most continuous suffering, and not a transitory plague by locusts, which can justify the call in i. 8: " Howl like a virgin girded with sackcloth for the husband of her youth." This verse forms the transition to ver. 9, where the sacrifice in the house of Jehovah appears as cut off, and connects Joel with Hosea, in whom the image, of which the outlines only are given here, appears finished. Zion has also lost the friend of her youth—the Lord; compare Prov. ii. 17: " Who forsaketh the friend of her youth, and forgot the covenant of her God " Is. liv. 6; Jer. ii. 2, iii. 4.—Of great

importance for the question under consideration are ver. 9:
"The meat-offering and drink-offering are cut off from the
house of the Lord;" and ver. 13: "Gird yourselves and lament,
ye priests, howl ye ministers of the altar, come, spend all night
in sackcloth, ye ministers of my God; for the meat-offering
and drink-offering are withholden from the house of your God."
It is quite inconceivable that the want of provisions, resulting
from a natural devastation by real locusts, could have been the
reason that the meat-offering and drink-offering, which, in a
material point of view, were of so little value, should have been
withheld from the Lord; inasmuch as the cessation of it appears
in these passages as the consummation of the national calamity.
During the siege of Jerusalem by Pompey, the legal sacrifices
existed, according to *Josephus* (*Arch.* xiv. 4, § 3), even amidst
the greatest dangers to life, during the irruption of the enemies
into the city, and in the midst of the carnage. It is true that,
during the last siege by the Romans, when matters had come
to an extremity, *Johannes* ordered the sacrifices to be discontinued. But this was done, not from want of materials, but
because there were none to offer them—from ἀνδρῶν ἀπορία,
as *Josephus* says (*Bell. Jud.* vi. 2, § 1; compare *Reland* in
Havercamp on this passage)—and to the great dissatisfaction
of the people in the city, ὁ δῆμος δεινῶς ἀθυμεῖ. The national
view is expressed in what *Josephus* says on this occasion to
Johannes, to whom he had been sent by Titus on account of
this event: "If any man should rob thee of thy daily food,
thou, most wicked man, wouldst certainly consider him as thine
enemy. Dost thou then think that thou wilt have for thine
associate in this war, God, whom thou hast robbed of His
eternal worship?" But the sound explanation readily suggests
itself, as soon as it is admitted that behind the locusts the
Gentiles are concealed. In that case, Dan. ix. 27, where the
destroyer makes sacrifice and oblation to cease, is parallel. The
destruction of the temple is also announced by the contemporary
Amos in chap. ix.; compare ii. 5: "And I send fire upon Judah,
and it devours the palaces of Jerusalem." Of a similar purport,
in the time after Joel, is the passage in Micah, chap. iii. 12.

The words in ver. 15—"Woe, for the day, for the day
of the Lord is at hand, and as destruction from the Almighty
does it come,"—point to something infinitely higher than a mere

desolation *by locusts in the literal sense*. This appears from a comparison of Is. xiii. 6, where they are taken, almost verbatim, from Joel, and used with a reference to the judgment of the Lord upon the whole earth. This is granted even by *Credner* himself, when he makes the vain attempt (compare S. 345) to refer them to a judgment different from the devastation by the locust. The same is the case with *Maurer* and *Hitzig*. How, indeed, is it at all conceivable that a national calamity, so small and transient as a devastation by real locusts would have been, *should have been considered by the prophet as the day of the* Lord κατ᾽ ἐξοχήν, as the conclusion and completion of all the judgments upon the Covenant-people? A conception like this would imply such low notions of God's justice, and such a total misapprehension of the greatness of human guilt, as we find in none of the Old Testament prophets, and, generally, in none of the writers of Holy Scripture. That which the men of God under the Old Testament, from the first—Moses—to the last, announce, is the total expulsion of the people from the *country which they defiled by their sins.*

The image suddenly changes in vers. 19 and 20 : "To thee, O Lord, do I cry. For fire devoureth the pastures of the wilderness, and flame burneth all the trees of the field. Even the beasts of the field desire for Thee; for the fountains of waters are dried up, and fire devoureth the pastures of the wilderness." The divine punishment appears under the image of an all-devouring fire. Now, since we cannot here think of a literal fire, it is certain that, in the preceding verses also, a figurative representation prevails. *Holzhausen* and *Credner* (S. 163), and others, attempt to evade this troublesome inference, by asserting that fire and flame are here used instead of the heat of the sun, scorching everything. But this assertion is, at all events, expressed in a distorted and awkward manner. Fire and flame are never used of the heat of the sun. According to this view, it ought rather to be said that the prophet represents the consuming heat, under the image of fire poured down from heaven. But even this cannot be entertained. For the parallel passage chap. ii. 3, "*Before him fire devoureth, and after him flame burneth*," shows that the fire, being immediately connected with the locusts, cannot be a cause of destruction independent of, and co-ordinate with, them. That the locusts are the sole cause of the devastation, and that there is not another cause besides them, viz., the heat, is evident also from the words: "As the garden of Eden is the land before them, and behind them a desolate wilderness, and nothing is left by them." The burning anger of God is represented under the image of a consuming and destroying fire, with a reference to the destruction of Sodom and Gomorrah, in which the divine wrath really manifested itself in that way. Under the image of fire, *war* also, one of the principal punishments of God, is often represented. Thus, fire means the fire of war in Num. xxi. 28; Amos i. 4, 7, 10, etc.; Jer. xlix. 27; Rev. viii. 8, 10. On the latter of these passages, my Commentary may be compared. If, then, the fire spoken of in this passage mean likewise the fire of war, and the locusts, the heathen enemies, the difficulty presented by the connection of these two things is solved. The comparison of Amos vii. here serves as a key. In vers. 1–3, the divine punishment is represented by the prophet under the image of a great army of locusts laying waste the country, which is just beginning to recover under Jeroboam II. after the former calamities inflicted by the Syrians; and then in ver. 4, under the image of a great fire devouring the sea (*i.e.*, the world), and eating up the holy land. This analogy is so much the more important, the more impossible it is to overlook, in other passages also, the points of agreement betwixt Joel and Amos. But the symbolical representation goes still further; it extends even to the details. The beasts of the field are the barbarous, heathen nations. In ver. 19, the desolations are described which the fire of war accomplishes among Israel; in ver. 20, those which it effects among the Gentiles: compare the antithesis between the beasts of the field and the sons of Zion in ii. 22. In Is. lvi. 9, the beasts of the field likewise occur as a figurative designation of the heathen. In Jer. xiv.—a prophecy which has been distorted by expositors through a too literal interpretation—the image is, in vers. 5, 6, individualized by the mention of particular wild beasts—the hind and the wild ass. Joel himself indicates that the beasts in this description must, in general, be understood figuratively, by using in ver. 18 the word נאשׁמו, which can be explained only by "become guilty," "suffer punishment." (Compare Is. xxiv. 6: "Therefore curse devoureth the land, and they that dwell in it become guilty;" and

Hos. xiv. 1.) The word נאנחה, which is never used of beasts, likewise leads us to think of men. "How do the beasts groan," is explained by "All the merry-hearted do groan," in Is. xxiv. 7. The words תערג אליך, in which there is an evident allusion to Ps. xlii. 2, must likewise appear strange, if the description be understood literally. But what is decisive in favour of the figurative interpretation is ii. 22 : "Be not afraid, ye beasts of the field, for the pastures of the wilderness are green with grass, for the tree beareth her fruit, the fig-tree and vine do yield their strength." The object of joy is here described, first, figuratively, and then, literally. The pastures of the wilderness are green with grass, *i.e.*, the tree, etc. It is only thus that the כי can be accounted for; it states the reason, only when the pastures of the wilderness are not understood literally. *The fruits of the trees are mentioned here as the ordinary food of the beasts of the field. Hitzig*, it is true, remarks on this : "That many beasts of the field feed upon fruits of trees which they gather up, and that, *e.g.*, foxes eat grapes also." But the point at issue here is the ordinary food; and Gen. i. 29, 30, where the trees are given to man, and the grass to the beasts, is decisive as to the literal or figurative interpretation. Under the image of unclean beasts—especially wild beasts—the Gentiles appear also in Acts xi. 6.—Nor can "the rivers of water" (ver. 20) be understood literally. The water of rivers, brooks, and fountains, is, in Scripture, the ordinary figure for the sources of sustenance, of thriving, wealth, and prosperity; compare remarks on Rev. viii. 10.

Chap. ii. 2 is to be considered as indicating the reason which induced Joel to choose this figurative representation. The words, "There hath not been anything the like from eternity, neither may there be any more after it, even to the years of all generations," are borrowed, almost verbally, from Exod. x. 14. The prophet thereby indicates that he transfers the past, in its individual definiteness, to the future, which bears a substantial resemblance to it. What was then said of the plague of locusts especially, is here applied to the calamity thereby prefigured. From among all the judgments upon the Covenant-people (for these alone are spoken of), this judgment is the highest and the last; and such the prophet could say, only if the whole sum of divine judgments, up to their consummation, represented itself to his inner vision under the image of the devastation by locusts. The absurdities into which men are led by the hypothesis of a later origin of the Pentateuch, are here seen in a remarkable instance—viz., in the assertion of *Credner*, that the passage in Exodus is an imitation of that of Joel. The verse immediately following, "As the garden of Eden (*i.e.*, Paradise) the land is before him," has an obvious reference to Genesis, not only to Gen. ii. 8, but also to xiii. 10, where the vale of Siddim, before the divine judgment, is compared to the garden of Jehovah—to Paradise.

In chap. ii. 6 it is said, "Before him nations tremble." That the mention of the *nations* here is but ill adapted to the literal interpretation, appears from the circumstance, that while *Credner* understands by the עמים, Judah and Benjamin, *Hitzig* attempts to explain it by people. But if, by the locusts, the heathen conquerors are designated, the עמים is quite in its place. When the powerful heathen empires overflowed the land, Israel always formed only a part of a large whole of nations; compare i: 19, ii. 22. Amos describes how the fire of war and of the desire of conquest raged, not only in Israel, but among all the nations round about, and consumed them. In addition to Amos chap. i. compare especially Amos vii. 4, 5, where, as objects of hostile visitation, are pointed out, first, the sea, *i.e.*, the world, and then, the heritage of the Lord. According to Is. x. 6, the mission of Asshur was a very comprehensive one. In Habakkuk and Jer. chap. xxv. the judgments which the Chaldeans inflicted upon Judah, appear only as a part of a universal judgment upon all nations.

According to chap. ii. 7–9, the locusts take the city by storm. They cannot be warded off by force of arms. They climb the wall. They fill the streets, and enter by force into the houses. Real locusts are not dangerous to towns, but only to the fields.

In chap. ii. 11, every feature is against the literal explanation. "And the Lord giveth His voice before His army; for His camp is very numerous, for he is strong that executeth His word; for the day of the Lord is great and very terrible, who can comprehend it?" There is not the remotest analogy in favour of the supposition which would represent an army of locusts as the host and camp of God, at the head of which He

Himself marches as a general, and before which He causes His
thunders to resound like trumpets. It is true that, in some
Arabic writer, this is mentioned as a Mosaic command: "You
shall not kill locusts, for they are the host of God, the Most
High;" see *Bochart* ii. p. 482, ed. *Rosenmüller* iii. p. 318. But
who does not see that this sentence owes its origin to the passage
under consideration? Is. xiii. 2–5, where the Lord marches at
the head of a great army to destroy the whole earth, may here
be compared; and on Joel ii. 10, "Before him the earth
quaketh, the heavens tremble, the sun and the moon mourn, and
the stars withdraw their shining," Is xiii. 10 and Jer. iv. 28
may be compared, where, in the view of threatening hostile inundation, the earth laments, and the heavens above mourn.

In ii. 17, "Give not Thine heritage to reproach, *that the
heathen should rule over them*" (לִמְשָׁל־בָּם גּוֹיִם), the prophet drops
the figure altogether, and allows the reality—the devastation of
the country by heathen enemies—to appear in all its nakedness.
(It is worthy of notice that by the term גּוֹיִם in this verse, our
remarks on גּוֹי in ii. 6 receive a confirmation.) The defenders
of the literal explanation have tried a twofold mode of escaping
from this difficulty. *Michaelis* explains thus: "Spare Thy
people, and deliver them from that plague of locusts. For if
they should continue to swarm any longer, the greatest famine
would arise, and Thy people, in order to satisfy the cravings of
hunger, would be compelled to flee into the territories of heathen
nations to serve them for bread, and to submit not only to their
sway, but to ignominy." But every one must at once see how
far-fetched this explanation is. In all history we do not find
any instance in which a devastation by locusts—which affects
the produce of one year only, and even this never completely
and throughout the whole country—has reduced a people to the
necessity of placing themselves under the dominion of foreign
nations. Modern interpreters—and especially *Credner*—take
refuge in another explanation: "Give not up Thine heritage to
the mockery of heathens over them." They assert that the signification "to mock" is required by the parallelism. But we
cannot see how, and why. The ignominy of Israel consisted
just in this, that they, the heritage of the Lord, were brought
under the dominion of the Gentiles. It is just by the parallelism
that the signification "to rule" is required. For it is the herit-

age of the Lord, and the dominion of the Gentiles, which form a striking contrast, and not their mockery. The very same contrast is implied in ver. 18, in the words: "Then the Lord was jealous for His land." In these, the prophet reports the manner in which the Lord put away that glaring contradiction. They are not natural locusts, but only the heathen enemies, who can be the objects of the jealousy of the Lord; *His* land, *His* people, He cannot give up as a prey to heathen nations. But *further*—and this alone is sufficient to settle the question—the explanation is altogether unphilological. The verb משל never has the signification "to mock;" the phrase מָשַׁל מָשָׁל, "to form a proverb," is altogether peculiar to Ezekiel, in whose prophecies it several times occurs. In the other books, nothing occurs which would be, even in the smallest degree, to the purpose, except that in the ancient language of the Pentateuch מּשלים occurs once, in Num. xxi. 27, in the signification "poets." The verb משל with ב means always, and without exception, "to rule over"—properly, "to rule by entering into any one." Thus it occurs especially in that passage which the prophet had in view, Deut. xv. 5, 6: "If thou wilt hearken unto the voice of Jehovah thy God . . . . . thou shalt rule over many nations, and they shall not rule over thee," ומשלת בגוים רבים ובך לא ימשלו. Compare also the very similar passages, Ps. cvi. 41: "And He gave them into the hand of the heathen, and they that hated them ruled over them," וימשלו בם; and Lament. v. 8: "Servants rule over us," משלו בנו. That it is from prejudice alone that the selection of the signification "to mock" can be accounted for, appears also from the circumstance that all the old Translators (the LXX., *Jonath.*, *Syr.*, *Vulg.*) render it by "to rule."

More than one proof is offered by ver. 20: "And I will remove from you the Northman, and will drive him into the land dry and desolate; his van into the fore sea, and his rear into the hinder sea; and his stench shall come up, and his ill-savour shall arise, for he has magnified to do."

1. If we understand this literally, and refer it to real locusts, then the designation by הצפוני, *i.e.,* "one from the North," "a Northman," is inexplicable. It is true that there is no foundation for the common assertion, that locusts move only from the South to the North (compare *Credner*, S. 284); but in all history there is not one instance known of locusts having come

to Palestine from the North—from Syria.   But even although occasionally single swarms, after having come to Syria from their native country, the hot and dry South, may have strayed thence to Palestine, such is not conceivable of so enormous a swarm as is here described, which, with youthful strength, devastated the whole of Palestine from one end to the other.   Is it, moreover, probable that the prophet, who, as we have already seen, prophesies things future, would mention a circumstance so accidental as the transient abode of a swarm of locusts in Syria? Such a residence, *besides*, would not justify the assertion.   The termination ־י added to common names, indicates origin and descent.   An inhabitant of a town, for example, who should reside for a short time in a village, could not for that reason be called a פרזי.—*Finally*—The native country of the real locusts is plainly enough indicated by the words: "And I will drive him into the land dry and desolate."   Who does not see that, by these words, the hot and dry southern countries are marked out, and that the prophet expresses the thought, "The enemies will be driven back to the place whence they came," by mentioning the country from which the real locusts used to come? Our opponents are here greatly embarrassed.   Some explain: "The locusts marching northward,"—*Hezel* and *Justi*, without the slightest countenance from the *usus loquendi*: "The dark and fearful host."   This opinion was approved of by *Gesenius* in the *Thesaurus;* but in opposition to it *Hitzig* may be compared, who himself gives the explanation, "The Typhonic." *V. Cöln* (*de Joelis aetate*, Marb. 1811, p. 10).   *Ewald* and *Meier* propose a change in the text.   With the reasons preventing us from referring the expression to the locusts in a literal sense, we may combine the fact that the North is constantly mentioned as the native land of the most dangerous enemies of Israel, viz., the Assyrians and Chaldeans.   And although this designation be, in a geographical point of view, inaccurate, this is outweighed by the circumstance, that enemies always invaded Palestine from Syria, after having previously made that land a part of their dominions.   Compare Zeph. ii. 13: "And the Lord stretches out His hand over the *North*, and destroys Assyria, and makes Nineveh a desolation—a dry wilderness;" Jer. i. 14: "And the Lord said unto me, Out of the *North* the evil shall break forth upon all the inhabitants of the land;" Jer. iii. 18, where the land of the North is mentioned as the land of the captivity of Judah and Israel; Jer. iv. 6, vi. 1, 22, x. 22, xlvi. 24, where the people of the North form the antithesis to Egypt, the African power; and Zech. ii. 10. *Jerome* long ago remarked: " The prophet mentions the North, that we might not think of real locusts, which are wont to come from the South, but might, by the locusts, understand the Assyrians and Chaldeans."

2. That we have here to do with a poetical description, and not with one of natural history, appears from a designation of the places to which the locusts are to be driven. Among these, the dry and hot southern country—the Arabian desert—is first mentioned; then, the anterior sea, *i.e.*, the Dead Sea, situated eastward of Jerusalem; and lastly, the hinder, or Mediterranean Sea. That, according to the view of the prophet, the dispersion in these different directions was to take place in a moment, appears from the circumstance that, according to his description, the van of the same army is driven into one sea, and the rear, into the other sea. Now, every one very easily sees that this is a physical impossibility, inasmuch as opposite winds cannot blow at the same time. *Credner's* explanation, according to which the פנים of the locusts is intended to be the swarm of those who first invaded Palestine, while סופו is their brood, deserves mention in so far only as it affords a proof of the greatness of the absurdities into which one may be deluded, after he has once adopted a groundless hypothesis.

3. The words, " For he has magnified to do," state the reason of the destruction of the locusts. They are *punished* in this manner, because they have *committed sin* by their proud haughtiness. Because they have magnified to do, the Lord now magnifies Himself to do against them, ver. 21; He glorifies Himself in their destruction, since, at the time of their power, they glorified themselves, and trampled God under foot. But sin and punishment necessarily imply responsibility; and it would be indeed difficult to prove that, in the way of a poetical figure, any prophet would ascribe such to irrational creatures; while, as regards the heathen enemies of Israel, the thought here expressed is of constant occurrence.

In chap. ii. 25, " And I restore to you the years (השנים) which the locusts have eaten," etc., *several* years of calamity are spoken of. But we cannot agree with *Ewald* in thinking that the land was, for several years, laid waste by locusts : we are prevented from doing so by the single word יתר in chap. i. 4. *Bochart* rightly remarks : " The produce of the new year cannot be called the residue of the former year. That word is much more applicable to the fruits of some fields, which are passed by, or to the residue left in a field, which should be eaten up in the same year." As little can we suppose, with *Ewald*, that the plural is here used with reference to the effects produced, by the devastation of one year, upon the ensuing years ; for it is not a possible loss which is here spoken of, but one which has actually taken place. The prophet then passes, here also, from the image to the thing itself,—to the hostile invasions extending over longer periods, which he describes under the image of a devastation by locusts which, at one time, took place.

Very strong arguments in favour of the figurative explanation are furnished, in addition, by chap. iv. (iii.). The whole announcement of punishment and judgment upon the heathen nations has sense and meaning, only when, in the preceding context, there has been mention made of the crime which they committed against the Lord and His people. In that case, we have before us the three main subjects of prophecy,—God's judgments upon His people by heathen enemies, their obtaining mercy, and the punishment of the enemies. At the very beginning of chap. iv. (iii.) the sufferings of Israel, described in chap. i. and ii., and the judgment upon the heathen, are brought into the closest connection. According to chap. iv. 1, 2, the gathering of the Gentiles is to take place at a time when the Lord will return to the captivity of Judah and Jerusalem, *i.e.*, according to the constant *usus loquendi* (compare my Commentary on Ps. xiv. 7), when He will grant them mercy, and deliver them from their misery.[1] But that this misery can be none other than that described in chap. i. and ii. appears simply from the fact, that this has been declared to be the close of all the judgments of God.—We must, *further*, not overlook the article

---

[1] The well ascertained *usus loquendi* must be here the less given up, as, in the preceding context, to which this verse carries us back, we are, it is true, told that the Lord will return and bestow mercy ; but the bringing back of the people is as little spoken of as the carrying of them away, inasmuch as the express mention of which did not suit the image of the devastation by locusts.

in את־כל־הגוים in chap. iv. 2, and, accordingly, must not translate, " I will gather all nations," but " all *the* nations." And how could this be explained in any other way than—all the nations which are spoken of in the preceding chapters under the image of locusts? But of special importance is the second part of the verse: " And I plead there with them concerning My people, and My heritage Israel, whom they have scattered among the nations, and distributed My land."[1] It is quite impossible that there should here be the mention of anything which happened before the time of Joel. Whatever period we may assign to him, he belongs, at all events, to a time in which a scattering of Israel among the Gentiles, and a distribution of their land, had not as yet taken place. *Credner*, indeed, believes that the calamities under Jehoram are sufficient to account for these expressions. " At that time," he says, " the Edomites revolted from Judah; Libnah, which belonged to Judah in the stricter sense, rebelled; the Arabs and Philistines invaded the kingdom and plundered its capital; those inroads did then not terminate without a diminution of the territory of Judah." But all this is irrelevant; the discourse concerns the distribution of the land of the *Lord*. The rebellion of a heathen tributary people does not, therefore, here come under consideration. Just as little can we see what Libnah has to do here. It belonged, it is true, to the kingdom of Judah; but the heathen nations had nothing to do with its rebellion;—for this, according to 2 Kings viii. 22, and 2 Chron. xxi. 10, proceeded from the inhabitants, who were dissatisfied with the bad government of the king, and was speedily brought to a close. It cannot then be proved, that even some small portion of the territory was lost at that time; far less, that the whole country was apportioned anew. It is quite the same as regards the dispersion among the Gentiles. The invasion of the Philistines cannot

---

[1] חִלֵּק means, not " to divide among themselves," but " to effect a new division," " to apportion the land anew," as, *e.g.*, Asshur distributed the territory of the ten tribes among the Aramean Colonists. חלק is used of the distribution of the land by Joshua, in Josh. xiii. 7, xix. 51. In Mic. ii. 4, when the captivity was impending, the people, in anticipation of it, utter their lamentation in the words, " He distributes our fields;" compare Ps. lx. 8.

x

here come into consideration, because, in ver. 4, these enemies are expressly distinguished from those who had effected the dispersion of the people, and the distribution of the land: "And ye also, what have ye to do with Me, O Tyre and Sidon, and all the borders of Palestine?" The prophet can thus not be speaking of something which had taken place at his time; but as little can he speak of something still future, which had not been touched upon by him when he threatened punishment upon the Covenant-people; for the devastation by the locusts appears as the highest and last calamity of the future. Nothing, therefore, remains but to suppose, that under the image of the devastation by locusts, the devastation of the country by heathen enemies, and the dispersion of its inhabitants, are described,—a supposition which is confirmed by the great resemblance of the passage under consideration to chap. ii. 17–19. *Vatke* (*Theol. des A. Th.* i. S. 462) founded upon the fact that the general exile is here predicted, the assertion that Joel had prophesied only after the captivity. No one, of course, has been willing to agree with him in this; but as long as the devastation by the locusts is understood literally, it will not be possible to undermine the grounds upon which he supports his views. It is altogether in vain that people spend their labour in disputing the fact, so obvious and evident, that the discourse here concerns the total occupation of the land by the heathen, the total carrying away of its inhabitants.

It may be further remarked, that this passage at the same time considerably strengthens the proof already adduced, that Joel foretells future things in chap. i. and ii. A devastation by the locusts is described in these chapters; but the substance of this figure does not refer to the time of Joel.

Finally—We must still direct attention to the words in iv. 17:—"And Jerusalem shall be a sanctuary, and there shall no strangers pass through her any more." This promise stands in evident contrast to the former threatening, and becomes intelligible only by it. In it, therefore, the *strangers* must be represented under the figure of the locusts.

And now, after all these single proofs have been enumerated —proofs which, if necessary, might easily have been strengthened and increased—let us look back to this survey of the contents of the book, and we shall see how, according to our view, and according to it alone, the prophecy of Joel forms an harmonious, complete, and well finished whole, and that the prophet adheres closely to the outlines already given by Moses, with the filling up and finishing of which all other prophets also are employed. And let us, finally, add, that exegetical tradition also bears a favourable testimony to the figurative interpretation.

We need not spend much time in considering the arguments advanced against the figurative interpretation by *Credner* (S. 27 ff.), *Hitzig*, and others. They all rest upon an almost incomprehensible ignoring of the nature of poetry, of the metaphor, and of the allegory. Thus, *e.g.*, *Credner* says, " What man of sound sense will ever be able to say of horses, horsemen and warriors, that they resemble horses and horsemen? Who has ever seen horses and horsemen climbing over walls? What shall we say concerning chap. ii. 20? Do land armies ever perish in the sea, and, moreover, in two different seas? What is the use of foretelling, in chap. ii. 22, 23, the ceasing of the drought, if the prophet here thought of real enemies?" But in opposition to all these and similar objections, let us simply keep in mind, that the prophet does not by any means view the enemies as such, and only incidentally compares them with locusts; but that in his inward vision they represented themselves to him as locusts. It is just the characteristic feature of the allegory, that the image becomes in it substantial, and has the thing represented, not *beside* it, but *in*, *with*, and *under* it. But it is just for this reason that many a feature must be introduced which does not belong to the *real* subject, *i.e*, the figure, but to the *ideal* only, *i.e*, the thing represented thereby. It is for this very reason also, that the metaphor, raised to the *ideal* subject, may again be compared with the *real* subject. After all this we may well judge what right *Ewald* has to call the figurative explanation " an error, which, in consideration of our present knowledge, becomes from day to day less pardonable."

We remark further, that, in chap. i. 4, it is distinctly indicated that Israel's visitation by the world's power will not be a simple one, but will present various aspects: " That which the *gnawer* has left, the *locust* devoureth; and that which the *locust* hath left, the *licker* devoureth; and that which the *licker* hath left, the *eater* devoureth." The opinion has been entertained, that " the prophet does not say, one cloud of locusts after another, or swarms of locusts of every description have come up ; but, on the contrary, that they are all contemporary, and that all of them devour the same things." But a succession is quite obvious. The four parties do not devour at the same time ; but the second devours what the first has left. It is true that the succession appears as very rapid ; but that is a peculiarity belonging only to the vision. If there be *at all* a succession of those extensive empires representing the world's power, there must in reality be considerable intervals between them. The question then arises, however, whether the number *four* is to be considered as a round number, so that the thought would only be this, that several nations are to visit the people of the Lord, or whether, on the contrary, importance is to be attached to the number *four* as such. According to *Jerome*, the Jews followed .the latter view. In accordance with their view, the first swarm denotes the Assyrians, together with the Chaldeans ; the second, the Medo-Persians ; the third, the Grecian kingdoms ; the fourth, the Romans. The analogies of the four horns in Zech. ii. 1–4 (i. 18–21), the four beasts in Daniel, the seven heads of the beast in Revelation—denoting the seven phases of the world's power opposed to God—are decisive in favour of the latter view; compare my *Commentary on Rev.* xii. 18, xiii. 1. Now, if we follow this view at all, we must, in determining the four swarms, certainly assent to the opinion of the Jews, as given in *Jerome ;* and this so much the more, as the four swarms are, in that case, exactly parallel to the four beasts in Daniel, which denote the Chaldean, Medo-Persian, Grecian, and Roman monarchies. The fact that the Assyrians are taken together with the Chaldeans can be the less strange, because, so early as in the prophecy of Balaam, Asshur and Babylon are comprehended under the common name עֵבֶר, *i.e.,* " that which is on the other side," —the power on the other side of the Euphrates ; and are contrasted with the new empire which pressed on from the West —from Europe. (Compare my *Dissertation on Balaam,* p. 593 ff.)[1] It was the less possible to ascribe to the Assyrians an independent position here, as Joel has to do mainly with Judah, upon which no judgment of real importance was inflicted by the Assyrians.

[1] In the volume containing the " *Dissertations on the Genuineness of Daniel,* etc.," published by T. and T. Clark.

ON CHAPTER II. 23.

" *And, ye sons of Zion, exult and rejoice in Jehovah your God;* *for He giveth you the Teacher of righteousness, and then He* *poureth down upon you rain, the former rain and the latter rain,* *for the first time.*"

The words, " In Jehovah your God," are an addition peculiar to the sons of Zion. In reference to the *earth*, which the locusts had devastated, it was in ver. 21 said only, " Fear not, exult and rejoice." In reference to the beasts, *i.e.*, to the heathen world, which was kept in subjection by the conquerors of the world, but which is delivered by the great deeds of the Lord, it is in ver. 22 said only : " Fear not." They are only the sons of Zion who know and love the Author of Salvation, and who receive from Him special gifts, besides the general ones.

There is considerable difference in the interpretations of this verse. The words, את־המורה לצדקה, are, by the greater number of interpreters, translated, " The Teacher of righteousness." Thus, *Jonathan,* the *Vulgate, Jarchi, Abarbanel, Grotius,* and almost all the interpreters of the early Lutheran Church translate them. Others take מורה in the signification of " rain," and לצדקה as qualifying its nature more accurately. Even in ancient times, this explanation was not at all uncommon. Among the Rabbinical interpreters, it was held by *Kimchi, Abenezra, S. B. Melech,* who explain it of a *timely* rain. *Calvin,* who rendered the לצדקה by *justa mensura,* defends it with great decision, and declares the other explanations to be forced, and unsuitable to the connection. It is translated by " rain " in the English[1] and Genevan versions, and by many Calvinistic interpreters, who differ, however, in the translation of לצדקה, and render it either : " In right time," or " in right measure," or " in the right place," or " for His righteousness," or " according to your righteousness." *Marckius* is of opinion that " rain " is necessarily required by the context; but that, on account of לצדקה, this rain must be understood spiritually of the Messiah with His saving doctrine, and His Spirit. Among the interpreters of the Lutheran Church, *Seb. Schmid* thinks of " a rain in due season."

---

[1] The English version has " a teacher of righteousness," as a marginal reading.—TR.

Among modern interpreters, the explanation by " rain " has become altogether so prevalent, that it is considered scarcely of any importance even to mention the other. לִצְדָקָה is explained by *Eckermann*: " In proof of His good pleasure ;" by *Ewald, Meier,* and *Umbreit*: " For justification ;" by *Justi*: " For fruitfulness ;" and by the others (*Rosenmüller, Holzhausen, Credner, Rückert, Maurer,* and *Hitzig*) by: " In right measure." We consider this explanation to be decidedly erroneous, and the other to be the sound one ; and this for the following reasons :—1. The great difference, on the part of the defenders of the current opinion, as regards the explanation of לִצְדָקָה, certainly indicates, with sufficient clearness, that, by this addition, a considerable obstruction is put in its way. The most current explanation, by " *justa mensura,*" " in right measure," " sufficiently," is certainly quite untenable. Even the fact, that it is not צֶדֶק but צְדָקָה which is used here, must excite suspicion. (On the difference betwixt these two words, compare *Ewald* in the first edition of his Grammar, S. 312–13.) But what is quite decisive is the fact that these two words, which occur with such extraordinary frequency, are never found in a physical, but always in a moral sense only. The only passage in which, according to *Winer*, צֶדֶק signifies " rectitude " in a physical sense, is Ps. xxiii. 3 : מַעְגְּלֵי צֶדֶק, which, according to him, means : " Straight, right ways." But that verse runs thus : " He restoreth my soul, He leadeth me in the paths of righteousness for His name's sake." The path is a spiritual one ; it is righteousness itself, which consists in the actual declaration of being just, and in justification, which are implied in the gift of salvation. With regard to צְדָקָה, *Holzhausen* (S. 120) maintains that it is used of a measure which has its due size in Lev. xix. 35, 36. The words are these : " Ye shall not do *unrighteousness* in judgment, in measure, in division. Balances of righteousness, weights of righteousness, ephas of righteousness, shall ye have : I am the Lord your God who brought you out of the land of Egypt." Even the contrast—so evident—with the *unrighteousness*, shows distinctly that balances, measures, and weights of righteousness are here such as belong to righteousness—are in harmony with it. Even the root צֶדֶק never occurs in a physical sense, but always, only in a moral sense. To this it must be added, that the explanation, " Teacher of righteousness," is recommended by the parallel passage in Hos. x. 12, where, also, teaching occurs in connection with righteousness: וירה צדק לכם, "And the Lord will come and teach you righteousness." This parallel passage is also opposed to *Ewald's* explanation, "for justification,"—the only explanation among those mentioned to which, it must be admitted, no philological objection can be raised. But the thought, "The early rain an actual justification of Israel," would be rather strange, and so much the more so, because the wrath of God had not manifested itself in a drought and want of water, but rather in the sending of the army of locusts.

2. That the giving of the מורה, in the first hemistich of the verse, must denote a divine blessing different from the giving of the מורה in the second, is evident for this reason :—that, otherwise, there would arise a somewhat meaningless tautology. They who assigned to מורה in the first hemistich, the signification of "rain in general," have felt how very unsuitable is the twofold mention of the early rain. To this must be added the use of the *Fut.* with *Vav convers.,* ויורד. By this form, an action is denoted which *follows* from the preceding one; but according to the current explanation, one and the same action would here be expressed, only in different words. It cannot be denied, indeed, that the form occurs by no means rarely in a weakened sense, and is used only to express a connection; and that for this reason, this argument is not, *per se,* conclusive. Yet the original signification so generally holds, that we can abandon it only for distinct and forcible reasons. In addition to this, it must be considered that the addition of גשם to the second מורה distinctly marks out the latter as being different in its meaning from the former. It must also be kept in mind that it is one of the peculiarities of Joel to use the same words and phrases, after brief intervals, in a different sense; compare *Credner's* remarks on ii. 20, iii. 5.

3. The explanation by "Teacher" is far more obvious for the reason that מורה always occurs with the signification of "teacher" (even in Ps. lxxxiv. 7, where the right translation is : "With blessing also the teacher covereth himself"), and never with that of "rain," or "early rain." This is rather the meaning of יורה ; and the verb also never occurs in *Hiphil,* as it does in *Kal,* with the signification "to sprinkle," "to water."

By this we are led to the supposition that Joel, in the second hemistich, made use of the uncommon form מורה with the meaning of "early rain," solely on account of the resemblance of the sound to the מורה occurring immediately before, with its usual signification; and that, at the same time, he added גשם for the purpose of avoiding ambiguity. What serves to confirm this supposition, is the circumstance that Jeremiah, alluding to the passage under consideration, has, in chap. v. 24, put יורה in the place of מורה; which proves that the second מורה in Joel ii. 23 has originated only from its connection with the first, which is altogether wanting in Jeremiah.

4. A causal connection, similar to that which exists here betwixt the sending of the Teacher of righteousness and the pouring out of the rain, occurs also in that passage of the Pentateuch which the prophet seems to have had in view, viz., Deut. xi. 13, 14: "And it shall come to pass, *if ye shall hearken unto my commandments* which I command you this day, that ye love the Lord your God, and serve Him with all your heart and with all your soul, that I will give you the rain of your land in due season, the first rain and the latter rain (יורה ומלקוש), and thou shalt gather in thy corn, and thy must, and thine oil." Here, as well as there, the righteousness of the people is the *antecedens;* the divine mercies and blessings are the *consequens.* Since the former does not exist, God begins the course of His mercies by sending Him who calls it forth. This remark removes, at the same time, the objection, that the mention of the Teacher of righteousness is unsuitable in a connection where the prophet speaks of temporal blessings only, and rises to spiritual blessings only afterwards, in chap. iii. There existed for the Covenant-people no benefits which were purely temporal; these were always, at the same time, signs and pledges of the divine favour, which depended upon the righteousness of the people, and this, in turn, upon the divine mission of a Teacher of righteousness.

5. The בראשון is also in favour of our explanation. It stands in close relation to אחרי־כן in chap. iii. 1, ii. 28. The sending of the Teacher of righteousness has two consequences;—*first,* the pouring out of the temporal rain—an individualizing designation of every kind of outward blessings, and chosen with a reference to the passage of the Pentateuch which we have just

cited, but with special reference to the description of the calamity, under the figure of a devastation by locusts;—and, *secondly*, the outpouring of the spiritual rain—the sending of the Holy Ghost. It needs only the pointing out of this reference, which has been overlooked by interpreters,[1] to set aside the manifold and different explanations of בראשן, which are, all of them, unphilological, or give an unsuitable sense.[2]

But if any doubt should still remain, it would be removed by a parallel passage in Isaiah, which depends upon the text under review, in a manner not to be mistaken, and which, therefore, must be regarded as the oldest commentary upon it. Isaiah is describing the condition of the people subsequent to their having obtained mercy, after a long time of deep misery, in chap. xxx 20: "And the Lord gives you the bread of adversity, and the water of affliction; and then thy *teacher* (מוריך is *singular*) shall no longer hide himself, and thine eyes shall see thy teacher; Ver. 21: And thine ears hear a word behind thee, This is the way, walk ye in it; do not turn to the right hand, nor to the left." Accordingly, after they have put away what was evil, ver. 22: "The Lord giveth the rain of thy seed, with which thou sowest thy land," etc., ver. 23. The teacher is not a human teacher, but God. *Human* teachers had not concealed themselves; but that the Lord had concealed Himself, is affirmed in the preceding verses. The words, "Behind thee" (ver. 21), suggest the idea of a teacher of such a glory that they could not look in his face (compare Rev. i. 10); and the words, "Thine eyes see thy teacher," ver. 20, imply the idea of the high majesty of the teacher, and suggest the idea of a revelation of the glory of the Lord; compare Is. xl. 5, lii. 8. The Lord must first manifest Himself as a Teacher, before He appears as a Saviour. In Isaiah, the Lord Himself appears as the Teacher; as also in Hos. x. 12: "It is time to seek the Lord, till He

---

[1] Since the appearance of the first edition of this work, it has been acknowledged also by *Ewald*, *Meier*, and *Umbreit*.

[2] *Hitzig* explains it: "In the first month." But altogether apart from the consideration that it is only in a chronological connection that "in the first" can stand for "in the first *month*," this explanation is objectionable on the ground that the early rain and the latter rain cannot, by any means, belong to the same month. There is the less difficulty in explaining it by "first," as בראשונה undeniably occurs, several times, in this signification; compare, *e.g.*, Zech. xii. 7.

come and teach you righteousness;" while in Joel, on the contrary, it is the Lord who giveth the Teacher. Both may be reconciled by the consideration, that in the Teacher whom the Lord gives, the glory of the Lord becomes manifest.

It now only remains to inquire who is to be understood by the Teacher of righteousness. (Teacher of righteousness is equivalent to: "Teaching them how they should fear the Lord," 2 Kings xvii. 28.) It is referred to the Messiah, not only by almost all those Christian interpreters who follow this explanation, with the exception of *Grotius,* who conjectures that Isaiah or some other prophet is to be thereby understood; but also, after the example of *Jonathan,* by several Jewish commentators; *e.g., Abarbanel,* who says: "This teacher of righteousness, however, is the King Messiah, who will show the way in which we must walk, and the works which we must do." Even on account of the article, it is not possible to refer it to a single human teacher; and this argument may, at the same time, be added to those which oppose the explanation of מורה by " an early rain." There can be only the choice betwixt the Messiah as the long promised Teacher κατ' ἐξοχήν, and the *ideal* teacher, —the collective body of all divine teachers. But the latter view requires to be somewhat raised, before it can be allowed to enter into the competition. That we have not here before us an ordinary collective body, is shown by the parallel passage in Isaiah, according to which the glory of the Lord is to be manifested in the Teacher. And this is as little applicable to a plurality of human teachers, as to a single individual. It is *further* proved by the fundamental passage in Deut. xviii. 18, 19, where, indeed, the prophetic order is comprehended in an *ideal* person. This, however, has its reason only in the circumstance, that the idea of prophetism was, at some future time, to find its realization in a *real* person. It is *further* seen from the state of the Messianic hopes at the time of Joel, and from the exceeding greatness of what is here connected with the appearance of the Teacher of righteousness. In addition to the allusion in Gen. xlix. 10 and Deut. xviii., the Messiah appears as a Teacher in the Song of Solomon also, chap. viii. 2; and in Is. lv. 4: "Behold, I give Him for a witness to the people, for a prince and a lawgiver to the people;" as also in those passages of the second part of Isaiah, in which He is declared to be the Prophet κατ' ἐξοχήν.

When thus understood, the explanation of the *ideal* teacher may be preferable to the reference to Christ exclusively. In favour of such a reference, there is the comprehensive character and the *ideal* import which are, in general, peculiar to the prophecies of Joel. Such a reference is, moreover, favoured by the expression itself, which points out only that which Christ has in common with the former servants of God, viz., the teaching of righteousness, and especially by a comparison with the fundamental passages, Deut. xviii.

EXPOSITION OF CHAP. III. (II. 28–32.)

Ver. 1. *"And it shall come to pass, afterwards, I will pour out My Spirit upon all flesh; and your sons and your daughters shall prophesy; your old men shall dream dreams, and your young men shall see visions."*

The communication of the Spirit of God was the constant prerogative of the Covenant-people. Indeed, the very idea of such a people necessarily requires it. For the Spirit of God is the only inward bond betwixt Him and that which is created; a Covenant-people, therefore, without such an inward connection, is an impossibility. As a constant possession of the Covenant-people, the Spirit of God appears in Isaiah lxiii. 11, where the people, in the condition of the deepest abandonment, say, in the remembrance of the divine mercies, "Where is He that put His Holy Spirit within him?" But it was peculiar to the nature of the Old Testament dispensation, that the effusion of the Spirit of God was less rich, His effects less powerful, and a participation in them less general. It was only after God's relation to the world had been changed by the death of Christ that the Spirit of *Christ* could be bestowed,—a higher power of the Spirit of God, standing to Him in the same relation as the Angel of the Lord to the incarnate Word. The conditions of the bestowal of the Holy Spirit were, under the Old Testament, far more difficult to obtain. The view of Christ in His historical personality, in His life, suffering, and death, was wanting. God, although infinitely nearer to the Jews than to the Gentiles, yet ever remained a God relatively distant. Since the procuring cause of the mercy of God—the merit of Christ—was not yet so clearly seen, it was far more difficult to lay hold of it, and the by-path of legalism was far nearer. It was thus only upon a few—especially upon the prophets—that the direct possession of the Spirit of God was concentrated; while the greater number, even among those of a better disposition, enjoyed a spiritual life derived only from a union with them, and hence it was less strong. It arose from the nature of the case that, at some future time, there must take place a richer and more powerful effusion of the Spirit of God; and it was just for this reason that it was the desire of Moses, that such might take place, and that the whole people might prophesy. Num. xi. 29, besides expressing such a desire, is, at the same time, a prophecy. He wished nothing else than that the people of God might attain to such a degree as to realize the idea of a people of God; and this must come to pass at some future time, because the omnipotent and faithful God could not leave His work unfinished. But Moses himself immediately subjoins the prophecy to the wish, as a clear proof, that behind the wish the prophecy is concealed: " Would God that all the Lord's people were prophets ! for the Lord will give His Spirit upon them," etc.; which is equivalent to : " At some future time, the whole people of the Lord shall be prophets, not against, but agreeably to, my wish; for," etc. It is this promise of Moses which is here resumed by Joel, with whom, subsequently, Is. in chap. xxxii. 15, " Until the Spirit be poured upon us from on high ;" chap. xi. 9, liv. 13; Jer. xxxi. 33, 34; Ezek. xxxvi. 26 ff., and Zech. xii. 10, connect themselves. The ultimate reference of the promise is to the Messianic time; but the reference to the preparatory steps must not, for this reason, be by any means excluded. The announcement of the pouring out of the Spirit rests upon the insight into the nature of God's relation to His kingdom. God's judgments, in which He draws near to His people, in which the abstract God becomes a concrete God, excite in the people a longing for a union with Him. Teachers sent by God give a right direction to this longing, and then an outpouring of the Spirit takes place. This proceeding does, and must continually, repeat itself in the history of the Covenant-people. The perfect fulfilment at the time of Christ could not at all have taken place, unless the imperfect fulfilment had already pervaded their whole earlier history; and that there is, in the prophecy under consideration, no reference at all to such imperfect fulfilments, could be maintained only, if there existed in the text any hint that the prophet intended to speak of only the last realization of the idea.   But as the exclusion of all the preliminary stages is entirely arbitrary, it is just as arbitrary to separate, from the events which make up the main fulfilment in the Messianic time, one particular event, viz., that which took place on the first day of Pentecost.   It is only to a certain extent that we can affirm that the prophecy found its final fulfilment in this event, viz., in as far as it formed the pledge of it,—in as far as the whole succeeding development and progress were already contained in it,—in as far as Joel's prophecy in words was then changed into an infinitely more powerful prophecy in deeds.   It is from overlooking the relation of the prophecy to the thought which animates it, and from the error arising from this, viz., that the fulfilment must necessarily fall within a particular, limited period, that the various opposite interpretations had their rise (compare the copious enumeration and representation of these in *Dresde, Comparatio Joelis de Effusione Spir. S. vatic. c. Petrina interpret. Wittemb.* 1782, *Spec.* 2), all of which are partially true, and are false only by their one-sidedness and exclusiveness.   1. Several interpreters think of an event at the time of Joel.   Thus Rabbi *Moses Hakkohen,* according to *Abenezra, Teller* on *Turrettine de interpret.* p. 59, *Cramer* on the *Scythische Denkmäler,* p. 221.—2. Others insist on an exclusive reference to the first Pentecost. Thus do almost all the Fathers of the Church—among whom, however, *Jerome* (on Joel iii. 1) felt the great difficulties in the way of this view, arising from the context—and most of the later Christian interpreters.—3. Others would refer it at the same time to the events in Joel's time, and to those at the first Pentecost.   Of this opinion are *Ephraem Syr., Grotius,* and *Turrettine.*—4. Others place the fulfilment altogether in the future.   Thus did the Jews as early as in the time of *Jerome,* and afterwards *Jarchi, Kimchi,* and *Abarbanel.*—5. Others, finally, find in the first Pentecost the beginning only of the fulfilment, and regard it as pervading the whole Christian time. Thus, *e.g., Calovius (Bibl. illustr. ad. h. l.)* says: " Although that prophecy began to be fulfilled in a remarkable manner on that feast of the Pentecost, yet its reference is not to that solemn event only, but to the whole state of these last, or New Testament times, *just after the manner of other general promises.*" These last words show that *Calovius* was very near the truth. But if the promise be a general one, by what are we entitled to place the beginning of its fulfilment only at the times of the New Testament, and to exclude all of that same gift which God bestowed in Old Testament times? The insufficiency of the foundation for such a limitation in the text itself is proved by the following confession of *Dresde* (l. c. p. 8), who even believes himself obliged to defend such a limitation from the authority of the Apostle Peter, and to whom it did not at all occur, that any other reference than to some particular event was even possible: "It appears, therefore," he says, "that the prophecy, considered in itself, is so expressed, that no one, except the first author of the prophecy, will be able convincingly to define the exact event to which it really refers." We shall afterwards see that the testimony of the New Testament to which *Dresde* here alludes, does not by any means demand such a limitation. We have seen that Joel points to a fourfold oppression of Israel by the world's power. The *main* fulfilment we must then expect at the time of the fourth; but this can scarcely be the first fulfilment; for we cannot imagine that the former calamities should have passed over the people altogether without effect; and the divine gift of the Spirit goes always hand in hand with the susceptibility of the people. By proving that fourfold oppression, we have also furnished the proof that the prophecy of the outpouring of the Spirit has a comprehensive character. —From the already established reference of the אחרי־כן to the בראשׁן in chap. ii. 23, it is obvious that it is not so much a determination of the succession of time, as of a succession in point of importance, which is thereby given. Among the two effects of the mission of the Teacher of righteousness, first, the lower, and then, the higher, presents itself to the view of the prophet. The determination of time is not the essential point; that serves only to illustrate the internal relation of these two events, the gradation of these divine blessings; although we are able to demonstrate that, even as regards time, the prophecy was fulfilled in this order. For after the destruction by the

Chaldeans, the temporal blessings were restored to the people, before the main fulfilment of the promise of the outpouring of the Holy Spirit took place; compare Ps. cvii. 33-42 with Joel ii. 25-27.—The words, "I shall pour out," refer to the rain in ver. 23. The idea of copiousness, opposed to the former scantiness, is indeed implied in it. Yet it must not be exclusively considered; the qualities of the rain alluded to in ver. 24 ff.—viz., the quickening of what was previously dead, the fructifying power—must not be overlooked.—The words, "Upon all flesh," are, by most of the Jewish interpreters (*e.g.*, *Kimchi*, *Abenezra;* compare *Lightfoot* and *Schöttgen* on Acts ii. 16, 17), referred to the members of the Covenant-people only; but by the Christian interpreters, whom even *Abarbanel* joins, to all men. So, still, does *Steudel* in the *Tübinger Pfingst-Programm*, 1820, p. 11. But in this latter explanation, one thing has been overlooked—as, among the older interpreters, has been well shown by *Calvin*,[1] and among the more recent, by *Tychsen* (*progr. ad h. l.* p. 5)—viz., that the subsequent words, "Your sons, your daughters, your old men, your young men, the servants, the handmaids," contain a specification of the בשר; so that the *all*, by which it is qualified, does not do away with the limitation to a particular people, but only with the limits of sex, age, and rank, among the people themselves. The participation of the Gentiles in the outpouring of the Holy Ghost did not, in the first instance, come into consideration in this place, inasmuch as the threatening of punishment, with which the proclamation of salvation is connected, had respect to the Covenant-people only. *Credner* has been led into a strange error, by pressing the words כל־בשר without any regard to the connection. He imputes to the prophet the monstrous idea, that the Spirit of God, the fountain of all which is good and great, well pleasing to God, and divine, is to be poured out upon all animals also, even upon the locusts.—The foundation for the promise of the Holy Spirit is formed by Gen. ii. 7, compared with i. 26. It supposes that the spirit of man, as distinguished from all other living things

---

[1] He says: "The sense in which the universality must be understood is clearly indicated by what follows. For, it is first said, in general, 'All flesh,' and afterwards, a specification is added, by which the prophet intimates, that age or sex will not constitute any difference, but that God will bring them all, without any distinction, into the communion of His grace."

on earth, is a breath from God.—There is here, moreover, the same contrast betwixt בשר and רוח as in Gen. vi. 3 and Is. xxxi. 3: "The Egyptians are men, and not God; their horses are flesh, and not spirit." (Compare other passages in *Gesenius' Thesaurus*, *s. v.* p. 249.) *Flesh*, in this contrast, signifies human nature with respect to its weakness and helplessness; the *spirit* is the principle of life and strength. As "your sons," etc., is a specification of all flesh, so, the words, "They prophesy, they dream dreams, they see visions," are a specification of: "I pour out My Spirit." From this, it is evident that the particular gifts do not here come into consideration according to their individual nature, but according to that essential character which is common to them as effects of the Spirit of God. Hence it is obvious also, that we are not at liberty to ask why it is just to the sons and daughters that the prophesying is ascribed, etc. The prophet, whose object it is only to individualize and expand the fundamental thought, *i.e.*, the universality of the effects of the Spirit, chooses for this purpose the extraordinary gifts of the Spirit,[1] because these are more obvious than the ordinary ones; and from among the extraordinary ones, again, those which were common under the Old Testament; without thereby excluding the others, or, as regards the real import, adding anything to the declaration, "I will pour out My Spirit." This appears also from ver. 2, where, in reference to the servants and handmaids, the expression returns to the former generality. In distributing the gifts of the Spirit among the particular classes, the prophet has been as little guided by any internal considerations, as, *e.g.*, Zechariah, when in chap. ix. 17 he uses the words, "Corn maketh the young men grow up, and must, the maids." The remark made by *Credner* and *Hitzig*, after the example of *Tychsen*, that visions are ascribed to vigorous youth, but dreams to feebler age, appears at once, from an examination of the his-

---

[1] The two parallel members prove, in opposition to *Redslob* and others, that the verb נבא here, as everywhere else, has reference to an ecstatic condition, to the speaking in the Spirit, although this is by no means limited to a revelation of the future. The closeness of the connection between prophesying, dreaming dreams, and seeing visions, is evident from Num. xii. 6, where visions and dreams appear as the two principal forms of revelation to the נביא.

torical instances, and from the comparison of Num. xii. 6, to be unfounded. "Your sons and your daughters prophesy," etc., is equivalent to: "Your sons and your daughters, your old men and your young men, prophesy, have *divine* dreams (a limitation to such is implied in their being the effects of the outpouring of the Spirit), and see visions;" and this again is equivalent to: "They will enjoy the Spirit of God, with all His gifts and blessings." In this, and in no other way, has the passage been constantly understood among the Jews. If it had been otherwise, how could Peter have so confidently declared the events on the feast of Pentecost, where there occurred neither dreams nor visions, to be a fulfilment of the prophecy of Joel? It is implied, however, in the nature of the case, that, in the principal fulfilments of the prophecy of Joel, the extraordinary gifts of the Spirit should be accompanied by the ordinary ones; for the former are the witnesses and means of the latter, although, at the same time, the basis also on which they rest; so that times like those which are described in 1 Sam. iii. 1, where the Word of God is precious in the country, and there is no prophecy spread abroad, must necessarily be poor in the ordinary gifts of grace also. It is not in the essence, but only in the form of manifestation, that the extraordinary gifts differ from the ordinary ones,—just as Christ's outward miracles differ from His inward ones.

Ver. 2. "*And upon the servants also, and upon the handmaids, I will pour out My Spirit in those days.*"

Credner refers this to the Hebrew prisoners of war, living as servants and handmaids among heathen nations, far away from the Holy Land. But if the prophet had this in view, he must necessarily have expressed himself with greater distinctness. Moreover, the relation to the preceding verse requires that, as the difference of sex and age was there done away with, so no allowance should here be made for the difference of rank. The גַּם shows that the extension of the gifts of the Spirit even to servants and handmaids, who, to the carnal eye, appeared to be unworthy of such distinction, is to be considered as something unexpected and extraordinary. That there is very little correctness in the assertion of *Credner*, that "there could have been scarcely any doubt as regards the participation of the Hebrew

Y

slaves," is sufficiently shown by the fact, that Jewish interpreters have attempted, in various ways, to lessen the blessing here promised to the servants and handmaids. Even the translation of the LXX. by, ἐπὶ τοὺς δούλους μου καὶ ἐπὶ τὰς δούλας μου, may be considered as such an attempt. In the place of the servants of men, who appeared to them unworthy of such honour, they put the servants of God. *Abarbanel* asserts that the Spirit of God here means something inferior to the gift of prophecy, which is bestowed only upon the free people. Instead of regarding the Spirit of God as the root and fountain of the particular gifts mentioned in the preceding verse, he sees in Him only an isolated gift,—that of an indefinite knowledge of God. But such a view is opposed even by the relation of the words, "I will pour out My Spirit," in ver. 2, to the same words in ver. 1; and also by Is. xi. 2, where "Spirit of God" is likewise used in a general sense, and comprehends within itself all that follows. It is not without design that the fact is so prominently brought out in the New Testament, that the Gospel is preached to the poor, and that God chooses that which is mean and despised in the eye of the world. The natural man is always inclined to suppose that that which is esteemed by the world must be so by God also. This is sufficiently evident from the deep contempt of the Pharisees for the ὄχλοι; compare, *e.g.*, John vii. 49.

Ver. 3. "*And I give wonders in the heavens, and on earth; blood, and fire, and vapour of smoke.*"

The mercy bestowed upon the Congregation of God is accompanied by the judgment upon her enemies. Since the Congregation has again become the object of His favour, especially in consequence of the Holy Spirit being poured out upon her, it cannot be but that He will protect her against the persecution of the world, and avenge her upon it. In vers. 3 and 4, the *precursors* of the judgment (*before* cometh, ver. 4) are described, and in chap. iv. throughout, the judgment itself. There is here an allusion to an event of former times, and which is now to be repeated on a larger scale, viz., the plagues inflicted upon Egypt in consequence of the same law. The prophet had specially in view the passage, Deut. vi. 22: "And the Lord gave signs and wonders, great and sore, upon Egypt, upon Pharaoh, and upon all his household before our eyes."—The wonders are divided into those which are in heaven, and those which are on earth ; then those which are on earth are in this verse designated individually ; and afterwards, in ver. 4, those which are in heaven. With regard to the former, many interpreters (the last of whom is *Credner*) understand by the " blood," bloody defeats of the enemies of Israel ; by " fire and smoke," their towns and habitations consumed by fire. But this interpretation cannot be entertained. The very designation by מופתים indicates that we have here to think of extraordinary phenomena of nature, the symbolical language of which is interpreted by the evil conscience, which recognises in them the precursors of coming judgment. This is confirmed also by the more particular statement of the signs in heaven, in ver. 4 ; for the signs on earth must certainly be of the same class as these. It is confirmed likewise by a comparison with the type of former times, which we have pointed out ; for it is from this, that the blood is directly taken. The first plague is thus announced in Exod. vii. 17 : " Behold, I smite with the rod in mine hand upon the waters in the river, and they are turned into blood." *Jalkut Simeoni* (in *Schöttgen*, p. 210) remarks : " The Lord brought blood upon the enemies in Egypt : thus also shall it be in future times ; for it is written, I will give wonders, blood and fire." The same is the case as respects the fire. Exod. ix. 24 : " And there came hail, and *fire mingled* with the hail." It is more natural to suppose that the prophet borrowed these features, as, in the former description of the judgment upon Israel, the plague of the locusts lies at the foundation, and as the contents of the following verse have likewise their prototype in those events. Compare Exod. x. 21 : " And the Lord said unto Moses, Stretch out thine hand toward the heaven, and let there be darkness over the land of Egypt." That it is not real blood which is here meant, but that only which, by its blood-red colour, reminds of blood (comp. *e.g.*, " Waters red as blood," 2 Kings iii. 22), is shown by the fundamental passage, Exod. vii. 17, where the water which had become red is called simply blood ; compare my work on *Egypt and the Books of Moses*, p. 106. Blood brings into view the shedding of blood ; the fiery phenomena announce that the fire of the anger of God, and the fire of war, will be enkindled ; compare remarks on i. 19, 20. —The word תימרות requires a renewed investigation. Interpreters uniformly explain it by " pillars,"—a signification which is altogether destitute of any foundation ; for the Chaldee תמרה, to which they refer, is not found with the signification " pillar." Such a meaning is quite inappropriate in the single passage quoted by *Buxtorf ;* the signification " smoke," or " cloud of smoke," is necessarily required in that place. As little are we at liberty to appeal to תמר, " palm," with which תימרה has nothing at all to do. The י, which would be without any analogy if derived from תמר (compare *Ewald* on *Song of Sol.* iii. 6), re- quires the derivation from ימר. The word תימרה is a noun formed from the 3d pers. *fem. Fut.* of this verb with ה affixed (compare, on these nouns, the remarks on Hos. ii. 14, and my work on *Balaam,* p. 434), and, as to its form, it corresponds exactly with תמורה, derived from the 3d *fem. Fut.* of the verb מור. There cannot now be any doubt regarding the significa- tion of ימר. Is. lxi. 6, and Jer. ii. 11, where המיר and הימיר occur in the same verse, show that it corresponds entirely with מור. Hence *Ewald* (l. c.) is wrong in identifying it with אמר, the alleged meaning of which is " to be high." Now in Hebrew, מור and ימר occur only in the derived signification of " to transform," " to change," " to exchange ;" but the primary signification is furnished by the Arabic, where it means : *huc illuc latus, agi- tatus fuit,—fluctuavit.* (Compare the thorough demonstration by *Scheid, ad cant. Hisk.* p. 159 sqq.) תימרות can accordingly signify only " clouds" or " *vortices.*" (In Arabic, מור means " dust agitated by the wind.") The connection of this signifi- cation with that of " *palpebrae,*" " eye-lids," in which it occurs in the Talmudic and Rabbinical languages, is very obvious. They were so called from their continual motion hither and thither. Such a connection, however, we must the more easily be able to prove, because that Talmudic and Rabbinical use of the word cannot be derived from any other root than an ancient Hebrew one. The ἀτμίς of the LXX. likewise leads to our interpretation, rather than to the prevailing one. The former is, in the only passage in which תימרות occurs, besides the one under consideration, and where it likewise occurs in the connection with עשן, viz., in Song of Sol. iii. 6, at least as suitable as the latter. We have to think here of such phenomena as those which are described in Exod. xix. 18 : " And Mount Sinai was altogether on a smoke, because the Lord had descended upon it in fire, and the smoke thereof ascended as the smoke of a furnace." Here, as well as there, the fire, and the accompanying smoke, represent, in a visible manner, the truth that God is πῦρ καταναλίσκον, Heb. xii. 29. The clouds of smoke are the sad forerunners of the clouds of smoke of the divine judgments upon the enemies, and of the fire of war, in the form of which the former commonly appear. Compare Is. ix. 18, 19: "And they mount up like the lifting up of smoke. . . . And the people became as the fuel of fire; no man spareth his brother." The belief — which pervades all antiquity — that the angry Deity announced the breaking in of judgments through the symbolical language of nature, is very remarkable. This belief cannot be a mere delusion, but must have a deep root in the heart. Nature is the echo and the reflection of the disposition of man. If there prevail within him a fearful expectation of things to come, because he feels his own sin, and that of his people, all things external harmonize with that expectation; and, most of all, that which is the natural image and symbol of divine punitive justice, which would not, however, be acknowledged as such, were it not for the interpreting voice within. Having regard to this relation of the mind to nature, God, previous to great catastrophes, often causes those precursors of them to appear more frequently and vividly, than in the ordinary course of nature. In a manner especially remarkable, this took place previous to the destruction of Jerusalem. Compare *Josephus, d. Bell. Jud.* iv. 4, 5. "For during the night, a fearful storm arose,—there arose boisterous winds with the most violent showers, continual lightnings and awful thunders, and tremendous noises, while the earth was shaken. It was, however, quite evident that the condition of the universe was put into such disorder for the destruction of men, and almost every one conjectured that these were the signs of impending calamity." A great number of other signs and precursors are mentioned by him in *B. J.* vi. 5, § 3. These will never be altogether absent, as certainly as punishment never comes without sin, and sin never exists without the consciousness, without the expectation, of deserved judgment. But the chief point in this mode of viewing things, is not the sign itself, but the disposition of mind which interprets it,—the consciousness of guilt, which fills the soul with the thought of an avenging God,—the *condition of things which brings into view the infliction of the judgment.* It is by this that we can account for the circumstance that, in the Old Testament, the darkening of the sun and moon, and other things, frequently appear as *direct images* of sad and heavy times.

Ver. 4. " *The sun is turned into darkness, and the moon into blood, before there cometh the great and terrible day of the Lord.*"

Among all interpreters, *Calvin* has given the most admirable interpretation of this verse : " When the prophet says that the sun shall be turned into darkness, and the moon into blood, these are metaphorical expressions, by which he indicates that the Lord will show signs of His wrath to all the ends of the earth, as if a whole revolution of nature were to take place, in order that men may be stirred up by terror. For, as sun and moon are witnesses of God's fatherly kindness towards us, as long as, in their changes, they provide the earth with light, so will they, on the other hand, says the prophet, be the messengers of the angry and offended God.—By the darkness of the sun, by the bloody appearance of the moon, by the black cloud of smoke, the prophet intended to express the idea, that wheresoever men should turn their eyes, upwards or downwards, many things would appear to fill them with terror. Hence the language of the prophet amounts to this :—that never had the state of things in the world been so miserable,—that never had there appeared so many and so terrible signs of the anger of God."—We have already seen that the prophet has before his eye the Egyptian type. The darkness upon the whole land of Egypt, while there was light in the dwellings of the Israelites, represented, in a deeply impressive manner, the anger of God in contrast with His grace, of which the symbol is the shining of His heavenly lights. The extinction of these is, in Scripture, frequently the forerunner of coming divine judgments, or an image of those which have been already inflicted ; compare the remarks on Zech. xiv. 6. Thus it has already occurred in the Book of Joel itself, in the description of the former judgment ; compare ii. 2 : " Day of darkness and gloominess, day of clouds and mist ;" ii. 10 : " Before Him quaketh the earth, and trembleth the heaven ; the sun and the moon mourn, and the stars withdraw their shining." Thus it returns in iv.

14, 15 : "The day of the Lord is near in the valley of judgment. The sun and the moon mourn, and the stars withdraw their shining." The passages in which, as in the one before us, the extinction has not a *figurative*, but a *typical* character, must not be limited to a single phenomenon. Everything by which the brightness of the heavenly luminaries is clouded or darkened, eclipses of the sun or moon, earthquakes, thunderstorms, etc., fill with fear those in whose hearts the sun of grace has set.

Ver. 5. "*And it comes to pass, every one who calls on the name of the Lord is saved; for in Mount Zion and in Jerusalem shall be such as have escaped, as the Lord hath said, and amongst those who are spared is whomsoever the Lord calleth.*"

We must first determine the signification of פליטה. The greater number of interpreters explain it by "deliverance;" but it means rather "that which has escaped." This appears, 1. from the form. It is the fem. of the Adj. פליט, the ִי— of which has arisen from ִ— by means of lengthening; hence it is that פְּלֵטָה is thrice formed without ִי—. It is, then, an adjective of intransitive signification. Now it is true that, by means of the feminine termination, adjectives are changed into abstract nouns, but never into such as indicate an action ; but always into such only for which, in Latin and Greek, the neuter of the adjective might be used. This, however, is here inadmissible. 2. To this must be added the constant use; as in Is. xxxvii. 31, 32 : "And *that which has escaped* (פליטת) of the house of Judah, the *remnant*, taketh root downward, and beareth fruit upward. For out of Jerusalem shall go forth a *remnant* (שארית), and *that which has escaped* out of Mount Zion,"—a passage exactly parallel to the one under consideration (compare also the following words in Is. xxxvii. 32 : "For the zeal of the Lord will do this," with "As the Lord hath said," here). Is. iv. 2 : "To that which has escaped," with which, "That which is left in Zion, and that which remaineth in Jerusalem," in the following verse, is identical; Is. x. 20 : "The remnant (שאר) of Israel, and that which has escaped of the house of Jacob;" Obad. ver. 17 : "And upon Mount Zion shall be that which has escaped,"—which forms an antithesis to ver. 9 : "And man shall be cut off from the Mount of Esau;" and *finally*— Gen. xxxii. 9 (8) : "And the camp which has been left is for

the escaped." There does not thus remain a single passage
in which the signification "deliverance" is even the probable
one. The passages in Jeremiah, where שריד ופליט occur together (xlii. 17, xliv. 14; Lam. ii. 2), show that פליטה here is
not different from שרידים in the subsequent clause of the verse.
—The expression קרא בשם יהוה never is used of a merely outward invocation, but always of such as is the external expression
of the faith of the heart; compare the remarks on Zech. xiv. 9.
Even on account of this stated condition, it is not possible to
think of the deliverance of the promiscuous multitude of Israel,
in contrast with that of the Gentiles; for the condition is one
which is purely internal, and it affords an important hint for
the right understanding of what follows. The כי by which it
is connected remains inexplicable, if Mount Zion and Jerusalem
be considered as a place of safety and deliverance for all who
are there externally. The same thing is evident from פליטה.
The sense is not by any means that all the inhabitants of Zion
and Jerusalem shall be delivered; but that there shall be some
who have escaped—viz., those who call on the name of the
Lord; while those who do not, shall be consumed by the divine
judgment. The second condition stated by the prophet—that
of being called by the Lord—is in like manner internal. The
words אֲשֶׁר יְהוָֹה קֹרֵא have so evident a reference to אֲשֶׁר־יִקְרָא בְּשֵׁם
יְהוָֹה, that we cannot at all suppose, as *Credner* does, that they
refer to other subjects. On the contrary, they who *call on* the
Lord, are also they whom *He calls* from the general calamity
into His protecting presence; and the prophet has endeavoured,
by the choice of the words, to bring out into view the close connection of these two parties. They who call on the Lord, and
they whom the Lord calls (*Maurer's* explanation: " And among
those who have escaped is every one who calls on the Lord"
[compare Ps. xiv. 4], gives a very feeble tautology), are the
very same upon whom, according to vers. 1 and 2, the fulness
of the Spirit has been poured out.—The words, " As the Lord
has said," indicate, that the faithful ones may safely take comfort from this promise; inasmuch as it is not the word of men,
but of God. We may see, from such parallel passages as
Is. i. 20, xlv. 5, lviii. 14, how little reason we have for thinking
that the prophet here refers to some other prophecy. That the
prophet, and not the Lord Himself, is speaking in this verse,

is evident from the words: "Who calls on the name *of the Lord.*" It was, therefore, very suitable to show, that it was by immediate, divine commission that the prophet had given utterance to the consolatory promise, that the people of God would escape in these great and heavy judgments which were to come upon the world. That it is very natural for believers to fear that the punishments which threaten the world should fall upon them also who are living *in* the world, is shown by Rev. vii., the aim of which is, throughout, to allay the anxious fear which might arise in believers when considering the judgments which threaten the world. The relation of the whole verse to what precedes and follows is this:—In vers. 3 and 4, the prophet had stated the signs and forerunners of the great and fearful day of the Lord. Now he points to the only, and the absolutely sure means of standing on that day. Then, in chap. iv., which is connected by כִּי, he describes the judgment itself.

If, now, we endeavour to discover the historical reference of vers. 3–5, we are met by a great variety of opinions. It is referred to the destruction of Jerusalem by the Chaldeans, by *Grotius, Cramer, Turrettine (de Scrip. s. interpret.* p. 331); among the Socinians, in the *Raccovian Catechism,* p. 22, and by *Oeder;* and among the Arminians, by *Episcopius* in the *Instit. Theol.* p. 198. Others (as *Jerome*) think of the resurrection of the Lord; others (as *Luther*) of the outpouring of the Holy Spirit; others (as *Münster, Capell, Lightfoot, Dresde,* l.c. p. 22) of the destruction by the Romans. It is referred to the judgment upon the enemies of the Covenant-people soon after the return from the Babylonish captivity, by *Ephraem Syrus;* to the impending overthrow of Gog, at the time of the Messiah, by the Jewish interpreters; to the general judgment, by *Tertullian, Theodoret,* and *Crusius,* in *Theol. Prophet.* i. p. 621; and to the destruction of Jerusalem, and the general judgment at the same time, by *Chrysostom* and others.

The great variety of these references has arisen solely from the circumstance, that the prophecy has not been reduced to its fundamental idea. This fundamental idea is:—The manifestation of God's punitive justice upon all which is hostile to His kingdom, which runs parallel with the manifestation of His grace towards the subjects of His kingdom. This idea appears here, in all its generality, without any temporal limitation whatsoever. Not one of these interpretations, therefore, can be absolutely right. They differ only in this, that some of them are altogether false, inasmuch as they assume a reference to events which do not at all fall under the fundamental idea; while others are only limited and partial views of the truth.

To the first of these classes belong evidently the references to the resurrection, and to the outpouring of the Holy Ghost. It is only by detaching these verses from the following chapter that such a view could arise. These events stand in no relation whatsoever to the animating thought of the passage. There is a certain relation to that thought in the reference to the destruction by the Chaldeans, in so far as this was really a manifestation of divine punitive justice. But the reference to this event would be admissible here, only if the prophet were describing the manifestation of divine punitive justice *in general*. But such is not the case. The comparison of chap. i. and ii. shows that the subject of the prophecy is rather the manifestation of divine justice in reference to those who are enemies to the kingdom of God. The defenders of such a view have altogether misunderstood the structure of the prophecy of Joel; for, otherwise, they would have seen that that event belongs to the threatening of judgment in chap. i. and ii., where the judgment upon the house of God is described; while, here, there is a description of the judgment upon those who are without.

The same argument seems, at first sight, to apply also to the destruction by the Romans. But on a closer examination, there appears to be a difference betwixt these two events, and one which brings the latter far more within the scope of the prophecy. The destruction by the Romans was much more intimately connected with a total apostasy and rejection, than was that by the Chaldeans. Even before the former destruction, and immediately after the death of Christ, the former Covenant-people had sunk down to the rank of the Gentiles. They were no more apostate children, who were, by means of punishment, to be brought to reformation, but enemies, who were judged on account of their hostile disposition towards the kingdom of God. Malachi, in chap. iii. 23 (iv. 5), shows that such a time would come when that, which they imagined to be intended only for the heathen by descent, should be realized upon Israel after the flesh. The verbal repetition of the words, "Before there cometh the great and dreadful day of the Lord," and their application to the judgment upon Israel, can be accounted for only by his intention to oppose the prevailing carnal interpretation of the prophecy under consideration.

It will now be seen also, what the relation is which the phenomena at the death of Christ, the darkening of the sun, the quaking of the earth, the rending of the rocks (compare Matt. xxvii. 45, 51; Luke xxiii. 44), occupy to the passage before us. They were like the מופתים here, actual declarations of the divine wrath, and forerunners of the approaching judgment; and they were recognised as such by the guilty, to whom this symbolical language was interpreted by their consciences; compare Luke xxiii. 48: Καὶ πάντες οἱ συμπαραγενόμενοι ὄχλοι ἐπὶ τὴν θεωρίαν ταύτην, θεωροῦντες τὰ γενόμενα, τύπτοντες ἑαυτῶν τὰ στήθη, ὑπέστρεφον.

But we must not limit ourselves to the obduracy of the Covenant-people. This we are taught, not only by the relation of chap. i. and ii. to iv. 2, but, with especial distinctness, by the renewal of this threatening in Rev. xiv. 14–20, where the image of the vintage and winepress, in particular, is borrowed from Joel; see iv. 12, 13. The objects of judgment are there the heathen nations on account of their hostility to the people of God, who, by Christ, and by the outpouring of the Spirit procured by Him, have fully attained to that dignity. Nor is the judgment there an isolated one. On the contrary, all which, in history, is realized in an entire series of judicial acts, to be at last consummated in the final judgment, is there comprehended in one great harvest—in one great vintage.

We have still to make a few remarks upon the quotation in Acts ii. 16 ff. Nothing but narrow-mindedness and prejudice could deny that Peter found, in the miracle of Pentecost, an actual fulfilment of the promise in vers. 1 and 2. This becomes probable, not only from the circumstance, that the reference of this prophecy to the Messianic time was the prevailing one among the Jews (compare the passages in *Schöttgen*, S. 413), but also from the translation of אחרי־כן by ἐν ταῖς ἐσχάταις ἡμέραις, by which, in the New Testament, the Messianic time is always designated. To this must also be added the express declaration in ver. 39, that the promise was unto the generation then present. How could Peter have uttered such a declaration, if his view had been that the promise had found its fulfilment in a time long gone past? At the same time, it is equally certain, that Peter was so far from considering all the riches of the promise to be completely exhausted by that Pentecostal miracle, that he rather considered it to be only a beginning of the fulfilment,—a beginning, indeed, which implies the consummation, as the germ contains the tree. This is quite obvious from ver. 38 : μετανοήσατε καὶ βαπτισθήτω ἕκαστος ὑμῶν. . . . καὶ λήψεσθε τὴν δωρεὰν τοῦ ἁγίου πνεύματος. How could Peter, referring to the prophecy, promise the gift of the Holy Spirit, promised in the prophecy to those who should be converted, if the prophecy was already completely fulfilled? But it is still more apparent from ver. 39 : Ὑμῖν γάρ ἐστιν ἡ ἐπαγγελία καὶ τοῖς τέκνοις ὑμῶν, καὶ πᾶσι τοῖς εἰς μακρὰν, ὅσους ἂν προσκαλέσηται Κύριος ὁ Θεὸς ἡμῶν. The question is, who are to be understood by those εἰς μακράν? No one could have doubted that the Gentiles are thereby to be understood, unless two things altogether heterogeneous had been confounded, viz., the uncertainty of Peter concerning the *fact* of the reception of the Gentiles into the kingdom of God, and his uncertainty concerning the *mode* of their reception. Considering the condition of the Old Testament prophecy, the latter is easily accounted for ; but the former cannot. To state only one from among the mass of arguments which prove that Peter could not be ignorant of the *fact*, we observe that the very manner in which, in Acts iii. 25, he quotes the promise given to Abraham, that by his seed the nations should be blessed, proves that he regarded the Gentiles as partakers of the kingdom of Christ. This is rendered still more incontrovertible by the πρῶτον in ver. 26. To understand, by εἰς μακρὰν, foreign Jews, is inadmissible, for the single reason that these were present in great numbers, and hence, were included in the term ὑμῖν. Now Peter, throughout, addresses all those who were present. How then could he have here confined himself, all at once, to a portion of these? There is, moreover, a plain allusion to the close of Joel iii. 5, which the LXX. translate οὒς Κύριος προσκέκληται. This allusion contains, at the same time, a proof of the concurrent reference to the Gentiles, which is not in express words contained in the prophecy, provided we do not put an arbitrary interpretation upon בשׂר. Attention is thereby directed to the fact, that, in that passage, salvation, which requires, as its condition, a participation in the outpouring of the Spirit, does not depend upon any human cause, but solely upon the call of God—upon His free grace. In a manner entirely similar, does St Paul, in Rom. x. 12, 13, prove, from the beginning of Joel iii. 5, the participation of the Gentiles in the Messianic kingdom : Οὐ γάρ ἐστι διαστολὴ Ἰουδαίου τε καὶ Ἕλληνος· ὁ γὰρ αὐτὸς Κύριος πάντων, πλουτῶν εἰς πάντας τοὺς ἐπικαλουμένους αὐτόν. Πᾶς γὰρ ὃς ἂν ἐπικαλέσηται τὸ ὄνομα Κυρίου, σωθήσεται. If the calling on God were the condition of salvation, access to it was as free to the Gentiles as to the Jews. But if the prophecy has a distinct reference to the still unconverted Jews, their children and the Gentiles, it is then evident, that, according to the view of the Apostle, it did not terminate in that one instance of its fulfilment, but that, on the contrary, it extends just as far as the thing promised—as the outpouring itself of the Holy Spirit. This clearly appears, also, from the allusions to the passage under consideration, in the accounts of later outpourings of the Spirit; compare, *e.g.*, Acts x. 45, xi. 15, xv. 8. How, then, was it even possible that Peter should have limited to the few who had already, at that time, received the Spirit, a prophecy, in which the idea of generality is, intentionally, made so prominent ? But, even if the universal character of the prophecy had been less distinct, Peter would certainly not have thought of confining it in such a manner. Such a gross and superficial view of the prophecies was far from Peter, as well as from the other Apostles.

Another question remains to be answered. For what purpose does the Apostle quote verses 3–5 also, inasmuch as, apparently, verses 1 and 2 alone properly served his purpose; and what sense did he put upon them? The answer is given in ver. 40 : Ἑτέροις τε λόγοις πλείοσι διεμαρτύρετο, καὶ παρεκάλει, λέγων· Σώθητε ἀπὸ τῆς γενεᾶς τῆς σκολιᾶς ταύτης. Even in the few words in which Luke communicates to us the brief summary of what Peter spoke in this respect, a reference to the passage under consideration has been preserved to us. Peter made use of the threatening which was, in the first instance, to be fulfilled upon the dark refuse of the Covenant-people, in order to induce them, by terror, to seek a participation in the promise which alone could deliver them from the threatened judgment. That he succeeded in this, is shown by the words, Ἐγένετο δὲ πάσῃ ψυχῇ φόβος, in ver. 43. Several interpreters have, by ver. 22, been led into a total misconception of the sense in which Peter quotes vers. 3–5. It is true, certainly, that the words τέρασι καὶ σημείοις are not used without reference to the passage in Joel. Peter directs attention to the circumstance, that they who, from their hardness of heart, do not acknowledge the τέρατα and σημεῖα with which God accompanied the manifestation of His grace, shall be visited by τέρατα and σημεῖα of a totally different nature, from the fearful impression of which they shall not be able to escape.

But let us now in addition consider some of the particulars. In substance, the quotation by Peter agrees with the LXX.; but deviations occur on particular points. At the very beginning, the LXX., adhering more closely to the Hebrew text, have: καὶ ἔσται μετὰ ταῦτα; whereas Peter says: καὶ ἔσται ἐν ταῖς ἐσχάταις ἡμέραις. The reason of this deviation is, that the Apostle intends to determine, by this deviation, the expression, which in itself is wider and more indefinite, in such a manner that the period to which the prophecy specially refers, and hence also its application to the case in question, should be rendered more obvious. In a case entirely similar, Jeremiah, in chap. xlix. 6, employs the wider term אחרי־כן, while in xlviii. 47 he makes use of the more definite באחרית הימים. By the latter term, Kimchi also explains the אחרי־כן in the passage before us; while Jarchi (compare Schöttgen, S. 210) explains it by the equivalent term לעתיד לבא. The words λέγει ὁ Θεός are wanting in the LXX., as well as in the original Hebrew text. They have been taken from ver. 5, and, contrasted with τὸ εἰρημένον διὰ τοῦ προφήτου Ἰωήλ, they direct attention to the divine source of prophecy, and hence to the necessity of its fulfilment. The two members, καὶ οἱ πρεσβύτεροι ὑμῶν ἐνύπνια ἐνυπνιασθήσονται, καὶ οἱ νεανίσκοι ὑμῶν ὁράσεις ὄψονται, Peter has reversed; probably in order to place the young men together with the sons and daughters, and to assign the place of honour to the old men. In the δούλους μου and δούλας μου, Peter follows the LXX., and that in a sense which only expressly makes prominent a point really contained in the prophecy, whether such was intended by the translators, or not; for the circumstance that the servants of men were, at the same time, servants of God, formed the ground of their participation in the promise. The same contrast is found, *e.g.*, in 1 Cor. vii. 22, 23 : Ὁ γὰρ ἐν Κυρίῳ κληθεὶς δοῦλος ἀπελεύθερος Κυρίου ἐστίν· ὁμοίως καὶ ὁ ἐλεύθερος κληθεὶς, δοῦλός ἐστι Χριστοῦ. Τιμῆς ἠγοράσθητε· μὴ γίνεσθε δοῦλοι ἀνθρώπων ; compare Gal. iii. 28 ; Philem. 10. Hence it is equivalent to : Upon servants and handmaids of men who are, at the same time, my servants and handmaids, and, therefore, in spiritual things of equal rank with those who are free. To give prominence to this perfect equality, is also the design of the additional clause : καὶ προφητεύσουσι, subjoined after ἐκχεῶ ἀπὸ τοῦ πνεύματός μου. The circumstance that Peter thought it necessary to add this clause, which, as we have proved, quite harmonizes with the design of the prophet, seems to prove that, even at his time, interpretations were current, in which an attempt was made to diminish, or altogether to take away, in the case of servants and handmaids, their participation in those blessings ;—interpretations similar to those of *Abarbanel*, and even of *Grotius*, who thus paraphrases the verse : "Even to those who seem to be lowest, I will certainly impart, although not prophesying and dreaming dreams, yet certain extraordinary and heavenly motions." The antiquity of this false interpretation is attested by *Jerome* also, who probably was, in this respect, altogether dependent upon his Jewish teachers. He interprets, indeed, the servants and handmaids spiritually, and of such as have not the spirit of freedom he says : "They shall neither have prophecies, nor dreams nor visions, but, satisfied with the outpouring of the Holy Spirit, they shall possess only the grace of faith and salvation."—In ver. 3, Peter adds ἄνω to ἐν τῷ οὐρανῷ, and κάτω to ἐπὶ τῆς γῆς, in order to make the contrast more obvious and striking. All the deviations from the LXX., and the original text, are thus of the same kind, and intended to bring out more distinctly what is implied in the passage itself. Not one of them need to be accounted for by the circumstance, that the Apostle quoted from memory.

THE PROPHET AMOS.

GENERAL PRELIMINARY REMARKS.

It will not be necessary to extend our preliminary remarks on the prophet Amos, since on the main point—viz., the circumstances under which he appeared as a prophet—the introduction to the prophecies of Hosea may be regarded as having been written for those of Amos also. For, according to the inscription, they belong to the same period at which Hosea's prophetic ministry began, viz., the latter part of the reign of Jeroboam II., and after Uzziah had ascended the throne in Judah.

The circumstances of the prophet we learn, generally, from the words in chap. i. 1: "Who was among the herdmen of Tekoah." If there existed no other statement than this, there might be truth in the remark made by many interpreters, that we cannot, from his having been a herdman, infer that he was poor and low. It is shown, however, by a statement in chap. vii. 14, that, by the "herdman," we are not to understand one who was also possessed of flocks, or, like David, the son of such, but a poor servant herdman. For, in that passage, the prophet replies to the command of the priest Amaziah to get himself out of the country, to which he did not belong, and to return to his native land: "I am no prophet, nor the son of a prophet, but I am a herdman; and *such an one as plucketh sycamores.* And the Lord took me from behind the flock, and the Lord said unto me, Go prophesy unto My people Israel." The fruit of the sycamores, called ἄτροφος and κακοστόμαχος by *Diosco-rides,* served as food for only the poorest and meanest. *Bochart* (*Hieroz.* t. i. p. 407 [385] *Rosenmüller*) remarks: "It is the same as if he had said, that he was a man of the humblest condition, and born in poor circumstances, so that he scarcely maintained his life by scanty and frugal fare; that he had never thought of obtaining the prophetical office in Israel, until a higher power, viz., divine inspiration, impelled him to undertake it."[1] But this passage merits our attention in another

---

[1] *Bochart* remains unrefuted by the assertions of *Hitzig, Baur,* and others, who make Amos the owner of a plantation of sycamores, which, according to them, made him a wealthy man. בלס can be understood only

point of view. In what sense is it that Amos here denies that he is a prophet? It is evidently in a very special sense that he does so. He obviously does not mean thereby to deny that he possessed the gift of prophecy, or held the prophetical office; for, otherwise, he would himself have furnished weapons to his enemy, to whom he wishes to prove his right. The following remarks will be found to contain the true answer.

It cannot be proved in any way, that the schools of the prophets, established by Samuel at a time when the circumstances of Judah and Israel were altogether similar, were continued in the kingdom of Judah. Every prophet there stands in an isolated position. The entire prophetic order and institute bears rather a sporadic character. But in the kingdom of Israel, where the prophetic order occupied a position altogether different from that which it held in the kingdom of Judah, inasmuch as, after the expulsion of the tribe of Levi, they had to watch over all the interests of religion, the schools of the prophets had a very important mission assigned to them. We must not by any means imagine that their constitution was such, that after a few years' training, the sons of the prophets attained to perfect independence. The greater number of them remained during all their lifetime in the position of sons. The schools of the prophets were a kind of monasteries. Even those who, in consequence of their peculiar circumstances, no longer remained there, but were scattered throughout the country, continued always under their authority. One needs only to read attentively the histories of Elijah and of Elisha, which afford us the fullest information regarding these institutions, to be speedily convinced of the soundness of the view which we have here presented. On the subject of the organization of the schools of the prophets in the kingdom of Israel, compare *Dissertations on the Genuineness of the Pentateuch*, i. p. 185. f.

of the plucking, or gathering of the fruits of the sycamores. The " cutting of the bark " is by no means obvious, and is too much the language of natural history. That the prophet's real vocation is designated by בוקר, and that בולם שקמים is not, by any means, something independent of, and co-ordinate with that, appears from ver. 15, where the בוקר is resumed. The fruits of the sycamores may, occasionally, not have a disagreeable taste, for him who eats them only as a dainty; but they are at all events very poor ordinary food; compare *Warnekros* in *Eichhorn's Repert.* 11. 256.

Z

But how can Amos adduce it as a proof of his divine mission, that he is neither a prophet, nor, in the sense explained, a prophet's son, *i.e.*, that he was neither a superior nor an inferior member of the prophetic order? The answer is,—It was the result of that organization of the prophetic order, that the relation to the Lord was one which was more or less mediate. To those who would not acknowledge the immediate divine influence, some ground was thereby afforded for doing so. Their training, their principles, the form of their prophecies, all admitted of a natural explanation. It is true that the *spirit* which animated them baffled any such attempt; but that spirit was not so easily perceived. In the case of any one, then, who appeared as a prophet, without standing in that connection, and yet in the full possession of all prophetic gifts,—in demonstration of the spirit and of power, a natural explanation was far more difficult; especially if, like Amos, he was, by his outward situation, cut off from all human resources for education. But was Amos, for that reason, an uneducated man? This is a question which one may answer either in the affirmative or negative, according to what he understands by education. So much is certain, that he was in possession of the essential part of a true Israelitish education—viz., the knowledge of the law. The most intimate acquaintance with the Pentateuch everywhere manifests itself; compare in proof of this the *Dissertations on the Genuineness of the Pentateuch*, i. p. 136 ff. There are too many instances, down to most recent times, of living piety breaking, in this respect, through almost impenetrable barriers, to allow us to consider this as a strange thing, and to make it necessary for us to excogitate the various ways and means by which Amos may have received this education. It is only on the lower ground of the mere forms of language, that the rank of Amos not unfrequently appears. In all the higher relations he shows himself a type of the Apostles, who, although they were uneducated fishermen of Galilee, exhibit the most distinguishing proofs of true education.

Amos belonged to that circle of prophets who received a commission to prophesy the ruin which was impending over the Covenant-people, before any human probability existed for it. *Baur*, on Amos, S. 60, is of opinion that " the definiteness with which he prophesies the destruction of the kingdom of

Jeroboam, although its power was at that time still flourishing, leads us to expect that he must have had distinct indications of its speedy decay." In a certain sense we may assent to this opinion. The prophet himself continually points to such indications. These indications are the sins of the people. But if *Baur* endeavours to put political indications in the stead of these moral ones; if he be of opinion that the Assyrians must, at that time, have stood in a threatening attitude in the background, we must give to his opinion a decided opposition. We can, in such an assertion, see only an effect of that naturalistic mode of viewing things, which would limit the horizon of the prophets to that of their own times.[1] Not the slightest allusion to the Assyrians occurs. The supposition that Calneh or Ktesiphon, in chap. vi. 2, appears as having already fallen (through the Assyrians), rests upon an incorrect interpretation, just as does the assertion that Hamath, in the same passage, is supposed to be conquered; concerning the latter point, compare *Thenius* on 2 Kings xiv. 28. In the announcement of the carrying away into captivity beyond Damascus, made in chap. v. 27, there appears nothing more than the knowledge, that the catastrophe will not be brought about by that heathen power which had hitherto brought ruin upon the kingdom of Israel But, everywhere, we may see that the prophet—whom we have no reason to think an especially ingenious politician—appeared at a time when no one expected any danger. Amos prophesied at a time when the morning-dawn had risen upon Israel, iv. 13, v. 8; " in the beginning of the shooting up of the grass, and behold the grass was standing, after the King (Jehovah) had caused to be mown," vii. 1; at a time when the prosperity of the kingdom of the ten tribes was again budding forth. In chap. viii. 9, the Lord threatens that He will cause the sun to go down at noon, and bring darkness over the land in the day of *light*. In chap. vi. 4-6, the prevailing careless luxury and

---

[1] The groundlessness of such a mode of viewing things is shown by the prophecy of events such as that mentioned in i. 15 : " The people of Aram are carried away to Kir, saith the Lord ;" compare the fulfilment in 2 Kings xvi. 9. They had originally come from Kir, Amos ix. 7. This circumstance furnished the natural foundation for the prophecy, and it was certainly this circumstance also which induced the conqueror to adopt his measures. But the supernatural character of the definite prophecy remains, nevertheless, unshaken.

joy are graphically described. Chap. v. 18 implies that the
people mocked at the threatening of the coming of the day of
the Lord, the coming of which could, therefore, not have been
indicated by any human probability. In chap. vi. 1, the prophet gives utterance to an exclamation of woe over them that
are secure in Zion, and that trust in the mountain of Samaria.
In chap. vi. 13, he opposes the delusion of those " who rejoice
in a thing of nought, who say, Have we not taken to us horns
by our own strength?"   The people in the kingdom of the ten
tribes must accordingly have imagined that they were living in
the golden age of the fulfilment of Deut. xxx. 17, and must not
have thought for a moment that the axe was already laid to the
root of the tree.

But we are not at liberty to seek the fulfilment of the prophecy of Amos, only in the visitation by the Assyrians.   That
which happens to the people of the ten tribes is, to the prophet,
only a part of a general visitation, which comes, not only upon
all the neighbouring nations, but upon Judah also, and which
brings utter ruin upon the latter, chap. ii. 4, 5, destroying the
temple at Jerusalem, and driving the house of David from the
throne, ix. 1, 11. According to prophecy and history, however,
this catastrophe came upon Judah, not by Asshur, but, in the
first instance, by Babylon.

The prophecy possesses a comprehensive character, such as
we should be led to expect from the close connection of Amos
with Joel. It comprehends everything which Judah and Israel,
along with the neighbouring people, had to suffer from the
rising heathen powers; compare vi. 14, v. 24, according to which,
judgment shall roll down as waters, and righteousness as a *continual* stream.[1]

In the case of Amos, also, interpreters have been at considerable pains in fixing the time and the occasion of the single
portions, but with as little success as in the cases of Hosea and
Micah. The very inscription proves that we have before us a
whole, composed at one time, and containing the substance of

---

[1] *Caspari* in his commentary on Micah, S. 69, is wrong in remarking :
" Joel beholds the instruments of punitive justice upon Israel, as numberless hosts only ; Amos, already, as a single nation." In Amos vi. 14 the גוי
as little means a single nation, as it does in the fundamental passage, Deut.
xxviii. 49 ff., beyond the definiteness of which Amos does not go.

what the prophet had uttered previously, and in a detached form. According to this inscription, the book was composed only two years after the prophet's personal ministry in the kingdom of Israel. But if there were such an interval betwixt the oral preaching of the prophet and its having been committed to writing, it is, *a priori*, not likely that the latter should have followed the former, step by step.

The words, "Two years before the earthquake," cannot be regarded as a chronological date, intended to fix more definitely the exact time within the more extended period previously stated, viz., "the days of Uzziah and Jeroboam." For such a purpose they are ill suited, inasmuch as the time of the earthquake is not fixed; and, moreover, any such more definite determination would have been without either significance or interest. This only was of importance, that the word of the Lord should have been uttered in the days of Jeroboam, and that the prophecy of the destruction should have been delivered at a time when the Israelites enjoyed an amount of prosperity, such as they had not known for a long time. It can scarcely be doubted that the earthquake under Uzziah, the fearfulness of which is testified by Zech. xiv. 5, comes under consideration only as the reason for the composition of the book,—for committing to writing what had formerly been delivered orally. The earthquake denotes, in the symbolical language of Scripture, great revolutions, by which the form of the earth is changed, and that which is uppermost, overturned; compare my remarks on Rev. vi. 12. To point to such an earthquake had been the fundamental thought of Amos' oral predictions. By the natural earthquake, he was induced to commit them to writing, that they might go side by side with the symbol, and serve as its interpreter.

There is a plan in the arrangement of the book, which indicates that the book is not a collection of separate discourses, but that it bears an independent character. It is distinctly divided into two parts,—the first, made up of naked prophecies, from chap. i. to chap. vi.; the second, of such prophecies as are connected with a symbol, which is always very simple, and very briefly described,—from chap. vii. to chap. ix.

In the first part, the prophet begins with the announcement of the wrath of the Lord, ver. 2. He then reviews, in their order, those kingdoms upon which it shall be poured out, viz., Damascus, Philistia, Tyrus, Edom, Ammon, Moab, and Judah: until at last the storm reaches to Israel, and, according to *Rückert's* striking remarks, remains suspended over it.

In addition to Israel, there are seven nations, and the seven are divided into three, and four; three not related to the people of the ten tribes, and four related to them; the brotherly people of Judah being introduced after three nations have been mentioned which are more distantly related to Israel.

According to *Rückert,* it is only in chap. ii. 6–16 that the storm which remained suspended over Israel is described; then in chap. iii.–vi. there follow four threatening discourses, which are not connected either with the preceding ones, or with each other. But the correct view rather is, that this stationary suspension is described in the whole of the first half,—in the main, indeed, even to the end of the book.

This is evident from the consideration that, if such were not the case, the treatment of the main subject would be, as regards the extent of the description, greatly disproportioned to the introduction; for chap. i. to ii. 5 must be considered to be, throughout, merely introductory. But as the ground on which we advance this assertion is made in opposition to an unsound view, it requires a more particular determination. It is assumed by many interpreters, that in the nations besides Israel, the prophet reproves "some haughty excesses, but, evidently, only as instances of the immorality prevailing" (*Jahn, Einl.* 2, p. 404). But this view, according to which the prophet might, instead of the various crimes mentioned, have noticed any other crime, *e.g.,* fornication, idolatry, etc., is certainly erroneous. It is rather a *theocratic* judgment of which he speaks throughout; they are crimes against the theocracy, the punishment of which he announces. These he considers as being more heinous than all others; for the guilt of the latter is diminished by the circumstance of their having been committed against the hidden God only, while the former have been committed against the God who has manifested Himself, and who is living among His people. For so much is evident, that the main cause of the hatred of all the neighbouring nations against Israel was, that Israel was the people of God. For where can an instance be found of a hatred betwixt any two of them, so inextinguishable, and continuing through centuries? How entirely different is, *e.g.*, the position of Edom against Moab, from that of Edom against Israel? Three reasons confirm the correctness of our assertion as to the purely theocratic nature of the judgment. 1. The general announcement of the judgment. "Jehovah roareth from Zion, and from Jerusalem He giveth His voice." The very use of the name Jehovah here deserves attention. A judgment of a general kind upon the heathen would belong to God as Elohim. It is Elohim who is the God of the heathen,—the Creator, Preserver, and Governor of the world, from whom blessings, as well as judgments upon it, proceed. Now it might be said that Jehovah is used in the case of the heathen also, for the sake of uniformity, because to Him belongeth the judgment upon Judah and Israel. But that this is not the case, is seen from the addition: "From Zion,—from Jerusalem." Every general judgment proceeds from heaven; it is only as a theocratic God, that God reigns in Zion and Jerusalem. This argument admits of no exception; all that God does from Zion is theocratic deliverance, or theocratic judgment.—2. The nature of the crimes themselves, which are cited by way of example. It can certainly not be merely accidental, that they are all such as were committed against the Covenant-people. There is one only which forms an apparent exception, viz., that of the Moabites, who are, in chap. ii. 1, charged with having burned into lime the bones of the king of Edom. But, with the consent of the greater number of interpreters, *Jerome* remarks on this: "In order that God might show that He is the Lord of all, and that every soul is subject to Him who formed it, He punishes the iniquity committed against the king of Edom." But in this remark of Jerome, the relation in which Idumea stood to the Covenant-people is altogether lost sight of. It is only as a vassal of their kings that the king of Edom here comes into view. This is sufficiently manifest from 2 Kings iii., although the event narrated there is different from that which is here alluded to, of which no record has been preserved in history.[1] The hatred against the Covenant-people, which the

---

[1] Scarcely any doubt can, however, be entertained that we have here before us a *consequence* of the war mentioned in 2 Kings iii., viz., the vengeance which the Moabites took for what they suffered on that occasion.

Moabites were too weak openly to exhibit, impelled them to this wicked deed against the king tributary to them.—3. It must be carefully observed how the prophet, when coming to Judah, introduces us, at once, into the centre of *theocratic* transgression, the forsaking of the living God, and the serving of vain, dead idols.

It will now be easily seen in what way the portion, chap. i.–ii. 5, serves as an introduction to what follows. The prophecies against foreign nations do not, as elsewhere, serve as a consolation, or as a proof of the love of God towards His people, and of His omnipotence, or as a means for destroying confidence in man's power, in man's help; they are, on the contrary, intended, from the very outset, to give rise in Israel to the question : If such be done in the green tree, what shall be done in the dry ? That question the prophet answers at large. If severe punishment be inflicted, even upon those who have trespassed against the living God, with whom they came into contact only distantly, what will become of those to whom He manifested Himself so plainly and distinctly,—among whom He had, as it were, gained a form,—before whose eyes He had been so evidently set forth ? The declaration, " You only do I know of all the families of the earth ; therefore I shall visit upon you all your iniquities " (iii. 2), forms the centre of the whole threatening announcement to Israel. And could it indeed be introduced in any better way than by pointing out, how even the lowest degree of knowledge was followed by such a visitation ? But now, that which under the Old Testament was the highest degree, becomes, under the New Testament, only a preparatory step. The revelation of God in Christ stands in the same relation to that made to Israel under the Old Testament, as the latter stands to the manifestation of His character and nature to the heathen, who came into connection with the Covenant-people. Thus the fulfilment becomes to us a new prophecy. If the rejection of God, in His inferior revelation, was followed by such awful consequences to the temporal welfare of the people of the Old Covenant, what must be the consequences of the rejection of the highest and fullest revelation of God to the temporal and spiritual welfare of the people of the New Covenant ? This is a thought which is further expanded in Heb. xii. 17 ff., and it forms the essential feature of the description of the judgment of the world in the New Testament. This judgment has been but too often thus misunderstood, as if it concerned the world as the world,—a misunderstanding similar to that of the section before us. The Gospel shall first be preached to every creature, and according as every one has conducted himself towards the *living* God, so he shall be judged. —But it is not to the heathen nations only, but to Judah also that, by way of introduction, destruction is announced. The circumstance that not even the possession of so many precious privileges, as the temple and the Davidic throne, could ward off the well-merited punishment of sin, could not but powerfully affect the hearts of the ten tribes. If God's justice be so energetic, what have *they* to expect?

If we continue the examination of *Rückert's* view, it will soon appear that the phrase, "Hear this word," in iii. 1, iv. 1, and v. 1, can alone be considered as the foundation on which it rests. But these words do not at all prove a new commencement, but only a new starting-point. This appears sufficiently from the absence of these words at the alleged fourth threatening discourse in chap. vi.; and likewise from a comparison of Hosea iv. 1 and v. 1: "Hear the word of the Lord, ye children of Israel," and "Hear this, ye priests, and hearken, ye house of Israel, and give ear, house of the king;" while nothing similar occurs in the following chapters. That such an exhortation was appropriate, even in the middle, is clearly seen from Amos iii. 13. It cannot then, *per se*, prove anything in favour of a new beginning. If it is to be regarded as such, the discourse must be proved, by other reasons, to have been completed. But no such reasons here exist. We might as reasonably assume the existence of ten threatening discourses, as of four. The circumstance that we can nowhere discover a sure commencement and a clearly defined termination, shows that we are fully justified in considering the whole first part, chap. i. to vi., as a connected discourse.

The second part, which contains the visions of the destruction, is composed, indeed, of various portions,—as might have been expected from the nature of the subject. Each new vision, with the discourse connected with it, must form a new section. Chap. vii., viii., and ix., form each a whole. From the account which is added to the first vision, and which relates to the transactions between Amos and the high priest Amaziah, which were caused by the public announcement of this vision (chap. vii. 12–14), we are led to suppose that these visions were formerly delivered singly, in the form in which we now possess them. But that, even here, we have not before us pieces loosely connected with each other in a chronological arrangement, is evident from the fact, that the promises stand just at the end of the whole collection. The prophet had rather to reprove and to threaten than to comfort; but yet he cannot refrain, at least at the close, from causing the sun to break through the clouds. Without this close there would be wanting in Amos a main element of the prophetic discourse, which is wanting in no other prophet, and by which alone the other elements are placed in a proper light.

It also militates against the supposition of a mere collection, that in the last vision the prevailing regard to the kingdom of the ten tribes disappears almost entirely, and that, like the third chapter of Hosea, it relates to the whole of the Covenant-people, —in agreement with the reference to the earthquake mentioned in the inscription, which the prophet had experienced in Judah, and which brought into view, not a particular, but a general, judgment.

The symbolical clothing, however, forms the sole difference betwixt the second part and the first. As the "real centre and essence of the book" the second part cannot be regarded; the threatening is as clear and impressive in the first part.

That which is common to Amos with the contemporary prophets, is the absolute clearness with which he foresees that, before salvation comes, all that is glorious, not only in Israel, but in Judah also, must be given over to destruction. Judah and Israel shall be overflowed by the heathen world, the Temple at Jerusalem destroyed, the Davidic dynasty dethroned, and the inhabitants of both kingdoms carried away into captivity. But afterwards, the restoration of David's tabernacle (ix. 11), and the extension of the kingdom of God far beyond the borders of the heathen world (ver. 12), take place. The most characteristic point is the emanation of salvation from the family of David, at the time of its deepest abasement.

CHAPTER IX.

The chapter opens with a vision. The temple, shaken by the Angel of the Lord in its very foundations, falls down, and buries Judah and Israel under its ruins. Without a figure,—the breach of the Covenant by the Covenant-people brings destruction upon them. The prophet endeavours to strengthen the impression of this threatening upon their mind, by breaking *down the supports of false security by which they sought to evade it.* There is no deliverance, no escape, vers. 2–4, for the Almighty God is the enemy and pursuer, vers. 5, 6. There is no mercy on account of the Covenant, for Israel is no more the Covenant-people. They shall not, however, be altogether destroyed; but the destruction of the sinful mass shall be accompanied by the preservation of a small number of the godly, vers. 7–10. This great sifting is followed, however, by the restoration; the tabernacle of David which is fallen, the kingdom of God among Israel, *connected with the family of David,* shall be raised up again, ver. 11; rendered glorious by its extension over the heathen, ver. 12; and blessed with the abundance of the divine gifts, vers. 12–15.

Ver. 1. "*I saw the Lord standing over the altar; and He said, Smite the chapiter, and make the thresholds tremble, and break them upon the heads of all; and I will kill their remnant by the sword: he that fleeth away of them shall not flee away, and he that escapeth of them shall not be delivered.*"

The principal question which here arises is :—Who is here addressed,—to whom is the commission of destruction given by the Lord? As, in accordance with the dramatic character of the prophetical discourse, the person is not more definitely marked out, we can think of Him only who, throughout, executes God's judgments upon the enemies of His kingdom. But He is the same to whom the preservation and protection of the true members of His kingdom are committed, viz., the Angel of the Lord. It was He, who, as המשחית, the destroying Angel, smote the first-born of Egypt, Exod. xii. 2, 3, compared with 12, 13. It was from Him that the destruction of the

Assyrians proceeded, 2 Kings xix. 34, 35; Is. xxxvii. 35, 36. After the numbering of Israel, when the anger of the Lord was kindled against them, it was He who inflicted the punishment, 2 Sam. xxiv. 1, 15, 16. As He encampeth round about them who fear the Lord, so He is, in regard to the ungodly, like the wind which carries away the chaff, Ps. xxxiv. 8, xxxv. 5, 6.— In opposition to the objection raised by *Baur*,—"That, with the exception of the passage in Is. vi., nowhere, in the books composed before the Chaldee period, do angels appear to act as mediators in the execution of the divine commands,"—it is sufficient to refer to Joel iv. (iii.) 9–11, and, as regards *the* Angel of the Lord, to Hosea xii. 5 (4). But we have, in addition, a special reason for thinking here of the Angel of the Lord. This is afforded to us by the ninth chapter of Ezekiel, which must be considered, throughout, as a further expansion of the verse under consideration, and as the oldest and most trustworthy commentary upon it. In that chapter, there appear (at the command of the Lord who is about to avenge the apostasy of His people) the servants of His justice—six in number—and in the midst of them, "a man clothed with linen;"—the former, with instruments of destruction; the latter, with writing materials. They step (the scene is in the temple) by the side of the brazen altar. Thither there comes to them out of the holy of holies, to the threshold of the temple, the glory of the Lord, and gives to Him who is clothed with linen the commission to preserve the faithful, while the others receive a commission to destroy the ungodly, without mercy. But now, Who is the man clothed in linen? None other than the Angel of the Lord. This appears from Daniel x. 5, xii. 6, 7, where Michael = the Angel of the Lord (compare *Dissertations on the Genuineness of Daniel*, p. 135 ff.) is designated in the same way,—a remarkable coincidence in these two contemporary prophets, to which we omitted to direct attention in our work on Daniel. It is *further* evident from the subject itself. The dress is that of the earthly high priest (*Theodoret* remarks: "The dress of the seventh is that of the high priest, for he was not one of the destroyers, but the redeemer of those who were worthy of salvation"); compare Lev. xvi. 4, 23. It is especially from the former of these passages that the plural בדים is to be accounted for. According to it, the various parts of the high prest's dress are of linen. But the heavenly Mediator, High Priest, and Intercessor, is the Angel of the Lord; compare, *e.g.*, Zech. i. 12, where He makes intercession for the Covenant-people, and the Lord answers Him with good and comfortable words. Concerning the earthly high priest as a type of Christ, and hence a type of the Angel of the Lord, compare the remarks on Zech. iii. But we must not imagine that He who is clothed with linen is commissioned solely for the work of delivering the godly, and hence stands contrasted with the six ministers of justice. On the contrary, these are rather to be considered as being subordinate to Him, as carrying out the work of destruction only by His command and authority. From Him, punishment no less than salvation proceeds. This is sufficiently evident for general reasons. The punishment and deliverance have both the same root, the same aim, viz., the advancement of the kingdom of God. We cannot by any means think of evil angels in the case of the six; such could be assumed only in opposition to the whole doctrine of Scripture on the point, which is always consistent in ascribing the punishment of the wicked to the good angels, and the temptation of the godly, with the permission of God, to the evil angels. In proof of this, we have only to think of Job's trial, of Christ's temptation, and of the angel of Satan by whom Paul was buffeted. This subject has already been very well treated by *Ode*, who, in his work *De Angelis*, p. 741 ff., says : " God sends good angels to punish wicked men, and He employs evil angels to chasten the godly."[1] But if this be established, it is then established at the same time, that the judgment here belongs to the Angel of the Lord. For to Him, as the Prince of the heavenly host, all inferior angels are subordinate, so that every-

[1] *Hofmann, Schriftbeweis* I. S. 312, objects : " If this were correct, Paul ought to have delivered that fornicator at Corinth (1 Cor. v. 5), or Hymeneus and Alexander (1 Tim. i. 20), not to Satan, but to the good angels." But the individuals mentioned were members of the Church of Christ, and they were delivered to Satan, not for their absolute destruction, but for their salvation : ἵνα τὸ πνεῦμα (which of course was still in existence ; and it is just the πνεῦμα that separates between the world and the Church, compare Ps. li. 13) σωθῇ ἐν τῇ ἡμέρᾳ τοῦ Κυρίου, ἵνα παιδευθῶσι μὴ βλασφημεῖν. It is, as in the case of Job, a punishment with a view to purification, for which power is given to Satan, Heb. xii. 6. These passages, then, serve only to confirm the view which we have expressed.

thing which they do belongs to Him.—To these general reasons, we may, however, add special reasons which are altogether decisive. That He who is clothed with linen is closely connected with the six, is indicated by the number seven. He also appears at the side of the altar, and comes in the midst of the others, who follow after Him, ver. 2. But of conclusive significance are the words in chap. x. 2 and 7 : "And the Lord spake unto the man clothed with linen, and said, Go in between the wheels under the cherubim, and fill Thine hand with coals of fire from between the cherubim, and scatter them over the city. And He went in, in my sight. And a cherub stretched forth his hand from between the cherubim, unto the fire that was between the cherubim, and took, and put it into the hands of Him who was clothed with linen. And He took it and went out." The *fire* here is not the symbolical designation of wrath, but natural fire ; for it is the setting on fire and burning of the city which is here to be prefigured. The wheels denote the natural powers,—in the first instance, the wind, chap. x. 13, but the fire also ; while the cherubim denote the living creation. The Angel of the Lord is here expressly designated as He who executeth the judgments of divine justice.

The importance of the preceding investigation extends beyond the mere clearing up of the passage under consideration. We have here obtained the Old Testament foundation for the New Testament doctrine, that all judgment has been committed to the Son, while the harmony of the two Testaments is exhibited in a remarkable instance. Compare with the already cited Old Testament declarations, such passages as Matt. xiii. 41 : Ἀποστελεῖ ὁ υἱὸς τοῦ ἀνθρώπου τοὺς ἀγγέλους αὐτοῦ, καὶ συλλέξουσιν ἐκ τῆς βασιλείας αὐτοῦ πάντα τὰ σκάνδαλα, καὶ τοὺς ποιοῦντας τὴν ἀνομίαν· and xxv. 31 : Ὅταν δὲ ἔλθῃ ὁ υἱὸς τοῦ ἀνθρώπου ἐν τῇ δόξῃ αὐτοῦ, καὶ πάντες οἱ ἄγγελοι μετ᾽ αὐτοῦ, τότε καθίσει ἐπὶ θρόνου δόξης αὐτοῦ. In order to be convinced of the identity of the Angel of the Lord and Christ (compare above, p. 107 sqq. and *Commentary on Rev.* i. p. 466), we may further direct attention to the fact that the Angel of the Lord, who meets us throughout the whole of the Old Testament, suddenly disappears in the New Testament, and that to Christ all is ascribed which was in the Old Testament attributed to the Angel of the Lord.

A second important question is:—What is to be understood by *the* altar, המזבח ? Several interpreters adopt the opinion of *Cyril*, and think of the altar at Bethel, or some other idolatrous altar in the kingdom of Israel. Others (*e.g.*, *Marckius*) are of opinion that the article stands here without meaning, and that it is the intention of the prophet only to represent God as appearing on some altar, leaving it undetermined on which, in order thereby to indicate that He required the blood of many men. But against such expositions the article is conclusive. *The* altar can be that altar only, of which every one would think, if an altar κατ' ἐξοχήν, and without a more definite designation, were spoken of. Such was the brazen altar, or altar of burnt-offering in the outer court of the temple at Jerusalem. That it was this altar, and not the altar of incense before the holy of holies, which received, in the common language of the people, the name of *the* altar, is easily explained from the circumstance that it stood in a much closer relation to the people than did the other which was withdrawn from their view. On this altar all the sacrifices were offered, and it must, throughout, be understood, when *the* altar of the Lord is spoken of; compare remarks on Rev. vi. 9. But that which removes all doubt is the comparison with the parallel passage in Ezekiel. There, the scene is the temple at Jerusalem. The ministers of justice step beside the brazen altar. At the threshold of the temple-building proper, the glory of the Lord moves toward them. This parallel passage, moreover, does not leave any doubt as to the reason why the Lord appears here beside the altar. *Jerome* remarks on this: " They are introduced standing beside the altar, ready for the order of their commander; so that they know every one whose sins are not forgiven, and who is liable, therefore, to the sentence of the Lord, and to destruction." The Lord's appearing beside the altar is a visible representation of the truth, that wheresoever the carcase is, there will the eagles be gathered together. The altar is the place of transgression; it is there that there lies accumulated the unexpiated guilt of the whole nation, instead of the rich treasure of love and faith, which alone should be there, embodied in the sacrifice. The Lord appears at the place of transgression, in order that He may be glorified in the destruction of those who would not glorify Him in their lives.

—Now several interpreters (*e.g., Michaëlis*), who have correctly
defined the meaning of the altar, would infer from the mention
of the temple at Jerusalem, that the whole prophecy refers to
the kingdom of Judah. But such an assumption is altogether
inadmissible. Even the general reason, that a prophecy which
refers exclusively to Judah cannot be at all expected from a
prophet who had received his special mission to Israel, militates
against it. *Further*,—The close of this prophecy, the proclamation of salvation, belongs, as we have already proved, to the
whole collection. If this be referred to Judah alone, there is
then an essential element awanting in that portion which is
addressed to Israel; we should then have judgment without
mercy, threatening without consolation,—a thing which could
not well be conceived of, and would be without analogy in any
of the prophets. To this we must *further* add the express references, or co-references to Israel throughout the whole chapter,—such as the mention of Carmel in ver. 3; of the children
of Israel, in ver. 7; of the house of Jacob, in ver. 8; of the
house of Israel, in ver. 9; of פְּרִיצֵהֶן, in ver. 11; of My people
Israel, in ver. 14. The whole assumption of an exclusive reference to Judah owes its origin to the circumstance, that features which are only symbolical have been erroneously interpreted as actual. But if they be viewed and explained as
symbols, every reason for denying the reference to Israel is
then at once removed. The temple symbolizes the kingdom of
God; its falling down upon the people is symbolical of the
punishment which is inflicted upon them, in consequence of this
kingdom. The destruction of the temple in the literal sense
is not, primarily, spoken of; although the latter, it is true, be
inseparable from the former. If the Covenant-people in general were outwardly desecrated, because they had desecrated
themselves inwardly, then also the outward sanctuary which
they had, by their wickedness, converted into a den of thieves,
was taken from them; compare the remarks on Dan. ix. 27.
If Israel then, at that time, still belonged to the kingdom of
God (and this can certainly not be doubted, and is sufficiently
proved by the very mission of our prophet to Israel), there
exists no reason at all for excluding it. For Israel also, the
temple at Jerusalem formed the seat and centre from which
it was governed,—the place from which blessings and punish-

ments proceeded. The prophet indeed, at the very opening of his prophecies, describes the Lord as roaring from Zion, and uttering His voice from Jerusalem. On the altar at Jerusalem the crimes of Israel were deposited, no less than those of Judah; for there was the place where the people of both kingdoms were to deposit the embodied expression of their godly disposition. It was there, then, that, in reality, the fruits of the opposite were lying, although, as regards the place, they were offered elsewhere.—So much indeed is certain, that the co-reference to Judah is necessarily required by the symbolical representation. The rejection of Israel alone could not be symbolized by the destruction of the temple. And no less does this appear from the announcement of salvation. For this does not by any means promise the re-establishment of the Davidic dominion among the people of Israel, but the restoration of the entire fallen Davidic government. The tabernacle of David that is fallen refers to the destroyed temple. Both signify, substantially, the same thing. With the destruction of the temple, the Davidic tabernacle also fell; and its fall included the overthrow of the kingdom of Israel; for, in this also, the Davidic race had still the dominion *de jure*, although it was suspended *de facto*.

The passage under consideration is remarkable also, inasmuch as it furnishes a proof for the custom of designating the kingdom of God from its existing seat and centre, and thus furnishes us, for other passages also, with the right of freeing the thought from the figurative clothing.

A *further* reason against referring *the* altar to the altar at Bethel, is, that the latter enjoyed no such pre-eminence in the kingdom of Israel. The temple at Bethel was, to the ten tribes, by no means what the temple at Jerusalem was to Judah. The law regarding the unity of the place of worship was, among the ten tribes, regarded as non-existing. Even in the verse immediately preceding, in viii. 14, Dan and Beersheba had been mentioned as the chief seats of the Israelitish worship; and in chap. iv. 4, Gilgal appears beside Bethel as possessing the same importance. In chap. v. 5, Bethel, Gilgal, and Beersheba are mentioned together. Hosea, in chap. viii. 11, reproves Israel for having made many altars to sin. Hence, there did not exist in Israel an altar κατ᾽ ἐξοχήν. Such an altar existed only in

2 A

Judah.   Nor had the sanctuary at Bethel such importance, as that it could be considered as the spiritual abode of the whole people.—*Hofmann* (*Weissagung u. Erfüllung*, S. 203) raises the following objection against the reference to the altar at Jerusalem :—" The prophet, it is true, reproves the sins in Judah as well as those in Israel ; but it is only to the kingdom of Jeroboam that he announces destruction, while to the house of David he promises that Jehovah would raise it up from its fallen condition." But in opposition to this objection, we need only refer to ii. 5 : "And I send fire in Judah, and it devours the palaces of Jerusalem." Passages such as i. 14, 15, ii. 3, absolutely forbid us to make an exception of the palace of the king ; and, by chap. vii. 9, where destruction is announced to all the sanctuaries of Isaac, we have as little warrant for excepting the temple. To assume any such exceptions, would be contrary to the analogy of all other threatenings. *Hofmann* further objects (l. c. S. 204), "As the threatening announcement of the prophet had last remained suspended over Israel, we are at liberty to think of the altar at Bethel only." But already, in the third chapter, all Israel is addressed, according to ver. 1 ; and we may further refer to v. 25, where likewise Israel can mean only the whole people,[1] while in vi. 1, Judah is expressly mentioned beside Israel. The prophet employs, throughout, the name of Israel with a certain ambiguity ; so that it would be vain to attempt to determine whether it be used in the wider, or in the more limited sense. Wherever he wishes to be distinctly understood as speaking of the ten tribes, he speaks of Joseph and Samaria. Still less would the prophet have employed the names of Jacob (iii. 13, vi. 8, vii. 2, 6) and of Isaac (vii. 9, 16), which were quite uncommon as a designation of the ten tribes,[2]

---

[1] The same is probably the case in vi. 14 : "For behold I raise up against you, O house of Israel, saith the Lord God of Hosts, heathen people ; and they shall afflict you from Hamath unto the river of the wilderness." The river of the wilderness can here be none other than the river of Egypt, which commonly appears as the boundary of the whole. Compare 1 Kings viii. 65 ; 2 Chron. vii. 8, where Solomon assembles the whole people from Hamath unto the river of Egypt ; Josh. xv. 4, 47 ; 2 Kings xxiv. 7 ; Is. xxvii. 12. They who think of the boundary of the kingdom of the ten tribes only, are at a loss, and have recourse to uncertain conjectures.

[2] In Micah i. 15 the entire people are called Jacob. The same occurs also in Hos. x. 11, xii. 3 (2).

if it had been of importance, and intentional on his part strictly
to separate the boundaries of Judah from those of Israel, and,
if there were not everywhere here, only a special application to
the ten tribes of that which concerned the whole who were connected by a common fate. But it is especially suitable, that
just the close of the whole should, in a remarkably distinct
manner, bring into view the two kingdoms, the destinies of
which were so intimately connected.—*Hitzig,* further, with a
view to favour the reference to the temple in Bethel, adduces
the consideration that this vision is connected with the close of
viii. 14, and forms a kind of explanation of it. But we have
here an entirely new beginning, just as in chap. viii. in its relation to chap. vii. The three visions are altogether independent
of, and co-ordinate with each other.—נצב with על is commonly
used of a prominent position *at the side of:* Gen. xviii. 2; 1 Sam.
iv. 20; compare עמד with על 1 Kings xiii. 1. In Ezek. ix. 1
also, the angels stand at the side of the brazen altar. נצב can,
of course, never signify "*to be suspended.*"—הכפתור is a species
of ornament at the top of the pillars; and הספים, "the thresholds," are contrasted with each other, in order to give expression to the thought that the building was to be shaken, and
destroyed from the highest part of it to the lowest,—from the
top to the bottom. The shaking of the thresholds occurs also
in Is. vi. to denote that the shaking extended to the deepest
foundations. The greater number of interpreters translate:
"Strike the knop *so that* . . tremble," etc.; but the וירעשו
must be viewed rather as co-ordinate with הך: "And they may
tremble," equivalent to "Make to tremble."—The suffix in בצעם
refers to the knops and threshold, or to the entire building,
which is marked out by the contrast of the highest and lowest
portions. According to *Ewald* and *Umbreit,* it is intended to
refer to the dashed pieces of the altar; but nothing has been
said about the destruction of the altar. In Ezek. ix. 2 likewise,
the altar is mentioned, not because it was to be destroyed, but
only because there the guilt is heaped up. The casting down
does not, in itself, imply the *breaking, dashing into pieces;* it
does so only by its being connected with the following בראש.
The passage in Jer. xlix. 20 is analogous: "He shall make
their habitation desolate over them;" instead of: "He shall
thus make it desolate that they are buried beneath its ruins;"

compare Jer. l. 45. בראש, properly understood, does not mean
"*upon* the head;" the head is rather represented as the recep-
tacle of the tumbling ruins; they fall into their heads and crush
them; compare Ps. vii. 17. In what precedes, there is no
definite noun to which כלם refers. This is to be explained by
the dramatic character of the whole representation which arises
necessarily from the opening phrase: "I saw." The same
reason accounts for the peculiarity of הך being employed without any designation of person. In his inward vision, the prophet
sees the whole people assembled before the Lord at the threshold
of the temple. The Lord appears before him as the judge,
at the place of the transgressions, at the side of the altar. At
His command, the whole assembled multitude are buried under
the ruins of the temple. From this also it is evident that a destruction of the temple in a literal sense cannot be entertained;
for how could a whole people be buried under its ruins? The
same appears also from ראיתי at the commencement. This,
then, shows that we have here before us a symbolical representation, corresponding altogether to that which we have in vii.
1, 4, 7, viii. 1. Hitherto, the Lord speaking to some one, had
given him the commission of destruction. He now continues
with: "I will kill." This also shows that the one who is addressed is the Angel of the Lord. The same occurrence takes
place in the greater number of the passages in which the Angel
of the Lord is spoken of. In the action there is constant alternation; it is ascribed, at one time to Him, at another, to Jehovah.—Several interpreters (*Marckius, De Wette, Rückert,* and
others) explain אחרית by "posterity;" others, after the example
of the Chaldee (שארהון), by "remnant;" and others, by "lowest
of the people." We must here enter into a closer examination
of the significations of this word. It is commonly supposed
(compare *Gesenius* and *Winer*) that, primarily and properly, it
signifies "the last and extreme part," and then "the end." But
that which is supposed to be the derived signification is rather
the original and proper one. The form of the word cannot
furnish any reason why this should not be the case, as is evident
from what has been remarked by *Ewald:* "As the feminine
termination, in general, forms abstract nouns, so also, not unfrequently, abstract nouns are derived from other nouns, by
means of the termination ית—; very frequently there is no

masculine in 'ָ— at all at the foundation, but ית— serves, in general, only as the sign of derivation." The following reasons prove that the signification "end" is the primary and proper one. 1. If the contrary were the case, the masculine 'ָ— would also occur, and the feminine would be met with as an adjective also. 2. ראשית forms the constant antithesis to אחרית; but it is universally admitted that the former is, originally and properly, an abstract noun, and signifies "beginning." The signification "end" must then be retained here also. The word never has another signification (compare my work on Balaam, p. 465 ff.); it means only "end" in its various relations. But the posterity cannot here be thought of as the end; for the whole action is concentrated in one point of time. Nor is the word ever used in the sense of "posterity." With as little propriety can "end" mean "the lowest of the people;" for one cannot see why just these should be given up to the sword. "End," here, rather denotes "remnant,"—all those who, at the overthrow of the temple, might escape. These, the Lord will pursue with the sword. They who were buried under the temple are the beginning, ראשית; the latter are the אחרית, end. Corresponding to the shaking of the temple from the knops to the thresholds, the thought is expressed in this manner, that from the first to the last, כלם מקצה they should be subjected to the divine punishment. An implied antithesis of quite the same kind, of אחרית to ראשית, occurs also in iv. 2 (where *De Wette* and *Rückert* have likewise mistaken the sense), and in viii. 10.—On the last words of the verse, which are to be considered as a further explanation of, "Their end, or remnant, I will kill by the sword," *Cocceius* remarks: "This slaughter becomes the more thorough, inasmuch as even they who flee, or seemed to have fled, are not excluded from it." The second member seems to contradict the first; for if none be allowed to flee away, how can any have escaped? Several interpreters have been thereby induced to give to the verb נוס, the first time, the signification "to escape,"—the second time, "to flee." But the contradiction is quite similar to that which occurs in the preceding context also, when all are dashed to pieces by the ruins, and yet a remnant is spoken of. It soon disappears when we consider that it is the intention of the prophet to cut off every possible way of escape, by which carnal security endeavoured to save and preserve itself against the impression of his discourse— that it is equivalent to : " *All* shall be buried under the ruins, and although some should succeed in escaping from this kind of destruction, yet the sword of divine vengeance would be behind them, and slay them ; flight shall not be possible to any man ; and even although it might be to some, it would be of no avail to them, for God would be their persecutor." But another apparent contradiction must not be overlooked. Even here, the destruction is most emphatically described as being quite general ; as such, it is minutely represented in vers. 2–4. One cannot fail to see how anxious the prophet is to cut off, from every individual, the idea of the possibility of an escape. On the other hand, it is announced in ver. 8, that the house of Jacob shall not be utterly destroyed ; according to ver. 9, all the godly shall be preserved ; according to ver. 10, the judgment is to be limited to the sinners from among the people,—a limitation which is also presupposed by the description in the 11th and subsequent verses. In iii. 12, the preservation of a small remnant amidst the general destruction had been promised. The greater number of interpreters, in order to reconcile this apparent contradiction, assume an hyperbole in vers. 1–4. But this assumption is certainly erroneous. The ground of this great copiousness,—the reason why the prophet represents the same thought in aspects so various,—is evidently to prevent every idea of an hyperbole, —to show that the words are to be taken in all their strictness of meaning. But the limitation may be arrived at, and effected in a different, and legitimate way. There is, in the nature of ungodliness, a levity which flatters every individual with the hope of escape, even although a threatened general calamity should take place. All the possibilities of deliverance are sought after in such a disposition of mind, and are, by imagination, easily changed into probabilities and realities, because just that is wanting which proves them to be improbable and unreal, viz., the consciousness of a living, omnipotent God. Thus men free themselves from fear, and with it, from the troublesome obligation of escaping from it in another and a legitimate way, viz., by true conversion. Now, it is this levity which the prophet opposes. He shows that whatever possibility of deliverance such levity may dream of, it never would become a reality, and this for the simple reason, that they had not to deal with human antagonists; from them an escape by human means would be possible, how powerful and wise soever they might be. But they have to deal with an omnipotent God, who, being also omnipresent, can arm all His creatures against His despisers, so that they cannot retreat to any place where He, who reigneth absolutely in heaven and on earth, has not ministers of His vengeance. Every thought, then, of an escape by *human means* is here cut off. But with this, every thought of deliverance in any way is taken from the *ungodly*, who are told by their own consciences that GOD will not deliver them. But, on the other hand, the same consideration could not but administer consolation to the godly. If no one, should he even hide himself in, heaven, can escape from God the Avenger, then no one, were he even in the midst of his enemies, and were the sword even already lifted up against him, can be lost from God the Deliverer.—Another question has been asked, which relates to the historical reference of the threatened punishment. It goes just as far as the thought which lies at its foundation: "You only have I known of all the families of the earth; therefore I shall visit upon you all your transgressions." Those interpreters who think exclusively of either the Assyrian, or the Chaldean, or the Roman destruction, are, in the same way, partly right and partly wrong, at the same time. All these events, and others besides, belong essentially to one whole. The difference as to time and circumstances is that which is unessential. That a prophet had exclusively in view any single one from among those divine manifestations of punishment, can be asserted, only where he himself has given express declarations to such an effect; and even then, the prophecy is limited to that single event, as to its *form* only: its *idea* is not lost by the single fulfilment.

Ver. 2. "*If they break through into hell, from thence My hand shall take them; if they ascend up into heaven, from thence I will take them down.*"

The Future must not, either here, or in what follows, be understood as *potentialis:* "Though they should conceal themselves;" but as the real Future: "If they are to conceal themselves." That אם with the Future is used only *de re dubia*, as *Winer* asserts, is as erroneous as to assert that, with the Preterite, it supposes the condition as existing. The correct view has been already given by *Gesenius* in the *Thesaurus*. By supposing the possibility of a condition, impossible in reality, the denial of the consequence becomes so much the more emphatic and expressive. That such a supposition is made here, is evident from ver. 4, where the prophet passes over to the territory of actual possibility, and where, therefore, we cannot translate : " Though they should go." Such a supposition is, in general, very frequent. It occurs, *e.g.*, Matt. v. 29, where *Tholuck* (*Comment. on the Sermon on the Mount*) has been led very far astray from the right understanding of εἰ δὲ ὁ ὀφθαλμός σου ὁ δεξιὸς σκανδαλίζει σε, κ.τ.λ., by overlooking this *usus loquendi*. We are not indeed at liberty to translate, " Though thy right eye should offend thee ;" but it must be decided by other arguments, whether the condition here *supposed* be one really possible ; and these arguments show that it is only for the sake of greater emphasis that there has here been supposed as possible, what is impossible.—Heaven and Sheol form a constant contrast between the highest height and the lowest depth. From a merely imagined possibility, the prophet descends to the real one. If, then, even the former be not able to afford protection, because God's hand reaches even where one has escaped far from any human power, how much less the latter !—חתר with the Accus. signifies " to break through," Job xxiv. 16 ; with בְּ, " to make a hole in anything ;" thus Ezek. viii. 8, xii. 7, 12 (חתר בקיר, " to make a hole in the wall "). These parallel passages show that the Sheol must be conceived of as being surrounded with strong walls,—by which is expressed its inaccessibility to all that is living. The fundamental passage is in Ps. cxxxix. 7, 8 : " Whither shall I go from Thy Spirit, and whither shall I flee from Thy presence ? If I ascend up into heaven, Thou art there ; if I make my bed in hell, behold, Thou art there." David does not here speak in his own person, but in that of his whole race. The Psalm is an indirect exhortation to his successors on the throne, and at the same time to the people. " If you are wicked," so he here addresses them, " you can never hope to escape from the punishing hand of the Almighty." And since they have become wicked, the words of David have acquired new emphasis.

Ver. 3. " *And if they hide themselves on the top of Carmel,*

from thence I will search and take them out; and if they hide them-
selves from My sight in the bottom of the sea, from thence I will
command the serpent, and he bites them."

The question here is :—Why is Carmel specially mentioned? Interpreters remind us of the numerous caves of this mountain, which make it peculiarly suitable for concealment. *O. F. von Richter*, in the *Wallfahrten im Morgenlande*, S. 65, remarks on this point : "The caves are extremely numerous in Carmel, especially on the west side. It is said that there are more than a thousand, and that they were inhabited in ancient times by monks, to whom, however, their origin cannot be ascribed. In one part of the mountain, called 'the caves of the members of the orders,' 400 are found beside each other. Farther down in the hard limestone mountain, there is one which is distinguished by its size, about 20 paces long, and more than 15 broad and high." Details still more accurate are given by *Schulz* in the *Leitungen des Höchsten*, Th. 5, S. 186, 303. According to him, the road is pure rock, and very smooth, and so crooked, that those going before cannot see those who follow them. "When we were only ten paces distant from each other, we heard each other's voices, indeed, but were invisible to each other, on account of the winding ways made in consequence of the intervening by-hills. . . . Everywhere there are caves, and their mouths are often so small that only one man can creep through at a time ; the approaches to them are so serpentine, that he who is pursued may escape from his pursuer, and step into such a small opening, of which there are frequently three or four beside each other, before his pursuer is aware of it. Hence, if any one should hide himself there, it is exceedingly difficult, yea, even impossible for the eyes of man to discover him who is pursued." But this circumstance alone does not exhaust the case, even if we still further add that the mountain was then, as it is now (*Richter*, S. 66), covered with trees and shrubberies up to the summit. The expression, " In the top," must not be overlooked, and the less so, since it stands in evident antithesis to the " *bottom* of the sea,"—like the contrast of height and depth in the preceding verse. Heaven and hell are represented on earth by the top of Carmel, and the bottom of the sea. The height of Carmel must, therefore, come also into consideration. This, it is true, is not very great ; *Bucking-*

ham estimated it at 1500 feet (*v. Raumer*, S. 40); but the prophet chose Carmel in preference to other higher mountains, partly on account of the peculiarity already stated; partly, and especially, on account of its position in the immediate neighbourhood of the sea, over which its summit hangs, and which can be seen to a great distance from it; compare 1 Kings xviii. 43, 44. Of corporeal things it holds true, as it does of spiritual things, that opposites, placed beside each other, become thereby more distinct. A lower elevation, placed by the side of a depth, appears to the unscientific eye to be much higher than another which is really so. Moreover, the position of Carmel at the extreme western border of the kingdom of Israel must also be considered. He who hides himself there, must certainly be ignorant of any safer place in the whole country; and if even then there be no more security, the sea alone is left.—צוה occurs frequently with the signification " to bid," to " command." The word is chosen on purpose to show, how even the irrational creatures stand in the service of the omnipotent God; so that it requires only a word from Him to make them the instruments of His vengeance. That the prophet had a knowledge of a very dangerous kind of sea-serpents (of which *Pliny* xix. 4 speaks), need not be supposed on account of the משם. That was not of the slightest consequence here. In v. 19 the serpent occurs in a particularizing representation of the thought that God is able to arm all nature against His enemies: " As if a man flees from the lion, and a bear meets him; and he comes home, and leans his hand on the wall, and a serpent bites him"—just the opposite of the assurance that " to those who love God, all things shall work together for good." So early as in Deut. xxxii. 24, apostates are threatened with the poison of the serpents of the dust, besides the teeth of wild beasts; and what this threatening implied, might have been well known to Israel from their former history; compare Num. xxi. 6: " And the Lord sent against the people serpents, and they bit the people, and much people of Israel died,"—a passage to which Jeremiah alludes in chap. viii. 17, where he says: " For behold I send against you serpents, basilisks, against which there is no charm, and they bite you, saith the Lord." It is very probable that to this the prophet also alludes in the passage before us.

Ver. 4. "*And if they go into captivity before their enemies, from thence will I command the sword, and it slayeth them; and I set Mine eyes upon them for evil and not for good.*"

בשבי means the state of exile. The circumstance of their being carried into captivity might awaken the hope that mercy will be granted to them; for, according to the natural course of things, he who is carried away into captivity may be sure of his life; but nothing can give security before God. The last words are strikingly illustrated by *Calvin*, who says: "There is an antithesis in this sentence, inasmuch as God had promised that He would be the protector of His people. But as hypocrites are always apt to appropriate to themselves the promises of God, without having either repentance or faith, the prophet here declares, that the eye of God would be upon them, not to protect them, as was His custom, but rather to add punishments to punishments. And this sentence is worthy of notice, inasmuch as we are thereby reminded, that although the Lord does by no means spare infidels, He yet observes us more closely in order to punish us the more severely, when He sees that we are utterly hardened and incurable." Under any circumstances, the people of the Lord continue to be the objects of special attention. They are more richly blessed; but they are also more severely punished.

Ver. 5. "*And the Lord, Jehovah, of hosts, who toucheth the earth, and it melteth, and all that dwell therein mourn; and it riseth up wholly like the stream, and it sinketh down as the stream of Egypt.*"

The prophet continues to cut off every false hope with which levity flatters itself. How can you think to escape, since you have the Almighty God for your enemy! "The prophet," remarks *Jerome*, "speaks thus, in order to impress them with the greatness of divine power, that they might not imagine that He would perhaps not do what He had threatened, or that His power was not equal to His will." Similar descriptions of the divine omnipotence, as opposed to unbelief and weak faith, are very numerous; *e.g.*, iv. 13, v. 8, 27; Is. xl. 22, xlv. 12. We are not at liberty to translate: "And the Lord Jehovah of hosts is He who toucheth." It is rather an abrupt mode of speech; and there must be supplied, either at the beginning, "And who is your enemy?" or at the end, "He is your opponent."

This abruptness of language is quite in accordance with the subject, and belongs, moreover, to the characteristic peculiarities of Amos. Altogether similar is v. 7, 8, where Israel and their God are simply placed beside each other, and every one is left to conclude for himself how such a God would act towards such a people: "They who turn judgment to wormwood, and cast righteousness to the earth. Making the Pleiades and Orion, and turning the shadow of death into the morning, and making the day dark with night, calling," etc. The accumulated appellations, Lord, Jehovah, of hosts, likewise serve to point out the omnipotence of God. The believer accumulates these appellations in his prayer in order to awaken his confidence and hope ; compare, *e.g.*, Is. xxxvii. 16, where Hezekiah begins his prayer to the Lord thus: "Jehovah, of hosts, God of Israel, Thou who art enthroned on Cherubim, Thou art God alone for all the kingdoms of the earth." But these appellations are held up to the unbelievers, to cast down all their hopes. We have separated, of hosts, from the preceding appellation of God by a comma. Ever since *Gesenius*, in his Commentary on Is. i. 9, has asserted that צבאות, when connected with Jehovah, must be considered as a Genitive depending upon it, his view has been pretty generally adopted. But it is certainly erroneous. The instances by which *Gesenius* endeavours to prove the possibility of such a connection of proper names with appellative names are not to the point. In "Bethlehem Jehudah" it is only by a false interpretation that Jehudah is considered as standing in the *status constr.* with Bethlehem (compare the remarks on Mic. v. 1 [2]) ; and with regard to ארם נהרים it is to be remarked that, in consequence of its many divisions, ארם loses the nature of a proper name. The two words, Jehovah Zebaoth, can no more be immediately connected with each other than Jehovah (which is as perfect a proper name as ever existed) ever has, or ever can have, the article. Let us only consider the phrase אלהים צבאות in Ps. lxxx. 15, and elsewhere, where a *status constr.* is out of the question ; and, *further*, the fact that wherever, as in the case under review, Adonai precedes, the Mazorets have always given to יהוה the points of אלהים, but never of אֱלֹהָי; and let us, *finally*, consider the far more frequent, full expression, יהוה אלהי הצבאות (*e.g.*, iii. 13, iv. 13, v. 14), and we shall be convinced, that even where the simple יהוה הצבאות occurs, not indeed אלהי is simply to be supplied (if such were the case, why is it that הצבאות never occurs alone?), but that the notion of the Lord is to be taken from the preceding designations of the sovereignty of God. Compare on צבאות the remarks in my Commentary on Ps. xxiv. 10, where those also are refuted who, like *Maurer* (in his Comment. on Is. i. 9), maintain that it had simply become a name of God.—The manifestations of God's omnipotence are, after the general intimations of it are given, just such as might now be expected; compare viii. 8. The *Fut. with Vav Conv.* ותמוג does not here denote the *Past*, "And it melted," but only the consequence of the preceding action, as continuous as that: "Who toucheth the earth, and it melteth." A dissolution of the earth is to be thought of,—similar to that condition in which it was before the days of creation, and similar to its condition during the great flood. Such a condition of dissolution takes place also when the earth is visited by mighty kings desirous of making conquests. "Who toucheth the earth, and it melteth,"—the truth of these words Israel had *first* to learn by sad experience when the wild hosts of Asshur were poured out over the West of Asia. The passage in Ps. xlvi. 7 is parallel, where it is said: "The heathen rage, kingdoms are shaken; He uttereth His voice (which corresponds with, 'Who toucheth the earth,' in the verse before us), and the earth *melteth*." The מוג, "to melt," "to dissolve," signifies, in that passage, the dissolving effect of the divine judgments, the instruments of which are the conquerors. *Further*,—Ps. lxx. 4: "The earth and all the inhabitants thereof are melted,"—by the success of the conqueror of the world, the earth is, as it were, dissolved, and sunk back into the chaotic state of primitive time.—The words, "And it riseth up," are to be explained from the fact that the earth, changed into a great stream, cannot be distinguished from the water which covers it. The earth rises up, it is overflowed,—the earth sinks down, the water subsides. The last clause of the verse must not be translated —as is done by *Rosenmüller, Gesenius, Maurer*—"It is overflowed as by the stream of Egypt." This explanation is unphilological, and contrary, at the same time, to the parallelism, which requires that כיאר be, both the times, understood in the same way. The verb שקע means only "to sink," "to sink down," and is used of the subsiding water, Ezek. xxxii. 14; of the subsiding flame,

Num. xi. 2; and of a sinking town, Jer. li. 64. The last words thus rather contain the opposite of the clause immediately preceding. But the sinking does not, by any means, signify a freedom from the waters, nor is it to be conceived of as remaining. All which is expressed is the change only,— the ebb takes the place of the flood, and *vice versa*. This, however, is, on the dry land, a very sad condition. The inundation is here an emblem of hostile overflowing. Water is frequently an emblem of enemies; compare Ps. xviii. 17, cxliv. 7. Overflowing streams are emblematical of the crowds of nations, who, with a view to conquest, overflow the whole earth, Is. viii. 7, 8, xvii. 12; Jer. xlvii. 2, xlvi. 7, 8, where Egypt rises as the Nile, just as, in the case before us, the earth; with this difference, however, that there the rising is an active, while here it is a passive one: "Who is this who riseth like the Nile, whose waters are moved as the rivers? Egypt riseth up like the Nile, and his waters are moved like rivers, and he saith, I will go up and cover the earth, I will destroy the city and the inhabitants thereof;" Ezek. xxxii. 14: "Then will I make sink their waters, and cause their rivers to run like oil," equivalent to: The conquering power of Egypt shall cease. Amos viii. 8 is a parallel passage, in which, after the description of the prevailing sin, it is said: "Shall not the earth tremble for this, and every one mourn that dwelleth therein? And it riseth up wholly like the Nile, and is agitated, and sinketh down like the Nile of Egypt." The earthquake is the symbol of great revolutions, by which that which is highest is turned upside down; compare Haggai ii. 21, 22: "I shake the heavens and the earth, and overthrow the throne of kingdoms, and destroy the strength of the kingdom of the heathen;" while the overflowing is emblematical of hostile inundation, of visitation by war, in which the ebb succeeds the flood, and *vice versa*.—In his negligent mode of writing—which frequently occurs in this book—the prophet wrote נשקה instead of נשׁקעה, corresponding to the שׁקעה in the verse under consideration, just as in the same verse he wrote כאר instead of כיאר. The Mazorets, who everywhere disregarded the peculiarities of the individual writers, have introduced the common form.

Ver. 6. "*Who buildeth His upper chambers in the heaven, and His vault—over the earth He foundeth it: who calleth the waters of the sea, and poureth them out over the earth—Jehovah His name."*

That מַעֲלוֹת is here equivalent to עֲלִיּוֹת, " upper chambers " (compare 1 Chron. xvii. 17, where מַעֲלָה occurs with the signification " high place "), is put almost beyond any doubt by the parallel passage, Ps. civ. 3 : " Who frameth with the waters His upper chambers." The fundamental passage is Gen. i. 7 : " God made the vault, and divided between the waters which are under the vault, and the waters which are above the vault." " The waters, viz., the upper ones "—thus we have remarked in our commentary on that passage from the Psalms—" are the material out of which the structure is reared. To construct, out of the moveable waters, a firm palace, the cloudy sky, firm as a molten looking-glass (Job xxxvii. 18), is a magnificent work of divine omnipotence. The palace of clouds, as the upper part of the fabric of the universe, gets the name *upper chambers of God*; the lower part is the earth." As all the other manifestations of divine omnipotence in vers. 5, 6, are such as are to be called into existence now, the upper chambers and the vault will here come into consideration, in so far as from thence the torrents of rain are poured forth ; compare Ps. civ. 13, according to which the rain cometh from the upper chambers of God; and Gen. vii. 11 : " The same day broke forth all the fountains of the great flood (the last member of our verse), and *the windows of heaven were opened.*" From the upper chambers of God, whence once, at the time of the deluge, the natural rain came down, the rain of affliction will now descend.—הקורא—שמו already occurred, *verbatim*, in v. 8. הקורא stands in the same relation to וישפכם, as in ver. 5 נוגע does to ותמוג, and is equivalent to : " Upon whose mere word the waters of the sea cover the surface of the earth ;" compare Gen. vi. 17 : " And, behold, I do bring the flood of waters upon the earth." The sea is the common emblem of the heathen world ; compare remarks on Ps. xciii., civ. 6-9. In chap. vii. 4, the " great flood " is contrasted with the " lot " in Deut. xxxiii. 9,—the heathen world, with the people of God. The fire of war, which the Lord kindles, devours both in the same way. Here, in contrast with the deluge, the conquering inundation of the earth proceeds from the midst of the heathen world, stirred up by the Lord, and destroys first of all unfaithful Israel, who, had they been faithful to the Covenant, would have been able to say, as in Ps. xlvi. 2-4, " God is our refuge and strength, a help in trouble He is found very much. Therefore will we not fear when the earth is overturned, and the mountains shake in the midst of the sea; its waters roar and foam, mountains tremble by its swelling."

Ver. 7. *"Are you not as the sons of the Cushites unto Me, O children of Israel? saith the Lord. Have not I brought up Israel out of the land of Egypt, and the Philistines from Caphtor, and Aram from Kir?"*

The prophet here deprives the people of another prop of false security. They boasted of their election, by which God Himself, as they imagined, had bound His hands. They considered the pledge of it—the deliverance from Egypt—as a charter of security against every calamity, as an obligation to further help in every distress, which God could not retract even if He would. A great truth lay at the foundation of this error, —a truth which has been disregarded by the greater number of interpreters, who have, in consequence, forced upon the prophet a sense which is altogether false.[1] The election of the people, and their deliverance from Egypt, were actually what they considered them to be. God Himself had in reality thereby bound His hands; He *was obliged* to deliver the people. He *could* not cast them off. The election was an act of free grace; the manifestation of it in deeds was an act of His righteousness. The people had a right to remind Him of His duty, when He seemed not to perform it. Their election was then a firm anchorage of hope, a rich source of consolation, the foundation of all their prayers. But the error consisted in this, that the election was usurped by those to whom it did not belong,—an error which is continually repeating itself, and which shows itself in a fearful form, especially in the case of those who believe in the doctrine of Predestination. We need, for example, refer only to *Cromwell,* who, in the hour of death, silenced, by this false consolation, all the accusations of his

---

[1] *Hitzig* says : With a disposition of mind different from that in iii. 2, the prophet says here, " You enjoy no privileges with me, you are to me like all others." A strange disposition of mind indeed for a prophet ! An interpretation which results in such thoughts, which cannot be entertained for a moment, is self-condemned.

conscience. Περιτομὴ μὲν γὰρ ὠφελεῖ, says the Apostle, in Rom. ii. 25, ἐὰν νόμον πράσσῃς· ἐὰν δὲ παραβάτης νόμου ᾖς, ἡ περιτομή σου ἀκροβυστία γέγονεν. The deliverance from Egypt stands on the same footing as circumcision. The former also was profitable; to those who showed themselves to be children of Israel, it afforded the certainty that God would prove Himself to be their God. For those, however, who had become degenerate, it entered altogether into the circle of ordinary events. For them, it became something that had altogether passed away—that did not carry within itself any pledge of renovation. This error is here laid open by the prophet, as he had already done in v. 14: "Seek good and not evil, that ye may live, and *thus* the Lord, the God of hosts, be with you." He directs their attention to the fact, that, in the Covenant-relation, which rests on reciprocity, the party who broke the Covenant had nothing to ask, nothing to hope for. "*Be not,*" etc.; the *tertium comparationis* is evidently the alienation from God. The "children of Israel" (the appellation expressive of their dignity is intentionally chosen in order to make more striking the contradiction between the appearance and the reality) have become so degenerate, that they are no more any nearer to God than the sons of the Cushites. Those interpreters who regard sin alone as the *tertium comparationis* (*Cocceius* says: "Ye are so alienated from Him, and so unfaithful, that every one of you may be called a Cushite"), give too limited a sense to the expression. "You are to Me," is rather equivalent to, "I have not any more concern in you, you stand not to Me in any other relation." But why are the Cushites alone mentioned as an example of a people alienated from God? Their colour, perhaps, is more to be considered in this, than their descent from Ham; the physical blackness is viewed as an emblem of the spiritual. Thus they appear in Jer. xiii. 23: "Will indeed the Cushite change his skin, and the leopard his spots? will you indeed be able to do good, who have been taught to do evil?" But the fundamental passage is the inscription of Ps. vii., where Saul, on account of his black wickedness, appears under the symbolical name of Cush.—The right explanation of these first words furnishes, at the same time, the key to the sound interpretation of the words which

2 B

follow: It is only for the Covenant-people that the deliverance from Egypt is a pledge of grace. But you are no longer the Covenant-people; your being brought up out of Egypt, there-fore, stands on the same line with the bringing up of the Philistines from their former dwelling-places in Caphtor to their present abodes, and with the bringing up of the Syrians from Kir, in which no one will see a pledge of divine grace, a pre-servative against every danger, and, especially, an assurance of the impossibility of a new captivity. The geographical in-quiries regarding Caphtor and Kir would lead us too far away from the subject which we are here discussing. The view which is now prevalent, and according to which Crete is to be understood by the former, is in contradiction to the old transla-tions, which have Cappadocia, and with Gen. x. 14,—as long as, in that passage, the Colchians are to be understood by the Casluhim. But that point would require a minute investigation, which may be more suitably carried on at some other place.

Ver. 8. "*Behold, the eyes of the Lord Jehovah are upon the sinful kingdom, and I destroy them from off the face of the earth, saving that I will not utterly destroy the house of Jacob, saith the Lord.*"

The sinful kingdom, whether its name be Israel or Judah, or whether it be called Egypt or Edom. The holy God has not by any means, as you in your blindness imagine, given you a privilege to sin. A difference exists between Israel and the others in this respect only, that utter ruin does not take place in the case of the former, as it does in that of the latter. For the distinction between the people of God and other nations consists in this, that in the former, there always remains a holy seed, an ἐκλογή, which the Lord must protect, and make the nursery of His kingdom, according to the same necessity of His nature as that by which He extirpates the sinners of His people. The "sinful kingdom" forms the contrast with the righteous kingdom; the article being here used in a generic sense. Similar are Is. x. 6: "*I send him against impious people, and against the people of My wrath* (wheresoever there are such) *I give him command;*" and Ps. xxxiii. 12: "Blessed is the nation whose God is the Lord, the people whom He hath chosen for His inheritance;" on which latter passage *Michaelis* remarks, "Blessed is the nation, whichsoever it may be." The eyes of the Lord are open upon *the* sinful kingdom, and hence also upon the house of Jacob; it must be destroyed as all others are, but it cannot be *destroyed like them*,—an idea which is prominently brought out by the prefixed Infinit. השמיד. That is an erroneous interpretation which understands by the sinful nation, Ephraim, and, after the example of *Grotius* ("I will destroy the kingdom, not the people"), assumes that, by the house, in contrast with the kingdom, the people are intended. Such a contrast betwixt the house and the kingdom would have required a more distinct intimation. The house of Jacob, when referred to the ten tribes, is identical with the kingdom. They were a house only in so far as they were a kingdom. But it is both against the words (in Obad. ver. 17, "house of Jacob" is likewise used of the whole of the nation), and against the connection, to refer it to the ten tribes. When, however, it is referred to the whole, a contrast betwixt people and kingdom can the less have place, as, according to ver. 11, the kingdom also shall be restored.—The first part of the verse is almost literally identical with Deut. vi. 15: "For a jealous God is Jehovah, thy God, in thy midst; lest the anger of Jehovah thy God be kindled against thee, and He destroy thee from off the face of the earth," והשמידך מעל פני האדמה. The prophet says nothing new; he only resumes the threatening of the revered lawgiver.—The construction of עיני יהוה with ב is explained by the circumstance that, according to the context, the eyes of the Lord can mean only His angry eyes—equivalent to the anger of the Lord in the passage quoted from Deuteronomy; and the verbs and nouns expressive of anger are connected by ב with the object on which the anger rests; compare Ps. xxxiv. 17.

Ver. 9. "*For behold I command and shake the house of Israel among all the nations, as one shaketh in a sieve, and not shall anything firm fall to the ground.*"

The figure in this verse is, upon the whole, plain; but some of the particulars require to be explained, and to be more accurately determined. The signification "sieve," commonly assigned to כברה, must be conceded to it. We must, however, here understand it of such a sieve as serves similar purposes as a winnowing shovel, in which the corn is violently shaken, and thus purified; and not of a sieve in which, by mere sifting, the corn is freed from the dust which has remained after the first and proper cleansing. The latter is assumed by *Paulsen* (*vom Ackerbau der Morgenländer*, S. 144), and, along with him, by the greater number of interpreters. Such a sieve—a kind of fan—is mentioned in Is. xxx. 24, in addition to the winnowing shovel. It occurs likewise in Luke xxii. 31, where συνιάζειν is *vanno agitare*. The LXX. also have here adopted the explanation, not of an ordinary sieve, but of an instrument which serves the same purposes as the winnowing shovel: διότι ἰδοὺ ἐγὼ ἐντέλλομαι καὶ λικμιῶ (Α. λικμήσω) ἐν πᾶσι τοῖς ἔθνεσι τὸν οἶκον τοῦ Ἰσραὴλ, ὃν τρόπον λίκμαται ἐν τῷ λικμῷ. *Hesych.* λικμῷ, πτύῳ. To this we are likewise led by the verb הניעותי, which is indicative of a violent procedure, and by the occurrence of the same figure in so many passages of Scripture; compare, *e.g.*, Jer. li. 2; "I will send against Babylon fanners that shall fan her, and shall empty her land;" Jer. xv. 7, and Matt. iii. 12; while the use of the ordinary sieve for such a purpose is never mentioned, nor is it ever employed for a figure.— בכל־הגוים is not to be translated, "*by* all nations," but, as the corresponding בכברה shows, "in," or "among all nations." The many people are the spiritual sieve,—the means of purging. The Lord, whose instruments they are, employs them for the destruction of the ungodly. They are taken away by His secret judgments, for the execution of which He employs the heathen; compare ver. 10. Even the godly are violently shaken; but the hand of the Lord secretly upholds them that they may not sink, but that the temptation may serve for their spiritual growth; compare Luke xxii. 31, 32, where the Lord distinctly alludes to the passage under consideration. The corn is shaken; dust and impurity fall to the ground, the chaff flies into the air. Many interpreters ascribe to צרור the signification, "corn;" others, "little stone." But these significations have been both assumed merely for the sake of the context. צרור, from צרר, *colligavit, constrinxit*, means, primarily, "that which is tightly bound together;" then, "bundle," "bag;" but here, as in 2 Sam. xvii. 13, "that which is compact, firm, and solid," as opposed to that which is loose, dissolved, and thin. That which is here meant is the solid, firm corn, as opposed to the loose chaff, and the dust which falls to the ground through the sieve.

Ver. 10. "*By the sword, shall die all the sinners of My people who say, The evil will not come near, nor advance to us.*"

In order that the preceding mitigation of the threatening of punishment might not be appropriated by those to whom it did not belong, the prophet, before passing on to the further detail of the promise, once more presents the threatening in all its severity. "The sinners who speak," etc., are they who usurped the promises of the Covenant without having truly fulfilled its conditions,—who boasted of, and trusted in, their belonging outwardly to the people of God (compare iii. 2), and their zeal in the external performance of the duties of worship (compare v. 21–23); and who therefore imagined that the judgments of the Lord could not reach them, while, by their sins, they did all in their power to draw them down upon them, v. 18, vi. 3.

Ver. 11. "*In that day I will raise up the tabernacle of David that is fallen, and wall up its breaches, and raise up its ruins, and build it as the days of eternity.*"

The words, "In that day," are to be understood quite generally, viz., as referring to a time after the divine judgments have broken in and have completed their work upon Israel. The μετὰ ταῦτα, by which James renders it in Acts xv. 16, completely expresses the sense. The assertion of *Baur*, "That the prophet must have conceived of the restoration of the tabernacle of David as being near at hand, because he recognised the instruments of judgment in the invading Assyrians," falls to the ground along with the supposition on which it rests. The prophet has nothing at all special to do with the invasion of the Assyrians.—The Partic. נפלת, according to the usual signification of the Partic., expresses a permanent condition. The very expression, "tabernacle," suggests the idea of a sunken condition of the house of David. The prophet sees the proud palace of David changed into a humble tabernacle, everywhere in ruins, and perforated. The same idea is expressed by a different image in Is. xi. 1. There the house of David is called the cut off trunk of Jesse, which puts forth a new shoot. *Hofmann* and others are of opinion that the prophet designates the house of David as a fallen tabernacle, on account of its abasement at the time then present. "At present," he says, "the lofty house of David is a סכה נפלת when compared with the power of Jeroboam; but the latter shall fall, and the former shall raise itself again from its decay." But this designation is certainly not applicable to the house of David under a king like Uzziah, nor, in general, to the whole time of the existing Davidic kingdom. The fact that Amos foresees the deep fall of Judah, is placed beyond all doubt even by ii. 5. It is impossible that the announcement of the restoration which is to *follow* only after this fall, should altogether ignore the latter. This is, moreover, proved by the parallel passages. The predictions of all the prophets are pervaded by the foresight of the Messiah's appearing at the time of the deepest debasement of the Davidic dynasty, and after the total loss of the royal dignity; compare the remarks on Mic. iv. 8, vi. (2); Is. xi. 1, liii. 2; Ezek. xvii. 22-24.—It might now appear as though the prophet here only supposed the ruin of the house of David, without having, in the preceding context, expressly mentioned it; but such is not the case. The whole of the preceding threatening of punishment relates to the ruin of the house of David; for when the kingdom suffers, the reigning family cannot but suffer also. This close connection of the two is pointed out by the prophet himself in the subsequent words. The change of the suffixes is there certainly not without a reason. The suffix in פרציהן refers to the two kingdoms; that in הריסתיו to David; and that in בניתיה to the tabernacle, while the subject of יירשו (ver. 12) is the people. By this it is intimated that David, his tabernacle, the kingdoms, and the people, are in substance one—that one stands and falls with the other. They who overlook the co-reference to Judah, in the preceding verses, do not know what to make of the suffix in פרציהן (compare the expression "these kingdoms," used of Judah and Israel in vi. 2), and, in their uncertainty, conjecture sometimes one thing and sometimes another.—ימי is Nominat., not Accusat. The comparison is merely intimated; compare remarks on Hos. ii. 17. The circumstance that the happy days of the times of David and Solomon are here spoken of as "days of eternity"—of the remotest past (compare Mic. vii. 14)—implies that the prophet sees a long interval between the present and the predicted event.—The foundation of this prophecy is the promise to David in 2 Sam. vii.; compare especially ver. 16: "And thine house and thy kingdom shall be sure in eternity before thee, and thy throne shall be firm in eternity." This reference has also been pointed out by *Calvin*, who remarks: "When the prophet says, 'as in the days of old,' he confirms the doctrine that the dignity of the house would not always flow in an equal current, but that, nevertheless, there would always be such a restoration as would make it easily perceptible that God's promise of an eternal dominion to David had not been in vain." The dominion of David had already suffered a considerable shock by the separation of the two kingdoms, existing at the prophet's time; but it was in future to sink even far more deeply, and the people along with it. But, with all these things, God's promise remains true. The judgments do not shut up the way for His mercy, but rather prepare it. That it was only through the family of David that the promised salvation could be imparted to the people, the prophet plainly declares. If it were not so, how could he have identified the tabernacle of David with the two kingdoms, and with the people? As to the person of the restorer, he does not more particularly designate it. The main thing with him, as with Hosea (compare the remarks on Hos. ii. 2, and iii. 5), is to impress upon the people of Israel the conviction, that salvation could come to them only from a reunion with Judah— from their joining again the house of David; compare Ezek. xxxvii. 22: "And I make them one nation in the land upon the mountains of Israel, and one king shall be king to them all; and they shall be no more two nations, and they shall be no more divided into two kingdoms." But if this was sure and established, there could then be no more any doubt as to the person. It was at that time generally known that the promise given to David would be finally fulfilled in the Messiah; and it was generally acknowledged by the ancient Jews, that the passages under consideration refer to the Messiah. *Jerome* remarks: "The Jews refer everything which, in this and the other prophets, is foretold concerning the building up of Jerusalem and the temple, and the happy condition of all things, to themselves, and foolishly expect that all shall be fulfilled in a carnal sense." It is from the passage under review that the Messiah received the name בר נפלים, *filius cadentium*—He who springs forth from the fallen family of David; compare *Sanhedrin*, fol. 96, 2: R. Nachman said to R. Isaac, Hast thou heard when בר נפילים is to come? The latter answered: Who is he? R. Nachman said: The Messiah. R. Isaac: But is the Messiah thus named? R. Nachman: Certainly, in Amos ix. 11:

"In that day I will raise up the tabernacle of David that is fallen." In *Breshith Rabbah*, sec. 88, we read: "Who would have expected that God should raise up again the fallen tabernacle of David? And yet we read in Amos ix. 11, 'In that day,' etc. And who could have hoped that the whole world could yet become one flock? And yet, such is declared in Zeph. iii. 9: 'Then will I turn to the people in pure lips, that they all may call upon the name of the Lord, and serve Him with one lip.' But all that is prophesied only in reference to the Messiah." See *Schöttgen*, p. 70, and other passages, especially from the *Sohar*, ibid. p. 111, 566.

Ver. 12. "*In order that they may possess the remnant of Edom, and of all the heathen upon whom My name is called, saith the Lord that doeth this.*"

Calvin remarks on this verse: "This main point is plainly declared to us, that there is here promised an extension of the kingdom under Christ; and it is just as if the prophet had said that the Jews were enclosed within narrow limits, even when the kingdom of David did most flourish, inasmuch as, under Christ, God is to extend their territory, so that they shall rule far and wide." There is here an evident allusion to the times of David, which, in the last words of the preceding verse, formed the subject of discourse. This is quite plain also from the mention of the Edomites. These had been made subject by David; but afterwards, availing themselves of the commencing fall of David's tabernacle, they had again freed themselves. Not only they, however, but all the other heathen nations, shall be again subjected to the raised up tabernacle of David. That former event served as a type and prelude to the latter, and formed moreover a prophecy of it in deeds, inasmuch as both rested on the same foundation, viz., God's protection of His Church, and His care for His kingdom. It is for this reason too, that, with an allusion to the former event, the verb יירשׁו is chosen. By this verb, expression is given only to the fact of their agreement, and to points in which those events agree; but it gives no indication of *how far* they agree, or in what respects they differ; this is to be declared in the subsequent words. The prophet, however, in speaking only of the *remnant* of Edom, looks back to the threatening in chap. i. They only who have been preserved in the judgment which is there announced, are to come under the blissful dominion of the kingdom of David. As Israel, so also the Gentiles, must be prepared for the coming of the kingdom of Christ by crushing judgments. The judgment upon Israel is only a single portion of a great judgment upon all nations. Into this connection it is brought by the very opening chapters of this book. In chap. v. 8, vii. 7, there is likewise an intimation of great calamities and shakings, which are to come upon the heathen world. The submission of the remnant of the heathen world, however, will not be an abasement, but, on the contrary, an exalting of them ; this is shown by the words, " Upon whom My name is called." These words do not allow us to think of such a relation of Edom and the other nations to Israel, as existed at the time of David in the case of the conquered nations. They are never used to designate a form of allegiance to the Lord so low and false, but always denote the relation of close and cordial allegiance. The heathen are in future to be considered and treated as those who are consecrated to the Lord, and who belong to His holy people, —just as Israel is now considered and treated. Compare, as to the use of these words with reference to Israel, Deut. xxviii. 9, 10 : " The Lord shall raise thee *an Holy people unto Him*, as He hath sworn unto thee . . . . and all people of the earth see that the name of the Lord is called upon thee, and are afraid of thee." In this verse, the expression, " The name of the Lord is called upon thee," corresponds with " holy people." Jer. xiv. 9 : " And Thou, O Lord, art in the midst of us, and Thy name is called upon us." Is. lxiii. 19 : " We are those over whom Thou hast not reigned from eternity, and upon whom Thy name has not been called." As regards the use of these words in reference to the temple, compare, further, Jer. vii. 10, 11 : " And ye come and stand before Me in this house, upon which My name is called. Is, perhaps, this house upon which My name is called, a den of robbers in your eyes ?" The exceeding greatness of their wickedness is denounced in these words ; and the ground why it is so great, is not by any means the fact, that the temple, as was indeed the case with that at Bethel, bore the name of the house of God only by the caprice of the people, but that it really was the house of God, and that God, in His gracious condescension, was there *really* present, as a type of His dwelling in Christ ; compare Deut. xii. 5 : " The place which the Lord your God shall choose out of all your tribes, to put His name there." *Finally,* These words are used in reference to single individuals, whom God, in a special sense, has made His own, His representatives, the bearers of His word, the mediators of His revelations, in Jer. xv. 16 : " I found Thy words and I did eat them, and Thy words became unto me the joy and rejoicing of my heart ; for Thy name was called upon me, Jehovah, God of hosts," etc., equivalent to, " For I was the messenger and representative of Thee, the Almighty God." —*Hitzig, Hofmann,* and *Baur* explain the expression, " Upon whom My name is called," by, " Upon all the nations who once, at the time of David, were in subjection to the people of God." The use of the Preterite has been urged in favour of this explanation ; but it is certainly very rash to assert, on the ground of this, that " this view alone is admissible according to the rules of grammar." The statement of *Ewald,* § 135 a, is exactly applicable to this case : " The *Perfectum,* when used with reference to some future event, either mentioned or conceived of, may as well indicate the past which *then* has taken place." The sense might thus be : " All the heathen upon whom then My name will be called." In the same sense, the Preterite is used in another passage, quoted by *Hofmann* for a different purpose—viz., 2 Sam. xii. 28 : " In order that I may not take (אלכד) the city, and my name be called (נקרא) upon it." It militates, however, against their view, that the name of the Lord being called upon any one, has, according to all the parallel passages, a sense too profound to admit of a relation to the Lord so loose and external being thereby designated. It is used only of such as are received into the condition of the people and sons of Jehovah, Hos. ii. 1 (i. 10). *Further,* The mere restoration of the Davidic dominion over the heathen is a very meagre thought, which is far from coming up to what Jacob had foretold in Gen. xlix. 10, and to what David and Solomon expected of the future ; compare, *e.g.,* Ps. lxxii. 11 : " And all kings worship Him, all the heathen serve Him."—The closing words, " Thus saith the Lord that doeth this," are intended to strengthen faith in a promise which appears to be incredible, by calling attention to the fact, that the person who promises is also the person who carries it out to its fulfilment ; compare Jer. xxxiii. 2 : " Thus saith the Lord that makes it, the Lord that forms it.

to carry it out, the Lord is His name." This closing formula is also very ill suited for so meagre a prediction as that of the restoration of the old borders, of which Israel, under the reign of Uzziah and Jeroboam, was not so very far short. It was, probably, solely from a false interpretation of the passage under review, that an important historical event had its rise. Hyrcanus compelled the Idumeans, who were conquered by him, to be circumcised, and in that way to be incorporated into the Theocracy; so that they lost entirely their national existence and name (*Jos. Arch.* xiii. 9, 1 ; *Prideaux Hist. des Juifs*, vol. v. p. 16). This proceeding differed so materially from that which was ordinarily followed—for David did not think it at all necessary to adopt a similar proceeding against the Idumeans, and the other nations which were conquered by him—that it necessarily requires some special reason to account for it; and such a reason is furnished by the passage under consideration. Hyrcanus wished to be instrumental in the fulfilment of the prophecy contained in it; but in this he failed. He did not consider, 1. That the reception of Edom into the kingdom of God is here brought into connection with the restoration of the tabernacle of David, and hence could be brought about only by a king of the house of David. He did not consider, 2. That the matter here in question is not such a reception into the kingdom of God as depends upon the will of man, but a spiritual reception, which carries along with it the full enjoyment of divine blessings. That it was, however, easy for Hyrcanus to fall into such a mistake, is shown by the example of *Grotius*, who confined himself to this merely apparent fulfilment, although he had the real fulfilment before his eyes. By a similar misunderstanding of Old Testament prophecies, other important events also were brought about; *e.g.*, according to the express testimony of Josephus, the building of the Egyptian temple, and, as we shall afterwards see, the building of the temple by Herod.

It now only remains to consider the quotation of this passage in the New Testament, in Acts xv. 16, 17. *Olshausen* has directed attention to a difficulty regarding it, which has been overlooked by the greater number of interpreters. He says that one cannot well see how the quotation bears upon the point at issue. Both parties were at one as to the duty of admitting the Gentiles into the kingdom of God. The only question was about the manner of their reception—whether with, or without, circumcision—and as to this, the prophecy, which confines itself to the fact only, does not contain any express declaration. But this difficulty has its sole foundation on the erroneous view that James was stating two reasons altogether independent of each other;—the first in ver. 14, God's declaration by facts, in His having given His Holy Spirit to the Gentiles, without their having been circumcised; and then, in vers. 16, 17, the testimony of the Old Testament. But the sound view rather is, that both together form only one reason. Apart from that testimony which God, the Searcher of hearts, had given to the Gentiles by the gift of the Holy Spirit, and by making no difference betwixt them and Israel, the prophetic declaration would have been without any significance; but it acquires this significance when combined with the testimony of God. It is now also that the silence of James, in reference to that condition which was demanded by those of a pharisaic tendency, gains significance. Simeon has declared how God at first was pleased to take a people for His name out of the Gentiles; and after the *fact* of their reception has been so expressively declared, the Old Testament passage, where this reception is spoken of, is not cognizant of any other *mode*. The Apostle does not content himself with quoting ver. 12; he first cites ver. 11, because it furnished the proof that the declaration contained in ver. 12 referred to that time. That event, with which the conversion of the Gentiles is here immediately connected, had already taken place in Christ, at least as to the germ, which contained within itself the whole substance which afterwards displayed itself. But it was the main thought only which came into consideration in ver. 11, and therefore it is somewhat abbreviated. In the quotation, the translation of the LXX. evidently forms the foundation.

The quotation of ver. 12 agrees, almost *verbatim*, with the LXX. It follows them in their important deviation from the Hebrew text. Instead of, "In order that they may occupy the remnant of Edom," the LXX. read, ὅπως ἂν ἐκζητήσωσιν οἱ κατάλοιποι τῶν ἀνθρώπων με (instead of με Luke has τὸν κύριον, which is found in the *Cod. Alex.* also, but has very likely come in from Luke). It is of very little consequence to determine in what manner the translation of the LXX. arose; whether they had a different reading, למען ידרשו שארית אדם,

before them ; or whether they merely read erroneously ; or whether, according to *Lightfoot* (in his remarks on Acts xv. 16, 17), they intentionally thus altered the words ; or whether it was their object to express the sense only generally and approximately (in the last two cases we should be obliged to suppose that, by a kind of play, and in order to represent, in an outward manner, the substantial agreement of the thought, they chose words exactly corresponding to the Hebrew text, with the exception of a change of a few letters,—a thing which frequently occurs in the Talmud, and even in Jeremiah when compared with the older prophets) ; only, we must set aside the idea of a really different reading,—a reading resting on the authority of good Manuscripts, inasmuch as such an idea would be irreconcilable with the deviations of the LXX. elsewhere, and with the unanimity of the Hebrew Manuscripts in the passage before us. The assertion of *Olshausen*, however, that, in the Hebrew form, the passage would not have been suitable for the purpose, and that therefore it is probable that, on this occasion, Greek must have been spoken in the assembly, does indeed deserve our attention.

Whether or not the latter was the case, we leave undecided. That it was probable, may be proved from other grounds, but it by no means follows from the reason stated by *Olshausen*. The passage was suited for the proof, as well according to the Hebrew text, as according to the Alexandrian version ; for the latter is quite correct and faithful in so far as the sense is concerned. The *occupying*, in the sense in which it is used by Amos, has the *seeking* for its necessary supposition. For how, indeed, can spiritual possession, spiritual dominion by the people of the Lord exist, unless the Lord has been sought by those who are to be ruled over ? Compare the declaration : " The isles shall wait for His law," Is. xlii. 4. The words, " And of all the heathen," following immediately after Edom, evidently prove that Amos mentions Edom, only by way of individualizing ; and the Idumeans, especially, as a people, only because their former, specially violent hatred to the Covenant-people (compare i. 11) made their future humble submission more evidently a work of the omnipotence of God, and of His love watching over His people ; and at the same time there may be a reference also to the former subjection by David. The LXX.

have done nothing more, than at once to substitute for the particular, the general which comprehends this particular,—a particular which is, by Amos too, designated as a part of the general.[1]

Ver. 13. "*Behold, days come, saith the Lord, and the ploughman reacheth to the reaper, and the treader of the wine-press to him that soweth seed. And the mountains drop must, and all the hills melt.*"

The fundamental thought in this passage is this :—Wheresoever the Lord is, there also is the fulness of His gifts.—The imagery in the first hemistich is taken from Lev. xxvi. 3–5 : "If ye shall walk in My laws, and keep My commandments and do them ; then I will give your rains in their seasons, and the land gives its produce, and the tree of the field gives its fruit. And your threshing *reaches* to the vintage, and the vintage *reaches to the sowing* time." After the Lord has purified His congregation by His judgments, then the joyful time of blessing, prophesied by His servant Moses, shall likewise come. *Cocceius* says : "One shall reap, the other shall immediately plough ; one shall scatter the seeds in the ploughed field, while another shall, at the same time, tread the grapes,—a work is wont to be done at the last time of the year. There shall be continual work, and continual fruit, and a fruitfulness such as that in the land of the Troglodytes which *Scaliger* (*Exercit.* 249, 2) thus describes : 'Throughout the whole year there is sowing and reaping at the same time; at one place the seed is committed to the fields, and at another the wheat shoots up, at another it gets ears, at another it is reaped, at another it is collected, and

---

[1] Whether, however, it was James or Luke who quoted these words according to the version of the LXX., this passage is one of the many hundreds which prove that the violent urging and pressing for an improvement in our (German) authorized version of the Scriptures, as it proceeded from *von Meier* and *Stier*, is exaggerated. The Saviour and His Apostles adopted, without hesitation, the version current at their time, when its deviations concerned not the thought but the words. If we proceed upon this principle, how will the mountain of complaints melt away which has been raised against *Luther's* translation of the Scriptures. But it is true that, even then, weighty objections remain. The revision of it is a want of the Church ; but it is not so urgent that we may not, and must not, wait for the time when it may be satisfied without danger. If it were undertaken at present, the disadvantages would far outweigh the advantages. To everything there is a season ; and it is the duty of the wise steward to find it out, and to know it.

brought to the threshing-places, and thence to the barn.' "—
The second hemistich agrees with Joel. iv. (iii.) 18 (which is
certainly not accidental; compare the introduction to Joel):
" At that time the mountains shall drop must, and the hills go
with milk." From a comparison of this passage it appears that
the melting of the hills can mean only their dissolving into
rivers of milk, must, and honey, with an allusion to the description of the promised land in the Pentateuch (Exod. iii. 8) as a
land flowing with milk and honey.

Ver. 14. "*And I turn Myself to the captivity of My people
Israel, and they build waste cities, and dwell, and plant vineyards,
and drink their wine; and they make gardens and eat their fruit.*"

The captivity is a figure of misery. With reference to שוב
שבות compare the remarks on Joel.

Ver. 15. "*And I plant them in their land, and they shall
no more be plucked up out of their land which I have given them,
saith the Lord thy God.*" Compare p. 227 seqq.

THE PROPHECY OF OBADIAH.

We need not enter into details regarding the question as to
the time when the prophet wrote. By a thorough argumentation, *Caspari* has proved, that he occupies his right position in
the Canon, and hence belongs to the earliest age of written
prophecy, *i.e.*, to the time of Jeroboam II. and Uzziah. As
bearing conclusively against those who would assign to him a
far later date, viz., the time of the exile, there is not only the
indirect testimony borne by the place which this prophecy occupies in the collection of the prophets which is chronologically
arranged, but there are also the following facts;—that those
who are to inflict the predicted calamity upon Judah are not
at all more definitely characterized than in the first part of
Hosea, in Joel, and Amos;—that, in like manner, the heathen
power from which the overthrow of Edom is to proceed, is
neither mentioned, nor more definitely pointed out in any other
way;—that Jeremiah already made use of Obadiah's prophecy;
and if such be denied, the older foundation would then be withdrawn from the prophecy of Jeremiah—which would be con-

trary to the analogy of Jeremiah's prophecies against foreign nations;—and, finally, that, in vers. 12–14, the prophet exhorts the Edomites neither to rejoice nor to co-operate in the destruction of Jerusalem, because, otherwise, they would certainly receive the well-merited reward of such wickedness committed against the Covenant-people, to whom they were so nearly related. Such an exhortation would have been out of place, after the wickedness had been committed.—The view of *Hofmann* (which was revived by *Delitzsch* in his treatise, "When did Obadiah prophesy?" [*Guerike's Zeitschrift* 51, *Hft.* 1])—according to which the capture of Jerusalem by the Philistines and Arabians under Jehoram (2 Chron. xxi. 16 ff.) was the occasion of the prophecy before us, and according to which Obadiah is thus made the oldest among all the prophets in the Canon, and separated by nearly a century from the three prophets who preceded him—overlooks the fact that only cogent reasons could induce us to assume so isolated a position, since it is certainly not a matter of accident that the written prophecy began its course under the reign of Jeroboam and Uzziah. The guilt and punishment of Edom are, in like manner, spoken of in the Preterite; and it is inadmissible to understand the Preterites as historical, in so far as they refer to the guilt, and as prophetical, in so far as they refer to the punishment. The words, "Day of their destruction," in ver. 12, are decisive against every other catastrophe upon Judah, but that of the Chaldean. Ver. 20, when rightly interpreted, supposes the carrying away of Israel and Judah, and hence allows us to think only of the Assyro-Chaldean catastrophe. In ver. 21, Mount Zion is forsaken, and "the saviours" return to it from the land of captivity.

In strict accordance with the position of the book in the Canon, is the fact, that Obadiah connects himself most closely with Joel, and, excepting him, among all the prophets, with Amos only; compare *Caspari*, S. 20 ff., 35; *Hävernick, Einleitung* II. S. 318. Of greater importance than the coincidences in particulars, is the fact that the prophecy of Obadiah, upon the whole, connects itself most closely and immediately with the fourth (third) chapter of Joel—that in the prophecy of Obadiah, we have indeed a *variation* on that chapter. The judgment upon Judah, which Joel announces in the first part, is here supposed to have already taken place; and this might be done so much the rather, because, even in Joel, the prophetic *Plerophory*, with which rationalistic interpreters are so much puzzled, has changed the Future into the Present and Past—as, even there, the destruction of Jerusalem, and the overflowing of the whole country by the heathen, are represented as already existing. It is only the judgment upon the heathen, and the restoration of Israel, which Obadiah represents in his prophetic picture.

Like Hosea (in the first three chapters), Joel, and Amos, so Obadiah also, received the mission to point out the catastrophe threatened by the world's power, even before the latter existed on the scene of history. It was to the Covenant-people a source of rich consolation that it was so clearly and distinctly foretold to them, even before it had an existence, and the points of view from which it must be regarded were opened up to them. He, however, distinctly points to one idea only, just because there were already predecessors to whose prophecies he could refer. He did not receive the mission to call to repentance, or to represent the judgment as a well-deserved punishment—although, *indirectly*, in him as well as in Joel, these thoughts also occur, as certainly as the supposed destruction of Judah and Israel could only be the punishment of their sin; he has to point out only the salvation subsequent to the overflowing by the heathen world, the conquering power of the kingdom of God which, in the end, will manifest itself, and deeply to impress upon the Covenant-people the words: θαρσεῖτε, ἐγὼ νενίκηκα τὸν κόσμον. The glaring contrast betwixt the *idea*—according to which the kingdom of God was to be all prevailing—and the *reality*, in which it is pressed into a corner, shall in future increase still more. Even from this corner, the people of God shall be driven. But death is the transition to life; the uttermost degree of sufferings, the forerunner of deliverance and salvation. Not a restoration only is in store for the people of God—they even obtain the dominion of the world; but to the heathen world, which is at enmity with God, their exaltation is a forerunner of destruction.

All which Obadiah had to say in reference to the heathen, God-hating world, and to the form which, in future, Israel's

2 C

relation to it would assume, has been exemplified by him in the case of Edom. For the fact, that it is only the heathen power individualized which we have before us, is shown by the transition to the heathen in general in ver. 15, according to which, Edom comes into consideration only as a part of the whole: "For near is the day of the Lord upon *all the heathen*." So also is it in ver. 16: "For as ye[1] have drunk upon My holy mountain, so shall *all the heathen* drink continually;[2] and they drink, and sup up, and they are as though they were not." When speaking of the guilt, he mentions Edom only; when speaking of punishment, he introduces all the heathen at once. According to ver. 17, Israel shall occupy the possessions of *all the heathen*. And even the last words of the whole prophecy, "And the kingdom shall be the Lord's," show that it bears a universal character,—that in the case of Edom, we have only a principle exemplified which applies to all the enemies of the kingdom of God. The leading thought is: The kingdom of God shall obtain universal dominion, which follows the deepest abasement of the people of God, and of which the fullest and most perfect realization must be sought in Christ.

The animating thought could be so much the better individualized in the case of Edom, as its natural relation to Israel was one of special nearness, and its hatred specially deep; and as, moreover, it at all times considered itself the rival of Israel, of whose advantages it was envious. That which Amos, the cotemporary of Obadiah, says of Edom in chap. i. 11—"He pursues his brother with the sword, and corrupts his compassions, and his anger tears perpetually, and he keeps his wrath for ever"— shows how exceedingly well he was fitted to be a representative of the enemies of the kingdom of God. It was so much the more obvious thus to represent Edom as a particular and individualizing exemplification of this principle, as the prophets of that period had not as yet received any more definite disclosures as to the threatening kingdoms of the future, while Edom, in his

---

[1] The fact that, *everywhere*, the discourse is addressed to the Edomites, proves that here also Edom is addressed. The כִּי and the כַּאֲשֶׁר in this verse, compared with those in the preceding verse, likewise suggest this. Compare, moreover, Joel iv. (iii.) 3, to which passage there is already an allusion in ver. 11.

[2] Namely, the cup of punishment, of divine wrath.

hatred against the people of God, stood before their eyes. The germ of this is to be found in Joel iv. (iii.) 19, where Edom already appears as a representative and type of the God-hating heathen world, which is to be judged by the Lord, after the judgment upon Judah.

In Obadiah, we find a fulness of remarkable glances into the future compressed within a narrow space. The chief events are the following:—1. The capture of Jerusalem, the total carrying away of the entire people, both of Judah and Israel, to a far distance, vers. 20, 21.   2. The return of Israel, the cessation of the separation of the two kingdoms, ver. 18 (compare Hos. ii. 2 [i. 11]; Amos ix. 11, 12), and his elevation to the dominion of the world by the "Saviours," ver. 21. 3. The judgment upon Edom by heathen nations, vers. 1–9. Jeremiah, in xxvii. 2 ff., compared with xxv., more distinctly points out the Chaldeans as the heathen instruments of the judgment upon Edom and all the people round about; and Matt. i. 3, 4, shows the weight of the sufferings which were inflicted by them upon Edom.   4. The occupation of the land of Edom by Judah. One realization of this prophecy took place in the time of the Maccabees; but we must not confine ourselves to this. As, in the main, Edom is only a type of the God-hating heathen world, the true and real fulfilment can be sought in Christ alone. Compare the remarks, p. 98, with reference to Moab in Balaam's prophecy.

The prophecy of Obadiah is divided into three parts:—the destruction of Edom by heathen nations summoned by Jehovah, vers. 1–9; the cause of it, his wickedness against Judah, vers. 10–16; Judah, on the contrary, rises with Joseph from this humiliation, and becomes a conqueror of the world, vers. 17–21. This last part claims our closer consideration.

Ver. 17. "*And upon Mount Zion shall be they that have escaped, and it is holy* (compare Joel iii. 5, iv. 17 [ii. 32, iii. 17]), *and the house of Jacob occupies their possessions.*"

The suffix in מוֹרָשֵׁיהֶם refers to all the heathen in ver. 16. The kingdom shall be the Lord's, according to ver. 16, and the dominion of His people extends as far as His own. We have here the general prophecy; and in what immediately follows, the application to Edom. The first two clauses serve as a foundation for the third. The holiness has, so to speak, not only a defensive, but also an offensive character. Its consequence is the dominion of the world.

Ver. 18. "*And the house of Jacob becomes a fire, and the house of Joseph a flame, and the house of Esau stubble, and they kindle them, and devour them; and there shall not be any remaining to the house of Esau; for the Lord has spoken.*"

Besides the whole of the people, that part of them (the house of Joseph, the people of the ten tribes) is specially mentioned which one might have expected to be excluded. That there is none remaining to the house of Esau (and to all who are like him) agrees with the declaration uttered by Joel in iii. 5 (ii. 32): "Amongst those who are spared, is whomsoever the Lord calleth." They, however, whom the Lord calls, are, according to the same verse, they who call on the name of the Lord. But the characteristic of Edom is his hatred against the kingdom of God,— and that excludes both the calling on the Lord, and the being called by the Lord. The single individual, however, may come out of the community of his people, and enter into the territory of saving grace, as is shown by the example of Rahab. In the further description of the conquering power, which the people of God shall, in future, exercise, we are, in ver. 19, first met by Judah and Benjamin.

Ver. 19. "*And they of the south possess the Mount of Esau, and they from the low region, the Philistines; and they (i.e., they of Judah, the whole, of whom they of the South and of the low region are parts only) possess the fields of Ephraim, and the fields of Samaria, and Benjamin—Gilead.*"

It is obvious that we have here before us only an individualized representation of the thought already expressed in Gen. xxviii. 14: "And thy seed shall be as the dust of the earth, and thou shalt break forth to the East and to the West, to the North and to the South; and in thee, and in thy seed, all the families of the earth are blessed;" compare also Is. liv. 3: "Thou shalt break forth on the right hand and on the left, and thy seed shall inherit the Gentiles."—נגב is the south part of Judea, at the borders of Edom; שפלה the low region on the West, at the borders of the Philistines. As, according to the vision of the prophet, the exaltation of Judah is preceded by his total overthrow and captivity (compare vers. 11–14, 20, 21), the tribe of Judah, which, before the catastrophe, was settled in the South and low region, is here meant. That את can be taken only as the sign of the Accus., and "Mount of Esau," accordingly, as the object only, appears from ver. 20, according to which the South is vacant. Judah thus extends in the South, over Edom, in the West, over Philistia, in the North, over the former territory of the ten tribes, and hence also over the territory of Benjamin, which formerly lay betwixt Judah and Joseph. Benjamin is indemnified by Gilead. The whole of Canaan comes thus to Judah and Benjamin. Joseph, to whose damage, according to ver. 18, this enlargement of Judah's territory must lead, must be transferred altogether to heathenish territory. We expect to find, in ver. 20, how he is indemnified.

Ver. 20. "*And the exiles of this host of the children of Israel* (shall possess) *what are Canaanites unto Zarephath, and the exiles of Jerusalem that are in Sepharad shall possess the cities of the South.*"

The circumstance that the Athnach stands below ספרד indicates that ירשו implies the common property of the exiles of this host, and of the exiles of Jerusalem. The "Sons of Israel," in this context, can only be the ten tribes; for they are here indemnified for their former territory, which, according to ver. 19, has become the possession of Judah. "The exiles of this host" is equivalent to: "This whole host of exiles,"—the whole mass of the ten tribes, carried away according to prophetic foresight (compare Amos v. 27: "And I carry you away beyond Damascus, saith the Lord, the God of hosts"), as opposed to a piecemeal carrying away, such as had once already taken place before the time of the prophet in respect to Judah, but not in respect to the children of Israel; compare Joel iv. (iii.) 6. That the "Canaanites unto Zarephath"—*i.e.*, the Phœnicians, whose territory formed part of the promised land, but had never, in former times, come into the real possession of Israel—are the objects of conquest, and that, hence, we cannot explain as *Caspari* does, "Who are among the Canaanites, even unto Zarephath," is evident from the circumstance, that all the neighbouring nations appear as objects of the conquering activity;—that the great mass of the Israelitish exiles were not among the Canaanites;—that the ב could, in that case, not have been omitted;—and that the South country is too small a space for the children of Israel, and of Jerusalem together. Sepharad, the very name of which is scarcely known, is mentioned as a particularizing designation of the utmost distance. The description becomes complete by its returning to the South country, from which it had proceeded. The South country penetrates to Edom; the inhabitants of Jerusalem extend beyond the South country.

Ver. 21. "*And saviours go up on Mount Zion to judge the Mount of Esau, and the kingdom shall be the Lord's.*"

עלי is to be accounted for from the consideration, that the deliverance and salvation imply the entire overthrow—the total carrying away of the people. The Saviour κατ' ἐξοχήν is hidden beneath the "saviours;" compare Judges iii. 9, 15; Neh. ix. 27. But even here, everything is connected with human individuals; and the more glorious the salvation which the prophet beholds in the future, viz., the absolute dominion of the Lord, and His people, over the world, the less can it be conceived that the prophet should have expected the realization of it by a collective body of mortal men without a leader. But the plural intimates that the antitype is not without types,—that the head cannot be conceived of without members. In Jer. xxiii. 4, we read: "And I raise up shepherds over them which shall feed them;" and immediately afterwards the one good shepherd—Christ—forms the subject of discourse.—"And the kingdom shall be the Lord's."—His dominion, till *then* concealed, shall now be publicly manifested, and the people of the earth shall acknowledge it, either spontaneously, or by constraint. The coming of this kingdom has begun with Christ, and, in Him, waits for its consummation. The opinion of *Caspari*, that the contents of vers. 19 and 20, as well as the close of this prophecy, belong altogether to the future, rests on a false, literal explanation, the inadmissibility of which is sufficiently evident from the circumstance that the Edomites, Philistines, and Canaanites have long since disappeared from the scene of history; so that there exists no longer the possibility of a literal fulfilment.

THE PROPHET JONAH.

It has been asserted without any sufficient reason, that Jonah is older than Hosea, Joel, Amos, and Obadiah,—that he is the oldest among the prophets whose written monuments have been preserved to us. The passage in 2 Kings xiv. 25, where it is said, that Jonah, the son of Amittai the prophet, prophesied to Jeroboam the happy success of his arms, and the restoration of the ancient boundaries of Israel, and that this prophecy was confirmed by the event, cannot decide in favour of this assertion, because it cannot be proved that the victories of Jeroboam belonged to the *beginning* of his reign. On the other hand, it is opposed, *first*, by the position of the book in the collection of the Minor Prophets, which, throughout, is chronologically arranged, and which is tantamount to an express testimony that Jonah wrote *after* Hosea, Joel, Amos, and Obadiah. *Then*,—the circumstance that Nineveh is mentioned here, and that too in a way which implies that, even at that time, the hostile relations of the Assyrians to the Covenant-people had already begun, while in the first part of Hosea, in Joel, Amos, and Obadiah, no reference to the Assyrians is as yet found. Even ancient interpreters, as *Chr. B. Michaelis*, *Crusius* (in the *Theol. Proph.* iii. S. 38), inferred from this mention of Nineveh, that the book had been composed in consequence of the first invasion of the Assyrians under Menahem, who ascended the throne 13 years after the death of Jeroboam II. *Finally*,—the book begins with *and*. Wherever else, in the canonical books of the Old Testament, such a beginning occurs, it indicates a resumption of, and a junction with, former links in the chain of sacred literature; compare Judges i. 1; 1 Sam. i. 1; Ezek. i. 1. That the expression, "And it came to pass," with which the book opens, is intended to establish the connection with the prophecy of Obadiah, which occupies the immediately preceding place in the Canon, is intimated by the internal relation of the two books to each other. The prophecy of Obadiah bears, throughout, a hostile aspect to the heathen world; it appears to him as the object only of God's judging activity. Jonah, on the other hand, received the mission, distinctly to point out the other aspect of the matter, and thereby, not indeed to correct, but certainly to supplement his predecessor.

The time was approaching when the heathen world was to pour out its floods upon the people of God. It was obvious that the position of Israel towards it became one altogether repulsive, that the susceptibility of the heathen for salvation was denied, and God's mercy was limited to Israel. Narrow-minded exclusiveness received a powerful support from the oppression and haughtiness of the heathen. Whilst other prophets opposed such exclusiveness by their words, by announcing the extension of salvation to the Gentiles, Jonah received the mission to illustrate, by a symbolical action, the capacity of the heathen for salvation, and their future participation in it. The effect of this must necessarily have been so much the greater, as the whole of the little book is exclusively devoted to this subject, as it appeared at the first beginning of the conflict, and as Nineveh is mentioned here, for the first time, in so peaceable and conciliatory a relation, and in close harmony and connection with the announcement of the willing submission of the heathen world to the dominion of Shiloh, spoken of in Gen. xlix. 10. It is remarkably impressive to see how spirit here triumphs over nature—a triumph which appears so much the brighter because the prophet himself pays his tribute to nature; for it was because he listened to the voice of nature, that, at first, he intended to flee to Tarshish. The reason why the commission of the Lord was so disagreeable to him, we learn from chap. iv. 2. He was afraid lest the preaching of repentance, which was committed to him, might turn away the judgments of the Lord from Nineveh, the metropolis of that country which threatened destruction to Israel. He knew the deep corruption of his own people, and foreboded the issue which the extension of the means of grace to the Gentiles might very easily bring about in the end. But yet, he felt almost irresistibly impelled to carry out the commission of God, and in order to cut himself off from the possibility of following the voice which called him to the east, he resolved to go to the far distant west. The voice, however, followed him even there; but the farther he advanced on his journey, the more difficult it became for him to follow it. At a later period, when the Lord granted mercy to Nineveh, he was angry and wished to die, not by any means because he

felt himself injured in his honour as a prophet (as was erroneously supposed, even by *Calvin*), but because he grudged to the
Gentiles the mercy which he considered as a prerogative of
Israel only, and because he was anxious for the destruction of
Nineveh as the metropolis of that kingdom which was destined
to be the rod of chastisement for his own people. He was thus
actuated by the same ardent love for his people which called
forth the wish of St Paul, that he might become an anathema
for his brethren,—by the same disposition of mind which prevailed in the elder brother at the return of the prodigal son
(Luke xv. 25 ff.), and which at first would manifest itself even
in Peter, Acts x. 14 ff. The Jewish sentence (*Carpzov. Introd.*
3, p. 149), "Jonah was anxious for the glory of the Son, but
he did not seek the glory of the Father," is very significant.
Jonah exhibits, in a very striking way, the thoughts of his old
man, in order that Israel might recognise themselves in his
image. But we are not at liberty to say that the prophet represented the people only. It is true that, as one of the people,
he also entertained those thoughts; but, besides these, he entertained other thoughts also. The voices of the Lord which he
heard were spiritual; and such voices can be heard only when
there is something akin in the heart. Not even with one step
did Jonah touch the territory of the false prophets, who prophesied out of their own hearts. He retained all his human
weakness to himself, and the Word of God stood by the side of
it in unclouded brightness, and obtained absolute victory.

There can be no doubt that we have before us in the Book
of Jonah the description of a symbolical action,—that his mission
to Nineveh has an object distinct from the mission itself,—that
it is not the result attained by it in the first instance which is
the essential point, but that it is its aim to bring to light
certain truths, and in the form of fact, to prophesy future
things. The truths are these:—*First*, that the Gentiles are by
no means so unsusceptible of the higher truth as vulgar prejudice imagined them to be. This was manifested by the conduct
of the sailors, who, at last, offer sacrifices and even vows to
Jehovah; but, in a more striking manner, by the deep impression which the discourse of Jonah produced upon the Ninevites.
In this we have the actual proof of Ezek. iii. 5, 6, where the
prophet represents his mission as one of peculiar difficulty—more

difficult, even, than it would have been if addressed to the
Gentiles: "Had I sent thee to them, surely they would have
hearkened to thee." *Further*,—that it is not in His relation to
Israel only, but in His relation to the Gentiles also, that the
Lord is "gracious and merciful, slow to anger and of great
kindness," chap. iv. 2. The view which these words, at once,
open up into the future, is, that at some future period the Lord
will grant to the Gentiles the preaching of His word, and admission into His kingdom. The glory of His mercy and grace
would have been darkened, if the revelation of them had been
for ever limited to a particular, small portion of the human
race. Nineveh, the representative of the heathen multitude,
is very significantly called the "great city" at the very outset,
in i. 2, and "a great city for God," in iii. 3, for which, as
Michaelis remarks, God specially cared, on account of the great
number of souls; compare iv. 11.

If the symbolical and prophetical character of the book be
denied, the fact of its having its place among the prophetical,
and not among the historical, books, admits of no explanation
at all. For so much is evident, that this fact cannot be satisfactorily accounted for by the circumstance that the book reports the events which happened to a prophet. The sound explanation has been already given by *Marckius*: "The book is,
in a great measure, historical, but in such a manner, that in
the history itself there is hidden the mystery of the greatest
prophecy, and that Jonah proves himself to be a true prophet,
by the events which happened to him, not less than by his
utterances." A similar explanation is given by *Carpzovius*:
"By his own example, as well as by the event itself, he bore
witness that it was the will of God that all men should be
saved, and should come to the knowledge of the truth," 1 Tim.
ii. 4.

We are led to the same conclusion by the representation itself. This differs very widely from that given in the historical
books. The objection raised by *Hitzig* against the historical
truth,—viz., that the narrative is fragmentary,—that it wants
completeness,—that a number of events are communicated only
in so far as is required by the object of gaining a foundation
for the graphic representation of the doctrinal contents,—cannot be set aside so easily as is done by *Hävernick* when he says:

"By arguments of a nature so flimsy, suspicions may be raised against the truth of every historical report." We cannot but confess that, to the writer, history is indeed a means only of representing a thought to which he is anxious to give currency in the Church of God. It is just for this reason that he abstains from graphically enlarging, because that would have been an obstacle to his purpose. The narrative of a symbolical action which took place outwardly, comes, in this respect, under the same law as the narrative of a symbolical action belonging to the internal territory, and to that of the parable. The narrative would lose the character of perspicuity which is so necessary for the whole matter, if it were complete in the subordinate circumstances.

It also tells in favour of the symbolical character of the history of Jonah, that the missionary activity on behalf of the Gentiles does not properly belong to the vocation of the prophets, their mission being to the two houses of Israel only. In the entire history, not even a single example is to be found of a prophet who, for the good of the heathen world itself, went out among them. The history of Elisha, in 2 Kings viii. 7 ff., has, without sufficient reason, been adduced by *Hävernick*. According to the visions of the prophets themselves, the conversion of the heathen is not to be accomplished *at present*, but in the Messianic time, and by the Messiah Himself. If, then, the book itself is not to stand altogether isolated, the symbolical character of Jonah's mission must be acknowledged. But then it is only in the form that it differs from the announcements of the extension of salvation to the heathen also,—announcements which occur in the other prophets also. That which these exhibited in words merely, is here made conspicuous by deeds. The influence thereby produced upon the heathen appears then only as the means, while the real purpose is to make an important truth familiar to the Congregation of God, and, by a striking fact, to remove the prejudices which prevailed in it.

Finally,—If the symbolical character of the facts be denied, the mission of Jonah appears to be almost divested of every aim; for the good emotions of the crew, and the repentance of the Ninevites, evidently did not lead to any lasting result. If anything else were aimed at than the prefiguring of future events, the prophet might better have stayed at home; an unassuming ministry in some corner among the Covenant-people would have carried along with it a greater reward.

If, on the other hand, the symbolical character of the history of Jonah be admitted, remarkable parallels in the history of Jesus present themselves. The Saviour, in the days of His flesh, was satisfied with the prophetic intimation of the future farther extension of His salvation. That which He Himself did for this extension, in those particular cases where the faith of non-Israelites obtruded itself upon Him, must, in its isolation, be viewed as an embodiment of that intimation,—as a prophecy by deeds. He says in Matt. xv. 24: "I am not sent but to the lost sheep of the house of Israel;" but if, nevertheless, He purposely makes His abode in the territory of Tyre and Sidon; if there He hears the prayer of the Canaanitish woman to heal her daughter, after having first tried her faith, then His purpose evidently is: That His prophecy in words concerning the extension of salvation to the Gentiles, might find a support in His prophecy in deeds. Jesus, prefiguring the future doings of His servants, passed over the boundaries of the Gentiles. Whilst the Jews had rejected the salvation offered to them, and forced Jesus to retire into concealment, the heathen woman comes full of faith, and seeks Him in His concealment. The Canaanitish woman is a representative of the heathen world, the future faith of which she was called to prefigure by sustaining the trial. From her example, the Apostles were to learn what might be expected from the Gentiles when the time should arrive for proclaiming the Gospel to them also. In Matt. x. 5, 6, the Lord speaks to the Apostles: "Go not in the way of the Gentiles, and into any of the cities of the *Samaritans* enter ye not; but go rather to the lost sheep of the house of Israel." His own conduct, however, as it is reported in John iv., stands in contradiction to this command to His Apostles, so long as its prophetical significance is not acknowledged. That which was, on a large scale, to be done by Christ in the state of glorification, was prefigured by Him, on a smaller scale, in the state of humiliation. The ministry of Christ in Samaria bears the same relation to the later mission among this people, that the single instances of Christ's raising the dead do to the general resurrection. The Lord afterwards did not foster the germs which had come forth among the Samaritans; He, in the meantime, left them altogether to their fate. That prelude was quite sufficient for the object which He then had in view, and nothing further could be done without violating the rights of the Covenant-people, to which, in the conversation as recorded by John, the Lord as expressly pays attention, as He does in Matt. x.

THE PROPHET MICAH.

PRELIMINARY REMARKS.

Micah signifies: "Who is like Jehovah;" and by this name, the prophet is consecrated to the incomparable God, just as Hosea was to the helping God, and Nahum to the comforting God. He prophesied, according to the inscription, under Jotham, Ahaz, and Hezekiah. We are not, however, entitled, on this account, to dissever his prophecies, and to assign particular discourses to the reign of each of these kings. On the contrary, the entire collection forms only one whole. At the termination of his prophetic ministry, under Hezekiah, the prophet committed to writing everything which was of importance for all coming time that had been revealed to him during the whole duration of that ministry. He collected into one comprehensive picture all the detached visions which had been granted to him in manifold repetition; giving us the sum and substance (of which nothing has been lost in the case of any of the men inspired by God) of what was spoken at different times, and omitting all which was accidental, and purely local and temporary.

This view, which alone is the correct one, and which contributes so largely to the right understanding of the prophet, has been already advanced by several of the older scholars. Thus *Lightfoot* (*Ordo temporum*, opp. i. p. 99) remarks: "It is easier to conceive that the matter of this whole book represents the substance of the prophecy which he uttered under these various kings, than to determine which of the chapters of this book were uttered under the particular reign of each of these kings." *Majus* also (*Economia temporum*, p. 898) says: "He repeated, at a subsequent period, what he had spoken at different times, and under different kings." In modern times, however, this view had been generally abandoned; and although, at present, many critics are disposed to return to it, *Hitzig* and *Maurer* still assert, that the book was composed at different periods.

We shall now endeavour to prove the unity of the book, *first*, from the prophecies themselves. If we were entitled to separate them at all, according to time and circumstances, we could form a division into three discourses only; viz., chap. i. and ii.; chap. iii.-v.; and chap. vi. and vii. For, 1. Each of these discourses forms a whole, complete in itself, and in which the various elements of the prophetic discourse—reproof, threatening, promise—are repeated. If these discourses be torn asunder, we get only the *lacera membra* of a prophetic discourse. 2. Each of these three discourses, forming an harmonious whole, begins with שמעו, *hear*. That this is not merely accidental, appears from the beginning of the first discourse, שמעו עמים כלם, "Hear, all ye people." These words literally agree with those which were uttered by the prophet's elder namesake, when, according to 1 Kings xxii. 28, he called upon the whole world to attend to the remarkable struggle betwixt the true and false prophets. It is evidently on purpose that the prophet begins with the same words as those with which the elder Micah had closed his discourse to Ahab, and, it may be, his whole prophetic ministry. By this very circumstance he gives intimation of what may be expected from him, shows that his activity is to be considered as a continuation of that of his predecessor, who was so jealous for God, and that he had more in common with him than the mere name. *Rosenmüller (Prol. ad Mich.* p. 8) has asserted, indeed, that these words are only put into the mouth of the elder Micah, and that they are taken from the passage under consideration. But the reason which he adduces in support of this assertion, viz., that it cannot be conceived how it could ever have entered the mind of that elder Micah to call upon all people to be witnesses of an announcement which concerned Ahab only, needs no detailed refutation. Why then is it that in Deut. xxxii. 1, Is. i. 2, heaven and earth are called upon to be witnesses of an announcement which concerned the Jewish people only? Who does not see that, to the prophet, Israel appears as too small an audience for the announcement of the great decision which he has just uttered; in the same manner as the Psalmist (compare, *e.g.*, Ps. xcvi. 3) exhorts to proclaim to the Gentiles the great deeds of the Lord, because Palestine is too narrow for them?—But now, if it be established that it was with a distinct object that the prophet employed the words, "Hear ye," does not the circumstance that they are found at the commencement of the three discourses, which are complete in themselves, afford sufficient ground for the assumption, that it was the intention of the prophet, not indeed absolutely to limit them to the beginning of a new discourse (compare, on the contrary, iii. 9[1]), but yet, not to commence a new discourse without them; so that the want of them is decisive against the supposition of a new section? 3. As soon as an attempt is made to break up any of these three discourses, many particular circumstances are at once found, upon a careful examination, to prove a connection of the sections so close, as not to admit of a separation without mutilating them. Thus chap. i. and ii. cannot be separated from each other, for the reason that the promise in ii. 12, 13, refers to the threatening in i. 5. That promise refers to all Israel, just as does the threatening in chap. i.; whilst in the threatening and reproof in chap. ii. the eye of the prophet is directed only to the main object of his ministry, viz., to Judah.

But even these three divisions, which hitherto we have proved to be the only divisions that do exist,[2] can be considered as such, in so far only as in them the discourse takes a fresh start, and enters upon a new sphere. They cannot be considered as complete in themselves, and separated from one another by the

---

[1] It must not, however, be overlooked, that there the term "hear" is only a resumption of "hear" in iii. 1 (and, to a certain extent, even of that in i. 2), intimating, that that which they are about to hear, will concentrate itself in a distinct and powerful expression,—the acme of the whole threatening in iii. 12.

[2] Besides the division into three sections, there is, to a certain extent, a division also into two. By וַאֹמַר in iii. 1, the first and second discourses, or the exordium and principal part, are brought into a still closer connection,—a connection founded upon the circumstance that the reproof and threatening of the first part are to be here resumed, in order that thus a comprehensive representation may be given. It is only in iii. 12 that the threatening reaches its height. But yet the tripartition remains the prominent one. This cannot be denied without forcing a false sense and a false position upon ii. 12, 13.

difference of the periods of their composition; for even in them
there are found traces of a close connection. Even the uniform
beginning by "Hear" may be considered as such. The second
discourse in iii. 1 begins with ואמר; but the *Fut.* with *Vav
convers.* always, and without exception, connects a new action
with a preceding one, and can never be used where there is an
absolutely new commencement. Its significance here, where it
is used in the transition from the promise to a new reproof and
threatening, has been very strikingly brought out thus, by *Ch.
Bened. Michaelis*: "But while we are yet but too far away from
those longed-for times, which have just been promised, I *say* in
the meanwhile, viz., in order to complete the list of the iniquities
of evil princes and teachers, begun in chap. ii." The words of
iii. 1, "Hear, I pray you, ye heads of Jacob, and ye princes of
the house of Israel," have an evident reference to ii. 12 : "I
will assemble Jacob all of thee, I will gather the remnant of
Israel." In the new threatening, the prophet chooses quite the
same designation as in the preceding promise, in order to prevent
the latter from giving support to false security. It is not by
any means Samaria alone, but all Israel, which is the object of
divine punishment. It is only a remnant of Israel that shall be
gathered. But the reference to the preceding discourse is still
more obvious in ver. 4 : "Then they shall cry unto the Lord,
and He will not answer; and may He hide[1] His face from them
at this time, as they have behaved themselves ill towards Him
in their doings." Now, as in vers. 1–3 divine judgments had
not yet been spoken of, the terms "then," and "at this time,"
can refer only to the threatenings of punishment in ii. 3 ff.,
which have a special reference to the ungodly nobles.

Thus the result presented at the beginning, is confirmed to
us by internal reasons. The inscription[2] announces the oracles

---

[1] The *Fut. apoc.* forbids us to translate: "He will hide." In order to
express his own delight in the doings of divine justice, the prophet changes
the prediction into a wish, just as is the case in Is. ii. 9, where the greater
number of interpreters assume, in opposition to the rules of grammar, that
אַל stands for לֹא.

[2] Against the genuineness of the inscription, doubts have been raised
by many, after the example of *Hartmann*, and last of all by *Ewald* and
Hitzig; but it is established by the striking allusions to, and coincidences
with it, in the text. With the mention of Micah's name in the former, the
allusion to this name in the *close* of the book, in chap. vii. 18, corre-

of God which came to Micah under the reign of three kings; while the examination of the contents proves that the collection forms a connected whole, written *uno tenore*. How, now, can these two facts be reconciled in any other way than by supposing that we have here before us a comprehensive picture of the prophetic ministry of Micah, the single component parts of which are at once contemporaneous, and yet belonging to different periods? This supposition, moreover, affords us the advantage of being allowed to maintain all the historical references in their fullest import, without being led to disregard the one, while we give attention to the other; for nothing is, in this case, more natural, than that the prophet connects with one another different prophecies uttered at different times.

The weight of these internal reasons is increased, however, by external reasons which are equally strong. When Jeremiah was called to account for his prophecy concerning the destruction of the city, the elders, for his justification, appealed to the

sponds. The circumstance of Micah being called the Morasthite, accounts for the fact that, in this threatening against the cities of Judah, in i. 14, it is Moresheth alone which is mentioned. In the inscription, Samaria and Jerusalem are pointed out as the objects of the prophet's predictions; and it is in harmony with this, that in i. 6, 7, the judgment upon Samaria is first described, and then the judgment upon Judah; that the prophet—although, indeed, he has Judah chiefly in view—frequently gives attention to the ten tribes also, and includes them,—as in the promise in ii. 12, 13, v. 1 (2), where the Messiah appears as the Ruler in Israel, and vers. 6, 7 (7, 8), of the same chapter; and that in iii. 8, 9, Judah is represented as a particular part only of the great whole. *Finally*—It is peculiar to Micah, that he thus views so specially the two *capitals*; and this again is in harmony with the inscription, where just these, and not Israel and Judah, appear as the subjects of the prophecy. It is in the capitals that Micah beholds the concentration of the corruption (i. 5); and to them the threatening also is chiefly addressed, i. 6, 7, iii. 12. Of the promise, also, Jerusalem forms the centre.—The statement, too, in the inscription—that Micah uttered the contents of his book under various kings—likewise receives a confirmation from the prophecy. The mention of the high places of Judah in i. 5, and of the walking in the statutes of Omri, and in all the works of the house of Ahab, refers especially to the time of Ahaz; compare 2 Kings xvi. 4; 2 Chron. xxviii. 4, 25; further, 2 Kings xvi. 3; 2 Chron. xxviii. 2; and *Caspari* on Micah, S. 74. On the other hand, the time of Hezekiah is suggested by v. 4, 5 (5, 6), which implies that already, at that time, Asshur had appeared as the enemy of the people of God,—and so likewise by the prophecy in iv. 9–14.

2 D

entirely similar prophecy of Micah in iii. 12 : " Therefore shall Zion for your sake be ploughed as a field, and Jerusalem shall become heaps of ruins, and the mountain of the house as the high places of the forest." In Jer. xxvi. 18, 19, it is said, " Micah prophesied in the days of Hezekiah, king of Judah, and spake to all the people of Judah, etc. Did Hezekiah, king of Judah, and all Judah, put him to death ? Did he not fear the Lord, and besought the Lord, and the Lord repented Him of the evil which He had pronounced against them ?" All interpreters admit that this passage forms an authority for the composition of the discourse in iii.–v. under Hezekiah; but we cannot well limit it in this way, we must extend it to the whole collection. For, even apart from the reasons by which we proved that the entire book forms one closely connected whole, it is most improbable that the elders should have known, by an oral tradition, the exact time of the composition of one single discourse, which has no special date at the head of it. Is it not a far more natural supposition, that they considered the collection as a whole, of which the component parts had, indeed, been delivered by the prophet at a former period, but had been repeated, and united into one description under Hezekiah; and that they mentioned Hezekiah, partly because it could not be determined with certainty whether this special prediction had already been uttered under one of his predecessors, and, if so, under which of them; and partly, because among the three kings mentioned in the inscription, Hezekiah alone formed an ecclesiastical authority ?

But just as that quotation in Jeremiah furnishes us with a proof that all the prophecies of Micah, which have been preserved to us, were committed to writing under Hezekiah, so we can, in a similar manner, prove from Isaiah, chap. ii., that they were, at least in part, uttered at a previous period. The problem of the relation of Is. ii. 2–4 to Micah iv. 1–3, cannot be solved in any other way than by supposing, that this portion of a prophecy which, in Jeremiah, is assigned to the reign of Hezekiah, was uttered by Micah as early as under the reign of Jotham, and that soon after it Isaiah, by placing the words of Micah at the head of his own prophecies, expressed that which had come to him also in inward vision; for, being already known to the people, they could not fail to produce their impression.

Every other solution can be proved to be untenable. 1. Least of all is there any refutation needed of the hypothesis which is now generally abandoned, viz., that the passage in Isaiah is the original one; compare, against this hypothesis, *Kleinert, Aechtheit des Jes.* S. 356; *Caspari,* S. 444. 2. Equally objectionable is another supposition, that both the prophets had made use of some older prophecy—one uttered by Joel, as *Hitzig* and *Ewald* have maintained. The connection in which these verses stand in Micah, is by far too close for such a supposition. We could not, indeed, so confidently advance this argument, if the connection consisted only in what is commonly brought forward, viz., that upon the *monitory* announcement of punishment in chap. iii., there follows, in chap. iv. 1 ff., the *consolatory* promise of a glorious future for the godly, and that the ו in ver. 1 evidently connects it with what immediately precedes. But the reference and connection are far more close. The promise in iv. 1, 2, is, throughout, contrasted with the threatening in iii. 12. "The mountain of the house shall become as the high places of the forest,"—hence, despised, solitary, and desolate. In iv. 1, there is opposed to it, "The mountain of the house of the Lord shall be established on the top of the mountains, and it shall be exalted above the hills, and upon it people shall flee together." "Zion shall be ploughed as a field, and Jerusalem become a heap of ruins." Contrasted with this, there is in iv. 2 the declaration : "For the law shall go forth of Zion, and the word of the Lord of Jerusalem." The desolate and despised place now becomes the residence of the Lord, from which He sends His commands over the whole earth, and of which the brilliant centre now is Jerusalem. In order to make this contrast so much the more obvious, the prophet begins, in the promise, with just the mountain of the temple, which, in the threatening, had occupied the last place; so that the opposites are brought into immediate connection. Nor is it certainly merely accidental that, in the threatening, he speaks of the mountain of the house only, while, in the promise, he speaks of the mountain of the house of the Lord; compare Matt. xxiii. 38, where "your house," according to *Bengel,* "is the house which, in other passages, is called the house of the Lord," just as the Lord, in Exod. xxxii. 7, says to Moses, "*Thy people.*" The temple must have ceased to be the house of the Lord, before it would be destroyed; for which reason, as we are told in Ezekiel, the Shechinah removed from it before the Babylonish destruction. And in point of form, the יהיה in iv. 1 so much the more corresponds with the תהיה in iii. 12, as from the latter יהיה must be supplied for the last clause of the verse; compare *Caspari*, S. 445. That ver. 5 must not be separated from the prophecy which Isaiah had before him, is seen from a comparison of Is. ii. 5: "O house of Jacob, come ye and let us walk in the light of the Lord." According to the true interpretation, "the light of the Lord" signifies His grace, and the blessings which, according to what precedes, are to be bestowed by it; and "to walk in the light of the Lord," means to participate in the enjoyment of grace. These words, accordingly, are closely related to those in Mic. iv. 5: "For all the people shall walk, every one in the name of his god, and we will walk in the name of the Lord our God for ever and ever:" *i.e.*, the fate of the people in the heathen world corresponds to the nature of their gods; because these are nothing, they too shall sink down into nothingness, while Israel shall partake in the glory of his God. There is the same thought, and in essentially the same dress, both in Isaiah and Micah,—only that the words which in Micah embody a pure promise, are transformed by Isaiah into an exhortation that Israel should not, by their own fault, forfeit this preference over the heathen nations, that they should not wantonly wander away into dark solitudes, from the path of light which the Lord had opened up before them. This transformation in Isaiah, however, may be accounted for by the consideration, that he was anxious to prepare the way for the reproofs which now follow from ver. 6; whilst Micah, who had already premised them, could continue in the promise. It is also in favour of the originality of the passage in Micah, that the text which, in Isaiah, appears as a variation, appears as original in Micah; so that both cannot be equally dependent upon a third writer. 3. There now remains only the view of *Kleinert*, according to which the prophecy of Micah, in chap. iii.–v., was first uttered under the reign of Hezekiah; and, under the reign of the same king, but somewhat later, the prophecy, in chap. ii.–iv. of Isaiah, who avails himself of it. But, upon a closer examination, this view also proves untenable. Isaiah's description of the condition of the people in a moral point of view, the general spread of idolatry

and vice, exclude every other period in the reign of Hezekiah
except the first beginning of it, when the effect and influence
of the time of Ahaz were still felt; so that even *Kleinert* (p. 364)
is obliged to assume, that not only the prophecy of Micah, but
also that of Isaiah, were uttered in the first months of the reign
of this king. But other difficulties—and these altogether insu-
perable—stand in the way of this assumption. In the whole
section of Isaiah, the nation appears as rich, flourishing, and
powerful. This is most strongly expressed in chap. ii. 7: "His
land is full of silver and gold, there is no end to his treasure;
his land is full of horses, and there is no end to his chariots."
To this may be added the description of the consequences of
wealth, and of the unbounded luxury, in iii. 16 ff.; and the
threatening of the withdrawal of all power, and all riches, as a
strong contrast with their present condition, upon which they,
in their blindness, rested the hope of their security, and hence
imagined that they stood in no need of the assistance of the
Lord, iii. 1 ff. Now this description is so inapplicable to the
commencement of Hezekiah's reign, that the very opposite of it
should rather be expected. The invasion by the allied Syrians
and Israelites, the oppression by the Assyrians, and the tribute
which they had to pay to them, the internal administration,
which was bad beyond example, and the curse of God resting
on all their enterprises and efforts, had exhausted, during the
reign of the ungodly Ahaz, the treasures which had been collected under Uzziah and Jotham, and had dried up the sources
of prosperity. He had left the kingdom to his successors in a
condition of utter decay. To these, other reasons still may be
added, which are in favour of the composition of it under
Jotham, while they are against its composition under Hezekiah;
especially the circumstance of their standing at the beginning
of the collection of the first twelve chapters (a circumstance
which is of great weight, inasmuch as these chapters are, beyond
any doubt, arranged chronologically), but still more, the indefiniteness and generality in the threatening of the divine judgments, which the prophecy of Micah has in common with the
nearly contemporaneous chapters i. and v. of Isaiah, whilst
the threatenings out of the first period of the reign of Ahaz
have at once a far more definite character. By these considerations we are involuntarily led back to a period when Isaiah still

pre-eminently exercised the office of exhorting and reproving, and had not yet been favoured with special revelations concerning the events of a future which, at that time, was as yet rather distant,—perhaps as far as the time when Jotham administered the government for his father, who was at that time still alive; compare 2 Kings xv. 5. By this hypothesis, Is. iii. 12 is more satisfactorily explained than by any other; and we are no longer under the necessity of asserting, that the chronological order is interrupted by chap. vi.; for this certainly could not have been intended by the collector. The solemn call and consecration of the prophet to his office, accompanied by an increased bestowal of grace, must be carefully distinguished from the ordinary ones which were common to him with all the other prophets. But if the prophecy of Isaiah was uttered as early as under Jotham (which has lately been most satisfactorily proved by *Caspari* in his *Beiträge zur Einl. in das Buch Jesaias*, S. 234 ff.), that of Micah also must have existed at that time, and must have been in the mouths of the people. And since its composition is assigned to the reign of Hezekiah, it follows that the prophet delivered anew, under the reign of this king, the revelations which he had already received at an earlier period.

It will not be possible to infer with certainty from vers. 6, 7, as *Caspari* does, that the book was committed to writing before the destruction of Samaria, and hence, before the sixth year of Hezekiah. Since the book gives the sum and substance of what was prophesied under three kings, all that is implied in vers. 6, 7, is, that the destruction of Samaria was foretold by Micah; but the prophecy itself may have been committed to writing even after the fulfilment had taken place. But, on the other hand, according to the analogy of Is. xxxix., and xiii. and xiv., we are led by iv. 9, 10, to the time of Sennacherib's invasion of Judea, in which the prophetic spirit of Isaiah likewise most richly displayed itself, and in which he was privileged with a glance into the far distant future.

The exordium in chap. i. and ii., and the close in vi. and vii., are distinguished by the generality of the threatening and promise which prevails in them. They have this in common with the first five chapters of Isaiah, and thus certainly afford us pre-eminently an image of the prophetic ministry of Micah, in the time previous to the Assyrian invasion; whilst the main body (especially from iv. 8) represents to us particularly the character of the prophecy during the Assyrian period.

We shall now attempt to give a survey of the contents of Micah's prophecy.

Upon Samaria and Jerusalem—the kingdom of the ten tribes, and Judah—a judgment by foreign enemies is to come. Total destruction, and the carrying away of the inhabitants, will be the issue of this judgment, and, as regards Judah more particularly, the total overthrow of the dominion of the Davidic dynasty.

Samaria is first visited by this judgment. This is indicated by the fact that it is first mentioned in the inscription, and that in i. 6, 7, the judgment upon Samaria is, first of all, described; but especially by the circumstance that Samaria, in i. 5, appears as the chief seat of corruption for the whole people, whence it flowed upon Judah also, i. 14, and particularly, vi. 16. We expect that where the carcases first were, there the eagles would first be gathered together.

As the first, and principal instrument of the destructive judgment upon Judah, Babylon is mentioned in iv. 10.

As the representative of the world's power, at the time then present, Asshur appears in v. 4, 5. If destruction is to fall upon the kingdom of the ten tribes *before* it falls upon Judah—which is most distinctly foretold by Hosea in i. 4–7—then, nothing was more obvious than to think of Asshur as the instrument of the judgment. That to which Micah, on this point, only alludes, is more fully expanded by Isaiah.

Judah is delivered from Babylon, but without a restoration of the kingdom, iv. 10, compared with ver. 14 (v. 1).

But a second catastrophe comes upon Judah, inasmuch as many heathens gather themselves against Jerusalem, with the intention of desecrating it, but yet in such a manner that, by the assistance of the Lord, it comes forth victoriously from this severe attack, chap. iv. 11–13. Then follows a third catastrophe, in which Judah becomes anew and totally subject to the world's power, iv. 14 (v. 1).

From the deepest abasement, however, the Congregation of the Lord rises to the highest glory, inasmuch as the dominion returns to the old Davidic race, iv. 8. From the little Bethlehem, the native place of David, where his race, sunk back again into the lowliness of private life, has resumed its seat, a new and glorious Ruler proceeds, born, and at the same time eternal, and clothed with the fulness of the glory of the Lord, v. 1, 3 (2, 4), by whom Jacob obtains truth, and Abraham mercy, vii. 20, compared with John i. 17 ; by whom the Congregation is placed in the centre of the world, and becomes the object of the longing of all nations, iv. 1–3, delivered from the servitude of the world, and conquering the world, v. 4, 5 (5, 6), vii. 11, 12 ; and at the same time lowly, and inspiring the nations with fear, v. 6–8 (7–9). To such a height, however, she shall attain after, by means of the judgment preceding the mercy, all that has been taken from her upon which she in the present founded the hope of her salvation, v. 9–14 (10–15).

CHAP. I. AND II.

The prophet begins with the words : " *Hear, all ye people, hearken, O earth and the fulness thereof, and let the Lord God be witness against you, the Lord from His holy temple. For, behold, the Lord cometh forth out of His place, and cometh down, and treadeth upon the high places of the earth. And the mountains are melted under Him, and the valleys are cleft, as wax before the fire, as waters poured down a steep place. For the transgression of Jacob is all this, and for the sins of the house of Israel.*" Vers. 2–5.

This majestic exordium has been misunderstood in various ways : *First*, by those who, like *Hitzig*, would understand by the people, עַמִּים, in ver. 2, the tribes of Israel. We shall show, when commenting on Zech. xi. 10, that this is altogether inadmissible. But in the present case especially, this interpretation must be rejected ; partly on account of the reference to the words of the elder Micah, and partly on account of the parallel terms, " O earth and the fulness thereof," which, according to the constant *usus loquendi*, lead us far beyond the narrow limits of Palestine. On the other hand, they who by the עַמִּים rightly understand the nations of the whole earth, are mistaken in this, that they consider them as mere witnesses, whom the Lord calls up against His unthankful people, instead of considering them as the very same against whom the Lord bears witness; and that they come into consideration from this point of view, clearly appears from the words, " The Lord be witness against you." As regards עד with ב following, compare, e.g., Mal. iii. 5.— Another mistake is committed in the definition of the way and manner of the divine witness. The greater number of interpreters suppose it to be the subsequent admonitory, reproving, and threatening discourse of the prophet. Thus, e.g., *Michaelis*, who explains: " Do not despise and lightly esteem such a witness, who by me earnestly and publicly testifies to you His will." But in opposition to this view, it appears from ver. 3, that here, as well as in Mal. iii. 5, " And I will come near to you in judgment, and I am a swift witness against the sorcerers, and against the adulterers, and against those that swear to a lie," the witness is a real one,—that it consists in the actual attestation of the guilt by the punishment, viz., by the divine judgment described in vers. 3, 4. The words, " The Lord cometh forth out of His place, and cometh down," there correspond to, " From His holy temple,"—from which it is evident, at the same time, that by the temple, the heavenly temple must be understood.

We have thus, in vers. 2–4, before us the description of a sublime theophany, not for a partial judgment upon Judah, but for a judgment upon the whole world, the people of which are called upon to gather around their judge—whom the prophet beholds as already approaching, descending from His glorious habitation in heaven, accompanied by the insignia of His power, the precursors of the judgment—and silently to wait for His judicial and penal sentence.[1]

But how is it to be explained that with the words, " For the transgression of Jacob is all this," etc., there is a sudden transition to the judgments upon Israel, yea, that the prophet

---

[1] The reference to the general judgment would indeed disappear, if we suppose בכם in ver. 2 to be addressed to *Israel*. It seems, indeed, to be in favour of this supposition, that, in 1 Kings xxii. 28, the people alone are called upon as witnesses, and that in Deut. xxxi. 28, xxxii. 1, and Is. i. 2, heaven and earth, and in Hos. vi. 1, the mountains also, are called upon only in order to make the scene more solemn. But the reference of בכם to the nations mentioned immediately before, is too evident.

goes on as if Israel alone had been spoken of? Only from the relation in which these two judgments stand to one another. For they are perfectly one in substance. They are separated only by space, time, and unessential circumstances; so that we may say that the general judgment appears in every partial judgment upon Israel. In order to give expression to the thought, that it is the *judge of the world* who is to judge Israel, the prophets not unfrequently represent the Lord appearing to judge the whole world; and in Israel, the *Microcosmos*, it was indeed judged. We have a perfectly analogous case, *e.g.*, in Is. chap. ii.–iv. It is only by means of a very forced explanation, that it can be denied that after the prophet has, by a few bold touches, from ii. 6–9, described the moral debasement of the Covenant-people, and marked out pride as its last source, the last judgment upon the whole earth forms the subject of discourse. In that judgment there will be a most clear revelation of the vanity of all which is created—a vanity which, in the present course of the world, is so frequently concealed—and that the Lord alone is exalted, and that those who now shut their eyes will then be compelled to acknowledge these truths. That Isaiah has this general judgment in view, is too clearly proved by the sublimity of the whole description, by the express mention of the whole earth, *e.g.*, ii. 19, and by not limiting, in the individualized description in ver. 12 sqq., the high and lofty which is to be brought low to Judah alone, but by extending it to the whole world. But in iii. 1 ff. the prophet suddenly passes over to the typical, penal judgment upon Judah; and the כי, at the commencement, shows that he does not consider this subject as one altogether new, but as being substantially identical with the preceding subject. This reminds us forcibly of the mode in which, in the prophecies of our Lord, the references to the destruction of Jerusalem, and to the last judgment, are connected with one another. In the "burden of Babylon" in chap. xiii. likewise, the judgment of the Lord upon the whole earth is first described. Nor is it only on the territory of prophecy that this close connection of the general judgment with the inferior judgments upon the Covenant-people appears. In Ps. lxxxii. 8, *e.g.*, after the unrighteousness prevailing among the Covenant-people has been described, the Lord is called upon to come to judge, not them alone, but the whole earth; compare my Commentary on Ps. vii. 8, lvi. 8, lix. 6.

The prophet thus passes over, in ver. 5, from the general manifestation of divine justice to its special manifestation among the Covenant-people, and mentions here, as the most prominent points upon which it will be inflicted, Samaria and Jerusalem, the two capitals, from which the apostasy from the Lord spread over the rest of the country. He mentions Samaria first, and then, in vers. 6, 7, he describes its destruction which was brought about by the Assyrians, before he makes mention of that of Jerusalem, because the apostasy took place first in Samaria, and hence the punishment also was hastened on. The latter circumstance, which is merely a consequence of the former, is in an one-sided manner made prominent by the greater number of interpreters, who therein follow the example of *Jerome*. It was at the same time, however, probably the intention of the prophet to be done with Samaria, in order that he might be at liberty to take up exclusively the case of Judah and Jerusalem —the main objects of his prophetic ministry.

He makes the transition to this in ver. 8, by means of the words: " *On that account I will wail and howl, I will go stripped and naked; I will make a wailing like the jackals, and a mourning like the ostriches.*" " *On that account*"—i.e., on account of the judgment upon Judah, to be announced in the subsequent verses. It is commonly supposed that the prophet here speaks in his own person; thus, *e.g.*, *Rosenmüller*: "The prophet mourns in a bitter lamentation for the number and magnitude of the calamities impending over the Israelitish people." But the correct view rather is, that the prophet, when, in his inward vision, he sees the divine judgments not remaining and stopping at Samaria, but poured out like a desolating torrent over Judah and Jerusalem, suddenly sinks his own consciousness in that of his suffering people. We have thus here before us an imperfect symbolical action, similar to that more finished one which occurs in Is. xx. 3, 4, and which can be explained only by a deeper insight into the nature of prophecy, according to which the dramatic character is inseparable from it. The transition from the mere description of what is present in the inward vision only, to the prophet's own action, is, according to this view, very easy. If we confine ourselves to the passage before us, the following

arguments are in favour of our view. 1. The predicates שׁילָל
and עָרוֹם cannot be explained upon the supposition that the prophet describes only his own painful feelings on account of the
condition of his people.   Even if עָרוֹם stood alone, the explanation by "naked," in the sense of "deprived of the usual and
decent dress, and, on the contrary, clothed in dirt and rags,"
would be destitute of all proof and authority. No instance
whatsoever is found of the outward habit of a mourner being
designated as nakedness.   But it is still more arbitrary thus to
deal with שׁילָל, whether it be explained by "deprived of his
mental faculties on account of the unbounded grief of his soul,"
—as is done by several Jewish expositors (who, in the explanation of this passage, would have done much better, had they
followed the Chaldee, in whom the correct view is found; only
that he, giving up the figurative representation, substitutes the
third person for the first, paraphrasing it thus : "On that account they shall wail and howl, they shall go stripped and
naked," etc.),—or by "badly clothed," as is done by the greater
number of Christian expositors.   The signification "robbed,'
"plundered," is the only established one; compare שׁולָל in Job
xii. 17–19.   The parallel passages, in which nakedness appears
as the characteristic feature of the captives taken in war, show
how little we are entitled to depart from the most obvious
signification, in these two words.   Thus we find immediately
afterwards, in ver. 11 : " Pass ye away, ye inhabitants of
Saphir, having your shame naked ;" on which *Michaelis* remarks : " With naked bodies, as is the case with those who are
led into captivity after having been stripped of their clothes."
Thus Is. xx. 3, 4 : " And the Lord said, Like as My servant
Isaiah walketh *naked* and *barefoot* three years, for a sign and
wonder upon Egypt and Ethiopia, so shall the king of Assyria
lead away the prisoners of Egypt, and the prisoners of Ethiopia,
young men and old men, *naked* and *barefoot*;" compare Is.
xlvii. 3.—2. The term הִתְפַּלַּשְׁתִּי, in ver. 10, is in favour of the
supposition, that the prophet here appears as the representative
of the future condition of his people.   The *Imperat. fem.* הִתְפַּלְּשִׁי
of the marginal reading is evidently, as is commonly the case,
only the result of the embarrassment of the Mazorets.   The
reading of the text can be pointed as the first person of the
Preterite only; for the view of *Rosenmüller*, who takes it as the

second person of the Preterite, which here is to have an optative signification, is, grammatically, inadmissible. *Rückert's* explanation, "In the house of *dust (zu Staubheim)*, I have strewed dust upon me," is quite correct. But if *here* we must suppose that the prophet suddenly passes over from the address to his unfortunate people, to himself as their representative, why should not this supposition be the natural one in ver. 8 also?

The correctness of the view which we have given is further strengthened, if we compare the similar lamentations of the prophets in other passages, in all of which the same results will be found. In Jer. xlviii. 31, *e.g.*, "Therefore will I howl over Moab, and cry out over all Moab, over the men of Kir-heres shall *he* groan," the "he" in the last clause sufficiently shows how the "I" in the two preceding clauses, is to be understood, —especially if Is. xvi. 7, "Therefore Moab howleth over Moab," be compared. But if this interpretation be correct in Jeremiah, it must certainly be correct in Is. xv. 5 also: "My heart crieth out over Moab,"—a passage which Jeremiah had in view; and this so much the more, that in Is. xvi. 9–11—where a similar lamentation for Moab occurs: "Therefore do I bewail as for Jazer for the vine of Sibmah; I water thee with my tears, O Heshbon and Elealeh. . . . Therefore my bowels sound like a harp for Moab, mine inward parts for Kirhareseth"—it is quite unsuitable to think of a lamentation of the prophet, which is expressive of his own grief. This was seen by the Chaldee, who renders "*my* bowels" by "bowels of the Moabites,"—a view the correctness of which has been strikingly demonstrated by *Vitringa*: "Although," he says, "the emotion of compassion be by no means unsuitable in the prophet, yet no one will be readily convinced that the prophet was so much concerned for the vines of Sibmah and Jazer, and for the crops of the summer-fruits of a nation hostile and opposed to the people of God, that it should have been for him a cause for lamentation and wailing." In Is. xxi., in the prophecy against Babylon, and in the lamentation in vers. 3, 4, "Therefore are my loins filled with pain, pangs take hold upon me as the pangs of a woman that travaileth, etc., the night of my pleasure has been turned into terror," it is clearly shown in what sense such lamentations are to be understood. By "the night of pleasure," we can, especially by a comparison of Jeremiah, understand only the night of the capture of Baby-

lon, in which the whole city was given up to drunkenness and
riot. But it is impossible that the prophet should say that this
night—the precursor of the long-desired day for Israel—had
been turned for him into terror. Either the whole lamentation
is without any meaning, or the prophet speaks in the name of
Babylon, and that, not of the Babylon of the present, but of
the Babylon of the future. This must be granted, even by
those who assert that this portion was composed at a later
period; so that, even from this quarter, the soundness of our
view cannot be assailed.

In ver. 9, the prophet returns to quiet description, from the
symbolical action to which he had been carried away by his
emotions. The subject of this description he states in the
words: *"It cometh unto Judah; it cometh unto the gate of my
people, unto Jerusalem."* By individualizing, he endeavours to
give a lively view of the thought, and to impress it. He begins
with an allusion to the lamentation of David over Saul and
Jonathan in 2 Sam. i. 17 ff., which is so much the more significant, that in this impending catastrophe, Israel also was to
lose his king (compare iv. 9), and that in it David was to experience the fate of Saul. He then indicates the stations by
which the hostile army advances towards Jerusalem, and describes how, from thence, it spreads over the whole country, even
to its southern boundary, and carries away the inhabitants into
exile. But, in doing so, he always chooses places, whose names
might, in some way, be brought into connection with what they
were now suffering; so that the whole passage forms a chain of
paronomasias. These, however, are not by any means idle
plays. They have, throughout, a practical design. The threatening is thereby to be, as it were, localized. The thought of a
divine judgment could not but be called forth in every one who
should think of one of the places mentioned. Jerusalem is first
spoken of in ver. 9 as the centre of the life of Judah: "The
gate of my people," etc., being tantamount to *"the* city or
metropolis of it." Then, it appears a second time in ver. 12,
in the middle between five Judean places preceding and five
following it,—the number ten, which is the symbolical signification of completeness, indicating that the judgment is to be
altogether comprehensive. The five places mentioned after
Jerusalem are all of them situated to the south of it. That the

five places, the mention of which precedes that of Jerusalem, are all to be sought to the north of it, and that, hence, the judgment advances from the north in geographical order, as is the case in Is. x. 28 ff. also, is evident from the fact that Beth-Leaphrah, which is identical with Ophrah, is situated in the territory of Benjamin, and that Beth-Haezel, which is identical with Azal in Zech. xiv. 5, was situated in the neighbourhood of Jerusalem. Hence, we cannot suppose that Zaanan here is identical with Zenan, which is situated in the south of Jerusalem, Josh. xv. 37, nor Saphir with Samir.

The question still arises, In what event did the threatening of punishment, contained in chap. i., find its fulfilment? *Theodoret, Cyril, Tarnovius, Marckius, Jahn*, and others, refer it to the Assyrian invasion. *Jerome* referred it to the Babylonish captivity: "The same sin," he says, "yea, the same punishment of sin which shall overturn Samaria, is to extend to Judah, yea, even unto the gates of my city of Jerusalem. For, as Samaria was overturned by the Assyrians, so Judah and Jerusalem shall be overturned by the Chaldeans." This opinion was adopted by *Michaelis* and others.

At first sight, it would appear as if the circumstance, that the judgment upon Judah is brought into immediate connection with that upon Israel, favoured the first view. But this argument loses its weight when we remark, that the events appear to the prophet in inward vision, and, therefore, quite irrespective of their relation in time; that the continuity of the punitive judgment upon Israel and Judah only, points out distinctly the truth, that both proceed from the same cause, viz., the relation of divine justice to the sin of the Covenant-people. It is this truth alone which forms the essence and soul of the prophetic threatenings; and with reference to that, the difference in point of time, which is merely accidental, is altogether kept out of view. Another argument in favour of the Assyrian invasion might be derived from the expression, "*to* Jerusalem," in ver. 9, inasmuch as the Chaldean invasion visited Jerusalem itself. But, because the calamity was not by any means to stop at Judah, but to overflow even it, it is shown by the preceding expression, "unto Judah," that עַד (compare on this word, *Dissertations on the Genuineness of Daniel*, p. 55 seq.) must, in both cases, be explained from a tacit antithesis with the expectation, that the judgment would either stop at the boundary of Judah, or, although this should not be the case, would at least spare the metropolis. The prophet contents himself with representing that this opinion was erroneous. Although this passage itself asserts nothing upon the point as to whether Jerusalem itself is to be thought of as the object of the divine punishment, or whether it will be spared, the following reasons show that the former will be the case. Even ver. 5 does not admit of our expecting anything else. Jerusalem is there marked out as the chief seat and source of corruption in the kingdom of Judah, just as is Samaria in the kingdom of Israel. The declaration which is there made forms the foundation of the subsequent threatening. How is it possible, then, that, while in the kingdom of Israel it is concentrated upon Samaria, in the kingdom of Judah the seducer should be altogether passed over, and punishment announced to the seduced only? That such is not the intention of the prophet, is clearly seen from ver. 12 : *"For evil cometh down from the Lord upon the gate of Jerusalem."* The כי alone is sufficient to prevent our limiting the sense of these words, so that they mean only that evil will come no farther than to the gate of Jerusalem, and will stop there. The *Particula causalis* proves that they are the ground of the declaration in ver. 11, and that the mourning will not cease at Beth-Haezel, "the house of stopping;" compare the remarks on Zech. xiv. 5. But, altogether apart from this connection, the words themselves furnish a proof. They contain a verbal reference to the description of the judgment upon Sodom and Gomorrha, Gen. xix. 24. Jerusalem is marked out by them as a second Sodom (compare Is. i. 10), upon which the divine judgments would discharge themselves. As a second mark of this extension to Jerusalem, the carrying away of the people into captivity is added (compare vers. 11, 15, 16), which, in the promise in chap. ii. 12, 13, is supposed to have taken place. It is not Israel alone, but the whole Covenant-people, who are in a state of dispersion, and are gathered from it by the Lord.

Now, both of these marks are not applicable to the Assyrian invasion; and if once we suppose the divine illumination of the prophet, it cannot be regarded as the real object of his threatenings. This, too, is equally inadmissible, if we consider the matter from a merely human point of view. The predictions

of the prophets with regard to Assyria are, from the very outset, rather encouraging. It is true that they are to be, in the
hand of the Lord, a rod of chastisement for His people, but
these are never to be altogether given up to them for destruction. By an immediate divine interference, their plan of cap-
turing Jerusalem is frustrated. Thus the matter is constantly
represented in Isaiah; thus also in Hosea i. 7. We can, moreover, adduce proofs from Micah himself, that his spiritual eye
was not pre-eminently, or exclusively, directed to the Assyrians.
In the prophecy from chap. iii. to v., where he describes the
judgment upon Judah in a manner altogether similar to that
in which he mentions it here, he passes over the Assyrians altogether in silence. Babylon is, in iv. 10, mentioned as the place
to which Judah is to be led into captivity.

Yet here, as well as everywhere else in the threatenings and
promises of the prophets, we must beware, lest, in referring
them to some particular historical event, we lose sight of the
animating idea. If this, on the other hand, be rightly understood, it will be seen that a particular historical event may indeed be pre-eminently referred to, but that it can never exhaust
the prophecy. Although, therefore, the main reference here
be to the destruction by the Chaldeans, we must not on that
account exclude anything in which the same law of retaliation
was manifested, either before, as in the invasion of the Syrians
and Assyrians; or afterwards, as in the destruction by the
Romans. The prophet himself points, in iv. 11–14 (iv. 11–v. 1),
to two other phases of the divine judgment which are to follow
upon that by the Chaldeans.

After the prophet has thus hitherto described the impending
divine judgment in great general outlines, he passes on, in chap.
ii., to chastise particular vices, which, however, must always be
at the same time, yea, prominently, considered as indications of
the wholly depraved condition of the nation, and of the punishments to follow upon it. One feature upon which he here
chiefly dwells, and which must, therefore, have been a peculiarly
prominent manifestation of the sinful corruption, consists in the
acts of injustice and oppression committed by the great, the
description of which presents striking resemblances to that in
Is. v. 8 ff. The prophet interrupts this description only in order

2 E

to rebuke the false prophets, who reproved him for the severity of his discourses, and asserted that they were unworthy of the merciful God. Such severity, answered the prophet, was true mildness, because it alone could be the means of warding off the approaching punitive judgment; that his God did not punish from want of forbearance—from want of mercy; but that the fault was altogether that of the transgressors, who drew down upon themselves, by force, His judgments.[1]

The prophecy closes with the promise in vers. 12, 13. It is introduced quite abruptly, in order to place it in more striking contrast with the threatening; just as, in iv. 1, there is a similar abrupt and unconnected contrast between the promise and the threatening.[2] It is only brief; far more so than in the subsequent discourses, and far less detailed than it is in them. The prophet desires first of all to terrify sinners from their security; and for this reason, he causes only a very feeble glimmering of hope to fall upon the dark future.

Ver. 12. " *I will assemble, surely I will assemble, O Jacob, thee wholly : I will gather the remnant of Israel. I will bring*

---

[1] Ver. 6 must be translated thus : " *Not shall ye drop* (prophesy),—*they* (the false prophets) *drop ; if they* (the individuals addressed, the true prophets) *do not drop to these* (the rapacious great), *the ignominy will not cease,* *i.e.,* the ignominious destruction breaks in irresistibly. The fundamental passage in Deut. xxxii. 2, and ver. 11 of the chapter before us, show that הטיף has not the signification, " to talk," which is assigned to it by *Caspari*. The false prophets must be considered as the accomplices of the corrupted great, especially as to the bulwark which they opposed to the true prophets, and their influence on the nation, and on their own consciences, —as indeed material power everywhere seeks for such a spiritual ally. If this be kept in view, the censure and threatening acquire a still greater unity.

[2] To a certain extent, however, verse 11 forms the transition: " If one were to come, a wind, and lie falsely : I will prophesy to thee of wine and of strong drink,—he would be the prophet of this people." Such a prophet Micah, indeed, is not ; but although he neither can nor dare announce salvation *without* judgment, he has, in the name of the Lord, to announce salvation *after* the judgment. The very singular opinion, that in vers. 12, 13, the false prophets are introduced as speaking, is refuted by the single circumstance that, in ver. 12, the gathering of the *remnant* of Israel only is promised, and hence the judgment is supposed to have preceded. It is no less erroneous if, instead of considering ver. 11 as introductory to vers. 12, 13, the latter be made to depend upon ver. 11, and be therefore considered as, to a certain extent, accidental.

them together as the sheep of Bozrah ; as a flock on their pasture, they shall make a noise by reason of men. Ver. 13. *The breaker goeth up before them; they break through, pass through the gate and go out, and their King marches before them, and the Lord is on the head of them."*

The remark, that almost all the features of this description are borrowed from the deliverance out of Egypt, will throw much light upon the whole description. In the midst of oppression and misery, Israel, while there, increased by means of the blessing of the Lord, hidden under the cross, to greater and greater numbers; compare Exod. i. 12. When the time of deliverance had arrived, the Lord, who had for a long time concealed Himself, manifested Himself again as their God. First, the people were gathered together, and then, the Lord went before them,—in a pillar of cloud by day, and in a pillar of fire by night: Exod. xiii. 21. He led them out of Egypt, the house of bondage: Exod. xx. 2. So it is here also. Ver. 12 describes the increase and gathering, and ver. 13 the deliverance. In both passages, Israel's misery is represented under the figure of an abode in the house of bondage, or in prison, the gates of which the Lord opens—the walls of which He breaks down. In this allusion to, and connection with, the former deliverance, Micah agrees with his contemporaries, Hosea and Isaiah. The deeper reason of this lies in the typical import of the former deliverance, which forms a prophecy by deeds of all future deliverances, and contains within itself completely their germ and pledge; compare Hosea ii. 1, 2 (i. 10, 11); Is. xi. 11 ff.: "And the Lord shall stretch forth His hand a *second time* to redeem the remnant of His people. . . . . And He sets up an ensign for the nations, and gathers together the dispersed of Israel, and assembles the scattered of Judah from the four corners of the earth. . . . . And the Lord smites with a curse the tongue of the Egyptian sea, and shakes His hand over the river, in the violence of His wind, and smites it to seven rivers, so that one may wade through in shoes. And there shall be a highway to the remnant of His people, ... like as it was to Israel in the day when he came up out of the land of Egypt." This reference to the typical deliverance clearly shows, that in the description we have carefully to separate between the thought and the language in which it is clothed.

Ver. 12. The *Infin. absol.*, which in both the clauses precedes the *tempus finitum*, expresses the emphasis which is to be placed on the *gathering*, as opposed to the carrying away, and the scattering formerly announced ; for the latter, according to the view of man, and apart from God's mercy and omnipotence, did not seem to admit of any favourable turn. By " Jacob" and " Israel," several interpreters understand Judah alone ; others, the ten tribes alone ; others, both together. The last view is alone the correct one. This appears from i. 5, where, by Jacob and Israel, the whole nation is designated. The promise in the passage before us stands closely related to the threatening uttered there. All Israel shall be given up to destruction on account of their sins ; all Israel shall be saved by the grace of God. This assumption is confirmed by a comparison of the parallel passages in Hosea and Isaiah, where the whole is designated by the two parts, Judah and Israel. Micah does not notice this division, because that visible separation, which even in the present was overbalanced by an invisible unity, shall disappear altogether in that future, when there shall be only one flock, as there is only one Shepherd. The expression, " remnant of Israel," in the second clause, which corresponds to, " O Jacob, thee wholly," in the first, indicates, that the fulfilment of the promise, so far from doing away with the threatening, rather rests on its preceding realization. The Congregation of God, purified by the divine judgments, shall be *wholly* gathered. Divine mercy has in itself no limits ; and those which in the present are assigned to it by the objects of mercy, shall then be removed.—The words, " I will bring them together," etc., indicate equally the faithfulness of the great Shepherd, who gathers His dispersed flock from all parts of the world, and the unexpected and wonderful increase of the flock ; compare Jer. xxiii. 3 : " And I will gather the remnant of My flock out of all countries whither I have driven them, and lead them back to their pasture-ground, and they are fruitful and increase ;" and xxxi. 10 : " He that scattereth Israel will gather him and keep him as a shepherd does his flock."—Bozrah we consider to be the name of a capital of the Idumeans in Auranitis, four days' journey from Damascus. The great wealth of this town in flocks appears from Is. xxxiv. 6 (although a slaughter of men is spoken of in that passage, yet evidently the wealth of Bozrah in natural flocks is there supposed), and can with perfect ease be accounted for from its situation. For, in its neighbourhood, there begins the immeasurable plain of Arabia, which, on one side, continues without interruption as far as *Dshof*, into the heart of Arabia, while, towards the North, it extends to Bagdad, under the name of *El Hamad*. Its length and breadth are calculated to amount to eight days' journey. It contains many shrubs and blooming plants; compare *Burkhardt* and *Ritter*.[1] Several interpreters consider בצרה to be an appellative, and assign to it the signification "sheepfold," " cote." But there is no reason whatsoever in favour of such a meaning of Bozrah, while there is this argument against it, that the probable signification of בצרה as the name of a town is "*locus munitus*" = מִבְצָר or בָּצְרוֹן. It can hardly be supposed that the word should at the same time have had the significations of "fortress" and "fold." It is, moreover, more in harmony with the prophetical character to particularize, than to use a general term. As is shown, however, by the last member (with which, according to the accents, the words, " As

---

[1] After the example of *v. Raumer, Robinson, Ritter* (*Erdk.* 14, 101), it has now become customary to distinguish between two Bozrahs,—one in Auranitis, and the other in Edom. But the arguments adduced for this distinction are not of very great weight. Nowhere is a "high situation" in reality ascribed to the Bozrah in Edom. The assertion, that Edom was always limited to the territory between the Dead Sea and the Red Sea, is opposed to Gen. xxxvi. 35, according to which passage, even in the time before Moses, the Edomitic king, Hadad, smote Midian in the field of Moab; and further, to Lam. iv. 21, according to which Edom dwells in the land of Uz, which can be sought for only in *Arabia Deserta*. We need to think only of that branch of the Midianites who had gone over to *Arabia Deserta*, whilst their chief settlement continued in *Arabia Petræa*. But the following arguments may be adduced *against* the distinction. 1. Bozrah is constantly and simply spoken of, without any further distinctive designation. 2. The Edomitic Bozrah must have been a great and powerful city, which agrees well with the "mighty ruins" in *Hauran*, but not with the much more insignificant ruins near *Busseireh* in *Dshebal*. 3. It is improbable that so important a city as that of Bozrah in Auranitis should never have been mentioned in Scripture.—But not satisfied with a double Bozrah, even a third, in Moab, has been assumed on the ground of Jer. xlviii. 24. But it is certainly strange that Bozrah, in that passage, is mentioned as the last of all the Moabitish towns, and that, immediately after its mention, there follow the words, "Upon all the cities of the land of Moab, far and near." It may be that Bozrah was conquered by the Edomites and Moabites in common, or that, in later times, the latter obtained a kind of possession of the town in common with the former.

a flock on their pasture," must be connected), the point of comparison is not the assembling and gathering, but the multitude, the crowd,—"As the sheep of Bozrah" being thus tantamount to, "So that in multitude they are like the sheep of Bozrah." הַדִּבְרוֹ, from דֹּבֶר, is, contrary to the general rule, doubly qualified, both by the article and by the suffix. This has been accounted for on the ground that the little suffix had gradually lost its power. But it is perhaps more natural to suppose that the article sometimes lost its power, and coalesced with the noun. The frequent use of the *Status emphaticus* in undefined nouns, in the Syriac language (compare *Hofmann, Gram. Syr.*, p. 290), presents an analogy in favour of this opinion.—The last words graphically describe the noise produced by a numerous, closely compacted flock. The plur. of the Fem. refers to the sheep.—מִן denotes the *causa efficiens*. They make a noise; and this noise proceeds from the numerous assembled people. The same connection of figure and thing occurs in Ezek. xxxiv. 31: "And ye (וְאַתֵּן) are My flock, the flock of My pasture are ye men;" compare Ezek. xxxvi. 38.

Ver. 13. The whole verse must be explained by the figure of a prison, which lies at the foundation. The people of God are shut up in it, but are now delivered by God's powerful hand. By the "breaker," many interpreters understand the Lord Himself. But if we consider, that in a double clause, at the end of the verse, the Lord is mentioned as the leader of the expedition if we look to the type of the deliverance from Egypt, where Moses, as the breaker, marches in front of Israel; and if, further, we look to the parallel passage in Hosea, where, with an evident allusion to that type, the children of Israel and of Judah appoint themselves one head; we shall rather be disposed to understand by the "breaker" the *dux* et *antesignanus* raised up by God. With the raising up and equipping of such a leader every divine deliverance commences; and that which, in the inferior deliverance, the typical leaders, Moses and Zerubbabel, were, Christ was in the highest and last deliverance. To Him the "breaker" has been referred by several Jewish interpreters (compare *Schöttgen, Horæ* ii. p. 212); and if we compare chap. v., where that which is here indicated by general outlines only is further expanded and detailed, we shall have to urge against this interpretation this objection only, viz., that it excludes the typical breakers,—that, in the place of the *ideal* person of the breaker, which presents itself to the internal vision of the prophet, it puts the individual in whom this idea is most fully realized. —The words ויעברו שער are, by several interpreters, referred to the forcing and entering of hostile gates. Thus *Michaelis*, whom *Rosenmüller* follows: " No gate shall be so fortified as to prevent them from forcing it." But this interpretation destroys the whole figure, and violates the type of the deliverance from Egypt which lies at the foundation. For the gate through which they break is certainly the gate of the prison.—The three verbs—" They break through, they pass through, they go out" —graphically describe their progress, which is not to be stopped by any human power.—The last words open up the view to the highest leader of the expedition; compare besides, Exod. xiii. 21; Is. lii. 12 : " For ye shall not go out in trembling, nor shall ye go out by flight. For the Lord goeth before you, and the God of Israel closeth your rear;" Is. xl. 11; Ps. lxxx. 3. In the exodus from Egypt, a visible symbol of the presence of God marched before the host, besides Moses, the breaker. On the return from Babylon, the Angel of the Lord was visible to the eye of faith only, as formerly when Abraham's servant journeyed to Mesopotamia, Gen. xxiv. 7. At the last and highest deliverance, the breaker was at once the King and God of the people.

As this prophecy has no limitation at all in itself, we are fully entitled to refer it to the whole sum of the deliverances and salvation which are destined for the Covenant-people; and to seek for its fulfilment in every event, either past or future, in the same degree as the fundamental idea—God's mercy upon His people—is manifested in it. Every limitation to any particular event is evidently inadmissible; but, most of all, a limitation to the deliverance from the Babylonish captivity, which, especially with regard to Israel, can be considered as only a faint prelude of the fulfilment. They, however, have come nearest to the truth who assume an exclusive reference to Christ,—provided they acknowledge, that the conversion of the first fruits of Israel, at the time when Christ appeared in His humiliation, is not the end of His dealings with this people.

CHAP. III.–V.

The discourse opens with new reproofs and threatenings.
It is *first*, in vers. 1–4, directed against the rapacious great, who
in ver. 2 are described as murderers of men (compare Sirach
xxxi. 21: "He who taketh from his neighbour his livelihood,
killeth him"), and in ver. 3, as eaters of men, because they turn
to their own advantage the necessaries of life of which they have
robbed the poor. The discourse *then* passes over to the false
prophets, vers. 5–7. Their character is described as hypocritical, weak, and selfish, and is incidentally contrasted with the
character of the true prophet, as represented by himself, whose
strength is always renewed by the Spirit of the Lord, and who,
in this strength, serves only truth and righteousness, and holds
up their sins to the people deluded by the false prophets, ver. 8.
This the prophet continues to do in vers. 9–12. The three orders
of divinely called rulers, upon whom the life or death of the
Congregation was depending,—the princes, the priests, and the
prophets (compare remarks on Zech. x. 1),—have become so
degenerate, that they are not at all concerned for the glory of
God, but only for their own interest. And while they have
thus inwardly apostatized from Jehovah, they are strengthened
in their false security by the promises which God has given to
His people, and which they, altogether overlooking the fact that
these are conditional, referred, in hypocritical blindness, to themselves. But God will, in a fearful manner, punish them for this
apostasy, and frighten them from their security. The Congregation of the Lord, which has been desecrated inwardly, shall be
so outwardly also. Zion shall become a corn-field; Jerusalem,
the city of God, shall sink into rubbish and ruins; the Temple-
hill shall again become what it was previous to its being the
residence of God, viz., a thickly wooded hill, which shall then
appear in all its natural lowness, and be considered as insignificant when compared with the neighbouring mountains.—In the
whole section, the twelve verses of which are equally divided
into three portions of four verses each, the prophet views chiefly
the great, and the civil rulers. The false prophets, whom he
takes up in the second of these subdivisions (vers. 5–8), come
under consideration as their helpers only. In the third subdi-

vision, the discourse is again directed to the great alone, in vers. 9, 10. The two other orders are added to them in vers. 11, 12 only; and the charges raised against them refer to their relation to the great. The *priests* are not by any means reproved because they made teaching a profession, from which they derived their livelihood, but because, for bribes, they interpreted the law in a manner favourable to the rapacious lusts of the great, and thereby, no less than the false prophets, assisted them in their wickedness.—The charge raised in ver. 10 against the great,—"Building up Zion with blood, and Jerusalem with iniquity,"—has been frequently misunderstood. The words must not be explained from Hab. ii. 12, but from Ps. li. 20, where David prays to the Lord, "Build Thou the walls of Jerusalem," which he had destroyed by his blood, ver. 16. The word "building" is used ironically by Micah, and is tantamount to: "Ye who are destroying Jerusalem by blood and iniquity (compare ver. 12: 'For your sakes Zion shall be ploughed as a field'), instead of building it up by righteousness." Righteousness builds up, because it draws down God's blessing and protection; but unrighteousness destroys, because it calls down the curse of God.

The unfaithfulness of the Covenant-people can nevertheless not make void the faithfulness of God. The prophet, therefore, passes suddenly from threatening to promise. *Calvin* thus expresses the relation of these two: "But I must now come to the little remnant. Hitherto I have spoken about the judgment of God, which is near at hand, upon the king's councillors, upon the priests and prophets, upon the whole people in short, because they are all wicked and ungodly, because the whole body is pervaded by contempt of God, and by desperate obstinacy. Let them receive, then, that which they all have deserved. But I now gather the children of God apart, for to them too I have a message to deliver."

The intimate relation of the first part of the promise to the preceding threatening has been already demonstrated, p. 420. The Mount of Zion, which forms the subject of vers. 1–7, shall, in future, not only be restored to its former dignity, but it shall be exalted above all the mountains of the earth. The kingdom of God, which is represented by it, shall, by the glory imparted to it by a new revelation of the Lord (compare ver. 7: "And the Lord shall be King over them on Mount Zion "), outshine all the kingdoms of the world, and exercise an attractive power upon their citizens; so that they flow to Zion, there to receive the commands of the Lord, vers. 1, 2. By the sway which the Lord exercises from Zion, peace shall have its dwelling in the heathen world, ver. 3, and, consequently, the Congregation of the Lord ceases to be a prey to injury from the world's power, ver. 4ᵃ. How incredible soever it may appear, this promise shall surely be fulfilled; for omnipotent faithfulness has given it, ver. 4ᵇ, and has given it indeed for this very purpose; for·it is altogether natural, and to be expected, that the glory of the Lord should in all eternity display itself in His dealings with His people, ver. 5. In vers. 6, 7, the promise receives a new impetus, by which it connects itself with ver. 4ᵃ. In that time of mercy, the Lord will put an end to all the misery of His people.

Ver. 1. "*And it shall come to pass at the end of the days, that the mountain of the house of the Lord shall be firmly established on the top of the mountains, and exalted above the hills, and people flow unto it.*"

The words, "And it shall come to pass," excite the attention to the great and unexpected turn which things are to take. The expression, באחרית הימים, is explained by many as meaning: "In times to come," "in future." But we have already proved, in our work on *Balaam*, p. 465 seq., that the right explanation is: "At the end of the days." This is the explanation given by the LXX. also, who commonly render it by ἐν ταῖς ἐσχάταις ἡμέραις; and by the Chaldee Paraphrast, who translates it by בסוף יומיא. The reasons which seem, at first sight, to favour the signification "in future," are invalidated by these two considerations:—*first*, that it is not at all necessary that the *end* be just absolutely the last, but only the end of those events which the speaker is reviewing; and, *second*, that it altogether depends upon the will of the speaker, what extent he is to assign to the beginning and to the end. The expression is used by the prophets in a manner different from that of the Pentateuch. The prophets use it almost exclusively with a reference to the Messianic times,—an *usus loquendi* which originated in Deut. iv. 30. They divide the whole duration of the kingdom of God into two parts, the beginning and the end,—the state of humiliation, and

the state of glorification. The line of demarcation is formed
by the birth of the Messiah, according to v. 2 (3) : " He will
give them up until she who is bearing brings forth."—"The
mountain of the house of the Lord " is, according to the common *usus loquendi*, not Moriah, but the whole mountain of Zion,
of which Moriah was considered as a part; compare Ps. lxxvi.
3, lxxviii. 68. In ver. 8, the prophet speaks of two parts only,
Zion and Jerusalem. In iii. 12, Zion only, as the better part, is
first spoken of; and then, in the second clause, Jerusalem and
the mountain of the house, the latter corresponding to Zion,
are contrasted with each other, or Jerusalem and Mount Zion
considered in its highest quality as the temple-mountain.—
נכון, " fixed," " firmly established," implies more than, simply,
" placed." It shows that the change is not merely momentary,
but that the temple-mountain shall be exalted for ever, and
that no earthly power shall be able to abase it. It thus goes
hand in hand with the declaration in ver. 7: " The Lord shall
be king over them from now *until eternity*." The same word
נכון is used in 1 Kings ii. 45 of the immutable firmness of the
throne of David : " The throne of David shall be firmly established before the Lord for ever;" compare 2 Sam. vii. 12, 13.
The commentary on נכון is given by Dan. ii. 44: " And in the
days of these kings shall the God of heaven set up a kingdom
which shall not be destroyed in all eternity . . . . it shall
break in pieces and destroy all these kingdoms, and it shall stand
for ever." That בראש ההרים does not mean, " at the head of
the mountains," *i.e.*, standing at the head, as the first among
them (as *Hitzig* and others think), but " on the summit of the
mountains" (the ב is used in a similar manner in Judg. ix. 7,
compared with 1 Sam. xxvi. 13), is evident from the fact that
בראש, in connection with הר, is constantly used of the summit
of the mountains, and, hence, cannot be used in a figurative
sense, in this connection. The sense can therefore be this
only : " Zion, in future, so pre-eminently stands out from
among the other mountains, that these serve, as it were, only
for its foundation." Now, the elevation of the temple-mountain is considered, by several interpreters, as a *physical* one.
Passages from Jewish commentaries, in which the expectation
is expressed that, in the days of the Messiah, Jehovah would
bring near Mount Carmel and Tabor, and place Jerusalem on

the summit of them, will be found in *Galatinus, de Arcanis Catholicæ Veritatis*, L. v. c. 3. The literal explanation has, in recent times, been defended by *Hofmann* and *Drechsler*. But *Caspari*, by pointing out the exact correspondence between the words, "The mountain of the house of the Lord shall be firmly established on the top of the mountains," and the words in ver. 2, "The law shall go forth of Zion, and the word of the Lord from Jerusalem," has proved in a very striking manner that the elevation is a moral one. " As 1^b corresponds to 2^a, so does 1^a to 2^b; ver. 1^a is the ground of ver. 1^b; ver. 2^a, by which ver. 1^b is further expanded, is the consequence of 2^b. Hence 2^b must be substantially identical with ver. 1^a; but 2^b speaks of something that points to the moral height of Mount Zion, and states something upon which it is based." To this it may be added, that height, in a moral sense, is often ascribed to the temple-mountain, even with reference to the ante-Messianic time, and that the passage under consideration could be disjoined from these by force only. It is upon such a view of it, indeed, that the use of עלה in reference to the journeys to Jerusalem rests, just as it is here used in ver. 2. We may, moreover, compare Ps. xlviii. 3; Ezek. xvii. 22, 33: "And I plant upon a mountain high and elevated. On the high mountains of Israel I will plant it;" but especially Ps. lxviii. 16: "Mountain of God is the mountain of Bashan, the top of mountains is the mountain of Bashan." Ver. 17. "Why do ye tops of mountains insidiously observe the mountain which God desireth for His residence? Yea, the Lord will dwell in it for ever." The mountain of God is, in these verses, an emblem of the kingdoms of the world, which are powerful through God's grace. In ver. 16, the Psalmist declares what the mountain of Bashan is. In ver. 17, he rejects the unfounded claims which it raises on account of its real advantages. Although it be great, yet Mount Zion is infinitely greater, and vain are all its efforts to overturn this relation. This passage, then, leads to another argument against the literal interpretation. We find in it the kingdoms represented under the figure of mountains,[1]—a mode of representation which is of very frequent occurrence in Scripture; compare my Commentary on

---

[1] We must not by any means suppose, as has been done last of all by *Caspari*, that the mountains are here regarded as places of worship.

Ps. lxv. 7, lxxvi. 5; Rev. viii. 8, xvii. 9. The more difficult it was to separate, according to the Israelitish conception, *mountain* and *kingdom*, the more natural it was to find, in the passage before us, expression given to the thought, that the kingdom of God would, in future, be exalted above all the kingdoms of the world. If we take into account the common practice of employing "mountain" in a figurative sense, it is natural to suppose that not the exaltation alone is to be understood figuratively, but that the mountain itself also is to be regarded chiefly in its symbolical signification,—as the symbol of the kingdom of God in Israel; although, in this aspect, we should expect, at least in the beginning of the relation, that the thing itself should still be connected with the symbol; afterwards they may be disjoined without any hesitation. The deep grief which must, of necessity, have been called forth by the announcement in iii. 12, did not regard the mountain as such. It had, for its real object, the condition of the kingdom of God which was prefigured by the condition of the mountain; and it is just this to which the consolation has respect.—But by what means is the exaltation of the temple-mountain to be effected? *Cocceius* has already directed attention to the circumstance, that it must not be supposed to consist in the flowing of the people unto it; for that is not the *cause*, but the *effect*. We find the correct answer in ver. 2: "The law goeth forth of Zion, and the word of the Lord from Jerusalem;" and in ver. 7: "And the Lord will be king over them on Mount Zion." The exaltation will, accordingly, be effected by a glorious manifestation of the Lord within His congregation; in consequence of which, Zion becomes the centre of the whole earth. That this manifestation is to take place in Christ, is brought out only subsequently; compare especially, v. 1, 3 (2–4). A parallel passage is also Ezek. xl. 2, where Mount Zion is likewise seen exalted in the Messianic time.

Ver. 2. "*And many nations go and say, Come and let us go up to the mountain of the Lord, and to the house of the God of Jacob, that He may teach us His ways, and that we may walk in His path; for from Zion the law shall go forth, and the word of the Lord from Jerusalem.*"

From the words, "And many nations go," to "paths," we have an expansion of—"People flow unto it." Zech. viii. 20–23 are founded upon, and serve as a commentary on the passage be-

fore us. The people go to one another, and send messengers to
one another; a powerful commotion pervades the heathen world,
which causes them to seek Zion, that had formerly been despised
by them. It makes no substantial difference whether the going
is to be understood physically or spiritually,—whether the people
flow to the literal Mount Zion, or to the Church, which is thereby
prefigured. All that is requisite is, that the commencement of
their going and flowing must belong to a time in which the
symbol and the thing symbolized were still connected,—when
the literal Zion was still the seat of the Church. The *plurality*
of nations forms a contrast with the *unity*, but not with the
universality, as is shown by a comparison of the parallel passage
in Isaiah, where the "many people" are preceded by the mention
of "all the heathens (כל־הגוים, *i.e.*, the whole heathen world)
flow unto it," instead of—"People flow unto it," as in Micah.
Formerly, *one* people only went to Zion, in order there to offer
to the Lord their worship, and to be taught His ways, Exod.
xxiii. 17, xxxiv. 23; Deut. xxxi. 10 sqq.; now, many people
flow thither. In the anticipation of this future glory of Mount
Zion, which will infinitely outshine that of the present, the sad
interval described in iii. 12, during which the mountain of the
house is altogether forsaken, may be more easily borne. · The
connection of הורה with מן, which is rather uncommon, may be
most simply explained by viewing the instruction as proceeding
from its object. "The ways of the Lord" are the ways in
which He would have men to walk,—that mode of life which is
well-pleasing to Him. The contrast of it is walking in one's
own ways, Is. liii. 6,—regulating of one's life according to the
desires of one's own corrupt heart.—The last words, "For from
Zion, etc.," are not to be conceived of as spoken by the people,
stirring up and encouraging one another, but by the prophet.
They state the reason why the people are so anxious to go to
Zion; and this accounts also for the circumstance that Zion is so
emphatically placed at the beginning. Zion shall, at that time,
be the residence of the true God, and proved to be such by
glorious revelations; and from it His commands go forth over
the whole earth. יצא, "to go out," stands here, as in ver. 1, in
the sense of "to go forth." As the sphere for the going forth of
the law from Zion is not limited, it must be considered in as
wide an extent as possible; in harmony with the preceding words,

according to which we must think of "people," "many nations," as being comprehended within this sphere.—We must not overlook the fact that the article is awanting before תורה, and that the law is not more strictly defined as the law of God. It is intended, in the first place, only to indicate that despised and desolate Zion is to be the seat of legislation for the whole earth. The law itself is then more strictly defined as the word of God. Many interpreters understand תורה here as meaning religion in general;[1] the going forth is explained by them of its spreading itself. From Zion, true religion is to extend over all the nations; and hence it is that to Zion the eyes of all of them are directed. Thus, e.g., *Theodoret*, who remarks: "This is the preaching of the Gospel, which began at Jerusalem, and from thence, as from its source, flowed over all the earth, offering drink to those who came to it in faith." But תורה never signifies "doctrine," "religion," any more than does משפט: it is always used as meaning "law;" and this sense of it can with the less propriety be departed from here, as the people, according to what precedes, flow to Zion not in order to seek religion in general, but laws for their conduct in life. But even if we were to follow *Caspari*, and to modify the explanation thus, "The law, which was formerly confined to Zion, and hence to a narrow circle, shall go forth from thence into the wide world,"—weighty objections to it would still remain. If "to go forth" were to be understood as meaning "to spread," the sphere of the going forth would have been more closely determined; as, e.g., in Is. xlii. 1: "He shall bring forth judgment *to the Gentiles*." In Is. li. 4, "Law shall *go out* from Me, and My judgment I will make for a light of the people," *to go out* is tantamount to, *to go forth*. "Mine arms shall judge the people," in li. 5, is parallel to it. יצא in itself does not mean "to go forth." *Further*—The circumstance that the law spreads from Zion, does not account sufficiently for the zeal with which the nations flow to Zion. If it *goes out*, there is then no need for their seeking for it at its home. In Zech. viii. 20–23, also, the thronging of the people to Zion, in order to enter there into a closer relation to the Lord, forms the subject of discourse. Zion, as the place where the Lord of

---

[1] Thus does *Calvin*, who says: "He speaks after the manner of the prophets, who under the term 'law' used to comprehend the whole doctrine of God."

the whole earth issues His orders, as if from His residence (Is. xi. 10), forms an appropriate contrast to "Zion shall be ploughed as a field,"—a suitable parallel to the exaltation of the temple-mountain above all the mountains of the earth, to which the prophet here returns, after having, in the first part of the verse, expanded the thought: "People flow unto it;" and to vers. 7, 8 also, where Zion appears likewise as the seat of dominion.

Ver. 3. "*And He judges among many people, and rebukes strong nations, even unto a distance. And they beat their swords into ploughshares, and their spears into pruning-knives; nation shall not lift up a sword. against nation, neither shall they learn war any more.*"

It appears strange to us that here we see ourselves transferred all at once to the sphere of the general description of the Messianic time; for, according to the whole context, and to the contrast with chap. iii., we expect such predictions as will serve especially for the consolation of the daughter of Zion, whose heart had been pierced by the announcement that the mountain of the house should become a wooded hill, and that she herself should be given into the power of the Gentiles. But this difficulty is removed by remarking that this verse only prepares the way for ver. 4, where there is a representation of the advantage which accrues to the daughter of Zion from the spirit of peace, which, through the powerful influence of Zion's God, has become prevalent in the heathen world. It is from failing to perceive the connection of the two verses, that the remark of *Hitzig* has arisen: "It is very probable that Micah, if he had been the (original) author, would rather have mentioned the change and restoration of Jerusalem, than the change of the arms."—The subject is the Lord. That it was through *Christ*, who as early as in the Song of Solomon appears as the true Solomon, that the Lord would carry out what is here announced, the prophet could, according to his plan, detail only afterwards. In chap. iv. 1–7, he describes how Zion is glorified by what the Lord does from thence; in ver. 8, by the restoration of the dominion of the Davidic race; and in v. 1 ff., by the appearance of the Messiah. It is especially from v. 3 (4), according to which the Messiah stands and feeds in the strength of the Lord, in the majesty of the name of the Lord His God,—and from v. 4 (5), according to which He is the Peace, that we infer with certainty that the judging also shall be done by His mediation. In Isaiah we meet the person of the Messiah in the prophecy of chap. iv., which, along with that in chap. ii., belongs to one discourse, and supplements it. The judging and rebuking (הוכיח with לְ, "to rebuke," "to reprove") refer to the strifes among the nations which hitherto could not be allayed, because there was wanting the counterpoise to selfishness which was productive of wrong. But such a counterpoise is now given in the word of God, which, carried home by His Spirit, penetrates deeply into the heart.—"*Strong* nations," who were hitherto most ready to seize the sword. The words, "And they beat," etc., refer to Joel iv. (iii.) 10, where the heathen beat their ploughshares into swords, their pruning-knives into spears; and they do so to the prejudice of the people of God, which the prophet, although apparently he speaks in general terms, has specially in view. By this allusion Micah indicates that, with reference to the disposition of the heathen world, Joel has spoken a word, true, indeed, but giving only a partial view. The words of *Justinus* in the *Dialogus cum Tryphone*—"For, having learned the fear and worship of God from the Law and Gospel which came to us through the Apostles from Jerusalem, we have fled for refuge to the God of Jacob, and the God of Israel; and we, who formerly were filled with war and murder, and every wickedness, have put away the instruments of war from the whole earth, and have, every one of us, changed the swords into ploughshares, and the spears into agricultural implements, and cultivate the fear of God, justice, brotherly love, faith, hope," etc.,—show that, even soon after the appearance of Christ, it was held that the fulfilment of this prophecy had commenced. But it was acknowledged by the prophet also, that even after the appearance of the salvation, this description would, in the meantime, give only a partial exhibition of the truth; inasmuch as not every one will submit to the judging activity of the Lord, how powerful soever may be the effect of the new principle which entered into the life of the nations; for in v. 4, 5 (5, 6) he speaks of the nations which, in the Messianic time, attack the people of God; in ver. 8 (9), of their adversaries and enemies; and in ver. 14 (15), of such as do not hear. But the

2 F

imperfect fulfilment is a pledge and guarantee for that which is perfect, as it will take place when, by the last judgment, they have been removed who have obstinately preserved within themselves the spirit of strife and hatred.   According to the predictions of the prophets—compare especially Is. xi. 6, 7—peace shall, at some future period, be extended even to the irrational creation, and the strife which has come upon earth by the fall, shall entirely cease from it.

Ver. 4. "*And they sit every man under his vine, and under his fig-tree, and none maketh them afraid; for the mouth of the Lord of hosts hath spoken it.*"

This verse contains a description of the happy consequences which the peaceful influence which goes forth from the Lord to the heathen world, shall have upon Israel.   For Israel is the subject in ישבו, and the verse does not at all pretend to give a description of "a Solomonic time for all the nations."   This is shown by what is stated, in the following verse, as to the ground of this happy change, as well as by a comparison of the fundamental passages, Lev. xxvi. 6: "And I give peace in the land, and ye lie down, and none maketh you afraid;" and 1 Kings v. 5 (iv. 25): "And Judah and Israel dwelt safely every man under his vine and fig-tree, from Dan to Beersheba, all the days of Solomon;" and of the parallel passages, Micah v. 4 (5); Zech. iii. 10. It is *further* shown by the connection with what precedes, where great calamity, and the devastation of their whole country had been predicted to Israel,—and by the mention of the vine and fig-tree, which are characteristic of the land of Israel.   The words, "For the mouth of the Lord," etc., point out the pledge, which the person of Him who promises affords for the fulfilment of the promise, which appears incredible.

Ver. 5. "*For all the nations shall walk, every one in the name of their God; and we will walk in the name of the Lord our God for ever and ever.*"

The causal particle כי states the ground of the fact that the Lord of hosts has spoken this, and given the promise of the final safety of Israel, and of his enjoying peace after the strife, in consequence of God's exercising dominion from Zion over the whole heathen world; while this peace after the strife is then more fully described in vers. 6, 7.   The lot of every people corresponds to the nature of their God.   And now, how could it be otherwise, than that all other nations should be humbled, because their gods are idols, while Israel, on the other hand, is exalted and endowed with everlasting salvation and prosperity, because his God is the only true God? Is. xlv. 16, 17 is parallel: "They shall be ashamed, and also confounded, all of them; they shall go to confusion, the makers of idols. Israel is saved by the Lord, with an everlasting salvation; ye shall not be ashamed nor confounded in all eternity."—"The name of the Lord" is the complex whole of His excellency which is revealed, and proved by deeds; compare Prov. xviii. 10: "The name of the Lord is a strong tower; the righteous runneth into it and is exalted." Inasmuch as the name of the Lord is to manifest itself in His dealings with His people, it represents itself as the way in which they are to walk: the prayer of the Psalmist in Ps. xxv. 5, that the Lord would lead him in His *truth*, forms a parallel to this; and so does also what he says in ver. 9 of the same Psalm, that "He guides the meek in *judgment*." But exactly corresponding is Zech. x. 12: "And I strengthen them in the Lord, and *in His name shall they walk*" = in the path of His name, so that the latter manifests itself in His dealings with them; compare the remarks on that passage. In favour of our exposition, moreover, is the comparison of the passage Is. ii. 5, the evidently requisite harmony of which with the passage under consideration is obtained, only if the latter be understood as we have explained it. The *light*, *i.e.*, the salvation of the Lord spoken of there, corresponds with the *name* of the Lord in the passage under review. Several interpreters explain: "They may walk, they may worship their gods. Although all nations should be idolaters, yet we, inhabitants of Judah, shall faithfully worship Jehovah." Against this explanation *Caspari* remarks, "An exhortation, or a resolution which implies an exhortation, is here not easily justified, because it would stand in the midst of promises." Moreover, the כִּי cannot be explained according to this interpretation, as appears with sufficient clearness from the remark of *Justi*: "This verse does not seem to be so closely connected with the preceding one." The connection is more firmly established by the explanation of *Tarnovius, Michaelis*, and others: "Surely so brilliant a lot must fall to us; for we are faithful worshippers of the true God, while all other nations walk after their idols."

But the objections to this explanation are : (1) the circumstance that it is rather unusual to found the salvation of the people upon their covenant-faithfulness (of which, from the preceding reproof, we cannot entertain very high notions), instead of founding it upon God's grace and faithfulness, compare vii. 18–20;[1] (2) the repeated use of the Future, while, according to it, we should have expected the Preterite, at least in the first member; and (3), and most decisive of all, the expression, "For ever and ever;" compare the expression, "From henceforth, even for ever," in ver. 7.

Ver. 6. *"In that day, saith the Lord, I will assemble that which halteth, and that which hath been driven out I will gather, and that which I have afflicted.* Ver. 7. *And I make that which is halting a remnant, and that which is far off a strong nation, and the Lord reigneth over them in Mount Zion from henceforth, even for ever."*

The expression "in that day" does not refer to "at the end of the days," in ver. 1, but is connected with, and resumes ver. 4ª. That the verb אסף has here the signification " to assemble," and not that " to receive," is shown by ii. 12, and especially by Ezek. xi. 17. The word refers to the announcement of Israel's being carried away, which was formerly made, and with which the scattering is connected. They are assembled for their return to the Holy Land. Such an assembling, however, is meant, as is connected with the full enjoyment of salvation, and in which the Congregation truly manifests itself in a close unity, as a kingdom of priests. In the passage, Zeph. iii. 19, which is founded upon the one under review, we find "I save" instead of "I assemble." Of such a description, the assembling under Zerubbabel was not; compare Nehem. ix. 36, 37. It can therefore come into notice only as a prelude to the true assembling.—"The Fem. sing. of the Partic.," says *Hitzig*, "must be understood collectively; and it is not several subjects, but predicates of the same subject, viz., of the whole of Israel,

---

[1] *Caspari*, indeed, is of opinion, that the walking in the name of the Lord is not to be considered as a merit, on account of which the salvation is granted, but as a mercy which has been bestowed upon Israel, and which forms the ground of the salvation. But this feature is not at all intimated; and we are the less at liberty to introduce it, as the walking in the name of the gods is parallel to the walking in the name of the Lord.

which are thereby designated." The "halting," which is a condition of bodily helplessness and weakness, occurs also in Ps. xxxv. 15, and xxxviii. 18, as a designation of adversity and misery.—The expression, "to make a remnant," forms the contrast to total annihilation. While these words show that a limit will be put to the *diminution*, the following words predict a vast *increase*. In the words, "In Mount Zion," the contrast with iii. 12 appears once more at the close of the section. As regards מלך יהוה, compare Ps. xciii. 1. It does not refer to the constant government of the Lord, but to a new and glorious manifestation of it—as it were to a new ascension to the throne. The expression, " From henceforth," refers to the *ideal* present. In spirit, the prophet is in that time when the Lord is just entering upon His government. The words, "The Lord reigneth . . for ever," are thus beautifully illustrated by *Calvin:* "Micah does not here mention the descendants of David, but Jehovah Himself; not as if he wished thereby to exclude that dominion of David, but in order to show that God would make it manifest that He was the author of that dominion, yea, that He Himself held all the power. For, although God governed the ancient people by the hand of David, and by the hand of Josiah and Hezekiah, *yet there was, as it were, a shadow placed between, so that God's government was then perceived darkly only.* The prophet, therefore, here expresses, that there would be some difference betwixt that shadowy government, and the future new dominion which He was openly to set up by the advent of the Messiah. And this was truly and solidly fulfilled in Christ's person. For although Christ was the true seed of David, yet He was also, at the same time, Jehovah, viz., God made manifest in the flesh." With respect to this promise, however, it must also be kept in mind that it will be finally fulfilled only in the future, when the kingdom and throne of glory (compare Matt. xix. 28) shall be set up.

The prophet had hitherto described the kingdom which was to be established anew, as a kingdom of GOD, without mentioning the channel through which His mercy was to be poured out upon the Congregation—the mediator who was to represent Him among them. His representation, therefore, was still defective; it still wanted the connection with the promise given to David, and so frequently celebrated by him, and by other

holy Psalmists and Prophets—the promise of the eternal dominion of David's house. According to this promise, every new,
great manifestation of grace, must be through some descendant
of this family as a mediator. This house must ever form the
substratum on which the divine power and the divine nature, in
its most complete manifestation, showed themselves. This blank
is supplied in ver. 8.

"*And thou tower of the flock, hill of the daughter of Zion,
unto thee it will come; and to thee cometh the former dominion, the
kingdom of the daughter of Zion.*" .

In the words immediately preceding it is said: "And the
Lord reigneth over them from henceforth, even for ever." We
have here, then, a prediction of the dominion of the house of
David, by whose mediation the Lord is to reign; compare v. 3
(4), where it is said of Him in whom the Davidic race is to
centre, "And He stands, and feeds in the strength of the Lord,
in the majesty of the name of the Lord His God." All interpreters agree that the Davidic race is designated by the "Tower
of the flock," and by "the hill of the daughter of Zion;" but,
with respect to the ground of this designation, they are very
much at variance. A great number of them (*Grotius*, and
among the recent interpreters, *Rosenmüller, Winer, Gesenius,
De Wette*) think of that Tower of the flock, in the neighbourhood of which Jacob, according to Gen. xxxv. 21, took up his
abode for a time. They say that, according to *Jerome*, this
Tower of the flock was situated in the immediate neighbourhood
of Bethlehem; that it is used here only by way of a *metalepsis*
for Bethlehem, and that Bethlehem again designates the Davidic
race; so that the passage agrees altogether with v. 1 (2). But,
upon a closer examination, this interpretation appears to be
objectionable, for the following reasons. 1. It is anything but
fixed that that Tower of the flock was situated in the immediate
neighbourhood of Bethlehem. It cannot be inferred from the
passage in Genesis, and as little can it be proved from *Jerome*.
In the *Quest. ad Genes. Opp.* iii. p. 145, Fref., he first mentions
the opinion of the Jews, according to which, by the "Tower of
the flock" is to be understood the place on which the temple
was afterwards built, and then says: "But if we follow the
direction of the road, we find, by Bethlehem, a 'place of the
shepherds,' which was so called, either because it was there

that, at the birth of the Lord, the angels sang their hymn of praise; or because Jacob fed his flock there, and gave this name to the place; or, which is more likely, because even then the future mystery was, by a revelation, shown to him." According to this, *Jerome* does not know anything of a "Tower of the flock" near Bethlehem. From the direction of the road which Jacob took, he only *surmises* that it was situated thereabouts; and since there was, in the neighbourhood of Bethlehem, a place called "the place of the shepherds," he, from a mere combination, declares this to be identical with the Tower of the flock; while, after all, he is so cautious as not at once to reject the only true derivation of this name from the shepherds at the birth of Christ. By this, the other passage in the book *de locis Hebr.* must be judged, where *Jerome* expressly delivers his supposition as if it were historical truth: "Bethlehem, the city of David . . . . and about a thousand paces (*passus*) distant is the tower *Ader*, which is called 'the Tower of the flock,' indicating that, by some vision, the shepherds had, beforehand, been made conscious of the birth of the Lord." That tradition knew but little of any "Tower of the flock" in the neighbourhood of Bethlehem, appears also from *Eusebius Onom.* s. v. *Gader.* p. 79, ed. *Cleric*: "The tower Gader . . . While Jacob dwelt there, Reuben went in to Bilhah." *Eusebius* evidently knew nothing more regarding the "Tower of the flock" than what we also may learn from the passage in Genesis. He does not venture to offer even a conjecture as to its position. The same ignorance is shown by the Jews, mentioned by *Jerome*, who certainly would not have thought of a reference to the temple, if a place called "Tower of the flock" had existed in the neighbourhood of Bethlehem. 2. But even assuming the existence of the Tower of the flock in the neighbourhood of Bethlehem, is it anything else than the assumption of a pure *quid pro quo*, to assert, without assigning any reason, that the "Tower of the flock" stands for Bethlehem? *Rosenmüller*, at least, has felt this. He makes the attempt to assign a reason: "In substituting, however, an unknown hamlet in the neighbourhood of Bethlehem, for Bethlehem itself, he intended to indicate that the dominion of David would be altogether weakened and brought low." But this reason is certainly not by any means sufficient; Bethlehem was, in itself, so small, that no further diminution was required; compare v. 1 (2). It had, moreover, been always small, and had not by any means sunk down in the course of time from former greatness. Hence, such a designation, in contrast with its former glory, would be entirely out of place; and even supposing that it were not, the mode of this designation would always be inexplicable, unless we could assume a closer reference of the "Tower of the flock" to the Davidic family. It is only by establishing such a reference, that the whole explanation can be saved and confirmed. For this purpose, it would be necessary to suppose that Bethlehem, and the district belonging to it, were the general designation of the native place of the Davidic family, while the "Tower of the flock" was the special one. But there is not the slightest ground on which to support this hypothesis. Everywhere, Bethlehem itself appears as the residence of Jesse, the father of David (compare 1 Sam. xvi. 1, 18, 19, xvii. 12), and likewise of Boaz, Ruth ii. 4.

The incorrectness of another explanation is still more evident. According to it, we are, by the "Tower of the flock," to understand a tower which is alleged to have stood at Jerusalem, near to the Sheep-gate. But the existence of such a tower is supported by no evidence whatsoever, and does not become even probable by the existence of a sheep-gate; for a Tower of the flock is not a tower which stands near the Sheep-gate, but a tower which is erected for the protection of the flock, as is clearly seen from *Migdal Eder* in Genesis. But, even supposing that such a tower existed, is there anything which could somehow make it a suitable designation of the Davidic family?

Let us now proceed to the establishment of our own opinion, by which the arguments advanced against the other explanations will be considerably strengthened. Concerning the situation of Jerusalem, *Josephus, de B. J.* i. 6, c. 13, remarks as follows: "It was built on two hills fronting each other, separated by a chasm running between, down to which the houses were situated. One of the hills, on which the upper part of the city lay, was much higher and longer than the other. And, because it was fortified, it was called the Citadel of King David," etc. These two hills are Akra and Zion. The city situated upon the latter, is, in other passages also, described by Josephus to be very high and steep; *e.g.*, vi. 40: τὴν ἄνω πόλιν περίκρημνοι οὖσαν. The sight afforded by the towers in this steep height is, by him, compared with that of the beacon at Alexandria from the sea (*B. J.* vi. c. 6: "It resembled in shape the light-house as seen by people sailing up to Alexandria"). Compare the similar representation of *Tacitus, Lib.* 5. *Histor.* c. 11 (*Reland* ii. p. 848 sqq.).

On the summit of this high and steep hill, in the upper town, was situated the royal castle, called the "upper house of the king," Neh. iii. 25. Its situation could not fail to afford to it extraordinary security. This is sufficiently shown by the ridicule of the Jebusites, when David, who did not build, but only enlarged it, was about to besiege it. They were of opinion that the lame and the blind would be sufficient for its defence, 2 Sam. v. 7–9; compare *Faber's Archæol.* p. 191.

Far above this royal castle, which David first selected for his residence (compare 2 Sam. v. 9: "And David dwelt in the castle and called it the City of David, and built it round about"), a tower jutted prominently out, and afforded a majestic sight. It is frequently mentioned in Scripture. The principal passage is Neh. iii. 25: "Opposite the tower which standeth out from the upper house of the king (appositely the Vulgate: *quæ eminet de domo regis excelsa*) in the court of the prison;" compare ver. 26, where the tower standing out, and elevated far above the king's castle, is likewise spoken of. Concerning the words, "In the court of the prison," we obtain some information from Jer. xxxii. 2: "Jeremiah the prophet was shut up in the court of the prison, בחצר המטרה, which is in the house of the king of Judah;" compare Jer. xxxviii. 6, according to which the pit into which the prophet was let down, was in the court of the prison. According to these passages, the court of the prison formed, agreeably to the customs of the East, part of the royal castle on Zion; and it was in this court that the tower rose. The other principal passage is in the Song of Solomon iv. 4: "Thy neck is like the tower of David built for arms; a thousand bucklers are hanging on it, all arms of heroes." According to this passage, the majestic appearance which the tower afforded was still further increased by the glittering arms which covered it. *Döpke* and others think of the armour of conquered heroes; but that we must rather think of the armour of David's own heroes, appears from Ezek. xxvii. 10, 11, where it is said of the hired troops of the Tyrians, "Shield and helmet they hanged up in thee," and is confirmed by the constant designation of David's faithful ones, as *his heroes;* compare Song of Sol. iii. 7: "Threescore heroes stand around the bed of the king, of the heroes of Israel;" and 1 Chron. xii. 1: "These were among the heroes, helpers in the war." The expression in the Song of Solomon iv. 4, "All shields of the heroes," indicates that the armour of all those who were received into the number of the heroes, was hung up on that tower, as an outward sign of this reception, as a kind of diploma of it. The circumstance that this tower, which is certainly quite identical with the tower mentioned by Nehemiah, is called the tower of David, refutes the supposition of *Clericus*, on Nehemiah, *l.c.*, according to which, it is not the castle of David or Zion which is spoken of in that passage, but another castle and its tower in the lower town, supposed to have been built by Solomon. This hypothesis is refuted, moreover, by that passage itself, inasmuch as the castle is there designated as the upper, or high one.

Now, it is this tower which Micah considers as the symbol of the Davidic house; and in so doing, he follows the example of the Song of Solomon, where it is the symbol of the lofty elevation of Israel, the centre and life-blood of which was the Davidic family. It scarcely needs any lengthened demonstration to show how well suited it was for this signification, how very naturally it represented the thing signified. It was indeed the most elevated part of the castle, the main-mast, as it were, of the ship, which, since the elevation of the Davidic family to the royal dignity, had been for centuries, and was still to be, the seat of the Davidic race. Its height was a symbol of the royal dignity and authority. Its relation to the whole of the rest of the city, which it overlooked and commanded, and which looked up to it with astonishment, symbolized the relation of the subjects to their king.

Micah calls this tower the "Tower of the flock." The main reason for this appellation must be sought in what immediately precedes, in vers. 6 and 7. As in chap. ii. 12, 13, so here also, Micah represented the Covenant-people under the figure of a flock that was to be gathered from its dispersion and estrangement, and protected against every hostile attack. Could anything then be more natural than that, continuing the image

which he had begun, he should call the tower, which, to him,
symbolized the family by whom, under the guidance of the
Lord, that gathering should be accomplished, the "Tower of
the flock?"[1] It is just this close connection with what precedes
which furnishes an important proof for the correctness of our
explanation, for which the way was prepared by all those expositors who, like *Jerome, Theodoret, Cyril, Cocceius*, and *Paulus*
(*über die Evang.* i. p. 189), understand מגדל עדר as an appellative,
and regard, as the ground of the appellation, the protection and
the refuge. In the East, they look out from the towers of the
flock, whether beasts of prey or hostile bands be approaching.
It is into these that the flocks are driven, in those regions where
there are no towns and villages, as soon as danger appears;
compare the proofs in *Faber*, l.c., p. 192 ff. There was so
much the stronger reason for Micah's choosing this figurative
mode of representation, as he had the type immediately before
his eyes. According to 2 Chron. xxvi. 10, xxvii. 4, Uzziah and
Jotham erected, in the woods and pasture grounds, castles and
towers for the protection and refuge of the flocks. But, besides
this main reason, there seems to have existed a secondary one
for choosing this appellation. They who adhere so firmly to
the "Tower of the flock," mentioned in Genesis, are not altogether wrong. Except in that passage, מגדל עדר nowhere occurs
in precisely the same manner as it stands here. If, then, we
consider that, besides this reference, there occur in Micah other
plain references to the Pentateuch (and very numerous they
are, compared with the extent of his prophecies; compare, *e.g.*,
ii. 12, 13 [vide supra], vi. 4, 5, vii. 14, where the words שכני לבדד
receive light from Num. xxiii. 9 only[2]); and still more, if we
consider that, in v. 1 (2), the appellation Bethlehem Ephratah
is likewise taken from Gen. xxxv. 19, and that it is in ver. 21 of
the same chapter that the "Tower of the flock" is mentioned,
—we shall certainly not be guilty of trifling, if we assert that
there is a suspicion of error and unsoundness against all those
interpretations which cannot connect the "Tower of the flock"

[1] *Caspari* very properly refers here to v. 3 (4), where the Messiah, in
whom the former dominion is to come to the Tower of the flock, is represented as a shepherd.

[2] Micah's references to the Pentateuch are made the subject of a most
thorough disquisition by *Caspari*, S. 419 ff.

in Micah with that which is spoken of in Genesis. But the explanation which we have given is not liable to this charge. For why should not Jacob, and the tower which he built for the protection of his literal flocks, serve the prophet as a type and substratum for the relation of a spiritual Shepherd? We must not overlook the truth, that the main and secondary reasons which we have adduced, do not stand beside each other, but run into each other,—are related to each other as the general and particular. For the reason why the prophet had specially in view the "Tower of the flock" which had been built by Jacob was certainly this only: that it partook of the nature of all such towers of the flocks. The *tertium comparationis* is not thereby changed; the figure is only more individualized, and, therefore, more striking and impressive. A reference to the pastoral life of the Patriarchs is certainly one of the reasons of the frequent use of images taken from pastoral life. In a different way, *Hitzig* endeavours to come to the same result. He supposes that the "Tower of the flock" mentioned in Genesis was not situated in the neighbourhood of Bethlehem, but is identical with the tower of the castle on Zion, and of the castle of Millo which David already found existing, and which was only more strongly fortified by him and by Solomon, 2 Sam. v. 9; 1 Kings ix. 15, 24, xi. 27. The figure of the "Tower of the flock" was so much the more appropriate in the passage under consideration, as the founder of the royal dynasty had been, for a long time, a shepherd of the lambs, before he was elected to be a shepherd of the people, and had thus himself prefigured his future relation—a circumstance to which allusion is frequently made in Scripture itself; compare 2 Sam. v. 2, vii. 8; 1 Chron. xi. 2; Ps. lxxviii. 70–72.

After having thus ascertained what is to be understood by the "Tower of the flock," there can be no great difficulty in explaining the "hill of the daughter of Zion." The daughter of Zion is Zion itself, personified, and represented as a virgin; and if her hill be spoken of, what else can be meant, than Mount Zion in the more restricted sense—the Mount κατ' ἐξοχήν, before which Akra and Moriah are changed into plains? We have thus a most appropriate relation of the two appellations to each other,—the tower of the flock being the particular, and the hill of the daughter of Zion, the general.

Further,—We obtain the most perfect harmony and agreement with the last words of the verse. The hill which, morally and physically, commands the daughter of Zion, is the same which obtains dominion over the daughter of Jerusalem. *Finally,*— We see the most striking contrast with iii. 12, and the most admirable connection with iv. 1–7, in which, everywhere, Mount Zion is spoken of, and the exaltation is described which, after its deep abasement, it shall obtain in the future, by the flowing of the heathens to it, and by the dominion of the Lord to be there exercised.

It is only in appearance that our explanation is contradicted by passages of the Old Testament, and of *Josephus,* where *Ophel* is mentioned as a particular place; compare *Bachiene* 2. 1, § 76; *Hamelsveld* 2, S. 35 ff. The supposition of several interpreters, that this *Ophel* is some particular hill (compare, *e.g., Vitringa de Templo Ezech.* L. i. c. iii. p. 159, and his *Commentary on Isaiah* xxxii. 13), has already been invalidated by *Reland* (p. 855), and *Faber* l.c., p. 347, who rightly remark, that *Josephus,* in enumerating the hills of Jerusalem, makes no mention of *Ophel,* but speaks always only of the place *Ophel.* All the difficulties, however, which stand in the way of the other assumptions, are removed by the following view of the matter. Mount Zion was called הָעֹפֶל, the Hill κατ᾽ ἐξοχήν, and this word became, by and by, a *nomen proprium,* and, in this state, as well as in its transition to the *nomen proprium,* was used without the Article. From this it followed—and numerous analogies everywhere occur—that the foot of the mountain, the place where it was connected with the lower part of the temple-mountain by means of a deep valley, acquired this name in preference, and received it, as it were, as a *nomen proprium.* At this foot of Zion—and hence over against the temple, and near it—dwelt the Nethinim, the temple servants, Neh. iii. 26; and *Josephus* says, that the wall surrounding Mount Zion extended on the east side to the place which was called *Ophel,* and ended at the eastern porch of the temple (*de Bell. Jud.* vi. 6).

The view which we have taken, not only of *Ophel,* but of this whole passage, receives an important confirmation by Is. xxxii. 13, 14: "Upon the land of My people come up thorns and briars, for they shoot up in all the houses of joy, in the joyous city. For palaces are forsaken, tumult of the city is forsaken, *hill* and *tower* are around caves (*i.e.*, it is only this which they have to protect) for ever, a joy of wild asses, a pasture of flocks." In this threatening of punishment, *hill*, עֹפֶל, and *tower*, בֹחַן (properly "a watch-tower," corresponding to מִגְדָל), are joined, just as in Micah's promise; and this is a certain proof of the unsoundness of all those explanations which would sever the two in Micah. Perhaps there is, in that passage of Isaiah, the addition of a third object, standing in the middle between the two, viz., the castle of the king which was situated on Zion, and of which the highest and strongest part was formed by the tower. There seems, at least, to be better ground for understanding this by אַרְמוֹן than the temple, as is done by *Vitringa*. It will, nevertheless, be better to understand the palace collectively, and to view it as being parallel to the houses of joy in ver. 13. So much is, at all events, evident, that here also, *Ophel* cannot be understood of the lowest part of Mount Zion, inasmuch as it had nothing distinguished about it that could account for its being mentioned in this context; and to this, the circumstance of its being connected with the tower, must, moreover, be added. *Faber*, l.c., has convincingly proved, that *Ophel*, in the stricter sense, neither had, nor could have, any fortifications.

עָדֶיךָ, "unto thee," seems here to have that emphasis which originally belongs to עַד. It indicates that the object in motion really reaches its goal, while אֶל originally expresses only its direction towards the goal. It points to all the obstacles which seem to render it impossible for the dominion to reach its goal, and represents them as such as shall be overcome by divine omnipotence. This is quite in accordance with the scope of the whole representation, which *Calvin* thus appositely points out: "The prophet endeavours to confirm the faith and hope of the godly, that they might look forward to the distant future, and not dwell only upon the present destruction; that they might rather believe that the matter was in the hands of God, who had promised, that He who raised the dead, would also restore the kingdom of David, which had been destroyed."

Several interpreters, *e.g.*, *Rosenmüller*, connect תֵּאתֶה immediately with what follows: "The kingdom shall come and attain." But, in opposition to this, there are not only the *accents* (*Michaelis:* "The *Athnach* is intended to keep the mind

of the reader in suspense for some time, and to direct his attention to what follows"), but also the change of the tenses, which
is intended just to prevent this connection, and the weak sense
which would be the result, inasmuch as one of the verbs would
be a pleonasm. It must rather be supposed, therefore, that the
subject in תאמה is indefinite. The remark which *Hävernick*, in
his *Commentary on Daniel*, S. 386, makes on the omission of
the indefinite subject, is here fully applicable, although he
himself makes a wrong application of it to that passage: "The
indefinite subject," he says, "has a special emphasis. By the
omission of the definite idea, it is, as it were, left to the reader
to supply everything possible (in the passage under consideration, the compass of all that is glorious), for which the writer
cannot find language."

The "first," *i.e.*, former, or ancient "dominion," refers to
the splendid times under David and Solomon; but, at the same
time, it supposes a period when the dominion is altogether taken
away from the dynasty of David. Such a period had already
been announced by the prophet, in his first discourse, inasmuch
as it is implied in the carrying away of all Judah into captivity;
and still more distinctly in iii. 12, according to which, Zion, the
seat of the Davidic dominion, is to be ploughed as a field. This
announcement, with the express mention of the king, returns
in ver. 9, and, contrasted with it, the announcement of the restoration of the Davidic dominion in v. 1 (2).

The last words of the verse are, by many expositors (*Calvin,
Michaelis*, and *Rosenmüller*), translated thus: "And the kingdom, I say, shall belong to the daughter of Jerusalem;" so that
Jerusalem would here be, not the *object*, but the *subject* of dominion. The sense, according to this explanation, is best
brought out by *Calvin*: "The prophet here distinctly mentions
the daughter of Jerusalem, because the kingdom of Israel had
obscured the glory of the true kingdom. The prophet hence
testifies, that God was not unmindful of His promise, and would
so arrange it that Jerusalem should recover its lost dignity, and
the whole people be gathered unto one body." But this explanation must be rejected on philological grounds. ממלכת is
status constr.; the ל serves, therefore, only as a circumlocution
of the genitive; and it is not admissible to supply the Verb
Substant. To this, moreover, there must be added the refer-

ence to what precedes. The dominion over the daughter of Jerusalem is to come to the tower which commands the daughter of Zion, not, by any means, to the daughter of Zion herself. The prophet makes Jerusalem to represent the kingdom of God; and, in so doing, he probably has regard to the relation of Zion and of the king's castle to the town, by which was symbolized the relation which the Davidic dynasty occupied to the kingdom of God.

CHAP. IV. 9–14.

At the close of the last chapter, the prophet had announced severe judgments. In the verses immediately preceding, he had given glorious promises. In that which follows, he now combines these two elements; and it is only in chap. v. that the promise again appears, purely, and by itself. The judgments are thus introduced into the middle of the proclamation of salvation, in order that the faithful might thus be preserved from forming any vain hopes, which, if not confirmed by the result, are apt to be exchanged for much deeper despondency. But this same circumstance contained within it an indirect consolation; for it is certain that He who causes future events to be foretold, overrules them also; and "He who sends them, can also turn them." For the greatest cause of our despondency under the cross is certainly the doubt which we entertain as to whether it really comes from God. The prophet, however, affords *direct* consolation also. Whensoever he speaks of any calamity, he immediately subjoins the announcement of divine deliverance. The intimation of the sufferings, in this section, differs essentially from the former ones. It is not, like these, in a threatening, but in an affectionate character; indeed, in vers. 11–13, the consolation preponderates even outwardly. From this, it is sufficiently evident, that it must have a different destination. Whilst the threatening was intended chiefly for the ungodly, it has, just as much as the preceding pure promise, the truly godly members of the Theocracy also in view, and aims at strengthening them in the manifold temptations into which they must fall, in consequence of the sufferings which always come upon them also at the same time, on account of their outward, and therefore also their inward, connection with the wicked.

A glance at the great catastrophes, which were to precede the appearance of Christ, was here just in its proper place. In the preceding context, the prophet had mentioned the restoration of the former dominion. Here, he describes how the dominion is lost ("There is no king in thee," ver. 9), and what shall happen during the period of this loss. He then further details, in v. 1 (2) sq., in what manner the dominion is to be restored.

It is a threefold suffering, joined with deliverance from it, which presents itself to the prophet in his inward vision, and which he describes accordingly. This is evident from the three-fold עתה, compare vers. 9, 11, 14, which, each time, indicates when a new scene presents itself to the prophet. This, further, appears from the different character which each one bears. In the case of the announcement in vers. 9 and 10, viz., the carrying away to Babylon, it is alone the Lord's hand which delivers His people. In the calamity described in vers. 11–13, He grants to Israel courage in war, and victory to his *arms*. The plans of the enemies to destroy Zion are frustrated, while in the former calamity they succeeded. In ver. 14, Zion is anew represented as sorely pressed by enemies, and captured by them. According to v. 1, which is closely connected with what precedes, the deliverance is accomplished by the Messiah, in whom the promise of the restoration of the dominion of the house of David over the daughter of Zion is fulfilled.

———

Ver. 9. "*Now why dost thou raise a cry? Is there no king in thee, or is thy councillor gone? For pangs have seized thee as a woman in travail.*"

Zion, mourning at the time of the carrying away into captivity, stands before the prophet's spirit, and is addressed by him. This ought never to have been overlooked. But since, nevertheless, it has been so, we quote from the multitude of analogous instances, at least one which is altogether incontrovertible, and where the writer likewise transfers himself into the time of the captivity, viz., the passage in Hos. xiii. 9–11, which, in other respects also, shows a great resemblance to the one under consideration : "This has destroyed thee, O Israel, that thou wast against Me, against thine help. Where is now thy king? Let him deliver thee in all thy cities. And where are thy judges? Surely thou didst say : Give me kings and princes. And I gave thee a king in Mine anger, and took him away in My wrath." It is quite impossible to entertain, even for a moment, the thought that, in this passage, Hosea speaks of the real past and present, inasmuch as he prophesied before the destruction of the kingdom of the ten tribes. Micah opens his representation just with the moment that Jerusalem is captured by the enemies ; and he announces to her that her sufferings are not yet at an end,—that she must wander into exile. The progress of the thought in the verse under consideration is this :—The prophet sees Zion dissolved in grief and lamentation. Full of sympathy, he asks of her the cause of this mourning,—whether, it may be, it was caused by the loss of her king ; and he himself answers this question in the affirmative, because such a cause could alone account for such a grief. Now, in order fully to realize the mourning of Zion over her king, we must bear in mind that the visible head was a representative of the invisible one,—the mediator of His mercies : that hence, his removal was a token of divine anger, and an extinction of every hope of salvation. Every other king is, indeed, likewise an anointed of the Lord ; but the king of Israel was so in a totally different sense. How deeply, from this point of view, the loss of the king was felt, at the time when that which is here merely the *ideal* present became the *real* present, is seen from Lam. iv. 20 : " The breath of our life, the anointed of the Lord, is taken a prisoner in their pits, he of whom we said, Under his shadow we shall live among the heathen." In Zech. iv. the civil magistrates, along with the ecclesiastical authorities, appear as the greatest gift of God's grace ; henceforth these two shall again be the medium through which the Lord communicates His gracious gifts to the Congregation, just as they had been before the captivity. It must further be borne in mind, that all the promises for the future were bound up with the regal institution. With its extinction, therefore, everything seemed to be lost ; every prospect of a better future seemed to have disappeared. The reference in

Jer. viii. 19, where the king is the Lord Himself, to the passage before us, is very beautiful, and full of deep meaning. It points out the truth, that the loss of the earthly king is a consequence of their having forced the heavenly King to withdraw from the midst of them.—The "councillor" is preeminently the king himself; compare Is. ix. 5, where Christ, in whom the Davidic dynasty is to attain to the full height of its destination, appears as the councillor in the highest sense. Other councillors, it is true, are not thereby excluded; they form, however, only a group around the king as their centre; compare Is. iii. 3.

Ver. 10. "*Travail and break forth, O daughter of Zion, like a woman who bringeth forth; for now shalt thou go forth out of the city, and thou dwellest in the field, and comest till to Babylon: there shalt thou be delivered, there the Lord shall redeem thee out of the hand of thine enemies.*"

The consolation begins with the words שם תנצלי only; the whole remaining part of the verse is of a mournful character. In the words, "Travail and break forth," one aspect only of the figure of the parturient woman is brought into view, viz., the pain; but not the joy following upon the pain; compare remarks on v. 2. The Imperative is thus not, as some interpreters erroneously assume, an *Imper. consolationis*, but an intimation that the pain would reach its height, put into the form of an exhortation to submit to it. Much more satisfactorily than by many of the later expositors, the sense of this verse has been thus fixed by *Calvin:* "The sum and substance is, that although God would, according to His promise, take care of the people, the faithful should have no reason from this to indulge in joy, as if they were to be exempt from all troubles; on the contrary, the prophet exhorts them that they should rather prepare themselves to undergo all kinds of misery, so that, when driven out of their own land, they should not only, like straying people, wander about in the fields, but should be driven to Babylon as into a grave. But while he thus prepares the faithful to bear the cross, he subjoins the hope of salvation, viz., that God would deliver them, and redeem them from thence out of the hands of their enemies."—The חלי resumes the preceding, where the prophet had, at the point of time where he had taken his stand, viz., the capture of the city, represented that calamity of this people, under the image of the pains of child-bearing. It thus becomes equivalent to—Thou shalt be obliged to bear, not only the pains which precede the birth, but also the highest of all pains, viz., the pains of the birth itself. What the latter are in relation to the former, that, in the view of the prophet, is the carrying away out of the Holy Land,—the expulsion from the face of God (an expulsion similar to that of Cain when he was obliged to flee from Eden), when compared to the mere capture. Hence the close connexion with what follows, by means of כִּי. The word וְגֹחִי (the o is, for the sake of euphony, employed instead of u; just as in ver. 13 דּוֹשִׁי) is, by most interpreters, translated, " And lead out." But we must object to this, on the ground that נוח has always an intransitive signification only, viz., " to break forth ;" and this signification is here quite suitable, more so even than the transitive ; for it marks more emphatically the *pain* during the birth, which is here the only point: Jer. iv. 31. It is, as it were, a dissolution of the whole nature, a violent breaking of it into pieces. The " now," just as the " now " at the commencement of the description of the scene, belongs to the *ideal* standing-point, where the carrying away is just at hand : for this is the period of the future into which the prophet has been carried. The " dwelling in the field " is the intervening station between the " going forth " and " the coming to Babylon." In the open air, exposed to all the inclemencies of the weather (compare the expression, " Under the dew of heaven," in Dan. iv. 22, 30 [25, 33]), the prisoners were collected for the purpose of being afterwards carried away. The word עַד, as well as the twofold שָׁם, are emphatic. Irresistibly, the divine *judgment* advances to its last goal ; but as irresistibly does divine *mercy* wrest from the enemies the prey which seemed to have been given to them even for ever.—The futility of all attempts to explain away the distinct prophecy of the Babylonish captivity in this passage has been shown in the *Dissertations on the Genuineness of Daniel*, p. 151 sqq. How even *Caspari* could join in these attempts, it is difficult to explain. Even he is of opinion that the prophet had expected the catastrophe to come from Asshur. Chap. v. 4, 5 (5, 6) cannot be decisive *for* the reference to Asshur. For the circumstance that Asshur appears there as the type of the future enemies of the kingdom of God, implies, indeed, that he occupied the first place among the ene-

mies at the time of the prophet; but it by no means implies that
he must occupy a place in the outline of the future catastrophes
of the people of God. Such a catastrophe was not to proceed
from him, but rather from an enemy who had not yet at that
time appeared on the scene, although his power was already ger-
minating, as is shown by Is. xxxix. and other passages. The
oppression of Judah by Asshur was indeed a heavy one; but
it was transitory, and did not by any means constitute an era.
From the relation in which vers. 9–14 (iv. 9–v. 1) stands to
ver. 8, it sufficiently appears that the oppression by the Chaldeans must here form the commencement, although the Assyrian
oppression must be added to it as an introduction and a prelude.
According to this relation, the point at issue here can be only
the cessation of the dominion of the Davidic family. From
Jer. xxvi. 18, 19, *Caspari* endeavours to prove that Micah had
in view, in the first instance, the Assyrians only. But that
passage of Jeremiah refers to Mic. iii. 12, where the prophecy
has a general character, and where the instruments of the divine
judgment are not expressly mentioned, as is the case here. On
the other hand, the following arguments are opposed to the reference to the Assyrians. 1. The prophet does not mention Asshur,
but Babylon. Nothing is, certainly, proved by the circumstance
that, at the time of the prophet, Babylon was still under the
Assyrian dominion; for Babylon comes here into consideration,
not so much as a place, but as a hostile power. The place, as
such, was of no consequence, and the mention of it was not
required by the character of the prophecy. 2. If the announcement referred to Asshur, the result would contradict the prophecy. *Caspari* says, that by the repentance and conversion of
the people, the fulfilment had been averted. But with such a
view of prophecy, the position of the prophetic institution becomes untenable, and historically incomprehensible. The Mosaic
regulation, that whosoever prophesied anything that did not
take place should be punished with death, would in that case
lose all practical significance; for there would always have been
at hand the excuse, that by the repentance the execution of that
sentence of punishment had been repealed. From the nature
of the case, and from that Mosaic regulation, it follows that
special announcements expressed absolutely must be fulfilled
absolutely; and not a single fact in the history of prophetism

stands in contradiction to this truth. Jonah's announcement to Nineveh, indeed, has been appealed to; but, in reply, we remark simply, that the words of that announcement have not been communicated to us, while we see from the result that it was conditional only. Such a decided repentance would scarcely have been called forth by it among the inhabitants of Nineveh, had repentance not been expressly declared in it as a means of deliverance. 3. Micah everywhere goes hand in hand with his contemporary Isaiah. But the latter always opposes energetically the despondency of Judah in the face of Asshur, and declares that his proud power would be broken at Jerusalem (as had been already prophesied by Hosea in i. 4–7), and that, while the kingdom of the ten tribes would be destroyed, Judah would experience the protecting hand of the Lord. *Caspari* contradicts himself in thus making these two men of God to differ in so essential a point. For a man like *Hitzig*, it may be quite befitting to say, " Micah did not possess the firm, courageous faith which was displayed by Isaiah." 4. It is quite impossible *to get rid of the obvious parallelism of the passage under con*sideration with Is. xxxix. 6, 7, where the rising of the Babylonish empire, the destruction of the Davidic kingdom by it, and the carrying away of Judah to Babylon, are clearly and distinctly predicted. And in a number of other prophecies, Isaiah likewise declares or supposes, that that which the Assyrians threatened in vain, would at some future period, when the iniquity of the people had become full, be carried out by Babylon with her Chaldeans. It is scarcely conceivable how *Caspari*, acknowledging as he does the genuineness of these prophecies of Isaiah, could think of dissevering from them the prophecy now under consideration.—Declarations like that before us, where, in clear and distinct outlines, a future event is foretold one hundred and fifty years before it takes place, inflict a death-blow upon the naturalistic view of the prophetic institution, as is sufficiently evident from *Hitzig's* embarrassment, and from his efforts to free himself from the bands of this troublesome fact.

Ver. 11. " *And now many nations assemble themselves against thee, that say : Let her be profaned, and let our eyes look upon Zion.*"

Israel, with its claim of being alone the people of the only true God, was a thorn in the eyes of the nations. These here burn with eager desire to prove, actually and by deeds, that this presumptuous claim was unfounded, and, by the destruction of the city, to take from it its fancied holiness, and the glory of holiness. Destruction and profanation are, in their view, inseparably connected. The contrast to the verse under review is formed by vii. 10: "And mine enemy shall see it, and shame shall come upon her who said, Where is the Lord thy God? Mine eyes shall behold her, now shall she be trodden down as the mire of the streets." The words, "Where is the Lord thy God?" entirely agree in substance with, "Let her be profaned!" But the desire of profaning Jerusalem must be conceived of as the human motive only. According to the view of Scripture generally, and of Micah particularly, all the distress of the people of God has its foundation in *sin;* and from the whole context, and especially from v. 2 (3), where this event also is comprehended within the time when God's people are given up, it clearly appears that, notwithstanding the happy issue, we have here before us a heavy calamity. By a new phase of sin, a new phase of judgment is brought about; and by a new phase of worldliness, a new phase of aggression by the world's power.— It is owing to a striving after variety, that the word "and" here stands before "now," while it is omitted in the third scene. It may stand, or it may be omitted, because the various catastrophes are independent of each other, and yet, at the same time, form a connected whole, as is evident from the words, "He will give them up," in v. 2 (3), by which they are connected together. The heavy oppression of Judah appears here under the form of a siege of its centre, in accordance with the scope of prophecy, which, everywhere, seeks to impart vividness and animation to the scene, by uniting into one picture that which is separated by time and space. The historical reference of the prophecy is thus very accurately stated by *Calvin:* "Although the Babylonish captivity has come to an end, and Israel has been restored from it, the promised kingdom shall not immediately come. Before that takes place, the neighbouring nations shall assemble themselves against Jerusalem, with the desire of profaning it, and of enjoying a pleasant spectacle. This took place under Antiochus." That to which the prophet here simply alludes, but yet in such a way that the right reference cannot possibly be mistaken (since a great hostile aggression is here described, which should happen after the people have returned from Babylon, and which is removed by the piety and courage of the people themselves; and since, after this second oppression, there follows a third, which is described in ver. 14, there certainly remains no other alternative: the times of the Maccabees are those which can alone be thought of), is further detailed by Zechariah in ix. 11 ff. At his time, the deliverance from the first calamity had already taken place; and he expressly states the names of the enemies; just as, in the prophecy under review, the authors of the first calamity are expressly named. That which is especially characteristic, and which points to the time of the Maccabees, is, moreover, the special mention of many nations, which are united in their decided hatred against Jerusalem as a city, and against Judah as the people of the Lord, taken in connection with the character of the war as a *religious war* in the strictest sense,—it being an attempt of heathenism to destroy the Congregation of the Lord as such. *These features are found in no other catastrophe during the time between Micah and Christ.* And that the aggression belongs to the period before the appearing of the Saviour, is evident from the whole context, as well as from v. 2 (3). In the time of the Maccabees, it was not with Syria alone that Judah had to do; but all the heathen nations without exception, with which Judah had any connection at that time, united themselves for a decisive stroke against the kingdom of God. Their purpose was to extirpate the whole race of Jacob, 1 Macc. v. 2. Striking remarks upon the real nature of the struggle at that period, as a struggle of faithful Judaism against Heathenism, the latter of which had gained a considerable party among the people themselves, are made by *Stark*, in " *Gaza und die Philistäische Küste,*" *Jena*, 52, S. 481 ff. Among other things, he says: "The national distinctions in the boundaries of Palestine had by no means ceased, but continued under the general cover of the Egyptian and Syrian administration in a varied, unyielding, and hostile manner. There were the Idumeans in the whole of the south of Palestine to near Jerusalem; then, the Philistines, or when called by their cities, the Gazeans and Ashdodians; the Phœnicians, the Samaritans or Chutteans, the mixed population of Galilee, the Arabs of Perea. . . . As soon as the Jewish people, who, up to that time, had been altogether insignificant in a political point of view, rose against the Syrian empire, at first for their religious peculiarities, then, for their political independence, and, finally, even for the recovery of the *ideal* possession of their country—an idea which had been kept alive by tradition,—it could not but be that those who were naturally the supports and centres of the Syrian operations, became the objects of the hostile Jewish operations; and that the whole national portion of the population, although not Greeks, were anew inflamed by their old hatred of, and opposition to, Judaism; so that they considered that Hellenic struggle as also a national one. This period thus produced at the same time a revival of the old national struggle of the inhabitants of Palestine, modified and increased by the struggle of Hellenism with the national reaction which served as a superstructure for it." The objection, raised even by *Caspari*, that a prophecy of the victorious struggles in the time of the Maccabees must be strange and surprising in a prophet of the Assyrian period, will not startle those who look at the analogies—such as the prophecy in Is. vi. In the latter prophecy, first the Chaldean, and then the Roman catastrophes, are described in sharp outlines, but without any mention of the names of the instruments of punishment. It is only in reference to the executors of the first of these judgments that more distinct disclosures were given to the prophet himself at a subsequent period. The announcement in Zech. ix., where the Greeks are expressly mentioned, is, in reality, not less miraculous. According to all prophetical analogies, it is *a priori* probable that this detailed prophecy of the Maccabean period, and the similar one in Daniel, should have been preceded by some older prophecy which refers to the same facts, but only in general outlines, such as we have in the passage under consideration. If any doubt should still remain, it would be removed by a glance at the conflicting interpretations. *Ewald* and *Hitzig* think of the Assyrian invasion, to which vers. 9, 10, are likewise referred by them, although such a reference is in opposition to the express words of these verses, —which, for a Naturalistic tendency, are rather inconvenient. The contradiction in these two prophecies *Ewald* endeavours to reconcile by the evidently erroneous supposition, that the carrying away in ver. 10 must be conceived of as only a partial one, —a supposition which is invalidated by a simple comparison of iii. 12. According to *Hitzig*, the prophet has, in vers. 11–13, overcome the despondency expressed in vers. 9, 10, and has raised himself to confidence in God. He thus makes the prophet distinctly contradict himself in one breath,—a supposition which does not even deserve a refutation. Even if we were entirely to separate this passage from its connection, how ill does the activity here ascribed to Judah agree with the oppression by the Assyrians! This activity of Judah supposes that it has to do with many small nations. Against the great Asiatic empires, a direct and immediate interposition of the Lord is *everywhere* referred to. The salvation, however, which is here announced to Judah, can be only an imperfect one, and cannot go beyond what they really received at the time of the Maccabees. This is sufficiently evident from the circumstance, that it belongs to a time in which Judah has no king of the Davidic house; for him they have already lost in ver. 9, and receive again only in v. 1 (2), in Christ; and it is certain that the Davidic house was the channel through which all the true and great mercies of the Lord were bestowed upon His people.

Ver. 12. "*And they know not the thoughts of the Lord, neither understand they His counsel; for He gathereth them as the sheaf for the threshing-floor.*"

The particle "and" is here used, where we, for the sake of a closer connection, would employ "but." The thoughts of the Lord are these,—that the sufferings, after having served their purpose as regards Zion, shall pass over to the enemies, so that they shall themselves be destroyed by Zion, while they so confidently thought to inflict destruction upon Zion. The כי introduces the reason of their not knowing the way of the Lord. If they knew it, they would not express such desire and hope; *for it is they themselves* whom the Lord gives over to destruction.

Ver. 13. "*Arise and thresh, O daughter of Zion, for I make thine horn iron, and thy claws brass; and thou crushest in pieces many people, and I consecrate their gain unto the Lord, and their strength to the Ruler of the whole earth.*"

The figure is based upon the Eastern mode of threshing; compare *Paulsen vom Ackerbau der Morgenl.* § 40–42; *Niebuhr, Reise* i. S. 151; and likewise Is. xxi. 10, xli. 15; Hab. iii. 12. Strictly speaking, one characteristic only of the threshing oxen is here considered, viz., the crushing power of their hoofs. The prophet, however, extends the comparison to that also in which the bullock is formidable, even when it is not engaged in the work of threshing, viz., to its horns. On this point 1 Kings xxii. 11 may be compared, where the pseudo-prophet Zedekiah makes to himself iron horns, and thus states the import of this symbolical action: "Thus saith the Lord, With these shalt thou push Aram until it is destroyed." The first person in החרמתי has perplexed several ancient translators (*Syr., Jerome*), as well as many modern interpreters, who, therefore, substitute the second person for it. But it is quite appropriate. As at the beginning, where the Lord gathers the sheaf on the threshing-floor, so at the close also, the prophet declares that the victory is the work of God. It is He Himself, the true God, the Lord of the whole earth, who reminds His rebellious subjects of their true relation to Him, by vindicating to Himself a part of the good things which He bestowed upon them; just as He once did in Egypt. This thought contains the reason why, instead of the pronoun of the first person, the noun is employed; so that it is equivalent to: To Me the only God, the Lord of the whole earth. But it is altogether distorted, if the first person here be changed into the second. With respect to the import of the word, we must by no means think only of the gifts of consecration which were brought to the temple. Such a view would be necessary, only if the goods of the Covenant-people, or the Covenant-people themselves, were introduced as that which is to be consecrated. In that case we could understand, by that which is consecrated, that only which is the exclusive property of the Lord, which has been dedicated to Him exclusively, and for ever withdrawn from the use of His subjects, and which, as far as they are concerned, is as good as annihilated; compare Lev. xxvii. 28: "Everything consecrated, which any one consecrates to the Lord, of man and of beast, and of the field of his possession, shall not be sold nor redeemed; every consecrated thing is most holy to the Lord." But here, where He who consecrates is the Lord, while the goods are those of the heathen, the latter only are to be considered as being excluded from the possession, and as those in reference to whom the goods are consecrated goods; while the people of God must, on the other hand, be considered as partaking in what He has acquired. The community of goods between these two is rendered prominent in other passages also where the object required it. Thus, *e.g.*,

Joel iv. (iii.) 5, where the Phœnicians and Philistines are charged: "My silver and My gold ye have taken, and My precious things, the goodly ones, ye have carried into your palaces." That we cannot here think of the temple-treasure is evident, not only from a comparison of ver. 4, where the attempts of these nations to avenge themselves on Israel on account of former injuries, are expressly represented as attempts to take vengeance upon God, but also from history, which knows nothing of the plunder of the temple by Phœnicians and Philistines. The mention of the *gain* points to the *male parta*,—and this is the more strictly applicable, the nearer the relation is in which he who is robbed stands to the Lord of the earth. With the *gain*, the substance in general is lost.—The fundamental thought of the verse, which is here expressed only with an application to a special case, is that of the victory of the Congregation of the Lord over the world. This was perceived by *Calvin*, who strikingly demonstrates how this declaration is ever anew realized, and how its complete fulfilment is reserved only for the second coming of Christ. He has erred, however, in this, that looking only to the eternal import of the thought, he overlooked the circumstance that it is here expressed with reference to a definite event in which it was to be realized.

Ver. 14. "*Now thou gatherest thyself in troops, O daughter of troops. They lay siege against us, they smite the judge of Israel with the rod upon the cheek.*"

A new scene presents itself to the prophet. Zion, victorious on the preceding occasion, appears here as powerless, and locked up within her walls. She is captured; and ignominious abuse is cast upon the leaders of the deeply abased people.—We need not here dwell for any length of time upon the numerous expositions of תתגדדי. There is only one, viz., "thou shalt press thyself together," which affords an appropriate contrast; while this contrast is lost when it is translated, as *Hofmann* does, by: "thou shalt lacerate thyself" (compare what *Caspari* has advanced against it). "Thou shalt press thyself together" does not, moreover, destroy the import of Hithpael, and has especially the use of the Hithp. of גדד, in Jer. v. 7, in its favour. The Hithpael in this signification is probably a Denominative of גדוד. The person addressed, the בת־גדוד, can be none other than the בת־ציון in ver. 13. For it is she who is addressed by the prophet

in each of the new scenes announced by עתה, and she is, generally, the only one to whom the discourse is, throughout the
whole section, addressed. The intentional paronomasia occasioned
by the designation "daughter of troops," *i.e.*, who appeared in
warlike array, evidently alludes to בת־ציון, and refers to the description of Zion as a brave victorious hero, in the preceding
verses. The *enemy* is immediately afterwards spoken of in
the third person. The words, "Siege (not by any means
'a wall,' as *De Wette* maintains) they lay, or direct against us,"
clearly indicate that the pressing of themselves together, which
forms a contrast with the former courageous excursions indicated by גדוד, is the consequence of fear, weakness, and hostile
oppression. The words are therefore strikingly paraphrased
by *Justi*, thus: "But now, why dost thou thus press thyself
together, thou who wast accustomed to press others?" This,
however, only must be kept in mind, that בת־גדוד implies an
allusion to the fact that the warlike disposition continues even
in the present, notwithstanding the feebleness forced upon her,
—a very characteristic feature. In saying, "They lay siege
against *us*," instead of "against *thee*," the prophet is carried
away by his emotions to show himself as one of the people
whom he sees to be oppressed by so heavy sufferings. As indicated by the word "now" also, he is, in spirit, in the midst
of them. The ignominious treatment of the judge of Israel
supposes that the prophet sees, in his inward vision, the capture
of the city as having already taken place; for it is impossible to
conceive of the judge, the soul of the city, as being outside of it.
This judge of Israel is an *ideal* person, formed by the prophet in
order that he might be able to contrast him with the Ruler of
Israel in v. 1 (2), who represents all the theocratic authorities;
compare, *e.g.*, Is. iii. 12, where the corrupted leaders of the
Theocracy present themselves to the prophet in the person of a
large child. To speak, in such a case, of a collective noun, as is
usually done, is out of place. But it may be observed that it is
not a king who is here spoken of, but, very significantly, a judge
of Israel only, probably with reference to the times before Saul,
when Israel was governed by judges. The royal dominion which,
according to the announcement in ver. 9, shall be destroyed by
Babylon, shall be restored by the Messiah only (compare v. 1
[2], iv. 8), who is not שפט ישראל, but, like His great ancestor

David, מושל בישראל ; compare 2 Sam. xxiii. 3. There can be no doubt that, in this connection, the *Judge* is spoken of as distinguished from, and contrasted with, the *King*. But even by itself, the mention of the *Judge* cannot but be startling. It would have been against the object of the prophet to have mentioned any inferior persons, when there existed a superior one; and if the *King* was thereby denoted, why should he have been designated thus?—It is on purpose that ישראל, which is the *nomen dignitatis* of the people, is here chosen. It more emphatically points out the unworthiness of the treatment, as well as the contrast between the reality and the idea in the destinies of the nation,—a contrast, it is true, which Israel has called forth by the preceding contrast between the reality and the idea with regard to his conduct. Since Israel has inwardly profaned himself by his own guilt, he is now, as a just punishment, profaned outwardly also.—With respect, now, to the historical reference of this disastrous announcement, its fulfilment cannot be sought for in any other event than the invasion by the Romans. Among the sufferings of the people, which are here described in general outlines, this is the only one recorded in history, with the exception of those already mentioned. Isaiah, the contemporary of Micah, likewise announced, as early as in chap. vi., that upon those who should return from the captivity a second judgment would be inflicted, by which the national independence should be destroyed. This judgment is described with remarkable clearness and distinctness by the post-exilic prophets, inasmuch as, to them, it appeared already more in the foreground; compare the remarks on Zech. v. and xi.; Dan. ix. The only plausible argument against this reference is this,—that the capture of the city by the Romans was subsequent to the appearance of the Messiah, and that it is, after all, the latter which forms the subject of the announcement of salvation in v. 1 (2), which, again, refers to the sufferings described in the verse before us. This argument, however, is set aside by the following considerations. 1. The prophet, indeed, designates the misery which was inflicted by those enemies upon the Covenant-people only according to its acme, viz., the siege and capture of the city; but he, nevertheless, views it in, and understands it of, its whole extent, and from its first beginnings. These, then, in so far as the Romans are concerned, fall in the time before Christ, for the Jewish people were already subjected to the Roman dominion by Pompey. 2. This alone, however, is not sufficient. If, with *Vershuir* (*de celebri oraculo Mic.* iv. 14, in the *Dissert. Philol. exeg.* Leuw. 1775), we confine ourselves to the capture by Pompey, we cannot, by any means, get rid of the feeling that that fulfilment does not exhaust the prophecy. But we are, on the other hand, quite entitled to add that highest point, viz., the destruction of Jerusalem by the Romans, along with all its still existing consequences, if only we consider, that the announcement of salvation in chap. v.—as is shown by its contents, and by its accordance with the analogy of all the Messianic prophecies—is not limited to the short period of the first appearance of Christ. That comes into consideration rather as the grain of seed only from which the tree grew up, under which all the fowls of heaven were to dwell. Hence it is, that the salvation, no less than the punishment, is a continuous one, until, at the end of the days, it appears in its glorious consummation. But if it be established that Christ is presented as the only Saviour from the calamity here described, then that calamity must still continue for those who reject Him, yea, it must still be increased. It is only by giving up their opposition that they can be delivered from the yoke which presses upon them. The election, on the other hand, is, from the very beginning, received into the communion of His kingdom, which extends over the whole world. Here, however, that which has been already remarked in reference to vers. 11–13 finds its application. The siege and capture of Zion are pre-eminently the means of representing the idea of the heavy oppression and deep abasement of Israel, and of the cessation of its political independence, although it must not upon any account be overlooked, that the natural form of the representation is, at the same time, the natural form of the realization of the idea that Judah could not be destroyed without the siege and capture of Jerusalem, its centre.

CHAP. V. 1.

" *And thou, Bethlehem Ephratah, too little to be among the thousands of Judah, out of thee shall come forth unto Me* (one) *to be Ruler in Israel; and His goings forth are the times of old, the days of eternity."*

The close connection of this verse with what immediately precedes (*Caspari* is wrong in considering iv. 9–14 as an episode) is evident, not only from the ו copulative, and from the analogy of the near relation of the announcement of salvation to the prophecy of disaster in the preceding verse (for if the connection with ver. 14 be overlooked, the announcement of disaster contained in it remains without a corresponding consolation,—and this would be against the analogy of vers. 9, 10, 11–13); but more strikingly so from the contrast of the מושל בישראל with the שפט ישראל. The *Judge* of Israel in his deepest abasement, is here contrasted with the *Ruler* of Israel in His highest divine glory. The connection is seen also in the indication of Bethlehem's natural littleness, as contrasted with the greatness to be bestowed upon it by God. What could have induced the prophet thus strongly to point out this circumstance, had it not been that he considered Bethlehem as the type of the Jewish people in their misery, described in the preceding verse, and the miraculous elevation of the former, to be accomplished by divine omnipotence, as the pledge of a like result for the whole people? There is, moreover, a reference to the *beginning* of the pretended episode. In iv. 9, it was said: "There is no king in thee;" here, it is announced that from Bethlehem there comes forth a glorious Ruler in Israel. But, on the other hand, there is also a close connection with ver. 8, as has been rightly perceived by *Caspari.* This connection and reference are sufficiently indicated by the like form. The address to Bethlehem here corresponds with the address to "the Tower of the flock" there,—the "Ruler," מושל, here, with the "dominion," ממשלה, there. There, the dominion returns to the house of David; here, the august person is described by whom this return is effected, after the events, described iv. 9–14, have come upon the Covenant-people. That the Ruler here comes forth out of Bethlehem, corresponds with iv. 8 in so far as there the dominion *returns* to the Tower of the flock, to the hill of the daughter of Zion, which implies the overthrow of the Davidic kingdom, and the return of the family of David to the condition in which it lived at Bethlehem before the time of David,—which must necessarily precede its final glory.—According to *Bachiene*

ii. 2, S. 7 ff., Bethlehem and Ephratah are to be distinguished, so that the former designates the town alone, and the latter at the same time its whole environs,—so that Bethlehem Ephratah would be equivalent to Bethlehem situated in Ephratah. But even if we were to agree with this opinion, we must not, by any means, consider the two words as standing in the *stat. constr.*, any more than the corresponding בית־לחם יהודה in Judges xvii. 9, xix. 1, 2, 18. For as a *Nomen proprium* is equivalent to a noun with the article, it can never stand in the *stat. constr.* with another noun. We should thus be obliged to assume that, by way of brevity, common in geographical designations, both appellations were placed unconnectedly beside each other, without any indication of their relation, just as in addressing a letter, we would simply write Berlin, Prussia. But if we compare Gen. xxxv. 19, where Ephratah is simply declared to be identical with Beth-lehem (אפרתה היא בית לחם);—and if we consider that the prophet had already alluded to the contents of that chapter (compare remarks on iv. 8), and that he regards the events which formerly happened in the neighbourhood of Bethlehem as a type of those which were to take place in future;—that in ver. 2 (3) he brings the new birth which is there to happen in parallelism with one which had formerly occurred in its nearest neighbourhood, and that it is just in the account of the latter that the designation occurs,—we shall have the strongest reason for understanding here also the two names as a designation of the town, without deciding whether the above-mentioned difference, as regards other passages, be well founded or not. Interpreters commonly assert that the sole ground of the twofold designation of the place is the intention of distinguishing it from another Bethlehem in the tribe of Zebulun; compare Josh. xix. 15. But in that case, we should rather have expected the common Bethlehem Judah, instead of Bethlehem Ephratah. There can be no doubt, that the prophet, in choosing this designation, was guided by a regard to that passage in Genesis. One might also suppose that the prophet wished to allude, at the same time, to the appellative significations of these nouns, viz., "house of bread," and "field of fruit," and to lay stress upon their typical import: the place, the blessing of which, as regards temporal things, is indicated by its name, shall, at some

future time, be blessed and fruitful in a higher sense. It is just
in Micah, who is fond of making significant allusions to names,
that such a supposition is very natural, as is shown, not only by
chap. i., but also by vii. 18, where he gives an interpretation of
his own name. As, however, the two names elsewhere also
occur thus connected, without any attention being given to
their signification, the prophet would not have omitted giving
a hint upon this point. It is not the way of Scripture to make
any allusions which cannot be understood with certainty. We
shall, therefore, be obliged to suppose that, after the common
name, the prophet mentions, in addition, the ancient name rendered sacred by memory from the time of the Patriarch, and
by the authority of the most ancient documents of revelation
(compare, besides Gen. xxxv. 19, Gen. xlviii. 7), in order thereby to impart greater solemnity to the discourse, and to intimate
what great things he had to say of Bethlehem. In accordance
with this designation by two names, is, then, the circumstance
that the address is directed to Bethlehem.—The word צעיר forms
an apposition to Bethlehem: "little to be," instead of, "who
art too little to be." If the sense were to be, "thou art little,"
the אתה would not have been omitted after צעיר. The circumstance that Bethlehem is addressed as a masculine (comp. אתה,
צעיר, and ממך) may be accounted for by the prophet's viewing
the town in the image of its *ideal* representative; compare remarks on Zech. ix. 7. In such a case, the gender may be
neglected; compare, *e.g.*, Gen. iv. 7, where sin, חטאת, appears
as a masculine noun, on account of the image of a ravenous
beast. Such personifications occur very frequently. Thus,
nothing is more common in the Mosaic law than that Israel is
addressed as one man. This has been frequently misunderstood,
and, in consequence, that which refers to the whole people has
been applied to the single individual. Thus it is even in the
Decalogue. In Is. v. 7, the people of Judah appear as the *man*
Judah.

The *littleness* of Bethlehem is sufficiently evident from the
circumstance of its being left out in the catalogue of the towns
of the tribe of Judah, in Joshua (compare *Bachiene*, § 192).
This induced the LXX. to insert it in Josh. xv. 60 along with
several other towns which had been omitted; and, in doing so,
they were probably guided, not so much by a regard to its out-

ward importance, as by the interest which attached to it from
the recollection of an event of former times (compare Gen.
xxxv.), from its being the birth-place of David, and still more,
from the prophecy under consideration, by which the eyes of
the whole nation were directed to this place, outwardly so unimportant. The assertion of *Jerome*, that the Jews omitted the
name in the Hebrew text, in order that Christ might not appear
as a descendant of the tribe of Judah, has received from *Reland*
(S. 643) a more thorough refutation than it deserved. *Keil*, in
his commentary on Joshua, has lately renewed the attempt to
prove, from internal reasons, the genuineness of the addition;
but, from the whole condition of the Alex. Version, it is very
dangerous to trust to such arguments. The very reasons which
Keil brings forward in support of the addition, are just those
which might have induced the LXX. to make it. The circumstance that they added to Bethlehem the name Ephratah, plainly
indicates the reason which induced them to introduce Bethlehem
specially. Bethlehem is likewise omitted in the catalogue of
the towns of Judah, in Neh. xi. 25 ff., and can therefore have
occupied among them a very low place only, although it is
mentioned in Ezra ii. 21, Neh. vii. 26. In the New Testament, it is called a mere village (κώμη, John vii. 42). *Josephus*,
indeed, occasionally gives it the title of a town (compare Luke
ii. 4, 11); but, in other passages, he designates it by χωρίον,
Ant. v. 2, 8.—צעיר להיות means properly, "little in reference to
being," instead of, "too little to be,"—the wider expression
being used to indicate the relations of the town to the being,
where we use the more limited expression.—Instead of the
"thousands of Judah," שׂרי אלפים ought to have been employed,
as it appears, in order strictly to maintain the personification.
The representative of Bethlehem is too small to be numbered
among the heads of Judah. Several expositors (*J. D. Michaelis,
Justi*) have thereby been induced to point בְּאַלְפֵי instead of בְּאַלְפֵי.
But this supposed emendation is set aside by the consideration
that אַלּוּף is only the special designation of the Edomitish
princes, and occurs in a general sense, only by way of *Catachresis*, in Zechariah, who lived at a time when the Hebrew
language was nearly extinct. The most simple explanation is,
that the prophet views the thousands, or the families of Judah,
no less than the town Bethlehem, as *ideal* existences; in which

case, the personification is maintained throughout. Moreover, there would not be any insurmountable difficulty in the way of supposing that the prophet had given up the personification; for these are frequently not strictly adhered to by the prophets, who constantly pass from the figure to the thing prefigured. This may be at once seen from the preceding verse, in the first clause of which, Zion appears personified as a woman, while immediately afterwards there follows, "against us."—אֶלֶף, "thousand," is frequently used for designating a family, because the number of its members usually consisted of about a thousand; compare Num. i. 16, where it is said of the twelve princes of the tribes: "Heads of the thousands of Israel are they;" Num. x. 4; Josh. xxii. 14, 21; Judg. vi. 15; 1 Sam. x. 19. On the division of Israel into thousands, hundreds, etc.—a division which existed before the time of Moses—compare what has been advanced in my *Dissertations on the Genuineness of the Pentateuch*, ii. p. 341 sqq. It is self-evident that the thought here is, that Bethlehem is too little to constitute a thousand *by itself*. Communities, however, which were not sufficiently numerous to constitute, by themselves, a generation or family, were reckoned with others, and formed with them an artificial generation, an artificial family; for the divisions of generations and families were, owing to the great significance which numbers had in ancient times, connected with numerical relations. An instance of this kind occurs in 1 Chron. xxiii. 11, 12, where it is said of four brothers that they had not sons enough, and were, for that reason, reckoned as one family only. Being merely *part* of a generation, Bethlehem had no place among the generations. The sense is clearly this: Bethlehem occupies a very low rank among the towns of the Covenant-people, —can scarcely show herself in the company of her distinguished sisters, who proudly look down upon her.—It is altogether a matter of course that יָצָא, "to go out," may be used also of "being born," of "descent," inasmuch as this belongs to the general category of going out; compare, *e.g.*, 2 Kings xx. 18. We must, however, confine ourselves to the general idea of "going forth," "proceeding," and not consider Bethlehem as the father of the Messiah. In opposition to *Hofmann*, this is proved by *Caspari*, from Jer. xxx. 21: "And their governor shall proceed from the midst of them;" and from Zech. x. 4.

—יֵצֵא is without a definite subject. It is best to supply "one," which is evidently implied,in what follows. The construction, which might otherwise appear somewhat strange, has been occasioned by the desire of making perceptible, by the very words, and their position, the contrast between the divine greatness and the natural littleness of Bethlehem :—

> Thou art little to be among the thousands of Judah ;—
> From thee shall come forth unto me, to be a Ruler in Israel.

From a place which is too little to form a single independent member of the body, the head proceeds. From this contrast appears also the reason why it is said, "Ruler in Israel," while we should have expected to hear of the Ruler of Israel κατ' ἐξοχήν,—a circumstance on which *Paulus* lays so much stress in opposing the Messianic interpretation.—Had the prophet adopted the latter expression, not only would this contrast have been less striking, but the other also, which is likewise intended, viz., the contrast with the judge of Israel, in the preceding verse, who loses his dignity. The prophet was, in the first instance, concerned more about the *genus* than the *individual*,—more about the idea of dominion in general, than about the mode and kind of it. The individual is, afterwards, however, partly in this verse itself, partly in the following verse, so distinctly characterized, that he cannot be by any means mistaken. Nothing more, it is true, is implied in these words, than that, at some future time, there would come forth from Bethlehem a Ruler over all Israel; and if these words stood isolated, and if it could be proved that, after the time of Micah, there came forth from Bethlehem a Ruler over all Israel, besides the Messiah—a thing which, however, cannot be proved—then, indeed, it might be questionable which of the two to choose. *Caspari's* exposition, "Will *he* come forth," has this against it, that, in the preceding verses, the Messiah was not yet spoken of, and, hence, that He cannot simply be supposed as known; and least of all—if the acquaintance with Him were to be supposed from other passages—could He have been introduced with a simple unaccented *he:* the הוא could not have been omitted in this case. The case in iv. 8 is but little analogous, for the subject in תֵאתֶה is there an indefinite one.—לִי is, by several interpreters, referred to the prophet. Thus *Rosenmüller,* following *Michaelis*, says, "*To me, i.e.*, for my good, the prophet says, in the name of his whole people." But the reference to God is required by the contrast between human littleness and divine greatness. *Calvin* remarks on it: "By this word, God declares that His decree to give up the people was not such, that He should not be willing to restore them after some time. He therefore calls the faithful back to Himself, and reminds them of His counsel, just as if He said, 'I have indeed rejected you for a time, but not so as that I am not filled with compassion for you.'" The import of the לְ, viz., that God could exalt that which was low, the believer saw, in a type, in David; and there is no doubt that the prophet was anxious indirectly to refer them to this type, and thereby to strengthen their faith in the promise, which appeared almost incredible. He (David) had been a native of the humble, little Bethlehem, the youngest among his brothers, without power, without renown. In order that the לְ might become the more evident, the Lord, at his election, gave such a direction to the circumstances, that this, his natural lowliness, might be most strikingly exhibited. It was God who raised him from being a shepherd of lambs, to be a shepherd of nations.

In contrast with the Messiah's human and lowly origin, His divine and lofty dignity is prominently brought out in the last words of the verse,—a contrast similar to that in the case of Bethlehem, to which the prophet thereby refers. Here also, the prophet has so clearly expressed the contrast by the words themselves, that, upon the *homines bonæ voluntatis* among the interpreters of all ages, it has most forcibly impressed itself. Thus, *e.g., Chrysostom, demonstratio adv. Judæos et Gentiles, quod Christus sit Deus*, opp. T. V., p. 739 : " He exhibits both Godhead and manhood. For in the words, ' His goings forth are from the beginning, from the days of eternity,' His existence from all eternity is revealed ; while in the words, ' Shall come forth the ruler who feeds My people Israel,' His origin according to the flesh is revealed." A more minute inquiry into the meaning of these words must begin with the investigation of מוֹצָאֹתָיו. The greater number of interpreters agree in this, that מוֹצָאָה, the feminine form of the more common מוֹצָא, here denotes the action of the going forth. But this is opposed by the following considerations. 1. The use of the plural. Those especially who here think of the eternal going forth of the Son from the Father, cannot by any means justify it. Several among them consider it as *plur. majest.* Thus, *e.g.*, do *Tarnovius* and *Frischmuth*, in the *Dissert. de Nativitate Messiæ*, in the remarks on this passage, Jena 1661. But although such a plural exists, indeed, in Hebrew, and many traces of it are to be found (compare my *Dissertations on the Genuineness of the Pentateuch*, i. p. 267 ff.), it could appear here, of course, in the suffix only, not in the noun. Others suppose that the plural stands here simply for the singular. Now, there are, it is true, three cases in which such does apparently take place:—the first, when a definite individual out of the multitude is meant,—when accordingly, not the *number*, but the general idea only is concerned;—the second, when a noun in the plural gradually loses its plural signification, because the etymology and original signification have become indistinct;—the third, when the plural stands for the abstract. Not one of these cases, however, is applicable here. Those interpreters have most plausibly removed the difficulty who understand מוצאתיו to be really a repeated act of going forth, and refer it to the Old Testament doctrine of the Angel of the Lord. Thus *Jerome:* "Because He had always spoken to them through the prophets, and became in their hands the Word of God." *Tremellius* and *Junius:* "The goings forth, *i.e.*, the declarations and demonstrations of, as it were, a rising sun; He from the very beginning revealed and manifested Himself to all created things, by the light of His word, and the excellency of His works· just as the rising sun manifests himself from the moment of his rising, by the light and its effects." *Cocceius:* "I cannot, however, be persuaded to believe that the plural מוצאתיו is here used without emphasis. For the Son has not gone forth from the Father, like a man from a man, who begins to exist only when he is brought forth from a man, and when he goes forth, ceases to be brought forth and to go out. In all the days of eternity, the Son proceeds from the Father, and is the eternal ἀπαύγασμα τῆς δόξης αὐτοῦ." But this circumstance is, in general, against this explanation, that the contrast with the going forth from Bethlehem, which is completed in one act, does not admit of the mention of a manifold going forth, and that, in this contrast, the arising, the origin of the existence of the Messiah, can alone be thought of; while, more specially, *Jerome,*

Tremellius, and *Junius,* who, with *Piscator* also, limit the going forth to the relation to created things only, are contradicted by מִימֵי עוֹלָם, by which the going forth is placed beyond the beginning of creation ; and *Cocceius,* by the fact that the מַלְאַךְ יְהוָה in the Old Testament, differently from the Λόγος in the New Testament, appears always as going forth from God, in relation to the world only.   But although the " time of old and the days of eternity" should be considered as the place of the going forth, yet the plural cannot be explained, as is done by *Caspari,* from the circumstance that " a person is always descended from several ;" for the transferring of such a *usus loquendi* to a relation, to which in itself it is not applicable, could be admitted only when it could be demonstrated to be altogether common and firmly established.   But the plural might indeed, although only with some difficulty, be vindicated and accounted for from the circumstance, that two points of going forth are mentioned, which, as it were, suppose a twofold act.   2. But even if the singular were used, the explanation of the act of going forth would not be admissible.   It is contrary to the idea of nouns with מ, that they could be used as *nomina actionis.*   It is only with writers living at a time when the language was dying out, that a few instances of this erroneous use can be found.   מ denotes the place where, the instrument wherewith, the time wherein, and perhaps the way and manner whereby, something is done, or is.   *Further*—It may signify also the thing itself which is done, or is ; but, in no writer of the living and flourishing language, does it ever denote the action itself.   *Caspari,* indeed, attempts to prove that " there occurs in the older books a number, by no means inconsiderable, of nouns with מ, which undeniably denote an action ;" but what he has advanced on this point requires still to be minutely sifted, and to be more closely examined ; compare, *e.g.,* on Num. x. 2, my pamphlet on " *The Day of the Lord,*" S. 32.   But we are quite satisfied with what is granted by *Caspari* himself (compare *Ewald's Lehrbuch d. Hebr. Spr.* § 160), that it is against the nature and common use of this form to denote the action.   Even by this concession, a presumption is raised against the correctness of an interpretation which would ascribe to מוֹצָא, here, and in other passages, the signification of going forth, viewed as an action.   The passages quoted by *Winer* in favour of the signification, *egressus,* are the following: 1. Hos. vi. 3, where it is said of the Lord כשחר נכון מוצאו, "firm like the morning-dawn is His going forth." But מוצא is there, not the action, but the place and the time of the going forth, as is evident from the word "firm" also. 2. Ezek. xii. 4: "And thou shalt go forth at even in their sight, כמוצאי גולה." Several interpreters agree that מוצא here signifies the kind and mode of the going forth. *Vatablus* says, "It denotes the deportment of him who goes forth, and means, Thou shalt go forth in sorrow, and indignant." But it is better, with *Hävernick*, to refer it to the time: "According to the goings forth of prisoners, at the time when emigrants of this kind prefer to go forth from their places." 3. Num. xxxiii. 2: "And Moses wrote down את מוצאיהם, 'the places of their goings out.'" 4. Ps. xix. 7, it is said of the sun: מקצה השמים מוצאו, "from the end of the heaven is his going forth," which is tantamount to—The end of the heaven is the place from which he goes forth. 5. 1 Kings x. 28: ומוצא הסוסים אשר לשלמה ממצרים, which *De Wette* translates, "And the export of the horses which Solomon had, (was) from Egypt." But a more accurate translation is, "And the place of coming forth of the horses which Solomon had was Egypt," or, more literally still, "from Egypt,"—a concise mode of expression for, "The place from which the horses of Solomon came forth was Egypt,"— just as in the preceding example. In proof of the signification, "action of going out," *Ch. B. Michaelis* refers, moreover, to 2 Sam. iii. 25, where *De Wette* translates, "Thou knowest Abner, the son of Ner; he came to deceive thee, and to see thy going out and thy coming in, and all that thou doest." But a more accurate translation would be, "The place from which thou goest out, and to which thou art going;" compare Ezek. xliii. 11. In all other passages—and these are rather numerous —the signification "place of going out," or "that which goes out," is quite obvious. Even *Caspari* grants that the signification "place of going out" has, *a priori*, the greatest probability in its favour.—To this it may be added, that the signification "place of going out" is recommended here, even by the contrast with what precedes, inasmuch as there Bethlehem is mentioned as the place from which the Ruler in Israel is to come forth. With this place of going out, another and a higher one is contrasted. This contrast also shows us how the מ

in מקדם and מימי עולם must be understood, viz., in the same manner as מן in ממך; for the evident reference of מוצאתיו to יצא ל shows that it must correspond with it. Hence the literal translation would be, " And His places of going out are from the times of old, from the days of eternity," which is equivalent to—The places from which He goes forth are the times of old, the days of eternity,—just as in the two passages, Ps. xix. 7; 1 Kings x. 28. The מן might very well have been omitted; but its insertion here has arisen chiefly from a desire to make the reference to the corresponding clause outwardly also more perceptible. This reference shows also, that the explanation of מן by *præ*, which was proposed by *Pococke* and others, is inadmissible, besides involving an absurdity, inasmuch as nothing can be *before* eternity; while, on the other hand, this reference alone affords a satisfactory explanation of the plural. According to it, the words, " From the time of old, from the days of eternity," contain a gradation. *First*, the existence of the Messiah before His birth in time, in Bethlehem, is pointed out in general; and *then*, in contrast with all time, it is vindicated to eternity. This could not fail to afford a great consolation to Israel. He who hereafter, in a visible manifestation, was to deliver them from their misery, was already in existence,— during it, before it, and through all eternity.

HISTORY OF THE INTERPRETATION.

1. AMONG THE JEWS.

This History, as to its essential features, might, *a priori*, be sketched with tolerable certainty. From the nature of the case, we could scarcely expect that the Jews should have adopted views altogether erroneous as to the subject of the prophecy in question; for the Messiah appears in it, not in His humiliation, but in His glory—rich in gifts and blessings, and Pelagian self-delusion will, *a priori*, return an affirmative answer to the question as to whether one is called to partake in them. But, on the other hand, the prophecy contains a twofold ground of offence which had to be removed, and explained away at any expense. One of these, the eternity of the Messiah—which was in contradiction to the popular notions, and conceivable only from a knowledge of His Godhead—could not but exist at all times; while the second of these—the birth at Bethlehem—made its appearance, and exercised its influence, only after the birth of Christ. That this should be set aside, was demanded by two causes. *First,* there was the desire of depriving the Christians of the proof, which they derived from the birth at Bethlehem, for the proposition that He who had appeared was also He who was promised. And, *secondly,* there was the difficulty of any longer deriving from Bethlehem the descent of Christ, after, by an ordinance of Hadrian (compare *Reland,* S. 647), all the Jews had been expelled from Bethlehem and its neighbourhood. This difficulty was strongly urged against them by Christian controversialists; compare *Tertullian cont. Jud.* c. xiii., "How then can the Ruler be descended from Judah, and how can He come forth from Bethlehem, as, in the present day, there is not one of Israel left there, of whose family Christ may be born?" The actual history furnishes facts and details which only confirm and enlarge what, in its essential features, we have sketched *a priori.*

1. The reference to the Messiah was, at all times, not the private opinion of a few scholars, but was publicly received, and acknowledged with perfect unanimity. As respects the time of Christ, this is obvious from Matt. ii. 5. According to that passage, the whole Sanhedrim, when officially interrogated as to the birth-place of the Messiah, supposed this explanation to be the only correct one. But if this proof required a corroboration, it might be derived from John vii. 41, 42. In that passage, several who erroneously supposed Christ to be a native of Galilee, objected to His being the Messiah on the ground that Scripture says: ὅτι ἐκ τοῦ σπέρματος Δαβὶδ καὶ ἀπὸ Βηθλεὲμ τῆς κώμης, ὅπου ἦν Δαβίδ, ὁ Χριστὸς ἔρχεται. But even after Christ had appeared, the interest in depriving the Christians at once of the arguments which, in their controversies, they derived from this passage, was not sufficiently strong to blind the Jews to the evident indications contained in this passage, or to induce them to deprive themselves of the sweet hope which it afforded. This, it is true, would be the case nevertheless, if we were to rely upon, and believe in the assertion of *Chrysostom (Hom.* 7,

in Matt. c. 2, in *Nov. Test.*, t. i. p. 80, ed. Frcf.) : "Some of them, in their impudence, assert that this prophecy has a reference to Zerubbabel;" of *Theodoret* (on this passage): "The Jews have tried to refer this to Zerubbabel, which evidently fights against the truth;" of *Theophylact* (on Matt. ii.); and of *Euthymius Zigabenus* (in iv. *Evang.* t. 1, p. 61, ed. Mat.). But the supposition is here forced upon us—a supposition which, in another case also (compare remarks on Zech. ix. 9, 10), we must acknowledge to be well-founded—that the Fathers, having in their controversies with the Jews sometimes met a reference to Zerubbabel, forced it upon the Jews, even when the latter themselves refused it. And there can be the less difficulty in admitting this supposition, as the apparently fourfold testimony may be easily reduced to a single one, viz., to that of *Chrysostom*. If these statements had any truth in them, some traces, at least, of this interpretation must be found among the Jews themselves. This, however, is not the case. All the Jewish interpreters adhere to the Messianic interpretation, and in this they are headed by the Chaldee, who paraphrases the words יצא לי ממך in this way : מנך קדמי יפק משיחא, *i.e.*, From thee Messiah shall go out before me.

2. A twofold method has been tried to remove the first ground of objection mentioned above. In ancient times, they gave their full sense to the words, "Of (or from) the days of eternity," but substituted the name of the Messiah for His person. This we meet with as early as in the Chaldee, who says : דשמיה אמיר מלקדמין מיומי עלמא, *i.e.*, "Whose name is said (or called) from the days of old, from the days of eternity." Thus also the *Pirke R. Elieser*, ch. iii., where, with a reference to the passage before us, the name of the Messiah is mentioned among the seven things created before the world existed, viz., along with the Law, Hell, Paradise, the Throne of Glory, the Temple, Repentance; compare *Schöttgen* ii. S. 213. According to *Eisenmenger* i. S. 317, the same, with some change, is found in the Talmud, *Tract. Pesachim*, fol. 54, col. i., and *Nedarim* f. 39, c. 2. We cannot, in that explanation by the Chaldee, understand "name" in its emphatic signification, in which it often occurs in Scripture, viz., as an expression and image of the substance, —a signification in which the "name" of the Messiah would be equivalent to "the glory of the Messiah," or to "the Messiah

in His glory." This is evident from the אמיר, *i.e.*, "said" or "spoken," of the Chaldee, which does not allow of our thinking of the creation of a substance; and not less from the consideration, that if this signification of "name" were assumed, the aim and object which he had in view in substituting "name" for "person" at all, would have been missed. The name of the Messiah expresses His nature, the idea of His existence. The creation or pronouncing of this name marks, accordingly, the rise of this idea in God,—His forming the decree of redemption by the Messiah. By this explanation—which we again meet with, afterwards, in *Calvin,* and which we shall then consider more minutely—a mere existence in thought, was substituted for the real existence of the Messiah,—His predestination, for His pre-existence.—But in aftertimes they came still further down. To supply "the name," was too arbitrary to admit of their resting satisfied with such an explanation. Almost unanimously they now came to the supposition, that the words of the passage under consideration merely marked the descent of the Messiah from the ancient, royal house of David. Thus *Aben-ezra:* "All this is said of David; the words also, 'His *goings out* are of old,' refer to David." *Aberbanel (Praec. Sal.* p. 62): "The goings out of the family from which that Ruler is to be descended are of old, and of the days of eternity, *i.e.*, of the seed of David, and the rod of Jesse, which is of Bethlehem-Judah." On the similar expositions of *Kimchi* and others, compare *Frischmuth l.c.,* and *Wichmannshausen, Dissert. on the pass.,* Wittenb. 1722, S. 6 ff. We could not urge against this exposition that מוצאות is erroneously understood either as "going out," or, as "family;" and that, in the latter signification, the *usus loquendi,* as well as the evident reference to יצא, are disregarded. For that might be given up, and yet the explanation would stand as to its substance. Even then, it might be translated: "His goings out (in the signification of 'places of going out') are the days of old, the days of eternity," *i.e.*, the very ancient times; so that there would be ascribed to the time something which belongs to that which exists in it, viz., to the family of David. But the following reason is decisive against it. Every one will admit that the eternal origin of the Messiah forms a far more suitable contrast with His temporal origin from Bethlehem, than His descent from the ancient family of

David. The latter would come into consideration here, only on
account of its antiquity; a reference to its dignity is not made
by even a single word, nor is the family itself mentioned at all
in the text; but the attribute of antiquity, and that alone, is
nevertheless taken from it, and ascribed to the Messiah. But
now, we cannot at all see what pre-eminence in this respect the
family of David enjoyed above other families, and how, therefore,
it could have been an honour for the Messiah to be descended
from it. How strange would, according to this explanation, be
the words, "of the days of eternity," which, as a climax, are
added to, "of days of old!" What reason could there have
existed for the prophet to exalt, by a hyperbolical expression, a
limited time to eternity? As regards His human origin, the
Messiah had not the slightest advantage over other mortals, as
far as the age of the family was concerned. What, then, was
the use of such a hyperbole in a matter which, in this connection, was of no consequence, and which could not in any way
serve for His exaltation? It is just this, however, which after
all is required by the contrast. What kind of consolation would
thereby have been afforded to the people? Certainly no one
doubted that the Messiah would have parents, and ancestors
reaching back to a hoar antiquity. But was there anything
gained by this, since He had it only in common with the lowest
and feeblest among the people? How does this shallow, un-
meaning, and yet so much pretending contrast in reference to
the Messiah, suit the other contrast in reference to Bethlehem,
which is so brilliant and exalted? And now what reason is
there for preferring that explanation which is so unnatural, to
the other, which is so natural, so obvious, which presents a
contrast so beautiful, and opens up to the Covenant-people a
source of consolation so rich? Is it this, perhaps, that the
eternity of the Messiah is not mentioned anywhere else in the
Old Testament? But the eternity of the Messiah is only a
single feature of His divine nature, and just that feature which,
according to the context, came here into special consideration.
Caspari very correctly remarks: "The prophet pointed out just
the feature of the pre-existence, and of the eternal existence of
the Messiah, and these only, because the announcement of His
origin from the little Bethlehem led just to this, and to this
alone." The intimation of the divine nature of the Messiah is,

however, as old as the Messianic prediction in general; compare, concerning this, my remarks on Gen. xlix. 10. In a more definite shape, and in a more distinct form, it appears as early as in the Messianic Psalms. But it is found, in sharply defined outlines, in Isaiah, and specially in ix. 5, where, just as in the passage before us, the divine glory of the Messiah is contrasted with the lower aspect of His existence; and the closer the points of contact are between Isaiah and Micah, the less can we refuse to acknowledge such here. This circumstance also must prevent us from doing so, that immediately afterwards, in ver. 3 (4), the divine dignity and nature of the Messiah meet us anew. This passage requires, as its foundation, the one upon which we are now commenting. Moreover, the eternity which, in contrast with His birth in time, is here ascribed to the Messiah, corresponds with the eternity of His existence and dominion after His birth, which is repeatedly ascribed to the Messiah, and, most prominently, in Is. ix. 5, where He receives the name "Father of eternity," *i.e.*, He who will be Father in all eternity. —Some one, perhaps, would infer from the subjoined words, "of the days," that עולם is here to be understood in a limited sense. But who does not know that, when eternity is predicated in contrast with a limited duration of time, just to make the contrast the more striking, those measures of time, which are properly applicable to the latter only, are transferred to the former? For in order to be able to compare things, a certain resemblance between them must necessarily be first established. Thus in Dan. vii. 9, God is called "the Ancient of Days;" thus it is said of Him in Ps. cii. 28, "Thy years have no end;" and the New Testament frequently speaks in the same way of eternal times. We are, in our thoughts, generally so much bound to time, that we can conceive of eternity only as "time without time." It cannot by any means be satisfactorily or incontrovertibly proved from vii. 14, 20, that קדם and ימי עולם here designate merely the ancient time. All which that passage proves is, that such a sense is possible—and this, no one probably has ever doubted—but not that it is applicable in this connection. If the connection be considered, Prov. viii. 22, 23, will then be acknowledged to be parallel,—a passage in which the eternal existence of Wisdom is spoken of in a similar manner.

3. That, in the prophecy under consideration, Bethlehem is

marked out as the birth-place of the Messiah, was held as an undoubted truth by the ancient Jews. This appears from the confident reply of the Sanhedrim to the question of Herod as to the birth-place of Christ. And it is not less evident from John vii. 42. The circumstance that, after the tumult raised by Barcochba, not only Jerusalem, but Bethlehem also, was, by the Emperor Adrian, interdicted to the Jews as a residence, renders it probable that this interpretation was not given up immediately after the death of Christ. But even after this edict of Adrian, and after the difficulty had appeared in all its force, they did not, for a considerable time, venture to assert that the prophecy knew nothing of Bethlehem as the birth-place of the Messiah. It is with the later Rabbinical interpreters only, who were better skilled in the art of distorting, that this assertion is found. The ancient Jews endeavoured to evade the difficulty by the fable, dressed up in various ways, that the Messiah was indeed born at Bethlehem, on the day of the destruction of the temple, but that, on account of the sins of the people, He was afterwards carried away by a storm, and had, since that time, remained, unknown and concealed, in various places. Thus speak the Talmud, the very ancient commentary on Lamentations, *Echa Rabbati*, and the very old commentary on Genesis, *Breshith Rabba* (compare the passages in *Raim. Martini*, S. 348–50; *Carpzovius* and *Frischmuth*, l.c.). Indeed, we can trace this fiction still farther back. Closely connected with it is the explanation of עפל בת־ציון by "darkness of the daughter of Zion" (עפל being confounded with אפל), *i.e.*, hidden on account of Zion. This explanation is found as early as in Jonathan. The concealment of the Messiah is only an isolated feature of this fiction. The fiction itself, indeed, has its roots, not only in the passage under review, but also in the endeavour to remove the contradiction between the destruction of the temple, and the firm expectation of the Messiah's appearing during the time of its existence,—an expectation founded on passages of the Old Testament. This concealment of the Messiah is mentioned as early as in the *Dialogus cum Tryphone* (No. 8 *Bened. Ven.*; compare also p. 114): "Christ, even if he be born, and exist anywhere, is unknown, and neither manifests himself in any way, nor has he any power until Elijah come, etc." In order to be convinced that, at the time when this book was composed,

and hence in the second century, the fiction was already fully
developed, we need only compare the account in *Breshith Rabba*.
After Elijah, at the time of the birth of the Messiah, had visited
his mother in Bethlehem Judah, and consoled her who was
afflicted on account of the destruction of the temple, which was
contemporaneous with her delivery, he withdraws. "After five
years had elapsed, he said, I will go and see the Saviour of Israel,
whether he be nursed up in the manner of kings or of minister-
ing angels. He went and found the woman standing at the
door of her house, and said to her : My daughter, in what state
is that boy ? And she answered him : Rabbi, did I not tell thee
that it is a bad thing to nurse him, because, on the day on which
he was born, the temple was destroyed ? But this is not all; for
*he has feet and walks not, he has eyes and sees not, he has ears and
hears not, he has a mouth and does not speak at all, and there he
lies like a stone.*"

The Rabbinical interpreters felt, however, that this fiction,
being destitute of all warrant, was of no use to them in their
controversies with Christians ; and it was to these that their
view was chiefly directed. Hence they sought to remove the
difficulty by means of the interpretation; and as all had the same
interest, the result was that the distorted explanation became
as generally prevalent, as the correct one had formerly been.
Kimchi, Abenezra, Abendana, Abarbanel, and, in general, all the
later Rabbins (compare the passages in *Wichmannsh.* l. c. S. 9),
maintain that Bethlehem is mentioned here as the birth-place of
the Messiah indirectly only,—in so far only as the Messiah was
to be descended from David the Bethlehemite. There cannot
well be a prepossession in favour of this exposition. The circumstance that, formerly, no one ever thought that it was even
possible to explain the passage under review in any other way
than that, in it, Bethlehem is spoken of as the birth-place of the
Messiah, and that this exposition was discovered and introduced,
only at a time when the other could no longer be received, raises,
a priori, strong suspicions against it. And this suspicion is fully
confirmed by a closer examination. *Cæteris paribus,* that explanation which here finds Bethlehem mentioned as the birth-
place of the Messiah, would deserve the preference, even for
this reason, that the passage, as thus understood, fills up a blank

in the Messianic prophecy,—and that from the whole analogy, we are led to expect that no such blank would be left. Should the family from which Christ was to descend, the time at which He was to appear, the part of the country which was pre-eminently to enjoy His blessings, and so many other things concerning Him, have been so minutely foretold, and not the place where He was to be born? Even the question of Herod, ποῦ ὁ Χριστὸς γεννᾶται; shows how much reason we have, *a priori*, to expect such a prediction. He supposes that, as a matter of course, the birth-place of the Messiah must have been determined in the Old Testament; he only inquires about the place where. But the matter is not so, that there could be any choice at all betwixt the two explanations. If we suppose that it is only the descent of the Messiah from the family of David which is here announced, the contrast between the natural littleness of Bethlehem, and its divine greatness, would be very far from being appropriate. After the family of David had, for centuries, resided and ruled at Jerusalem, the natural littleness of Bethlehem came very little into further consideration. It was not this which could render improbable the appearance of the Messiah. It was only the downfall of Jerusalem, and the destruction of the King's Castle, which were in opposition to the belief in the Messiah's appearance. And, in like manner, the glory, resulting from His appearance, was not imparted to Bethlehem, but to Zion. Hence it is that, in iv. 8, where the prophet wishes to declare the descent of the Messiah from the family of David, he contrasts the glorification of Zion, and especially of the King's Castle, with its previous degradation.— *Further*—There is not a single instance to be found of a place, in which the ancestors of some one resided centuries ago, being spoken of as the place of his descent. Is there a single passage in which Bethlehem is mentioned as the native place of any of the kings from the Davidic dynasty who were born at Jerusalem, or as the native place of Zerubbabel who was born at Babylon? For further details concerning this argument, *Huetius, dem. Evang.* p 579 *ed. Amstel.* 1680, may be compared. —*Further*—The relation of the passage under review to the parallel passage Is. viii. 23 (ix. 1) must not be overlooked. As in the latter text, the *province* is marked out which, by the appearance of the Messiah, is to be raised from the deepest degradation to the highest glory, so, in the passage under consideration, the *place* is designated.—*Finally*—If any doubt yet remained, it must surely be removed by the fulfilment,—by the fact that Christ was actually born at Bethlehem ; and this so much the more, that this fact cannot be looked upon as an accidental circumstance, for Bethlehem was not the residence of His parents.

But the Jews endeavoured, in another way, to wrest from Christian controversialists the advantage afforded by this passage. They denied altogether that Christ was born at Bethlehem. Thus *Abr. Peritsol* (compare *Eisenmenger*, l. c. S. 259): "Since they called Him Jesus the Nazarene, and not Jesus the Bethlehemite, it is to be inferred that He was born at Nazareth, as it is written in the *Targum* of Jerusalem." Upon this point, however, there existed no unanimity among them. *David Gans*, in the Book *Zemach David*, mentions, without any remark, Bethlehem as the birth-place of the Messiah (S. 105 of *Vorst's* translation).

2. AMONG THE CHRISTIANS.

The conviction that Christ is the subject of the prophecy under consideration was so much the prevailing one in the Christian Church, that the mention of any of its defenders is altogether superfluous. It were more interesting to learn who were the opponents of it. The assertion of *Huetius*, l. c., that *Chrysostom*, *Theophylact*, and *Euthymius Zigabenus* attempted an explanation by which it was referred to Zerubbabel, rests on a misapprehension resulting from want of memory. *Huetius* himself ascribes to them that very view which they most decidedly oppose as the one alleged to be held by the Jews. But this interpretation was actually advanced by *Theodorus* of *Mopsueste*, whose exegetical tendencies it admirably suited. Along with several other interpretations, it was condemned by the Council at Rome, under Pope Vigilius; compare *H. Prado* on Ezek. *prooem. Sect.* 3, and *Hippol. a Lapide in prophet. min. prooem.*, and in the remarks on this passage. The immediate successor of *Theodorus* was *Grotius*. His book *de veritate relig. Christ.*—where in i. 5, § 17 (p. 266, ed. Oxon. 1820), he proves against the Jews the Messianic dignity of Christ, from the circumstance that He was, in accordance with the passage, born at Bethlehem—might, indeed, entitle us to infer that he was not confirmed in this opinion. But perhaps he only imagined that, in a popular work, he needed not to be so careful, and that, even according to his own views, he had retained a certain right to this use of the passage, inasmuch as he considered Zerubbabel as a type of Christ, and the birth of the latter at Bethlehem as an outward representation of His descent from the Davidic family. It was at the commencement of the Rationalistic period, when an easier mode of evading the reference to Christ had not as yet been discovered, that the reference to Zerubbabel was seized upon. It is found in *Dathe* and *Kuehnöl* (*Mess. Weissagungen*, S. 88). The latter, however, changed his opinion (compare Commentary on Matt. ii.), after such a mode had been discovered, by referring the prophecy to the *ideal* Christ. From that time onwards, the reference to the *ideal* Christ is found in almost all the Rationalistic interpreters. The distinctness with which the marks here given, viz., the birth in time at Bethlehem, and the eternity of the origin, lead to the *historical* Christ; and the difficulty of explaining these when the prophecy is referred to the *ideal* Messiah, are rendered sufficiently evident by the efforts which all these interpreters, without exception, have made to explain these marks away. Who does not discover, in these very efforts, a confession of their force, on the supposition that they can be, as they have already been, demonstrated to have an actual existence? God Himself has borne witness by facts against this explanation; for He ordered the circumstance in such a manner that, by the birth of Christ at Bethlehem, the prophecy was fulfilled. But how can a fulfilment be spoken of by those who do not believe in prophecy, but see in it human conjectures only, since the very idea of prophecy necessarily implies divine inspiration? How should God have impressed His own seal upon mere human conjectures, as He would have done by effecting an apparent fulfilment? He would Himself have surely become the author of error by so doing. *Finally,*—We shall afterwards see that, in the New Testament, this passage has been explained in the strictest sense, of the historical Christ; and the attempts of the Rationalistic interpreters to divest that quotation of its import, will furnish us with a proof, that it is not truth for which they are concerned, but the removal only, at any rate and cost, of a fact which is irreconcilable with their system. All that has been advanced by them (*e.g.*, by *Justi* and *Ammon*) against the reference to the historical Christ, rests on their misapprehension of Christ's Regal office. The Regal office of Christ is by no means a poetical image, but the most *real* among all kingly offices; yea, His kingdom is that from which all others derive their existence and reality. It rests, *further*, on their ignorance as regards the final history of the Messianic kingdom. Of the whole history of Christ, they know a single fragment only, viz., His first appearance in His humiliation; and even this they know, and can know, only very imperfectly. His invisible dominion existing even now, they do not recognise, because it is beheld with the eye of faith only; and His future visible manifestation of it they do not believe, because they have not experienced in their own hearts the invisible power of Christ, which is a pledge and earnest of this visible success. It rests, *finally*, on their ignorance of the prophetic vision, which necessarily requires that the kingdom of God under the Old Testament should serve as a substratum for the description of the kingdom of Christ. It can be demonstrated, from the intimations contained in this passage, in which the Messiah appears in His glory, how little it is contradictory to others, in which He is represented in His lowest humiliation. Through humiliation to glory,—this is the proposition which lies at the foundation of the announcements of the prophet concerning the destinies of the Covenant-people, and which he distinctly expresses in regard to Bethlehem. That this proposition is applicable to the Head not less than to the members, —to Him who was born, not less than to the place where He was born, appears from the circumstance that He was to be born at the time of the deepest degradation of the Davidic dynasty, iv. 8, and not at Jerusalem, where His Royal ancestors resided, but at Bethlehem.

2. As regards the last words of this verse, the same twofold false interpretation which we noticed among Jewish interpreters, is found among Christian expositors also. One of these, which, besides in other Jewish interpreters, occurs in *Jarchi* ("*and His goings out*, etc.; just as in Ps. lxxii. 17, it was said that His name

should continue as long as the sun ;—thus *Jonathan* also translated it"), changes the eternal origin of Christ into an eternal predestination. This view was held by *Calvin:* "These words," he says, "signify that the rising of the Prince who was to rule the nations would not be something sudden, but long ago decreed by God. I know that some pertinaciously insist that the prophet speaks here of Christ's eternal essence, and as far as I am concerned, I *willingly* acknowledge that Christ's eternal Godhead is here proved to us ; but as we shall never succeed in convincing the Jews of this, I prefer to hold that the words of the prophet signify that Christ would not thus suddenly proceed from Bethlehem, as if God had formerly decreed nothing concerning Him." He speaks indeed of his "*willingly* acknowledging ;" but that he was not very much in earnest in his willingness, appears from what follows : "Others advance a new and ingenious view," etc. It is only from the relation of *Calvin* to the earlier interpreters, that we can account for his advancing an exposition so very arbitrary. These had, *ad majorem Dei gloriam*, advanced a multitude of forced expositions. *Calvin*, who very properly hated such interpretations ("I do not like such distorted explanations," he says, in his commentary on Joel ii.), always regarded them with suspicion ; and whensoever there was the appearance of any motive which may possibly have guided them in adopting a certain explanation, he himself, rather than concur with them, falls upon the most unnatural explanations in return. The best refutation of his exposition is to be found in *Pococke.* It is absurd to suppose that the actual going forth of Christ from Bethlehem is here contrasted with one which is merely imaginary,—the action, with a mere decree. It is without any analogy that some one should be designated as actually existing, or going forth, who exists merely in the divine foreknowledge, or the divine predestination.—The other view, which regards the last words of this verse as referring to the Messiah's descent from the ancient family of David, is found among all interpreters who, from some cause, were prevented from adopting the sound one. It is thus with the Socinians (compare, *e.g., Volkel de vera religione,* 1. 5, c. 2), some of whom, in order the more surely to set aside a passage so damaging to their system, supposed that, according to its proper sense, it did not refer to Christ at all ; *e.g., Jo. Crellius,* who, in his exposition of Matt. ii., asserts that it refers indefinitely to some one of the family of David who, after the Babylonish captivity, was to rule the nation. It is thus with *Grotius* also, who says: "He (Zerubbabel) has his origin from the days of old, from ancient times, *i.e.*, he has descended from a house, illustrious from ancient times, and governing for five hundred years." Thus it is with all the Rationalistic interpreters. Among recent faithful Christian expositors, *Jahn* also (*Vatic. Mess.* 2, p. 147) has been led away to the adoption of this opinion. But that he felt strongly, at least, one of the difficulties which stood in its way, viz., that if the reference to the family of David be assumed, it is the mere age of the family, apart from every preference on the ground of its dignity, which is mentioned to magnify the Messiah—appears from the strange exegetical process which he employs for the purpose of removing it. He supplies at the end, *celebris est :*—" His origin or His family (thus he erroneously explains מוצאתי) is *celebrated* from ancient times." One may see in this case how much, in particulars, an individual still remains dependent upon a community, even although, upon the whole, he may have freed himself from such dependence. For it is certainly from this dependence alone that the fact can be accounted for, that this commentator rejected an exposition which must have been to him the most agreeable, which has everything in its favour, and nothing against it,—and chose another instead, the nakedness of which he was obliged to cover as well as he could, while, in so doing, he was violating his *exegetical convictions*. *Ewald* also permits himself to introduce into the passage what is necessary for the sense which he has made up his mind to adopt. In place of the simple antiquity, he puts: "Descended from the ancient, venerable royal family of David." The view taken by *Hofmann* is peculiar : " He comes from the family of David, just as it had happened long ago, when that family still belonged to the community of Bethlehem,—from the community of Bethlehem does He come." *Weiss. u. Erf.* 1, S. 251. In order to get at this rather superfluous repetition, he has substituted the manner in which the family of David formerly existed, for " the days of old, and eternity." The " origins " (this is the sense which he gives to מוצאתי) cannot be attributed to that portion only of David's family which dwelt at Bethlehem; for He was descended from them indirectly only, through the royal family of David.

3. The Jewish assertion, that in the prophecy there is no allusion to the birth at Bethlehem of Him who was to come, could not fail to be repeated by *Grotius* and his supporters, inasmuch as Zerubbabel was not born at Bethlehem. "Zerubbabel," he says, "is rightly said to have been born at Bethlehem, because he was of the family of David which had its origin there." This is, in like manner, repeated by the Rationalistic interpreters, in order to avoid the too close coincidence of the prophecy with the actual history of Christ, *e.g.*, by *Paulus* and *Strauss* (both, in their "Life of Jesus"), and by *Hitzig*. It is remarkable, however, that, in order the more securely to attain this object, some have gone so far even as to follow the example of several Jews, and of the infamous *Bodinus* (*de abditis rerum sublimium arcanis*, l. 5, compare the refutation by *Huetius*, l.c. p. 701), and to characterize the evangelical account concerning the birth of Christ at Bethlehem as unworthy of credit. Such has been the case with *Ammon* especially.

THE QUOTATION IN MATT. II. 6.

Several interpreters, *Paulus* especially, have asserted that the interpretation of Micah which is here given, was that of the Sanhedrim only, and not of the Evangelist, who merely recorded what happened and was said. But this assertion is at once refuted when we consider the object which Matthew has in view in his entire representation of the early life of Jesus. His object in recording the early life of Jesus is not like that of Luke, viz., to communicate historical information to his readers. The historical event which he could suppose to be already known to *his* readers, comes into his view only in so far as it served for the confirmation of Old Testament prophecies. Hence it is that he touches upon any historical circumstance, just when the mention of it can serve for the attainment of this purpose. Thus, the design of the genealogy is to prove that, in accordance with the prophecies of the Old Testament, Christ was descended from Abraham, through David. Thus all which he mentions in chap. i. 18–21, serves only to prepare the way for the quotation of the prophecy of Isaiah, that the Messiah was to be born of a virgin, which is subjoined in ver. 22, with the words: τοῦτο δὲ ὅλον γέγονεν ἵνα πληρωθῇ. Even the ὅλον proves that all which precedes is mentioned solely with a view to the prophecy. The παρερμηνεία of *Olshausen* which refers the ὅλον to the whole, in contrast with the particular, can be accounted for only from the embarrassment into which this commentator could not here avoid falling by his interpretation of the prophecy of Isaiah, according to which a semblance of agreement is, with the utmost difficulty, made out betwixt it, and the event in which Matthew finds its fulfilment. Moreover, all the single features of the account have too distinct a reference to the prophecy which is to be afterwards quoted. It is from a regard to it, that he is most anxious to point out that Christ was conceived by a pure and immaculate virgin, that, in ver. 25, he expressly adds that before the birth of Jesus, Mary had had no connubial intercourse with Joseph, because Immanuel was not only to be conceived, but born of a virgin. The words, καλέσεις τὸ ὄνομα αὐτοῦ Ἰησοῦν, correspond exactly with καὶ καλέσουσι τὸ ὄνομα αὐτοῦ Ἐμμανουήλ. The Evangelist explains the latter name by μεθ' ἡμῶν ὁ Θεός, which, again, cannot be without an object, for the name of Jesus (*Gottheil, God-Salvation*) has, with him, the same signification. We pass over, in the meantime, the section ii. 1–12. In ver. 13 there follows the account of the flight into Egypt with a reference to Hos. xi. 1. This passage refers, in the first instance, to Israel; but Israel does not here come into view according to its carnal condition, but only according to its divine destination and election,—as is evidently shown by the designation "Son of God." Israel was called to preserve the truth of God in the midst of error, to proclaim among the Gentiles the mighty acts of God, and to be His messenger and ambassador. In this respect Israel was a type of the Messiah, and the latter, as it were, a concentrated and exalted Israel. It is from this relation alone that many passages in the second part of Isaiah can be explained; and in Is. xlix. 3, the Messiah is expressly called Israel. If, then, there existed between Israel and the Messiah such a relation of type and Antitype;—if this relation was not accidental, but designed by God, it will, *a priori*, appear to us most probable that the abode of the children of Israel in Egypt, and the residence of Christ in the same country, have a relation to each other. This supposition rests upon the perception of the remarkable coincidence which, by divine Providence, generally exists betwixt the destinies of typical persons, and those of the Antitype, so that the former may be considered as an actual prophecy of the latter. But this coincidence must here not be sought in the stay in the same country only; this circumstance served only to direct attention to the deeper unity, to represent it outwardly. It was not from their own choice, but from a series of the most remarkable dispensations of Providence, and on the express command of God, that Israel went to Egypt. They thereby escaped from the destruction which threatened them in the land for which they were really destined. They were there prepared for their destiny; and when that preparation was finished, they were, agreeably to the promise of God, which was given to them even before they went down into Egypt, introduced into that land in which their destiny was to be realized. The same providence of God which there chose the means for the preservation of His kingdom, which was at that time bound up with the existence of the typical Israel, chose the same means now also when their hopes concentrated themselves in the person of their future Head. It was necessary that Egypt should afford Him a safe abode until the danger was over.—There then follows, in vers. 16–19, the account of the murder of the children of Bethlehem, with a sole reference to Jer. xxxi. 15, and just on account of it. Here, too, we must not think of a simple simile only. In Jeremiah, the mother of Israel laments over the destruction of her children. The Lord appears and comforts her. Her grief is, at some future time, to be changed into joy. She is to see the salvation which the Lord will still bestow upon her sons. That which, therefore, constitutes the essence of that passage is the contrast of the merited punishment which Israel drew down upon themselves by their sins, with the unmerited salvation which the mercy of the Lord will bestow upon them. Now, quite the same contrast is perceptible in the event under consideration. In the same manner as the tyranny of the Chaldeans, so that of Herod also was a deserved punishment for the sins of the Covenant-people. Herod, by birth a foreigner, was, like Nebuchadnezzar, a rod of correction in the hand of the Lord. The cruel deed which, with divine permission, he committed at the very place in which the Saviour was born, was designed actually and visibly to remind the Covenant-people of what they had deserved by their sins,—was intended also to be a matter-of-fact prophecy of the impending more comprehensive judgment, and thus to make it manifest that so much the more plainly, the sending of the Messiah was purely a work of divine mercy, destined for those only who would recognise it as such. From this it appears that the Old Testament event, to which the prophet, in the first instance, refers, viz., the carrying away into captivity, and the deliverance from it, were prophecies by deeds of those New Testament relations (in which, however, the typical relation of the murder of the children at Bethlehem, as we have stated it, must not be overlooked);—that both were subject to the same laws, that both were a necessary result of the working of the same divine mercy, and that hence, a declaration which, in the first instance, referred to the first event, might at the same time be considered as a prophecy of the second.—Vers. 19 and 20 have for their foundation Exod. iv. 19, where the Lord, after having ordered Moses to return to Egypt, subjoins the words: τεθνήκασι γὰρ πάντες οἱ ζητοῦντές σου τὴν ψυχήν. That which the Lord there speaks to Moses, and that which, here, He speaks to Joseph, proceed from the same cause. Like all servants of God under the Old Testament, Moses is a type of Christ. There is the same overruling by divine Providence, the same direction of all events for the good of the kingdom of God. Moses is first withdrawn from threatening danger by flight into distant regions. As soon as it is time that he should enter upon his vocation, the door for the return to the scene of his activity is opened to him. Just so is it with regard to Christ.—Vers. 21—23 have for their sole foundation the prophetic declaration: ὅτι Ναζωραῖος κληθήσεται (compare, on these words, the remarks on Is. xi.). The particular circumstances which are mentioned, viz., that Joseph had the intention of settling in Judea, but received from God the command to go into Galilee, are designed only to make it more perceptible that the fulfilment of this prophecy was willed by God.

From this summary it sufficiently appears that the object of Matthew in chap. i. and ii. was by no means of an historical, but rather of a doctrinal nature; and since this is the case, all the objections fall to the ground, which *Sieffert*, solely by disregarding this object of the writer, has lately drawn from these chapters against the genuineness of Matthew's Gospel. And if we apply this to the question before us, it follows that the section ii. 1–12 must likewise have an Old Testament foundation. That this foundation can, in the first instance, be sought for only in the prophecy of Micah, becomes evident from the circumstance, that Bethlehem is, in ver. 1, mentioned as Christ's birth-place. If we now take into consideration the fact that the Evangelist does not mention at all that the parents of Jesus formerly resided at Nazareth, just because it had no reference to any prophecy of the Old Testament (it is merely by designating, in the account of the birth of Jesus, Bethlehem as the place of His parents, that he intimates that that which had been previously reported had happened in a different place),—and that, on the other hand, he mentions the residence of the Holy Family at Nazareth, after their return from Egypt, evidently for the sole purpose of bringing it into connection with a prophecy,—it becomes quite evident that it is not from any historical interest that this circumstance, which was known to all his readers, is mentioned. To this it may be further added, that the account given in vers. 1–6, especially the communication of the answer of the Sanhedrim to the question of Herod, would, according to the proved object and aim of Matthew, stand altogether without a purpose, unless he had considered the answer of the Doctors as being in harmony with the truth, and hence as superseding his usual formula, ἵνα πληρωθῇ. In order to show how much Matthew was guided by a regard to the Old Testament, and how frequently, at the same time, he contented himself with a mere allusion, supposing his readers to be acquainted with the Old Testament—as is quite evident from vers. 20 and 23—we must further consider the second Old Testament reference which he has in view in vers. 1–12. The passages to which he refers are Ps. lxxii. 10: "The kings of Sheba and Seba shall offer gifts;" and Is. lx. 6: "All they from Sheba shall come, they shall bring gold and incense, and they shall show forth the praises of the Lord." The representation, in these and other similar passages, is, in the first instance, a figurative one. Gifts are in the East a sign of allegiance. The fundamental thought is this: "The most distant, the wealthiest, and the most powerful nations of the earth shall do homage to the Messiah, and consecrate to Him themselves and all that they have." But that which is prophesied by a figurative representation in these Old Testament passages began to be fulfilled by the symbolical action of the Magi, by which the image was represented externally; for the gold, incense, and myrrh which they consecrated to the new-born King of the Jews symbolized the homage which they offered to Him; and these gifts are certainly expressly mentioned by Matthew for this reason, that they occur in the Old Testament passages. As this event formed, in one respect, the beginning of the fulfilment, so, in another, it formed a new prophecy by deeds,—the type of a new, greater, and more proper fulfilment. The Apostles considered these Magi as the types and representatives of the whole mass of heathen nations who were, at a subsequent period, to do homage to the Messiah. They were the ambassadors, as it were, of the heathen world, to greet the new-born King, just as the shepherds, whom God Himself had chosen, were the deputies of the Jews. In my work on Balaam, pp. 480-482, I have proved that, even with these references, the contents of the passage are not yet exhausted,—that there still remains a prominent point, viz., the star which the Magi saw, and that this refers to Balaam's prophecy of the star proceeding from Jacob.

But if it be established that the view of the prophecy under consideration, which the Evangelist reports as that of the Sanhedrim, must, at the same time, be considered as his own, we must also suppose that the quotation, even in its particulars, is approved by him, and that the view which was first advanced by *Jerome* ("I believe that he wished to exhibit the negligence of the scribes and priests, and wrote it down as it had been spoken by them"), and recently by *Paulus*, cannot be made use of in order to justify the deviations,—if any should indeed be found. In order to ascertain this, we must examine more closely the quotation in its relation to the original text of the passage, Matt. ii. 6: Καὶ σὺ Βηθλεέμ, γῆ Ἰούδα οὐδαμῶς ἐλαχίστη εἶ ἐν τοῖς ἡγεμόσιν Ἰούδα· ἐκ σοῦ γὰρ ἐξελεύσεται ἡγούμενος, ὅστις ποιμανεῖ τὸν λαόν μου, τὸν Ἰσραήλ. The first thing which demands our attention is γῆ Ἰούδα for the Ephratah of the original. The reason of this deviation is to be sought for in the circumstance, that the place appears as Bethlehem Judah in 1 Sam. xvii. 12, where it is mentioned with a reference to David. The deviation at the beginning has, accordingly, the same purpose

as that at the close. As regards the grammatical exposition of
γῆ 'Ιούδα, it stands for: Bethlehem situated in the land of
Judah,—a short mode of expression which is common in geographical and other similar designations, just as in the Old Testament also we find בית־לחם יהודה, for: Bethlehem situated in
the land of Judah. The assertion of many interpreters, that
γῆ has here the signification "town," is as objectionable as the
attempt to change the text, made by *Fritzsche*, who advances
nothing on the whole verse that can stand examination. The
Evangelist here as little follows the LXX. as he does the
Hebrew text. The former has here: καὶ σὺ Βεθλεέμ, οἶκος
'Εφραθά (thus without an article, *Cod. Vatic.*). *Fritzsche* thinks
that οἶκος had been brought into the text from the margin.
But the translator evidently considered "Ephratah" to be the
proper name of Caleb's wife (1 Chron. ii. 19, 50, iv. 4), from
whom others also, *e.g.*, *Adrichomius* (compare *Bachiene* ii. 2, §
190), derived the name of the place, and did nothing else than
express more definitely, by the subjoined οἶκος, the relation of
dependence which, as he supposed, was indicated by the Genitive.
The apparent contradiction, that the prophet calls Bethlehem
small, whereas the Evangelist speaks of it as by no means small,
has already been so satisfactorily explained by ancient and
modern interpreters (compare, *e.g.*, *Euthymius Zigabenus l. c.* p.
59 : "Although in appearance thou art small, yet, truly, thou
art by no means the least among the principalities of the tribe
of Judah ; " *Michaelis* : "Micah, looking to the outward condition, calls it small ; Matthew, looking to the birth of the Messiah, calls it by no means small, inasmuch as, by that birth, that
town was in a wonderful manner adorned and exalted "), that
we need not dwell upon it. We only remark, that the supposition of *Paulus*, that the members of the Sanhedrim understood
the verse interrogatively—"Art thou, perhaps, too small," etc.—
receives no confirmation from the passage in *Pirke Eliezer*, c. 3,
which he quotes in favour of it, but which he saw only in the
Latin translation of *Wetzstein ;* for, in the original text, the
verse is quoted in literal agreement with the Hebrew original ;
compare *Eisenmenger*, i. p. 316. A comparison with the Chaldee,
who with similar liberty paraphrases, " Thou, Bethlehem Ephratah, shalt soon be numbered," clearly shows that the deviation
has arisen rather from an endeavour to express the sense more

clearly and definitely. On such deviations, *Calvin* strikingly remarks: "Let the reader always attend to the purpose for which the Evangelists quote Scripture passages, that they may not scrupulously insist upon single words, but be satisfied with this,—that the Scriptures are never distorted by them to a different sense."—Micah introduces Bethlehem in the person of its representative; but this figure Matthew has dropped at the beginning. Instead of the Masculine צעיר he puts the Feminine ἐλαχίστη; and, on the other hand, he renders באלפי by ἐν τοῖς ἡγεμόσι, which, in a way not to be mistaken, suggests this representation. *Fritzsche* announces himself as the man who would heal this *fœdum solœcismum* which had not hitherto been remarked by any one. He proposes to read: Καὶ σὺ Βεθλεὲμ τῆς Ἰουδαίας οὐδαμῶς ἐλαχίστη εἶ ἐν τοῖς ἡγεμόσιν Ἰούδα,— "and thou Bethlehem, by no means the smallest part of the land of Judah, art," etc. But altogether apart from the arbitrary change of γῆ Ἰούδα,—which certainly no one could ever have been tempted to put for the more simple τῆς Ἰουδαίας,—the personification could even then not have been maintained, and the *fœdus solœcismus* would still remain. Even although the ἐλαχίστη be understood in accordance with the "*elegantissimus Grœcorum usus*," Bethlehem must, after all, be treated as a thing —as a town. Nor is the case much improved by the assistance which *Fritzsche* immediately afterwards endeavours to give to the text: καὶ σὺ Βεθλεέμ, γῆ Ἰούδα, οὐδαμῶς ἐλαχίστη εἶ ἐν ταῖς ἡγεμόσιν Ἰούδα, "among the principal towns of the families in Judea." Is there an instance in which αἱ ἡγεμόνες means the "principal towns?" Moreover, the relation of ἡγεμόσιν to the subsequent ἡγούμενος, which requires the Masculine, has been overlooked. — Micah personifies Bethlehem from the outset. Matthew first introduces Bethlehem as a town, but afterwards passes to the personification by speaking of the ἡγεμόνες instead of the tribes. For this he had a special reason in the regard to the subsequent ἡγούμενος. Bethlehem, although outwardly small, is, notwithstanding, when regarded from a higher point of view, even in the present by no means small among the *leaders* of Judah, for, from it, in the future, the great *leader* of Judah shall proceed. This relation, which is so evident, must the rather be assumed, that in Micah also a contrast occurs which, as to the sense, is altogether similar. It serves, at the same time, for a proof against the assumption that the Gospel of Matthew was originally written in the Aramean language,— a view which is, generally, opposed also by the free handling of the Old Testament text in the whole quotation. The inconsistency in the use of the personification is, further, the more easy of explanation, since it is altogether of an *ideal* character, and, substantially, person and town are not distinguished.—The last words in Micah, "And His goings forth," etc., have been omitted by Matthew, because they were not needed for his purpose, which was to show that, according to the prophecies of the Old Testament, the Messiah was to be born at Bethlehem. On the other hand, the בישראל of Micah is paraphrased by: ὅστις ποιμανεῖ τὸν λαόν μου, τὸν Ἰσραήλ. These words refer to 2 Sam. v. 2: "And the Lord says to thee, *Thou shalt feed My people Israel,* and thou shalt be a prince over Israel." They point out the typical relation between the first David who was born at Bethlehem, and the second David, the Messiah.

With respect to the relation betwixt prophecy and its fulfilment, we must here still make a general remark. It is everywhere evident (compare the remarks on Zech. ix. 9), that the fulfilment of the prophecies of the Old Testament forms a secondary purpose of the events of the New Testament, but that in none of the latter this fulfilment is the sole object. Every one, on the contrary, has its significance apart from the prophecy; and it is by this significance that prophecy and history are equally governed. This general remark is here also confirmed. The birth of Christ at Bethlehem testified, in one respect, for the divine origin of the prophecy of the Old Testament, and, in another, that Jesus is the Christ. But its main object, altogether independent of this, was to represent, outwardly also, the descent of Christ from David. This was recognised by the Jews even, at the time of Christ, as appears from the addition ὅπου ἦν Δαβίδ, John vii. 42. Of the two seats of the Davidic family, viz., Bethlehem and Jerusalem, the former is chosen, partly, because, from its external littleness, it was, generally, very suitable for prefiguring the lowliness of the Messiah at the outset—a circumstance which is expressly pointed out by the prophet himself—and partly, because it was peculiar to the family of David during its obscurity; whilst Jerusalem, on the contrary, belonged to their regal condition,—and the Messiah was to be born in the fallen tabernacle of David, to be a rod from the cut off stem of Jesse, Is. xi. 1. That this reference also was in the view of the prophet, seems to be evident from a comparison of iii. 12, and iv. 8, 9, 14. At all events he considered the family of David as having altogether sunk at the time of the Messiah's appearing. The very threatenings in chap. i.–iii. imply the destruction of the Davidic kingdom. This meets us, very distinctly, in chap. iv.

———

Ver. 2. "*Therefore will He give them up until the time that she who is bearing hath brought forth; and then the remnant of his brethren shall return unto the sons of Israel.*"

The description of what the Messiah is to bestow upon the Covenant-people begins in this verse, and is carried on through the whole chapter. By לכן the close connection of v. 1 with vi. 9–14 is indicated. *Michaelis* remarks: "Because this is the counsel of God, first to afflict Zion, on account of her sins, and, afterwards only, to restore her through the Messiah to be born at Bethlehem." In chap. iv. 9–14, it is implied that the giving up will not terminate *before* His birth; in v. 1, that it will come to an end *with* His birth. The whole time described in iv. 9–14 is a time of affliction, of giving up Israel to the world's power in a threefold form of its manifestation. In iv. 14, however, the affliction has reached its highest point, and the lucid interval, mentioned in vers. 12, 13, has fully expired. It is only when we look back to v. 1 alone, that the "therefore" with which our verse opens is not explained, inasmuch as there it is said only, that with the Messiah deliverance and salvation would come, but not that the affliction would continue until He should come. —נתן is similarly used in 2 Chron. xxx. 7: "And be not ye like your fathers, and like your brethren who trespassed against the Lord God of your fathers; therefore He gave them up to desolation (ויתנם לשׁמה), as you see." With respect to the words, "Until the time that she who is bearing hath brought forth," there is an essential difference of opinion as to the explanation of the main point. One class of interpreters—comprehending *Eusebius* and *Cyril*, and by far the greatest number of the ancient Christian expositors; and among the more recent, *Rosenmüller, Ewald, Hitzig, Maurer,* and *Caspari*—understand

by " her who is bearing," the mother of the Messiah. Another
class understands thereby the Congregation of Israel. The
latter, however, differ from each other as to the signification and
import of the figure of the birth. Some—*Abendana, Calvin,* and
Justi—suppose the *tertium comparationis* to be the joy following
upon the pain. Others—*Theodoret, Tarnovius* (" until Israel,
like a fruitful mother, has brought forth a numerous progeny"),
Vitringa (in his *Commentary on Revel.* S. 534)—suppose it to be
the great increase. Let us first decide between these two modifications of that view which refers the words to the Congregation of Israel. The former—the joy following after the pain—
appears to be inadmissible for this single reason, that among the
very numerous passages of the Old Testament where the image
of a birth is employed, there does not occur even one, in which
the joy following after the pain is made prominent, as is the case
in the well-known passage in the New Testament. On the contrary, in all the passages which come into consideration on this
point, it is rather the pain accompanying the birth which is considered. Thus Mic. iv. 10 ; Is. xxvi. 17 ; Jer. iv. 31 : " For I
hear a voice as of a woman in travail, anguish as of her that
bringeth forth her first-born child, the voice of the daughter of
Zion, she groaneth, spreadeth her hands : Woe to me, for my
soul is wearied, through them that kill;" xxx. 6, xlix. 24; Hos.
xiii. 13. To consider the pain alone, however, as the *tertium
comparationis,* is inadmissible, because, in that case, we would
obtain the absurd meaning : the suffering shall continue until
the suffering cometh. It is likewise impossible to understand
the bringing forth as the highest degree of affliction,—so that
the sense would be : the Lord will give them up until the distress reaches its highest point,—because this meaning could
apply only in the event of the lower degrees, the pains before
the birth, being also mentioned. They who hold and defend
the second modification of this view, can indeed refer to, and
quote, a large number of parallel passages—almost all of them
from the second part of Isaiah—where this image occurs with a
similar signification. Thus, *e.g.,* Is. liv. 1 : " Shout for joy, O
barren, thou that didst not bear ; break forth into shouting and
exult, thou that didst not travail ; for more numerous are the
sons of the desolate than the sons of the married wife, saith the
Lord ;" xlix. 21, 22, lxvi. 7-9. But we must nevertheless pre-

fer to this explanation, that which refers the words to the mother
of the Messiah, for the following reasons. 1. If the words were
to be referred to the Congregation of Israel, we should expect
the Article before יולדה. For the Congregation of Israel is substantially mentioned in what immediately precedes; she is only
a personification of those who are to be given up. 2. It is true
that, frequently, the personification is not consistently carried
out; but the circumstance that here, in the same sentence, the
children of Israel are spoken of in the plural ("He will give
them up"), and that no trace of a personification is found in
what follows, but that, on the contrary, the children of Israel
are mentioned expressly, makes the pretended personification
appear in rather an abrupt manner, so that such an assumption
would be admissible in a case of necessity only. 3. If referred
to the Congregation of Israel, the relation of the Messiah to
that great event, and epoch, is not intimated by a single
word. Of Him ver. 1 speaks, and of Him vers. 3–5. How
then can it be that in ver. 2 there should all at once be a transition to the general Messianic representation? 4. The suffix
in אחיו, which refers to the Messiah, requires that He should be
indirectly mentioned in what precedes; and such is the case,
only when the יולדה is she who is to bring forth the Ruler announced in ver. 1. 5. It appears from the reference to Gen.
xxxv., which we have already pointed out and proved, that the
prophet has in view one who is to bring forth in Bethlehem.
Bethlehem, which had in ancient times already become remarkable by a birth, is in future to be ennobled by another
birth, infinitely more important. 6. The comparison of Is. vii.
14, where likewise the mother of the Messiah is mentioned;
compare the remarks on that passage. 7, and lastly—The evident reference of " Until the time that she who is bearing hath
brought forth" to "From thee shall come forth," suggests
the mother of the Messiah. That she is designated as "she
who brings forth," may be explained from the circumstance
that she comes into view here in a relation which is altogether
one-sided, viz., only as regards the one event of the birth of the
Messiah.—Among the blessings which the Messiah is to confer
upon the Congregation of the Lord, there is first of all viewed
the fundamental blessing, the condition of all others, viz., the
change which He is to effect in the disposition of the Covenant-

people. It is this which, above and before everything .else, needs to be changed, if Israel is not any more to be given up; for Israel which is so only by name and in appearance, is the legitimate prey of the world.—By the Brethren of the Messiah, the members of the Old Covenant-people, His brethren according to the flesh, can alone be understood. There is no Old Testament analogy for referring the expression to the Gentiles. We are led to the reference to Israel by the connection with the first member of the verse. The brethren are such as have become the Messiah's brethren by the circumstance that He has been born of the Bethlehemitish woman "who is to bring forth." (*Caspari*). We are led to it, *further*, by v. 1, according to which, the Messiah is to be Ruler in Israel; and, *still further*, by the fundamental passage in Ps. xxii. 23: "I will declare Thy name unto my brethren," where, according to the address in ver. 24, the brethren are all the descendants of Israel, among whom a great awakening is to be produced.—The construction of שוב with על may be explained by the remark of *Ewald:* "על stands in its primary local signification with verbs also, when the thing moves to another thing, and remains upon it." Of a material return the verb שוב with על is thus used in Prov. xxvi. 11, Eccles. i. 6;—of a spiritual return, 2 Chron. xxx. 9: בשובכם על יהוה "when ye return to the Lord," properly, "upon the Lord;" and Mal. iii. 24 (iv. 6): "And he makes return the hearts of the fathers to the sons, על בנים,"—which latter passage has a striking resemblance to the one under review. In the latter signification שוב must be taken here also.—By the "sons of Israel," here, as ordinarily, the whole of the Covenant-people are signified, and that by its highest and holiest name. From this holy communion, the wicked—the souls which, according to the expression of the Lord, are cut off from their people—are separated and dissevered; compare my commentary on Ps. lxxiii. 1. The whole description of the prevailing corruption, and especially vii. 1, 2, show us to what an extent this separation existed at the time of the prophet. But, by the Saviour, this separation is to be abolished, and the lost and wandering are to be brought back to the communion of the church,—a work which, according to Rom. xi., will be perfected in the future only.[1]

[1] After the example of *Hofmann, Caspari* gives this exposition : " And

Ver. 3. "*And He stands and feeds in the strength of the Lord, in the majesty of the name of the Lord His God; and they dwell, for now shall He be great unto the ends of the earth.*"

In this verse we are told what the Saviour shall do for awakened and, thus, inwardly united Israel. "He stands," has here not the signification of "He abides," but belongs merely to the graphic description of the habit of the shepherd; compare Is. lxi. 5: "And strangers stand and feed your flocks." The shepherd stands, leaning upon his staff, and overlooks the flock. The connection of "He feeds" with "in the strength of the Lord," we cannot better express than *Calvin* has done in the words: "The word 'to feed' expresses what Christ will be towards His people, *i.e.*, towards the flock committed to Him. He does not exercise dominion in the Church like a formidable tyrant who keeps down his subjects through terror, but He is a Shepherd, and treats His sheep with all the gentleness which they can desire. But, inasmuch as we are surrounded on all sides by enemies, the prophet adds: 'He shall feed in the strength,' etc.; *i.e.*, as much power as there is in God, so much protection there will be in Christ, when it is necessary to defend and protect His Church against enemies. We may learn, then, from this, that we may expect as much of salvation from Christ as there is strength in God." The great King is so closely united to God, that the whole fulness of divine power and majesty belongs to Him. Such attributes are never given to any earthly king. Such a king has, indeed, strength in the Lord, Is. xlv. 24; "The Lord giveth strength to His king, and exalteth the horn of His anointed," 1 Sam. ii. 10; but the whole strength and majesty of God are not his possession. The pas-

the remnant of His brethren, viz., the inhabitants of Judah, shall return from the captivity to Canaan, along with the sons of Israel, *i.e.*, the ten tribes." But the return from the captivity never appears in the prophets, as a work of the Messiah. It has here taken place long before His appearing: chap. iv. 10, iv. 11-14 supposes it to have taken place, and Zion to be in existence. The "brethren of the Messiah" can neither be the inhabitants of Judah especially, nor the sons of Israel, the ten tribes, unless the antithesis to Judah be distinctly expressed. It is absurd to suppose that the ten tribes should appear as those chiefly who are to be redeemed. שוב, which means "to return," cannot be used simply of a return to the country, while שוב with על can, according to the *usus loquendi*, be understood only in the sense of "to return to," etc., etc.

sage in Is. ix. 5 (6) is parallel,—where the Messiah is called אֵל גִּבּוֹר, God-hero.—The "name of God" points to the rich fulness in deeds, by which He has manifested the glory of His nature. The Messiah will be the brightness and image of this His glory,—a glory which is manifested by acts, and not a glory which is inactive and concealed. "They dwell" forms a contrast to the disquietude and scattering, and we are, therefore, not at liberty to supply "safely" before it. The last words are deprived of their meaning and significance by explanations such as that of *Dathe*: "His name shall attain to great renown and celebrity." The ground of the present rest and safety of the Congregation of the Lord rather is this,—that her Head has now extended His dominion beyond the narrow limits of Palestine, over the whole earth; compare iv. 3.—2 Sam. vii. 9 cannot here be compared, as there the *name* of the Lord is not spoken of as it is here. That the "being great" here implies real dominion (*Maurer: auctoritate et potentia valebit*), which alone can afford a pledge for the dwelling in safety, is shown also by the fundamental passages Ps. ii. 8, lxxii. 8; compare Zech. ix. 10. In Luke i. 32 the passage before us is referred to. The "now" does not by any means form a contrast with a former condition of the Messiah, but with the former condition of the Congregation when she did not enjoy so powerful a Ruler.

Ver. 4. "*And this* (man) *is peace. When Asshur comes into our land, and when he treads in our palaces, we raise against him seven shepherds, and eight princes of men. Ver. 5. And they feed the land of Asshur with the sword, and the land of Nimrod in its gates; and He protects from Asshur when he comes into our land, and when he treads within our borders.*"

"And this man (He whose glory has just been described) is peace,"—He bestows that which we have so much needed, and longed for with so much anxiety in these troublous times before His appearing. In a similar manner, and with reference to the passage before us, it is said in Ephes. ii. 14: αὐτός ἐστιν ἡ εἰρήνη ἡμῶν; compare also Judges vi. 24: "And Gideon built an altar there unto the Lord, and called it Jehovah-Peace, יְהוָה שָׁלוֹם." Abandoning this explanation, which is so natural, *Jonathan, Grotius, Rosenmüller,* and *Winer* explain: "And *there* will be peace to us,"—an interpretation, however, which is inadmissible even on philological grounds. זֶה is nowhere used, either as Adverb. loci ᴤ "here," or as Adverb. temp. = "then." As regards the latter, such passages as Gen. xxxi. 41—"These are to me twenty years," instead of, "twenty years have now elapsed"— are, of course, not at all to the purpose. But of such a kind are almost all the examples quoted by *Nolde.* In Esther ii. 13 בזה is used. The verb המשיל in ver. 5 is likewise in favour of understanding זה personally; compare also Zech. ix. 10: "And He shall speak peace unto the nations."—There can scarcely be any doubt that the words allude to the name of Solomon, and that the Messiah is represented in them as the Antitype of Solomon. Upon this point there is the less room for doubt, because even Solomon himself called the Messiah by his name in the Song of Solomon; and in Is. ix. 5 (6) also, He is, with an evident allusion to the name of Solomon, called the Prince of Peace.—All which follows after these words, to the end of ver. 5, is only a particularizing expansion of the words: "And this (man) is peace." Interpreters have almost all agreed, that Asshur, the most dangerous enemy of the Covenant-people at the time of the prophet, stands here as a type of the enemies of the Covenant-people. Even *L. Baur* has translated: "And though another Asshur," etc., with a reference to the passage in *Virgil* to which allusion had already been made by *Castalio: "Alter erit tum Tiphys et altera quæ vehat Argo delectos heroas."* That the prophet, however, was fully conscious of his here using Asshur typically, appears from iv. 9, 10. For, according to these verses, the first of the three catastrophes which preceded the birth of the Messiah, proceeds from a new phase of the world's power, viz., from the Babylonian empire, the rising of which implies the overthrow of the Assyrian. But the figurative element in the representation goes still farther. From ver. 9 ff.—according to which the Lord makes His people outwardly defenceless, before they become, in Christ, the conquerors of the world—it is obvious that the spiritual struggle against the world's power is here represented under the image of the outward struggle, carried on with the sword. One might be tempted to confine the thought of the passage to this: "The Messiah affords to His people the same protection and security as would a large number of brave princes with their hosts," inasmuch as the bestowal of these was, under the Old Testament, the ordinary means by which the Lord delivered His people. If, however, the spiritual character of the struggle only be maintained, there is no sufficient reason for considering the seven and more shepherds and the princes as mere imagery, because, in the kingdom of Christ also, the cause of the kingdom of God is carried on by human instruments, whom He furnishes with His own strength. The words, "This (man) is peace," and "He protects," in ver. 5, show indeed with sufficient distinctness, that, in the main, Christ is the only Saviour,—the shepherds, His instruments only,—and their world-conquering power, a derived one only. The apparent contradiction of the passage before us to iv. 1–3, vii. 12—according to which the heathen nations shall, in the time of the Messiah, spontaneously press towards the kingdom of God—is removed by the remark, that we have here before us two different streams which may as well flow together in prophecy as they do in history. The zeal with which the nations press towards the kingdom is, in part, greatly called forth by the fact, that, in attacking the kingdom of Christ, they have experienced its world-conquering power. The circumstance that the words, "This (man) is peace," stand at the beginning, proves that the main idea is the security of the kingdom of God against all hostile attacks. For the like reason it is, towards the end, resumed in the words, "And He protects," etc. But this affords no reason for saying, with *Caspari:* "It forms part of the defence, it is indeed its consummation, that the war is carried into Asshur." In the first hemistich of ver. 5, it is intimated rather, that, in the time of the Messiah, the positions of the world and of the people of God are changed,—that the latter becomes world-conquering; and for this reason, every thought of their own insecurity must so much the rather disappear. "The land of Nimrod" is, according to Gen. x. 11, Asshur. The "gates" are those of the cities and fortresses, corresponding with, "When he treads in our palaces," in ver. 4. It weakens the sense to think of the gates of the country, as such, *i.e.*, the borders. The attack, on the contrary, is directed against, and strikes the real centre of the seat of the world's power, just as, formerly, the stroke was always directed against Zion.

With regard to the remaining part of the chapter, we content ourselves with a mere statement of the contents. The Congregation of the Lord shall, at that time, not only be lovely and refreshing, ver. 6 (7), (this is the constant signification of the image of the dew, compare Ps. cx. 3, cxxxiii. 3, lxxii. 6 ; the relative pronoun אשר must be referred to the grass, mentioned immediately before; that which the dew descending from heaven is to the grass, Israel will, in his heavenly mission, be to the heathen world), but at the same time fearful and irresistible, vers. 7, 8 (8, 9) ; the latter of these qualities shall show itself not only as a curse in the case of obstinate despisers, but also as a blessing in the case of those who are estranged from the kingdom of God, through ignorance only. Resuming then the last words of ver. 8 (9), "All thine enemies shall be cut off," the prophet declares that before this word shall be fulfilled, the destructive activity of the Lord will be manifested in Israel itself. He will cut off by His judgments, and by the catastrophes described in iv. 9–14, everything in which, in the present, they placed a carnal confidence, everything by which they became externally strong and powerful (*Caspari:* "A cutting off, in the first instance, of all wherewith elsewhere enemies are commonly cut off"), and so likewise all idolatry, to which the Chaldean catastrophe already put a violent end. It is only of such a termination by force, and not of a purely inward effect of the "gentle power of the Spirit then poured out upon them," that the words here, as well as in reference to the horses, etc., permit us to think. The two kinds of objects of false confidence are then, in conclusion, in ver. 13 (14) once more summed up,—when the cities, just as in ver. 10 (11), come into view as fortresses only. If thus the path be cleared and prepared for the Lord, He will, on behalf of His people, execute vengeance upon the heathen world.

CHAP. VI. VII.

We shall now, in conclusion, give a survey of the third and closing discourse of the prophet. After an introduction in vi. 1, 2, where the mountains serve only to give greater solemnity to the scene (in the fundamental passages Deut. xxxii. 1, and in Is. 1, 2, "heaven and earth" are mentioned for the same purposes, inasmuch as they are the most venerable parts of creation ; "contend *with* the mountains" by taking them in and applying to

them as hearers), the prophet reminds the people of the benefits
which they have repaid with ingratitude, vers. 3–5. (In ver. 5
those facts also which served as a proof of its truth, are considered
as part of Balaam's answer.)   He then, in vers. 6–8, shows the
fallacy of the imagination that they could satisfy the Lord by
the observance of the mere outward forms of worship, though
such should be increased to the utmost, and performed in a manner totally different from that in which it was in the present, and
points out the spiritual demands already made even by the law,
and especially by Deut. x. 12, a compliance with which could
alone be pleasing to the Lord.   From vi. 9–vii. 6, he shows to
how limited an extent these demands are complied with by the
people,—how true and cordial piety and justice have disappeared
from the midst of them,—and how, therefore, the threatenings
of the law must, and shall be fulfilled upon them.   The reproof and threatening are then followed by the announcement
of salvation, which refers indeed to the Messianic times, but
without any mention in it of the person of the Messiah, the
brightness of which meets us only in the main body of the prophecy.   The main thought here also is the entirely altered
position of Israel in their relation to the heathen world.   " A
day is coming"—so it is said in ver. 11—"to build thy walls ;
in that day shall the law be far removed."   גדר is used especially
of the walls and fences of vineyards ; and under the image of a
vineyard, Israel appears as early as in the Song of Solomon.
The wall around the vineyard of Israel is the protection against
the heathen world ; Is. v. 5.   The " law " is, according to the
context, in which the heathen oppressors are spoken of, that
which is imposed by them upon the people of God ; Ps. xciv. 20.
Ver. 12. " *A day it is when they shall come to thee from Asshur,
and from the cities of Egypt, and from Egypt to the river, and to
sea from sea, and to mountain from mountain.*"   It is not enough
that the people of God are freed from the servitude of the
world.   They shall become the objects of the longing of the
nations, even the most powerful and hostile.   They become the
magnet which attracts them ; compare iv. 1, 2.   From among
the heathen nations Asshur and Egypt are first specially mentioned, as the two principal representatives of hostility against
the kingdom of God in the present and past, and, at the same
time, as the two most powerful empires at the time of the pro-

phet—the latter quality being indicated by the circumstance of Egypt's appearing under the name מָצוֹר, "fortress." But then, by the expressions "from sea to sea," "from mountain to mountain," which are equivalent to "from every sea to every sea," etc., all barriers in general are completely removed; compare in v. 3 (4) the words: "He shall be great unto the ends of the earth." (The subject in יָבוֹא can only be the inhabitants of these countries themselves, not the Jews living there. If the latter had been intended, a more distinct indication of it would have been required. The Masculine Suffix עָדֶיךָ "to thee," *i.e.*, not to Zion but to Israel, is opposed to such a reference. This shows clearly that they who come are different from Israel. In entire harmony with this prophecy is Is. xix. 18-25.) But, before such glory can be bestowed upon the people of God, the irrevocable judgment must first have done its fearful work, ver. 13; compare the fundamental passage Lev. xxvi. 33, and Is. i. 7. In ver. 14 the announcement of salvation takes a new start. Vers. 18–20 form the sublime close, not only of the last discourse, but also of the whole book, as is clearly indicated by the coincidence of the words, "Who is, O God, like unto Thee?" ver. 18, with the mention of Micah's name in the inscription. The name of the prophet, by which he is dedicated to the incomparable God, has been confirmed by the contents of his prophecy. The New Testament parallel passage is Rom. xi. 33–36: "*Who is, O God, like unto Thee; pardoning iniquity, and remitting transgression to the remnant of His heritage? He retaineth not His anger for ever, because He delighteth in mercy.*" "Who is, O God, like unto Thee?" so the people once already sang after the redemption from Egypt: Thus it resounds still more loudly in the view of the antitypal redemption, by which the fundamental definition of the divine nature in Exod. xxxiv. 6, 7, and David's praise of divine mercy in Ps. ciii., are fully realized. "He will return and have compassion upon us (according to the promise in Deut. xxx. 3), will overcome our iniquities (which, like a cruel tyrant, like Pharaoh of old, subjected us to their power, Ps. xix. 14), and cast all their sins into the depth of the sea," as once He cast the proud Egyptians, Exod. xv. 5–10. "Thou wilt give truth to Jacob, and mercy to Abraham, as Thou hast sworn unto our fathers from the days of old."

DATE DUE

A~~~~		
~~NOV~~ ~~1975~~		
~~		
~~		
~~MAR 3 1990~~		
~~		
NOV 8 0		

Lightning Source UK Ltd.
Milton Keynes UK
UKOW06f1911260713

214468UK00010B/563/P